Handbook of Special Education

Research and Practice

Volume 2

Other titles of related interest

WANG *et al.*	Handbook of Special Education, Volume 1: Learner Characteristics and Adaptive Education
WANG *et al.*	Handbook of Special Education, Volume 3: Low Incidence Conditions
DUNKIN	The International Encyclopedia of Teaching and Teacher Education
PSACHAROPOULOS	Economics of Education and National Systems of Education
POSTLETHWAITE	The Encyclopedia of Comparative Education and National Systems of Education
LEWY	The International Encyclopedia of Curriculum
THOMAS	Encyclopedia of Human Development and Education
WALBERG & HAERTEL	The International Encyclopedia of Educational Evaluation
ERAUT	International Encyclopedia of Educational Technology
TITMUS	Lifelong Education for Adults
KEEVES	Educational Research, Methodology, and Measurement
WANG *et al.*	Special Education: Research and Practice: Synthesis of Findings

Handbook of Special Education
Research and Practice
Volume 2

Mildly Handicapped
Conditions

Edited by
MARGARET C. WANG
Temple University, Philadelphia, USA

MAYNARD C. REYNOLDS
University of Minnesota, Minneapolis, USA

HERBERT J. WALBERG
University of Illinois at Chicago, USA

PERGAMON PRESS

Member of Maxwell Macmillan Pergamon Publishing Corporation

OXFORD · NEW YORK · BEIJING · FRANKFURT
SÃO PAULO · SYDNEY · TOKYO · TORONTO

U.K.	Pergamon Press plc, Headington Hill Hall, Oxford OX3 0BW, England
U.S.A.	Pergamon Press Inc., Maxwell House, Fairview Park, Elmsford, NY 10523, U.S.A.
PEOPLE'S REPUBLIC OF CHINA	Pergamon Press, Room 4037, Qianmen Hotel, Beijing, People's Republic of China
FEDERAL REPUBLIC OF GERMANY	Pergamon Press GmbH, Hammerweg 6, D-6242 Kronberg, Federal Republic of Germany
BRAZIL	Pergamon Editora Ltda, Rua Eça de Queiros, 346, CEP 04011, Paraiso, São Paulo, Brazil
AUSTRALIA	Pergamon Press Australia Pty Ltd, P.O. Box 544, Potts Point, N.S.W. 2011, Australia
JAPAN	Pergamon Press, 5th Floor, Matsuoka Central Building, 1-7-1 Nishishinjuku, Shinjuku-ku, Tokyo 160, Japan
CANADA	Pergamon Press Canada Ltd, Suite No. 271, 253 College Street, Toronto, Ontario, Canada M5T 1R5

First edition 1988
Reprinted 1990

Library of Congress Cataloging in Publication Data

Handbook of special education.
Contents: v. 1. Learner characteristics and adaptive education—
v. 2. Mildly handicapped conditions.
1. Special education literature—United States. I. Wang, Margaret
C. II. Reynolds, Maynard Clinton. III. Walberg, Herbert J.,
1937- .
LC3965.H263 1987 371.9 88-18965

British Library Cataloguing in Publication Data

Handbook of special education: research and practice.
Vol. 2: Mildly handicapped conditions
1. Special education —— United States
I. Wang, Margaret C. II. Reynolds, Maynard C.
III. Walberg, Herbert J.
371.9'0973 LC3981

ISBN 0-08-033384-2

Information included in this publication is the result of a project
funded at least in part through Federal funds from the U.S.
Department of Education under contract number 300-84-0194.
The contents of this publication do not necessarily reflect the
views or policies of the U.S. Department of Education; nor does
the mention of trade names, commercial products or organizations
imply endorsement by the U.S. Government.

Printed in Great Britain by BPCC Wheatons Ltd, Exeter

Contents

Contents

Preface

In the United States, as in many other parts of the world, we are engaging in a new wave of education reform efforts, particularly the improvement of schools' capabilities to serve students who have greater-than-usual needs for educational support but were often either left out of earlier reform movements or kept on the sidelines. The term "students with special needs" is used here to refer to students with physical, behavioral, or cognitive disabilities; students from economically, culturally, or language disadvantaged backgrounds; and students with chronic low achievement or those who otherwise can be considered academically at risk.

Significant progress has been made, especially in the past decade, in providing equal access to free and appropriate schooling for students. At this point in our history, nearly all school-age children in the United States and other industrialized countries attend school. This effort to achieve universal and effective education is based on a recognition of the rights of children to basic education that enables them to thrive in a complex society, as well as a realization that technological and economic growth is facilitated by increasing the numbers of students, even those with poor academic prognoses, who are, in fact, successful in school learning. Thus, recent and current efforts to improve schooling serve both private and social interests.

This three-volume publication. *The Handbook of Special Education: Research and Practice*, represents a commitment to examine the research base, broadly defined to represent current knowledge or the "state of the art," that can be used in formulating plans to improve the chances of schooling success for all students, especially students with special needs. Each of the 45 chapters comprising the *Handbook* summarizes the well-confirmed knowledge in a particular area, giving attention first to the research literature, broadly defined, and then to the tested experience and practices of leading professionals. The authors include in their reviews estimates of the state of practice in their respective topic areas and then proceed to recommend improvements for effectively linking practice with the state of the art. Thus, the research syntheses provide state-of-the-art standards against which the state of practice can be judged.

Several perspectives provided the specific context for this *Handbook*. First, the reviews of research and practice mark the impact of a decade of intensive research and program development in the United States aimed at improving the chances of educational success for students with special needs. Since 1975, the year of the enactment of The Education for All Handicapped Children Act (PL 94-142), schools have made major advances in providing for handicapped students and others with special needs. Consequently, there is reason to celebrate the 10th anniversary of what has proven to be an extremely powerful and influential piece of legislation. During the same period, there have been important advances in educational research, thus adding to the impetus for careful review of both research and practice at this time.

The second perspective derives from the movement to provide more inclusive arrangements for disabled persons and for others who often find themselves at the margins of schools and other institutions. These efforts are variously described as deinstitutionalization, normalization, and mainstreaming. Even persons with severe impairments are less often segregated in special enclaves and more often mainstreamed into ordinary community situations. As a result, it is critical that the findings from research on persons with special needs be made available to broader groups than ever before, and that the future research be conducted in new settings and on the specific processes of change involved in implementing new policies. In a sense, research needs to be "mainstreamed." Accordingly, the reviews reported here join the work of special education researchers with that of the broader community of researchers in general education and human behavior.

The need to coordinate services across a wide range of caretakers and agencies provided a third perspective for the research syntheses. Specifically, special education must be coordinated with services such as health and welfare, family services, correction, rehabilitation, and employment assistance. Many of the "new morbidities," such as child abuse, drug addiction, and the erosion of "natural" support systems as a consequence of broken family structures and incomplete mother-child attachments, have grave effects on school children. Often, children who are referred to special education programs came from unsupportive families and disordered communities. Schools must respond by linking up with other community agencies in order to construct high-quality, broadly coordinated programs for students and families with special needs. At the same time, it is necessary to recognize and delimit the special functions of the schools. In this context, the research reviews reported in this *Handbook* were designed to be instructionally relevant, while also acknowledging the larger networks of service to which educational processes can be linked.

The dependence of special education on public policy and legal imperatives is yet another perspective that guided the research syntheses. Several reports, court decisions, and policies have enlarged this perspective in recent years. Examples include Nicholas Hobb's 1975 work entitled, *The Futures of Children* (San Francisco, CA: Jossey-Bass); and the 1982 report by the National Academy of Sciences Panel on Selection and Placement of Students in Programs for the Mentally Retarded, entitled *Placing Children in Special Education: A Strategy for Equity* (K. A. Heller, W. H. Holtzman, and S. Messick, Editors, Washington, DC: National Academy Press). These and other reports by leading scholars cast doubt on some of the traditional practices of special education.

The courts, moreover, have had far-reaching effects on educational policy. For instance, the 1972 decision of *Larry P. v. Riles* (Civil action N.L.-71-2270, 343 F. Supp. 1306, N.D. Cal., 1972) held that the use of intelligence tests as a prime determiner of the classification and placement of children as educable mentally retarded is unconstitutional. Similar court decisions have been the basis for many program changes. Clearly, the field of special education is held accountable to the procedural standards and practices outlined by binding court decisions. Thus, the research reviews reported in this work were sensitive to studies of policy and policy related developments.

Finally, the research syntheses took account of the rising public concern over the general quality of schools, as expressed in the widely heralded 1983 report by the National Commission on Excellence in Education entitled, *A Nation at Risk: The Imperative for Educational Reform* (Washington, DC: U.S. Department of Education), as well as at least a dozen other recent and significant national reports. They reflect growing public demand for better instruction and for a greater focus on all forms of school accountability, including a commitment to provide the greater-than-usual educational interventions required by students who are difficult to teach. Because recent developments in special education (e.g., more individualized planning, closer partnerships with parents, better measurements of instructional outcomes) are congruent with the increasing general demands made of schools, it should be possible, as we see it, for special educators to complete the necessary reforms. To this end, the authors of the chapters in these volumes sought to define the knowledge base and extend its application in the field of special education in the broadest and most helpful way. Just as students with special needs are no longer isolated in the schools, research in special education should no longer be treated in isolation.

As we have noted, 1986 is a year in which schools in the United States entered into a second decade under the mandates of changed national policy concerning special education and related services for students with special needs. However, the authors of the research syntheses were also mindful of the international scope of the research literature and of the similarity in trends and problems surrounding special education throughout the world.

This publication was initiated, in part, as a culminating activity of a project entitled, "Research Integration of Selected Issues in the Education of Handicapped Children," which was funded by the Office of Special Education and Rehabilitative Services of the United States Department of Education. The forty-five chapters are organized in three volumes under nine major topic areas or sections. Volume I includes chapters in the topic areas, Learning Characteristics of Handicapped Students and the Provision of Effective Education, Effectiveness of Differential Programming in Serving Handicapped Students, and Noncategorical Programming for Mildly Handicapped Students. Volume II consists of writings in the areas of Mild Mental Retardation, Behavioral Disorders, and Learning Disabilities. The chapters in Volume III focus on the topic areas, Education of Deaf Children and Youth, Education of Visually Handicapped Children and Youth, and Handicapped Infants.

An eight-member advisory board played a major role at important stages in the substantive development and preparation of the research syntheses. They participated in the initial selection of areas of research in special education and related fields, in the identification of authors who would conduct the research syntheses, and in the reviewing of manuscripts. The members of the advisory board were Joseph Fischgrund from the Lexington School for the Deaf in New York; James Gallagher from the University of North Carolina; Reginald Jones from the University of California, Berkeley; Stephen Lilly from Washington State University; Daniel Reschly from Iowa State University; Judy Schrag from the Washington State Department of Education; Phillip Strain from the University of Pittsburgh; and Martha Ziegler from the Federation for Children with Special Needs based in Boston, Massachusetts.

A group of scholars, each of them nationally and internationally known and active in research, provided substantive leadership to the authors in the nine topic areas. these scholars assisted the editors of this *Handbook* in overseeing the quality and breadth of the content coverage. They also wrote Introductions that provide overviews of the topics addressed in the nine areas. The names of these individuals and the topic areas in which they worked are Verna Hart from the University of Pittsburgh—Handicapped Infants; Kenneth Kavale from the University of Iowa—Effectiveness of Differential Programming in Serving Handicapped Students; Barbara Keogh from the University of California, Los Angeles—Learning Disabilities; Daniel Reschly from Iowa State University—Mild Mental Retardation; Maynard Reynolds from the University of Minnesota—

Noncategorical Programming for Mildly Handicapped Students; Geraldine Scholl from the University of Michigan—Education of Visually Handicapped Children and Youth; E. Ross Stuckless from the National Technical Institute for the Deaf—Education of Deaf Children and Youth; Margaret Wang from Temple University—Learning Characteristics of Handicapped Students and the Provision of Effective Education; and Frank Wood from the University of Minnesota—Behavioral Disorders.

The chapters were reviewed during various draft stages by persons representing a broad range of expertise in research, personnel preparation, curriculum development, and educational practice. The contributions of these reviewers helped to enhance the comprehensiveness and relevance of the individual research syntheses. Lists of reviewers for the chapters included in individual volumes are provided at the end of the volumes.

The comprehensiveness of the research syntheses was further enhanced by making available to all authors the findings from computerized literature searches. These covered the two major indices of the Educational Resources Information Center (ERIC)—the Resources in Education Index and the Current Index to Journals in Education. In addition, the authors made use of technical reports and other documentation on more than 100 research projects in special education that were conducted in the United States in recent years.

As a final note, we wish to acknowledge the contributions of several others who played important roles in facilitating the development and production of this *Handbook*. Funding from the Office of Special Education and Rehabilitative Services provided the necessary support to commission the writing of most of the chapters. Judy Fein and Nancy Safer from that agency's staff were the source of continuing advice and encouragement. Special acknowledgements go to Mary Kay Freilino for her efficient orchestration of the myriad administrative details involved in the manuscript reviewing process and her efforts in overseeing the substantive and technical details of conducting computerized literature searches for authors; to K. Charlie Lakin whose substantive input during the reviewing of many of the manuscripts was consistently insightful; to Rita Catalano for her editorial and administrative leadership throughout the preparation of this work; to Jackie Rubenstein for her technical editing expertise and her diligence in monitoring the details of a Herculean editing assignment; and to Regina Rattigan for her contribution as a member of the technical editing team. Finally, we are grateful to Barbara Barrett from Pergamon Press for her constant support and guidance throughout the editing and production process.

Margaret C. Wang
Maynard C. Reynolds
Herbert J. Walberg
Editors

SECTION 1

Mild Mental Retardation

Introduction

DANIEL J. RESCHLY

Iowa State University

Mild Mental Retardation has fallen on hard times. There has been a precipitous decline in the number of students classified as mildly mentally retarded over the past decade. The chapters in this section represent an attempt to make sense out of the confusing array of such social, political, educational, and research trends.

Mild mental retardation is one of four levels of mental retardation specified in the American Association on Mental Deficiency (AAMD) classification scheme. Various terms are used to refer to mild mental retardation, including educable mentally retarded, mentally handicapped, mentally disabled, and so on. Despite the confusion over terminology, there is a set of fundamental characteristics typically found among mildly retarded students. These fundamental characteristics, which lead to teacher referral, are very low achievement, usually accompanied by other classroom problems such as difficulties in social skills; and performance on individually administered measures of general intellectual functioning in the IQ range of about 50 to 75. Although IQ is perhaps the most prominent feature of the mild mental retardation diagnosis, it is by no means the only, nor the most important, feature.

The recent decline by one third in the number of mildly mentally retarded students is somewhat surprising in view of the distinguished history of mild mental retardation programs in the United States. Special classes for mildly mentally retarded students were first established in the 1890s in several large cities, primarily in the Northeast and the upper Midwest. These special class programs gradually expanded throughout the first 6 decades of the 20th century, so that by the time of the passage of the landmark Education for All Handicapped Children Act of 1975, the mild mental retardation classification had the highest incidence of the exceptional child diagnoses. Over the past decade, the one-third decline in the incidence of mild mental retardation has led to substantial changes in the nature of the students included in this diagnostic construct. As noted in several of the chapters in this section, the decline in numbers clearly implies caution in interpreting the older research in the area.

Despite this caution, however, seven persistent themes have been apparent in the literature throughout the 20th century. These themes are briefly described in this Introduction; they are discussed in greater detail by the authors of the five chapters that comprise this section. In some instances, entire chapters are devoted to a specific theme, such as in the chapter by Zetlin entitled "Adult Development of Mentally Retarded Students: Implications for Educational Programs." In other instances, more than one chapter deals with a specific theme, or a single chapter may deal with two or more themes. The seven themes provide a sense of order to current efforts to understand basic phenomena associated with mild mental retardation as well as efforts to design, implement, and evaluate better educational programs for mildly mentally retarded students.

The first major theme reflects the significant changes that have occurred in the mild mental retardation construct over the past two decades. Debates over the fundamental meaning of mild mental retardation are not new. The basic question continues to be whether or not mild mental retardation requires permanence (i.e., it is lifelong) and a biological origin. Although the current AAMD system clearly indicates that neither permanence nor biological origin is required, earlier conceptions did indeed include these attributes and some persons wishing to reform the present system would reserve the mild mental retardation classification for those who are permanently disabled due to, or at least associated with, some kind of biological anomaly. Related to questions about the fundamental meaning of the diagnostic construct are persistent issues concerning classification criteria such as the relative importance of adaptive behavior and general intellectual functioning. Two of the chapters in this section discuss these issues in considerable detail. They are "Current Status of the Mild Mental Retardation Construct: Identification, Placement, and Programs," by Polloway and Smith, and "Minority Mild Mental Retardation Overrepresentation: Legal Issues, Research Findings, and Reform Trends," by Reschly.

Another prominent theme throughout the 20th century has been the degree to which the basic intellectual and cognitive deficits exhibited by mildly mentally retarded students might be prevented through early intervention programs or remedied through cognitive or intellectual training activities. Efforts to prevent or remediate fundamental cognitive deficits are more vigorous and prominent in the professional literature today than at any previous time. These efforts are extremely complex, but they are enormously promising in their implications, both for the fundamental understanding of cognitive development and the delivery of services that might markedly change the course of the lives of mildly mentally retarded individuals. This literature is discussed by Kramer, Piersel, and Glover in their chapter on "Cognitive and Social Development of Mildly Retarded Children," and by Taylor in his chapter entitled "Psychological Intervention with Mildly Retarded Children: Prevention and Remediation of Cognitive Deficits." It should come as no surprise that much of this research is confounded with methodological problems. The complexities of the prevention or remediation of something as fundamental as mild mental retardation practically guarantee methodological difficulties.

A theme closely related to prevention and remediation is found in the research on fundamental cognitive processes associated with mild mental retardation. Kramer and his colleagues provide an excellent review of this literature; and other reviews of basic research closely related to this theme appear in Volume III of this Handbook, in the section on "Learning Characteristics of Handicapped Students and the Provision of Effective Education." The critical and still unsolved problem in cognitive training of mildly mentally retarded students appears to center on the involvement of more complex than simple cognitive processes. Although considerable advances have been achieved, particularly in demonstrating that mildly mentally retarded students can learn to use strategies to solve complex problems, the basic difficulties of the generalization of strategies to other situations and the spontaneous use of appropriate strategies remain. Further developments in this literature have vast potential for prevention and remediation as well as for effective educational programming.

Educational programming for mildly mentally retarded students has been highly controversial for at least 20 years. The major concern has been with the effectiveness of self-contained special classes, the most commonly used special education option for this diagnostic construct. Efficacy data concerning these special classes have been disappointing. Although enormous problems exist with this literature, the lack of clear-cut, positive results demonstrating the benefits of special classes has been at least part of the dynamics leading to the decline in incidence of mild mental retardation over the past decade. Polloway and Smith discuss the efficacy

literature and provide an insightful treatment of different curricular models. The fundamental question here is: What kind of special programming is most appropriate for mildly mentally retarded students who, as nearly everyone agrees, need educational services beyond those typically provided in regular education?

The fifth persistent theme in the literature focuses on the fundamental and far-reaching implications of mildly mentally retarded adult adjustment for the development of educational programs. Adult adjustment is enormously difficult to study for a variety of reasons. In her chapter, Zetlin notes that mildly mentally retarded adult adjustment has been studied since at least 1919 in the United States, but that only a handful of longitudinal studies have been completed. Moreover, each of these longitudinal studies is open to criticism due to methodological problems. Nevertheless, key issues in the adult adjustment of mildly mentally retarded persons have become much clearer in recent years through research by Zetlin and others. Their findings need to be considered by educators in the development of educational programs for this population.

Social competence, particularly in the realms of everyday independent functioning in the community, interpersonal skills, avoidance of problem behaviors, and acquisition of fundamental self-help skills is perhaps the most crucial issue in the education of mildly mentally retarded persons. Indeed, ample literature suggests that failure to acquire these social competencies is probably more important than deficits in general intellectual functioning in adult vocational adjustment. Further, social competence difficulties contribute significantly to whether or not a person with low general intellectual functioning is actually referred: a prerequisite step in the complex process whereby a student may be classified as mildly mentally retarded. Although acquisition of social competencies has not been studied to the same degree as has cognitive functioning, some very important initial work has been done. Again, the results of research in this area have vast implications for the development of educational programs, particularly in view of the nearly universal objective of mild mental retardation programs to stimulate the development of skills that allow individuals to be self-supporting and function independently as adults. Several chapters in this section address various aspects of social competence.

A final theme apparent in several of the chapters is the link between extreme poverty and mild mental retardation. This link is complex. The overwhelming majority of mildly mentally retarded persons do come from poverty circumstances; however, the overwhelming majority of persons in poverty circumstances do not become mildly mentally retarded. These two generalizations have been reported throughout the 20th century for numerous population groups, both white and minority, throughout the Eastern and Western worlds. The link of poverty and mild mental retardation provides an explanation for the overrepresentation of minority students in educational programs for this diagnostic construct, a phenomenon that continues to exist despite extensive and controversial litigation throughout the 1970s and 1980s. Reschly discusses this litigation and related issues in his chapter, along with the enormous subsequent influence on the diagnostic construct of mild mental retardation.

Although the themes discussed here are far from new, the character and substance of recent research have been markedly influenced by the change dynamics in mild mental retardation. These dynamics of change over the past 10 years are prominent in several of the chapters and implicit in others. They include the factors of (a) litigation; (b) labeling effects; (c) doubts about the efficacy of programs; (d) concerns about equity to minorities; and (e) the development of alternatives in the classification system, particularly for the learning disability classification. It is important to recognize these dynamic factors and to evaluate the character and sub-stance of each in this research synthesis. For example, doubt about the efficacy of programs has substantially influenced research and the provision of services. It is clear that this debate would have been very different if the efficacy data for special class programs in mild mental retardation were more positive. Numerous other examples of how these dynamics have shaped current research and service provision will become apparent as the reader examines the chapters that follow in this section.

The dynamics of the past 10 years, as well as the persistent themes in mild mental retardation for the past 8 decades, provide the context for these five chapters. The authors have attempted to clarify much of the present confusion while also providing direction for the future of research and services for the beaten and battered, but still distinguished, diagnostic construct of mild mental retardation.

Current Status of
the Mild Mental Retardation Construct:
Identification, Placement, and Programs

EDWARD A. POLLOWAY, Ed.D.

Professor of Education
Lynchburg College
Lynchburg, VA 24501

J. DAVID SMITH, Ed.D.

Professor of Education
Lynchburg College

Abstract—The construct of mild retardation is discussed through a review of past and current practices and by presenting recommendations for the future. After an examination of the origins of the construct in the work of Goddard and of service delivery patterns which have been traditional in the field, specific influences that have subsequently affected the mild retardation population are identified and analyzed. The recent reduction in the number of students served in mild retardation programs is documented with reference to recent governmental prevalence studies. Implications are drawn for this smaller and lower functioning population for characteristics, placement, and curriculum. Needs and recommendations relative to identification, programming, and research are presented.

The field of mild mental retardation is struggling with a crisis of identity. Despite a proud professional history as the training ground for many eminent special educators, over the last 20 years a variety of challenges have had a significant impact on its status. Today there is an increasing need for resolution of this crisis through attention to the central issues of identification, eligibility and placement of students who are mildly retarded.

The factors which have been most important within the field of educable mental retardation (EMR) in the last decade have been the significant change in the population served and the redefinition of the concept of mild retardation. These changes have coincided with decreased professional interest and research in this field (Bartlett, 1979; Haywood, 1979). The interplay between the trend toward reduced professional involvement and the trend toward changes in the population has resulted in a rather dramatic lack of attention to demographic, programmatic, and research concerns about this population especially when compared to its relative status in special education in the early 1970s. As an example of this phenomenon, Prehm (1985) recently reported that 1984 manuscript submissions focused on mild retardation accounted for approximately 10% of the papers sent to the professional journal *Education and Training of the Mentally Retarded*, as against 90% in moderate, severe, or profound retardation.

The purpose of this chapter is to evaluate the mild mental retardation construct as it has evolved in recent years. In particular it will discuss historical and contemporary trends in definition and identification, the effects of these changes on the mildly retarded population and the implications of these changes for both placement and curriculum in special education. The chapter concludes with the presentation of a set of recommendations for the future.

Historical Perspectives

The chapter begins with a brief historical review in order to provide appropriate background both to the origins of the construct of mild retardation and to the traditional practices related to service delivery for this population. The discussion in this section addresses these two respective historical concerns.

7

Origins of the Mild MR Construct

The history of the construct of mild mental retardation in the United States can be traced directly to the work of Henry Goddard. While serving as Director of Research at the Training School for Feeble-Minded Boys and Girls in Vineland, New Jersey, Goddard coined the term "moron," derived from a Greek word meaning foolish. His intention in using this label was to designate children and adults who were "high grade defectives." Although many of Goddard's ideas have since been disproven (see Gould, 1981; Smith, 1985), his work provides an apt starting point for the consideration of the mild retardation construct.

The term moron came to be widely applied to people who were not retarded seriously enough for it to be obvious to the casual observer and who had no clearly discernible brain damage from disease, injury, or birth defect. Morons were characterized by Goddard as being intellectually dull, socially inadequate, and morally deficient (Smith, 1985). Goddard used his study of the Kallikak family to argue that mild retardation was primarily hereditary in origin. Therefore he hypothesized that reproduction among mildly retarded people posed a significant threat to social order and to the advancement of civilization (Goddard, 1912).

Goddard, like other psychologists and educators who subscribed to the eugenic philosophy, initially felt that the only solution to the problems presented by morons in society was institutionalization. By segregating them their reproduction could be curtailed. The question of education for these mildly retarded people was moot; they were considered incapable of substantial academic achievement. Institutions were charged only with protecting mildly retarded persons from the pitfalls and dangers of living in society and, more importantly, with protecting society from the ills which the mildly retarded would create if not controlled (Goddard, 1912).

Goddard eventually modified his views and came to believe that mildly retarded persons existed in such great numbers that they could not, and probably should not, all be housed in institutions. He argued that they could be taught to become useful "hewers of wood and drawers of water" with the correct kind of educational techniques (Goddard, 1928). He helped establish training programs for public school teachers of mentally retarded children at Vineland, in New York City, and in several other locations. His influence added force to an already growing movement for the establishment of public school special classes for mentally retarded children (Smith, 1985). This movement is further discussed below.

Traditional Service Delivery Practices

The history of public school services for mildly retarded students has been traced to 1896 with the first class for retarded children initiated in Providence,

Rhode Island (Hoffman, 1972). Early efforts to establish programs have been portrayed both as positive developments (MacMillan, 1982) and as mere responses to the emergence of compulsory school attendance and the subsequent need for segregated programs to deal with students difficult to teach in the regular classroom (Dunn, 1968; Hoffman, 1972).

Regardless of the motivation behind the creation of these first special programs, the concept clearly became an attractive one. Increasing financial support for special programs in the 1920s and 1930s ushered in a period of rapid growth in services available for educable mentally retarded students (Gardner & Nisonger, 1962; Johnson, 1962). During this time, the placement question of primary importance was that of separate special school versus regular school enrollment in special classes. Special educators in the 1930s and early 1940s were thus concerned with the question of integration on a fundamental level: Would handicapped students profit more from being schooled along with or apart from their nonhandicapped peers? Goldberg and Blackman (1965) summarized the arguments in favor of regular school placement as: closer conformity to democratic principles; academic and social benefits to retarded children from frequent association with their nonhandicapped peers; an increase in the appreciation by normal children of individual differences. They identified the following points that had been cited as supportive of special schools: more efficient, higher quality services; facilitation of the availability of auxiliary services; the absence of an unhealthy competitive environment.

In spite of the limited research on this issue, the consensus of professional thought moved toward the favoring of regular school-based programs which then provided impetus for the growth in the numbers of special classes. Data indicate an impressive increase in their prevalence during the middle of the century. By 1957, 46 states provided support for such classes (Mullen & Itkin, 1961). The number of retarded students served in the public schools increased by 400% between 1948 and 1966. By this latter date, 89.5% of all school divisions provided educable mentally retarded programs in the public schools with the vast majority being in the form of self-contained classes (Mackie, 1969).

Although the special class was clearly the most popular choice as a form of service delivery wherever special programs had been established, the question raised on a regular basis was: Are educable mentally retarded students' needs better met in special classes than in regular classrooms? Without question, the 1950s and 1960s were the zenith of research on this question of more efficacious placement; during this time a major effort was undertaken by numerous professionals to provide empirical resolution to the key question of the effectiveness of special classes (Polloway, 1984). Several comprehensive reviews (e.g., Cegelka & Tyler, 1970) analyzed the research published on this issue; the discussion below highlights some illustrative findings.

The efficacy studies primarily focused on the areas of academic achievement, personal-social adjustment, and postschool adjustment. The research on academic achievement can best be summarized as producing either insignificant findings or data in support of regular class placement. For example, Elenbogen (1957) reported more substantial gains for regular class educable mentally retarded students in both reading and arithmetic with several specific achievement subtests reflecting significantly higher levels of improvement. Similarly, Cassidy and Stanton (1959) reported superior achievement for regular class educable mentally retarded children with the caveat that this conclusion was most valid for relatively high IQ (70–75) students.

In terms of personal-social adjustment, a common assumption was that special classes were more beneficial. The data reported in the efficacy studies were not, however, consistent on this point. This was partially due to the inherent difficulties in studying the many facets of this domain. Several examples illustrate this point. Johnson and Kirk (1950) provided data on two studies of the social acceptance of mentally retarded students placed in regular classrooms. In both cases, the number of retarded children classified as *isolates* was nearly double that of their nonhandicapped peers while the number classified as *rejectees* was 10 times or greater. Thus integration in the regular class did not overcome segregation from peers; they concluded that the reason was primarily behavioral rather than academic or intellectual. Other studies reported varied results: positive findings for special classes (e.g., Elenbogen, 1957; Cassidy & Stanton, 1959), mixed results (e.g., Blatt, 1958; Mullen & Itkin, 1961), or data supportive of regular class placement (e.g., Meyerowitz, 1962).

In terms of postschool adjustment, research was generally supportive of special class training at the secondary level (e.g., Elenbogen, 1957; Porter & Milazzo, 1958). However, the studies collectively did not produce a great degree of confidence regarding the future of retarded students and, as Dunn (1973) later stated, the lack of success experienced by many handicapped students left special educators with little reason for optimism or complacency concerning the fate of their graduates.

The absence of consistent research supportive of special classes led Johnson (1962) to outline what he termed the paradox of special education: Educable mentally retarded students failed to make more significant progress in the special classroom despite better trained teachers, more money, lower student-teacher ratios, and uniquely designed programs. Clearly frustration had developed not only with the special class as primary service delivery model but also with the construct of mild retardation. These frustrations and concerns were most notable in the early 1970s during what Polloway (1984) identified as the abolitionist movement in special education.

Several reports and reviews typified the sentiments of the time (e.g., Lilly, 1970; Milazzo, 1970), with Dunn's (1968) classic treatise often credited with sounding the loudest of the many death knells for special classes. His stated purposes in writing the article included the desire to communicate the fact that: ". . . a large proportion of this so-called special education in its present form is obsolete and unjustifiable from the point of view of the pupils so placed" (Dunn, 1968, p. 6). While Dunn's focus was specifically on socio-culturally deprived students who had been labeled educable mentally retarded, others expanded on his concerns about special class programs.

The results of this trend toward the denigration of special classes affected not only the question of service delivery but also that of the concept of mild retardation itself. These cries for the abolition of special classes coincided historically with significant events in the process of identification in mild retardation that have ultimately modified the educable mentally retarded population while questioning the entire construct. These key trends and other related factors are discussed in the next section.

Variables Influencing Population Changes

In the past 15 years, a number of factors have influenced the diagnostic process in the field of mild retardation. This is particularly true of identification procedures. These factors have been most significant in their impact upon the subpopulation which Dunn (1973) referred to as "adaptive EMRs," that is, those individuals with a higher level of functioning, more advanced academic skills, and greater prospects for success in the regular classroom. The focus of this section is on how recent events have determined the nature of the population in educable mentally retarded programs by essentially reconceptualizing the construct and the identification of mild retardation.

Definitional Changes

The most obvious starting point for an analysis of the changes in the construct of mild retardation is the series of definitions of retardation advanced by the American Association on Mental Deficiency, which have clearly contributed to the current state of affairs. The publication of the 1973 classification manual (Grossman, 1973) as a replacement for the previous edition (Heber, 1959, 1961) resulted in the technical declassification of approximately 13% of the total population by lowering the ceiling IQ score from 85 to 70 (Wechsler scales). Despite the fact that the AAMD intended this ceiling score to be considered as a guideline subject to clinical judgment rather than as an absolute requirement (Begab, 1981), in practice the educable mentally retarded category increasingly became reserved for those with an IQ of 65 or lower (Gottlieb, 1981). The importance of considering the ceiling IQ of 70 as an approximation subject to clinical judgment has been reaffirmed in the AAMD's most recent revised definition (Grossman, 1983). This manual has advocated the removal of the use of standard deviations and has emphasized the use of 70 as an estimation of the IQ ceiling.

While the more recent AAMD definitions restricted the practice of identifying as mentally retarded students who had IQs in the upper 70s, probably of greater significance was their endorsement of the importance of adaptive behavior (AB), a position reflected in the regulations of *PL 94–142* and slowly acknowledged in educational practice. By complementing IQ with this second dimension, the definition clearly decreased the potential number of individuals who could accurately be identified as mentally retarded.

Litigation

Litigation has also played a major role in the change in the mildly retarded population, particularly by questioning the placement of minority group children. The two most significant cases, *Diana v. State Board of Education* (1970) and *Larry P. v. Riles* (1972), were concerned with the educational rights of Mexican-American and black children, respectively, in the California public school system. The basic assumption in both cases was that the placement of these children was based on discriminatory procedures and that such placement had a negative effect on their educational progress. Clearly discrimination was the major concern in the court's deliberations. As Reschly (1982) has pointed out, in *Larry P.* and related cases the key issue should have been the effectiveness of the programs, but the focus instead was primarily limited to criteria for placement. The specifics of these and related cases and their importance for the field of mild retardation will be further discussed in the next chapter. It is sufficient to note that MacMillan and his colleagues (MacMillan, 1982; MacMillan, Meyers, & Morrison, 1980) have reported that subsequent to the decisions in these cases 11,000 to 14,000 individuals were declassified from California educable mentally retarded programs, a trend which has continued to the present (Forness, 1985). Similar, though less dramatic results have been noted elsewhere, although substantial variance in prevalence figures between states has continued to be common (Gerber, 1984; Patrick & Reschly, 1982).

Early Intervention and Population Shifts

Another important factor which has influenced population trends in mild retardation has been early intervention. These efforts have included programs designed for poverty level, technically nonidentified children (and their parents) as well as for identified young handicapped children.

Early intervention programs for disadvantaged children have among their goals the prevention of mild retardation from psycho-social sources. These programs

have been well-documented and are fully discussed in volumes edited by Begab, Haywood, and Garber (1981). The evidence supporting such programs points to the alterability of intellectual levels for children deemed to be at high risk for mild retardation and related learning difficulties in school (e.g., Ramey & Haskins, 1981). The most impressive results have been limited to specific projects, but the data suggest that the application of these principles and procedures to poor families in general could significantly reduce the prevalence of retardation in the schools.

Although changes in identification and effective preschool programming reduced the prevalence of higher functioning, adaptive educable mentally retarded children in special education programs, there has been an increase in educable mentally retarded class enrollment of those children traditionally served in programs created for a lower functioning population. As MacMillan, Meyers, and Morrison (1980) accurately pointed out, the openings in such classes due to the decertification of former educable mentally retarded students have often been filled by children with more serious handicaps who previously would have been labeled moderately retarded and placed in trainable classes.

The most encouraging reason for this change has been the success of early intervention programs with preschool handicapped children. The work of Rynders, Spiker, and Horrobin (1978), for example, alerted professionals to one aspect in the shift in population in groups from trainable to educable classes. After reviewing data on Down syndrome children who participated in early intervention programs, Rynders et al. indicated a "temptation" to predict a 30-55% likelihood that such a child would subsequently function in the educable mentally retarded range. Their review of 29 studies of Down syndrome children indicated that for all three karyotypes (trisomy 21, translocation, and mosaicism), specific case examples were found with IQ scores above 70.

Conceptual Changes

Another major factor which has greatly influenced the identification of mild retardation and thus the nature of the population, has been the changes in the way that this handicap is conceptualized. The sociological perspective, often associated with the work of Mercer (e.g., 1970, 1973), has encouraged a more restrictive concept of retardation as a comprehensive impairment involving permanent incompetence. Such a concept is quite inconsistent with the typical picture of persons who have traditionally been classified as educable mentally retarded. This perspective is also inconsistent with the Grossman manual's (1983, p. 15) specification that retardation refers to current life status, which "carries no connotation of chronicity or irreversibility." The implications of this perspective are relevant to the discussion here.

As an alternative to the traditional use of IQ scores, Mercer developed the System of Multicultural Pluralistic Assessment (SOMPA) as an attempt to control bias in assessment (Mercer & Lewis 1977). The acceptance of the rationale underlying the SOMPA (with or without the use of the tool itself) would have some obvious effects on identification procedures in programs for mildly retarded students. First, it encourages the adjustment of IQ scores based on socio-cultural status, an effort that would dramatically increase scores for most minority children. Second, it emphasizes adaptive behavior outside of school while downplaying difficulties experienced within the school setting. Such procedures warrant careful scrutiny. If an assumption can be made that students are initially referred primarily by teachers for academic and behavioral deficits, then we must conclude that students are not adapting well within this environment and that IQ tests are not being used by psychologists to ". . . attempt to catch unwitting victims in their psychometric nets" (Reschly, 1982, p. 23). Thus, while changes in identification procedures stemming from the operationalizing of a sociological perspective would decrease the number of students eligible for services, they would not decrease the number of individuals who are in need of educational support services.

The consequences of such a decrease in population have been researched in several studies. Reschly (1981) estimated that the use of the measures and criteria built into SOMPA would result in a prevalence figure of less than 0.5% for mild mental retardation, clearly having a major effect on children no longer eligible for services. He concluded that while one half of those declassified were eligible for other special education services, the other students were not, in spite of continuing intellectual limitations and academic deficiencies. Similar consequences stemming from changes in identification criteria have been reported by Childs (1982), Fisher (1977) and Mascari and Forgnone (1982); data related to the results of these changes will be discussed later in the chapter.

Any shift in conceptualization as described above would result in a focus on a more seriously disabled group. An increasing number of states and local school divisions have begun the search for the so-called "truly retarded," that is, those demonstrating low competence across all social roles (Reschly, 1981). If declassification of individuals included only those previously misdiagnosed, a positive step toward the elimination of the major discriminatory effects of special education would be achieved. However, efforts to remove pupils who demonstrate primarily school-based problems ignores the initial reason for referral for services. As Reschly (1981) stated, ". . . the interest of declassification stems from concerns for social equity. The consequences of the methods required in order to achieve this social equity may extend far beyond what was anticipated" (p. 18).

Radical changes in the concept of mild retardation deserve close attention. Although courts, legislatures, or professionals can encourage such a shift, ". . . learning problems cannot be mandated or legislated away" (MacMillan, 1982, p. 316). Thus while a more restrictive concept of mild retardation (for example, one requiring an out-of-school focus for adaptive behavior deficits) might reduce the prevalence of identified educable mentally retarded students, the question remains as to whether such a change is in the best interests of those children who no longer are deemed eligible for services.

Professional Reluctance

The final, and arguably the most significant, factor which has influenced the construct by affecting the nature of the population in educable mentally retarded programs, has been the reluctance of professionals to place students in such programs. Perhaps due in part to a history of abuses in special class identification procedures as well as the fear of stigma stemming from labeling a child "mentally retarded," there has been substantial reduction in the willingness of school personnel to classify students. This reluctance may reflect at times a healthy fear of diagnostic error. The unfortunate consequence, however, has often been to deny special services to students with demonstrated need or to label the child as learning disabled and fit the individual's needs to the curriculum in programs in that area. Given the increasing disparity between the levels of functioning of the new, less adaptive educable mentally retarded students and of learning disabled students, placement in learning disabled programs may become as untenable as would the denial of services altogether.

Population Description

Several major implications for the "new EMR" population derive from the factors discussed above. First, the number of individuals identified as mentally retarded has decreased dramatically on the national level (Polloway & Smith, 1983; Gerber, 1984). Second, the general functioning level of the remaining educable mentally retarded population has decreased and thus the specific characteristics often ascribed to this population warrant further evaluation to verify their continued accuracy. Finally, any changes in functioning levels of students would dictate reconsiderations of placements and curricular choices.

Prevalence Trends

Polloway and Smith (1983) presented data from the Department of Education, Office of Special Education related to the overall decrease in numbers of students in mental retardation programs between the school years of 1976–77 and 1980–81. Given the fact that these years followed the passage of *PL 94–142* and thus that this reduction came in spite of an apparent federal mandate for increased identification efforts, it is significant to note that all but eight states and territories showed a decrease in the number of children served during this five-year period and furthermore that six of these eight did show a drop-off between 1979–80 and 1980–81. During the years covered by these data, the overall percentage decrease in retardation for the nation was 12.9%.

More recently Gerber (1984) and Algozzine and Korinek (1985) have evaluated population trends in specific categories of exceptional individuals. Gerber (1984) presented data from the annual report to Congress on *PL 94–142* on prevalence figures for the states for the years 1976–77 through 1982–83. Using the first and last years as parameters, the overall national prevalence for retardation dropped with decreases noted in 33 states, no change in 6 states and increases in 11 states. In several of the states with no change or increases however there was actually an initial increase subsequently followed by a trend toward reduction. Of related interest is the fact that the incidence of learning disabilities increased in every state during this period.

Data from the same governmental report was used by Algozzine and Korinek (1985) in their analysis. They reported an approximate 1.85% decrease yearly (for 1978–1982) in the national incidence of mental retardation. In addition they projected that the mentally retarded population would decrease by 20% over a 10-year period if the current rate continued.

In states where the reduction in numbers has occurred, it has had the direct effect of declassifying those students previously termed the most "adaptive" and of making the determination of eligibility unlikely for other children considered borderline cases. As a consequence, programs in states where major changes in identification have taken place have been left to serve what MacMillan and Borthwick (1980) termed "a more patently disabled group" (p. 155). Such a change clearly has implications for the specific characteristics found in mildly retarded students.

Characteristics of "New EMRs"

Polloway and Smith (1983) discussed emerging characteristics of the "new EMRs" by utilizing a comparison with a list of general characteristics provided by Dunn (1973) as an elaboration on Rothstein (1971). Although such a comparison presents a somewhat superficial analysis, it does provide a point of orientation.

Rothstein (1971) initially identified a series of generalizations that were considered to be more accurate for students classified as educable mentally retarded than for students within the general school population. As Dunn (1973) presented the list, students who were mildly retarded were more likely:

(1) to have met defeat, frustration, and rejection in the regular grades where they were first placed; (2) to have exhibited substantial behavior disorders in general education; (3) to be from racial or ethnic minority groups; (4) to have parents who place little value on education; (5) to have inadequate health and nutritional provisions; (6) to be unclean and unkempt; (7) to live in poverty and deprivation; (8) to be boys rather than girls; (9) to come from broken or disorganized homes; (10) to be seriously retarded in school achievement; (11) to have restricted oral language skills in Standard English; (12) to have obtained IQ scores ranging between 65 and 78 on individualized tests of verbal intelligence administered in Standard English. (p. 131)

Dunn (1973) accurately predicted the fact that dramatic changes in the 1970s would greatly affect the nature of the population. In terms of the 12 specific characteristics listed above, the following observations appear justifiable.

Although the number of children from poverty backgrounds remains high in educable mentally retarded classes, the cultural-familial stereotype fostered by a number of the above characteristics has increasingly become a misconception of this population. While the disproportionate number of minority children in educable mentally retarded classes is still being reported (e.g., Polloway, Epstein, Patton, Cullinan, & Luebke, 1986), the designation of mildly retarded children collectively as cultural-familial, suggesting the interaction of genetic and environmental factors in the absence of specific pathological causes (Heber, 1961), is now less accurate. Anecdotal reports also indicate that the population of children served in educable mentally retarded classes is increasingly composed of individuals affected by other etiological factors (e.g., chromosomal anomaly).

The first characteristic concerning regular class failure should be reviewed in light of the fact that a larger number of educable mentally retarded children are likely to enter such programs directly from preschool handicapped programs or to at least have been referred earlier in their school careers. Such a change would seem to suggest re-analysis of the classic data on outer-directedness and failure set (see Zigler, 1966), which have been traditional foundations for an understanding of the learning styles of children who are mildly retarded.

The reference to substantial behavior disorders was a reflection of the fact that, given deficiencies in intellectual and academic functioning, the referral of a given child was more likely to have been made when he or she had experienced difficulty with conforming to rules in the regular classroom (Polloway & Patton, 1986). The advent and growth of programs for disturbed or disordered children has probably decreased the prevalence of such behavioral problems in educable mentally retarded classes, although it is likely that concomitant behavioral disorders may continue to increase chances for referral and thus continue to bias identification procedures. Several recent studies have investigated the presence of behavior problems in this population and reported inconsistent findings.

Polloway, Epstein, and Cullinan (1985) reported data that confirmed that mildly retarded students are more likely to exhibit behavioral and emotional problems than their non-handicapped peers. These researchers analyzed a total of 330 such comparisons based on teacher reports on the Behavior Problem Checklist (Quay, 1977) and found that 40.6% (or 134) of the comparisons were indicative of significantly more problems in educable mentally retarded students. Overall, elementary school educable mentally retarded pupils differed from their non-handicapped same-sex peers on the most items with a significant difference found for this group on 30 of 55 items for males and 36 of 55 items for females.

Two direct observational studies provide another perspective on this issue. Forness, Guthrie, and MacMillan (1981) reported that levels of on-task behavior were quite high for educable mentally retarded children and compared favorably with data previously reported on non-handicapped children. In a related study, Russell and Forness (1985) reported that over 90% of the educable mentally retarded (and TMR) students exhibited infrequent disruptive behavior. Although these studies are difficult to compare to the data reported by Polloway et al. (1985), clearly additional attention is warranted to further clarify the behavioral characteristics of students with mild retardation.

Given the assumption of a more handicapped population, the generalization focused on deficits in school achievement should be of greater concern. The discrepancy between chronological age and achievement level would be expected to be greater, thus presenting a challenge to teachers concerning the possibilities of having students who are mildly retarded reach at least a level of partial literacy.

With regard to oral language development, the shift toward a lower functioning educable mentally retarded population would likely be related to increased probability of substantial language delay in this group such as reported, for example, with Down syndrome children even after successful early intervention (e.g., Hayden & Dmitriev, 1975; Rynders, et al., 1978). Considerations of the possible interaction between language delay and dialectical variance associated with cultural difference will be critical in the educational assessment of the population and in the subsequent development of intervention programs.

The most obvious change between the set of characteristics framed in 1973 and the current status is in terms of intellectual level. The range of IQ scores within programs for students who are mildly retarded has been limited significantly by the more widespread adoption of the cut-off established by the American Association on Mental Deficiency (Grossman, 1973). Although in practice this figure has not been universally adopted by all states (Huberty, Killer, & ten Brink, 1980; Patrick & Reschly, 1982), the fact remains that accepted cut-off scores above 70 are currently far less common. A frequent result of this change has been the creation of an educational no-man's land where students whose scores are between 70 and 80 or 85 are not eligible for any special services (Forness & Kavale, 1984; Forness, 1985; Smith, Polloway, & Smith, 1978).

Current Placement Alternatives

The preceding historical review of educational programs highlighted the fact that special classes had been the preferred service delivery model until being attacked in the 1960s and 1970s. Much of the negative rhetoric of the early 1970s was eventually replaced by efforts to determine the appropriate niche for the individual within the expanding variety of options available to exceptional children and adolescents in the public schools. It is this more recent concern regarding placement that serves as a basis for evaluating placement practices as they relate to the characteristics of the current educable mentally retarded population.

Cascade of Services

Consistent with the spirit of *PL 94-142*, the concept of cascade of services reflects the assumption that all students must be viewed as individuals and served in the least restrictive environment specifically determined for them. However the focus on individualization belied reality as defined by many educators; the mainstream was regularly touted as the most efficacious placement for the majority of educable mentally retarded students. This sentiment was clearly expressed by Heller (1982): ". . . the interpretation of ambiguous and weak results as support for mainstreaming (or, more accurately, evidence against the value of self-contained classrooms) is consistent with the thrust of *PL 94–142* toward education in the least restrictive environment" (p. 49).

The last decade has been a period of increased emphasis on resource and consultation models as a basis for service delivery to mildly handicapped students. In a comprehensive review, Sindelar and Deno (1978) reviewed 11 studies of resource rooms, four of which dealt with the question of resource versus special class placement of students with mild retardation. Results were mixed in studies of achievement gains with one study favouring the special class setting, two the resource room, and one other reporting comparable gains for both placements. Although some data indicated social adjustment benefits from resource programming (e.g., Walker, 1974), Sindelar and Deno indicated that no generalizable conclusions could be made in that domain. Again, as had been true of the original research on the efficacy of special versus regular class placement, design problems hindered interpretation. Based on the limited research relative to resource programming, Sindelar and Deno (1978) urged caution. They concluded that ". . . while resource programming in service delivery multiplies, the efficacy of programs and program variables has not been established" (p. 18).

The relative absence of research in the last decade underscores the fact that the placement issue in this era was clearly not predicated on a strong empirical base. Given the spirit of *PL 94–142*, it had become somewhat indefensible to argue for a given placement option for any *group* of students since program decisions were to be reached on an *individual* basis. This concern also ethically interfered with the option of using alternative designs for research; for example, the stress on the importance of random assignment of students to placement alternatives would now have to be considered as a possible violation of the rights of the individual child to be placed in the most appropriate educational setting.

Decision-Making Concerns

The essential placement concern at the current time is whether the population of students remaining after the legal, sociological, and educational challenges to educable mentally retarded programs of the early 1970s, could be successful in the integrated placements inspired by the implementation of *PL 94–142*. Several points are relevant to resolution of this issue.

Research on declassification is particularly illustrative of this placement concern. As noted earlier, Reschly (1981) estimated that implementation of the measures and criteria built into SOMPA (Mercer & Lewis, 1977) would result in a prevalence figure of under 0.5% for mild mental retardation, thus having a major effect on those children no longer eligible for services. Similarly Childs (1982) determined that the use of third percentile point cut off on SOMPA's *Adaptive Behavior Inventory for Children* in conjunction with deficits in measured intelligence would result in the declassification of 80% of the educable mentally retarded population which he researched. Although use of the SOMPA is not currently widespread, nevertheless these data do illustrate the effects of a shift in the meaning of the construct of mild retardation.

A recent study reported by Mascari and Forgnone (1982) followed the status of students in Florida four years after 44% of the total educable mentally retarded population had been declassified. They reported that 58% of the children studied had since been re-referred with 17% returning to educable mentally retarded classes. Reschly's (1981) review of relevant studies indicated that of those removed from educable mentally retarded programs one half were eligible for other special services while the remaining individuals were not, despite continuing intellectual and academic limitations.

It is also important to consider what data are available on programs for educable mentally retarded students who remain eligible. MacMillan and Borthwick (1980) reported that the "new EMRs," identified under a restrictive diagnostic construct and thus remaining after the effects of declassification in California in the 1970s, were being successfully mainstreamed only in nonacademic subjects. Polloway et al. (1986) reported that in

Illinois only approximately 10% of educable mentally retarded students were in regular classes for greater than 50% of the school day and that a substantial percentage of the group were integrated for only very brief periods of time. Of course these data need to be qualified due to local and regional variance in terms of the type of children being identified (Patrick & Reschly, 1982). This point is particularly important in states like California that have adopted more stringent eligibility guidelines. As noted earlier, in these instances the educable mentally retarded population is likely to be more severely debilitated and thus less likely to be successfully mainstreamed for a significant portion of the instructional day.

The shift in population toward a lower functioning group offers an interesting historical perspective. As Meyers, MacMillan, and Yoshida (1980) noted, the relatively high IQ students who tended to fare better in regular classes as reported in the early efficacy studies are now unlikely to be identified. The low IQ students who performed better in special classes in several studies (e.g., Myers, 1976; Goldstein, Moss, & Jordan, 1965; Thurstone, 1959) may more closely resemble the students remaining in current programs. Thus the higher functioning population that many individuals (e.g., Budoff & Gottlieb, 1976; Luftig, 1980; Robinson & Robinson, 1965; Stanton & Cassidy, 1964) expressed greatest concern about vis-à-vis the appropriateness of special class placement are simply no longer identified as mildly retarded in many states. As Forness and Kavale (1984) noted, these students "may indeed be mainstreamed, but in the poorest sense" (p. 241), that is they simply are not eligible for support services.

Curricular Considerations

Recent years have seen greater attention in special education to the importance of differentiated curricular approaches. This emphasis on the selection of appropriate models for curriculum is characterized by the work of Alley and Deshler (1979) and Vergason (1983) and reflects the need for selecting a model best suited to meet the needs of individual students. Such a focus is particularly important for students who are mildly retarded, especially for those who represent the "new EMR" population. The focus of this section is on key considerations that should be addressed in curriculum building for these students.

Curricular Models

Although many professionals have for years stressed the importance of training for educable mentally retarded students that is focused on critical daily living skills or persistent life problems (see Kolstoe & Frey, 1965), the more recent emphasis on integrated placements has influenced the nature of the curriculum to which students are exposed. Thus in spite of the discrediting of the validity of the "watered down" curriculum, mainstreaming in effect has encouraged emphasis on the skills dominant in the regular class curriculum. Bartlett (1979) concluded that a primary outcome of this change was a questionable emphasis on a purely academic curriculum. Given the needs of the current population, this curricular orientation has become even less warranted. Clearly now there is a great need to evaluate the balance between an academic focus which may facilitate mainstreaming with a practical orientation concerned more with postschool adjustment (Forness & Kavale, 1984).

One important contributing factor to the academically-oriented curriculum has been the trend in some states toward noncategorical special education programs. Assumptions of overlap in characteristics between mild retardation, learning disabilities, and emotional disturbance have provided a basis for the related assumption that these individuals have similar curricular needs. Those areas of categorical overlap that have been noted in the literature (e.g., Hallahan & Kauffman, 1977), are based, however, on suppositions which require renewed scrutiny.

This need for reevaluation stems directly from the central assumption on which noncategorical programming is based. As Hallahan and Kauffman (1977, p. 147) stated ". . . grouping according to behavioral characteristics is more advisable than grouping according to traditional categories." The merits of such an orientation are apparent; however, consideration must be given to whether behavioral characteristics may be more discrepant across categories than previously hypothesized and thus whether there is an increased degree of difference between representatives of these three categorical groupings.

The significant increase in the number of children being served under the learning disabled label (Gerber, 1984; Algozzine & Korinek, 1985) certainly includes many children previously identified as mildly retarded. Thus many "retarded" students to whom the noncategorical movement most appropriately applied have already been subsumed within the learning disabled category. Research attention should be focused on determining whether the curricular needs of remaining educable mentally retarded students correspond to those of the majority of learning disabled students, particularly in light of the frequent remedial emphasis of learning disabled programs.

The implication for teacher education programs has more to do with the content of training programs than with their identification by categorical as opposed to generic labels (e.g., mildly handicapped). Effective teaching methods selected according to task requirements and individual student responses certainly cut across categories and especially across mild retardation, learning disabilities, and behavior disorders. It is rather in the area of curriculum that differences potentially present the most significant concern. Noncategorical training programs, such as those generically identified for mildly handicapped students, need to eschew a narrow focus on academic and remedial concerns in favor

of a more comprehensive focus. Several aspects of curricular development are dicussed below.

Curricular Focus

The orientation of curriculum in programs for students who are mildly retarded requires attention to two premises that derive from the previous discussions. First, the importance of social skills training must be considered both for its facilitation of mainstreaming as well as for its postschool benefits for handicapped individuals. Second, the focus within special education programs must reflect an appropriate blending of academic and career skills that are relevant to success beyond the school setting.

Social Skills

It is illustrative to reconsider the study reported by MacMillan and Borthwick (1980). They indicated that mainstreaming did not appear to be feasible when applied to educable mentally retarded children identified under a very restrictive definition; integration efforts were generally limited to nonacademic periods during the school day. These findings can be interpreted as support for the importance of social skills training as a complement to academic instruction as a key factor in the establishment of successful integrated progams. Research on social variables relative to integrated programs is critical to an understanding of the contribution of such training.

Reese-Dukes and Stokes (1978) reported on a program in which 33 educable mentally retarded students were completely mainstreamed into regular classes. Social acceptance of integrated mildly retarded and non-retarded students was determined through a sociometric scale. In all areas evaluated, the mildly retarded children received significantly lower social acceptance scores than did the nonretarded students. Two possible conclusions were implicit in the study: mainstream placement should be reconsidered or training must be provided to assist in the adjustment and acceptance of educable mentally retarded students when mainstreamed.

Luftig (1980) reviewed research on the effects of placement on the self-concept of retarded students and indicated that students with higher IQ scores (71–85) were more successful in the regular class while a lower IQ group (49–70) with poor reading skills maintained higher levels of self-concept in special classes. Given that students representing the former group would now rarely be placed in educable mentally retarded programs, the key finding for our discussion concerns the latter, lower IQ group. Luftig concluded ". . . to place a child in an educational environment in which he cannot maintain feelings of self-worth may actually increase rather than decrease the restrictiveness in the school environment" (p. 14).

Gottlieb and Leyser (1981) reviewed the literature on the social aspects of mainstreaming and concluded that unless formal measures were taken to involve students in daily school activities, it was unlikely that they would become accepted members of the class. They indicated that the absence of active interaction would result in an education that was not an improvement on what was available in the special class. Similarly Kehle and Barclay (1979) indicated that integrative efforts were more likely to be successful after students learned prosocial behaviors and corrected inappropriate behaviors; they asserted that teachers should not assume that exposure to nonretarded peers alone would be sufficient. Semmel and Cheney (1979) suggested structured group interactions and an increase in positive social behavior by teachers toward retarded students as ways to promote social acceptance in the regular class. In reference to handicapped students in general, Gresham (1982) pointed to the inability of past mainstreaming efforts to achieve increased social interaction, social acceptance, and behavioral modeling by handicapped students. Consistent with the reports cited above, he also stressed that systematic efforts at social skills training are requisite to student success in these areas and thus in mainstream environments.

Functional Skills

If the assumption that educable mentally retarded students, at least those identified under a relatively restrictive construct of retardation, are unlikely to be served primarily in regular class-based programs (i.e., resource programs) is correct, then special class programs must be tailored to meet the reality of their needs. This focus would be consistent with instruction in functional daily living skills and career preparation.

A primary career education orientation presents some difficulties for implementation in some schools since it is not consistent with the emphasis in regular education on "back-to-the-basics." As Smith and Dexter (1980) noted, this emphasis could have negative effects on curriculum for students who are mildly retarded if it resulted in a fixation on academic skills, and, thus, a possible exclusion of life skills orientation within the more comprehensive curriculum needed for most educable mentally retarded students. In a similar way, the functional orientation can also prove problematic if recent national calls for excellence in education lead to a more strictly academic focus with less room for curricular individualization.

The question of an appropriate curriculum is most critical for adolescents since it is at this level that training for postschool adjustment must proceed in earnest. However curriculum development for adolescents is often hindered in many states by the requirement of minimum competency tests. While secondary programs can be most effective by focusing on vocational and practical considerations, an emphasis on tests with unproven relevance for adult success are likely to have a negative

impact on educable mentally retarded programs by encouraging more restrictive curricular alternatives (Cohen, Safran, & Polloway, 1980).

The ultimate measure of effectiveness of instruction and appropriateness of curriculum must come from an evaluation of adult outcomes. Edgerton has demonstrated convincingly that the concept of the "six-hour retarded child" must be carefully examined since he has reported (Edgerton, 1984; Koegel & Edgerton, 1984) that mildly retarded children do not typically grow up and simply disappear into normal community life. Rather they often remain socially isolated, set apart by the same limitations that handicapped them while in school. Their continuing difficulties in reading, writing and calculating disables them socially and vocationally. Finding the means of articulating the curriculum of educable mentally retarded programs within the realities of the prospective adult lives of the students they serve must be a critical concern and thus must lead professionals toward the careful consideration of adult goals as a basis for programming especially at the secondary level.

Needs and Recommendations

This chapter has dealt with a variety of topics concerned with the construct of mild mental retardation and corresponding identification issues and concerns relative to appropriate placement and curricular needs. The purpose of this section is essentially to summarize this information while providing specific recommendations for the future of this field. The specific points to be discussed are divided into the three areas of: construct and identification, programming, and research. In each area specific recommendations are made and/or needs are identified.

Construct and Identification

The following points target relevant concerns that deal with the refinement of the construct of mild retardation specifically as they relate to operationalization within the identification process.

INTELLECTUAL FUNCTIONING LEVEL

Adherence to level of intellectual functioning as stated in the definition within the most recent edition of the AAMD manual (Grossman, 1983) is recommended because it eliminates adherence to a rigid cutoff point for IQ while reflecting the importance of careful professional judgment. As stated in the manual:

Significantly subaverage is defined as IQ of 70 or below on standardized measures of intelligence. This upper limit is intended as a guideline; it could be extended upward through IQ 75 or more, depending on the reliability of the intelligence test used. This particularly applies in schools and similar settings if behavior is impaired and clinically determined to be due to deficits in reasoning and judgment. (p. 11)

The flexibility implicitly recommended in establishing this ceiling score yields the additional advantage of recognition of the importance of potential measurement error inherent in the specific test used. It also represents a move away from the artificial and unwarranted use of standard deviations as cutoff points both as a ceiling for retardation as well as for subclassification according to levels of functioning. These positive moves which represent greater flexibility than present in previous AAMD definitions (Grossman, 1973, 1977) are consistent with the sentiments expressed by others in the field (Kidd, 1984). While the use of an IQ score of 70 still remains arbitrary, it nevertheless has practical benefits of which the foremost is its general familiarity and wide acceptance by professionals (Zigler, Balla, & Hodapp, 1984; Zigler, 1984).

Adaptive behavior

The concept of the six-hour retarded child (President's Committee on Mental Retardation, 1970) has often been cited as a basis for declassifying children who are apparently adapting well outside of the school setting. However, what must not be overlooked is that many students who are reasonably successful in relatively unstructured social or recreational activities may nevertheless have significant difficulty in school in the areas of academic achievement, social skill development, and coping abilities. Therefore, assessment of adaptive behavior must be considered to be twofold in nature and thereby inclusive of both in and out-of-school concerns. While the latter may respond at least reasonably well to assessment via currently available commercial adaptive behavior scales such as the AAMD Adaptive Behavior Scales or the Adaptive Behavior Inventory for Children (see Reschly, 1982), it is apparent from the most cursory review that the assessment of in-school adaptive behavior is not a primary feature of these instruments. Rather this aspect must be evaluated on formal and informal academic achievement tests, direct behavioral observation measures, and teacher rating scales.

Relationship of IQ and AB: The relative weighting to be given to intelligence test scores and adaptive behavior data respectively is perhaps the most difficult feature of the identification process to operationalize. These two dimensions were represented as equal concerns in Grossman's 1973 and 1977 definitions. However a relatively minor wording difference between the 1977 and the 1983 definitions concerning the relationship between intelligence and adaptive behavior is noteworthy. While the 1973 and 1977 definitions indicated that adaptive behavior deficits *exist concurrently* with low intelligence,

the 1983 manual indicated that adaptive behavior deficits *result from or are associated with* low intelligence. Although the change is a relatively subtle one, it tends to reinforce the apparent primary importance of the IQ dimension. In addition it has been clear in research practices that equality between the duel dimensions has rarely been realized (Smith & Polloway, 1979) and that in the diagnostic process IQ has continued to play the more significant role. This practice is due not only to the fact that IQ scores are more often viewed as "clean" since they are more objective measures but it also reflects the inherent limitations in the AB construct (Zigler et al., 1984).

While the question of whether subaverage intelligence or deficient adaptive behavior is most central to the essence of retardation will no doubt continue to be argued, the practical reality is that IQ will remain the primary determinant of retardation perhaps until other, more defensible assessment tools are developed (Zucker, Polloway, 1987). Adaptive behavior can thus best be viewed as functioning within the identification process by serving a confirming role in one of the following ways: by justifying eligibility for services for individuals with IQs above 70 who have significant adaptive behavior deficits which interfere with school performance or postschool adjustment; by encouraging scrutiny of the accuracy of the mental retardation label for individuals with IQs below 70 who have demonstrated adequate adaptive skills thus serving as a "check against excessive reliance upon measures of intelligence" (Sargent, 1981, p. 3); and, by making a primary contribution to educational decisions regarding both placement (e.g., special versus regular class programs) as well as curricular orientation (Polloway, 1985).

Programmatic Concerns

The second area to be addressed is that of program considerations. Three specific factors warrant attention in this area: school placement, labeling, and teacher preparation.

Educational Placement

Given the change in the population of students who are mentally retarded as discussed throughout this chapter, the emphasis on mainstream programs that was fairly common in the 1970s clearly merits closer attention in the 1980s (MacMillan & Borthwick, 1980; Polloway, 1984). It seems increasingly likely that special class programs are now more appropriate for the majority of remaining educable mentally retarded students especially in those states where declassification of educable mentally retarded students has been most vigorous since in those instances the more adaptive students would no longer be found eligible for such programs.

This assumption is particularly valid for older students due to the increased discrepancy in ability between educable mentally retarded and nonhandicapped students and due to the more common subject- (as against child-) orientation of secondary teachers (Reschly, 1984). This conclusion should not, however, be interpreted as a retreat from integration efforts. This is important since social skills must ultimately be refined through structured interaction with nonhandicapped students. Flexible service delivery arrangements that reflect a true range of alternative placements may not only facilitate this learning process but also may assist in the alleviation of the possible stigma related to special class placement. As Forness and Kavale (1984) noted, mainstreaming as an effective procedure must be separated from mainstreaming as a policy.

LABELING

The search for a new label has been an ongoing process in this field and a task that continues to receive attention (Sobsey, 1984; Zigler & Balla, 1981). While the success of such an effort is perhaps doomed from the outset, the potential effects of labels should be minimized by practices in the schools. Efforts must be made to avoid overt labeling of children while rather stressing the functions of programs. At the same time it is important to acknowledge the limited data base that exists on the deleterious effects of the mental retardation label on students (see MacMillan, Jones, & Aloia, 1974; Reschly & Lamprecht, 1979), to accept the fact that most discussions on the issue have not been based on research (Reschly, 1982), and to consider the often underemphasized advantages stemming from labeling such as effective interventions and social services (Zigler, 1984).

Two approaches to the labeling process might be worthy of consideration. One approach would be to develop a system based on the labeling of services instead of children, in the way that was initially proposed in the field of learning disabilities (Lilly, 1982). Providing programs under a designation such as academic and adaptive-skills training could provide a beginning point in serving those students who no longer meet the more stringent educable mentally retarded identification criteria or for whom there is serious professional reluctance to label. Recognition by federal and state agencies that this type of alternative approach is an appropriate one for children who have experienced educational retardation would certainly be preferable to the two current alternatives: requiring that the label "mentally retarded" be inappropriately affixed as a condition for eligibility or failing to provide programs for those whose educational needs are not being met satisfactorily in the regular classroom.

A second approach to current labeling practices also merits consideration. For students who remain in educable mentally retarded programs or who are otherwise likely to be destaffed primarily because of professional and parent fear of the label a new term may be in order. Consistent with Zigler and Balla's (1981, p. 198) call for ". . . some term in the area of intelligence that is analogous to the term 'short' when referring to height," we suggest consideration of the term *educationally delayed*. While it encourages a comprehensive view of the deficits of the population, it refrains from the powerful connotations that have come to be associated with "mentally retarded." For similar reasons the terms educationally retarded, educationally handicapped, and academic aptitude handicap have been suggested (Reschly, 1982, 1984).

PERSONNEL PREPARATION

Discussion earlier in this chapter touched on some implications for teacher education of current trends related to the construct and identification of mild retardation. To reiterate, we do not advocate the necessity of a strictly categorical approach to training for future teachers of mildly retarded students; rather the concern should be for the breadth of training for these individuals. In particular prospective teachers must: be aware of the concept of differentiated curricular approaches and be able to evaluate facets of the child and the school situation in order to decide on the most appropriate alternative; be competent to teach career-oriented portions of the curriculum in addition to the academic domains within a comprehensive special class program; and, be able to design placement alternatives which acknowledge the benefits of the integrated environment for the student along with the need of students for preparation before being placed in such environments.

Research

The recency of changes in the mild retardation field has not yet allowed for the appropriate evaluation of common practices related to eligibility for services, educational placement, and curricular design. This absence of critical research analysis is of particular concern given the revision that this population has undergone in many states. Due to these changes the rich research foundation developed in prior decades has been rendered seriously dated and of questionable merit for contemporary evaluation of programmatic issues (Gottlieb, 1982; MacMillan, Meyers, & Morrison, 1980).

Polloway and Smith (1983) identified the following areas of significant research need directly related to these recent population changes:

> comparison of the cognitive and functional levels of the "new" EMR student with "traditional" EMR students; the effectiveness of mainstream procedures with this population; the result of destaffing procedures on former EMR students with attention to where they are placed and how they fare; analysis of changes in the frequency of clinical types (e.g., Down syndrome) of retardation within EMR classes; and analysis of the relative benefits and potential effects of the focus on out-of-school versus in-school adaptive behavior. (p. 157)

Some other areas which present important research questions include the evaluation of remedial versus other curricular models for students who are mildly retarded and the replication of the classic studies on the learning of educable mentally retarded students (Forness & Kavale, 1984). Finally, cogent to this concern, in a recent survey of professionals concerning critical research issues facing the field (Polloway & Epstein, 1985), the two most often selected topics were vocational and career education and postschool adjustment. Both reflect a concern for the success of mildly retarded individuals after current school placement. Many professionals strongly feel that the most critical need for research in special education for mildly retarded students is in the development and evaluation of programs to insure that individuals maximize their level of functioning beyond the school experience.

References

Algozzine, B., & Korinek, L. (1985). Where is special education for students with high prevalence handicaps going? *Exceptionl Children, 51*, 388–394.

Alley, G. R., & Deshler, D. D. (1979). *Teaching the learning disabled adolescent: Strategies and methods.* Denver, CO: Love Publishing.

Bartlett, R. H. (1979). Mental retardation—Where does the future lie? *Education and Training of the Mentally Retarded, 14*, 3–4.

Begab, M. J. (1981). Issues in the prevention of psychosocial retardation. In M. J. Begab, H. C. Haywood, & H. L. Garber (Eds.), *Psychosocial influences in retarded performance: Issues and theories in development* (Vol. 1 pp. 3–28). Baltimore, MD, University Park Press.

Begab, M. J., Haywood, H. C., & Garber, H. L. (Eds.). (1981). *Psychosocial influences in retarded performance: Issues and theories in development* (Vol. 1). Baltimore, MD, University Park Press.

Blatt, B. (1958). The physical, personality, and academic status of children who are mentally retarded attending special classes as compared with children who are mentally retarded atending regular classes. *American Journal of Mental Deficiency, 62*, 810–818.

Budoff, M., & Gottlieb, J. (1976). Special-class EMR children mainstreamed: A study of an aptitude (learning potential) × treatment interaction. *American Journal of Mental Deficiency, 81*, 1–11.

Cassidy, V. M., & Stanton, J. E. (1959). An investigation of factors involved in the educational placement of mentally retarded children: A study of differences between children in regular and special classes in Ohio. Columbus, OH: Ohio State University. (ERIC Document Reproduction Service No. ED 002 752).

Cegelka, W. J., & Tyler, J. L. (1970). The efficacy of special class placement for the mentally retarded in proper perspective. *Training School Bulletin, 67* (1), 33–67.

Childs, R. E. (1982). A study of the adaptive behavior of retarded children and the resultant effects of this use in the diagnosis of mental retardation. *Education and Training of the Mentally Retarded, 17*, 109–113.

Cohen, S. B., Safran, J., & Polloway, E. A. (1980). Minimum competency testing and its implications for retarded students. *Education and Training of the Mentally Retarded,* 15, 250–255.

Diana v. State Board of Education (1970). C–70–37 (RFP, District Court for Northern California).

Dunn, L. M. (1968). Special education for the mildly retarded: Is much of it justifiable? *Exceptional Children, 35*, 5–22.

Dunn, L. M. (1973). Children with mild general learning disabilities. In L. M. Dunn (Ed.), *Exceptional children in the schools,* (p. 126–188). New York: Holt, Rinehart, & Winston.

Edgerton, R. N. (Ed.) (1984). *Lives in process: Mildly retarded adults in a large city.* Washington, D.C.: AAMD Monographs, No. 6.

Elenbogen, M. L. (1957). A comparative study of some aspects of academic and social adjustment of two groups of mentally retarded children in special classes and in regular grades. (Doctoral dissertation, Northwestern University, 1975). *Dissertation Abstracts International, 17*, 2496. (Microfilms No. 57–4033).

Fisher, A. T. (1977). *Adaptive behavior in non-biased assessment: Effects on special education* (Report No. CG 012 181). San Francisco, CA: American Psychological Association. (ERIC Document Reproduction Service No. ED 150 514).

Forness, S. R. (1985). Effects of public policy at the state level: California's impact on MR, LD, and ED categories. *Remedial and Special Education, 6* (3), 36–43.

Forness, S. R., Guthrie, D., & MacMillan, D. L. (1981). Classroom behavior of mentally retarded children across different classroom settings. *Journal of Special Education, 15*, 497–509.

Forness, S. R., & Kavale, K. A. (1984). Education of the mentally retarded: A note on policy. *Education and Training of the Mentally Retarded, 19*, 239–245.

Gardner, W. I., & Nisonger, H. W. (1962). *A manual on program development in mental retardation.* Washington, D.C.: American Association of Mental Deficiency.

Gerber, M. M. (1984). The Department of Education's sixth annual report to Congress on PL 94–142: Is Congress getting the full story? *Exceptional Children, 51*, 209–224.

Goddard, H. H. (1912). *The Kallikak family: A study in the heredity of feeblemindedness.* New York: MacMillan.

Goddard, H. H. (1928). Feeblemindedness: A question of definition. *Journal of Psycho-Asthenics, 33*, 219–227.

Goldberg, I. I., & Blackman, L. S. (1965). The special class: Parasitic, endophytic, or symbiotic cell in the body pedagogic. *Mental Retardation, 3* (2), 30–31.

Goldstein, H., Moss, J. W., & Jordan, L. J. (1965). *The efficacy of special class training on the development of mentally retarded children.* U.S. Office of Education Cooperative Research Project No. 619. Urbana: University of Illinois. (ERIC Document Reproduction Service No. ED 002 907)

Gottlieb, J. (1981). Mainstreaming: Fulfilling the promise? *American Journal of Mental Deficiency, 86*, 115–126.

Gottlieb, J. (1982). Mainstreaming. *Education and Training of the Mentally Retarded, 17*, 79–82.

Gottlieb, J., & Leyser, y. (1981). Facilitating the social mainstreaming of retarded children. *Exceptional Education Quarterly* 1 (4), 57–69.

Gould, S. J. (1981). *The mismeasure of man.* New York: W. W. Norton.

Gresham, F. M. (1982). Misguided mainstreaming: The case for social skills training with handicapped children. *Exceptional Children* 48, 422–433.

Grossman, H. J. (1973, 1977). *Manual on terminology and classification in mental retardation.* Washington, D.C.:

American Association on Mental Deficiency, Special Publication No. 2.

Grossman, H. J. (1983). *Classification in mental retardation*. Washington, D.C.: American Association on Mental Deficiency.

Hallahan, D. P., & Kauffman, J. M. (1977). Labels, categories, and behaviors: ED, LD, and EMR reconsidered. *Journal of Special Education*, **11**, 139–149.

Hayden, A. H., & Dmitriev, V. (1975). The multi-disciplinary program for Down's syndrome at the University of Washington. In B. Z. Friedlander, G. M. Sterritt, & G. E. Kirk (Eds.), *Exceptional infant: Assessment and intervention* (Vol. 3). New York: Brunner/Mazel.

Haywood, H. C. (1979). What happened to mild and moderate mental retardation? *American Journal of Mental Deficiency*, **83**, 429–431.

Heber, R. (1959, 1961). A manual on terminology and classification in mental retardation. Monograph Supplement, *American Journal of Mental Deficiency*.

Heller, K. A. (1982). Effects of special education placement on educable mentally retarded children. In K. A. Heller, W. H. Holtzman, & S. Messick (Eds.), *Placing children in special education: Equity through valid educational practices*. Washington, D.C.: National Academy Press. (ERIC Document Reproduction Service No. ED 217–618)

Hoffman, E. (1972). *The treatment of deviance by the education system*. Ann Arbor, MI: Institute for the Study of Mental Retardation and Related Disabilities.

Huberty, T. J., Koller, J. R. & ten Brink, T. D. (1980). Adaptive behavior in the definition of the mentally retarded. *Exceptional Children*, **46**, 256–261.

Johnson, G. O. (1962). Special education for the mentally handicapped: A paradox. *Exceptional Children*, **29**, 62–69.

Johnson, G. O., & Kirk, S. A. (1950). Are mentally handicapped children segregated in the regular grades? *Journal of Exceptional Children*, **17**, 65–68, 87–88.

Kehle, T. J., & Barclay, J. R. (1979). Social and behavioral characteristics of mentally handicapped children. *Journal of Research and Development in Education*, **12**(4), 46–56.

Kidd, J. W. (1984). The 1983 AAMD definition and classification of mental retardation: The apparent impact of the CEC-MR position. *Education and Training of the Mentally Retarded*, **18**, 243–244.

Koegel, P., & Edgerton, R. B. (1984). Black "six-hour retarded children" as young adults. In R. B. Edgerton (Ed.), *Lives in process: Mildly retarded adults in a large city*. Washington, D.C.: AAMD Monographs, No. 6.

Kolstoe, O. P., & Frey, R. M. (1965). *A high school work-study program for mentally subnormal children*. Carbondale, IL: Southern Illinois Press.

Larry P. V. Riles (1972). C–71–2270 (RFP, District Court for Northern California).

Lilly, M. S. (1970). Special education: A teapot in a tempest. *Exceptional Children*, **37**, 43–49.

Lilly, M. S. (1982), April). Divestiture in special education: A personal point of view. Paper presented at the 60th International CEC Convention, Houston, T.

Luftig, R. L. (1980). The effect of differential educational placements on the self-concept of retarded pupils. Paper presented at the annual meeting of the American Educational Research Association. (ERIC Document Reproduction Service No. Ed 196 198)

Mackie, R. (1969). *Special education in the United States: Statistics 1948–1966*. New York: Teachers College Press.

MacMillan, D. L. (1982). *Mental retardation in school and society* (2nd ed.). Boston: Little, Brown.

MacMillan, D. L., & Borthwick, S. (1980). The new educable mentally retarded population: Can they be mainstreamed? *Mental Retardation*, **18**, 155–158.

MacMillan, D. L., Jones, R. L., & Aloia, G. F. (1974). The mentally retarded label: A theoretical analysis and review of research. *American Journal of Mental Deficiency*, **79**, 241–261.

MacMillan, D. L., Meyers, C. E., & Morrison, G. M. (1980). System-identification of mildly mentally retarded children: Implications for interpreting and conducting research. *American Journal of Mental Deficiency*, **85**, 108–115.

MacMillan, D. L., Meyers, C. E., & Yoshida, R. K. (1978). Regular class teachers' perceptions of transition programs for EMR students and their impact on the students. *Psychology in the Schools*, **15**, 99–103.

Mascari, B. G., & Forgnone, C. (1982). A follow-up study of EMR students four years after dimissal from the program. *Education and Training of the Mentally Retarded*, **17**, 288–292.

Mercer, J. R. (1970). Sociological perspectives on mild mental retardation. In H. C. Haywood (Ed.), *Social-cultural aspects of mental retardation: Proceedings of the Peabody-NIMH Conference* (p. 378–391). New York: Appleton-Century-Crofts.

Mercer, J. R. (1973). *Labeling the mentally retarded*. Berkeley, CA: University of California Press.

Mercer, J. R., & Lewis, J. P. (1977). *System of multicultural pluralistic assessment: Parent interview manual*. New York: Psychological Corporation.

Meyerowitz, J. H. (1962). Self-derogations in young retardates and special class placement. *Child Development*, **33**, 443–451.

Meyers, C. E., MacMillan, D. L., & Yoshida, R. K. (1980). Regular class education of EMR students, from efficacy to mainstreaming: A review of issues and research. In J. Gottlieb (Ed.), *Educating mentally retarded persons in the mainstream*. Baltimore, MD, University Park Press.

Milazzo, T. C. (1970, April). Special class placement or how to destroy in the name of help. Paper presented at the 48th annual international convention of the Council for Exceptional Children, Chicago. (ERIC Document Reproduction Service No. ED 309 383)

Mullen, F. A., & Itkin, W. (1961). *Achievement and adjustment of educable mentally handicapped children in special classes and in regular classes*. Chicago, IL: Chicago Board of Education.

Myers, J. K. (1976). *The special day school placement of high IQ and low IQ EMR pupils* (Report No. EC 090 431). Chicago, IL: The Council for Exceptional Children. (ERIC Document Reproduction No. ED 125 197)

Patrick, J. L., & Reschly, D. J. (1982). Relationship of state educational criteria and demographic variables to school-system prevalence of mental retardation. *American Journal of Mental Deficiency*, **86**, 351–360.

Polloway, E. A. (1984). The integration of mildly retarded students in the schools: An historical review. *Remedial and Special Education*, **5**(4), 18–28.

Polloway, E. A. (1985). Identification and placement in mild mental retardation programs: Recommendations for professional practice. (Position paper of the Division on Mental Retardation of the Council for Exceptional Children). *Education and Training of the Mentally Retarded*, **20**,

218–221

Polloway, E. A., & Epstein, M. H. (1985). Current research issues in mild mental retardation: A survey of the field. *Education and Training of the Mentally Retarded*, **20**, 171–174

Polloway, E. A., Epstein, M. H., & Cullinan, D. (1985). Prevalence of behavior problems among educable mentally retarded students. *Education and Training of the Mentally Retarded*, **20**, 3–13.

Polloway, E. A., Epstein, M. H., Patton, J. R. Cullinan, D., & Luebke, J. (1986). Demographic, social and behavioral characteristics of students with educable mental retardation. *Education and Training of the Mentally Retarded*, *21*, 27–34.

Polloway, E. A., & Patton, J. R. (1986). Biological causes of mental retardation. In J. S. Payne, J. R. Patton, M. Beirne-Smith, *Mental retardation* (2nd ed.). Columbus, OH: Charles E. Merrill.

Polloway, E. A., & Smith, J. D. (1983). Changes in mild mental retardation: Population, programs, and perspectives. *Exceptional Children*, **50**, 149–159.

Porter, R. B., & Milazzo, T. C. (1958). A comparison of mentally retarded adults who attended a special class with those who attended regular school classes. *Exceptional Children*, **24**, 410–412, 420.

Prehm, H. J. (1985, January). *Education and Training of the Mentally Retarded*: Mid year report to the Board of Directors, CEC-MR.

President's Committee on Mental Retardation (1970). *The six-hour retarded child*. Washington, D.C.: U.S. Government Printing Office.

Quay, H. C. (1977). Measuring dimensions of deviant behavior: The behavior problem checklist. *Journal of Abnormal Child Psychology*, **5**, 277–287.

Ramey, C. T., & Haskins, R. (1981). The causes and treatment of school failure: Insights from the Carolina Abecedarian project. In M. J. Begab, H. C. Haywood, & H. L. Garber (Eds.), *Psycho-social influences in retarded performance: Strategies for improving competence* (Vol. II) (p. 89–112). Baltimore, MD: University Park Press.

Reese-Dukes, J. L., & Stokes, E. H. (1978). Social acceptance of elementary educable mentally retarded pupils in the regular classroom. *Education and Training of the Mentally Retarded*, **13**, 356–361.

Reschly, D. (1979). Nonbiased assessment. In G. Phye & D. Reschly (Eds.), *School psychology: Perspectives and issues*. New York: Academic Press.

Reschly, D. J. (1981). Evaluation of the effects of SOMPA measures on classification of students as mildly mentally retarded. *American Journal of Mental Deficiency*, **86**, 16–20.

Reschly, D. J. (1982). Assessing mild retardation: The influence of adaptive behavior, sociocultural status, and prospects for nonbiased assessment. In C. R. Reynolds & T. B. Gutkin (Eds.), *The handbook of school psychology*. New York: John Wiley.

Reschly, D. J. (1984). Beyong IQ test bias: The National Academy Panel's analysis of minority EMR overrepresentation. *Educational Researcher*, **13**, 15–19.

Reschly, D. J., & Lamprecht, M. J. (1979). Expectancy effects of labels: Fact or artifact? *Exceptional Children*, **46**, 55–58.

Robinson, H. B., & Robinson, N. M. (1965). *The mentally retarded child: A psychological approach*. New York: McGraw-Hill.

Rothstein, J. H. (Ed.) (1971). *Mental retardation: Readings and resources* (2nd ed.). New York: Holt, Rinehart & Winston.

Russell, A. T., & Forness, S. R. (1984). Behavioral disturbance in mentally retarded children in EMR and TMR classrooms. *American Journal of Mental Deficiency*, **89**, 338–344.

Rynders, J. E., Spiker, D., & Horrobin, J. M. (1978). Underestimating the educability of Down's syndrome children: Examination of methodological problems in recent literature. *American Journal of Mental Deficiency*, **82**, 440–448.

Sargent, L. R. (1981, Jan.). *Assessment, documentation and programming for adaptive behavior: An Iowa task force report*. Des Moines, IA: State of Iowa, Department of Instruction.

Semmel, M. I., & Cheney, C. O. (1979). Social acceptance and self-concept of handicapped pupils in mainstreamed environments. *Education Unlimited*, *I*(2), 64–68.

Sindelar, P. T., & Deno, S. L. (1978). The effectiveness of resource programming. *Journal of Special Education*, **12**, 17–28.

Smith, J. D. (1985). *Minds made feeble: The myth and legacy of the Kallikaks*. Rockville, MD: Aspen.

Smith, J. D., & Dexter, B. L. (1980). The basics movement: What does it mean for the education of mentally retarded students? *Education and Training of the Mentally Retarded*, **15**, 72–79.

Smith, J. D., & Polloway, E. A. (1979). The dimension of adaptive behavior in mental retardation research: An analysis of recent practices. *American Journal of Mental Deficiency*, **84**, 203–206.

Smith, J. E., Polloway, E. A., & Smith, J. D. (1978). The continuing dilemma of the mildly handicapped. *Special Children*, **4**(2), 52–63.

Sobsey, D. (1984). Stigma and words of obscure origin. *TASH Newsletter*, **10**(2), 1, 8.

Stanton, J. E., & Cassidy, V. M. (1964). Effectiveness of special classes for educable mentally retarded. *Mental Retardation*, **2**(1), 8–13.

Thurstone, T. G. (1959). *An evaluation of educating mentally handicapped children in special classes and in regular classes*. Chapel Hill, N.C.: University of North Carolina. (ERIC Document Reproduction Service No. 002 798)

Vergason, G. A. (1983). Curriculum content. In E. L. Meyen, G. A. Vergason, & R. J. Whelan (Eds.), *Promising practices for exceptional children: Curriculum implications*. Denver, CO: Love Publishing.

Walker, V. S. (1974). The efficacy of the resource room for educating retarded children. *Exceptional Children*, **40**, 288–289.

Zigler, E. (1966). Research on personality structure in the retardate. In N. R. Ellis (Ed.), *International review of research in mental retardation*. Vol. 1 (p, 77–108). New York: Academic Press.

Zigler, E. (1984). A developmental theory of mental retardation. In B. Blatt & R. J. Morris (Eds.), *Perspectives in special education: Personal orientations* (pp. 173–209). Glenview, IL: Scott, Foresman and Company.

Zigler, E., & Balla, D. (1981). Issues in personality and motivation in mentally retarded persons. In M. J. Begab, H. C. Haywood, & H. L. Garber (Eds.), *Psychosocial influences in retarded performance: Issues and theories of development* (Vol. 1) (p. 197–218). Baltimore, MD: University Park Press.

Zigler, E., Balla, D., & Hodapp, R. (1984). On the definition and classification of mental retardation. *American Journal of Mental Deficiency*, **89**, 215–230.

Zucker, S., & Polloway, E. A. (1987). Issues in identification and assessment in mental retardation. *Education and Training in Mental Retardation*, **22**, 69–76.

Minority Mild Mental Retardation Overrepresentation: Legal Issues, Research Findings, and Reform Trends

DANIEL J. RESCHLY

Department of Psychology
Iowa State University
Ames, IA 50011

Abstract—Mild or educable mental retardation (MMR) was the first category of handicapped students served in most United States schools and, until recently, had the highest prevalence of any handicapping condition (Doll, 1962, 1965; MacMillan, 1982; Meyers, Sundstrom, & Yoshida, 1974). Despite this early history and venerable past, mild mental retardation is one of the most controversial and least understood of the present exceptional child classifications. In this chapter the central problem of minority overrepresentation in programs for the mildly retarded will be discussed with special attention devoted to litigation, research findings, and reform trends.

Overview

First, a brief consideration of the diagnostic construct of mild mental retardation (MMR) is needed. The mildly retarded typically come from low socio-economic status circumstances. This is true regardless of race or ethnicity, and has been reported in studies conducted throughout the Western world (Heber, 1970; Richardson, 1981). Minority students in the United States, especially black, hispanic, and native American Indian, are more likely to experience poverty circumstances. Minority students have been overrepresented in school programs for the mildly mentally retarded, but as will be analyzed carefully later, this overrepresentation is often exaggerated and misunderstood.

Typically, students classified as mildly mentally retarded are not recognized as handicapped until they enter the public schools. They do not exhibit any physical stigmata suggestive of mental retardation or any other handicap. They are usually regarded as functioning within broadly defined normal limits by other members of their family. The first indication of mild retardation typically is repeated failure in educational settings, usually experienced over two to three years. Most have been retained one or more times prior to being formally classified as mildly mentally retarded. When classified as mildly mentally retarded, using state department of education criteria, IQ scores are important. That alone is a controversial issue. Most students classified as mildly mentally retarded obtain IQ scores between about 55 and 75, although that, too, varies considerably. When placed in special education, mildly mentally retarded students are more likely than other mildly handicapped students to be in self-contained classes which may involve relatively little contact with regular education students and programs. Finally, most persons classified as mildly mentally retarded during the school-age years are not formally classified as mildly mentally retarded during the adult years. However, the earlier belief that mildly mentally retarded persons disappear into the adult population without being recognized as exceptional is probably overly optimistic.

The modal characteristics presented in the previous paragraph do not, of course, apply to every single individual classified in public school settings as mildly mentally retarded. Furthermore, nearly every one of the modal characteristics is subject to further limitations and, frequently, is the source of considerable controversy.

Changes in Mild Mental Retardation

Vast changes have occurred over the past 25 years in the diagnostic construct of mild mental retardation (MMR). These changes involve the diagnostic criteria, amount of research, prevalence, and educational programming. Numbers of students classified as mildly mentally retarded have declined markedly since 1976. As indicated in Table 1, mildly mentally retarded numbers in the school population declined by about one-third from 1976 to 1983 (United States Department of Education, 1985). This decline is even more remarkable because over that period, substantial numbers of more

23

severely retarded students were served in the public schools for the first time. The decline in mildly mentally retarded students was probably even greater than indicated in the official child count. This decline in MMR numbers has been overshadowed by the dramatic increase in learning disabilities numbers, a phenomenon causing considerable controversy (Algozzine & Korinek, 1985; Gerber, 1984). The changes in mild mental retardation are large enough for serious questions to have been raised about whether older literature still applies to the current mildly mentally retarded population (MacMillan & Borthwick, 1980; MacMillan, Meyers, & Morrison, 1980; Polloway & Smith, 1983, in press). The declining numbers almost certainly also mean substantial changes in the population of mildly mentally retarded students which, in turn, constitutes a change in the overall diagnostic construct.

TABLE 1
[1]Mental Retardation and Learning Disability Child
Count Data, 1976–1983

	1976–77	1983–84	Change	Per Cent
MR	969,547	650,534	−319,013	−33%
LD	797,213	1,811,489	+1,014,276	+127%

[1]Based on December 1 child counts in the 1976–77 and 1983–84 school years (United States Department of Education, 1985).

The vast changes that have occurred have been the result of a variety of factors, with litigation serving as a catalyst for changes advocated by strong critics of conventional practices (Dunn, 1968; Mercer, 1973). Two additional indications of the turmoil in the field of mild mental retardation are the frequent changes in mild mental retardation classification criteria as well as efforts to develop markedly different assessment procedures (Feuerstein, Rand, & Hoffman, 1979; Mercer, 1979). These factors, especially litigation, have prompted substantial changes. The irony of recent events in this area, particularly the litigation, is illustrated by two dilemmas described in the next section.

Dilemmas in Mild Mental Retardation

In addition to the factors mentioned above, one further indication of serious problems with the mild mental retardation diagnostic construct are two dilemmas which are symptoms of serious problems. The first dilemma has to do with the anomaly of districts and state departments of education being sued in federal district courts due to overrepresentation of minority students in programs which, under normal circumstances, would be seen as providing highly desirable characteristics, namely, expenditure of one and a half to two times the amount spent on education of students in regular programs, an individualized program which is updated periodically, sharply reduced class size, and a teacher with special training. These very positive characteristics were not sufficient to overcome the concerns related to minority overrepresentation in several court cases. On the face of this situation, it clearly does not seem logical that state departments and districts have been sued, incurring litigation costs in the millions of dollars, for placing students in programs that would appear to offer several advantages.

Further indications of serious problems in the area of mild mental retardation are apparent from the reasoning in a landmark court decision forbidding certain uses of standardized ability tests. An opinion rendered by Federal Court Judge Peckham (*Larry P.*, 1979) reached the following three conclusions: First, IQ tests are biased. Second, IQ and standardized achievement tests autocorrelate, that is, they measure the same thing. Third, the customary uses of achievement tests are acceptable. That reasoning, like the apparent anomaly of a special program with greater resources being unacceptable, makes no sense without consideration of broader controversies and implicit issues impinging on the diagnostic construct of mild mental retardation.

The purview of this chapter will be restricted to issues related to minority overrepresentation in programs for the mildly mentally retarded. Other chapters in this section have addressed more general issues with the mildly mentally retarded including programming, implications of longitudinal studies for curriculum, and learning characteristics. The topic of socio-cultural differences and the effects of poverty on learning and educational achievement will not be discussed extensively in this chapter due to space limitations as well as an excellent chapter in another section of these volumes by Guskin and Brantlinger. This chapter will deal extensively with litigation. Numerous judicial decrees or opinions are cited as primary references as well as several articles and book chapters which analyze these basic cases. Major attention will be devoted to the implicit issues in these cases which will be regarded as more important, in numerous instances, than the ostensible reasons for the litigation. The problem of overrepresentation, particularly overrepresentation statistics, will be analyzed with a strong recommendation that greater care and more precision be devoted to analyses of this problem. Finally, various reforms will be discussed along with recommendations for changes in public policy.

Litigation

Two distinctly different kinds of court case have exerted profound influences on the development of educational programs for handicapped students (Bersoff, 1982a; Turnbull, 1978). The various right to education cases, the classic cases being *Mills* (1972) and *PARC* (1971), established the right of handicapped students to educational services. These cases are generally well-known and their profound effects on establishment of educational programs are widely recognized (e.g., Turnbull, 1978). Another kind of case, considerably less well-known but just as important, has dealt with alleged placement bias due to overrepresentation of minority students in special education programs. Two essential features of the placement bias cases must be noted. Firstly, nearly all of the cases to date have involved the classification of mild or educable mental retardation. Secondly, nearly all of the cases have involved placement of students in self-contained special classes, an educational program which is relatively segregated from regular education. Overrepresentation of minority students in other programs for the mildly handicapped, or overrepresentation in the mildly mentally retarded category with part-time special education placement, such as resource rooms, have not been addressed by the courts.

The minority students involved in this litigation include black students in urban and rural settings, Hispanic students in urban and rural settings, and native American students in rural settings. The overrepresentation data, often misunderstood, has typically involved placement rates such as: 10% of the total population in a state was black, but perhaps 25% of the enrollment in mildly mentally retarded special class programs was black. These cases have been filed in Federal District Courts in all regions of the United States on the basis of constitutional and statutory law. Several cases are still pending resolution at various stages of the judicial process. One case, *Larry P.*, appears to be headed for the United States Supreme Court for final resolution. However, the nature of the cases, the legal bases for filing the court action, and the method to resolve issues has varied, with at least two distinct phases apparent in the last 15 years.

Pre-1975 Placement Bias Cases

The cases resolved prior to about 1975 generally involved a variety of poor, and sometimes clearly unethical, practices. The *Diana* case in California and the *Guadalupe* case in Arizona are excellent examples of this early litigation (*Diana*, 1970; *Guadalupe*, 1972). Hispanic students were involved in both cases, with native American students also involved in Guadalupe. In both of these cases plaintiffs argued that the overrepresentation of minority students occurred because of inappropriate assessment procedures. In both, plaintiffs were prepared to offer evidence that placement decisions were made with billingual children, and still worse, some monolingual Spanish language children, with verbal IQ scales apparently administered in English. Furthermore, there was little or no effort to assess adaptive behavior, which was by then regarded nearly universally as an important aspect of the diagnosis of mild mental retardation (Grossman, 1973). The plaintiffs also alleged other bad practices such as poorly trained teachers, poorly administered programs, inadequate related services personnel, poorly trained school psychologists, and so on. In the pre-1975 cases these bad practices were not disputed in court by the defendant school districts and state departments of education. The cases were settled by consent decrees in which the

defendant school districts and state departments of education agreed to a number of reforms designed to eliminate the bad practices cited earlier. These court consent decrees required that: 1) less emphasis was to be placed on IQ tests in classification and placement of minority students; 2) nonverbal tests were to be used with bilingual minority students; 3) adaptive behavior must be assessed; and 4) due process protections were to be established (further discussion of these cases is provided in Reschly, 1979).

The pre-1975 cases cited above are perhaps best understood as reflecting bad practices arising in part from very limited resources. It is significant that the defendant school districts and state departments of education made no effort to defend their programs in court. Rather, defendants agreed to institute nearly all of the reforms advocated by plaintiffs. It should also be noted that the pre-1975 cases did not attack fundamental notions of mental retardation, nor was there any effort to ban IQ tests. These latter issues became increasingly prominent in the post-1975 placement bias litigation which continues today (Bersoff, 1982a, b; Prasse & Reschly, 1986; Reschly, 1987).

Post-1975 Placement Bias Cases

The placement bias litigation resolved since 1975 has been different on a number of very important dimensions. First, there have not been allegations of unethical practices, nor suggestions of incompetence among the personnel involved with the classification/placement decisions. Rather, the major issues have revolved around the nature of mild mental retardation and the fairness of IQ tests to black students. All of these cases have involved the same essential characteristics, that is, overrepresentation of minorities in special class programs for the mildly mentally retarded.

Larry P.

The most famous of the placement bias cases is *Larry P. v Riles*, which may be appealed to the United States Supreme Court. *Larry P.* has been before the federal courts in one form or another since 1971. *Larry P.* was settled by an opinion by District Court Judge Robert Peckham in October, 1979. Peckham's opinion was rendered after a very lengthy trial which extended from about October, 1977 through May, 1978. In the *Larry P. Opinion*, Peckham banned the use of IQ tests with black students if the outcome of test use was classification as mild or educable mentally retarded. Moreover, Peckham ordered that overrepresentation of black students in programs for the mildly mentally retarded be eliminated. Peckham reached his decision on the basis of evidence which he was convinced proved that: 1) IQ tests were biased against black students; 2) mild mental retardation was no more common among the economically disadvantaged; 3) the California State Department of Education intentionally discriminated against black students; and 4) adaptive behavior had not been assessed appropriately with these students. The *Larry P.* case, particularly the ban on the use of IQ tests, even though it is technically a very narrow ban, may have profound influences upon psychological assessment and special education in the future. The case was appealed by the State of California to the Circuit Court of Appeals where the original decision was upheld on a 2 to 1 vote by a three-judge panel in a decision rendered on January 23, 1984 (*Larry P.*, 1984).

Pase

Another post-1975 bias case dealing with the same issues as *Larry P.* was *PASE v Hannon* (1980). In *PASE*, an advocacy group brought the Chicago Public Schools to a federal district court where they alleged biased IQ tests caused overrepresentation of minority students in special classes for the mildly retarded. The plaintiffs in this case requested a ban on IQ tests, much like the *Larry P.* court resolution, as well as an elimination of overrepresentation in special class programs. This case was also heard by a federal district court judge, John Grady, and decided by a lengthy opinion. However, the conclusions of the *PASE Opinion* were opposite to those of *Larry P.* Judge Grady concluded that IQ tests were only part of the process whereby a student might be classified as mildly retarded and that, in any event, the IQ tests were largely unbiased. The method by which he reached this conclusion concerning bias, his own subjective impression of the items, has been severely castigated by Bersoff (1982b). Further legal steps in *PASE* are unclear at this time since the Chicago Public Schools voluntarily banned IQ tests one year later after winning the *PASE* decision. The fundamental issues in *PASE* are therefore moot, and further judicial activity regarding *PASE* is not expected.

Marshall

In another potentially landmark decision, a federal district court in Georgia ruled in *Marshall v Georgia* (1984) that overrepresentation of black students in special class programs for the mildly retarded did not constitute discrimination. In *Marshall*, the court was not asked to rule on the very complicated issue of whether or not IQ tests are biased. Rather, the court was asked to determine whether disproportionate classification and placement across a variety of educational programs, specifically underrepresentation of minorities in gifted programs and in programs for students classified as learning disabled, and overrepresentation in lower ability tracks in regular education and in mildly mentally retarded programs in special education, constituted discrimination. In the portion of the case involving mild mental retardation, the primary issues were whether or not mild mental retardation was found more frequently in lower socio-economic status circumstances; whether the association of mild mental retardation with lower

socio-economic status circumstances explained the over-representation of black students; whether an appropriate conception of adaptive behavior was used by the state and by the defendant districts, particularly whether adaptive behavior for school-age children should include academic performance; and whether the state IQ criteria which allowed some flexibility in the IQ cut-off was appropriate. In *Marshall*, Federal District Court Judge Edenfield, in an opinion rendered on June 28, 1984, rejected plaintiffs' claims of discrimination. Edenfield ruled that mild mental retardation did occur more frequently with lower socio-economic status circumstances, and that the relative conditions of poverty among blacks in Georgia provided sufficient explanation for overrepresentation of black students in programs for the mildly retarded. Furthermore, Judge Edenfield agreed with defendant's testimony that adaptive behavior within the educational setting needed to be considered in deciding whether or not students were properly classified as mildly mentally retarded.

Summary

The early placement bias litigation exerted enormous influence on subsequent legislation including Public Law 94–142 (Bersoff, 1982a; Reschly, 1981a, 1983, 1987; and Turnbull, 1978). The future impact of these cases, particularly those still before the Federal Courts, is difficult to forecast, but a comprehensive ban on the use of IQ tests in classification of students as mildly retarded is a distinct possibility. That sort of ban might be part of the aftermath of a Supreme Court Decision upholding the original trial opinion in *Larry P.* Although these kinds of events are difficult to foresee, it is clear that placement bias litigation has had a significant influence on the mildly mentally retarded diagnostic construct. However, the most important aspect of this litigation has been the assumptions made about mild mental retardation and about special education programs for the mildly retarded. It is to these assumptions that attention is now turned.

Underlying Issues and Implicit Assumptions

The placement bias litigation reflected a number of underlying issues and implicit assumptions which, in total, are probably more important than the central issues in the cases (overrepresentation and IQ test bias). These implicit issues and assumptions were important in all of the cases, but are most apparent in *Larry P.* where the opinion by Judge Peckham clearly reflects the influence of these issues and assumptions. Due to space limitations these issues and assumptions are not discussed thoroughly here, but the interested reader is referred to Reschly (1979, 1981a, 1984, 1987) and to Prasse & Reschly (1986). Elliott (1987) has developed an excellent analysis of *Larry P.* based on a review of the opinion, the transcript from the trial, and interviews with key figures including the attorneys for both sides.

Nature-Nurture

The very old debate concerning the relative effects of nature and nurture as determinants of individual differences in ability has intensified over the past 15 years due to Jensen's assertion of racial differences in hereditary potential (Jensen, 1969). Nature-nurture was a crucial underlying issue in *Larry P.* and influential in the other cases as well. A court challenge to hereditarian views does not, of course, directly address the scientific merits of that view, but, in all likelihood, provides an extremely effective mechanism to refute the hereditarian view, at least in a broader sociopolitical realm. The *Larry P.* court decision now serves as a way for attacks to be made on the basic Jensen hypothesis. However, this enormously complex issue, now debated for decades, is not central to *educational* programming for students classified as mildly retarded. Nevertheless, the nature-nurture debate has moved into the special education arena with enormous potential impact on the future of mild mental retardation as a diagnostic construct.

Meaning of IQ

Another implicit issue in the placement bias cases has been misunderstanding of the meaning of IQ test results. Despite all of the expert testimony from all of the placement bias cases agreeing that IQ test results are not fixed, are not predetermined by heredity, and do not reflect innate ability, federal court judges have continued to suggest that a good, legally acceptable IQ test would measure innate potential (*Hobson v Hansen*, 1967; *Larry P.*, 1979). This apparent misunderstanding of what IQ does represent, despite the unanimity in expert testimony, many reflect inherent limitations in the term IQ which now has the connotations of global, fixed, and predetermined ability. A more appropriate term, such as *school functioning level* or *academic aptitude* might reduce some of these misconceptions. However, misunderstanding of the meaning of IQ and the inherent limitations of psychological tests has been a complicating factor in this litigation.

Role of IQ Tests

Much of the litigation reflects an assumption that IQ tests are the primary, if not the sole, basis for classifying students as mildly mentally retarded (Mercer, 1973, 1979). Mercer and others have undoubtedly exaggerated the role of IQ tests in the entire referral/evaluation/classification/placement process. Initial referral is probably a much more important factor (Ysseldyke, Thurlow, Graden, Wesson, Algozzine, & Deno, 1983).

The *Larry P.* court was convinced that IQ tests were the primary basis for mildly mentally retarded classification as well as the principal culprit causing overrepresentation. In contrast, the trial judge in *PASE* concluded that IQ tests had a subordinate role in the overall classification/placement process and that any biases in such tests were compensated for adequately by due process procedural protections and by consideration of a broad variety of information prior to classification/placement. The role of IQ tests in classification/placement continues to be an important underlying issue in the placement bias litigation.

Labeling Effects

Implicit in all of the placement bias litigation has been the assumption that classification as mildly mentally retarded was stigmatizing and humiliating with probable permanent negative effects. This underlying assumption involves the enormously complex theory and research on self-fulfilling prophecy and other effects of labels. Although direct effects of labels on the behavior of children or adults have been very difficult to document (Gibbons, 1981; MacMillan, 1982; MacMillan, Jones, & Aloia, 1974), quite justifiable concerns about the impact of these labels continue to be prominent in the literature. These concerns have also been quite prominent in the litigation and have, quite properly, prompted the courts to suggest that great care must be taken in classification/placement decision making.

Six-Hour Retardation

The term *six-hour retardation* was first used in the President's Committee on Mental Retardation Report (1970) to refer to what scholars have seen as the classic pattern of mild mental retardation. This classic pattern for the mildly retarded involves little or no recognition of any handicapping condition during the preschool years; Increasing incidence of mild mental retardation during the school years up to about age 14; decreasing frequency of mild mental retardation from age 14 on, with most persons earlier classified as mildly retarded during their school years adjusting sufficiently to adult demands so that they are no longer regarded as retarded. Although relatively little is known about the adult adjustment of "six-hour" mildly mentally retarded students, most are not officially classified as mildly mentally retarded as adults.

The critical question in the litigation, prominent also in theory and research, was whether mild mental retardation is an appropriate classification for persons whose handicapping condition is largely restricted to a particular context, the public school, and a particular age, roughly ages 6 or 7 to about age 17, and to a particular social role, performing as a student with demands to demonstrate literacy skills and abstract thinking. This underlying issue raises questions about the fundamental meaning of the mild mental retardation diagnostic construct, a question discussed in the last section of this chapter.

Efficacy of Self-Contained MMR Classes

The most important implicit assumption in the placement bias litigation is the view that mild mental retardation special education programs are ineffective and, perhaps, even inferior to placement in regular education classes for mildly mentally retarded students. In *Larry P.*, Judge Peckham excoriated the efficacy of special classes no less than 27 times in his Opinion through comments such as "deadend," "inferior," "stigmatizing," and so on. An obvious point is that if these programs were as bad as alleged by plaintiffs, no students, quite apart from race or ethnic considerations, should be placed in the programs. The efficacy issue is by far the most important and, by far, the most difficult to address (see Polloway & Smith, this volume, and Taylor, this volume). Efficacy or program outcomes relate to the validity of a diagnostic construct (Cromwell, Blashfield, & Strauss, 1975). Valid constructs need to have known relationships to treatment or programming for which effectiveness data are available. The efficacy issue should have been a more prominent issue in the testimony and in the various consent decrees and opinions. Efficacy is far more important and fundamental than IQ test bias or overrepresentation. The importance of assumptions about mild mental retardation program outcomes will be illustrated in several later sections.

Concepts of Test Bias

Test bias is a very complicated issue that has attracted considerable attention in theory and research (e.g., Flaugher, 1978; Jensen, 1980; Reschly, 1979; and Reynolds, 1982). The placement bias litigation has not reflected the sophisticated theory and research on test bias. Two of the major cases, *Larry P.* and *PASE*, reached sharply different conclusions concerning IQ test bias. Both were equally remiss in not accurately reflecting the available theory and research (Bersoff, 1982b). In *Larry P.*, the conclusions about test bias were regarded by Bersoff as unsophisticated and inconsistent with empirical research (much of which was presented by expert witnesses in testimony). However, Bersoff was even more critical of *PASE*, characterizing Judge Grady's method of resolving the issue of item bias as "embarrassingly devoid of intellectual integrity." (p. 88) For a variety of reasons, including the complexity of the issues, limitations in the judicial approach to problem solving, and inadequacies in expert testimony (Reschly, 1987), the placement bias litigation has not adequately reflected theory and research on test bias.

Summary

Implicit issues and underlying assumptions in the placement bias litigation were crucial. Far more than IQ tests and overrepresentation were represented in these cases. These issues and assumptions are crucial to this chapter in that they represent fundamental concerns about mild mental retardation, which must be considered in efforts to identify needed research and special education programming reforms that maximize opportunities for students.

The Overrepresentation Problem

Minority social scientists, including psychologists and educators, have been increasingly harsh in their criticism of special education programs in which minority students are overrepresented. These harsh criticisms need to be acknowledged. Their assumptions about the fairness of special education classification and placement procedures and the effectiveness of special education programs with minority students must be considered carefully. Although a National Academy panel took a somewhat different approach to this problem (Heller, Holtzman, & Messick, 1982), asking why overrepresentation is a problem rather than why it exists, it is important to understand and analyze both questions, that is, why it exists and why it is a problem. In some cases views of critics reflect inadequate understanding of special education classification, placement, and programming. In other instances overrepresentation data are exaggerated or distorted. These problems will be pointed out in subsequent sections. Despite these limitations it is essential to be responsive to the points of view expressed by minority critics. These points of view represent an important reality concerning perception of special educational programs. Future progress in educational programming for persons now diagnosed as mildly mentally retarded will depend in large part on effective responses to this criticism.

Minority Views

Minority social scientists and representatives of student advocate groups have been extremely skeptical of the benefits of special education programs for minority students. Although their criticisms are often directed generally at all special education programs, the mildly mentally retarded classification and the self-contained special classes are seen as the most objectionable programs by a large margin. Many of these criticisms are summarized well in Jones (1976) as well as in recent papers published by advocate groups (e.g., Edelman, 1980). Some representative views are:

Williams (1970):
Ability testing is being utilized to dehumanize, damage, and destroy black children and youth through improperly labelling and classifying them. (p. 5)

Samuda (1976):
The implications and consequences of testing for minority group individuals are real, drastic, and pervasive in their effects at all stages in the lives of minority individuals. (p. 69)

Johnson (1969):
The latest attempt at system maintenance is the generation of data to show blacks may actually be genetically less intelligent, and, therefore, less able to learn. Special education is implicated for it has cheerfully accepted the charge with little or no scrutiny of either the faulty conception upon which the IQ is grounded or the sociocultural environment of its clientele. (p. 244)

Marino (quoted in Jones, 1976) advocated:
. . . that school districts place Mexican Americans in special classes at the same proportion or percent that the school districts are placing majority students in special classes. School districts will claim that it is possible that some very needy children will be excluded from special education. We must remember that we are willing to take the chance that some children may be excluded from the program, but that the risk of a few children is far superior than living with a system that is misplacing thousands of our children every year. (p. 8)

Edelman (1980):
Large numbers of black students are misclassified as mentally retarded and put in inappropriately segregated classes. (p. 29)

Watson (1981):
. . . the fact remains that today, right now, it is the almighty test score that condemns minority students in disproportionate numbers to classes for the mentally retarded. It is the "objective," "scientific," "democratic" test score that helps perpetuate the myth of the intellectual inferiority of blacks. (p. 44)

Jones (in press), a social scientist with solid credentials in special education, suggested the overrepresentation of minority students in special class programs for the mildly retarded represented systemic discrimination. Such overrepresentation was seen as part of an overall pattern of discrimination, pervasive in public schools at all ages and in all programs. Similar views have been expressed by Hilliard (1980) and by Jones & Wilderson (1976).

The harsh criticism of minority social scientists is directed at several aspects of special education programming including classification procedures (especially IQ tests) and the effectiveness of programs. Many of these criticisms suggest special education overrepresentation is merely part of a system-wide and society-wide pattern of discrimination. Perhaps the most impressive comments are those suggesting that minority students with serious educational problems would be better off without special education services, presumably designed to meet those problems, due to the stigma associated with special education as well as the presumption that special education programs are ineffective. These criticisms are quite similar to the underlying issues and implicit assumptions in the litigation discussed earlier.

Overrepresentation Data

Percentage data reflecting proportions of students from various groups in different educational programs are easily and frequently misunderstood. This is especially the case with the data reflecting minority representation in various special education programs. The somewhat surprising conclusion is that minority students often are not overrepresented in special education programs when overall percentage of minority students classified as handicapped is considered or when classification of minority students across all special education categories is compared with general population rates. However, minorities are overrepresented in programs for mildly retarded students.

The actual percentage data reflecting minority placement in various special education programs must be carefully analyzed. Careful distinction must be made between: 1) the percentage of minority students in the total school population, 2) the percentage of special education students that are minority, and 3) the percentage of minority students in special education programs. In the landmark *Larry P.* case, black students constituted 10% of the total school-age population in California and approximately 25% of the students placed in mild mental retardation special education classes. The totally incorrect assumption that apparently has been made by some critics was that perhaps as many as 25% of all black students were placed in special class programs for the mildly mentally retarded students. In fact, as shown in Table 2, at the time of the *Larry P.* trial only about 1% of all school-age blacks were placed in special class programs for mildly retarded students.

TABLE 2
[1] Overrepresentation Data From California 1968–69 and 1976–77

Group	Percent of Total Population	Percent of MMR Enrollment		Percent of Each Group in MMR classes	
		1968–69	*1976–77*	*1968–69*	*1976–77*
White	72%	43%	—	0.8%	0.4%
Black	10%	25.5%	25.4%	3.2%	1.1%
Hispanic	15%	29%	—	2.6%	

[1]Based upon estimates derived from data reported in *Larry P.* (1979), Yoshida et al. (1976), and personal communication with the California State Department of Education in 1979.

Similar data are available from other sources such as the Riverside, California Public Schools (Mercer, 1973), and for the State of New Jersey (Manni, Winikur, & Keller, 1980). These data are summarized in Table 3. In all of these situations, an entirely erroneous impression of the degree of overrepresentation might be developed from merely looking at the simple percentages of minorities in the total population and the percentage of the mild mental retardation special education program that was minority. In all instances, simple comparisons of these percentages suggest a high degree of overrepresentation with the implication that a large percentage of minority children are placed in self-contained special classes for mildly mentally retarded students. However, in all instances, the actual percentage of minority students classified and placed in these programs is a relatively low proportion of the total population of minority students.

In recent years data have become available concerning the percentages of minority and majority students placed in all types of special education programs. National data gathered by the Federal Office for Civil Rights in 1978 were summarized in the National Academy Panel Report (Heller, Holtzman, & Messick, 1982). Similar data from New Jersey (Manni, Winikur, & Keller, 1980) and the Chicago Public Schools (*Caught in the Web*, 1982) are summarized in Table 3. When all special education categories are considered there was little or no overrepresentation of minority students. Generally, there are slight variations with no systematic trend across all special education programs and categories except for mild mental retardation and learning disability. Black students are typically underrepresented in programs for learning disabled students and overrepresented in programs for mildly retarded students. However, some exceptions to this trend have been reported (Tucker, 1980). The National Academy Report (Heller, Holtzman, & Messick, 1982) concluded that approximately 3% of all black students are classified as mildly retarded in the United States while only 1% of all white students are so classified.

TABLE 3
Overrepresentation Data From Riverside, California, Chicago, and New Jersey

[1]*Riverside, California, about 1965*

	White	Black	Hispanic
Percent of Total Enrollment	82	9.5	7
Percent of MMR Program	53	32	12
Percent of Group in MMR	0.6	3.4	1.7

[2]*State of New Jersey, 1979–80*

	White	Black	Hispanic
Percent of Total Enrollment	73	18	7
Percent of Total Handicapped Enrollment	71	21	7
Percent of MMR Enrollment	43	43	13
Percent of Group in MMR	0.5	1.9	1.4
Percent of Group in ED	0.8	2.3	0.7
Percent of Group in LD	2.8	2.3	1.4
Percent of Group in LD + Ed + MMR	4.1	6.5	3.5
Percent of Group in Special Education	10.4	12.5	10.1

Chicago

	1980–81		1983–4	
	White	Black	White	Black
Percent of Total Enrollment	18.7	60.7	15.6	60.6
Percent of Group in MMR	1.7	3.8	1.3	2.9
Percent of Group in LD	4.2	2.4	4.8	3.1
Percent of Group in LD + MMR	5.9	6.2	6.1	6.1
Percent of group in Special Education	11.0	9.7	11.4	10.4

National Projections From 1978 OCR Survey (Finn. 1982)

Group	Minority %	White %	Hispanic %	Black %
Classification Mildly Mentally Retarded	2.54	1.07	0.98	3.46
Seriously Emotionally Disturbed	0.42	0.29	0.29	0.50
Learning Disabled	2.29	2.32	2.58	2.23
Speech impaired	1.82	2.04	1.78	1.87
Totally (Mildly Handicapped)	7.07	5.72	5.63	8.06

[1]Based on data reported by Mercer (1973) and personal communication from Mercer in 1979 indicating that the total enrollment in the Riverside Public Schools in the mid-1960s was about 25,000 students, of which about 1% were in special classes for the mildly retarded.
[2]Data from Table 1, p. 10 of Manni, Winikur & Keller, 1980.
[3]From Finn (1982), Table 1, p. 324.
[4]From Finn (1982), Table 3, p. 330.

The available data indicate that minority overrepresentation is not pervasive throughout special education but, rather, is specific to mild mental retardation programs. If the percentage of white and minority students is combined for mild mental retardation and learning disability programs, there typically is little or no difference. Although superficial, one possible solution to the overrepresentation problem is to combine programs for mildly handicapped students, particularly mildly mentally retarded and learning disabled, which would then eliminate overrepresentation. Cross-categorical programming for the mildly handicapped has been debated in the literature for a number of years (Gajar, 1979; Hallahan & Kauffman, 1977; Kavale, 1980; Reschly, 1986).

The major problem with this superficial solution is that nothing is addressed nor resolved concerning the effectiveness of special education programs. It is essential to understand the minority criticisms. Their criticism is not just overrepresentation, but also the implicit assumption of ineffective programming leading to unequal educational opportunities. The fact that overrepresentation per se is not the entire problem is even more apparent when consideration is given to proportions of students placed in other kinds of programs. The minority overrepresentation in Chapter 1 and Head

Start, both fairly popular compensatory education problems, is at least as great as overrepresentation in programs for the mildly retarded. However, that overrepresentation has never been the subject of litigation nor is it criticized by minority social scientists. Why is overrepresentation in one situation acceptable but not in another? The obvious answer to this question has to do with assumptions about the nature of the programs, their effectiveness, as well as the degree of stigma associated with placement in mild mental retardation programs. This perspective though, that is, that effectiveness of programs is the main problem, not overrepresentation per se, is extremely important as we attempt to develop more appropriate procedures.

Poverty, Minority Status, and MMR

Prior to discussing the characteristics of minority mildly mentally retarded students, some cautionary statements regarding the relationships between poverty, minority status, and mild mental retardation need to be emphasized. These complex relationships are frequently misunderstood. First, there is a strong link between poverty and mild mental retardation (Reschly, 1986; Richardson, 1981; Robinson & Robinson, 1976). Middle and upper socio-economic status circumstances are very rarely found among mildly mentally retarded students. The presumed etiology of most mild mental retardation, regardless of race or ethnicity, is psycho-social disadvantage (Grossman, 1983; Robinson & Robinson, 1976). The characteristics which must exist for mild mental retardation to be attributed to psycho-social disadvantage are: 1) significantly subaverage general intelligence and deficits in adaptive behaviour; 2) no evidence of biological anomaly or physical cause; 3) poverty circumstances during the developmental period; and 4) evidence of borderline level intelligence or mild mental retardation among other family members (Robinson & Robinson, 1976).

Poverty is a correlate of mild mental retardation. Causal links among specific variables are very difficult to establish. Poverty alone clearly is not sufficient. The fact is that the vast majority of the very poor, of all races and/or ethnic groups, are not mildly mentally retarded. Degree of poverty increases risk, but does not, in and of itself, cause mild mental retardation (Heber, 1970). Poverty involves a host of variables, ranging from prenatal health care to quality of educational opportunities, which combined can, apparently, produce mild mental retardation. The complex interaction of various risk factors associated with poverty is beyond the scope of this chapter. Additional information is provided in Guskin and Brantlinger (in press), Reschly (1986), and Richardson (1981).

Poverty circumstances are associated with a higher incidence of low educational achievement and school failure (Chan & Rueda, 1979; Chinn, 1979; Kavale, 1980). The overlap of characteristics associated with disadvantaged circumstances (e.g., Deutsch, 1967 or Havighurst, 1964) and learning disabilities was discussed well by Kavale (1980). These learning characteristics are not uniform, nor well understood. However, the fact of lower overall achievement is well known. Compensatory education programs such as Head Start, Follow Through, and Chapter 1 were designed to address these achievement problems and thereby improve educational opportunities for disadvantaged students. Economically disadvantaged students, who are disproportionately minority, are overrepresented in various educational programs designed to ameliorate low achievement or learning problems. From the perspective of the traditional mild mental retardation literature, this overrepresentation of minorities in poverty circumstances would be expected to, as it does, lead to overrepresentation in the classification of mild mental retardation. Another National Academy Report (Wigdor & Garner, 1982, p. 176) reached the following conclusion concerning minorities and special education, "An unbiased count of the children who are expected to have severe difficulty with instruction at the regular pace would surely find a greater proportion of poor children, including minority children, in that category."

This relationship is obviously quite controversial (Mercer, 1973, 1979; Reschly, 1986). To date, there has been no definitive analyses of this overrepresentation to determine whether the primary factor is socio-economic status, socio-economic status and race or ethnicity, or primarily race or ethnicity. Unraveling those associations would bear on the question of whether minority students are overrepresented primarily due to poverty circumstances or, alternatively, due primarily to biases in conventional assessment procedures. The latter explanation was central to the litigation cited earlier as well as the criticisms voiced by various minority critics.

Before leaving this topic some further cautions are essential. The proportions of persons in various classifications, minority and majority, need to be clarified. Although poverty is more common in minority families, the vast majority (probably two-thirds or more) of minority families are not poor according to official government data (Chan & Rueda, 1979). The majority of the poor in the United States are white. Likewise, although minorities are overrepresented in mild mental retardation programs, the vast majority of minority students are not classified as handicapped, in mild mental retardation or any other classification. Finally, the vast majority of the very poor of all groups are not mildly mentally retarded. It is also important to note the limitations of research comparing minority students and families to the general population. There are definite limitations in the modal traits or group characteristics often reported. Henderson (1980, 1981) provided excellent discussions illustrating how these modal characteristics lead to unfortunate stereotypes that are not true for most minority children or families. The longstanding caveat in individual differences research, that is, greater overlap than dispersion in distribution of traits for different groups, applies to the relationship of poverty, sociocultural group, and learning characteristics.

Characteristics of Minority MMR Students

Surprisingly, relatively little has been reported concerning the characteristics of minority mildly mentally retarded students. What has been written suggests rather clearly that such students are, by and large, very similar to non-minority mildly mentally retarded students. The most common characteristics are very low educational achievement, leading to referral, followed by individual assessment which verifies very low achievement and then the finding of low general intelligence. The outcome of this pattern is mild mental retardation classification and special education placement.

A landmark study concerning the characteristics of minority mildly mentally retarded students was reported by Mercer (1973). The monograph, based on an epidemiological study of mental retardation in Riverside, California, concluded that minority overrepresentation in mild mental retardation programs reflected the effects of bias and discrimination, not merely poverty circumstances. Mercer recommended dramatic changes in mental retardation classification criteria, in how IQ test results are interpreted, and in the assessment of adaptive behavior. These are discussed in a subsequent section on attempted solutions. Mercer also reported information on the characteristics of Hispanic and black students classified as mildly retarded in the Riverside Public Schools. These characteristics suggest that mild mental retardation classification was not the first nor the only solution attempted to resolve *chronic* educational difficulties. For example, nearly all students classified as mildly retarded in Riverside were referred by teachers and most had been retained one or more years prior to classification and placement.

A major question with Mercer's findings and the subsequent reforms she advocated has to do with conception of adaptive behavior and procedures for assessing adaptive behavior. If academic competence and school learning are at least part of what is regarded as adaptive behavior, then the students described by Mercer in the Riverside Epidemiological Study did, indeed, have adaptive behavior deficits which, along with low scores on individually administered intelligence tests, provided the basis for mild mental retardation classification.

Mercer's other findings were quite in line with the traditional literature on mild mental retardation. Students classified as mildly retarded in the Riverside studies typically were not regarded as handicapped in their home, neighborhood, or community; they were not identified as mildly mentally retarded prior to school entrance; the overwhelming majority of them did not have physical disabilities or developmental histories suggestive of biological anomalies which might account for mild mental retardation.

The implicit question in Mercer's work, even more apparent in Mercer (1979) is the nature and meaning of the diagnostic construct of mild mental retardation. If mental retardation requires a biological etiology as well as a prognosis of permanent incompetence, then the students described by Mercer in the Riverside Epidemiological Study were not mildly mentally retarded. The overwhelming majority of students classified as mildly mentally retarded, regardless of race or ethnicity, do not now and have never met those criteria. However, the diagnostic construct of mild mental retardation does not require specification of etiology or prognosis. Mental retardation refers to current functioning level (Grossman, 1973, 1977, 1983; Heber, 1959, 1961), a point often ignored or not comprehended by critics of conventional school programs.

Other recent studies of minority students classified as mildly retarded suggests that they perform substantially below average for the general population, and substantially below average for minority students on a wide variety of ability, achievement, adaptive behavior, and social skills measures (Reschly, Gresham, & Graham-Clay, 1984; Reschly & Kicklighter, in press). These differences typically are large, usually ranging from 1.5 to 2.5 standard deviations. It is especially important to note, particularly in regard to the question of equitable treatment, that there are substantial differences between average levels of performance of minority students in regular education and minority students classified as handicapped and placed in special education. The critical question is not simply declassifying minority students now placed in special education programs. Although that declassification can be carried out through a variety of procedures to be described in the next section, the underlying educational and social competence difficulties would remain unchanged. The critical question is the most appropriate method to deliver compensatory and remedial educational services to minority students who perform markedly below classroom averages, and markedly below typical levels of performance of disadvantaged students in Chapter 1 and other remedial/compensatory educational programs that currently exist.

Attempted Solutions to MMR Overrepresentation

A number of solutions have been attempted to resolve problems with overrepresentation of minority students in mild mental retardation programs in response to litigation and other influences. These solutions have generally placed heavy emphasis on changes in the assessment process or in the criteria used to classify students as mildly mentally retarded. These reforms have been part of the reason for drastic changes in conception, students served, and research in mild mental retardation over the past 15 years. Although these reforms were often directed specifically at rectifying overrepresentation of minorities, they often had little or no effect on actual degrees and patterns of overrepresentation and, in some instances, led to virtual elimination of programs for the mildly retarded.

Reevaluation/Declassification Orders

Perhaps the most drastic reforms have been instituted as a result of consent decrees in the late 1960s and early 1970s (*Diana*, 1970; *Guadalupe*, 1972). As noted earlier, the early placement bias litigation involved a number of poor professional practices. The aftermath of these early cases, particularly in California, was a number of requirements which: 1) committed the state department and school districts to immeediate reevaluation of bilingual minority students who earlier were classified as mildly retarded; 2) use of alternative assessment procedures; 3) application of more stringent IQ requirements; 4) reliance on nonverbal measures with bilingual students; and 5) more emphasis on adaptive behavior. These reevaluation orders as well as the more stringent criteria adopted by the legislature and implemented through California State Department of Education Rules and Regulations led to massive declassification of students from mild mental retardation special class programs to, by and large, regular education programs with relatively little additional services. The declassification order in *Diana* had to be carried out within a relatively short period of time. Studies of samples of declassified students indicated that the students were originally placed properly according to the criteria in place at that time. However, the more stringent criteria led to literally thousands of students being declassified. According to Meyers, MacMillan, & Yoshida (1978) the total number of students classified as mildly retarded in the California Public Schools declined from about 50,000 to just under 30,000 over the course of a few years in the early 1970s. Another study by the same authors (Yoshida, MacMillan, & Meyers, 1976) indicated that most declassified students performed at the bottom or near the bottom of the regular classrooms in which they were placed. However, most were receiving passing marks which, if true for the long term, suggests questions about the need for special education. However, no long-term follow-up was conducted with these or other declassified students. Clearly, these students had problems with school achievement, but the services might better have focused on supporting their involvement in regular education rather than placement in the more restricted, segregated special education program.

Other declassification orders for immediate reevaluation decrees have been issued by the courts in *Guadalupe* (1972) and *Larry P.* (1979). However, the effects of these decrees on numbers of students placed in programs and follow-up on the fate of students placed out of special education programs have not been published. Such studies would yield very useful information for anticipation of possible problems in the development of less restricted, noncategorical special education programs.

Reevaluation Projects

A number of studies have been conducted in recent years of the effects of various reevaluation projects undertaken as a result of anticipated legal pressure or changes in policies instituted by state or local officials. Generally reevaluation projects have led to significant reductions in numbers of students classified as mildly retarded if different, more stringent, criteria were imposed or if markedly different assessment procedures were applied. In other instances, without markedly different assessment procedures or classification criteria, relatively little change resulted from the reevaluation efforts.

An ambitious reevaluation project was carried out, and studied carefully, in Corpus Christi, Texas. The impetus for the reevaluation project came, at least in part, from pressure from the Federal Office for Civil Rights concerning overrepresentation of minority students in special class programs for the mildly retarded. In addition to stringent IQ and achievement criteria, the reevaluations were conducted using the pluralistic assessment procedures and the adaptive behavior measure developed by Mercer and her associates as part of the System of Multicultural Pluralistic Assessment (SOMPA) (Mercer, 1979). The result of using the alternative assessment procedures, particularly the use of Mercer's Adaptive Behavior Inventory for Children (ABIC), was massive declassification of both minority and majority students. The effect was virtual elimination of the population previously classified as mildly mentally retarded because hardly anyone, despite meeting stringent IQ and achievement criteria, qualified according to the adaptive behavior of pluralistic measures (Fisher, 1978, 1979). A later study of the declassified students (Fisher, 1979; Scott, 1979) indicated that about half of them could be deemed as eligible for other special education programs, usually learning disability or emotionally disturbed. This suggests that declassification has often involved reclassification in some other special education area, either when the reevaluation was done or within a few months after its completion. Tucker (1980) noted the burgeoning numbers of minority students classified as learning disabled in Texas, probably as a result, at least in part, of the pressure to reevaluate and eliminate overrepresentation of minority students classified as mildly mentally retarded.

Other reevaluation projects have been reported in recent years. In Chicago, an innovative assessment battery designed to assess cognitive processes and learning potential was developed locally in response to the Chicago Board of Education mandate to eliminate IQ tests and to reevaluate all students placed in special education programs as mildly mentally retarded. The use of this experimental battery to make classification placement decisions about students sparked considerable controversy (*Caught in the Web*, 1982). Use of the experimental battery resulted in a small decline in absolute numbers of students classified as mildly mentally retarded, but no substantial impact on the pattern of overrepresentation.

Still another reevaluation project was reported recently from Champaign, Illinois where black students constituted 25% of the district population, but 73% of the mildly mentally retarded population (Mahon, First, & Coulter, 1981). This project also applied SOMPA criteria and instruments. In results almost identical to those reported in Texas, use of the SOMPA instruments and criteria led to the virtual elimination of the population of students classified as mildly mentally retarded.

Although the research record is rather sparse, the available studies would suggest reevaluation of minority students classified as mildly mentally retarded leads to substantial changes in the population if markedly different criteria are applied or if substantially different assessment procedures are utilized. Clearly, overrepresentation can be eliminated. However, elimination of overrepresentation often results in elimination of the entire population of mildly mentally retarded students which may or may not be in the best interests of children depending, again, on the crucial question of the outcomes of mild mental retardation classification and placement.

Alternative Criteria and Assessment Procedures

Several studies have been reported, in addition to those involving large scale reevaluations of already classified populations, of the effects of alternative criteria and assessment procedures on new referrals or on randomly selected samples of students. One of the changes in the area of mild mental retardation over the past 15 years has been the application of more stringent classification criteria in many states, particularly those states where placement bias cases have mandated changes in practices or states where pressure from the Federal Office for Civil Rights has prompted voluntary change. It appears that more stringent classification criteria, for example, in California where the top IQ score which could be used for classification of a student as mildly retarded was changed from 79 to 70, sharply reduces the number of students potentially eligible for the classification of mild mental retardation. It is instructive to note that approximately 4.7% of all persons would be expected to obtain IQs below 75, but only 2.3% are expected to obtain scores below 70. Thus, what may seem to be a relatively small change in the IQ criterion, from 75 to 70, potentially reduces by half the number of students who might be classified as mildly retarded.

The record on the effects of changing the IQ criteria is unclear. The apparent effect on overrepresentation in California was minimal as noted earlier. However,

Reschly & Jipson (1976) reported moderate reduction in degree of overrepresentation at an IQ score of 70 as opposed to 75 for Hispanic, black, and native American students. Use of more stringent IQ criteria certainly reduces numbers of students and, perhaps, exerts influence on degree of overrepresentation as well. However, other changes in classification criteria and procedures have more substantial effects on overrepresentation.

The use of nonverbal or performance measures of ability as well as the application of an IQ score of 70 rather than 75 virtually eliminated overrepresentation for Hispanic students and markedly reduced overrepresentation for native American students as well (Reschly & Jipson, 1976). Use of nonverbal measures, with bilingual children and youth, seems to be an obvious best practice now widely adopted as a result of the Diana & Guadalupe Consent Decrees, as well as the Rules and Regulations Implementing Public Law 94–142 (Reschly, 1987). Although this appears to be an obvious best practice, the use of verbal ability tests with bilingual children and youth, even with some monolingual, non-English-speaking students, occurred with disturbing frequency prior to the reforms prompted by the pre-1975 litigation. The widespread adoption of these reforms may account for the absence of overrepresentation among economically disadvantaged Hispanic students in recent analyses (Heller, Holtzman, & Messick, 1982).

The most drastic change in the mild mental retardation population results from application of alternative assessment procedures, particularly the system developed and strongly advocated by Mercer (1979). Mercer's influence on this area through the Riverside Epidemiological Study (1973), numerous journal articles and book chapters, literally hundreds of workshop and convention presentations, and through publication of the System of Multicultural Pluralistic Assessment (SOMPA) should not be underestimated. Mercer also, implicitly, strongly advocated a different conception of mental retardation. For Mercer, mental retardation should be reserved for persons who exhibited biological anomalies, and for whom the prognosis was likely life-long status as handicapped. Moreover, Mercer would argue that people should not be classified as mentally retarded unless they are deficient in most, if not all, social roles and community settings. In order to understand Mercer's influence, as well as the logic underlying the development of SOMPA instruments and criteria, it is necessary to recognize her view of mental retardation. This view is significantly different from the semi-official classification system published by the American Association on Mental Deficiency over the past 25 years (Grossman, 1973, 1977, 1983; Heber, 1959, 1961).

The alternative assessment procedures as well as the decision rules recommended by Mercer were applied in several studies including the Corpus Christi, Texas research reported above, where massive declassification resulted for all groups. Talley (1979) reported on the effects of applying SOMPA instruments and criteria to all new Hispanic and white referrals in the Pueblo, Colorado Public Schools over a one-year period. The effect was dramatic. Of the small number of students who met the standard IQ criterion of less than or equal to 69, nearly all failed to meet either the SOMPA adaptive behavior criterion or the SOMPA pluralistic IQ criterion. The largest effect was with the ABIC which, alone, declassified virtually all of the Hispanic and white students who obtained IQ scores below 70 and who had been referred, presumably, due to chronic poor achievement.

Similar results were reported by Reschly (1981b) in a large randomly selected sample of white, black, Hispanic, and native American students. Nearly all the students, from all socio-cultural groups, were declassified using Mercer's SOMPA instruments and criteria, most often by the SOMPA adaptive behavior measure. Clearly, SOMPA procedures do not eliminate overrepresentation as much as they abolish mild mental retardation as a diagnostic construct. The critical question is whether this drastic change is in the best interests of students, which requires consideration of effects of special education programs for the mildly retarded.

Transition Programs

The record to date concerning the nature and effects of transition programs is, unfortunately, very sparse. Transition programs for students formerly classified and placed in special education mild mental retardation programs involve use of academic support services and small group or individual tutoring to ease the adjustment to regular education and to enhance the likelihood of success. The evidence on these programs to date is largely anecdotal or testimonial (Adkisson, 1981, Cantalician, n.d.). As noted earlier, results from California decertification studies, where the transition programs were not particularly intense, comprehensive, or of long duration, indicated that the overall adjustment of the decertified students in regular class programs was relatively positive. They certainly were not regarded as average, nor anywhere close to average, on indices of achievement or on everyday classroom work. However, most apparently had not been referred again, at least up to the time they were studied.

Much more needs to be known about transition programs and about different alternatives for providing support services within regular education to students traditionally classified as mildly mentally retarded. Alternatives to special classes and resource programs need to be designed, implemented, and evaluated. The usefulness and effectiveness of non-special education programs need to be evaluated at different ages. It seems likely, but remains to be established, that regular education programs will be increasingly insufficient at later grades. It also should be remembered that the very sparse record to date concerning transition programs is based on studies of the "old" mildly mentally retarded

population, many of who would not meet current mild mental retardation criteria.

Social Competence

Much of the current debate over various issues in the field of mild mental retardation should be considered within the broad framework of social competence. Social competence along the lines suggested by Greenspan (1979) or Zigler and Trickett (1978) provides a basis for re-analyzing several issues, including conception of mild mental retardation in educational settings, classification criteria, assessment procedures, educational program goals, and program outcomes. The debate to date has focused on narrow issues which have relatively little to do with the broad purpose of socialization: preparation of children and youth for adult roles. Biases in IQ tests or whether or not overrepresentation is discriminatory, the foci of debates to date, are relatively unimportant to the broader socialization purpose. Questions concerning what should be done in educational settings, from a social competence perspective, regarding students with very low levels of achievement and academic aptitude, namely, mildly mentally retarded students, are central to future developments in this field.

Social Competence Criteria

Social competence criteria regarding adult adjustment are, in general terms, fairly easy to establish. A normal, fully functioning adult must be capable of: 1) self-support, suggesting vocational/career development as crucial; 2) functioning independently in the community without care and supervision; and 3) functioning in a socially responsible manner so as not to be a threat to oneself or unacceptable to others. These criteria are essentially the major facets of adaptive behavior emphasized in the American Association on Mental Deficiency classification schemes (Grossman, 1983). These broad domains need to be the basis for reconsideration of the mild mental retardation diagnostic construct. Several additional issues should be analyzed within this framework.

Adult Adjustment

Zetlin, in another chapter in this section, discusses the longitudinal studies of students classified as mildly mentally retarded during the school-age years. Her review as well as other sources, see especially Edgerton (1984), indicates that mildly mentally retarded persons do not magically disappear as normal adults into the community. Mildly mentally retarded students as adults have serious adjustment problems, often related to the specific domains of behavior that led to the initial referral, classification, and placement. These domains of behavior have to do with abstract thought, application of concepts of time and number, and literacy skills.

These data from studies of adults need to be organized in a rational manner and then used as the basis for a new conception of what we now call mild mental retardation. This new conception needs to be grounded within social competence as the primary dimension of behavior rather than intelligence which continues to be, despite the efforts of many people, the principal consideration in the area of mild mental retardation. It should be noted here that much of what has been assumed about biases in IQ tests is simply wrong. However, the problem with IQ tests and intelligence as the pre-eminent dimension in mild mental retardation is not bias as much as it is relevance: relevance to adult functioning, to school programming, and to the conception of a diagnostic construct that meets the criterion of instructional validity.

Social Competence Domains

Domains of social competence for school-age children and youth need to be clearly established, as part of conception of mild mental retardation, in classification criteria, and as programming goals. The crucial domains need to be based on the adult longitudinal data (Baller, 1936; Baller, Charles, & Miller, 1967; Edgerton, 1967, 1984; Edgerton & Bercovici, 1976; Edgerton, Bollinger, & Heir, 1984; Zetlin, this volume). This date base, though far from perfect, provides the basis for much greater consideration of social competence in all aspects of mild mental retardation. Literacy skills and competencies with concepts of time and number are essential to adult social competence. There is little doubt about that. Those skills and competencies should form the basis for conception, classification/placement, and programming with mildly mentally retarded students. Persons who have mastered those and related skills should not be classified as handicapped; those without those skills due to chronic academic failure need special education programming.

Adaptive Behavior Conception and Assessment

In other work I have argued that conception is the crucial problem with adaptive behavior; also that assessment is relatively uncomplicated if agreement on a clear conception of adaptive behavior can be establish (Reschly, 1985).

The major issue is the degree to which academic performance and the school setting is important to the conception of adaptive behavior for school-age children. On the basis of several lines of evidence, including the expectations and aspirations of parents from diverse socio-cultural groups, I have argued that school performance should be a major component of our conception of adaptive behavior for school-age children. Other scholars in this area for whom I have considerable respect, for example, Mercer, have quite different views on this matter. And adaptive behavior measures vary

markedly with respect to inclusion of academic performance, literacy skills, and conceptions of time and number. If scales are used which place very little or no emphasis on these competencies, as in the Adaptive Behavior Inventory for Children (ABIC) (Mercer, 1979), there are very few if any students who have adaptive behavior deficits (see earlier discussion on declassification studies). Although other problems with Mercer's approach should be noted here such as the inappropriate use of exact cutoff scores and single measures in assessment of adaptive behavior (Reschly, 1985), the primary issue in this discussion is conception of adaptive behavior.

In Table 4 a conception of adaptive behavior is provided which suggests emphasis on both in-school and out-of-school settings. This conception can also be used in choice of placement option, with self-contained classes used only for those students who experience significant adaptive behavior deficits in both settings. Further discussion of this approach is provided in Reschly (1982, 1985).

TABLE 4
Conception of Adaptive Behavior for School-Age Children

Adaptive Behavior: School Based

Rationale:
1) Mastery of literacy skills is a key developmental task for persons between the ages of 5 and 17.
2) The expectation for and emphasis on educational competencies is common to most if not all major socio-cultural groups.

Assessment:
1) Collection and consideration of a broad variety of information including teacher interview, review of cumulative records, examination of samples of classroom work, classroom observation, results of group standardized achievement tests, results of individual achievement tests, diagnostic achievement tests, and other informal achievement measures.

Adaptive Behavior: Outside of School

Rationale:
1) Mastery of a variety of nonacademic competencies also is expected, and a key developmental task between the ages of 5 and 17.
2) The expectations for and opportunities to develop nonacademic competencies may vary among socio-cultural groups.

Assessment:
1) Collection of information on social role performance outside of school in areas such as: peer relations, family relationships, degree of independence, responsibilities assumed, economic/vocational activities, etc.
2) Method of collecting data may include formal measures, interviews with parents, interview with student, etc.

Outcomes Criterion

Prior to consideration of reforms in the field of mild mental retardation in the last section, the criteria for usefulness of a diagnostic construct need to be identified. Cromwell, Blashfield and Strauss (1975) argued persuasively for the importance of effective treatment or programming and outcome data in determining the validity of a diagnostic construct. Considerable work is needed in the field of mild mental retardation in order to meet those essential criteria.

All of the problems with mild mental retardation discussed to this point would have radically different character if the outcome data concerning mild mental retardation classification and special education programming were more positive. There are long standing debates regarding efficacy (Carlberg & Kavale, 1980; Dunn, 1968; Johnson, 1962; Kolstoe, 1976) which are not easily resolved. Two things are quite clear in this debate. Students classified as mildly mentally retarded have persistent, severe academic problems, but the special education programming despite the additional resources is not definitively better than regular education with no special services. That is oversimplified. But the lack of a clear advantages in special education cannot be dismissed.

Further evidence of how assumptions about efficacy would change this discussion is implicit in Cegalka's argument that young women are discriminated against because they are underrepresented in mild mental retardation high school work study programs. Cegalka (1976, p. 327) argued that, "Retarded females should be given the same opportunities as retarded males to participate in special vocational programs." High school work study programs appear to be effective, hence students who are probably eligible, but not identified and placed, were regarded as the victims of discrimination on the basis of sex.

Outcomes criteria are essential to fair and useful programming for minority students (Reschly, 1979). It is not sufficient to defend mild mental retardation programs on the basis of needs of students, which surely are great for mildly mentally retarded students. Program effectiveness is essential, especially in view of the stigma attached to persons classified as retarded. The absence of good outcome data and the relatively greater stigma attached to mild mental retardation (in comparison to other mildly handicapping classifications) sets the stage for the argument in the next section for classification system reform, noncategorical or cross categorical classification and programming, and greater use of regular education options with students now classified as mildly mentally retarded.

State of Art, State of Practice, and Future Directions

The diagnostic construct of mild mental retardation has been and will continue to be under substantial pressure for a variety of reasons. The underlying reality which the diagnostic construct of mild mental retardation reflects is unlikely to change substantially. That underlying reality, based on the fact that a sizable percentage, perhaps three or more percent of the school-age population, has very low academic aptitude, chronically low achievement, as well as significant deficits in social competence, will bring these students to the attention of regular and special educators whether or not they are ultimately classified as mildly mentally retarded. The critical challenge before us is to devise, carefully implement, and then rigorously evaluate promising alternatives for meeting the very real needs of these persons. I hope the device of the largely segregated special class will become increasingly rare in the future and that the term educable or mild mental retardation will become extinct. Substantial changes in the classification system are long overdue and a variety of alternatives for addressing the educational needs of these students need to be developed.

Changes in Classification

A major theme in the volumes of which this chapter is a part is the need for classification system reform. The noncategorical classification system advocated in volume 1 in this series would probably benefit mildly retarded children and youth more than any other group (Reynolds & Lakin, 1987). The reason for greater benefit is that the classification mild mental retardation is by far the most objectionable of the mildly handicapping classifications. Reactions of various persons including those classified as mildly retarded suggests that the classification of learning disability or emotional disturbance/behavior disorder are considerably less objectionable (Edgerton, 1967; Leinhardt, Bickel, & Pallay, 1982). A noncategorical classification system which included the mildly retarded would also eliminate the current disproportionate classification of minorities across learning disability and mild mental retardation which has prompted so much costly and divisive litigation to date. It is important to note that the questions involved with these public policies are more complex than mere change in names attached to symptom complexes. However, the naming problem is significant.

Because the sweeping changes advocated in several chapters in these volumes are likely to occur slowly, and may not occur everywhere, it is important to consider changes in the mental retardation classification system. The need and rationale for this change has been recognized by others, particularly Polloway and Smith (1983). The critical problem with the present system is that all levels of mental retardation are represented by the same basic terminology in the American Association on Mental Deficiency scheme (Grossman, 1983). Experience with that scheme over the past 25 years indicates that students classified as mildly retarded are inappropriately stigmatized by implicit use of the same continuum for all levels of mental retardation. A much clearer distinction is needed between the mild or educable level and the other levels (moderate, severe, and profound). Mild mental retardation is vastly different from the other more severe levels on three crucial dimensions. In contrast to the other levels, mild mental retardation is not permanent, not comprehensive in the sense of influencing most or all social roles, and not due to physical or biological anomaly. One of the reasons the mild mental retardation classification is so aversive is that most people, including many professionals from a variety of areas, confuse mild with the other levels. Thus, the attributes of the other levels, permanence, biological basis, comprehensive incompetence, are incorrectly attributed to the mildly retarded. Separation of the mild or educable level from the other levels is needed, preferably with terminology that describes and is restricted to their salient problems. A term like *educational handicap* would be considerably more accurate in describing the salient symptoms and, at the same time, potentially effective in avoiding incorrect attributions to the mildly retarded. This change should be undertaken by the American Association on Mental Deficiency and, regardless of what that very influential organization decides, could be implemented by states and districts. It is important to acknowledge that changing names does not change reality and new terminology can acquire negative connotations with surprising rapidity. However, these inevitable problems are substantially exacerbated when the system itself invites confusion and widespread misconceptions.

Alternative Educational Programming

In too many instances, in the past and today, educable or mild mental retardation is automatically assumed to result in *special class* placement. States and local districts vary considerably in this regard. In some places, the least restrictive environment concept is realized in that students classified as mildly retarded may be served by related services personnel without special education placement, may be served through resource teaching programs varying in duration from as little as one or two hours per week to as much as half of each school day, or, when necessary, in largely self-contained special classes. In other districts, the decision to classify a student as mildly retarded means, almost automatically, placement in a special class. A minimal reform, necessary to comply with legislation and rules and regulations of the past 10 years, is to ensure and carry out the development of a variety of placement alternatives for serving mildly retarded students.

Another crucial theme in the volumes in which this chapter appears is the development of regular education programs for the mildly handicapped. Students now classified as mildly retarded need to be included in these experimental programs. Although the programs to date appear to have been implemented and evaluated primarily with mildly handicapped students classified as learning disabled, inclusion of the mildly retarded is essential. Careful studies of student progress may indicate that, at some point, some kind of "pull-out" program such as special education resource may be essential. In fact, largely self-contained special classes may be required by the high school level where it is likely that the discrepancy between educational achievement levels of students now classified as mildly retarded and classroom averages will be so large that regular education alternatives will be insufficient. That, however, remains to be seen. We do not know that now and we need to find out what degree of separation from regular education, if any, is necessary.

Prevention

Results of efforts to prevent the development of mild mental retardation, although preliminary and controversial, deserve wider implementation, larger funding, and intense research evaluation attention (Garber & Heber, 1981; Ramey & Campbell, 1984). The prevention efforts described and evaluated in Taylor's chapter in this section have considerable promise.

Two kinds of preventive efforts need to be undertaken, at least at the level of funding for several model projects. The first kind of project should focus on early preschool interventions which are sufficiently intensive, persistent, and structured to enhance the likelihood of beneficial results (Garber & Heber, 1981; Ramey & Campbell, 1984). Another kind of prevention effort would be early implementation of programs such as Feuerstein's Instrumental Enrichment (Feuerstein, Rand, & Hoffman, 1979). Instrumental Enrichment, particularly if instituted relatively early in the school career, may prevent much of the later educational failure and special education referral and placement now observed with students classified as mildly retarded. It should be noted that the instrumental enrichment techniques are related to alternative assessment practices, all of which were designed for economically disadvantaged children and youth. Again, the findings here are enticing and sufficient to justify several well funded model programs.

Summary

Mild mental retardation has served as the lightning rod for increasing dissatisfaction with traditional special education practices. The effects of various problems with traditional special education, particularly concerns over disproportionate classification and placement of minority students as mildly retarded, have fostered substantial changes over the past 15 years. Thus far, many of the changes have been cosmetic. There are fewer students classified as mildly retarded but the relative proportions of minority and majority students remain about the same. The fewer students now classified as mildly retarded are still, by and large, served in self-contained classes with part-time programming unavailable or difficult to establish in many districts. In the foreseeable future we need to move beyond these cosmetic changes toward more fundamental classification system reform, and toward the development of educational alternatives ranging from prevention to implementation of a variety of degrees of special services assistance. Minority overrepresentation has served to illuminate problems in special education generally and in mild mental retardation specifically. The best response to the controversies associated with minority overrepresentation is the development of better services for children and youth, minority and majority, who experience significant learning problems. We have a sufficient data base to begin that process, particularly the development of a number of model projects involving efforts to prevent or to establish early remediation of cognitive deficits associated with mild mental retardation.

References

Adkisson, R. M. (1981). Declassified EMH students make gains. *Integrated Education*, **18**, 20–22.

Algozzine, B., & Korinek, L. (1985). Where is special education for students with high prevalence handicaps going? *Exceptional Children*, **51**, 388–394.

Baller, W. R. (1936). A study of the present social status of a group of adults who, when they were in elementary schools, were classified as mentally deficient. *Genetic Psychology Monographs*, **18**, 165–244.

Baller, W., Charles, D., & Miller, E. (1967). Mid-life attainment of the mentally retarded. *Genetic Psychology Monographs*, **75**, 235–329.

Bersoff, D. N. (1982a). The legal regulation of school psychology. In C. R. Reynolds & T. B. Gutkin (Eds.) *The Handbook of School Psychology*. New York: John Wiley.

Bersoff, D. N. (1982b). Larry P. and PASE: Judicial report cards of the validity of individual intelligence tests. In T. Kratochwill (Ed.) *Advances in School Psychology, Volume II*. Hillsdale, NJ: Lawrence Erlbaum Associates.

Cantalician Foundation (N.D.) *Technical assistance on alternative practices related to the problem of the overrepresentation of black and minority students in classes for the educable mentally retarded*. Buffalo, NY: Cantalician Foundation, Inc.

Carlberg, C., & Kavale, K. (1980). The efficacy of special vs. regular class placement for exceptional children: A meta-analysis. *Journal of Special Education*, **14**, 295–309.

Caught in the Web: Misplaced children in Chicago's classes for the mentally retarded. (1982), Chicago, IL: Designs for Change.

Cegalka, P. T. (1976). Sex role stereotyping in special education: A look at secondary work study programs. *Exceptional Children*, **42**, 323–326.

Chan, K. S. & Rueda, R. (1979). Poverty and culture in education: Separate but equal. *Exceptional Children*, **45**, 422–428.

Chinn, P. C. (1979). The exceptional minority child: Issues and some answers. *Exceptional Children*, **45**, 532–536.

Cromwell, R., Blashfield, R., & Strauss, J. (1975). Criteria for classification systems: In N. Hobbs (Ed.) *Issues in the classification of children*. San Francisco: Jossey-Bass.

Deutsch, M. (1967). Learning in the disadvantaged. In M. Deutsch (Ed.) *The disadvantaged child*. New York: Basic Books.

Diana vs. State Board of Education (1970). C.A No. C-70-37 (N.D. Cal., July 1970) (consent decree).

Doll, E. E. (1962). A historical survey of research and management of mental retardation in the United States. In E. P. Trapp & P. Himmelstein (Eds.) *Readings on the exceptional child*. New York: Appleton-Century-Crofts.

Doll, E. E. (1965) (Ed.). Historical review of mental retardation, 1800–1965: A. Symposium. *American Journal of Mental Deficiency*, **72**, 165–189.

Dunn, L. (1968). Special education for the mildly retarded: Is much of it justifiable? *Exceptional Children*, **35**, 5–22.

Edelman, M. W. (1980). *Portrait of Inequality: Black and white children in America*. Washington, D.C.: Children's Defense Fund.

Edgerton, R. (1967). *The cloak of competence: Stigma in the lives of the mentally retarded*. Berkeley, CA: University of California Press.

Edgerton, R. B. (Ed.) (1984). *Lives in process: Mentally retarded adults in a large city*. Washington, D.C.: American Association on Mental Deficiency.

Edgerton, R., & Bercovici., S. (1976). The cloak of competence: Years later. *American Journal of Mental Deficiency*, **80**, 485–497.

Edgerton, R. B., Bollinger, M., & Heir, B. (1984). The cloak of competence: After two decades. *American Journal of Mental Deficiency*, **88**, 345–351.

Elliott, R. (1985).

Feuerstein, R., Rand, T., & Hoffman, M. (1979). *The dynamic assessment of retarded performers: The learning potential assessment device, theory instruments, and techniques*. Baltimore, MD: University Park Press.

Finn, J. D. (1982). Patterns in special education placement as revealed by the OCR surveys. In K. A. Heller, W. Holtzman, & S. Messick (1982) *Placing children in special education: A strategy for equity*. Washington, D.C.: National Academy Press.

Fisher, A. T. (1978). Four approaches to classification of mental retardation. Revised version of paper presented at A.P.A. Annual Convention, Toronto.

Fisher, Alan T. (1979). Administrative interventions to provide educational services for declassified students. APA Paper, New York.

Flaugher, R. (1978). The many definitions of test bias. *American Psychologists*, **33**, 671–679.

Gajar, A. (1979). Educable mentally retarded, learning disabled, and emotionally disturbed: Similarities and differences. *Exceptional Children*, **45**, 470–472.

Garber, H. L., & Heber, R. (1981). The efficacy of early intervention with family rehabilitation. In M. J. Begab, H. C. Haywood, & H. L. Garber (Eds.), *Psychosocial influences in retarded performance, Volume II: Strategies for improving competence*. Baltimore, MD: University Park Press.

Gerber, M. M. (1984). The Department of Education's sixth annual report to Congress on PL 94-142: Is Congress getting the full story? *Exceptional Children*, **51**, 209–224.

Gibbons, F. X. (1981). The social psychology of mental retardation: What's in a label? In S. S. Brehm, S. M. Kassin, & F. X. Gibbons (Eds.), *Developmental social psychology*. New York: Oxford University Press.

Greenspan, S. (1979). Social intelligence in the retarded: In N. R. Ellis (Ed.), *Handbook of mental deficiency, psychological theory and research*. (2nd Ed.). Hillsdale, NJ: Lawrence Erlbaum Associates.

Grossman, H. J. (Ed.) (1973, 1977). *Manual on terminology and classification in mental retardation*. Washington, D.C.: American Association on Mental Deficiency.

Grossman, H. J. (Ed.) (1983). *Classification in mental retardation*. Washington, D.C.: American Association on Mental Deficiency.

Guadalupe Organization vs. Tempe Elementary School District No. 3, No. 71–435 (D. Ariz., January 24, 1972) (consent decree).

Guskin, S. L., & Brantlinger, E. A. (1951). Ethnocultural and social psychological perspectives on learning characteristics of handicapped students. In M. C. Wang & M. C. Reynolds (Eds.) *Research integration of selected issues in special education*.

Havighurst, R. (1964). Who are the socially disadvantaged? *Journal of Negro Education*, **33**, 210–217.

Hallahan, D. P., & Kauffman, J. M. (1977). Labels, categories and behaviors: ED, LD and EMR reconsidered. *Journal of Special Education*, **11**, 139–149.

Heber, R. (1959). A manual on terminology and classification in mental retardation. *American Journal of Mental Deficiency Monograph Supplement*, **64** (2).

Heber, R. (1961). Modifications of the "Manual on terminology and classification in mental retardation." *American Journal of Mental Deficiency*, **65** (4), 499–500.

Heber, R. (1970). *Epidemiology of mental retardation*. Springfield, IL: Charles C. Thomas.

Heller, K. A., Holtzman, W. H. & Messick, S. (Eds.) (1982). *Placing children in special education: A strategy for equity*. Washington, D.C.: National Academy Press.

Henderson, R. (1980). Social and emotional needs of culturally diverse children. *Exceptional Children*, **46**, 598–605.

Henderson, R. W. (1981). Nonbiased assessment: Sociocultural considerations. In T. O. Oakland (Ed.) *Nonbiased assessment*. Minneapolis, MN: University of Minnesota, National School Psychology Inservice Training Network.

Hilliard, A. (1980). Cultural diversity and special education. *Exceptional Children*, **46**, 584–588.

Hobson vs. Hansen, 269 F. Supp. 401 (D.D.C. 1967).

Jensen, A. R. (1969). How much can we boost IQ and scholastic achievement? *Harvard Educational Review*, **39**, 1–123.

Jensen, A. R. (1980). *Bias in mental testing*. New York: The Free Press.

Johnson, G. O. (1962). Special Education for the mentally handicapped: A paradox. *Exceptional Children*, **29**, 62–69.

Johnson, J. (1969). Special education and the inner city: A challenge for the future or another means of cooling the mark out. *Journal of Special Education*, **3**, 241–251.

Jones, R. (Ed.) (1976). *Mainstreaming and the minority child*. Reston, VA: Council for Exceptional Children.

Jones, R. (1987). Institutional bias and prejudice. In M. Brassard, R. Germain, & S. N. Hart (Eds.) *The psychological maltreatment of children and youth*. New York: Pergamon.

Jones, R., & Wilderson, F. (1976). Mainstreaming and the minority child: An overview of issues and a perspective. In R. Jones (Ed.) *Mainstreaming and the minority child*. Reston, VA: Council for Exceptional Children.

Kavale, K. (1980). Learning disability and cultural-economic disadvantage: The case for a relationship. *Learning Disability Quarterly*, **3**, 97–112.

Kolstoe, O. P. (1976). *Teaching educable mentally retarded children* (2nd ed.). New York: Holt.

Larry, P. vs. Riles (1979). 495 F. Supp. 926 (N. D. Cal 1979) (decision on merits).

Larry, P. vs. Riles (1984). United States Court of Appeals, Ninth Circuit, No. 80–427. January 23, 1984. Trial Court Decision Affirmed.

Leinhardt, G., Bickel, W., & Pallay, A. (1982). Unlabeled but still entitled: Toward more effective remediation. *Teachers College Record*, **84**, 391–422.

MacMillan, D. L. (1982). *Mental retardation in school and society*. (2nd ed.) Boston: Little, Brown.

MacMillan, D. L., & Borthwick, S. (1980). The new educable mentally retarded population: Can they be mainstreamed? *Mental Retardation*, **18**, 155–158.

MacMillan, D. L., Jones, R. L., & Aloia, G. F. (1974). The mentally retarded label: A theoretical analysis and review of research. *American Journal of Mental Deficiency*, **79**, 241–261.

MacMillan, D. L., Meyers, C. E., & Morrison, G. M. (1980). System-identification of mildly mentally retarded children: implications for interpreting and conducting research. *American Journal of Mental Deficiency*, **85**, 108–115.

Mahon, H. J., First, J. M., & Coulter, W. A. (1981). An end to double jeopardy: The declassification/transition of minority EMH students. *Integrated Education*, **18**, 16–19.

Manni, J. L., Winikur, D. W., & Keller, M. (1980). *A report on minority group representation in special education programs in the state of New Jersey*. New Jersey State Department of Education, 225 W. State Street, Trenton, NJ 08625. (ERIC No. ED 203 575).

Marshall et. al. vs. Georgia. (1984). U.S. District Court for the Southern District of Georgia, CV482–233, June 28, 1984.

Mercer, J. R. (1973). *Labeling the mentally retarded*. Berkeley, CA: University of California Press.

Mercer, J. R. (1979). *System of multicultural pluralistic assessment technical manual*. New York: Psychological Corporation.

Meyers, C. E., MacMillan, D. L., & Yoshida, R. K. (1978). Validity of psychologists' identification of EMR students in the perspective of the California decertification experience. *Journal of School Psychology*, **16**, 3–15.

Meyers, C. E., Sundstrom, P., & Yoshida, R. K. (1974). The school psychologist and assessment in special education: A report of the Ad Hoc Committee of APA Division 16. *Monographs of Division 16 of the American Psychological Association* **2**(1), 3–57.

Mills vs. Board of Education. (1972). 348 F. Supp. 866 (D.D.C. 1972).

(PARC) (Pennsylvania Association for Retarded Children vs. Commonwealth of Pennsylvania, (1972). 343 F. Supp. 279 (E.D. Pa. 1972).

PASE (Parents in Action on Special Education) vs. Joseph P. Hannon, (1980). U.S. District Court, Northern District of Illinois, Eastern Division, No. 74 (3586), July, 1980.

Polloway, E. A., & Smith, J. D. (1983). Changes in mild mental retardation: Population, programs, and perspectives. *Exceptional Children*, **50**, 149–159.

Polloway, E. A., & Smith, J. D. (1987). Current status of the mild mental retardation construct: Identification, placement, & programs. In M. C. Wang & M. C. Reynolds (Eds.) *The Handbook of Special Education Research and Practice, Volume II*.

Prasse, D., & Reschly, D. (1986). *Larry P.* A case of segregation, testing, or program efficacy? *Exceptional Children,* **52**, 333–346.

President's Committee on Mental Retardation (1970). *The six hour retarded child,* Washington, D.C.: United States Government Printing Office.

Ramey, C. T., & Campbell, F. A. (1984). Preventive education for high risk children: Cognitive consequences of the Carolina Abecedarian project. *American Journal of Mental Deficiency,* **88**, 515–523.

Reschly, D. (1979). Nonbiased assessment. In G. Phye & D. Reschly (Eds.), *School psychology: Perspectives and Issues.* New York: Academic Press.

Reschly, D. (1981a). Psychological testing in educational classification and placement. *American Psychologist,* **36**, 1094–1102.

Reschly, D. (1981b). Evaluation of the effects of SOMPA measures on classification of students as mildly mentally retarded. *American Journal of Mental Deficiency,* **86**, 16–20.

Reschly, D. (1982). Assessing mild mental retardation: The influence of adaptive behavior, sociocultural status, and prospects for nonbiased assessment. In C. R. Reynolds & T. B. Gutkin (Eds.) *The Handbook of School Psychology.* New York: Wiley.

Reschly, D. (1983). Legal issues in psychoeducational assessment. In G. Hynd (Ed.) *The school psychologist: Contemporary perspectives.* Syracuse, NY: Syracuse University Press.

Reschly, D. J. (1984). Beyond IQ test bias: The National Academy Panel's analysis of minority EMR overrepresentation. *Educational Research* **13(3)**, 15–19.

Reschly, D. (1985). Adaptive behavior. In A. Thomas & J. Grimes (Eds.) *Best practices in school psychology.* Kent, OH: National Association of School Psychologists.

Reschly, D. (1987). Assessing educational handicaps. In A. Hess & I. Weiner (Eds.) *Handbook of forensic psychology.* New York: Wiley.

Reschly, D. (1986). Economic and cultural factors in childhood exceptionality. In R. Brown & C. Reynolds (Eds.) *Psychological perspectives on childhood exceptionality.* New York: Wiley.

Reschly, D. J., Gresham, F. M., & Graham-Clay, S. (1984). *Multi-factored nonbiased assessment: Convergent and discriminant validity of social and cognitive measures with black and white regular and special education students.* Final Project Report. Department of Psychology, Iowa State University, Ames, IA 50011. (ERIC No. ED 252 034).

Reschly, D. J., & Jipson, F. J. (1976). Ethnicity, geographic locale, age, sex, and urban-rural residence as variables in the prevalence of mild retardation. *American Journal of Mental Deficiency,* **81**, 154–161.

Reschly, D. J., & Kicklighter, R. J. (1985). *Comparison of black and white EMR students from Marshall vs. Georgia.* Paper presented at the Annual Convention of the American Psychological Association, Los Angeles. (ERIC No. ED. 271 911).

Reynolds, C. R. (1982). The problem of bias in psychological assessment. In C. R. Reynolds and T. B. Gutkin, (Eds.) *The Handbook of School Psychology.* New York: Wiley.

Richardson, R. (1981). Family characteristics associated with mild mental retardation. In M. Begab, H. C. Haywood, and H. Garber, *Psychosocial influences in retarded performance,* Volume I. Baltimore, MD: University Park Press.

Robinson, N., & Robinson, H. (1976). *The mentally retarded child* (2nd Ed.). New York: McGraw-Hill.

Samuda, R. J. (1976). Problems and issues of minority group children. In R. Jones (Ed.) *Mainstreaming and the minority child.* Reston, VA: Council for Exceptional Children.

Scott, Leigh S. (1979). Identification of declassified students: Characteristics and needs of the population. Annual Convention of the American Psychological Association, New York.

Talley, R. (1979). *Evaluating the effects of implementing SOMPA.* Bloomington, IN: Center for Innovation in Teaching the Handicapped, University of Indiana.

Tucker, J. (1980). Ethnic proportions in classes for the learning disabled: Issues in nonbiased assessment. *Journal of Special Education,* **14**, 93–105.

Turnbull, H. (1978). The past and future impact of court decisions in special education. *Kappan,* **60**, 523–527.

United States Department of Education (1985). *Seventh Annual Report to Congress on the Implementation of Public Law 94–142: The Education for all Handicapped Children Act.* Washington, D.C. Office of Special Education.

Watson, B. (1981). The social consequences of testing: Another view. In W. Schrader (Ed.) *Admissions Testing and the Public Interest: Proceedings of the 1980 ETS Invitational Conference.* San Francisco: Jossey-Bass.

Wigdor, A. K., & Garner, W. R. (Eds.) (1982). *Ability testing: Uses, consequences, and controversies.* Washington, D.C.: National Academy Press.

Williams, R. (1970). Danger: Testing and dehumanizing the black child. *Clinical Child Psychology Newsletter,* **9**, 5–6.

Yoshida, R., MacMillan, D., & Meyers, C. E. (1976). The decertification of minority group EMR students in California: Student achievement and adjustment, in R. Jones (Ed.), *Mainstreaming and the Minority Child,* Reston, VA: Council for Exceptional Children.

Ysseldyke, J. E., Thurlow, M., Graden, J., Wesson, C., Algozzine, B., & Deno, S. (1983). Generalizations from five years of research on assessment and decision making: The University of Minnesota Institute. *Exceptional Education Quarterly,* **4**, 75–93.

Zigler, E., & Trickett, P. (1978). IQ, social competence, and evaluation of early childhood intervention programs. *American Psychologist,* **33**, 789–798.

Cognitive and Social Development of Mildly Retarded Children

JACK J. KRAMER, WAYNE C. PIERSEL, AND JOHN A. GLOVER

University of Nebraska-Lincoln

Abstract—This paper presents a review of the cognitive and social development research with mildly retarded children and youth. Within the cognitive domain the focus is on the processing differences that exist between mildly retarded and normal children, while in the social area the development of social competence and social cognition in mildly retarded children are emphasized. The implications of these research efforts for educational practice are examined. Finally, an agenda for future research is provided.

The purpose of the present chapter is a simple one. We will attempt to provide a review and synthesis of recent research related to the cognitive and social development of mildly retarded children.

Although our goals are simple, the size of the task is enormous. The amount of research in the general area of mental retardation has grown dramatically during the last two decades (Detterman, 1979) and there appears to be no let-up in sight. To this literature we must also add the current research on the cognitive and social development of normal, or nonhandicapped, populations. This addition is necessary if we are to be able to: (a) compare retarded with normal development in a manner that will allow for a cogent analysis of the differences that exist, and (b) develop an understanding of the strategies and skills that should serve as models in our attempt to train efficient, adaptive skills to retarded learners. Clearly, an exhaustive analysis of the entire research literature is beyond the scope of this chapter.

Indeed we make no attempt to review every piece of research, but instead try to bring some order to the field through selective and integrative analysis of the most definitive studies. We acknowledge that others who would be asked to complete this same review might well identify other research or even choose to take a completely different approach to the task.

As indicated in the title, this chapter focuses on the research with mildly retarded individuals (IQ scores 50–75, educable mentally retarded, familial retarded, etc). Comparisons will be made with other populations; however, in the final analysis the emphasis is always on the retardation literature and the implications for the retarded learner. In the cognitive domain our goal is to focus on the process differences that exist between mildly retarded and normal children, while in the social area we emphasize the development of social competence. An examination of the implications of the cognitive and social literature for practice is provided with the suggestion that the findings in these two areas have similar impact on our future training efforts. Finally, we explore an agenda for future research.

Cognitive Development

The existence of differences in the cognitive development of mildly retarded and normal children is such a frequently made observation that it hardly bears mention. Indeed, the old ratio IQ was based on the fact that patterns of children's chronological and cognitive development diverge. Subsequent research comparing retarded and normal populations has dramatized the extent of the differences that exist. Mentally retarded individuals are, as a group, inefficient learners. It is this characteristic more than any other that distinguishes them from their nonretarded peers. Regardless of whether we explore particular domains such as competence, adaptive behavior, cognitive processing, or other clusters of variables, we find ourselves ultimately examining the results of inefficient learning. Not only are retarded individuals less efficient in formal learning situations, many believe that these individuals are especially deficient in acquiring information and skills in informal or naturally occurring situations. Our purpose here is not to reiterate the obvious differences in achievements in cognitive development. Rather we present an approach for understanding *process* differences between mildly retarded and normal children.

A Framework for Viewing Cognitive Processes

Our view of cognitive development is based on a general information processing paradigm and, more specifically, the theoretical work of Siegler (e.g., 1976,

1984), Case (1978, 1984a), and Sternberg (1982, 1984b). Central to the perspective is the use of a computer analog for human thought processes. And, although Siegler, Case, and Sternberg differ in how they have utilized this analog in their work, a brief review of an information processing model of human cognition is necessary before we can turn to a discussion of research focusing on processing differences between mildly retarded and normal children.

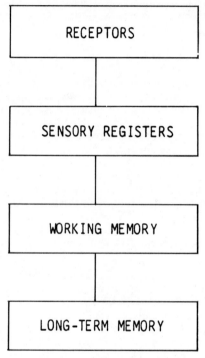

Figure 1–1 pictures a simple information processing model.

The model consists of four basic interactive elements. Below, we will examine each of these components in brief.

The sense receptors. Information from the external world enters the processing system through children's sense receptors (eyes, ears, nose, tongue, etc). The model does not make the empiricist assumption that all information comes from the external world. Instead, the model presumes an interaction between the child's extant knowledge structure and incoming information. Although issues related to sensory disabilities are beyond the scope of the current chapter, it is important to note that the model presumes that the information acted on in the processing system can be no better than the quality of information received and transmitted by the sense receptors. Hence, any sensory impairments

have powerful implications for the quality of the information processing system (e.g., Morariu & Bruning, 1984).

Sensory registers. The sensory registers (there apparently is one for each sense) serve as brief holding systems for maintaining representations of incoming stimuli so that cognitive activities can begin to be performed on them. Each sensory register has a limited capacity and can hold information for very circumscribed periods of time (e.g., the iconic register is estimated to hold information for up to 0.5 seconds; the echoic register for as long as 2.5 seconds). The sensory registers are critical to the process of perception. In the general information processing view, perception is more than simply sensing that something is present. Rather perception is defined as the assignment of meaning to incoming stimuli. The distinction between sensing and perceiving is analogous to the difference between feeling something in one's coat pocket and knowing that what has been felt is the car key.

In contrast to Gibson's views (e.g., Gibson & Spelke, 1983), information processing theorists (e.g., Tighe & Shepp, 1983; von Wright, 1972) argue that perception is not an instantaneous process. Before a child can determine the meaning of stimuli, a number of cognitive processes must be carried out and each of these processes takes time. In brief, the stimulus must be attended to, passed to working memory, matched to information in long-term memory, and a decision reached in working memory. As we will see later in this section, research focusing on individual differences in the capacity and duration of memory in the sensory registers (which would directly influence what and how much could be perceived in the environment) seems to indicate that this component of the model may be a critical source of individual differences in cognitive development.

The working memory. In the current model, the working memory is both a short-term repository of information and the system's executive. Similar to the sensory registers, the working memory has limited capacity (e.g., Britton & Tesser, 1982) and, unless certain processes are invoked (i.e., rehearsal), a limited duration.

Beyond serving as a short-term repository of information (e.g., briefly remembering a phone number while you walk across the room to the phone), the working memory is that part of the system in which executive control is exerted. In working memory decisions are made (e.g., what to attend to, whether or not to reread a sentence), information is manipulated, long-term memory and new information interplay, and so on. Research on individual differences in working memory has focused on the speed with which information can be manipulated (e.g., Benton, Kraft, Glover, & Plake, 1984; Hunt, 1978, in press), the amount of information that can be held (Benton et al., 1984; Case, 1984a; Hunt, 1978; Humphreys, Lynch, Revelle, & Hall, 1983), and the various executive processes involved in problem solving (e.g., Case, 1984a; Hunt, 1978, in press; Sternberg, 1984c).

Long-term memory. In our simple model, long-term memory is the relatively permanent repository of knowledge (e.g., the square root of 5, the capital of Delaware). Long-term memory is accessed in perception and is necessary for the executive processes in working memory (that is, the "programs" are stored in long-term memory and are "called-up" by the working memory). Not all of the information from the working memory will be passed on to the long-term memory. Further, access to information in long-term memory is affected by many variables and so the availability of long-term memories varies as a function of the context in which recall is attempted.

Sources of Individual Differences

Research on the individual differences in information processing is based on the observation that there are several "bottlenecks" in the processing system (Broadbent, 1958; Hunt, Frost, & Lunneburg, 1973). For example, far more information in the environment is available to children than can be held in the sensory registers (see Sperling, 1960, 1963). Further, only a fraction of what is held in the sensory registers can be accessed by the working memory (Darwin, Turvey, & Crowder, 1972; Sperling, 1960; von Wright, 1972). As we have noted, working memory has a limited capacity (Britton & Tesser, 1982; Miller, 1956; Murdock, 1961; Postman, 1975; Simon, 1974), and only a portion of the information held in working memory is passed on to long-term memory (see Klatzky, 1980). These "bottlenecks" in the processing system taken with the obvious differences in cognitive achievement led several theorists (e.g., Case, 1974; Ellis, 1970; Hunt, 1978; Sternberg, 1984b) to propose that differences in cognitive abilities could be accounted for on the basis of differences in individuals' information processing systems.

In particular, Hunt and his colleagues (e.g., Hunt, 1978, in press; Hunt, Lansman, & Davidson, 1981; Hunt et al., 1973) have suggested that there are three potential sources of individual differences in information processing: knowledge, mechanics of information processing, and elementary information processing programs. Differences in knowledge (contained in long-term memory) clearly influence what will be attended to, what will be perceived, and the likelihood of passing new information into long-term memory. For example, a child faced with a word problem in mathematics who has knowledge of how to solve such problems will likely attend to relevant aspects of the problem, assign appropriate meanings to various aspects of the problem, and is very likely to append any new information to his or her already existing store of knowledge in long-term memory. In contrast, a child who does not know about such problems is unlikely to know what to focus on, will not assign appropriate meanings to several aspects of the problem, and will have little likelihood of tieing his or her experience with the problem into relevant knowledge structures in long-term memory.

Hunt's second source of individual variations in cognition, the mechanics of information processing, refers to the "hardware" component of the information processing system. Hunt proposed that there were capacity and duration differences in the sensory registers, capacity, duration, and speed of manipulation differences in working memory, and speed of access to long-term memory differences. Hunt (1978) also suggested, however, that "hardware" differences had to be considered in light of differences among individuals' elementary information processing programs. In Hunt's (1978) view human beings must possess:

> simple strategies that are used as steps in virtually every larger problem. Examples are the strategy of repeating names that are to be remembered or the strategy of checking an answer after it has been developed but before it is publicly enunciated . . . much of what we refer to as general intelligence is based on the facility with which one uses such general information processes. (p. 128)

Of the sources of cognitive ability differences Hung describes, knowledge has been most frequently investigated in psychometric studies, albeit from a perspective very different than that of information processing. Here, we focus on information processing oriented research.

Individual Differences in Cognition

A review of all the work that has examined individual differences in information processing is beyond the scope of our current chapter. In this section, we briefly recount general approaches in the area and then review in greater depth work specific to differences between mildly retarded and normal children.

Two traditions of research. Two rather different traditions have developed for research on individual differences in cognition. The cognitive-developmental approach grows out of attempts to understand the process of cognitive development in terms of the development of human information processing systems. In contrast, the "intelligence" approach is based on more traditional psychometric approaches to the assessment of intelligence and has focused on identifying cognitive processes associated with individual differences in intelligence. We will describe each below.

The cognitive-developmental approach (e.g., Case, 1984; Sternberg, 1984a, 1984b) has centered primarily on differences in working memory, the very clear observation that children's working memory capacity increases with age. Case's emphasis (e.g., 1984a) has been on the efficiency of elementary information processing programs used in working memory. In general, he has argued that the capacity of working memory does not increase with development. That is, he does not perceive a change in "hardware." Instead, children's executive processes become more and more efficient through practice and increased knowledge, requiring less and less space in working memory. The analog to computer programs is direct: highly efficient programs can do the same job that inefficient programs do but require less working memory space and work more speedily. In Case's view, changes in working memory capacity (and the consequent changes in the cognitive products children produce) result from the development of better and better elementary information processing programs (see Case, 1974, 1978, 1985).

Sternberg's (1982, 1984b, 1984c, 1984d) developmental approach has also emphasized working memory as the source of individual differences in cognition, although Sternberg clearly is working on a more comprehensive theory of intelligence. To date, Sternberg's major focus has been on his *componential subtheory* growing out of his larger "triarchic" theory of intelligence. The emphasis in this subtheory is primarily on what we have called elementary information processing programs. Like Case, Sternberg suggests that cognitive development proceeds as a function of the development of more and more efficient elementary information processing programs.

In contrast to the cognitive-developmental approach, the "intelligence" approach grew out of attempts to meld experimental cognitive psychology and psychometrics (Hunt, in press; Jensen, in press). Beginning with Cronbach's (1957) call for experimental and psychometric psychology to work together, this approach has centered on identifying information processing tasks related to psychometric measures.

For example, Hunt and his colleagues (e.g., 1978, in press) typically have identified diverse groups of subjects on the basis of psychometric instruments and have then attempted to determine whether these groups also differed in their performance on information processing tasks. In general, Hunt has found that groups differing on measures of verbal ability also differ significantly in the capacity of iconic register, the capacity of working memory, the speed with which information can be manipulated in working memory, the duration of information in working memory, and the speed with which long-term memory can be accessed (see Hunt, 1978, in press, for reviews). Unlike the developmental approach, the "intelligence" approach has focused on all elements of the information processing system and, as discussed below, considerable emphasis has been given to "hardware"-"software" distinctions.

Contrasts of Retarded and Normal Individuals

Research examining processing differences between normal and mildly retarded individuals has proceeded largely from the "intelligence" perspective (e.g., Butterfield & Belmont, 1975; Ellis, 1970; Krupski, 1980; Nettlebeck & Brewer, 1981). The typical procedure is to identify a mildly retarded group and either an age-matched or a mental age-matched group of normal subjects and then to compare them on a series of information processing tasks (e.g., Caruso, 1985). The majority of such research has been conducted on adults and adolescent retarded subjects, although recent work has begun to focus on children (e.g., Bos & Tierney, 1984).

The general findings of this line of research fit well within the results provided by Hunt in contrasts of normal and highly capable students (see 1978). For example, the size of the iconic register appears to be smaller in mildly retarded than in normal subjects (Hornstein & Mosley, 1979; Libkuman, Velliky, & Freidrich, 1980; Pennington & Luszca, 1975; Ross & Ward, 1978; Saccuzzo, Kerr, Marcus, & Brown, 1979). Although the data are less clear, it also seems that the duration of iconic store may be shorter among the mildly retarded (Saccuzzo et al., 1979) and that the accessibility of information from iconic store is poorer (Libkuman et al., 1980; Saccuzzo et al., 1979).

An example of iconic register research can be seen in a study by Pennington and Luszca (1975) in which they contrasted the iconic register capabilities of normal and retarded young adults in a series of four experiments. In this study, arrays of letters were presented to the subjects via a tachistoscope for 50 milliseconds. Subjects then reported the letters seen after varying delay intervals. Confirming Sperling (1960), normal subjects reported about four items per array. The retarded subjects, however, consistently reported an average of about one less item per array (see Pennington & Luszca, 1975, pp. 296–297).

The Pennington and Luszca (1975) study has served as the prototype of sensory register research contrasting normal and retarded individuals. The reliability with which iconic store processing deficits are observed in mildly retarded individuals taken together with the widely held position that no executive processes operate at the level of sensory registers (see Averbach & Coriell, 1961; Sperling, 1960) have been often cited reasons for concluding that at least part of the information processing deficit in mildly retarded individuals is due to structural ("hardware") limitations (see Saccuzzo & Michael, 1984), perhaps located in the visual cortex.

As important as the capacity of the sensory registers are to information processing, several types of deficits have also been reported in working memory. For instance, the capacity of working memory (in "chunks" of information) is lower among retarded individuals than among normal persons (Brown, 1974; Spitz, 1973), the speed of information manipulation is slower (Saccuzzo & Michael, 1984), the availability of elementary information processing programs is more limited (e.g. Borkowski & Cavanaugh, 1979), access to long-term memory (see, for example, Saccuzzo & Michael, 1984) is more restricted, and there seem to be more constraints on specific executive processes (e.g., Nettlebeck, Hirons, & Wilson, 1985). Although at this point it is not possible to determine the relationship of sensory register deficits on working memory functions, it is clear that sensory register capabilities have a powerful effect on working memory (Saccuzzo & Michael, 1984) and must be considered in conjunction with observed deficits in working memory.

Given the diversity of the field, it is difficult to identify a characteristic study among the many that have focused on working memory. Here, the recent study by Ellis, Deacon, and Woolridge (1985) will serve as our example. Across four experiments, Ellis et al. compared the performance of normal and mildly retarded young adults' ability to recall sets of pictures after 0, 5, 15, and 30 seconds with the use of an intervening task (counting backwards) designed to eliminate executive processing (and thereby to reduce the potential that executive processes would influence recall). The overall results mirrored typical findings on studies of normal adults in that recall decreased as the delay after encoding increased, suggesting that executive processes had effectively been blocked. When retarded and normal subjects were compared, both groups showed similar patterns of forgetting as delay time increased. However, the normal group recalled significantly more pictures than the retarded group at each of the delay intervals.

Ellis et al. (1985) interpreted their results as confirming a structural deficit in working memory among the retarded and have addressed what seems to be the major controversy in information processing abilities research: whether working memory deficits are due to elementary information processing program shortcomings or to structural problems. Research on cognitive processes has proceeded beyond the point at which the "bottlenecks" in retarded people's information processing capabilities are disputed. It is clear that there are deficits at each point in the processing system (although, curiously, no work has been done to determine if different people suffer different deficits at different points in their system). Currently the argument revolves not around whether or not there are information processing deficits but rather why these deficits occur.

Early work on memory deficits in the mentally retarded was based on a belief in structural shortcomings (see Ellis, 1963). By the late 1960s and early 1970s, however, the emphasis shifted more and more toward executive process inadequacies (see Belmont & Butterfield, 1969, 1977; Detterman, 1979; Ellis, 1970). Very recent work (e.g., Ellis et al., 1985) has again emphasized structural deficits. It seems to us that neither of the extreme positions (structure only or executive processes only) can be totally accurate. The results of research

on iconic memory are strongly suggestive of structural deficits as are studies based on minimal strategy paradigms (e.g., Ellis & Meador, 1985). However, it also seems beyond question that there are very real executive control deficits (e.g., Bos & Tierney, 1984; Luftig & Johnson, 1982). Further, the lack of research focusing on possible different sources of information processing deficits among the retarded leave us without any data on which to draw a firm conclusion about relative "hardware"-"software" contributions. Given the current status of research in the area, it appears that a middle-ground position (e.g., Campione & Brown, 1977; Fisher & Zeamon, 1973; Zeamon & House, 1979) will be most fruitful for future research and the development of practical applications.

Summary

In this section of the chapter, we presented a framework for viewing cognitive processes based on a computer analog. The model includes sense receptors, sensory registers, a working memory, and a long-term memory. There are "bottlenecks" at each part in this system: capacities are limited in the sensory registers and working memory, speed is limited in working memory, and passage and access to long-term memory is restricted.

We followed Hunt's reasoning in describing three sources of individual differences in information processing: knowledge, mechanics of information processing (structure), and elementary information processing programs (executive processes). Each of these sources of potential individual differences helps account for differences in cognitive performance. Knowledge influences all of the executive processes in working memory. The mechanics of information processing influence the capacity and speed of processing in the system. Elementary information processing programs directly affect the speed and quality of processing in the working memory.

Two traditions of research have developed in work on individual differences in cognitive processes: the cognitive-developmental and the "intelligence" approaches. The cognitive-development approach focuses on the unfolding of the human information processing system across time, while the "intelligence" approach has emphasized the identification of processing tasks related to observed psychometric differences among individuals. Research contrasting mildly retarded and normal subjects has been performed almost exclusively from the "intelligence" perspective.

The results of research contrasting mildly retarded and normal individuals has evidenced differences in the capacity of the iconic register and working memory. In addition, deficits among the retarded have been observed in elementary information processing programs and in access to long-term memory. These deficits fit into the continuum of individual processing differences observed in research on normal and highly capable individuals.

Social Development and Competence

As we have already noted, when we examine the learning of mentally retarded students, the absence of and/or inefficient use of cognitive processes is readily apparent. Although cognitive processes underly all aspects of a behavior, including the behavior of individuals we choose to call mentally retarded, social intelligence or social competence is viewed by many as the most important aspects of an individual's development. The ultimate adequacy of social development determines, in a very real way, the quality of life that the individual will attain. Thus, the inefficient learning of mentally retarded students have definite implications for their social development.

A major requirement for acceptance by society is appropriate social behavior. One of the major problems in individuals with intellectual deficits is a parallel deficit in social behavior. Indeed, for many mildly and moderately retarded individuals, it is the lack of social competencies rather than intellectual deficits which bring unwanted attention. Although there is a lack of consensus on the meaning of social competence (Schiefelbusch, 1981), there is general agreement that socially adequate individuals have developed skills and capabilities in interpersonal awareness and communicative competence.

Social intelligence or awareness has long been recognized as among the most important variables determining retardation and in determining the types of services available as well as where the services will be provided (institution, group home, family). Unfortunately, most research has focused on investigating age-related changes with only a limited number of studies attempting to examine interrelations among the various factors or dimensions that comprise social awareness or social cognition.

Greenspan (1979, 1981) has developed a model of social awareness components that consists of three groupings with further refinements. The clusters are: (a) social sensitivity, to include role-taking and social inference; (b) social insight, to include social comprehension, psychological insight, and moral judgment; and (c) social communication, to include referential communication and social problem solving. To Greenspan's conceptual scheme, we would add the cluster (d) self-awareness or self-understanding, to include dimensions of self-concept, expectancies, and motivation. It is around these four clusters (a—d) that we discuss social competence in the mildly retarded.

Social Versus Cognitive Development

Social and cognitive skills are interrelated such that the development of such skills as role-taking, self-awareness, interpersonal skills, social communication skills reflect both social and cognitive development. In many ways the development of cognitive skills create the foundation and make possible the acquisition of more complex social skills and related affective behaviors. In a very real sense, cognitive development is prerequisite to the attainment of adequate social development.

It is also important to distinguish between social cognition and affect. Many writers such as Affleck (1976) and Parrill-Bernstein (1979) view social development or social cognition as the strategy of social behavior while viewing affect as the emotional reaction or feeling underlying the problem solving process. Thus, social interactions provide the setting in which social problems are posed, strategies are developed and utilized and emotional responses are learned or unlearned. It therefore follows that social interactions within the family, peer groups, or school setting become the primary setting to investigate the development of social cognition and affect.

Self-awareness

The vast majority of what we know about how mentally retarded students perceive themselves has been derived or inferred from how these children and youth have responded to stimulus situations such as self-statments and role-play situations. The limitations in their language and communication skills has made examination of self-awareness particularly difficult. While other individuals can explain their cognitive responses, the mentally retarded people have a more difficult time organizing and expressing their thoughts.

Self-Concept. Self-concept refers to the evaluative view that an individual has regarding himself or herself. Self-concept is thought to relate to a person's life experiences and to the degree of positive acceptance by other individuals in the person's life. Research with mildly retarded children (Zigler, Balla, & Watson, 1972) suggests that mentally retarded children have lowered expectations indicating more limited aspirations and a less positive view of self. There does appear to be a relationship between successful experiences and self-concept. This relationship may explain some of the contradictory findings regarding the effect of self-contained and regular class placement on self-concept. Those regular classrooms and self-contained classrooms that structure positive experiences may be more likely to produce more positive self-descriptions (Hayes & Prinz, 1976).

Thus, those environments that have a high ratio of successful to unsuccessful experiences and enable mentally retarded individuals to perceive themselves as successful facilitate positive feelings about self. This finding may well explain the often repeated result that mentally retarded students in self-contained classes have a more positive view of self than mentally retarded individuals who are mainstreamed into regular classes (e.g., Gruen, Ottinger, & Ollendick, 1974).

Expectancies. This attribute of social development relates to the expectation on the part of an individual that an event will or will not happen. We typically think of expectations in terms of mutually rewarding social interactions or in terms of being successful or unsuccessful on a particular task (i.e., arithmetic test, completion of an art assignment). Popular belief indicates that mentally retarded students are more likely to expect to fail because of the belief that they encounter a higher rate of failure in their natural environments and a lower rate of success than normal children of the same age. In addition, elaborate psychological theories regarding pathological processes such as hostility, increased withdrawal, and increased use of defense mechanisms have been postulated for mentally retarded individuals based on the belief that they experience a high rate of failure. Indeed, research by Cromwell (1963) and discussion by Logan and Rose (1982) indicate that mentally retarded individuals are more likely to decrease their efforts on tasks following failure experiences. Research by Ollendick, Balla, and Zigler (1971) suggests that successful experiences lead to increases in performance and expectations of success. Gruen, Ottinger, and Ollendick (1974) found that mildly retarded students in regular classrooms had lower expectations for success than did comparable individuals in self-contained classes.

While it is obvious that avoidance behaviors may develop and reflect a "failure expectation," it is not so obvious that not to experience failure may also be undesirable. Studies with nonretarded students have consistently shown that being signaled following correct and incorrect responses results in more efficient learning than just being informed of correct responses (Meyer & Offenbach, 1962; Whitehurst, 1969). Harter, Brown, & Zigler (1971) found that both retarded and nonretarded children demonstrated better learning when tangible rewards were combined with tangible penalties. To the extent that failure experiences possess a stimulus cue value and are followed by successful experience, the undesired effects of failure experiences may be minimized and the educational advantages may be maximized.

Motivation. Given that experiential factors for mentally retarded children differ substantially from that of normal children, it is not surprising that a retarded individual's motivation differs from that of a nonretarded individual of the same mental and chronological age. Stated differently by Zigler and Balla (1981) the position of various reinforcers in the hierarchy differ for the two groups. This is a potentially important event since more reinforcement in natural environments are of the intangible nature (e.g., information about the correctness of a response, verbal compliments). Research has consistently demonstrated that tangible reinforcers such as food or trinkets are more effective for mentally retarded students. Further, the conclusions of researchers concerning the "rigidity" of the response patterns of mentally retarded individuals may also have been a function of using intangible reinforcers. Indeed, Stevenson and Zigler (1957) found that when tangible reinforcers were employed in studies comparing retarded and nonretarded children the retarded were no more rigid than the nonretarded on a discrimination reversal learning task.

Social Sensitivity

Role-taking skills. Role-taking is the ability to recognize and coordinate thoughts, feelings, and beliefs of self and others during a social interaction (Feffer, 1970). Research by Affleck (1975a, 1975b, 1976) has contributed significantly to our knowledge of role-taking skills in the mentally retrded.

The investigation of role-taking skills in children typically involves a series of tasks in which the child is requested to assume the perspective of another and engage in some course of action. Although research appears to link perspective-taking with maturational age, the methodologies employed prevent definitive statements. What is clear is that mentally retarded children display a significant delay in demonstrating the ability to take another person's point of view and act from the assumed point of view. One of the more important findings to emerge from studies on role-taking has been reported by Affleck (1975a, 1975b, 1976) who notes that role-taking was strongly related to interpersonal skills and problem solving skills. In particular, utilizing Feffer's (1970) Role Taking Task and Role Playing Assessment Technique, Affleck found that the presence of interpersonal communication skills and problem solving strategies were a prime factor in successful role-taking. Although delay in role-taking ability has been tied to mental age (DeVries, 1970), Volpe (1970) reported that orthopedically handicapped children with normal ability demonstrated inferior role-taking skills when compared to nonhandicapped age mates. The importance of experiencing varied roles and perspectives and having access to appropriate models is highlighted by these studies.

A series of studies by Affleck (1975a 1975b, 1976) provide considerable understanding of the relationship between cognitive strategies and role-taking. In the first study by Affleck, a group of retarded young adults (mean age of 22) were asked to develop a story from a scene depicted in a picture. The subjects were then asked to relate their story from the point of view of each of the individuals pictured in the scene. A second task required the subjects to act out a part in a social conflict situation with another nonretarded adult. The results of both experiments indicated that there was a strong relation between both types of role-taking tasks. Overall ability as measured by IQ was significantly related to successful role-taking. Age and role-taking and IQ and self-concept were not significantly correlated. In a second study, Affleck (1975b) examined the role-taking ability of mentally retarded students with a mean age of 13 and a mean IQ of 66. The procedures involved the storytelling task in study one and a two person game. The game involved a series of cards that reflect a choice of intended actions on the part of the other player. The goal was to choose the card that would match the card of the other player thereby indicating a correct description of the individual's intent. Again a significant relationship between role-playing and mental age was obtained but not for chronological age. A third study (Affleck, 1976) utilized the storytelling task and a social problem solving task with a group of 50 mildly retarded students with a mean age of 13. Again role-taking ability was correlated with mental age but not with chronological age. Comparing this research with that involving retarded adults seems to suggest that the key variable may be the availability of interpersonal problem solving strategies. These strategies are routinely found with successful role-taking and are absent with unsuccessful role-taking. These findings have been confirmed by other studies using slightly differing tasks and student samples. Lack of experimental manipulation of significant variables limits strong conclusions.

Social inference/person perception. Studies of how mentally retarded individuals perceive or develop opinions of other individuals is limited. The literature that does exist is based on studies of mentally retarded adults. One such study was conducted by Monson, Greenspan, & Simeonsson (1979). Monson and Simeonsson asked 20 mildly and moderately retarded adults to describe an individual that they liked and an individual that they did not like. Their descriptions were scored on three dimensions of: (a) amount of unique information concerning the person being described, would the information permit the selected person to be differentiated from others: (b) amount of person information in the description, such as "he talks to me," "he yells at me;" and (c) the depth of the descriptions (i.e., reference to individuals thoughts and motives, situational determinants). The response patterns for distinctiveness and personal involvement resemble that of five- and six-year-old normal children (Secord & Peeves, 1973). The responses on the third dimension of depth resembled 12- and 13-year-olds. An earlier study by Wooster (1970) found that retarded teenage boys utilized simpler and less differentiated social perception systems.

As mentioned, the research on person perception is very limited. It does appear that mentally retarded children and youth do not perceive others in as many ways, view others in more egocentric terms, and demonstrate limited insight into the motives and characteristics of others. However, mentally retarded individuals may be much more sensitive to the behavior of others. Research has suggested for example that the level of cognitive development, relative frequency of success experienced

by the individual in social interaction situations, and the degree of positive relation to adults directly influence mentally retarded individuals' awareness of other individuals. The finding that mentally retarded individuals are more "outer directed" or sensitive to other adults in the environment has been linked to their more frequent failure experiences. Hence, the need to be more vigilant.

Social Insight

Social insight may be defined as the ability of an individual to identify and understand the processes that underly social interactions and to make evaluative judgments regarding those situations. Three areas are included within this category: (a) social comprehension; (b) psychological insight; and (c) moral judgment. Social comprehension includes the individual's understanding of society's institutions and social processes. Psychological insight refers to the individual's understanding of how and why people differ from each other and why they behave the way they do. Moral judgment relates to the individual's ability to consider society's rules and to think about ethical issues.

Social comprehension. Social comprehension has received only minimal attention with retarded populations. The limited research has focused on adult populations. Variables that could be investigated include the child or youth's understanding of social class, political processes, monetary exchange systems, operation of systems such as schools or other agencies, and friendship, to name a few (Greenspan, 1981). There appears to have been no research conducted in this area with mildly retarded individuals.

Psychological insight. Psychological insight involves the student's ability to understand personal characteristics and motivational processes of other individuals.. Two areas that thave been investigated in a limited manner as they related to mentally retarded people's social competence are *person perception* and *psychological causality*. A third variable posited by Greenspan (1981) is what one could refer to as *social foresight*. Social foresight is used to describe an individual's ability to predict how an individual or group will respond in a given situation.

Moral judgment. Moral judgment refers to the individual student's ability to evaluate a person's behavior in a given situation in relation to moral rules and ethical principles. This has been a frequently researched area within child development. Generally, the research procedure has involved some variation of the *moral dilemma paradigm* used in Piaget's (1932) early work as well as Kolbert's research (Kohlberg, 1981). What research there is concerning moral judgment has been related with cognitive reasoning, such as the research by Kahn (1976). Using three groups consisting of non-retarded, mildly retarded, and moderately retarded individuals with all subjects matched on mental age, Kahn found that the moderately retarded group was inferior to the normal and mildly retarded groups in terms of both cognitive reasoning and moral reasoning. There were, surprisingly, no difference between the nonretarded and mildly retarded group. Bender (1980), using three groups of second graders (normal, mildly, and moderately retarded), examined moral judgment relative to intent and outcome interpretations of a set of stories. All subjects indicated what they perceived to be the intent of the story rather than the outcome of the story. As with other areas of social development, mildly retarded individuals have demonstrated difficulty in developing moral judgment and are perceived to have difficulties dealing with more than one aspect of a moral dilemma.

Social Communication

Social communication refers to the student's ability and skill in understanding how to intervene effectively in social settings and to influence the behavior of others in the desired manner. The areas of referential communication and social problem solving fall within this category. Referential communication involves the capability planfully to meet the informational needs of another individual and to communicate to other individuals what one is perceiving or thinking. Social problem solving includes the ability to change another's way of thinking better to meet one's own needs.

Referential communication. There is a general consensus that language skills and related communication skills are an essential component of social competence. The importance of communication skills has been discussed by Blout (1969) and Simeonsson (1978). Of particular note is the repeated finding that richness of vocabulary is less important than the manner in which the vocabulary is used (Halpern & Equinozzi, 1969). The referential process is the situation in which the speaker selects the most appropriate communication components (words, gestures, intonation) to communicate to the listener, and the listener correctly identifies those referents. Effective referential communication depends to a substantial degree upon the speaker's skill in identifying the viewpoint and informational needs of the listener (Rosenberg, 1972).

Studies on referential communication have typically employed a two person communication situation that is used to investigate the flow of behavior between two individuals. A representative study involving the classic two person communication task was conducted by Longhurst (1974). He assigned speaker and listener roles to individuals of three levels of mental retardation

using a group of adolescents. Comparing the results to data from normal adolescents, Longhurst found that communication was only about 50% effective. The effectiveness was directly related to IQ. Additionally, an analysis of speaker-listener combinations revealed that impaired communication was apparently due to inadequate, idiosyncratic speaker skills. Longhurst and Berry (1975) essentially replicated earlier findings regarding the role of perspective taking and communication skills in referential communication competence. Thus, referential communication requires skills in taking the perspective of the potential listener as well as communication or language skills. Mentally retarded individuals have a generalized deficit in both of these areas. These two skills have positive relationship to level of retardation and degree of cognitive skill. Referential communication has a much stronger relation to IQ than does role-taking (Monson, Greenspan, & Simeonsson, 1979). Again, social developmental deficits appear to have a direct link to a lack of sophisticated cognitive strategies.

Social problem solving. The limited research with mildly retarded individuals and social problem solving has been focused on persuasive skills. In one of the few studies undertaken to examine how mentally retarded children would go about influencing another individual, Affleck (1976) had 50 mildly and moderately retarded children, ranging in age from 8 to 17, attempt to influence another individual (friend or individual's counselor) to let them watch their favorite television show. The distribution of responses was found to be related to the individual's level of role-taking ability. In particular, children above the mean in role-taking ability tended to use positive inducements which is a more sophisticated tactic (Wood, Weinstein, & Parker, 1967). Low ability role-taking children were more likely to utilize simple request to achieve their goal. Role-taking seems to be positive related to utilization of more effective problem solving strategies.

In addition to the limited repertoire of interpersonal problem solving strategies, mentally retarded individuals may not generate startegies in any organized manner. Nor do they appear to perceive the sequential relationship between a series of interactions (Asher & Renshaw, 1981). Further, mentally retarded individuals perform more poorly on communication tasks that require editing and/or comparison processes (Rueda & Chan, 1980).

Summary

It is becoming increasingly obvious that we need to consider not only the referent communication skill but also the strategic modes of thinking and reacting when viewing social development of mentally retarded children and youth. Self-regulatory processes which are essential to cognitive problem solving strategies are also necessary for effective interpersonal interactions (Campione & Brown, 1978). However, to date much of the empirical research has been focused on identifying the critical elements that facilitate or hinder interpersonal competence in nonhandicapped children. The research with mentally retarded children and youth generally has been confined to examining: (a) the problems that these individuals encounter in social interactions, and (b) how this population differs from normal children in problem solving in social situations. The considerable effort expended in attempts to identify critical aspects of social development and to develop approaches of measuring social development does put us in a position to begin vigorously pursuing effective instructional/intervention strategies.

Current Research: Implications for Training and Practice

In the following sections an attempt is made to examine current research from the perspective of those who will ultimately have the responsibility for developing instructional programs for mildly retarded children. Much research has been completed and our knowledge of the cognitive and social development of this group has been improved substantially. The value of this information, however, must be judged by the extent to which it improves our ability to facilitate the adaptation of mildly retarded individuals to complex societal demands.

Throughout this chapter we have constantly emphasized the importance of understanding the cognitive processing abilities of retarded individuals in an attempt more clearly to understand their cognitive and social development. We have detailed the nature of the information processing deficits which exist and made reference to the impact of those deficits on social development. We are not alone in believing that an important component of any training program designed to improve the adaptive skills of retarded learners will need to address these cognitive deficits (see e.g., Winschel, Ensher, & Blatt, 1977). This is not meant to imply that all training programs must involve a cognitive instruction component, but that the degree to which training will be successful will be influenced by the cognitive abilities of the population being trained and the extent to which training remediates any limitations which exist. During the last two decades there has been a tremendous expansion in the number of individuals interested in investigating the ability of exceptional children to use cognitive strategies. In the sections which follow we examine a portion of the cognitive instruction research with retarded learners. As stated earlier, we examine that literature with an eye towards the implications of current research for the design and implementation of educational and remedial programs for educable retarded students.

Training and Maintenance of Basic Skills

There is solid evidence that educable mentally retarded students can learn and maintain task-specific cognitive strategies. In fact, during the last two decades a great deal of cognitive instruction research has been aimed at evaluating the extent to which retarded children can learn to use information processing strategies to improve performance on a wide variety of tasks. An excellent example of the benefits and limitations of this type of training of mentally retarded individuals is provided by the early work in the mnemonic strategy training literature.

The failures of retarded individuals spontaneously to use mnemonic strategies has long been apparent (e.g., Ellis, 1970; Luria, 1961; Reese, 1962). Early training efforts revealed that retarded subjects could learn to use different strategies to facilitate performance on a variety of memory tasks (Ashcraft & Kellas, 1974: Brown, Campione, Bray, & Wilcox, 1973). Subsequent research revealed that with very limited training often lasting no more than two or three hours, mildly retarded children could not only be trained to use mnemonic strategies effectively, but could be expected to maintain the use of the strategy for periods of two weeks (Reichhart, Cody, & Borkowski, 1974), to six months (Brown, Campione, & Murphy, 1974) and to a year after training (Brown, Campione, & Barclay, 1979). The accumulated evidence made it clear that strategies such as verbal elaboration, repetitive rehearsal, visual imagery, and self-instruction could be learned and used to improve performance on specific tasks (Kramer, Nagle, & Eagle, 1980).

The results of the line of investigation described above generated a great deal of enthusiasm. There were immediate calls for the utilization of mnemonic instruction approaches in classrooms (Borkowski & Cavanaugh, 1979; Kramer et al., 1980; Winschel & Lawrence, 1975) and research indicating that mnemonic instruction could be used to teach adaptive information and skills (e.g., Taylor, Thurlow, & Turnure, 1977) was completed. (This type of research continues today, e.g., Scruggs, Mastropieri, & Levin, 1985.)

Despite these successes researchers were not satisfied and quickly began to look for more efficient methods of training. The problem was that attempts to train strategic behavior to retarded learners required detailed strategy training for each area being investigated. Tasks needed to be analyzed, information processing strategies evaluated (and eventually trained) and this process needed to be repeated for every task and every time training was to be undertaken. Furthermore, this approach had not been successful in promoting evidence of generalization of trained skills.

Although it was not often explicitly stated, these early training studies were conducted with the hope that they would result in new methods of teaching generalizable skills that would be translated in more efficient classroom instruction (Kramer et al., 1980). The difficulty of obtaining transfer of training had long been recognized in the cognitive instruction literature (Brown, 1978). This failure to obtain transfer has been true regardless of whether the focus was on generalization of the use of the information processing skill itself (Kramer & Engle, 1981) or the generalization of trained skills to new task domains (e.g., social competence, Kneedler, 1980). If one adheres strictly to the notion that generalization is demonstrated only when individuals use a trained skill on a task (or in a new situation) that is clearly different from that encountered in training, the evidence for generalization of trained cognitive skills among mentally retarded people is scarce (O'Leary, 1980). Thus the success of the early training studies in teaching new cognitive skills, combined with the failure of this approach to result in generalization, caused researchers to look beyond simple instructional effects and to begin to assess the effects of other forms of training on the ability of mildly retarded students to generalize trained strategies.

The Limits of Training: Generalization and Executive Control

The most appropriate solution to the problem of obtaining mnemonic strategy generalization, as envisioned by some researchers, was to focus on the training of the memory-monitoring skills that were common to most memory tasks. It was assumed that these monitoring skills would be most helpful to retarded learners in their attempts to generalize trained skills to new tasks or novel situations. Research during the last few years has focused on these higher-order skills which have been broadly construed as executive function or *metacognitive* skills.

Metacognition refers to an individual's knowledge about his or her cognitive processes: an "awareness of what you know about how you know" (Borkowski, Reid, & Kurtz, 1984, p. 55), or "knowing about knowing" (Brown, 1978). Efficient problem solvers use metacognitive knowledge to select, monitor, and create problem solving strategies. Although there is some uncertainty regarding the nature of the metacognition-problem solving connection (Borkowski & Cavanaugh, 1979), there is reliable evidence that children's knowledge of their memory system does begin to develop and expand during the elementary school years (Kreutzer, Leonard, & Flavell, 1975).

In a recent review of the literature, Belmont, Butterfield, and Ferrati (1982) provided some evidence of the potential importance of metacognitive functioning (or in this case "*metamemorial*" functioning). They found that generalization of trained cognitive skills occurred only in studies which included training in metamemory. However, only a handful of successful strategy generalization studies has been reported in the retardation literature (e.g., Belmont, Butterfield, & Borkowski, 1978; Brown, Campione, & Barclay, 1979; Kendall, Borkowski, & Cavanaugh, 1980; Pray, Kramer, &

Camp, 1984) and instruction in metamemorial functioning is no guarantee that strategy generalization will result (Brown, 1978). Even in some cases where generalization has been inferred, there has been evidence of substantial variability in the extent to which individual subjects have exhibited strategy generalization (Brown et al., 1979; Pray et al., 1984). Further, there are numerous examples of failure to obtain trained strategy generalization with mildly retarded subjects (e.g., Kramer & Engle, 1981) and we can only assume that other examples exist that have not been published. If all this were not discouraging enough, it is also important to note that when generalization has occurred it has been "largely restricted to other laboratory-type tasks that differ minimally from the original training context in both stimuli and task demands" (Blackman & Lin, 1984, p. 257).

While it is true that we have concentrated on the memory training literature, it is clear that attempts to train mildly retarded individuals' cognitive strategies to improve social skills (e.g., Kneedler, 1980), academic skills (e.g., Lloyd, 1980), or general problem-solving skills (e.g., Pray, et al., 1984) have encountered the same problems noted above. It is also apparent that recent entrants into the cognitive instruction field (as with Instructional Enrichment, Feuerstein, 1980) have met a similar fate (at least as it relates to retarded individuals, see Blackman & Lin, 1984). Although many of the training studies completed during the last few years have been couched in the current language of metacognition (e.g., executive function or control, metamemory, mnemonic awareness, etc.), it is nonetheless true that these studies have been aimed at improving the intellectual abilities of mildly retarded students. It is also obvious that they have failed in that regard. Retarded students can be trained to use task-specific cognitive strategies and they will continue to use these strategies when presented with the training task. Attempts to modify more general memory monitoring or problem solving skills have met with little success.

Implications for Practice

A number of years ago one of us (in Kramer et al., 1980) ended a paper with hopeful comments about the likelihood of the cognitive instruction field providing insights about training the retarded "how to think." There followed the following quotation from Winschel et al., (1977):

> . . . teachers, knowledgeable in science and humanities—spend endless hours training children to button coats, shake hands, and read preprimers. While this type of education may lead to children who are more "acceptable" and more "manageable," the retarded are defeated inevitably by the multitude of specific skills necessary for minimal functioning in society. The efforts are laudable but the central objective, increased problem-solving

behavior, is largely ignored. Clearly, we need to develop educational approaches which, in addition to teaching children to know more, help them to think better (p. 26).

Unfortunately, analysis of the cognitive instruction literature with educable retarded individuals leaves one with the depressing realization that there is not really much new information to report to the classroom teacher. The last half-decade of research has contributed little to our ability to teach retarded people how to think.

A decade ago Brown and Campione (1977) suggested that there were two types of situations where retarded children might benefit from the detailed analysis and training of cognitive instruction. They recommended training educable retarded children specific task/strategy relationships when either (a) mastery of the experimental task/materials is itself of great value (e.g., vocabulary skills); or (b) when the trained skill is applicable in a wide range of settings (e.g., measurement or time management). So it remains today.

At this juncture our conclusions are not particularly optimistic ones. After two decades of intensive investigation there is little evidence that this line of study has produced ecologically valid techniques for improving the learning skills of retarded learners. Analysis of the literature leads to the conclusion that our attempts to train mildly retarded individuals must be tempered by the knowledge that individuals are capable of demonstrating improvements only within the limits defined by their structural capabilities. Research investigating the educability of retarded learners must continue and in the final section of this chapter we provide suggestions for future efforts. We must remain cognizant, however, of the limited success of past efforts.

An Agenda for Future Research

Research on information processing differences between retarded and normal individuals has made great strides in the past few years, adding tremendously to our understanding. Not only do we understand more about the specific capabilities of mildly retarded students, we have also learned a great deal from our efforts to train new skills. Although training efforts have not proved to be unequivocally successful, these efforts should continue. Further, there are some very real shortcomings in the literature that need to be addressed in future work.

1. First, research needs to be focused specifically on mildly retarded individuals. The studies we cited included mildly retarded individuals in their samples but often lumped them together with moderately retarded or nonretarded (e.g., slow learners) subjects. Hence, deficits specific to mild retardation are impossible to disentangle in many studies.

2. Research should be focused on children. As it now stands, the vast majority of work has been done on adolescents and young adults, individuals whose processing systems have presumably matured. Even though the generalizability of work with young adults seems reasonable, a specific focus on the development of processing deficits seems warranted.

3. Greater care needs to be taken in the selection of target populations for study. To our knowledge, one cannot assume that processing deficits in, say, Down's syndrome subjects are identical to those that could be observed in subjects suffering retardation for other reasons. Studying groups of children categorized together on the basis of IQ alone may yield misleading results. As there are several causes of mental retardation, there may be several different processing deficits. Different processing deficits, of course, could yield similar IQ measures but for different reasons. The potential that different causes of retardation could yield different processing deficits should be explored. Perhaps some of the process-structure debate can be addressed in syndrome-specific research.

4. Sensory register research needs to be expanded to include work on the echoic register. Even though we would expect the results to be highly similar to those obtained in studies of the iconic register, the experimental work remains to be completed.

5. Research should focus on the entire processing system of subjects rather than on specific elements. To this point, subjects have been carefully scrutinized for one or another processing deficit without examining for the possibility of several different deficits. Hunt's (e.g., 1978) research contrasting highly capable and normal subjects could serve as a model for such multiple-task processing research.

6. Educational relevant/training relevant processing research (e.g., Bos & Tierney, 1984) should be explored. There exists a large literature on information processing differences in reading and smaller literatures on differences in writing and solving math problems. Research focusing on differences in how information is processed between mildly retarded and normal children in reading, writing, and math may have important implications for education and training. To date, most of the research with retarded children has dealt with analysis of information processing abilities on rather sterile, laboratory-type tasks.

7. Greater care should be taken to integrate work contrasting retarded and normal subjects with that contrasting normal subjects and highly capable subjects. Our understanding of the human information processing system requires a full knowledge of the total spectrum of human abilities.

8. Attempts should be made better to integrate the cognitive-developmental approach (e.g., Case, 1984a; Sternberg, 1984a) with what we have termed the "intelligence" approach. Such an integration seems especially pertinent as we begin to focus more and more on children and educational relevant processing differences.

9. Care should be taken to analyze individual subject performance in all cognitive instruction research. Although this line of investigation has not proven overwhelmingly successful with retarded individuals, some training studies have demonstrated evidence of transfer of trained skills to new tasks in some subjects. Individual analysis of subject performance may result in the discovery of specific subject characteristics that increase the probability of generalization. It may be that our current methods of subject categorization (see recommendation #3 above) are too gross and these methods may obscure individual differences of importance.

Obviously, although much progress has been made, much remains to be done.

References

Affleck, G. (1975a). Role-taking ability and interpersonal conflict resolution among retarded young adults. *American Journal of Mental Deficiency*, **80**, 233–236.

Affleck, G. (1975b). Role-taking ability and the interpersonal competencies of retarded children. *American Journal of Mental Deficiency*, **80**, 312–316.

Affleck, G. (1976). Role-taking ability and the interpersonal tactics of retarded children. *American Journal of Mental Deficiency*, **81**, 667–670.

Ashcraft, M. H., & Kellas, G. (1974). Organization in normal and retarded children: Temporal aspects of storage and retrieval. *Journal of Experimental Psychology*, **103**, 502–508.

Asher, S. R., & Renshaw, P. D. (1981). Children without friendships: Social knowledge and social skill training. In S. R. Asher & J. M. Gottman (Eds.), *Development of children's friendships*. New York: Cambridge University Press.

Averbach, E., & Coriell, A. S. (1961). Short-term memory in vision. *Bell System Technical Journal*, **40**, 309–328.

Belmont, J. M., & Butterfield, E. C. (1969). The relations of short-term memory to development and intelligence. In L. P. Sipsitt & H. W. Reese (Eds.), *Advances in child development and behavior*, **4**, New York: Academic Press.

Belmont, J. M., & Butterfield, E. C. (1977). The instructional approach to developmental cognitive research. In R. V. Kail, Jr., & J. W. Hagen (Eds.), *Perspectives on the development of memory and cognition*. Hillsdale, NJ: Lawrence Erlbaum.

Belmont, J. M., Butterfield, E. C., & Borkowski, J. G. (1978). Training retarded people to generalize memorization methods across memory tasks. In M. M. Gruneberry, P. E. Morris, & R. N. Sykes (Eds.), *Practical aspects of memory*. London: Academic Press.

Belmont, J. M., Butterfield, E. C., & Ferrati, R. P. (1982). To secure transfer of training, instruct self-management skills. In D. K. Detterman and R. J. Sternberg (Eds.), *How and how much can intelligence be increased?* Norwood, NJ: Ablex Publishing.

Bender, N. N. (1980). Intent and outcome in the moral judgment of mentally and non-retarded children. *Mental Retardation*, **18**, 39–40.

Benton, S. L., Kraft, R. G., Glover, J. A. & Plake, B. S. (1984). Cognitive capacity differences among writers. *Journal of Educational Psychology*, **76**, 820–834.

Blackman, L. S., & Lin, A. (1984). Generalization training in the educable mentally retarded: Intelligence and its educability revisited. In P. H. Brooks, R. Sperber, & C. McCauley (Eds.), *Learning and cognition in the mentally retarded* (pp. 237–263). Hillsdale, NJ: Lawrence Erlbaum.

Blout, W. R. (1969). A comment on language, socialization, acceptance, and the retarded. *Mental Retardation*, **7**, 33–35.

Borkowski, J. G., & Cavanaugh, J. C. (1979). Maintenance and generalization of skills and strategies by the retarded. In N. R. Ellis (Ed.), *Handbook of mental deficiency*: Psychological theory and research. Hillsdale, NJ: Lawrence Erlbaum.

Borkowski, J. G., Reid, M. K., & Kurtz, B. E. (1984). Metacognition and retardation: Paradigmatic, theoretical, and applied perspectives. In P. H. Brooks, R. Sperber, & C. McCauley (Eds.), *Learning and cognition in the mentally retarded* (pp. 55–75). Hillsdale, NJ: Lawrence Erlbaum.

Bos, C. S., & Tierney, R. J. (1984). Inferential reading abilities of mildly mentally retarded and nonretarded students. *American Journal of Mental Deficiency*, **89**, 75–82.

Britton, B. K., & Tesser, A. (1982). Effects of prior knowledge on use of cognitive capacity in three complex cognitive tasks. *Journal of Verbal Learning and Verbal Behavior*, **21**, 421–436.

Broadbent, D. E. (1958). *Perception and communication*. London: Pergamon Press.

Brown, A. L. (1974). The role of strategic behavior in retardate memory. In N. R. Ellis (Ed)., *International review of research in mental retardation*, **7**, New York: Academic Press.

Brown, A. L. (1978). Knowing when, where, and how to remember: A problem of metacognition. In R. Glaser (Ed.), *Advances in instructional psychology*. Hillsdale, NJ: Lawrence Erlbaum.

Brown, A. L., & Campione, J. C. (1977). Training strategic study time apportionment in educable retarded children. *Intelligence*, **1**, 94–107.

Brown, A. L., Campione, J. C., & Barclay, C. R. (1979). Training self-checking routines for estimating test readiness: Generalization from list learning to prose recall. *Child Development*, **50**, 501–512.

Brown, A. L., Campione, J. C., Bray, N. W., & Wilcox, B. L. (1973). Keeping track of changing variables: Effects of rehearsal training and rehearsal prevention in normal and retarded adolescents. *Journal of Experimental Psychology*, **101**, 123–131.

Brown, A. L., Campione, J. C., & Murphy, M. D. (1974). Keeping track of changing variables: Long-term retention of a trained rehearsal strategy by retarded adolescents. *American Journal of Mental Deficiency*, **78**, 446–453.

Butterfield, E. C., & Belmont, J. M. (1975). Assessing and improving the executive cognitive functions of mentally retarded people. In I. Bialer & Sternlicht (Eds.), *Psychological issues in mental retardation*. New York: Academic Press.

Campione, J. C., & Brown, A. L. (1977). Memory and metamory development in educable retarded children. In R. V. Kail, Jr. & J. W. Hagen (Eds.), *Perspectives on the development of memory and cognition*. Hillsdale, NJ: Lawrence Erlbaum.

Campione, J. & Brown, A., (1978). Toward a theory of intelligence: Contributions from research with retarded children. *Intelligence*, **2**, 279–304.

Caruso, D. R. (1985). Influence of item identification on the memory performance of mentally retarded and non-retarded adults. *Intelligence*, **9**, 51–68.

Case, R. (1974). Structures and strictures: Some functional limitations on the course of cognitive growth. *Cognitive Psychology*, **6**, 544–573.

Case, R. (1978). A developmentally based theory and technology on instruction. *Review of Educational Research*, *48*, 439–463.

Case, R. (1984a). The process of stage transition: A neoPiagetian view. In R. J. Sternberg (Ed.), *Mechanisms of cognitive development*. New York: W. H. Freeman.

Case, R. (1985). *Intellectual development: A systematic reinterpretation*. New York: Academic Press.

Cromwell, R. L. (1963). A social learning approach to mental retardation. In N. R. Ellis (Ed.), *Handbook of mental deficiency: Psychological theory and research*. New York: McGraw Hill.

Cronbach, L. S. (1957). The two disciplines of scientific psychology. *American Psychologist*, **12**, 671–684.

Darwin, C. T., Turvey, M. T., & Crowder, R. G. (1972). An auditory analogue of the Sperling partial report procedure: Evidence for brief auditory storage. *Cognitive Psychology*, **3**, 255–267.

Detterman, D. K. (1977). Is intelligence necessary? *Intelligence*, **1**, 1–3.

Detterman, D. K. (1979). Memory in the mentally retarded. In N. R. Ellis (Ed.), *Handbook of mental deficiency*. Hillsdale, NJ: Lawrence Erlbaum.

DeVries, R. (1970). The development of role-taking as reflected by behavior of bright, average, and retarded children in a social guessing game. *Child Development*, **41**, 759–770.

Ellis, N. R. (1963). The stimulus trace and behavioral inadequacy. In N. R. Ellis (Ed.), *Handbook of mental deficiency*. New York: McGraw-Hill.

Ellis, N. R. (1970). Memory processes in retardates and normals. In N. R. Ellis (Ed.), *International review of research in mental retardation*, **4**, New York: Academic Press.

Ellis, N. R., Deacon, J. R., & Woolridge, P. W. (1985). Structural memory deficits of mentally retarded persons. *American Journal of Mental Deficiency*, **89**, 393–402.

Ellis, N. R., & Meador, D. M. (1985). Forgetting in retarded and nonretarded persons under conditions of minimal strategy use. *Intelligence*, **9**, 87–96.

Feffer, M. H. (1970). A developmental analysis of interpersonal behavior. *Psychological Review*, **77**, 197–214.

Feuerstein, R. (1980). *Instructional Enrichment: An intervention program for cognitive modifiability*. Baltimore, MD: University Park Press.

Fisher, M. A., & Zeamon, D. (1973). An attention-retention theory of retardate discrimination learning. In N. R. Ellis (Ed.), *International review of research in mental retardation*, **7**, New York: Academic Press.

Gibson, E. J., & Spelke, E. S. (1983). The development of perception. In J. H. Flavell & E. M. Markman (Eds.), *Handbook of child psychology Vol. III*. New York: Wiley.

Goldstein, A. P. (1973). Structured learning therapy: Toward a psychotherapy for the poor. New York: Academic Press.

Greenspan, S. (1979). Social intelligence in the retarded. In N. R. Ellis (Ed.), *Handbook of mental deficiency: Psychological theory and research*. Hillsdale, NJ: Lawrence Erlbaum.

Greenspan, S. (1981). Defining social competence in children: A working model. In B. K. Koegh (Ed.). *Advances in special education (Vol. 3): Socialization influences on exceptionality* (pp. 1–40). Greenwich, CT: JAI Press.

Gruen, G., Ottinger, D., & Ollendick, T. (1974). Probability learning in retarded children with differing histories of success and failure in school. *American Journal of Mental Deficiency*, **70**, 417–423.

Halpern, A. S., & Equinozzi, A. M. (1969). Verbal expressivity as an index of adaptive behavior. *American Journal of Mental Deficiency*, **74**, 180–186.

Harter, S., Brown, L., & Zigler, E. (1971). Discrimination learning in retarded and nonretarded children as a function of task difficulty and social reinforcement. *American Journal of Mental Deficiency*, **76**, 275–283.

Hayes, C. S., & Prinz, R. J. (1976). Affective reactions of retarded and non-retarded children to success and failure . . . *American Journal of Mental Deficiency*, **81**, 100–102.

Hornstein, H. A., & Mosley, J. L. (1979). Iconic-memory processing of unfamiliar stimuli by retarded and nonretarded individuals. *American Journal of Mental Deficiency*, **84**, 40–48.

Humphreys, M. S., Lynch, M. J. Revelle, W., & Hall, J. W. (1983). Individual differences in short-term memory. In R. F. Dillon & R. R. Schmeck (Eds.), *Individual differences in cognition*. New York: Academic Press.

Hunt, E. (1978). Mechanics of verbal ability. *Psychological Review*, **85**, 109–130.

Hunt, E. (in press). Science, technology and intelligence. In R. Ronning, J. A. Glover, & J. Conoley (Eds.), *Cognitive psychology and measurement*. Hillsdale, NJ: Lawrence Erlbaum.

Hunt, E., Frost, N., & Lunneburg, C. (1973). Individual differences in cognition: A new approach to intelligence. In G. Bower (Ed.), *The psychology of learning and motivation*, **7**, New York: Academic Press.

Hunt, E., Lansman, M., & Davidson, J. (1981). Individual differences in long-term memory access. *Memory & Cognition*, **9**, 599–608.

Jensen, A. (in press). The g beyond factor analysis. In R. R. Ronning, J. A. Glover, & J. Conoley (Eds.), *Cognitive psychology and measurement*. Hillsdale, NJ: Lawrence Erlbaum.

Kahn, J. V. (1976). Moral and cognitive development in moderately retarded, mildly retarded, and non-retarded individuals. *American Journal of Mental Deficiency*, **81**, 209–214.

Kendall, C., Borkowski, J. G., & Cavanaugh, J. C. (1980). Maintenance and generalization of an interrogative strategy by EMR children. *Intelligence*, **4**, 255–270.

Klatzky, R. L. (1980). *Human memory: Structures and processes* (2nd ed). San Francisco: W. H. Freeman.

Kohlberg, L. (1981). *The philosophy of moral development: Moral stages and the idea of justice (listed.)*. San Francisco: Harper & Row.

Kneedler, R. D. (1980). The use of cognitive training to change social behaviors. *Exceptional Education Quarterly*, **1**, 65–73.

Kramer, J. J., & Engle, R. W. (1981). Teaching awareness of strategic behavior in combination with strategy training: Effect on children's memory performance. *Journal of Experimental Child Psychology*, **32**, 513–530.

Kramer, J. J., Nagle, R. H., & Engle, R. W. (1980). Recent advances in mnemonic strategy training with the mentally retarded: Implications for educational practice. *American Journal of Mental Deficiency*, 85, 306–314.

Kreutzer, M. A., Leonard, C., & Flavell, J. H. (1975). An interview study of children's knowledge about memory. *Monographs of the Society for Research in Child Development*, 4 (1, Serial No. 159).

Krupski, A. (1980). Attention processes: Research, theory and implications for special education. In B. K. Keogh (Ed.), *Advances in special education, Vol. I: Basic constructs and theoretical orientations*. Greenwich, CT: JAI Press.

Libkuman, T. M., Velliky, R. S., & Freidrich, D. D. (1980). Nonselective read-out from iconic memory in normal, borderline and retarded adolescents. *Intelligence*, 4, 363–369.

Lloyd, J. (1980). Academic instruction and cognitive behavior modification: The need for attack strategy training. *Exceptional Educational Quarterly*, 1, 53–64.

Logan, D. R., & Rose, E. (1982). Characteristics of the mentally retarded. In P. T. Cegelka & H. J. Prehm (Eds.). *Mental retardation: From categories to people* (pp. 149–185). Columbus, OH: Charles E. Merrill.

Longhurst, T. M. (1972). Assessing and increasing descriptive communication skills in retarded children. *Mental Retardation*, 78, 42–44.

Longhurst, T. M. (1974). Communication in retarded adolescents. *American Journal of Mental Deficiency*, 78, 607–618.

Longhurst, T. M., & Berry, G. W. (1975). Communication in retarded adolescents: Response to listener feedback. *American Journal of Mental Deficiency*, 80, 158–164.

Luftig, R., & Johnson, R. (1982). Identification and recall of structurally important units in prose by mentally retarded learners. *American Journal of Mental Deficiency*, 86, 495–502.

Luria, A. R. (1961). *The role of speech in the regulation of normal and abnormal behavior*. New York: Liveright.

Meyer, W. J., & Offenbach, S. I. (1962). Effectiveness of reward and punishment as a function of task complexity. *Journal of Comparative and Physiological Psychology*, 55, 532–534.

Miller, G. A. (1956). The magical number seven, plus or minus two: Some limits on our capacity for processing information. *Psychological Review*, 63, 81–97.

Monson, L. B., Greenspan, S., & Simeonsson, R. J. (1979). Correlates of social competence in retarded children. *American Journal of Mental Deficiency*, 83, 637–630.

Morariu, J., & Bruning, R. H. (1984). Cognitive processing by prelingual deaf students as a function of language context. *Journal of Education Psychology*, 76, 844–856.

Murdock, B. B. (1961). The retention of individual items. *Journal of Experimental Psychology*, 64, 618–625.

Nettlebeck, T., & Brewer, N. (1981). Studies of mental retardation and timed performance. In N. R. Ellis (Ed.), *International review of research in mental retardation* (Vol. 10). New York: Academic Press.

Nettlebeck, R., Hirons, & Wilson, C. (1985). Mental retardation, inspection time, and central attentional impairment. *Intelligence*, 9, 91–98.

O'Leary, S. G. (1980). A response to cognitive training. *Exceptional Educational Quarterly*, 1, 89–94.

Ollendick, T. H., Balla, D., & Zigler, E. (1971). Expectancy of success and the probability learning performance of retarded children. *Journal of Abnormal Psychology*, 77, 275–281.

Parrill-Bernstein, M. (1979) Social-cognitive and affective development. In T. L. Miller and E. E. Davis (Eds.), *The mildly handicapped student* (pp. 165–183) New York: Grune and Stratton.

Pennington, F. M., & Luszca, M. A. (1975). Some functional properties of iconic storage in retarded and nonretarded subjects. *Memory & Cognition*, 3, 295–301.

Piaget, J. (1932). *The moral judgement of the child*. New York: Free Press.

Porter, R. B. (1965). A comparative investigation of the personality of educable mentally retarded children and those of norm group of children. *Exceptional Children*, 31, 457–463.

Postman, L. (1975). Verbal learning and memory. *Annual Review of Psychology*, 26, 291–335.

Pray, B. S., Jr., Kramer, J. J., & Camp, C. (1984). Training recall readiness skills to retarded adults: Effects on skill maintenance and generalization. *Human Learning*, 3, 43–51.

Reese, H. W. (1962). Verbal mediation as a function of age level. *Psychological Bulletin*, 59, 502–509.

Reichhart, G. J., Cody, W. J., & Borkowski, J. G. (1975). Training and transfer of clustering and cumulative rehearsal strategies in retarded individuals. *American Journal of Mental Deficiency*, 79, 648–658.

Renshaw, P., & Asher, S. (1981). Social competence and peer status: The distinctions between goals and strategies. In K. H. Rubin & H. S. Ross (Eds.). (In press). *Peer relationships and social skills in childhood*. New York: Springer-Verlag, in press.

Rosenberg, S. (1972). The development of referential skills in children. In Schiefelbusch (Ed.), *The language of the mentally retarded*. Baltimore, MD: University Park Press.

Ross, L. E., & Ward, T. B. (1978). The processing of information from short-term visual store: Developmental and intellectual level differences. In N. R. Ellis (Ed.), *International review of research in mental retardation*, 9, New York: Academic Press.

Rueda, R., & Chan, K. (1980). Referential communication skills levels of moderately retarded adolescents. *American Journal of Mental Deficiency*, 85, 45–52.

Saccuzzo, D. P., Kerr, M., Marcus, A., & Brown, R. (1979). Input capability and speed of processing in mental retardation. *Journal of Abnormal Psychology*, 88, 341–345.

Saccuzzo, D. P., & Michael, B. (1984). Speed of information processing and structural limitations by mentally retarded and dual-diagnosed retarded-schizophrenic persons. *American Journal of Mental Deficiency*, 89, 187–194.

Schiefelbusch, R. (1981). Development of social competence and incompetence. In M. J. Begab, H. C. Haywood, & H. L. Garber (Eds.), *Psychosocial influences in retarded performance (Vol. 1): Issues and theories in development*. Baltimore, MC: University Park Press.

Scruggs, T. E., Mastropieri, M. A., & Levin, J. R. (1985). Vocabulary acquisition by mentally retarded students under direct and mnemonic instruction. *American Journal of Mental Deficiency*, 89, 549–551.

Secord, B. H. & Peeves, P. F. (1973). Developmental changes in attributions of descriptive concepts to persons. *Journal of Personality and Social Psychology*, 27, 120–128.

Siegler, R. S. (1976). Three aspects of cognitive development. *Cognitive Psychology*, 8, 481–520.

Siegler, R. S. (1984). Mechanisms of cognitive growth: Variation and selection. In R. J. Sternberg (Ed.), *Mechanisms of cognitive development*. New York: Freeman.

Simeonsson, R. J. (1978). Social competence. In J. Wortis (Ed.), *Mental retardation and developmental disabilities:*

Annual review X (pp. 130–171). New York: Brunner/ Mazel.

Simon, H. A. (1974). How big is a chunk? *Science*, **183**, 482–488.

Sperling, G. (1960). The information available in brief visual presentations. *Psychological Monographs*, **74**, 1–29.

Sperling, G. (1963). A model for visual memory tasks. *Human Factors*, *5*, 19–36.

Spitz, H. H. (1973). Consolidating facts into the schematized learning and memory system of educable retardates. In N. R. Ellis (Ed.), *International review of research in mental retardation*, **6**, New York: Academic Press.

Sternberg, R. J. (1982). A componential approach to intellectual development. In R. J. Sternberg (Ed.), *Advances in the psychology of human intelligence*, **1**, Hillsdale, NJ: Lawrence Erlbaum.

Sternberg, R. J. (1984a). What should intelligence tests test? Implications of a triarchic theory of intelligence for intelligence testing. *Educational Researcher*, **13**, 5–15.

Sternberg, R. J. (1984b). Mechanisms of cognitive development: A componential approach. In R. J. Sternberg (Ed.), *Mechanisms of cognitive development*. New York: Freeman.

Sternberg, R. J. (1984c). Toward a triarchic theory of human intelligence. *The Behavioral and Brain Sciences*, **7**, 269–315.

Sternberg, R. J. (1984d). *Beyond IQ: A triarchic theory of human intelligence*. New York: Cambridge University Press.

Stevenson, H. W., & Zigler, E. (1957). Discrimination learning and rigidity in normal and feebleminded individuals. *Journal of Personality*, **25**, 699–711.

Stevenson, H. W., & Zigler, E. (1958). Probability learning in children. *Journal of Experimental Psychology*, **56**, 185–192.

Taylor, A. M., Thurlow, M. L., & Turnure, J. E. (1977). Vocabulary development of educable retarded children. *Exceptional Children*, **43**, 444–450.

Tighe, T. J., & Shepp, B. E. (1983). *Perception, cognition, and development: Interactional analysis*. Hillsdale, NJ: Lawrence Erlbaum.

von Wright, J. M. (1972). On the problem of selection in iconic memory. *Scandinavian Journal of Psychology*, **13**, 159–171.

Whitehurst, G. J. (1969). Discrimination learning in children as a function of reinforcement condition, task complexity, and chronological age. *Journal of Experimental Child psychology*, **7**, 314–325.

Winschel, J. F., Ensher, G. L., & Blatt, B. (1977). Curriculum strategies for the mentally retarded: An argument in three parts. *Education and Training of the Mentally Retarded*, 26–31.

Winschel, J. F., & Lawrence, E. A. (1975). Short-term memory: Curricular implications for the mentally retarded. *Journal of Special Education*, **9**, 395–408.

Wood, J. R., Weinstein, E. A., & Parker, R. (1967). Children's interpersonal tactics. *Social Inquiry*, **37**, 129–135.

Wooster, A. D. (1970). Formation of stable and discrete concepts of personality by normal and mentally retarded boys. *Journal of Mental Subnormality*, **16**, 24–28.

Zeamon, D., & House, B. J. (1979). A review of attention theory. In N. R. Ellis (Ed.), *Handbook of mental deficiency*. Hillsdale, NJ: Lawrence Erlbaum.

Zigler, E., & Balla, D. (1981). Issues in personality and motivation in mentally retarded persons. In M. J. Begab, H. C. Haywood, & H. L. Garber (Eds.), *Psychosocial influences in retarded performance (Vol. 1): Issues and theories in development*. Baltimore, MD: University Park Press, 197–218.

Zigler, E., Balla, D., & Watson, N. (1972). Developmental and experimental determinants of self-image disparity in institutionalized and noninstitutionalized retarded and normal children. *Journal of Personality and Social Psychology*, **23**, 81–87.

Psychological Intervention with Mildly Retarded Children: Prevention and Remediation of Cognitive Deficits

RONALD L. TAYLOR

Florida Atlantic University

Abstract—A comprehensive review of early intervention programs designed to prevent mild mental retardation as well as remediation programs designed to modify cognitive skills and strategies are presented. Results of a number of early intervention projects are discussed and analyzed, including Head Start, the report from the Consortium for Longitudinal Studies, the Milwaukee Project, and the Abecedarian Project. Remediation approaches developed by Budoff, Feuerstein, Campione and Brown, and Butterfield and Belmont, among others, are presented and critiqued. Issues such as maintenance and generalization of both prevention and remediation programs are highlighted.

The prevention and/or remediation of cognitive deficits is an extremely important area that has educational, psychological, sociological, and economic implications. Inherent in such prevention and remediation programs is the goal of altering the presence and/or reducing the degree of mental retardation. In 1972, the President's Committee on Mental Retardation made the (somewhat optimistic) statement that the incidence of mental retardation could be reduced 50% by the year 2000, given the current technology in the biological and behavioral sciences. This statement represents the optimism associated with, and the priority assigned to, early intervention in the past quarter of a century.

PREVENTION vs. REMEDIATION

There is a clear distinction between prevention and remediation of severe and profound retardation. Severely retarded children are usually identified early in life, and the etiology of their retardation is usually biological in nature. With increased medical technology, improved methods of preventing severe retardation have been developed. Stark (1983) noted, for example, several *primary* prevention techniques that result in the total prevention of the handicapping condition. These include intrauterine fetal surgery for hydrocephaly and

vitamin B_{12} treatment for methylmalonic acid deficiency identified through amniocentesis. He also noted the presence of *secondary* prevention techniques (e.g., Guthrie test with subsequent dietary management for phenylketonuria) that can reverse the condition. For individuals for whom prevention is not possible, the remediation usually involves an attempt to minimize the residual handicap and maximize the potential for future development.

The distinction between prevention and remediation of mild retardation is not as clear cut. The issue is largely age related. Ramey and Bryant (1983) suggested age two as the marker that distinguishes between prevention and remediation. They noted that at this age, children from different socio-economic backgrounds begin to demonstrate cognitive differences. Typically, however, infant intelligence test scores are not good predictors of later cognitive scores (e.g., Page & Grandon, 1981).

Mildly retarded children are frequently not identified until they reach school. At this time, they are placed into situations where peer comparisons are necessary. Those lagging behind in certain skills are frequently referred, and many classified as mildly retarded. For this reason, the cut-off for differentiating prevention and remediation programs is approximately age five to six (i.e., the beginning of formal school training) in this chapter. This is consistent with a large portion of the literature. Therefore, those programs/approaches that focus on children prior to school age (and who usually are not labeled mildly retarded) are classified as *prevention* or *early intervention* programs and those used after a child is in school and has been identified as mentally retarded are considered *remedial*.

PREVENTION/EARLY INTERVENTION

The history of early intervention programs aimed at preventing mild mental retardation has had a rocky, controversial, and confusing first half-century. Beginning with the classic study by Skeels (Skeels & Dye,

1939; Skeels, 1966), and continuing with Kirk's (1958) research, Head Start, the Milwaukee Project, and current early intervention programs, the results have been anything but straightforward. Argued and debated are such issues as the relative effects of early intervention programs, cost-effectiveness, appropriateness of IQ as an outcome measure, and the possible variables that account for program effects.

There have been literally hundreds of programs developed to provide early intervention for high-risk children. These programs have been evaluated in depth and reported on in the professional literature. There have also been several major syntheses of this information in the past 10 years. In this section, the major findings are integrated and critiqued. First, however, a brief discussion of the target populations and the outcome measures for these programs are presented.

Early Intervention: The Target Population

As mentioned earlier, mildly retarded children are usually not identified until they reach school. At this time they start to fall behind their peers in language, preacademic/academic, and conceptual skills. Mild retardation in a very real sense is an educational diagnosis. Early intervention (before the school years) must therefore involve some degree of prediction as to who is high risk for subsequent problems.

There has been much interest in the area of early identification of mild retardation. Approximately 80% of all individuals labeled as retarded fall into the mild range, and most of them have no known medical/biological problem to explain their deficiency (Ramey & Bryant, 1983). The "causes" of mild mental retardation are constantly debated and are undoubtedly complex. Those espousing hereditarian positions are in considerable disagreement with those who favor an environmental explanation. Although this nature-nurture controversy regarding intelligence continues, most researchers pragmatically have attempted to identify environmental variables associated with later mental retardation. Investigators, therefore, have examined a number of variables, including demographic, child-rearing factors, and child status (Finkelstein & Ramey, 1980) that are associated with later cognitive and school problems of this population in an attempt to improve predictive accuracy.

Environmental information has been proven to be valuable and, in fact, has been found to be more effective than infant intelligence scales in predicting subsequent school performance (Elardo, Bradley, & Caldwell, 1975). Also, environmental variables seem to have greater *predictive* validity than *concurrent* validity when preschool and infant intelligence measures are used as the criterion variables (Gottfried, 1984). In a series of studies (Finkelstein & Ramey, 1980; Ramey & Brownlee, 1981), Ramey and his colleagues have demonstrated that relatively accurate predictions can be

made of subsequent school functioning by using demographic and other information available on the child's birth certificate. Approaches such as this have cost-effective appeal for relatively large screening programs. A high-risk index (see Figure 1) has also been developed and used to predict which children are more likely to have cognitive deficits. Ramey and Bryant (1983) noted that in the Abecedarian Project (discussed later in this chapter), the high-risk index was used to identify a group of children that were six times more likely than the national average to receive scores that would lead to a label of retardation.

The issue of which specific environmental variable(s) account for later cognitive development is somewhat controversial and difficult to determine. Recently, Gottfried (1984) reported the results of a series of longitudinal studies designed to focus on the relationship of home environment and cognitive development. He noted that socio-economic status (SES) historically has been associated with later intellectual performance. He also noted, however, that there are other home environmental factors that are important, including maternal involvement, amount and type of play materials, and opportunity for a variety of stimulating activities. Although SES is associated with home environment, there are other home environment factors that are related to cognitive development even after the effects of SES are partialled out. Thus, home environmental factors contribute significantly to cognitive development, independent of their relationship with SES, and SES is associated with cognitive development independent of home factors (Gottfried & Gottfried, 1984; Seigel, 1984). This somewhat confusing finding indicates the complexity and apparent interaction of the variables involved in cognitive development. It is an understatement to say that a variety of environmental factors, including SES, can have both a positive or a negative effect on subsequent cognitive development.

The target populations for the majority of the early intervention programs have been children of low SES who are frequently from a minority ethnic background and inner-city neighborhoods. A large percentage of these children are at risk for school failure. Again, one must be careful not to overlook the complexities in identifying specific risk factors. The fact that the majority of children chosen as high risk were of miniority background and from inner-city areas does not necessarily mean that ethnic group status or neighborhood type by themselves are risk factors. Again, the SES variable cannot be ignored. For example, Bradley and Caldwell (1984) found that differences in home environment was a function of SES and not race. This led Gottfried (1984) to conclude that:

> . . . it is an empirical fact that children from relatively higher SES families receive an intellectually more advantageous home environment. This finding holds for white, black, and Hispanic children, for children within lower- and middle-SES families as

FIGURE 1. High Risk Index

Factor	Weight
Mother's educational level[a]	
6	8
7	7
8	6
9	3
10	2
11	1
12	0
Father's educational level[a]	
6	8
7	7
8	6
9	3
10	2
11	1
12	0
Family income (per year)	
1,000	8
1,001–2,000	7
2,001–3,000	6
3,001–4,000	5
4,001–5,000	4
5,001–6,000	0
Father absent for reasons other than health or death	3
Absence of maternal relatives in local area (i.e., parents, grandparents, or brothers or sisters of majority age)	3
Siblings of school age who are one or more grades behind age-appropriate grade or who score equivalently low on school-administered achievement tests	3
Payments received from welfare agencies within past 3 years	3
Record of father's work indicates unstable and unskilled or semi-skilled labor	3
Records of mother's or father's IQ indicate scores of 90 or below	3
Relevant social agencies in the community indicate that the family is in need of assistance	3
One or more members of the family has sought counseling or professional help in the past 3 years	1
Special circumstances not included in any of the above that are likely contributors to cultural or social disadvantage	1

Note: Criterion for inclusion in high-risk sample is a score of 11.

[a]Last grade completed.

well as for children born preterm and full-term. (p. 330)

One final note of caution is in order in a discussion of the risk factors associated with mild mental retardation. The previous discussion has focused on the relationship of SES and other environmental variables with *lowered*

school and test performance. This, of course, does not mean that all, or even most, of the low SES and environmentally deprived children were eventually labeled as mildly retarded at subsequent followups. Many of these predictive studies (e.g. Finkelstein & Ramey, 1980) used one standard deviation (*SD*) below average on psychometric instruments as the criterion for an educational deficit. Obviously, not all children with such scores will be classified as mentally retarded. Zigler and Cascione (1977) adamantly made this point when they responded to Clarke and Clarke's (1977) assertion that Head Start failed to prevent mild mental retardation. On the other hand, Robinson (1976) noted that the war on poverty was concomitantly a war on borderline and mild mental retardation. Perhaps this issue is best summarized in the following manner. Although there is a higher probability that lower SES children will be classified as mildly retarded than will higher SES children, the percentage of low SES children who are classified is relatively small.

Outcome Measures

One important issue related to the effects of prevention or early intervention programs is the nature of the outcome measure. This issue focuses on the types of skills that are meant to be altered or changed by the prevention/intervention programs. Most programs have focused on developing cognitive, social, and achievement skills using traditional intelligence test results as well as later achievement/academic scores, and measures of social competence as the measure of program effectiveness. There is some question as to whether or not these variables are the most appropriate measures to use to evaluate the effectiveness of such programs, however. For example, Miller and Davis (1981) noted that intelligence tests have limited validity and are somewhat narrow in their scope. They suggested that the intelligence construct should be broadened to include measures of real-life situations. They also suggested a shift from a *static* to a *dynamic* assessment model (the dynamic assessment model is discussed later in this chapter). Other critics (e.g., Stedman, 1977) have noted the numerous shortcomings of using gain scores to measure program effectiveness.

Despite criticisms, IQ is perhaps the most widely used criterion measure and is the variable evaluated (as well as criticized) in this section of the chapter. The IQ still plays an extremely important role in the identification and classification of mental retardation, and any alteration of a child's IQ could have a subsequent effect on the prevalence of mild mental retardation.

IQ: The Misunderstood Concept

Much has been written about the pros and cons of intelligence testing as well as the various meanings and limitations of IQ. Recent litigation (e.g., Larry P. vs. Riles, PASE vs. Hannon) has literally put intelligence testing and IQ on trial with varying, and in some cases, opposite conclusions being drawn. There are those who believe steadfastly that IQ is an extremely important score indicating the potential for subsequent learning. Conversely, there are those who believe that IQ has no relationship to educational performance and has no place in the schools. Perhaps a more logical belief is that the meaning and use of IQ falls somewhere between these two extremes. It has been documented on numerous occasions that IQ is a fairly good predictor of school achievement and school performance (e.g., Reschly & Reschly, 1979; Oakland, 1977), yet IQ is not a stable score reflecting learning potential; IQs can and do change.

It is not surprising that IQ is chosen as the outcome measure for determining the effectiveness of many early intervention programs. First, it is a variable that can be altered. Second, IQ, to a large extent, measures information to which a child has been exposed. If the goal of early intervention programs is to increase stimulation and provide exposure to an enriched environment, then IQ is a natural choice as an outcome measure. One must also look at the limitations of the IQ, however. Increasing IQ in an experimental group does not mean that permanent changes have been made or that there have been increases in learning potential. Unfortunately, many have misinterpreted the results of early intervention studies when increases in IQ are demonstrated.

Description of Early Intervention Programs

The use of early intervention programs for children who are mentally retarded or at high risk for later problems in cognitive areas is certainly not new. For years the effects of such programs has been a source of constant debate. In one classic experiment focusing on early intervention with retarded children, Skeels (1966) followed two groups of institutionalized subjects over a 30-year period. Thirteen children were placed in the foster care of female institutionalized mother-substitutes, and the control group stayed in an orphanage setting. During the 1.5-year program, the experimental group showed an IQ increase of 28 points (from 64 to 92), whereas the control group showed a decrease of 26 points. Thirty years later, all the experimental subjects were self-supporting; all the control subjects had either died or were still institutionalized. Although this study, like so many others of its type, had methodological flaws and no control over a host of factors that could account for the results, it demonstrated that early intervention was at least possible. Kirk (1958) extended this research and found that IQ could be altered through systematic intervention but that the results were not permanent. Shortly after the children entered school, the gap between the experimental and control group narrowed. These findings (initial gains, lack of permanence) have been well substantiated in recent years and have been referred to as the "freshman effect" (Bloom, 1964) and

the "fadeout theory" (Bronfenbrenner, 1976), respectively.

With the introduction of the widely publicized Head Start Program in 1965, the debate became even more heated, with the issue of cost-effectiveness becoming a central concern. Other programs also emerged, many with greater care being taken to improve experimental methodology. Long-term projects were also undertaken. Two of the more widely publicized were the Milwaukee Project and the Abecedarian Project. A description and critique of these early intervention programs follows.

Head Start

Politically and socially, the time was right in the 1960s for new and innovative psychological and educational intervention programs. It seemed only fitting that the focus of such programs in the Great Society would be the disadvantaged and the poor. Certainly the most ambitious early intervention program was Head Start. Although there had been some smaller scale programs in the late 1950s and early 1960s, Head Start represented a significant commitment by the Federal government to focus on preventing cognitive, emotional, and educational deficits. In the first summer program in 1965, there were half a million children enrolled. There was (and still is) some misunderstanding and uncertainty about the specific objectives and goals of Head Start. The following were identified and recommended by a task force as being realistic objectives for Head Start:
1) to improve the child's physical health and physical abilities,
2) to foster emotional and social development,
3) to improve the child's mental processing and skills,
4) to establish patterns and expectations of success,
5) to increase the child's capacity to relate positively to family members and others, and to strengthen the family stability,
6) to develop a responsible attitude toward society as well as to foster constructive opportunities for the family to work together to solve problems, and
7) to increase the sense of dignity and self-worth of the child and the family (Hodges and Cooper, 1981).
Although no specific mention of the prevention of mental retardation was made, there is somewhat of an implicit assumption that this should be at least a by-product of Head Start. Because there were so many Head Start sites around the United States, it is difficult to characterize the type of instructional program that the children received. In general, however, they are probably best described for the most part as traditional nursery school programs (Hodges and Cooper, 1981).

Even with the optimism surrounding Head Start, there were a number of skeptics who questioned the efficacy and cost-effectiveness of such a massive, intense program. Indeed, there was relatively little empirical research to support such an extensive program.

Skepticism grew into pessimism with the publication of the Westinghouse/Ohio University study (Cicirelli, 1969), which reported that the summer programs were ineffective in producing gains that persisted into the early school years. It was also reported that although the full-year programs produced some gains in cognitive development, they appeared to be ineffective in developing affective skills. In addition, it was noted that Head Start children still scored considerably lower than the national average on standardized readiness and achievement tests. Although this study has been criticized for methodological flaws (Lazar, 1981), there was a sharp reaction to these results. A task force was immediately appointed to interpret their possible explanations. After careful investigation two hypotheses were generated. The first was that Head Start was initiated too late in the child's life. The second was that Head Start was producing immediate gains, but because of the lack of continuity between Head Start and the schools, the gains eroded (Hodges & Cooper, 1981). Two recommendations followed. The first suggested the use of parent-child centers so that children could be worked with younger in life. The second was the development of Follow-Through Projects that allowed for more continuity between the preschool and school-based programs. Many of these projects (e.g., Perry Preschool Project, Parent Education Program) were included in the report of the Consortium for Longitudinal Studies (discussed in the next section).

Contrary to the findings of the Westinghouse study, more recent studies have provided somewhat different conclusions. Mann, Harrell, and Hurt (1978) reviewed Head Start research since 1969 (the year of the Westinghouse study). The post-1969 Head Start Programs became known as Head Start Planned Variation (Hodges & Cooper, 1981) and were characterized by more experimental control. Mann et al. found that the majority of studies indicated that Head Start was effective in preparing children for later school life and that IQs were increased. In fact, 22 of the 27 studies found positive results.

Taken as a whole, these results seem to indicate that carefully planned intervention programs can be effective (at least on a short-term basis) if experimental methodology is appropriate and there is a sound theoretical base; simply providing early intervention with little structure of consistency will provide minimal gains, at best.

Perhaps the current state of the art on the effects of Head Start (and possibly other early intervention programs) is best summarized by Hodges and Cooper (1981):

> One of the original objectives of Head Start was to improve the child's mental processes and skills. Based on this objective, many scientists have concluded that Head Start was a failure while other scientists have professed that it was a success. Both views can be found expressed in unequivocal terms.

When cogent investigators can disagree so dramatically about the results of a program, it must indicate that the truth lies somewhere between the extremes of absolute failure and total success. (p. 228)

Consortium for Longitudinal Studies

At the same time that Head Start and Follow Through were implemented, there were several independent ongoing projects that examined various early intervention models. Some of these were, in fact, parts or extensions of Head Start/Follow Through. The most comprehensive summary and extension of the early intervention studies of the 1960s was produced by the *Consortium for Longitudinal Studies*. In 1974, Lazar and Gratburg designed a study to investigate the long-term effects of early intervention programs. This study was designed primarily as a reaction to the public criticism aimed against such programs. First, Lazar and Gratburg attempted to find researchers and research projects that dealt with early intervention but who had a relatively low attrition ratio. They identified 12 research groups (for a total of 11 projects) who met this criterion. Each group agreed to provide data for analysis and reanalysis and to allow collection of follow-up data to determine the long-term effects of the program.

The justification behind the longitudinal study was that it would broaden the base for generalization (if there were consistent data across projects). The Consortium also felt that it would be effective in analyzing the gross variables that cut across studies. They did note, however, that specific variables (such as site-specific variables) were difficult to analyze (Lazar & Darlington, 1982) and that because of this fact, generalization of the data to massive programs such as Head Start in which multiple sites were used was not appropriate.

In analyzing the projects' data, the Consortium balanced Type I and Type II errors so that there was little chance that a false hypothesis of a lasting effect would be accepted; that is, they wanted to make sure that if a long-term effect was noted, that it was, in fact, a true long-term effect.

Description of Relevant Projects

The 11 projects included in the longitudinal study involved both *home-based programs*, in which intervention was aimed primarily at the parents of the high-risk child, and *center-based programs*, in which the intervention was aimed more at the high-risk child. (Several projects included a combination of these.) Of the 11 projects (see Table 1 for summary) 7 were analyzed to determine the long-term effect on IQ. These were the (a) Philadelphia Project, (b) Parent Education Program, (c) Early Training Project, (d) Mother-Child Home Program, (e) Experimental Variation of Head Start Curriculum, (f) Harlem Training Project, and the (g) Perry Preschool Project. Dependent on the research design employed, these projects were classified by the

TABLE 1

Characteristics of Early Education Programs and Ages of Subjects for Each Data Set

Principal Investigator	Project Name and Location	Delivery System	Birth Year	Age at Entry	Program Length	Years of Program
Beller*	Philadelphia Project, Philadelphia	Center	1959	4 yrs	1 yr	1963–64
Deutsch	Institute for Developmental Studies, New York	Center	1958–66		5 yrs	1963–71 (8 waves)
Gordon/Jester	Parent Education Program, North Central Florida	Home	1966–67	3–24 mos	1–3 yrs	1966–70 (3 waves)
Gray	Early Training Project, Tennessee	Center/home	1958	3.8 or 4.8 yrs	14 or 26 mos	1962–65
Karnes	Curriculum Comparison Study, Champaign-Urbana, Ill.	Center	1961–63	4 yrs	1–2 yrs	1965–67 (2 waves)
Levenstein	Mother-Child Home Program, Long Island, N.Y.	Home	1964–68	2 or 3 yrs	1–2 yrs	1967–72 (5 waves)
Miller	Experimental Variation of Head Start Curricula, Louisville, KY.	Center and center/home	1964	4 yrs	1 yr	1968–69
Palmer	Harlem Training Project, New York	Center	1964	2 or 3 yrs	1 or 2 yrs	1966–68
Weikart	Perry Preschool Project, Ypsilanti, Mich.	Center/home	1958–62	3 or 4 yrs	1 or 2 yrs	1962–67 (5 waves)
Woolman	Micro-social Learning System, Vineland, N.J.	Center	1966–68	4–5 yrs	1–4 yrs	1969–73
Zigler	New Haven Follow-Through Study, New Haven, Conn.	Center	1962–64	5 yrs	4 yrs	1967–71 (2 waves)

*Beller used a different designation of program group from the one shown here. In his own study, this group received 2 years of preschool while his second group received 1 year of preschool (i.e., kindergarten).

Consortium as "more nearly randomized designs" or "less randomized designs." The Parent Education Program, Early Training Project, Harlem Training Project, and the Perry Preschool Project were considered more randomized and the Philadelphia Project, Mother-Child Home Program, and the Experimental Variation of Head Start, less randomized. A brief description of the projects (summarized from Lazar & Darlington, 1982) follows.

Philadelphia Project. (Beller) The Philadelphia Project was developed to determine the effects of length of formal schooling prior to first grade on later cognitive and social development. The subsequent performances of children who entered school at nursery school (age 4), kindergarten (age 5) and first grade (with no earlier formal program) were compared. The children came from predominantly low-income black neighborhoods. The nursery school program was conducted by Temple University faculty. The kindergarten and first-grade groups used the curricula and materials provided by the regular school system.

The Parent Education Program. (Gordon & Jester) This project was aimed at developing children's skills through family intervention. The children included were as young as 3 months. A Piagetian model was used in the development of curriculum materials. Paraprofessionals were trained to work with parents on a once-a-week basis. The activities and materials were presented to the parents, who were trained to work with their child. After the project was initiated, a Home Learning Center approach was added in which groups of five children and their mothers met periodically with a teacher.

Early Training Project. (Gray & Klaus) This project was designed to develop low-income children's later

cognitive and social development. It included a highly sequenced instructional program aimed at nursery-school-aged children and involved an intense 10-week summer program in which the children worked 20 hours a week. Included in each group were 20 children, a teacher, and 20 assistant teachers. During the rest of the year, project staff would meet with the family for one hour a week.

Mother Child Home Program. (Levenstein) This home-based program was designed for children aged 2 and 3. Project staff would visit the home, work with educational materials, and encourage verbal interaction between the mother and children.

Experimental Variation of Head Start. (Miller) In this program four specific preschool programs were compared and evaluated: a traditional Head Start Program, the Demonstration and Research Center for Early Education (DARCEE), a program following the Montessori philosophy, and a program following the Bereiter-Englemann approach. Children participating in this program entered at age 4 and received one of the four programs or acted as a control group (participating only in the traditional kindergarten program).

Harlem Training Project. (Palmer) This program was designed to determine the effects of minimal early intervention (i.e., 2 hours per week for 8 months) on the developmental level of children. Children aged 2 and 3 were presented with two modes of intervention to increase later cognitive skills. These two approaches, the concept training approach and discovery approach, were quite different. The concept training approach taught basic concepts through the use of relatively structured environment in a one-to-one setting. The children in the discovery program were given toys used to teach the concepts but without formal training.

Perry Preschool Project. (Weikert). This project was focused on the development of cognitive skills of low SES children (age 3) through the use of Piagetian curricula, including the interplay of content, levels of representation, and levels of operation. This theoretical framework was translated into a workable curriculum by teachers who provided appropriate activities and materials for the children.

Findings of the Consortium

In general, an analysis of the early intervention programs indicated that measurable and dramatic changes in IQ were found. In addition, the children exposed to such programs had a reduced probability of receiving a special education label. In fact, Lazar and Darlington (1982) stated that, "The conclusion that a well run, cognitively oriented early education program will increase the IQ scores of low income children is one of the least disputed results in educational evaluation" (p. 44). After subjecting the IQ data to statistical regression controlling for background variables, they found that the average IQ difference between the experimental and control groups was 7.42. The Consortium also reported that the change in IQ lasted for at least 2 years following the intervention program. After 3 or 4 years, the results were not as obvious, and at the follow-up in 1976 there was virtually no difference between the IQs of the experimental and control groups. Ramey (1982), in fact, noted that for the four projects listed as having a nearly randomized design, both the experimental and control groups had IQs about ½ SD below average at follow-up.

What are some of the possible explanations for the lack of permanent effects on IQ? There are actually several possibilities, some philosophical, some economic, and some methodological. Perhaps the most obvious and potentially most devastating is that cognitive skills cannot be modified, at least on a long-term basis. Another is that after the intervention programs are stopped, the children go back into the lower socio-economic environment that was associated with their high-risk status to begin with. In other words, unless permanent environmental changes can be made, permanent cognitive skill development can not be expected. Another possible explanation for the lack of permanence, however, are the various methodological problems found in many of the studies. Figure 2 shows the results of the four projects classified as having nearly randomized designs. As can be seen, the experimental groups scored higher than did the control group at every age. It is noted, however, that the experimental group also scored approximately 2 to 10 points higher than did the control group at the *pretest level* (the Parent Education Program did not have a pretest because of the age of the subjects). In fact, the pattern of changes

(increases and decreases) are markedly similar for both the experimental and control groups.

One potentially confounding effect is the use of different instruments to measure intelligence at various stages of the projects. For example, the four projects used the Stanford-Binet Intelligence Scale and the Wechsler Intelligence Scale for Children (WISC) for the pretest and during the intervention program, yet the Wechsler Intelligence Scale for Children-Revised (WISC-R) was used in the follow-up testing for all the projects except for the Perry Preschool Project (which used the WISC). This difference in instrumentation could have had an effect. Among other reasons, it is well documented that individuals score lower on the WISC-R than on the WISC (e.g., Quattrochi & Sherrets, 1980). Therefore, the changes in IQ over time could have been due, at least in part, to test differences, which could account for the drop in IQ but not for the lack of differences between the experimental and control groups.

A somewhat different trend in scores was found for the three projects that were classified as having less randomized designs (see Figure 3). These studies resulted in greater experimental/control group differences during follow-up. The methodological shortcomings were even more evident in these studies, however. For example, the Peabody Picture Vocabulary Test (PPVT) was used as the intelligence measure for the pretest and age 6 data for the Mother-Child Home Program. A visual inspection of these data in Figure 3 in relation to the other scores shows how the overall trends can be misinterpreted as a function of instrument difference. In addition, the use of the PPVT as an intelligence measure is, in itself, making a tenuous assumption (e.g., Salvia & Ysseldyke, 1985; Taylor, 1984).

The Consortium also examined the project data to determine whether certain types of children (e.g., ethnic status, sex) benefited more from the early intervention programs. Their analysis indicated that there was no relationship between program effectiveness and type of children. They acknowledged, however, that such a relationship could have been washed out by collapsing the individual project's data.

In summary, the results of the Consortium for Longitudinal Studies answered some questions and raised others. Regarding the effects of the intervention programs on modifying IQ, the conclusions are fairly obvious. The programs do have an initial impact on modifying traditional intelligence scores, at least on a short-term basis. The maintenance of these effects over time are much less well documented, and after a period of 7 to 10 years, there appears to be a regression back to the pretest level. Research in this area, however, is fraught with methodological problems. Only four of the seven projects that used IQ as an outcome measure were classified by the Consortium as having nearly randomized experimental designs. Only three of those four included a pretest measure. Further, the follow-up measure used in three of the four projects was different

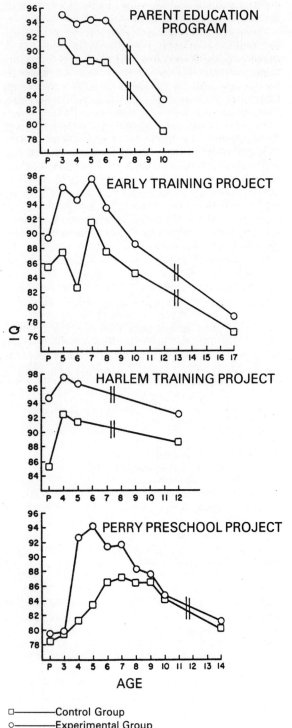

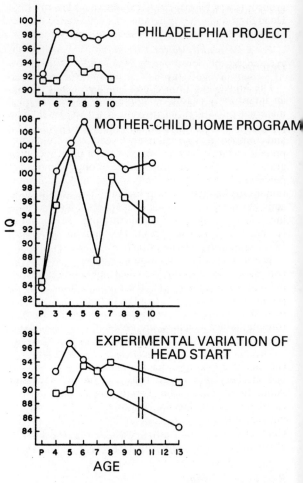

Figure 3. Results of projects classified as having less randomized designs

Control Group
Experimental Group
P = Pretest Score
Figure 2. Results of projects classified as having nearly randomized designs

from the measures used during other aspects of the projects. Thus, although the data indicating a loss of IQ over time appear overwhelming, these methodological considerations should be taken into account.

The Milwaukee Project

The Milwaukee Project was an extremely controversial program whose reported results started somewhat of a media event. The project was initially formulated to study the effects of an early, direct, intensive, family-oriented program on the cognitive development of high-risk children. It was one of the first attempts to design a "true experiment" to measure the effects of a prevention program for mild retardation of sociocultural etiology (Page & Grandon, 1981). In terms of the number of children served (20 in the experimental group), it was an extremely expensive endeavor. Like Head Start and other programs, the Milwaukee Project was funded at a time of great social optimism.

Description

The Milwaukee Project had two main components, an infant early childhood stimulation program and a maternal rehabilitation program (Garber, 1975). The programs were to begin shortly after the child's birth and continue for approximately 6 years. The child component included both an infancy and a preschool program. The infancy program provided opportunities for perceptual-motor, cognitive/language, and social/emotional development. The preschool program included activities designed to enhance perceptual-motor, reading, language, math, and social/emotional development (Heber, Garber, Harrington, Hoffman, & Falander, 1972). Both programs had structured, all-day schedules.

The maternal rehabilitation component consisted of two phases. The first involved the training of basic reading and math skills to give the mothers the necessary prerequisites for job training (Heber et al., 1972). The second phase involved vocational, primarily on-the-job, training, which included the areas of nursing, housekeeping, food service, and laundry.

The 20 experimental subjects and 20 control subjects came from a low SES area in Milwaukee. All of them had mothers who scored below 75 on the Wechsler Adult Intelligence Scale. Previous research had indicated that maternal IQ is an important factor in identifying high-risk children (Garber & Heber, 1977). The children (and families) were subsequently assigned to either the experimental or the control group.

Results and Critique

The results of the Milwaukee Project reported by Heber and his associates were very impressive. The mothers gained self-confidence and became more verbally interactive with their children. The children's gain was remarkable. At 72 months of age, the experimental group had a mean IQ of 123, compared to 87 for the control group (Garber & Heber, 1977). These data were impressive for two reasons. First, they suggested that early intervention could increase IQ, in fact as much as two *SD*s. The second was that the early intervention could produce superior, or at least above average, IQ results. Previous studies (e.g., Consortium) found that the intervention programs only brought the IQ up to the average.

These results fueled the heated environmentalist debate. They were frequently taken out of context and overgeneralized. In addition, they were scrutinized and criticized. Perhaps the sharpest criticism came from Page (1972), and Page and Grandon (1981). Specifically, they focused on methodological inadequacies and inconsistencies. For example, they questioned whether or not the subjects were actually randomly assigned to the

experimental and control groups and provided evidence that the physical measures (e.g. height) were statistically different for the two groups. They also questioned the lack of information about attrition. Perhaps their most significant criticism was that the tasks taught during the project were similar to the test items on the developmental and intelligence scales that were used to determine program effectiveness. Thus, there was little generalization of the gains to real-life situations.

Yet another criticism was aimed at the lack of scientifically appropriate dissemination of the data. Specifically, this criticism was focused on the lack of published reports in scholarly journals where the data could be subjected to rigorous review. Sommers and Sommers (1983) noted that the Milwaukee Project and its reported findings are frequently mentioned in psychology textbooks. The primary resources cited in these texts, however, consist only of progress reports, technical reports, and chapters. This led them to question "the ease with which tentative information may become virtual fact." (p. 983)

Carolina Abecedarian Project

The Abecedarian Project has been an integral part of the Frank Porter Graham Child Development Center at the University of North Carolina since 1972. This project is a well-designed longitudinal study focusing on the effects of an intensive child-centered day care program for high-risk children. Specifically, the four objectives of the project are to (a) demonstrate that socio-cultural retardation can be prevented, (b) develop an infant curriculum, (c) investigate which psychological and other processes are affected by early intervention, and (d) determine the relationships among psychological, biological, and family attributes during the preschool child's life (Ramey, Holmberg, Sparling, & Collier, 1977).

Like the Milwaukee Project, the Abecedarian Project was focused on children immediately after birth. Therefore, the subjects were chosen by identifying potentially high-risk mothers at prenatal clinics and through social services. After potential mothers were identified, the high-risk index (discussed previously) was administered to them. They were also interviewed and administered an individual intelligence test. A total of 107 subjects were included. Children and their families were placed in pairs according to their score on the high-risk index and then randomly assigned to either the experimental or the control group (Ramey & Campbell, 1984).

Description

The curriculum given to the experimental group consisted of a variety of language, social, motor, and cognitive areas (Ramey & Campbell, 1984). The curriculum was presented individually to the infants and in small groups to the older children. A traditional preschool curriculum was also used after the children reached 3 years of age. Particular emphasis was placed on communication skills and language development. The program went from 7:45 a.m. to 5:30 p.m., 5 days a week, 50 weeks per year.

One interesting and potentially valuable characteristic of the Abecedarian Project is the attempt at controlling the internal validity of the experimental design; that is, there was some attempt at analyzing the effects of the child care program per se by controlling for some other environmental factors that could account for the experimental effect. As a result, both the experimental and control subjects received a number of services that are typically needed by low-income families, including nutritional supplements, medical care, diaper service, and family support. In addition, both groups were paid for their participation. Thus, the major factor on which the experimental and control group differed was the child-centered program and the curriculum.

Results and Critique

Perhaps the best summary of the results of the Abecedarian Project was presented by Ramey and Campbell (1984). They noted that differences between the control and experimental groups on the Bayley Scales of Infant Development were found as early as 18 months. There were also statistical differences on the Stanford-Binet and the McCarthy Scales of Children's Abilities at various intervals between the ages of 2 and 5 years. One interesting result of the analysis of the separate Indices from the McCarthy Scales was reported. As expected, there were significant differences between the groups on the Verbal Index. There were also differences on the Perceptual-Performance and the Quantitative Indices. The differences between the groups on the Memory and Motor Indices were not as great, however.

Ramey and Campbell also noted that, similar to other programs, the IQs of the experimental group were near the national average and not in the superior range (as was found in the Milwaukee Project). They acknowledged that the treatment effect in the Abecedarian Project was not as large as that reported in the Milwaukee Project and attributed this to program intensity. Two other explanations are also possible, however. First, the control of some of the other experimental factors in the Abecedarian Project could have eliminated some of the experimental effect found in the Milwaukee Project. Second, the parent component included in the Milwaukee Project could have accounted for the difference. This latter possibility is currently being investigated by the project staff in another program called project CARE (Ramey, Sparling, Bryant, & Wasik, 1982).

Summary and Implications of Early Intervention Studies

As noted previously, there have been many questions answered, but perhaps more questions raised by research involving early intervention programs. There is little doubt that the initiation of a well-designed program will result in increases in cognitive skills (particularly when traditional IQ measures are used as the criterion). There is also sufficient evidence to suggest that these effects are not maintained after the program is terminated. As previously mentioned, there have been many syntheses of intervention program research in the past 10 years. In one of the more systematic studies, Stedman (1977) reported the results of his evaluation that was commissioned by the Department of Health, Education, and Welfare. Among other conclusions, he noted that (a) the strength of the intervention programs is increased by parent involvement; (b) effects seem to last longer in home-training studies than in school-based programs; and (c) that successful programs are successful regardless of age of entry, sex, or race. He also noted that the alteration of IQ in these programs was a function of the initial IQ (lower initial scores resulted in more gains) as well as the duration and intensity of the program. Beyond these fairly general statements, there remains a number of unanswered questions and conflicting results.

There are two obvious (and frustrating) findings in the early intervention literature. First, there is continued debate over the appropriateness and cost-effectiveness of these programs. Many times, researchers will take dichotomous positions when interpreting the same data. Clarke and Clarke's (1977) and Zigler and Cascione's (1977) argument about the results (and even the goals) of Head Start is a prime example. The second finding is that research in this area is both difficult and, for the most part, methodologically unsound. It is indeed difficult to plan and implement studies in this area because of the usual problems in doing field-based research plus the additional problem of dealing with high-risk subjects. Issues of randomization and subject selection take on added significance. Many of the programs have focused on external validity, or the generalization of the findings to other populations. What seems to have resulted is a subsequent lack of internal validity; we simply do not know what factor(s) accounted for the effects.

There are several implications of these findings that might help us avoid ambiguous results and provide meaningful interpretative data. The first is the need for increased research in the area of *prediction* of children who are at high risk for becoming mildly retarded. This might require longitudinal studies aimed at identifying known and hypothesized predictor variables and using statistical procedures (e.g., regression and discriminant function analysis) to predict criterion variables (e.g., school performance, test scores, educational label) at various age levels. Such studies would allow us to have much better controlled samples for future early intervention studies.

Another need relates to the lack of carefully controlled studies that focus on the specific variables that affect cognitive growth. Early intervention studies are both time consuming and costly. This implies that we might have to abandon temporarily the notion that "the larger the sample the better the sample." It also implies that we must refrain from using a "shotgun approach" of modifying numerous variables in an attempt to demonstrate program effects. Demonstrating dramatic gains (as in the Milwaukee Project) that cannot be replicated is of little importance in the long run.

A final need focuses on the insufficiency of the dependent measures used to evaluate program effectiveness. As noted earlier, IQ has been, and will probably remain, a major variable under investigation. Although controversy and debate have resulted in close scrutiny of (and hopefully improvement in) intelligence tests, further development of the concept and its measurement should be emphasized. Other dependent variables, such as social skills, that have been used are equally difficult to define and measure. Perhaps with the growing interest in adaptive behavior and the development of new instruments to measure this construct, more attention can be paid to this variable as a viable dependent measure.

Preventing mild retardation for the first few years of life is undeniably an important concern. It loses importance, however, if those same children become retarded in later life because of the lack of maintenance effects of the prevention program. Again, if we could isolate those independent variables or combinations of variables that are important, these could be built into a maintenance program. Further, we might find that a carefully planned program might not have to be as intensive, time consuming, and costly as many that have been employed.

REMEDIATION

Early intervention/prevention programs for high-risk children have focused on developing cognitive skills so that the label of mental retardation ultimately can be avoided. As such, researchers are interested in the effects of these programs on subsequent IQ (one criteria for labeling) as well as on academic and social competence. As noted previously, there is a certain amount of statistical error involved in such programs because it is not clear whether the children identified as high risk and given an intervention program would have been labeled retarded if the program had not been initiated. A certain amount of the guesswork is taken out of the experimental paradigm when focusing on remediation programs designed to increase cognitive skills. The subjects have already been labeled as mentally retarded (or at least they are performing below average on intellectual and academic measures). Thus the issue of subject selection and randomization takes on less significance as a potential source of misinterpretation.

There are literally hundreds of remediation programs available that attempt to modify cognitive skills. This is true primarily because there are so many theories and models related to cognition. As Brooks and McCauley (1984) stated, there are almost as many ways of studying

cognition as there are researchers doing the investigations. These approaches range in focus from strictly behavioral to developmentally-based Piagetian. In recent years the programs that have been receiving the most attention are those that combine a cognitive-behavioral model and are based on sound cognitive and learning theory principles. Even so, there are still a large number of programs that meet these criteria (Sternberg, 1981).

Most of the more popular and accepted theories of cognition view intelligence as a dynamic, multifaceted construct (e.g., Das, Kirby, & Jarman, 1979; Sternberg, 1980). These theories stress the importance of the ability to process information effectively and efficiently. The Sternberg model, for example, includes five components that demonstrate these points: the *metacomponent*, which emphasizes the person's ability to plan and use strategies for problem solving, *performance* components to execute the strategies, and *acquisition, retention, and transfer* components to learn, remember, and generalize new strategies. Thus the acquisition and use of appropriate strategies necessary to learn and generalize information is a hallmark of many of these cognitive theories.

In addition to the available theoretical models, there is a vast amount of learning theory literature that is available about the mentally retarded population. Much of this literature focuses on the characteristic cognitive/learning deficits associated with mental retardation. Many of these remedial programs have as their goal the development of these deficient skills. It is important, therefore, to look at some of these characteristics that are associated with retardation and serve as a basis for both the focus of the remediation program and the nature of the outcome measure.

Cognitive Characteristics

In addition to the general reduction in ability to learn, there are a number of specific characteristics that have been noted among mentally retarded individuals. These include attentional deficits (Zeaman & House, 1963) and memory problems, particularly related to short-term memory (Robinson & Robinson, 1976). Investigators have speculated that these problems are tied to retarded persons' inability to use appropriate learning strategies such as mediation (Hallahan & Kauffman, 1982).

Another area in which retarded individuals have difficulty is metacognitive processing. This refers to the ability to define, attend to, monitor, and use one's own sets of cognitive operations and strategies (Brooks & McCauley, 1984). Campione and Brown (1977) noted, for example, that retarded children do not use strategic behaviors spontaneously and have difficulty selecting, modifying, and sequencing strategies. In a series of research studies, Borys (e.g., 1979) has demonstrated that retarded children have problems in the area of self-questioning. In fact, the inability to use strategies effectively is a seldom disputed characteristic of retarded individuals.

Another related issue is that of generalization. The difficulty that retarded individuals have in generalizing new information is well documented (MacMillan, 1982; Robinson & Robinson, 1976). Borkowski and Varnhagen (1984) found that for generalization to occur, the effective use of the executive skills such as strategy selection and monitoring are necessary. As a result, many investigators have attempted to train the generalization of strategic behavior. Many of these approaches are discussed later in this chapter. As will be seen, the effects of these training programs are somewhat unclear at this time.

Focus of Programs and Nature of Outcome Measures

Given the various information-processing models of cognition and the documented deficiencies of mentally retarded individuals in that area, it is not surprising that the majority of remediation programs designed to increase cognitive performance are aimed at developing, maintaining, and applying cognitive strategies. In other words, cognitive training is concerned with teaching an individual how to think, solve problems, and so on, whereas traditional content approaches are more concerned with teaching knowledge, facts, and so on. Certainly, both approaches serve important purposes. Until recently, however, the training of cognitive *processes* as opposed to the teaching of *specific information* has been largely overlooked.

Even though cognitive strategy training approaches are relatively similar in their goals, many have historical roots that can be traced to different theoretical models as well as differences in the specific strategies that are trained. For example, there are those that are heavily tied to an assessment model using a test-train-test paradigm. This approach would be characterized by the work of Budoff as well as Feuerstein and his associates. There are other approaches such as cognitive behavior modification and attack strategy training that borrow heavily from the behavioral model. Still other approaches have been developed out of a series of long-term, laboratory studies. These include the contributions of Butterfield and Belmont, and Campione and Brown, among others. All of these approaches represent only a small proportion of the available techniques. They are, however, some of the more popular and/or methodologically sound.

Feuerstein's and Budoff's Approaches

Feuerstein's Instrumental Enrichment

One of the more popular, and increasingly controversial, approaches to remediating cognitive deficits has been proposed by Feuerstein and his associates. Their approach, *instrumental enrichment*, has been used widely in Israel and has been receiving increased attention in the United States in the last few years. Although the approach was developed initially for culturally deprived children, its application with retarded individuals has also been persued.

Feuerstein borrowed heavily from Vygotsky (1978) and his notion of the proximal zone of development. Vygotsky's approach emphasizes the importance of mediation (by other individuals) that ultimately leads to internalization (by the subject). According to the instrumental enrichment model, learning occurs as a function of direct exposure to the environment as well as through *mediated learning experiences* (MLE). Mediated learning occurs when a mediator (another individual) intervenes between the learner and the environment and interprets the world to the learner (Feuerstein, Miller, Hoffman, Rand, Mintzker, & Jensen, 1981).

Inherent in the instrumental enrichment program is an assessment battery that serves as the stimulus for the mediated learning. This assessment instrument, the *Learning Potential Assessment Device* (LPAD), is used first to test the subject, then to train (mediate), and finally to retest to determine the effect of the remediation (Feuerstein, 1979). According to Feuerstein, the LPAD is intentionally content-free, although several researchers (e.g., Brown, Campione, & Ferrara, 1982) have questioned this by noting that they are essentially variants of traditional intelligence test items. According to its originators the LPAD is used primarily as a vehicle to achieve the goals of the intervention program. Those six goals are:

1. The correction of deficient cognitive functions;
2. The teaching of specific concepts, operations, and vocabulary required by the instrumental enrichment exercises;
3. The development of an intrinsic need for adequate cognitive functioning and the spontaneous use of operational thinking by the production of crystallized schema and habit formation;
4. The production of insight and understanding of one's own thought process that produce success and are responsible for failure;
5. The production of task-intrinsic motivation that is reinforced by the meaning of the program in a broader social content; and
6. A change in orientation towards oneself from passive recipient and reproducer to active generator of information. (Feuerstein et al., 1981, p. 275)

These goals emphasize that in addition to the training and development of cognitive skills, the development of metacognitive skills is stressed. This includes the internalization of the learned cognitive processes that lead to the use of self-regulation and the independent use of appropriate cognitive strategies.

Perhaps one of the more debated aspects of the instrumental enrichment model is the content-free nature of the stimulus materials. In other words, the *content* of the materials used to train cognitive skills is unimportant, or are at least secondary to the *process* of training. Feuerstein et al. (1981) argued that through instrumental enrichment, structural changes occur that should result in increased effects over time. They further argued that by using task-bound materials, any effects will either remain stable or diminish; the child might learn a task but be unable to generate problem solving strategies for novel tasks. The key issue becomes one of generalization. In other words, can one expect the results of cognitive strategy training to generalize to novel tasks?

Campione and Brown (1977) represent the alternate opinion regarding this issue and feel that generalization must be built into the training procedure, and that the training task can and should be content-rich. They argue that teaching a specific skill actually enhances generalization.

Budoff's Learning Potential Assessment Strategy

Budoff and his associates developed a procedure that also uses the test-train-retest paradigm. Their procedure is like Feuerstein's in that it uses IQ type test materials and is based on Vygotsky's work (Brown, Campione, & Ferrara, 1982). Unlike Feuerstein, Budoff was interested primarily in differentiating mildly retarded individuals from those who scored poorly on traditional intelligence test measures but were not, in fact, retarded. The rationale was to offer relevant learning opportunities (called "coaching") in a systematic, structured, format designed to teach nonverbal reasoning skills (Sewell & Severson, 1974). Budoff used the Kohs Block Design Test, the Raven Progressive Matrices, and a Series Learning Potential Test to evaluate and coach the individual. The coaching consisted of giving more and more explicit prompts until the person could solve the problem. The individual was encouraged to check his or her work throughout the task (Brown, Campione, & Ferrara, 1982). This part of the coaching was done to encourage the individual to use a systematic, planned work approach and to provide concrete reinforcement for task achievement (Budoff, 1974).

Cognitive Behavior Modification

In recent years, the use of cognitive behavior modification (CBM) has been popularized. Although there is little consensus on an exact definition, certain characteristics are usually associated with CBM. Ledwedge (1978) noted that it usually includes some type of self-statement, such as self-instruction, and relies heavily on internal speech as a therapeutic instrument. Lloyd (1980) listed five characteristics of CBM: (a) the use of some form of self-treatment; (b) the use of verbalization; (c) the identification of a general strategy to help a student solve a problem; (d) the use of modeling to instruct the student; and (e) the emphasis on training students to delay responding and reflect on various alternative strategies/answers. Thus, CBM is used to train certain cognitive skills with the emphasis on *self-management* of those learned cognitive strategies.

Although CBM shows promise in terms of controlling disruptive behavior (e.g., Turkewitz, O'Leary, & Ironsmith 1975), impulsive behavior (e.g., Finch & Spirito, 1980), and attention to task (Kneedler & Hallahan, 1981), the effects of CBM on cognitive and academic skill development is unclear. On the one hand, there is some evidence that CBM increases reading skills (e.g., Lloyd, Kosiewicz, & Hallahan, 1982) and arithmetic and handwriting skills (e.g., Hallahan, Lloyd, Kosiewicz, Kauffman, & Graves, 1979). On the other hand, other researchers (e.g. Robin, Armel, & O'Leary, 1975; Wozniak and Nuechterlein, 1973) have found that CBM has a minimal effect on academic skills. Lloyd (1980) stated that, in general, more CBM research has been focused on behavior related to academic performance rather than on academic performance specifically. Few investigators have dealt specifically with cognitive skill development. Research aimed directly at measuring the effects of CBM on the acquisition of cognitive and academic skills is necessary and might shed some light on many unanswered questions.

Attack strategy training is similar to CBM except that *specific* strategies are taught for specific types of problems, and self-management is not required (Lloyd, 1980). Perhaps due to the task-specific nature of the cognitive strategies in this approach, research related to academic skill development is promising. Researchers have demonstrated that specific attack strategies are particularly relevant for both arithmetic skills (e.g., Carnine, 1980) and to a lesser degree beginning reading skills (e.g., Carnine, 1977). Similar to CBM, attack strategy training has not been investigated adequately with regard to the development of cognitive skills.

Laboratory Training Studies

There are a number of investigators who have studied the cognitive processing problems of mentally retarded individuals and designed instructional programs to improve those deficits. These individuals have attempted to manipulate certain independent variables experimentally (e.g., number and types of cues, length of task) in order to evaluate the subsequent effect on learning. These laboratory approaches also use a test-train-retest paradigm, but were designed more for theoretical investigation than remediation per se (Campione, Brown, & Ferrera, 1982). This is not to say, however, that the approaches do not have tremendous implications for remediation. Such tightly controlled studies might in the long run have the most significant implications.

As noted previously, the majority of these investigators have taken advantage of the vast amount of learning theory literature available about the mentally retarded population. Subsequently, their programs have focused on increasing a variety of skills, including memory, language, and the generation and use of cognitive strategies. Glidden (1979) reviewed the various experimental approaches that have been used to improve learning. Those included labeling and item repetition, grouping of stimulus materials, cueing, cumulative rehearsal, imagery formation, and verbal elaboration. That these approaches can be used to increase performance is a relatively undisputed supposition. Most of these approaches, however, have trained specific skills related to a specific task (subordinate training). Recently more attention has been paid to the importance of transfer and generalization of these skills to novel tasks (superordinate training). This issue is discussed later in this section.

The *types* of training programs have also been reviewed. Brown, Campione, and Day (1981) classified the existing training programs as blind, informed, or self-control. In a blind study, the retarded performer is not told or cued that any strategy is being employed. In an informed study, feedback is provided to the subjects who are aware that strategies are being manipulated. In self-control studies, the subject is not only taught a strategy but encouraged to monitor and regulate the use of the strategy. The earlier training programs were primarily of the blind type and were used to determine what if any strategy deficits existed. Later studies have been either the informed or self-control type. This has occurred because we know that the deficits exist and that they can be trained. Again, the current interest in transfer and generalization of strategy use is emphasized.

Of the many available approaches, those by Butterfield and Belmont and Campione and Brown perhaps have received the most scrutiny in the mental retardation literature. Butterfield and Belmont's theoretical position focuses on the metacomponential aspects of cognition (Sternberg, 1981). Noting Ellis's (1970) finding of rehearsal deficits among mentally retarded persons, they have found that retarded individuals' difficulty in learning new material is due largely to their inability to rehearse. Further, this failure to rehearse is due, in part, to their difficulty in applying new strategies (Belmont & Butterfield, 1971). As a result of these findings, they incorporated an *instructional approach* into their strategy training (Belmont & Butterfield, 1977). This includes three components, the direct measurement of the individual's strategy use, an analysis of the task demands and the strategies necessary for successful completion, and standards of evaluation to judge treatment gains. In other words, the instructional approach requires that the experimenter observe individuals solving a problem and at the same time provide them with a way to complete it (Borkowski & Cavanaugh, 1979). In a series of studies Butterfield and Belmont have demonstrated that when retarded individuals are taught specific strategies to facilitate rehearsal, their improvement on specific learning tasks is significant (e.g., Belmont & Butterfield, 1977).

Similar to Belmont and Butterfield, Campione and Brown have developed remedial approaches that have focused on strategy training. While Butterfield and Belmont focus on executive processes, Campione and

Brown are interested in the selection, retention, and transfer of strategies (Sternberg, 1981). They were one of the first groups of researchers interested in the transfer of these strategies to new situations. As Sternberg (1981) noted, the difference between Belmont and Butterfield and Campione and Brown is more a function of emphasis than theoretical position. In general, Butterfield and Belmont, by focusing on executive control, train using more general tasks. Campione and Brown, on the other hand, are more willing to train specific tasks, at least initially. This difference in emphasis is due, in part, to their differing opinions about generalization and the most effective method of promoting it. Brown (1978) downplayed the difference in their approaches and noted that one can not really separate the training of specific and general tasks. In other words, both training programs have both components. More recently, Butterfield (1983) also noted the similarities in their training programs. As previously noted, virtually everyone in the strategy field agrees that the important empirical question at this time is how to promote generalization of strategic thinking.

In reviewing the literature on maintenance and generalization of skills and strategies, Borkowski and Cavanaugh (1979) made several important observations. First, they noted that successful maintenance of the trained skills could be facilitated by following a few guidelines that have surfaced consistently in the experimental literature. These include extended training, fading of experimental prompts, and feedback on the value of the strategy. They also made several suggestions that represent a somewhat optimistic viewpoint towards training generalization or executive processing. These include training children on several strategies, making sure that the training and generalization contexts are evident, promoting self-instructional procedures, instructing retarded individuals so that they use the skills they do possess, and reinforcing successful executive functioning. Borkowski and Cavanaugh further note that a synthesis of methodology from cognitive psychology, behavior modification, and the instructional approach might be the necessary approach to train the elusive construct of generalization.

Summary and Implications of Remediation Approaches

The remediation of cognitive deficits would be a potentially significant contribution to the area of psychology and education. To date, there has been much optimism surrounding this topic. Although remediation programs have been developed from a number of theoretical bases, emphasized a variety of experimental methodologies, and attempted to modify different skills, one finding is fairly straightforward. Skills and strategies can be taught to retarded persons, and under the right conditions can be maintained over time.

As more research is generated regarding the use of

cognitive strategies, an important educational issue arises. How much time should be spent "remediating" the cognitive abilities of mentally retarded students and how much time should be spent teaching them specific skills necessary for survival outside the school environment?

Historically, special education has been a cyclical field. Approaches come and go, only (usually) to return with modifications and (hopefully) improvements. At this point in time we appear to be at a crossroads. The functional approach of teaching skills necessary for independent living, while still in vogue, has been at least supplemented by cognitive approaches. At first glance this might seem to be a poor marriage (as most "pure"behaviorists or cognitivists would attest). In fact, however, just the opposite is true; both approaches are concerned with making a mentally retarded person self-sufficient. Perhaps we are at a point where we should consider both in the educational programming of a retarded student. Rather than attempting to prove that one approach is superior to another, we should focus on ways in which the program can be combined. We might then be able to move forward to focus on the important, and as yet unanswered, question of how these skills and strategies can be trained so that they generalize to new and different situations. Only then will retarded persons become truly self-sufficient.

References

Belmont, J., & Butterfield, E. (1971). Learning strategies as determinants of memory deficiencies. *Cognitive Psychology, 2,* 411–420.

Belmont, J., & Butterfield, E. (1977). The instructional approach to developmental cognitive research. In R. Kail and J. Hagen (Eds.), *Perspectives on the development of memory and cognition*. Hillsdale, NJ: Erlbaum.

Bloom, B. (1964). *Stability and change in human characteristics*. New York: Wiley.

Borkowski, J., & Cavanaugh, J. (1979). Maintenance and generalization of skills and strategies by the retarded. In N. Ellis (Ed.) *Handbook of mental deficiency* (2nd ed.). Hillsdale, NJ: Erlbaum.

Borkowski, J., & Varnhagen, C. (1984). Transfer of learning strategies: Contrast of self-instructional and traditional formats with EMR children. *American Journal of Mental Deficiency, 83,* 369–379.

Borys, S. (1979). Factors influencing the interrogative strategies of mentally retarded and nonretarded students. *American Journal of Mental Deficiency, 84,* 280–288.

Bradley, R., & Caldwell B. (1984). 174 children: A study of the relationship between home environment and cognitive development during the first 5 years. In A. Gottfried (Ed.), *Home environment and early cognitive development: Longitudinal research*. New York: Academic Press.

Bronfenbrenner, U. (1976). Is early intervention effective? In M. Guttentag & E. Struening (Eds.), *Handbook of evaluation research* (Vol. 2). Beverly Hills, CA: Sage Publications.

Brooks, P., & McCauley, C. (1984). Cognitive research in mental retardation. *American Journal of Mental Deficiency, 88,* 479–486.

Brown, A. (1978). Knowing when, where, and how to remember: A problem of metacognition. In R. Glaser (Ed.) *Advances in instructional psychology*. (Vol. 1). Hillsdale, NJ: Erlbaum.

Brown, A., Campione, J., & Day, J. (1981). Learning to learn: On training students to learn from texts. *Educational Researcher, 10,* 14–21.

Budoff, M. (1974). *Learning potential and educability among the educable mentally retarded* (Final Report Project 312312). Cambridge, MA: Research Institute for Educational Problems, Cambridge Mental Health Association.

Butterfield, E. (1983). To cure cognitive deficits of mentally retarded persons. In F. Menolascino, R. Newman, & J. Stark (Eds.), *Curative aspects of mental retardation*. Baltimore, MD: Paul Brookes.

Campione, J., & Brown, A. (1977). Memory and metamemory development in educable retarded children. In R. Kail and J. Hagen (Eds.), *Perspectives in the development of memory and cognition*. Hillsdale, NJ: Erlbaum.

Campione, J., Brown, A., & Ferrara, R. (1982). Mental retardation and intelligence. In R. J. Sternberg (Ed.), *Handbook of human intelligence*. New York: Cambridge University Press.

Carnine, D. (1977). Phonics vs. look-say: Transfer to new words. *Reading Teacher, 30,* 636–640.

Carnine, D. (1980). Preteaching versus concurrent teaching of the components skills of a multiplication problem-solving strategy. *Journal for Research in Mathematics Education, 11,* 375–379.

Cicirelli, V. (Ed.). (1969). *The impact of Head Start:An evaluation of the effects of Head Start on children's cognitive and affective development*. Washington: National Bureau of Standards, Institute for Applied Technology.

Clarke, A. D. B., & Clarke, A. M. (1977). Prospects for prevention and amelioration of mental retardation: A guest editorial. *American Journal of Mental Deficiency, 81,* 1–12.

Das, J., Kirby, J., & Jarman, R. (1979). *Simultaneous and successive cognitive processes*. New York: Academic Press.

Elardo, R., Bradley, R., & Caldwell, B. (1975). The relation of infant's home environment to mental test performance from six to thirty-six months. A longitudinal analysis. *Child Development, 46,* 71–76.

Ellis, N. (1970). Memory processes in retardates and normals. In N. Ellis (Ed.), *International review of research in mental retardation* (Vol. 4). New York: Academic Press.

Feuerstein, R. (1979). *The dynamic assessment of retarded performers: The learning potential device, theory, instruments and techniques*. Baltimore, MD: University Park Press.

Feuerstein, R., Miller, R., Hoffman, M., Rand, Y., Mintzker, Y., & Jensen, M. (1981). Cognitive modifiability in adolescence: Cognitive structure and the effects of intervention. *The Journal of Special Education, 15,* 269–287.

Finch, A., & Spirito, A. (1980). Use of cognitive training to change cognitive processes. *Exceptional Education Quarterly, 1,* 31–40.

Finkelstein, N., & Ramey, C. (1980). Information from birth certificates as a risk index for educational handicap. *American Journal of Mental Deficiency, 84,* 546–552.

Garber, H. (1975). Intervention in infancy: A developmental approach. In M. Begab & S. Richardson (Eds.), *The mentally retarded and society*. Baltimore, MD: University Park Press.

Garber, H., & Heber, R. (1977). The Milwaukee Project: Indications of the effectiveness of early intervention in preventing mental retardation. In P. Mittler (Ed.), *Research to Practice in Mental Retardation*. Baltimore, MD: University Park Press.

Glidden, L. (1979). Training of learning and memory in retarded persons: Strategies, techniques, and teaching tools. In N. Ellis (Ed), *Handbook of mental deficiency: Psychological theory and research*. Hillsdale, NJ: Erlbaum.

Gottfried, A. (1984). Home environment and early cognitive development. Integration, meta-analyses and conclusions. In A. Gottfried (Ed.), *Home environment and early cognitive development: Longitudinal research*. New York: Academic Press.

Gottfried, A., & Gottfried, A. (1984). Home environment and cognitive development in young children of middle socioeconomic status families. In A. Gottfried (Ed.) *Home environment and early cognitive development: Longitudinal research*. New York: Academic Press.

Hallahan, D., & Kauffman, J. (1982). *Exceptional Children* (2nd Ed.) Englewood Cliffs, NJ: Prentice-Hall.

Hallahan, D., Lloyd, J., Kosiewicz, M., Kauffman, J., & Graves, A. (1979). *A comparison of the effects of self-recording and self-assessment on the on-task behavior and academic productivity of a learning disabled boy*. Charlottesville, VA: Learning Disabilities Institute, (No. 13).

Heber, R., Garber, H., Harrington, S., Hoffman, C., & Falander, C. (1972). *Rehabilitation of families at risk for mental retardation*. Madison: WI. Rehabilitation Research and Training Center in Mental Retardation.

Hodges, W., & Cooper, M. (1981). Head Start and Follow Through: Influences on intellectual development. *The Journal of Special Education, 15*, 221–238.

Kirk, S. (1958). *Early education of the mentally retarded: An experimental study*. Urbana, IL: University of Illinois Press.

Kneedler, R., & Hallahan, D. (1981). Attacking the strategy deficits of learning disabled children: Research on self-monitoring. *Exceptional Education Quarterly, 2*, 73–82.

Lazar, I. (1981). Social research and social policy. In R. Haskins & J. Gallagher (Eds.). *Family policy*. Chapel Hill, NC: University of North Carolina Press.

Lazar, I., & Darlington, R. (1982). Lasting effects of early education. *Monographs of the Society for Research in Child Development, 47*, (2–3, Serial No. 195).

Ledwedge, B. (1978). Cognitive behavior modification: A step in the wrong direction? *Psychological Bulletin, 85*, 353–375.

Lloyd, J. (1980). Academic instruction and cognitive behavior modification: The need for attack strategy training. *Exceptional Education Quarterly, 1*, 53–63.

Lloyd, J., Kosiewicz, M., & Hallahan, D. (1982). Reading comprehension: Cognitive training contributions. *School Psychology Review, 11*, 35–41.

MacMillan, D. (1982). *Mental retardation in school and society* (2nd ed.). Boston, MA: Little-Brown.

Mann, A., Harrell, A., & Hurt, M. (1978). A review of Head Start research since 1969. In B. Brown (Ed.), *Found: Long term gains from early intervention*. Boulder, CO: Westview Press.

Miller, T. & Davis, E. (1981). Can change in intelligence be measured by contemporary techniques? *The Journal of Special Education, 15*, 185–200.

Oakland, T. (1977). *Pluralistic norms and estimated learning potential*. Paper presented at the annual meeting of the American Psychological Association, San Francisco.

Page, E. (1972). Miracle in Milwaukee: Raising the IQ. *Educational Research, 1*, 8–16.

Page, E., & Grandon, G. (1981). Massive intervention and child intelligence: The Milwaukee Project in critical perspective. *The Journal of Special Education, 15*, 239–256.

President's Committee on Mental Retardation (1972). *Entering the era of human ecology*. Washington: Dept of Health Education and Welfare Publication No. (05) 72–7.

Quattrochi, M., & Sherrets, S. (1980). WISC-R: The first five years. *Psychology in the Schools, 17*, 297–312.

Ramey, C. (1982). Commentary. In I. Lazar & R. Darlington (Eds.), *Monographs of the Society for Research in Child Development, 47* (2–3 Serial No. 195).

Ramey, C, & Brownlee, J. (1981). Improving the identification of high-risk infants. *American Journal of Mental Deficiency, 85*, 504–511.

Ramey, C., & Bryant, D. (1983). Early intervention. In J. Matson & J. Mulick (Eds.), *Handbook of mental retardation* (pp. 467–478). NY: Pergamon.

Ramey, C., & Campbell, F. (1984). Preventive education for high-risk children: Cognitive consequences of the Abecedarian project. *American Journal of Mental Deficiency, 88*, 515–523.

Ramey, C., Holmburg, M., Sparling, J., & Collier, A. (1977). An introduction to the Carolina Abecedarian Project. In B. Caldwell & D. Stedman (Eds.), *Infant education for handicapped children*. New York: Walker and Co.

Ramey, C., Sparling, J., Bryant, D. & Wasik, B. (1982). Primary prevention of developmental retardation during infancy. *Prevention in Human Services, 1*, 61–93.

Reschly, D., & Reschly, J. (1979). Validity of WISC-R factor scores in predicting teacher ratings of achievement and attention among four groups. *Journal of School Psychology, 17*, 355–361.

Robin, A., Armsel, S., & O'Leary, K. (1975). The effects of self-instruction on writing deficiencies. *Behavior Therapy, 6*, 178–187.

Robinson, N. (1976). *Prevention: The future society. The future of very early intervention and education*. Paper presented at the AAMD meeting, Chicago, IL.

Robinson, N., & Robinson, H. (1976). *The mentally retarded child* (2nd ed.). New York: McGraw-Hill.

Salvia, J., & Ysseldyke, J. (1985). *Assessment in special and remedial education* (3rd Ed.). Boston MA: Houghton-Mifflin.

Seigel, L. (1984). Home environmental influences on cognitive development in preterm and fullterm children during the first 5 years. In A. Gottfried (Ed.), *Home environment and early cognitive development: Longitudinal research*. New York: Academic Press.

Sewell, T., & Severson, R. (1974). Learning ability and intelligence as cognitive predictors of achievement in first-grade children. *Journal of Educational Psychology, 66*, 948–955.

Skeels, H. (1966). Adult status of children from contrasting early life experiences. *Monographs of the society for research in child development, 31*, (Serial No. 105).

Skeels, H., & Dye, H. (1939). A study of the effects of differential stimulation on mentally retarded children. *Proceedings and addresses of the American Association on Mental Deficiency, 44*, 114–136.

Sommers, R., & Sommers, B. (1983). Mystery in Milwaukee: Early intervention, IQ, and psychology textbooks. *American Psychologist, 38*, 982–985.

Stark, J. (1983). The search for cures of mental retardation. In F. Menolascino, R. Neman, & J. Stark (Eds.), *Curative aspects of mental retardation*. Baltimore, MD: Paul Brookes.

Stedman, D. (1977). Important considerations in the review and evaluation of educational intervention programs. In P. Mittler (Ed.), *Research to Practice in Mental Retardation* (vol. 1). Baltimore, MD: University Park Press.

Sternberg, R. (1980). Sketch of a componential subtheory of human intelligence. *Behavioral and Brain Sciences, 3*, 573–584.

Sternberg, R. (1981). Cognitive behavioral approaches to the training of intelligence in the retarded. *The Journal of Special Education, 15*, 165–183.

Taylor, R. (1984). *Assessment of exceptional students: Educational and psychological procedures*. Englewood Cliffs, NJ: Prentice-Hall.

Turkewitz, H., O'Leary, K., & Ironsmith, M. (1975). Generalization and maintenance of appropriate behavior through self-control. *Journal of Consulting and Clinical Psychology, 43*, 577–583.

Vygotsky, L. (1978). Mind in society: The development of higher psychological processes. Cambridge, MA: Harvard University Press.

Wozniak, R., & Nuechterlein, P. (1973). *Reading improvement through verbally self-guided looking and listening: Summary report*. Minneapolis, MN: University of Minnesota Research, Development and Demonstration Center in Education of Handicapped Children.

Zeaman, D., & House, B. (1963). The role of attention in retardate discrimination learning. In N. Ellis (Ed.), *Handbook of Mental Deficiency*. New York: McGraw-Hill.

Zigler, E., & Cascione, R. (1977) Headstart has little to do with mental retardation: A reply to Clarke and Clarke. *American Journal of Mental Deficiency, 82*, 246–249.

Adult Development of Mildly Retarded Students:
Implications for Educational Programs

ANDREA G. ZETLIN

University of Southern California
School of Education
Waite Phillips Hall–303
University Park
Los Angeles, CA 90089–0031

Abstract—This chapter reviews the body of literature which reports on the community adaptation patterns of mildly retarded adults. Longitudinal and follow-up studies in four general areas of community functioning are described: vocational, economic, social and personal adjustment, and the success or failure of two mildly retarded populations are presented: those raised and trained in the community and former institutional residents. Problems inherent in these studies including flawed research designs, superficiality of data gathering techniques, and single point in time follow-up are discussed and conclusions as to the implications of this research are drawn.

Since the mid 1960s, the social policy directives of deinstitutionalized care and normalization have had a profound impact on the social development of mildly retarded adults. Resulting efforts to provide mentally retarded persons with an enhanced quality of life and opportunities for the individual to maximize his or her potential, have led to the shift of institutionalized mentally retarded adults to various community residential arrangements and to the virtual halt of new placements in institutional settings. Today, most mildly retarded individuals begin their adult lives in their parents' homes. Some remain there, but many soon move to a group home where they live with other retarded persons under varying degrees of supervision. Still other mildly retarded adults live independently, moving into their own residences and managing their lives with minimal assistance (Baker, Seltzer, & Seltzer, 1977; Edgerton, 1979).

A considerable body of research has now accumulated examining how well these mildly retarded persons cope and adapt to varying levels of responsibility and self-sufficiency and what their adaptations to the many demands and opportunities of adult life are like. These investigations, often characterized as community adjustment studies, generally distinguish between two mildly retarded populations: those persons who at one time lived in public institutions for the mentally retarded and those individuals who, as children, resided in the community and received training in community-based programs.

Reports of persons released from institutions have either described the postinstitutional adjustment of ex-patients or attempted to derive variables which predict their success or failure in community living. Studies of the community-trained retarded have traced these individuals into adult life and examined the characteristics of their vocational and social adjustments. The adults in these studies were all identified as mildly mentally retarded at some point during the developmental period. At that time, their handicap had been so impairing as to bring it to the attention of family members and/or social agencies who sought special services for them. All displayed some degree of functional intellectual deficit and impaired adaptive behavior; however, they were far from homogeneous in terms of etiology and life experiences. Throughout most of the investigations reported here, subjects tended to range in IQ from 50 to 75. Males and females were studied in equal numbers. Chronological age ranged from 18 to 70 years, with most studies concentrating on subjects in their mid-twenties and mid-thirties. Mostly Anglos of varying SES levels were examined and nonwhites were included if they appeared in the particular population being investigated: all those who had been discharged from a state hospital or had graduated from a special education school program. In the first section of this chapter, we will review some of the early studies which report on community living patterns and which attempt to isolate variables distinguishing those who succeeded and those who failed (see Cobb, 1972; Goldstein, 1964; Heal,

Sigelman, & Switzky, 1978; McCarver & Craig, 1974; and Windle, 1962 for more extensive reviews of the early studies in community adjustment).

The Assessment of Community Adaptation

The conclusion drawn from these early follow-up studies is that in terms of the criteria of employment, marriage, and law-abiding behavior, the majority of mildly retarded persons, whether ex-patients or community-trained, make satisfactory adjustments and that many disappear into the community and become indistinguishable as a social group. Fernald (1919) conducted the first significant institutional follow-up of all patients who had left Waverly State School during the years 1890–1914. He found that of 1,537 persons discharged (most of whose release had not been recommended by the institutional administration), only 612 had been readmitted to some type of custodial institution. The males who remained in the community (64%) appeared to have adjusted better than the female population, with only 18% arrested for unlawful behavior. Of the females found in the community (51%), 58% showed no problems while 42% had records of sexual, alcohol, or theft problems. Most of the ex-patients were employed, although in unskilled jobs; those who held jobs were the least retarded, while those who remained unemployed were among the most retarded. For both men and women, their community adjustment appeared related to the amount of guidance and support available either from the retarded person's relatives or from others in the community. Other studies that followed Fernald similarly indicated that a sizable proportion of mildly retarded persons could adequately adapt to life outside the institution, especially when training, selection, placement and supervision were at an optimum (Cobb, 1972; Goldstein, 1964).

Kennedy (1948, 1966) and Baller, Charles, and Miller (1966) conducted the best examples of longitudinal studies of community-based persons who had been identified during the school years as mildly retarded. Kennedy examined at two points in time, the outcome in adult life of former special education students (i.e., in terms of marital adjustment, economic adjustment, antisocial behavior and social participation). The first study contrasted the adjustment patterns of 265 mildly retarded persons (age range 20–30; IQ range 45 to 75 during school years) with 129 adults of normal IQ matched for age, sex, and socioeconomic status (Kennedy, 1948). The findings indicated that although more retarded subjects than controls had unsatisfactory work records and had been in trouble with the police, overall they were "economically independent and self-supporting and not serious threateners of the safety of society" (p. 52). Sixteen years later, 70% of the original retarded sample and 80% of the control sample were studied a second time and again Kennedy (1966) concluded that: (1) the overwhelming majority of both subjects and control made acceptable and remarkably similar adjustments . . . the main differences were of degree rather than kind, (2) in the sphere of personal and familial behavior, subjects showed no striking divergencies from what was generally attained by the normal controls, (3) both groups showed an upward mobility in economic functioning although the control exceeded retarded subjects, (4) the retarded subjects showed more irregularity of behavior than controls, but were not in any respect a threat to society.

The other major long-term study was conducted by Baller and his associates and spanned a 30-year period. Baller's (1936; 1939) three samples of former students from the Lincoln, Nebraska public schools: a Low Group of 206 mentally deficient individuals (IQs of 70 and below) who were at least 21 years old at the time of the study, a High Group of intellectually normal persons matched on the basis of age, sex, and race, and a Middle Group of dull individuals with tested IQs of 75 to 85, were recontacted in the 1950s by Charles (1953) and again in the 1960s by Baller, Charles and Miller (1966). The findings of the final study confirm the evidence of early reports that the members of the Low Group fared much better than anyone ever expected. Not only did they make reasonably good social adjustments, but the majority of them no longer behaved or tested at the intellectual level ascribed to them during their school years. In comparison with the groups originally identified as dull and normal (i.e., in terms of marital status, economic status, law conformity, social and recreational activities), the Low Group continued to be in an inferior position in most respects with the normal group generally faring best.

The optimism of these early studies was subsequently challenged by investigators in the 1960s and beyond. Questions about the quality of the lives of community-based mildly retarded adults were raised as was their vulnerability to economic recession (Heber & Dever, 1970). Goldstein (1964) pointed out that the occupational success of various mentally retarded samples has often been marginal at best and others noted that compared to nonretarded controls, retarded adults tend to live in deteriorated housing, to be socially isolated, and to commit more violations of the law (Edgerton, 1983; MacMillan, 1977).

Edgerton (1967) attempted one of the first studies which focused specifically on the quality of life of former residents of a state hospital. He studied intensively 48 ex-patients who had been released from Pacific State Hospital and were living in the community for an average of 6 years. Considerable time was spent with each of the subjects, interviewing and observing them in order to describe their everyday lives and the problems they faced in living independently. Most subjects were found to be highly marginal economically and living in "lamentable" conditions in downtown commercial or slum areas of a large city. The majority were in debt, few had any appreciable job security, and fewer still had marketable skills. Most striking of all was the discovery that if it were not for the ssupport of benefactors who assisted the adults in coping with everyday problems, at least 21 of the ex-patients would have required reinstitutionalization. In fact, Edgerton estimated that only 3 of the 48 could be judged as independent. He concluded that their experiences at the state hospital did not equip them for life in the community and that their training concerning money, time, work attitudes, transportation, and frustration tolerance was deficient.

Edgerton's subjects were recontacted 12 years after the first contact and again 10 years after the second follow-up to determine the effects of time and changes in life situations on social adaptation (Edgerton & Bercovici, 1976; Edgerton, Bollinger & Herr, 1984). While the general level of community adaptation tended to become more positive over time, the findings of the follow-up studies did not conclusively support the notion that the passage of time improves the social adaptation of retarded persons. Most important was the finding that the lives of mildly retarded persons in the c mmunity are characterized by frequent and often dramatic fluctuations. Edgerton (1979) speculated that this may be so because most mentally retarded people have few reliable resources that can stabilize them in times of crises. With no job security, few marketable skills and no network of reliable friends or relatives, the loss of a job, benefactor or spouse can precipitate a major change in their level of adaptation. Edgerton cautioned that unless the course of their adaptation is monitored more or less continously, any attempt to assess success or failure risks producing both false negative and false positive findings depending on whether assessment occurs during a peak or a valley.

While Edgerton took issue with the reliance by most community adjustment researchers on a single point in time for follow-up as well as the superficiality of the techniques employed for data gathering, others have criticized the ambiguous nature of the criteria used to measure success (Cobb, 1972; Heal, Sigelman, & Switzky, 1978; McCarver & Craig, 1974). Some investigators have defined success in its most simple terms: remaining in the community versus being remanded to an institution (Fernald, 1919; Windle, 1962). Others have held that success is more complex and that, "adjustment is a matter of degree and of personal preference which may vary from time to time and from one area of life to another" (Lakin, Bruininks, & Sigford, 1981, p. 47). Edgerton (1983) for one, contended that:

> . . . judgments about success and failure are relative to the various environments that retarded persons inhabit: group homes, sheltered workshops, neighborhood markets, buses, public parks, and streets. Not only do these environments require different competencies, it is often true that success in one environment (e.g., a group home that requires dependency) may increase the probability of failure in another environment (e.g., a job that requires independence) (p. 139).

Edgerton also argued that the simple objective criteria of reemaining in the community or returning to an institution are relative to shifting sociocultural circumstances. To illustrate, he described how today, reinstitutionalization is no longer a useful criterion for failure because the contemporary restraints against institutional placement are so imposing.

The net result is that little has come of the various investigative efforts for predicting success or failure in adjustment to community life. In part, lack of agreement over what constitutes adjustment and the tendency to oversimplify a complex process bear some responsibility for the inconclusive findings. Perhaps even greater problems have been flawed research designs, lack of experimental control, and heavy sample attrition which characterize a major portion of these investigations (Heal, Sigelman, & Switzky, 1978; Windle, 1962).

The next section will focus on recent studies which report on various aspects of the community adaptation of mildly retarded adults. The presentation will be organized in terms of four general areas of community functioning: vocational adjustment, economic adjustment, social adjustment and personal adjustment. Each is viewed as an important facet of community adjustment and most authors agree that inadequate performance in one or more areas leads to community failure.

Vocational Adjustment

Reports on the vocational adjustment of mildly retarded adults comprise the bulk of the literature on community adaptation. This is so because vocational success is generally regarded as an essential feature of community adjustment. In turn, this has led to vocational training figuring heavily in the habilitative programming of retarded persons at all levels (Edgerton & Bercovici, 1976; Rosen, Clark, & Kivitz, 1977; Wolfensberger, 1972). Three basic types of studies have been conducted: (1) follow-up studies which examine the extent to which former institutional residents and graduates of special education and vocational programs have made successful vocational adjustments; (2) studies which assess various characteristics of mildly retarded individuals, their employers, and the work environment to derive variables that predict vocational success and failure; and (3) studies which describe assessment procedures and vocational program curricula designed to promote placement of retarded adults in work settings and job tenure.

Follow-up Studies. Follow-up studies of former institutional residents generally have shown high rates of employment with job success or failure related to conditions of supervision, work efficiency, home support, and emotional stability (Birenbaum, 1975; Craft & Craft, 1979; Edgerton, 1967; Fernald, 1919; McDevitt, Smith, Schmidt, & Rosen, 1978; Windle, 1962). Similarly, longitudinal reports of those who received training in community programs indicated that as adults, the majority were employed full-time or at least marginally (Baller, Charles, & Miller, 1966; Deno, 1965; Kennedy, 1966; Kernan & Koegel, 1984). Unemployment rates as low as 10% to 38% have been reported for both populations and in studies which included nonretarded control groups, retarded subjects were found to be employed in numbers similar to their normal peers (Baller, et al., 1966; Brickey, Browning, & Campbell, 1982; Cobb, 1972; Kennedy, 1966; Richardson, 1978).

The type of employment held by mildly retarded adults ranged from competitive to sheltered workshop employment. Those employed competitively have been found mostly in semiskilled or unskilled positions. In general, follow-up investigations of former institutional residents have found high rates of employment among resettled adults (i.e., those residing on their own or in community residences). Positions had been obtained in competitive industry (e.g., institutional or industrial housekeeping, custodial kitchenwork, simple machine operation) or at sheltered workshops, and most took pride in their accomplishments at the workplace (Birenbaum, 1975; Birenbaum & Re, 1979; Gollay, Freedman, Wyngaarden, & Kurtz, 1978; McCarver & Craig, 1974; McDevitt, et al., 1978).

Of the 48 ex-patients Edgerton (1967) followed, 21 were full-time employees working in sanitariums, doing kitchen work in restaurants or holding other semiskilled or unskilled jobs (e.g., handyman, ground maintenance, door-to-door salesman); another 21 were married women who viewed their role as a housewife as an acceptable alternative to employment (although four continued to work a few hours a week); and the remaining six were unemployed. Edgerton felt that for many of the 48 former patients, work served as, "one of the central facts of their lives and provided the quintessential means of proving themselves to be normal worthy human beings" (p. 152). Twelve years later, of the original 30 subjects who had been relocated, Edgerton and Bercovici (1976) found that 35% had either full- or part-time employment which had been more or less continuous since discharge, 38% were supported by spouses, and 27% were unemployed and receiving welfare assistance. Although the vocational record of the subjects appeared to have declined over the years, the authors argued that, "given that marriage is a more important goal for some than employment, given the aging and illness of some subjects, and given the worsening economic conditions, the changing picture of vocational adaptation is not as bleak as it first appears" (p. 490).

Craft and Craft (1979) reported on the employment status of 45 mentally handicapped married couples, some of whom lived in married quarters in a mental hospital, some in hostels, and some independently in the community. Just over half of the husbands (54%) and one-third of the wives (35%) were found to have some form of employment, full-time, part-time or sheltered (another 20% of the women were full-time mothers caring for children under the age of 12). Of those employed competitively, jobs held by men included gardener, road sweeper, dustman, and arcade attendant; jobs held by women included caretaker and housekeeper. Those in sheltered employment (50% of the employed men; 40% of the employed women) worked on assembly lines in adult training centers doing collating, sealing, assembling, and packaging jobs.

The effects of special education on postschool adjustments were examined by Deno (1965) who followed up over 90% of former educable mentally retarded students who had attended the Minneapolis School system from 1957 to 1960 (mean chronological age = 20; mean IQ = 73). In terms of employment, 54% were employed full-time, were in the armed service or were housewives; 15% were marginally employed, 27% were unemployed and 4% were incarcerated, institutionalized, under day-care or deceased. Especially noteworthy was that the unemployment rate did not differ greatly from that of normal youth in the same general neighborhoods.

Richardson (1978) too, focused on community-trained retarded persons in an extensive longitudinal study in which the entire population of mentally retarded persons born during a 5-year period, who were residents of a British city, were followed up to age 22. One topic of investigation was the comparison of post-school careers of mildly retarded sample members and nonretarded matched controls. Richardson found that only 8% of the retarded group were unemployed as compared to 2% of all the controls; the retarded group held positions requiring lower levels of skills with less take home pay (and fewer dealings with people than objects) than the controls, and fewer retarded members than controls expressed discontent with the particular work they were doing.

Although these research efforts, conducted on independent populations, indicated that a high proportion of mildly retarded persons made reasonably favorable vocational adaptations, other investigations which monitored the retarded adults' employment records, either retrospectively or prospectively, were less positive in their evaluations. A second part of Deno's study (1965) sought to examine the outcome of a demonstration project which had provided prevocational assessment, planning and training to those special education students considered by their school counselor as ready or about to leave school. At the time of research contact, 3 years after the project had ended, 52% of the 325 students served by the project were found working in competitive employment. Examination of the students' employment histories, however, revealed frequent changes in employment status which was not always in the expected direction. For example, while some students had moved from part-time to full-time positions or from sheltered to regular employment, others had moved from not employed and seeking work to not employed and not seeking work.

Kernan and Keogel (1984) also found a great deal of instability in the employment status of individual sample members which was not reflected in the overall group average. Their sample was comprised of 48 mildly retarded community-based individuals who had been followed intensively over a 30-month period. Subjects ranged in age from 19 to 49 years and had been identified by professionals as having the potential for living independently. Some were already living on their own, others were living in residential facilities or at home with their parents. While more than half the group (54 to 60%) were found to be employed competitively, in sheltered workshops or were housewives, as with Deno's (1965) subjects frequent change in the work status of individuals was apparent. In fact, in terms of competitive employment, the average length of time a job was held was 10½ months with a range from one day to eleven years. Only 27% of the sample remained stably employed throughout the study's duration.

Predictor Studies. The second type of vocational adjustment studies are concerned with the identification of those variables which differentiated between mildly retarded adults who made successful adjustments and those who did not. Some of these studies sought to identify specific properties of the individual which appeared linked to vocational success such as personality factors (Domino & McGarty, 1972), emotional control (Foss & Peterson, 1981) and interpersonal competence (Greenspan & Shoultz, 1981). Other studies, having recognized that occupational adjustment was an interactive process between the individual and the environment, sought to determine the manner in which many interacting variables predicted success or failure (Stephens, Peck & Veldman, 1968; Krauss & McEachron, 1982). No clear message has emerged from these efforts to establish a predictive formula which will separate in advance those who will succeed from those who will fail. As Cobb (1972) has stated:

> If there is one conclusion to be drawn from this array of studies, it is that no simple formula for prediction is possible, that the relationships between predictors and criteria are enormously complex, and that the outcomes in terms of personal, social and vocational success are the product of manifold interactive determinants. (p. 138)

Stephens and her associates carried out one of the first investigations which recognized the multivariate nature of both success and the predictors associated with success (Stephens, 1964; Stephens, Peck, & Veldman, 1968). They conducted structured interviews with subjects, parents, and work supervisors which measured 80 criterion variables (judged by a panel of experts to constitute postschool adjustment). These variables were reduced through factor analysis to 17 basic success factors. In a like manner, 78 predictors of success, drawn from ratings on standardized instruments, were reduced through factor analysis to 21 basic predictor factors.

Techniques of hierarchical grouping and multiple discriminant analysis were then employed and eight success profiles were derived which characterized the major types of postschool performances among a sample of mildly retarded adult males and which related predictor factors to particular performance types. They were: (1) Parent Accepted Group; (2) Goal Achieving Group; (3) Passively Oriented Group; (4) Erratic Group; (5) Contented Group; (6) Subsidized Group; (7) Socially Oriented Group; and (8) Failure Group. From Stephen's research, it became clear that a variety of forms of adjustment could be considered "successful" and that a profile presentation is the most adequate way of describing successfulness of the individual in the various dimensions of adjustment.

Turner (1983) too, constructed adjustment profiles which reliably differentiated between four types of workers at a sheltered workshop. From time sampled observations of work behavior and social interaction and from ethnographic data collected over a 7-year period, members of the workshop population were sorted by factor analysis into four independent groups and described in terms of the qualities that characterized their adaptation to the workshop. They included: (1) the Elite, who were the best workers and most popular members of the workshop; (2) the Loners, who were good workers (comparable to the Elite) but the least talkative and sociable members of the workshop; (3) the Socialites, who were generally popular among peers but highly variable in their work attitudes and habits; and (4) the Nonconformers, who were the least reliable and most unproductive workers as well as the least popular among peers.

In Zetlin, Turner, and Winik's (1987) study of 46 mildly retarded adults living independently in the community, three characteristic employment patterns were identified which reflected the more general personal and social adaptation styles of sample members. Those who had the most stable employment records were the most likely to be employed competitively and the least likely to receive public assistance. They were also the most self-sufficient adults and those with the most positive relationships with parents, peers, and work supervisors. Those who preferred sheltered employment were the ones who relied heavily on parents and others for even basic maintenance needs, were the most socially immature adults and were heavily enmeshed in the service delivery system; three fourths received public assistance to supplement their meager workshop incomes. Those who were the most likely to be unemployed, to work on and off part-time jobs or to spend periods of time enrolled in various job training programs, were overall the least successful adults. Their employment records, independent living situations and friendship patterns were marked by instability, their relationships with parents and counselors were conflict-ridden, and all were dependent on welfare payments as their most stable means of financial support. In both these studies, as in Stephen's research, clusters of attributes were related to vocational outcomes and more than one successful profile was delineated.

More systematic examinations of the relationships between vocational adjustment and the family, the delivery system and the work environment, followed the recognition that success or failure is not inherent in the nature of the individual. Krauss and McEachron (1982) examined properties of the work environment to identify factors contributing to a 50% placement rate, the outcome of a 5 months competitive employment training program completed by 26 mildly retarded adults. Significant relationships were found between job placements and (a) the worker's skills and abilities (i.e., task performance, work behavior); (b) the worker's ability to meet the requirements of the job (i.e. productivity rate, attendance and ease of supervision); and (c) the presence of reinforcements within the employment setting (i.e., hourly wage, provision of bonuses, company commitment to hire).

Kernan and Koegel (1984) found that the extent to which mildly retarded sample members succeeded in achieving competive employment was to a large degree a function of the support available to them from family members and/or the service delivery system. Within their sample of 48 adults, variations in the strength of the two support systems (ranging from those who enjoyed the active aid of both family members and counselors to those who were isolated from their families and ignored their delivery system liaisons) were related to an individual's job-seeking strategies and job success: those individuals who had strong support systems sought and found more jobs in competitive employment while those who did not enjoy such a support system were far less active and successful. Even those who changed jobs frequently and suffered many setbacks, if supported in their search, eventually found job stability as well as job satisfaction. In studies conducted by Brickey and Campbell (1981). Brolin (1972), and Deno (1965), a positive relationship between delivery system involvement and client success in finding and maintaining competitive employment was also reported.

Family support systems, on the other hand, were found to inhibit placement of retarded adults in competitive employment at least some of the time. Kernan and Koegel (1984) identified one subgroup within their sample, whose parents believed competitive employment was psychologically taxing and might disturb their grown child's mental stability. They therefore discouraged any expressed interest in independent work by their son or daughter. Brickey, Browning and Campbell (1982), Brickey and Campbell (1981), and Koegel and Kernan (1983) found that while parents would permit their adult offspring to work in sheltered workshops or in Projects with Industry (i.e., sheltered workstations within factories and industrial plants), they objected to their placement in competitive jobs which would mean the loss of a guaranteed income through social security benefits (SSI). These parents held that given job instability in the competitive world as well as the rigid regulations

guiding the provision of federal support (i.e., that once people have been gainfully employed for at least 9 months, they are no longer eligible for SSI), sheltered employment and/or SSI stood as more viable choices.

Testing and Programming Studies. The third set of studies are those which describe testing procedures to assess vocational potential and programming efforts to improve the social-vocational skills of retarded trainees/clients. Cobb (1972) reviewed a number of studies which attempted to devise a battery of measures to predict vocational success and job level. He found that measures of manual dexterity such as the Purdue Peg Board showed some promise for predicting employability, but none of the personality or social behavior measures yielded significant predictive value.

Schreiner (1978) examined the role of intellectual capacity as a determinant of outcome in vocational adjustment. He found that IQ was not consistently aligned with work success but that performance on standardized work samples was indicative of later employability. Based on Schreiner's finding, Snart and Swann (1982) sought to increase the efficiency of vocational assessment by identifying specific types of cognitive processes which relate to widely used work samples. They examined three types of processes suggested by information-integration theory and found that successive processing ability was most clearly related to work sample performance. They concluded with the recommendation that, "in any training program, improvement in performance may occur due to both general improvement in the competence for successive processing as well as specific task related training in which successive processes are taught for tackling the essential components of the task" (p. 211).

Implications for vocational training were also noted by Greenspan and his associates who found low or marginal levels of social awareness among their mildly retarded clients especially with regard to making effective judgments about people and social situations (Greenspan & Shoultz, 1981; Greenspan, Shoultz & Weir, 1981).

Economic Adjustment

Studies of economic adjustment have focused on the degree to which former institutional residents and community trained individuals manage in day to day living. Specifically, they report on how mildly retarded adults have fared with respect to financial status, banking, money management, and shopping. Most notable across studies was that, "the handling of financial matters represented the most consistently problematic area and the one which elicited the greatest need for outside intervention" (McDevitt, et al., 1978 p. 23). In terms of overall adjustment level, variation was wide ranging from adults who were mostly self-sufficient and self-support-ing to adults who relied extensively on parents, benefac-tors or agency counselors for virtually all needs.

Edgerton (1967) found that of the 48 ex-patients he studied, most were marginal wage earners with little job security. At least one third had received welfare aid at one time or another since their discharge. With few exceptions, they had difficulty with all aspects of money management: "earning it, counting it, spending it, bank-ing it and owing it" (p. 165). Few were capable of hand-ling money and so found shopping baffling. Many had run up debts and were having difficulty repaying them. None could manage checking accounts, and those with a savings account had to be assisted in its use.

Of the former patients McDevitt, et al. (1978) fol-lowed up, all lived modestly, with money spent on daily living expenses and tangible items. Most showed only limited knowledge of their financial status, few were able to plan a monthly budget, and while many had saving accounts, credit and banking were felt to be too complicated, and so most paid everything in cash.

In other studies more diversity in adjustment level was observed among sample members. Craft and Craft (1979) found that over half of the married couples stud-ied handled their own affairs with reasonable com-petence. Of these, most managed their finances independent of outside help (with the more skilled part-ner assuming the major responsibility), but a few relied on assistance from family or friends for budgeting and shopping. The remaining couples required more struc-tured help from professional agency personnel who maintained control over their finances and saw that homes were stocked with food and such. Zetlin, Turner and Winik (1987) also found a sizable number of house-holds to be largely self-supporting and self-reliant. Of the 46 adults followed over an 18-month period, almost half were competent at budgeting, bill paying, and the everyday demands of community living. The remaining adults were dependent on family members, benefactors and/or delivery system counselors in varying degrees, for subsistence and monetary needs.

One aspect of economic adjustment, which has been singled out for attention, is how community-based retarded adults have fared as shoppers. Reports by Ed-gerton (1967) and Craft and Craft (1979) indicated quite strongly that shopping was an especially trying activity for mildly retarded adults who had little confidence in their ability to handle money. To cope, some adults had others compile shopping lists which they carefully fol-lowed, others relied on willing parents and neighbors to make purchases for them. In Williams and Ewing's (1981) study of marketing behavior, none of their 11 mildly retarded sample members demonstrated the necessary skills to be "prudent shoppers." The adults either chose items which were the most prominent on display or made some random selections. When asked why a particular item was picked, they showed no aware-ness of the various consumer factors which go into choosing the best product.

Levine and Langness (1985) also examined shopping strategies, including item selection, quantity selection, and payment strategy. They identified five types of mar-keting behavior among their 17 sample members which were related to background characteristics of the adults. Only one type consisted of efficient, flexible, and skills-based shoppers: those with elaborate calculation and comparative shopping skills. These adults were ident-ified as having been relatively independent for much of their adult lives. The other four types included shoppers who were mostly confused, disoriented or rigid orderly thinkers: some had trouble with item selection, some could not deviate from lists compiled by counselors, and many had trouble calculating costs and making change at the checkout stand. In most areas of day to day living, these individuals were judged to be largely dependent on their family members.

Social Adjustment

Reports on the social adjustment of mildly retarded adults have focused on five dimensions: (1) leisure activity, (2) friendship patterns, (3) sex, marriage and children, (4) social support, and (5) criminality. Within each of these, researchers have documented wide vari-ations in the patterns or modes of adaptation of commu-nity-based adults. At issue with regard to social adaptation in general is what constitutes adequate adjustment performance. While many investigators pre-fer objective judgments based on normative criteria, others hold that personal satisfaction and the retarded person's assessment of success should be considered foremost.

Leisure Activity. The use of leisure time has been examined as an indication of the richness or impoverish-ment of the lives of mildly retarded adults. Findings generally have indicated that few community-based adults make use of recreational facilities or participate in organized activities. Rather most watch television or listen to music for many hours each day, and a few pur-sue hobbies and other interests (Birenbaum & Re, 1979; McDevitt et al., 1978; McCarver & Craig, 1974). Some researchers have interpreted such leisure habits to mean that these adults lack awareness of recreational oppor-tunities and so have advocated enrollment in training programs which offer instruction in various social activi-ties (Corcoran & French, 1977; Jones & Moe, 1980). Other investigators observed that these recreational pat-terns do not differ greatly from those who live near them in lower socioeconomic status neighborhoods and that the majority of adults are personally satisfied with their lifestyles as evolved (Craft & Craft, 1979; Edgerton, 1967; Edgerton & Bercovici, 1976; Edgerton, Bollinger & Herr, 1984).

Birenbaum and Re's (1979) study illustrates the issues at hand. During a 4-year period since resettlement in a community residence, it was found that participation in outside recreational activities had dropped off sharply and that a "prosaic routine of work, sleep, and at-home recreation of a passive nature" (i.e. TV viewing, listening to music) characterized the lifestyles of most former patients. Although the researchers acknowledged that the adults had settled into comfortable and conventional routines, and that this picture of living was not too different from that of those who are nonretarded and marginally employed or mostly unemployed, alternative hypotheses were offered to explain what was perceived as a social regression: that perhaps the adults were not competent to engage in activities in the wider community, or that staff members had inadvertently discouraged such outside activity.

Friendship Patterns. Most studies report that the friendship relations of mildly retarded adults assume a variety of forms: some individuals are highly popular and enjoy a large network of friends, others prefer more limited interaction with a few close friends, and still others have the reputation as "troublemakers" or "babies" with few or no significant peer relationships. Turner (1983) observed in a sheltered workshop population, as did Zetlin and Turner (1984) in a sample of independently residing adults, that peer associations ranged from those which were positive, enduring and mutually satisfying to those which were shallow, problematic and relatively unstable. Friendships were mostly with individuals of comparable ability; however, some adults preferred contacts with nonhandicapped peers (although these associations tended to be nonreciprocal and situation-specific), and others enjoyed a mixed group of friends, both handicapped and nonhandicapped. In general, these relationships were based on common interests and concerns and provided the retarded adult with companionship, opportunities for enjoying conventional pasttimes and, in some cases, sources of support.

Craft and Craft (1979) also reported variation in the degree of social life which couples enjoyed as a pair. They found that a third of the couples engaged in "ordinary social activities" (i.e., attended social events, visited friends or had friends see them at home); another third associated mostly with family members or people that lived nearby, and a fourth had minimal associations and contacts outside the marital unit (i.e., their social isolation was self-imposed). In the remaining couples, only one member was socially active so that partners rarely went out together.

Kaufman (1984) was able to reduce the heterogeneity of friendship patterns within a sample of 46 independent adults to a four group typology based on two dimensions: sociality and satisfaction (hi social/hi satisfaction; lo social/hi satisfaction; hi social/lo satisfaction; lo social/lo satisfaction). Factors such as age, experience in living independently, employment status (i.e., workshop employment provided more social opportunities than competitive employment), attitude toward one's

peers (i.e., willingness to consider other retarded persons as potential friends), marriage and child-bearing, and the relationship with one's family of origin were found to be significantly related to an individual's satisfaction with the quality of his or her friendship situation. Kaufman concluded her study with the statement that, "sociality and satisfaction seen from the perspective of the mentally retarded adults themselves seem to be appropriate organizing concepts for describing and assessing their interpersonal adaptation." (p. 90)

Sex, Marriage and Children. Two early related beliefs: that mentally retarded persons are incapable of sexual control and that marital associations will naturally lead to an increase in the frequency of handicaps in the population, led to laws on sterilization and the prohibition of marriage. In fact, within most institutional settings, patients were denied the right to marry and surgical sterilization was routinely performed as a precondition to their discharge (Edgerton, 1967). Reports on the postinstitutional adjustment of former residents provided little support for such beliefs or policies. Only small numbers of adults were remanded to hospitals due to sexual problems. Even those who had originally been institutionalized for sexual misconduct presented fewer such problems when resettled in the community (McCarver & Craig, 1974). Edgerton (1967) found that only 5 out of at least 20 former patients who had been active sexual troublemakers before hospitalization, continued to exhibit similarly severe problems. Within the sample in general, remarkable diversity in sexual behavior was found from "extremely promiscuous men and women, through devoted and happy marriages, to fearful maidens dedicated to the avoidance of men." (p. 112) Craft and Craft (1979) noted that marital partnerships appeared to have answered the needs of seven husbands with histories of sexual misconduct; of 10 sample members convicted of sexual offenses before marriage, only two were convicted after their marriage.

Edgerton also observed a strong desire for marriage and children among the ex-patients (sterilization, however, had made childbearing impossible). Thirty of the 48 sample members did marry and more than half of these unions were with nonretarded spouses. Further, only four divorced or separated. In commenting on the successfulness of such marital unions, Craft and Craft (1979) noted that:

> in social and marital terms, the quality of life enjoyed by many of the couples was not to be envied, with substantial accommodation, hand-to-mouth management, and a high degree of social isolation. Yet in personal terms, the majority felt that marriages had brought them satisfaction which a single existence had not afforded" (p. 77)

Andron and Sturm (1973) also found that within their sample of 12 married couples, all but one married man held that married life was better than single life. The overwhelming reason given was the companionship that marriage provided in contrast to their previous social isolation.

Studies which explored the adequacy of retarded adults as parents, in general, have found that they are satisfactory parents and that their children are reasonably clean, within the normal range of intelligence, and exhibit no unusual behavior problems in school (Johnson, 1981; Whittemore & Koegel, 1978; Winik, 1981). When inadequacy was detected, it could be accounted for by factors other than retardation such as family size, socioeconomic status, marital status, and the harmoniousness of the marital relationship (Mickelson, 1947; Scally, 1973; Winik, 1981; Zetlin, Wiesner & Gallimore, 1985).

Both Winik's (1981) intensive study of two families and Johnson's (1981) observations of six families concluded that none of the families could be considered abusive or neglectful of their children, and although certain problems (e.g., bureaucratic tangles, marital conflicts) were experienced which tended to overwhelm the families and caused them to become temporarily less conscientious about their child care responsibilities, the availability of an extensive amount of support aided them in coping with the pressures of self-maintenance and child care. Similarly, Zetlin, Weisner and Gallimore (1985) found from intensive observation of 13 mildly retarded family units that a cooperative arrangement had evolved between family members and the retarded parents. In all instances, the extended family adapted to the perceived needs of the retarded persons. In those homes in which responsibilities were considered satisfactorily handled, minimal support was provided. When incidents arose which warranted additional assistance, appropriate accommodations were made. And when the situation necessitated intensive intervention, extended family members responded accordingly.

Social Support. With few exceptions, studies of the postinstitutional adjustment of mildly retarded adults have found that success in the community is significantly related to the amount of guidance and support available from others (Fernald, 1919; Goldstein, 1964; McCarver & Craig, 1974; McDevitt et al., 1978). Indeed, Edgerton (1967) had found that only 3 of his 48 sample members were completely independent while the vast majority required varying degrees of support and aid to maintain their independent status. He concluded that, "the ex-patient succeeds in his efforts to sustain life in the community only as well as he succeeds in locating and holding a benefactor." (p. 193) Craft and Craft (1979) also reported that less than one third of the married couples were independent in the community (i.e., unknown to social agencies or dropped from active files). The others lived in married quarters in a mental hospital where they received total care, in hostels or group homes where

staff monitored their needs on a daily basis, or in apartments in the community where they received regular support from relatives, landlords, neighbors or agency personnel.

In a like manner, studies of community-trained retarded adults have found familial and nonfamilial advocates providing vital assistance with the demands of everyday living (Koegel, 1983). Over an 18-month period, Zetlin and her associates observed the daily lives of 46 independent adults, most of whom had never been institutionalized. The most striking finding was the relative lack of self-maintenance displayed by all sample members. Even those who most resembled nonretarded counterparts in their competence and independence, required some assistance to cope with the exigencies of day to day living. With few exceptions, parents were the providers of such support. When parents were no longer accessible, other benefactors were located, from prior arrangements by parents (i.e., siblings, extended family members, family friends) or through the efforts of sample members themselves (i.e., more competent co-workers, friends, neighbors) to satisfy their ongoing support needs (Winik, Zetlin & Kaufman, 1985; Zetlin, Turner & Winik, 1987).

Across such studies, most researchers have stressed that these support systems were not fixed entities but were dynamic and constantly changing. Edgerton and Bercovici (1976) found, for example, that after 12 years of community living, the ex-patients' dependence on benefactors had been greatly reduced. Zetlin, Turner and Winik (1987) noted that there were shifts in both directions in the level of assistance needed by sample members as a result of experience in community living, a parent's or benefactor's death or relocation, marriage and/or the birth of a child. Finally, Koegel (1983) reported that over a 15-month period of research contact, approximately 83% of the 46 independent adults followed had experienced some kind of change in their social network, and that one third of these changes had had a damaging impact on the ability of the adults to cope with the routine aspects of community living.

Criminality. The bulk of the literature on criminality within the mentally retarded population has emphasized two points: (1) that a minority of mildly retarded adults are involved in antisocial behavior (i.e., that most mildly retarded adults are consistently law abiding), and (2) that mildly retarded adults are more likely to commit unlawful acts than their nonretarded counterparts (Edgerton, 1981). Follow-up investigations of deinstitutionalized mildly retarded persons have found with remarkable consistency that the most common cause of community failure and recidivism was antisocial behavior (McCarver & Craig, 1974; Pagel & Whitling, 1978; Windle, Stewart & Brown, 1961). Failure rates varied from study to study, but in at least one investigation, as many as 63% of the patients on leave to their parents' home were returned for antisocial behavior

(Windle et al., 1961). In Deno's (1965) and Baller, Charles and Miller's (1966) studies of community-trained retarded persons, delinquency rate was compared with that of nonretarded controls. Deno found that by the age of 18, 57% of former special class males had police records compared with 37% of all the males in Minneapolis where the research was conducted; the rate of special females was 24% compared with 11% in the general population. Baller et al., too, found that in all periods of research contact (1930s, 1950s, 1960s), former special education sample members were more likely to violate the law than were matched controls of normal intelligence, although less and less unlawful behavior was exhibited by both groups as the years passed.

While such investigations of criminal activity have mostly relied on police or court records, the studies of Craft and Craft (1979) and Edgerton (1981) are unique in their employment of more direct measures. From ongoing observations and self-reports by the subjects themselves, Craft and Craft found that 22% of their sample had been in trouble with the law at one time or another. While most of the offenses were of a minor nature (e.g., the theft of small items), there were some exceptions including arson, rape and indecent assault of children. Edgerton also used direct observation of the daily lives of sample members and found that over a 2-year period, approximately one third of his sample (18) had engaged in no serious deviance, another 20 persons had committed various kinds of minor victimless crimes, while a final group (10) had committed more serious offenses, often against other persons. Edgerton emphasized that this intrasample variation existed with respect to frequency of criminal acts (from never at all to an everyday occurrence) as well as to form and seriousness of these offenses (e.g., driving without a licence, occasional use of marijuana, theft, aggravated assault, etc.).

Personal Adjustment

The relationship between personal adjustment and success or failure in community living has been stressed by researchers throughout the years. In follow-up studies of postinstitutional adjustment, personality factors were among the most commonly mentioned reasons for failure in community placement (Cobb, 1972; McCarver & Craig, 1974; Windle, 1962). Similarly, unstable temperament, emotional disturbance, bizarre or aggressive behavior, and lack of maturity accounted for large numbers of retarded adults being terminated from jobs in competitive industry (Cobb, 1972; Domino & McGarty, 1972; Greenspan & Shoultz, 1981).

Investigations of personality characteristics and self-concept within the mentally retarded population have revealed that there is a higher prevalence of emotional disturbance among mentally retarded individuals than in persons of normal intelligence, and that the same disorders that are present in the general population (i.e.,

global personality types) are also present in the mentally retarded population (Koller, Richardson, Katz & McLaren, in press; MacMillan, 1977). Such findings have been questioned by Windle (1962) and others (McCarver & Craig, 1974) who strongly objected to the lack of adequate measures of personality and the failure of researchers to cross-validate their own results or those of others. Further, much of this research employed paper and pencil self-report instruments and ignored response bias problems including acquiescence, social desirability, evaluative apprehension, and lack of item comprehension (Sigelman, Budd, Spanhel & Schoenrock, 1981; Zetlin, Heriot & Turner, 1985).

Some researchers have focused on the subjective component of personal adjustment (the retarded person's sense of well-being), employing qualitative techniques to learn about the personal lives of mildly retarded adults. In-depth interviews with former institutional residents have revealed that almost all the adults hold in high regard their freedom and independence and prefer their community existence to institutional living (Birenbaum, 1975; Craft & Craft, 1979; Edgerton, 1967; McDevitt et al., 1978). In the same manner, those trained in the community and now living on their own are proud of their normative accomplishments (e.g., material possessions, managing their own homes, holding down jobs, being married) and their independent status (Zetlin & Turner, 1984; 1985). Edgerton (1967) used a form of participant observation and found that while his sample members valued their release into the community, they were also consumed by feelings of shame at having been hospitalized as mentally retarded. The stigma they felt dominated every aspect of their lives and led them to evoke passing and denial as self-esteem maintenance strategies. They lied about their institutional history, acquired and displayed material possessions as evidence of a "normal" existence (e.g., an inoperable car parked outside their home, photographs of fictitious family members, souvenirs from fabricated vacations), and enlisted the help of benefactors to maintain their deception and conceal their past. With the passage of time, however, most came to perceive their handicaps as insignificant, "never completely forgotten, but not an everyday concern either." (p. 491) They became devoted to enjoying life and what dominated their interests was not stigma or passing, but recreation, hobbies, leisure, good times, friends and family (Edgerton & Bercovici, 1976).

Zetlin and Turner (1984) used participant observation techniques with a community-trained sample of independent adults and found that some freely acknowledged their handicap while others denied having one. Some dwelled on their sense of stigma while others disclaimed having any such feelings, and many were inbetween, seeming to be ambivalent, conflicted or confused. Those ill-at-ease with their handicapped status evoked various esteem-maintenance strategies to project a nonretarded public image. They developed personas to project self-reliance (i.e., fabrication of accomplishments and other forms of self-aggrandizement), participated in on-going battles to discredit their supporters (i.e., dependence/autonomy struggles with parents), or dictated the terms of continuing their dependence on parents and others.

Turner (1983) employed a variety of ethnographic strategies (i.e., participant observation, small group discussions, informal questioning) within a sheltered workshop setting and also observed that for many of the clients "being retarded" was the most salient aspect of their social identity. Moreover, clients were so preoccupied with deviance disavowal that, "any verbalization, evaluative comparison or other public behavior that asserted or implied diminished competency was strictly taboo" (p. 169).

In a related study, Graffam and Turner (1984) found that boredom was another major concern among the clients and that the maintenance of self-esteem and the presentation of a positive social identity was related to the relative degree of boredom and eventfulness that they experienced. The researchers identified eight informal means used by clients to raise the level of eventfulness in their lives including grandiose claims of personal achievements or exploits, highly dramatized or emotional responses to apparently mundane events, and sometimes quite intense involvements in a fantasy life. They concluded that many of these means would have been seen as unacceptable, fantastic or even pathological in other social situations, yet in the workshop they appeared to be adaptive in increasing both a sense of eventfulness and self-esteem.

Boredom and lack of social opportunities were among the reasons given by professionals as to why some mentally retarded adults were abusers of alcohol (Krischef & DiNitto, 1981). Even so, only occasional heavy users have been reported within the mentally retarded population. Most of the evidence suggests that neither drug nor alcohol use pose significant problems for retarded persons. Edgerton (1986) examined observational data from four samples of retarded adults ranging from middle-class whites to inner-city Afro-Americans and living in a variety of community settings. He found that, "compared to their nonretarded parents, siblings, spouses and friends, these retarded individuals less often (1) used alcohol and drugs, (2) were labeled by others or themselves as abusers, and (3) engaged in deviant or criminal behavior associated with the use of alcohol or drugs." Negative role models and the influence of socialization practices were identified as the main reasons for sample members' avoidance of intoxicants and drugs.

Implications for Educational Programs

Throughout this review of research studies, several points have been emphasized that have important implications for educators and program developers. Each will be listed separately followed by some general comments about curricula implications.

(1) It is clear that within each area of community adjustment—vocational, economic, social, and personal—a high proportion of mildly retarded adults achieve satisfactory adjustments. These adjustments take a variety of forms and are not unlike those of their nonretarded neighbors in the community.

(2) Success or failure in community functioning is not inherent in the individual but the product of many interacting variables, including employment opportunities, public attitudes, welfare legislation, and so forth.

(3) The majority of community-based adults are able to maintain their independent status because of varying degrees of ongoing support and aid from parents, siblings, friends, benefactors, and social service agencies.

(4) Money management is the most consistently problematic area across samples of independent adults and the one which requires the greatest need for outside intervention.

(5) No simple formula for prediction has been established which can be relied upon to separate in advance those who will achieve satisfactory adaptations from those who will fail.

(6) Each environment has its own criteria of success so that different variables may be associated with maintaining an independent residence rather than are associated with client movement through an independent living training program; different variables may be associated with job performance than are associated with adapting to group home living.

(7) Instability in the various areas of adjustment and movement from less restrictive to more restrictive settings or circumstances are more appropriate criteria for judging failure in community functioning than reinstitutionalization. Subjective elements also must be considered including personal satisfaction and the retarded adults' assessment of their adaptation.

(8) Single point in time sampling provides insufficient and misleading evidence of success or failure in community living. Close monitoring of the progress of individuals over time allows for a more comprehensive understanding of the nature of their adaptation.

(9) Little is known about how nonwhite mildly retarded adults fare in the community and what their particular adaptations are like.

As is often the case in comprehensive reviews such as this, "the total bloc of research studies appears to contribute more to theory development than to the improvement of practice" (p. 138) (Cobb, 1972). Educators and program developers, however, look to research to determine what needs to be taught. They prepare educational curricula by seeking precisely which characteristics contribute to successfully adapting mildly retarded adults. They have as their objective the development of those skills needed to live fully and work effectively in modern society. Research thus far has not provided them with many answers. Rather they have learned that adjustment is an ongoing process affected both positively and negatively by many factors over time, that there is more than one pattern of community living acceptable for mildly retarded adults, and that there is no simple means to predict success or failure in community living.

Edgerton and Bercovici (1976) noted that, "the principle of normalization compels us to seek a better fit between a retarded person and the more nearly 'normal' life that normalization calls for" (p. 496). Before educators and program developers can effectively implement the goals of normalization, more information is needed on (a) the personality characteristics and life history experiences of mildly retarded persons which contribute to individual coping strengths and weaknesses, and (b) the features of natural environments in which retarded persons live and work including the structural aspects (i.e., task requirements, authority structure, rules) and the socioemotional aspects (i.e., opportunities for social support, a sense of belonging, a sense of self-worth). Since adaptation is a function of the interaction of individual characteristics and environment characteristics, an adequate understanding of each is required in order for the most desirable and optimal match to occur.

Educators and program developers also need to recognize that one of the most important aspects of environments is their interpersonal quality. It may be that efforts to move mildly retarded individuals into mainstreamed settings, independent living situations, or competitive employment inadvertently places them in environments which are not suited to their socioemotional needs (for friends, romances, group memberships, sense of belonging, etc.). As retarded adults are increasingly encouraged to live and work independently, we must be sure that they do not end up leading lonely and marginal lives, having little that could be called a support system, and vacillating between boredom and stress. As Turner (1983) emphasized, "this may be 'normal', but it is the lousy side of normalcy and reflects the priority often assigned to self-sufficiency at the expense of other equally compelling values" (p. 170). It is essential to listen to what retarded persons say about their lives, what *their* personally salient concerns are and what *they* think of their own adaptations. This, in conjunction with intensive, long-term study of the details of their everyday lives will help educators and program developers to plan better curricula and programs which reflect the diversity and interests of the mildly retarded population and which enhance their quality of life and sense of dignity and worth.

Acknowledgements

This research was supported by National Institute of Child Health and Human Development Grants HD-11944 and HD-19194. The author wishes to thank Dr. Jim Turner for his helpful comments during the writing of this manuscript.

References

Andron, L., & Sturm, M. L. (1973). Is "I do" in the repertoire of the retarded, *Mental Retardation*, **11**, 31–34.

Baker, B. L., Seltzer, G. B., & Seltzer, M. M. (1977). *As close as possible: Community residences for retarded adults*. Boston, MA: Little, Brown.

Baller, W. R. (1936). A study of the present social status of a group of adults, who, when they were in elementary school, were classified as mentally deficient. *Genetic Psychology Monographs*, **18**, 165–244.

Baller, W. R. (1939). A study of the behavior records of adults who, when they were in school, were judged to be dull in mental ability. *Journal of Genetic Psychology*, **55**, 365–379.

Baller, W. R., Charles, D. C., & Miller, E. l. (1966). *Mid-life attainment of the mentally retarded: A longitudinal study*. Lincoln, NE: University of Nebraska Press.

Birenbaum, A. (1975). The changing lives of mentally retarded adults. In M. J. Begab & S. A. Richardson (Eds.), *The mentally retarded and society: A social science perspective*. Baltimore, MD.: University Park Press.

Birenbaum, A., & Re, M. (1979). Resettling mentally retarded adults in the community: Almost 4 years later. *American Journal of Mental Deficiency*, **83**, 323–329.

Brickey, M., Browning, L., & Campbell, K. (1982). Vocational histories of sheltered workshop employees placed in Projects with Industry and competitive jobs. *Mental Retardation*, **20**, 52–57.

Brickey, M., & Campbell, K. (1981). Fast-food employment by moderately and mildly retarded adults: The MacDonald's project. *Mental Retardation*, **19**, 113–116.

Brolin, D. (1972). Value of rehabilitation services and correlates of vocational success with the mentally retarded. *American Journal of Mental Deficiency*, **76**, 644–651.

Charles, D. C. (1953). Ability and accomplishment of persons earlier judged mentally deficient. *Genetic Psychology Monographs*, 47, 3–71.

Cobb, H. (1972). *The forecast of fulfillment: A review of research on predictive assessment of the adult retarded for social and vocational adjustment*. New York: Teachers College Press.

Corcoran, E. L., & French, R. W. (1977). Leisure activity for the retarded adult in the community. *Mental Retardation*, **15**, 21–23.

Craft, A., & Craft, M. (1979). *Handicapped married couple: A Welsh study of couples handicapped from birth by mental, physical, or personality disorder*. London: Routlege & Kegan Paul.

Deno, E. (1965). *Final Report of Project VRA-RD-681*. Minneapolis, MN: Minneapolis Public Schools.

Domino, G., & McGarty, M. (1972). Personal and work adjustment of young retarded women. *American Journal of Mental Deficiency*, 77, 314–321.

Edgerton, R. B. (1967). *The cloak of competence: Stigma in the lives of the mentally retarded*. Berkely, CA: University of California Press.

Edgerton, R. B. (1979). *Mental retardation*. Cambridge, MA.: Harvard University Press.

Edgerton, R. B. (1981). Crime, deviance and normalization: Reconsidered. In R. H. Bruininks, C. E. Meyers, B. B. Sigford, & K. C. Lakin (Eds.), *Deinstitutionalization and community adjustment of mentally retarded people* (Monograph No. 4). Washington, D.C.: American Association on Mental Deficiency.

Edgerton, R. B. (1983). Failure in community adaptation: The relativity of assessment. In K. T. Kernan, M. J. Begab, & R. B. Edgerton (Eds.), *Environments and behavior: The adaptation of mentally retarded persons*. Baltimore, MD.: University Park Press.

Edgerton, R. B. (1984). The participant-observer approach to research in mental retardation. *American Journal of Mental Deficiency*, **88**, 498–505.

Edgerton, R. B. (1986). Alcohol and drug use by mentally retarded adults. *American Journal of Mental Deficiency*, **90**, 602–609.

Edgerton, R. B., & Bercovici, S. M. (1976). The cloak of competence: Years later. *American Journal of Mental Deficiency*, **80**, 485–497.

Edgerton, R. B., Bollinger, M., & Herr, B. (1984). The cloak of competence: After two decades. *American Journal of Mental Deficiency*, **88**, 345–351.

Fernald, W. E. (1919). After-care study of the patients discharged from Waverly for a period of 25 years. *Ungraded*, **5**, 25–31.

Foss, G., & Peterson, S. L. (1981). Social-interpersonal skills relevant to job-tenure for mentally retarded adults. *Mental Retardation*, **19**, 103–106.

Goldstein, H. (1964). Social and occupational adjustments. In H. A. Stevens & R. Heber (Eds.), *Mental Retardation: A review of research*. Chicago: University of Chicago Press.

Gollay, E., Freedman, R., Wyngaarden, M., & Kurtz, N. R. (1978). *Coming back: the community experiences of deinstitutionalized mentally retarded people*. Cambridge, MA.: Abt Books.

Grafnam, J., & Turner, J. L. (1984). Escape from boredom: The meaning of eventfulness in the lives of clients at a sheltered workshop. In R. B. Edgerton (Ed.), *Lives in process: Mildly retarded adults in a large city* (Monograph No. 6). Washington, D.C.: American Association on Mental Deficiency.

Greenspan, D. & Shoultz, B. (1981). Why mentally retarded adults lose their jobs: Social competence as a factor in work adjustment. *Applied Research in Mental Retardation*, **2**, 23–38.

Greenspan, S., Shoultz, B., & Weir, M. M. (1981). Social judgement and vocational adjustment of mentally retarded adults. *Applied Research in Mental Retardation*, **2**, 335–346.

Heal, L. W., Sigelman, C. K., Switzky, H. N. (1978). Research on community residential alternatives for the mentally retarded. In N. R. Ellis (Ed.), *International Review of research in mental retardation* (Vol. 9). New York: Academic Press.

Heber, R. F. & Dever, R. B. (1970). Research on education and habilitation of the mentally retarded. in H. C. Haywood (Ed.), *Socio-cultural aspects of mental retardation*. New York: Appleton-Century-Crafts.

Johnson, O. R. (1981, August). *Mildly retarded adults as parents*. Paper presented at the 89th Annual Convention of the American Psychological Association, Los Angeles, CA.

Jones, L. A., & Moe, R. (1980). College education for mentally retarded adults. *Mental Retardation*, **18**, 59–62.

Kaufman, S. (1984). Friendship, coping systems and community adjustment of mildly retarded adults. In R. B. Edgerton (Ed.), *Lives in process: Mildly retarded adults in a large city* (Monograph No. 6). Washington, D.C.: American Association on Mental Deficiency.

Kennedy, R. J. (1948). *The social adjustment of morons in a Connecticut city*. Willport, CT.: Commission to Study Resources in Connecticut.

Kennedy, R. J. (1966). The social adjustment of morons in a Connecticut city: Summary and conclusions, and abstract of a Connecticut community revisited: A study of social adjustment of a group of mentally deficient adults in 1948 and 1960. In T. E. Jordan (Ed.), *Perspectives in mental retardation*. Carbondale, IL.: Southern Illinois University Press.

Kernan, K. T., & Koegel, P. (1984). Employment experiences of community-based mildly retarded adults. In R. B. Edgerton (Ed.), *Lives in process: Mildly retarded adults in a large city* (Monograph No. 6). Washington, D.C.: American Association on Mental Deficiency.

Koegel, P. (1983, May). *Changing support systems and their impact on quality of life*. Paper presented at the Annual Convention of the American Association on Mental Deficiency, Dallas, TX.

Koegel, P., & Kernan, K. T. (1983). Issues affecting the involvement of mildly retarded individuals in competitive employment. In K. T. Kernan, M. J. Begab, & R. B. Edgerton (Eds.), *Environments and behavior: The adaptation of mentally retarded persons*. Baltimore, MD.: University Park Press.

Koller, H., Richardson, S. A. Katz, M., & McLaren, J. (in press). Behavior disturbance in childhood and the early adult years in populations who were and were not mentally retarded. *Journal of Preventative Psychiatry*.

Krauss, M. W., & McEachron, A. E. (1982). Competitive employment training for mentally retarded adults: The supported work model. *American Journal of Mental Deficiency*, **86**, 650–653.

Krischef, C. H., & DiNitto, D. M. (1981). Alcohol abuse among mentally retarded individuals. *Mental Retardation*, **19**, 151–155.

Lakin, K. C., Bruininks, K. H., & Sigford, B. B. (1981). Deinstitutionalization and community adjustment: A summary of research and issues. In R. H. Bruininks, C. E. Meyers, B. B. Sigford, & K. C. Lakin (Eds.), *Deinstitutionalization and community adjustment of mentally retarded people* (Monograph No. 4). Washington, D.C.: American Association on Mental Deficiency.

Levine, H. G., & Langness, L. L. (1985). Everyday cognition among mildly retarded adults: An ethnographic approach. *American Journal of Mental Deficiency*, **90**, 18–26.

MacMillan, D. L. (1977). *Mental retardation in school and society*. Boston: Little, Brown.

McCarver, R. B., & Craig, E. M. (1974). Placement of the retarded in the community: Prognosis and outcome. In N. R. Ellis (Ed.), *International review of research in mental retardation* (Vol. 7). New York: Academic Press.

McDevitt, S. C., Smith, P. M., Schmidt, D. W., & Rosen, M. (1978). The deinstitutionalized citizen: Adjustment and quality of life. *Mental Retardation*, **16**, 22–24.

Mickelson, P. (1947). The feebleminded parent: A study of 90 family cases. *American Journal of Mental Deficiency*, **51**, 644–653.

Pagel, S. E., & Whitling, C. A. (1978). Readmissions to a state hospital for mentally retarded persons: Reasons for community placement failure. *Mental Retardation*, **16**, 164–166.

Richardson, S. A. (1978). Careers of mentally retarded young persons: Services, jobs and interpersonal relations. *American Journal of Mental Deficiency*, **82**, 349–358.

Rosen, M., Clark, G. R., Kivitz, M. S. (1977) *Habilitation of the handicapped: New dimensions in programs for the developmentally disabled.* Baltimore, MD.: University Park Press.

Scally, B. G. (1973). Marriage and mental handicaps: Some observations in Northern Ireland. In F. F. de la Cruz & G. D. LaVeck (Eds.), *Human sexuality and the mentally retarded.* New York: Brunner/Mazel.

Schreiner, J. (1978). Prediction of retarded adults' work performance through components of general ability. *American Journal of Mental Deficiency, 83,* 77–79.

Sigelman, C. K., Budd, E. C., Spanhel, C. L. & Schoenrock, C. K. (1981). When in doubt, say yes: Acquiescence in interviews with mildly retarded persons. *Mental Retardation, 19,* 53–58.

Snart, F., & Swann, V. (1982). Assessment of intellectually handicapped adults: A cognitive processing model. *Applied Research in Mental Retardation, 3,* 201–212.

Stephens, W. B. (1964). *Success of young adult male retardates.* Ann Arbor, MI: University Microfilms.

Stephens, W. B., Peck, J. R., & Veldman, D. J. (1968). Personality and success profiles characteristic of young adult male retardates. *American Journal of Mental Deficiency, 73,* 405–413.

Turner, J. L. (1983). Workshop society: Ethnographic observations in a work setting for retarded adults. In K. T. Kernan, M. J. Begab, & R. B. Edgerton (Eds.), *Environments and behavior: The adaptation of mentally retarded persons.* Baltimore, MD.: University Park Press.

Whittemore, R. D., & Koegel, P. (1978). *Loving alone is not helpful: Sexuality and social context among the mildly retarded.* Working Paper no. 7, Socio-Behavioral Group, Mental Retardation Research Center, School of Medicine, University of California, Los Angeles.

Williams, R. D., & Ewing, S. (1981). Consumer roulette: The shopping patterns of mentally retarded persons. *Mental Retardation, 19,* 145–149.

Windle, C. D. (1962). Prognosis of mental subnormals. *American Journal of Mental Deficiency, 66,* 1–180.

Windle, C. D., Stewart, E., & Brown, S. J. (1961). Reasons for community failure of released patients. *American Journal of Mental Deficiency, 66,* 213–217.

Winik, L. (1981). *The mildly retarded as parents: A description and explication of the parenting practices of two mildly retarded couples.* Unpublished masters thesis, University of California, Los Angeles.

Winik, L., Zetlin, A. G., & Kaufman, S. (1985). Adult mildly retarded persons and their parents: The relationship between involvement and adjustment. *Applied Research in Mental Retardation, 6,* 409–419.

Wolfensberger, W. (1967). Vocational preparation and occupation. In A. A. Baumeister (Ed.), *Mental retardation, appraisal, education and rehabilitation.* Chicago: Aldine Publishing.

Wolfensberger, W. (1972). *Normalization: The principle of normalization in human services.* Toronto: Leonard Crainford.

Zetlin, A. G., Heriot, M. J., & Turner, J. L. (1985). Self-concept measurement: A microanalysis of response styles. *Applied Research in Mental Retardation, 6,* 113–125.

Zetlin, A. G., Turner, J. L., & Winik, L., (1987). Socialization effects on community adaptation of adults who have mild retardation. In S. Landesman & P. M. Vietze (Eds.), *Living environments and mental retardation.* Washington, D.C.: American Association on Mental Deficiency.

Zetlin, A. G., & Turner, J. L. (1984). Self-perspectives on being handicapped: Stigma and adjustment. In R. B. Edgerton (Ed.), *Lives in process: Mildly retarded adults in a large city* (Monograph No. 6). Washington, D.C.: American Association on Mental Deficiency.

Zetlin, A. G., & Turner, J. L. (1985). The transition from adolescence to adulthood: Perspectives of retarded individuals and their family. *American Journal of Mental Deficiency, 89,* 570–579.

Zetlin, A. G., Weisner, T. S., & Gallimore, R. (1985). Diversity, shared functioning, and the role of benefactors: A study of parenting by retarded persons. In K. Thurman (Ed.), *Children of handicapped parents: Research and perspectives.* New York: Academic Press.

SECTION 2

Behavioral Disorders

Introduction

FRANK H. WOOD

University of Minnesota

One of the goals of the research syntheses reported in this *Handbook* was to summarize what the available literature tells us about important issues of policy and practice in the education of students with special needs. When the disability of concern is behavioral disorders, or the related problem of emotional disturbance, an immediate matter of concern is the lack of consensus among researchers as to either label or definition. The authors of the five chapters in this section have been faced with decisions about the comparability of sample groups or populations as well as the quality of methodology in the studies reviewed. Many of their dilemmas are rooted in the problem of definition itself.

Which students in our schools are sufficiently behaviorally disordered to be considered elegible for special education services? A consideration of points raised in these chapters suggests that the "behaviorally disordered" or "emotionally disturbed" student group is characterized by several clusters of problem behavior, not all of which are present in every student. In turn, each of these problem behaviors is addressed by different interventions. Because most students show more than one problem behavior, they are typically the target of several interventions at the same time, not all of which may be described or even mentioned by the researchers who have contributed chapters to this section.

The following are major clusters of problem behavior that commonly are used to characterize behaviorally disordered students.

1. *Unsatisfactory academic achievement without evidence of sensory or cognitive disability.* Some degree of learning disability or mild mental retardation may be present. Diagnosis is by educators who are assisted by psychologists or other professionals in ruling out alternative explanations. Interventions are typically individualized instruction and the use of alternative curricula.
2. *Emotional disturbance.* Diagnosis of emotional disturbance is usually considered to require confirmation of an educator's preliminary evaluation by psychologists or psychiatrists. Interventions involve changes in the educational program to accommodate the emotional needs of the student and the use of cognitive-emotional interventions.
3. *Behavior excesses and deficits.* Diagnosis may be by either educators or psychologists. Interventions focus on training of adaptive behavior through the manipulation of contingent environmental events and use of some cognitive-emotional interventions such as modeling.
4. *Disruptive behavior.* Diagnosis is by educators with confirmation from other professionals. Interventions stress control and suppression, with occasional use of seclusion or other punishing consequences. Law-violating disruptive behavior leads to application of the label "delinquent."

It is noteworthy that the prerogative of certifying the applicability of a specific label rests with different professional groups and that the interventions typically employed differ greatly in character and degree of intrusiveness. Furthermore, most behaviorally disordered students probably show some degree of disability in each cluster area and are probably the target of more than one intervention procedure.

However, investigators reporting in the research literature are frequently forced by journal space requirements, and permitted through a history of acceptance of ambiguity by the field, to define population characteristics inadequately and to ignore the possible impact of interventions other than those which are being featured in their reports. The resulting weakness of the research literature has been condemned by the authors of the chapters that follow in this section. However, our criticism is cheap. Doing something about it may be very expensive. Readers are encouraged to bear in mind both this pervasive problem and the difficulty and cost of doing anything significant about it. Those who will be inconvenienced resist change. This is a behavioral tendency that is as characteristic of researchers as of those in other professions. Deeply rooted inertia must be overcome if progress is to be made in resolving the fundamental problems that have been noted in the areas of terminology and definition.

Issues of definition are among the topics addressed in the chapter by Smith, Wood, and Grimes entitled, "Issues in the Identification and Placement of Behaviorally Disordered Students." In their review, these authors focus on identification and placement decisions made in relation to students who are educationally handicapped by virtue of unacceptable behavioral patterns. The chapter includes discussions of the conceptual models for identification and placement of such students, the systems used to classify and label, and the decision-making practices that affect the students' identification and placement. The authors' conclusion that there are serious theoretical and applied problems in consistently implementing effective, nonbiased identification and placement procedures comes as little surprise to those working in the field. Their recommendations for more accurate descriptions of research populations and procedures, the coupling of research knowledge and clinical skills, and the improvement of decision-making practices, including the use of data from multiple sources, suggest some of the directions that should be taken in improving work in the area. Readers are encouraged to move beyond the documentation of cited problems and toward solutions.

In the second chapter, Nelson and Rutherford address the topic, "Behavioral Interventions with Behaviorally Disordered Students." Although the findings of research on behavioral interventions must be qualified, as already noted, Nelson and Rutherford demonstrate that, by deliberately restricting their focus to the parameters suggested as critical by one theoretical model of human behavior, behavioral researchers have made impressive progress in describing subject groups, intervention procedures, and outcomes. They have also shown commendable integrity in facing squarely the important issue of generalizability of effects. Whether or not they will be able to develop solutions to this problem and demonstrate broad, long-term effects of interventions without departing from their rigorous paradigm remains an open question for this writer. However, the behaviorists have established a solid base of literature from which to expand.

The overall picture regarding the literature on cognitive-emotional interventions is less encouraging. As discussed in the chapter by Carpenter and Apter entitled, "Research Integration of Cognitive-Emotional Interventions for Behaviorally Disordered Children and Youth," the issues surrounding the description of populations, interventions, and outcomes in this area have not been so effectively managed. Theoretical models and submodels compete with one another for heuristic and explanatory prominence. Their assumption regarding the complexity of human behavior may make these models more "true" in some ultimate sense, but it has not made them more useful for guiding the development of research methodologies that yield reliable results. Researchers concerned with cognitive-emotional interventions should be challenged by the Carpenter and Apter chapter to think more critically about their goals and how they propose to reach them.

With so much of the groundwork as yet incomplete, it may seem premature to seek useful information on the important policy issues of the training of teachers and the cooperation between schools and other agencies. In their respective chapters, Zabel, writing on "Preparation of Teachers for Behaviorally Disordered Students: A Review of Literature," and Huntze, writing on "Cooperative Interface of Schools and Other Child Care Systems for Behaviorally Disordered Students," find the literature on these topics to be characterized by much discussion and a limited amount of solid research. In a sense, this may be an appropriate state of affairs. In the absence of solid research findings on which to build policy, it may be best to rely on reasoned argument and response. Besides covering such research literature as exists, the authors of these two chapters provide an overview of the conceptual frameworks within which important political and economic decisions are being made at present. There is clearly a need to expand our knowledge base in both areas. To do so will require moving beyond the research methodologies that have been considered mainstream by American education and psychology and incorporating survey and field study methods.

These five chapters represent a thoughtful synthesis of the available literature in areas of importance for those with an interest in the education of students whose behavioral and emotional needs lead their teachers to view them with special concern. As the chapters demonstrate, there is much to be proud of in the literature that has developed in this field during the past 20 years. There is a solid foundation on which further research can be built. However, the vastness of what we do not yet understand, and of the studies for which we have not yet even developed satisfactory methods, is somewhat demoralizing. The recommendations of the authors in this section give us direction. We must give priority to understanding and solving the big problems rather than limiting ourselves only to admiring them or to demonstrating and redemonstrating our skills within the narrow spheres where we have developed some degree of mastery.

Dedication

The chapters in this section are dedicated to Steven J. Apter. With his untimely death, we lost not only a respected colleague but a good friend.

Issues in the Identification and Placement
of
Behaviorally Disordered Students

CARL R. SMITH

Buena Vista College, Iowa

FRANK H. WOOD

University of Minnesota

JEFF GRIMES

Iowa Department of Public Instruction

Emotional Disturbance and Behavioral Disorders

Definitions are usually clear and concise at the extremes of a condition . . . As one moves from the extreme of a handicapping condition toward the mean, one reaches a point where the waters are sufficiently muddied to cause serious definitional problems. If such controversies were relegated to academics, scientists, or interested philologists, it could be a merry and instructive debate. However, where such definitions limit or prescribe who may or may not receive services, the definitional problem becomes significant for children, their families, and school systems. (Bower, 1982, p. 55)

Beginning in California in the 1950s, E. M. Bower led an early and still exemplary effort to determine the prevalence of emotional disturbance/behavioral disorders in school children. His comment on the current situation regarding definitional issues and their implications for eligibility and placement summarized his 30 years of struggling with this complex problem. Faced squarely, the problem is seen to have no easy solution. The answer lies in developing and maintaining the sophistication of the definers and labelers rather than in the search for a user-proof formula. As Kauffman (1980) has said:

The choice of the Bureau of Education for the Handicapped [now Office of Special Education Programs] of one definition over another does not make it better; the choice only makes it the one that will be the standard in court. A definition does not remove the need for clinical judgment. It is true that clinical judgment is as capricious and arbitrary as any bureaucratic rule, but bureaucratic rules often become impenetrable barriers to rational action. To enshrine an arbitrary definition of social deviance by government decree and to make that arbitrary definition the basis of a bureaucratic mandate for special education is to invite disappointment. (p. 254)

The complexity of the situation for educational decision-making is increased by the fact that behavioral disorders (BD) accompany so many other educational disabilities. Bower (1982) cites a 1960 Los Angeles County Study report that 50% of the students in special education classes with other labels were also considered to be emotionally disturbed. One might expect that the number of students reported to be behaviorally disordered would be showing a rapid rate of increase. Yet, the behavioral disorders prevalence figures reported by states consistently average less than 1% of the total school population, and Algozzine and Korinek's (1985) summary of national trend data reveals that the number of students identified as such, reported as a percentage of all students with disabilities, remained relatively constant for the years 1978–82 despite marked increases in the number of learning disabled students and decreases in those labeled as mentally retarded, two of the higher prevalence groups of students with disabilities.

The situation that emerges is one of agreement in the existence of a widespread, subjectively defined, seriously disabling condition affecting the ability of students to benefit from their school experience, a condition that

95

is more frequently noted than labeled. In this chapter we will summarize the literature that describes this condition and explore the reasons for the seemingly reluctant use of the behaviorally disordered label for establishing eligibility for and planning special education services. We found that while the existence of some of the problems in this area is well-documented, generally accepted solutions remain elusive. For this reason, our recommendations may appear to some to be conservative. We were guided by what Donnellan (1984), writing about the equally perplexing but low prevalence condition of autism, calls "the criterion of the least dangerous assumption," which ". . . holds that in the absence of conclusive data educational decisions ought to be based on assumptions which, if incorrect, will have the least dangerous effect on the likelihood that students will be able to function independently as adults". (p. 141)

Terminology

Throughout this chapter, we will use the already introduced term, behavioral disorders, to refer to the educational disability of concern. It should be noted that we are using this term as synonymous to other terms such as emotional disturbance or emotional maladjustment. We remain sensitive to the fact that the label applies to a disability rather than a person. However, it is difficult to maintain this distinction at all times, and we fall back on the common practice of speaking of students for whom this is considered to be the primary reason for a failure to progress in school as "Behaviorally disordered students." Likewise, we speak of learning disabled students and educable mentally retarded students although we regret contributing to the tendency to view the disability as larger than the person.

None of these disability labels defines an exclusive or "pure" group of students. Many educable mentally retarded or learning disabled students also have behavioral disorder problems, and the converse is also true. Some of the literature exploring the extent and nature of the overlap will be discussed later in the chapter.

Boundaries of the Review/Subtopics

The scope of this review focuses on identification and placement decisions made by education professionals in relation to behaviorally disordered students. Of primary importance is the decision making process as related to determining when such students are handicapped in obtaining an education as specified in *P.L. 94–142*. The limited literature addressing these issues directly has been supplemented by the inclusion of material that the authors believe is relevant indirectly or by analogy.

This review is divided into several sections. Following an introduction that presents the models used to conceptualize such students, we discuss eligibility, prevalence, and classification systems. This is followed by discussion

of the reported characteristics of such students and two sections look at the labeling process. The latter section of this chapter deals with considerations affecting general decision making in special education, and a more specific look at practices in decision making in the identification and placement of behaviorally disordered students. A discussion of research, policy, and practice implications is presented at the conclusion of the chapter.

Educational Models of BD Behavior

What does a behaviorally disordered student look (or behave) like? Educators and those in related professions have considered this issue both practically and theoretically. Various educational models of behavioral disorders have been proposed. Such models have been important in the development of guidelines for determining eligibility and placement of such students. Wood and Lakin (1979a) edited a series of papers in which researchers discussed various aspects of the definitional problem and its history. A brief review of two major streams of thought on this problem follows.

Empirically Derived Models

One approach to the problem of definition is illustrated by the work of Bower (Bower, 1960). He and his colleagues undertook a study of students who were considered to be emotionally disturbed, determining the measures that appeared to discriminate this group from their nonlabeled peers. He summarizes the procedures used in a more recent article (1982):

> Based on the analysis of the approximately 6,000 returns (207 designated emotionally disturbed children and their classmates) the major differences between the designated emotionally disturbed children and their classmates were spelled out in the definition. The emotionally disturbed children were poor learners, although potentially able to learn; they had few if any satisfactory interpersonal relationships; they behaved oddly or inappropriately; they were depressed or unhappy and developed illnesses or phobias. It was also noted that one or more of these characteristics were true of almost all nondesignated students to some extent at different times. The crucial differentiation was based on the observation and assessment that in the emotionally disturbed child the characteristics existed to *a marked degree over a period of time*. (p. 57)

Bower's approach is typical of what we will call an empirical approach to model building: study of the characteristics of a previously labeled group to develop criteria to guide labeling of a nonlabeled group.

A group of researchers associated with Quay have also developed a model of the behaviorally disordered student using an empirical approach. Their research has involved the description of various student populations using the Behavior Problem Checklist (Quay & Peterson, 1979). Quay's (1978) summary of this research led to the definition of four basic clusters of problem behavior. Researchers like Cullinan, Epstein, and Kauffman (1984) are among those who have continued to add to knowledge of the characteristics of behaviorally disordered students rated on the Behavior Problem Checklist as compared to nonlabeled and other labeled disability groups.

Social Context Models

Empirically based models are subject to criticism for certain inherent biases. For one thing, they are circular in their approach to the issue of definition. The characteristics of those students who have already been defined are measured and those measurements are used to define the next population of students. The ultimate criterion for the definition is the judgment of adults in authority roles, teachers and mental health professionals. The focus of that judgment is the child.

Rhodes, in a paper (Rhodes, 1967) which grew from his work with Hobbs and others on Project Re-Ed (Hobbs, 1966), and continuing with his work on the Conceptual Project on Child Variance at the University of Michigan in the early 1970s, challenged this child-centered view of behavioral disorders. Rhodes argued that these students' behavior should be viewed in the context of the social interrelationships in which it occurs. The application of the behaviorally disordered label to the child is to be understood in the context of the power characteristics of that social system. Whereas the empirically derived model directs interventions at the behavior of the student, the social context model calls for interventions that affect the functioning of the disturbed social system as a whole.

Suchar (1978) uses a social context perspective to discuss an interesting variant of the child-focused model. He studied the processing of child referrals in mental health service organizations. He concluded that ". . . bureaucratic practitioners of child psychotherapy engage in *co-deviant labeling*, a labeling process which places responsibility for the child's pathology on the parents and casts the parent into the role of 'copatient' " (p. 76). Here the focus has moved beyond the individual child but still fails to take in the entire social system.

While the social context model does not translate into an easily applied set of procedures, it has provided a valuable theoretical antithesis to the dominant empirically based model of child psychopathology.

Alternative Definitions

Problems in the application of the definitions that have been mentioned and their numerous variations continue to invite efforts at their revision and operationalization. Revisionist papers by Bower (1982) (who writes with special authority because his 1960 definition

became the basis of the current federal definition), Kauffman (1980), and Wood and Lakin (1979a) have already been mentioned. Another thoughtful proposal was that put forward by Algozzine, Schmid, and Conners (1978). Their proposal differentiates two types of behaviorally disordered students along the dimensions of measurable alternate placements, behavior deviations, behavioral interference, and etiology. One type of student, described as the nonclinical type of student, is characterized by behavioral variability across settings and is responsive to structured behavioral interventions. The second type of student (clinical) demonstrates more behavioral consistency across settings, is less responsive to behavioral interventions, and is more likely to be affected by hypothesized physiological factors contributing to their deviant behavior.

It remains to be seen whether any of the numerous proposed revisions and refinements of current definitions and the associated labels would lead to more appropriate educational programming for behaviorally disordered students and be more useful to their teachers.

Eligibility/Prevalence Issues

Special educators are called upon to answer specific questions regarding who is eligible for special education programs and services on the basis of "serious emotional disturbance" or "behavioral disorders." Inherent to this concept is the question of what is the actual prevalence rate for this handicapping condition. Related concepts are the problems of differentiating behavioral disorders in special education from labels applied by other systems such as mental health and corrections, and the terminology best suited to describe this population. These issues are examined in this section.

Classification Systems Imposed by Law or Regulation

Despite the lack of consensus on what constitutes behavioral deviance, federal and state education agencies have been given the responsibility for monitoring procedures used by local school districts for identifying and appropriately serving school-age pupils who are handicapped by virtue of behavioral deviance. At the federal level such students are referred to as "seriously emotionally disturbed" (Federal Register, 1977). According to *P.L. 94–142* serious emotional disturbance is:

. . . a condition exhibiting one or more of the following characteristics over a long period of time and to a marked degree, which adversely affects educational performance:

(A) An inability to learn which cannot be explained by intellectual, sensory, or health factors;

(B) An inability to build or maintain satisfactory interpersonal relationships with peers or teachers;
(C) Inappropriate types of behavior or feelings under normal circumstances;
(D) A general pervasive mood of unhappiness or depression;
or
(E) A tendency to develop physical symptoms or fears associated with personal or school problems.

The term includes children who are schizophrenic. The term does not include children who are socially maladjusted, unless it is determined that they are seriously emotionally disturbed.

Although "seriously emotionally disturbed" is defined in *P.L. 94–142*, the definition is considered general and advisory. A variety of terms and/or definitions are currently being used at the state level (Epstein, Cullinan, & Sabatino, 1977; National Association of State Directors of Special Education, 1978; White, Beattie, & Rose, 1984). Such diversity in definition results in diversity in the means by which such pupils are identified from state to state. This conclusion is supported by the data gathered in a recent project conducted by the National Association of State Directors of Special Education (NASDSE, 1985). At this time there are no documents or position papers prepared at the federal level advocating or defining uniform identification procedures.

One particular problem with the present federal definition that has been pointed out is the exclusion of the "socially maladjusted" student (Bower, 1982; Neel & Rutherford, 1981). As noted by Grosenick and Huntze (1980, p. 27):

> Although many states are making valiant efforts to develop consistent and fair criteria for determining if given behavior problems are indicative of "social maladjustment" without "emotional disturbance," the prospect is bleak. There is no clear cut evidence or thought in the field which delineates the distinction between categories . . . Unless Congress or the Office of Special Education can provide states with a definition of social maladjustment that is clear, consistent and adequately differentiated from emotional disturbance, the current confusion will probably remain. (p. 27)

As of 1984, the majority of states (27) have definitions that do not specifically exclude socially maladjusted students who are not also emotionally disturbed from service (NASDSE, 1985).

Although the rules implementing *P.L. 94–142* do not impose their definition of "seriously emotionally disturbed" on the states, a state's definition must be judged as identifying an equivalent group of children to the federal definition in order for the state to be eligible for

federal funding. This discretionary authority has permitted the great diversity in the labels and definitions used throughout the states and territories.

While the issue of terminology may be less critical, use of fair, consistent, and verifiable identification procedures would appear to be a necessary prerequisite to securing a free appropriate special education for students handicapped by virtue of their behavior. Not to do so would appear to confirm the observations of Kauffman (1982).

> . . . it will be particularly difficult, if not impossible, to fulfill that guarantee (free, appropriate public education) for emotionally disturbed children because their identification is subjective and can be avoided by school officials when it is in their own best interest to do so. (p. 6)

Several studies have examined trends in state definitions of behaviorally disordered students. Epstein, Cullinan, and Sabatino's (1977) analysis of state definitions resulted in specification of 11 different components. No state definition contained every component; some had as few as two. Most had at least five. Some had as many as nine components. At that time, and in a later review, these researchers concluded that there was not a national consensus regarding the characteristics of the behaviorally disordered population (Cullinan, Epstein, & Lloyd, 1983).

More recently, Mack (1980) examined state definitions. She concluded that there were many discrepancies between state and federal definitions of the behaviorally disordered population. Among her major conclusions were: (1) Only seven states were using the term "seriously emotionally disturbed," (2) only twelve states' criteria addressed all of the criteria contained in the federal definition of behavioral disorder, (3) over two thirds of the states did not mention the term "social maladjustment" although the federal definition specifically mentions that disability is excluded from the behaviorally disordered category.

Bower (1982), whose own definition of serious emotional disturbance in 1960 formed the basis for the current federal definition, made several observations regarding the *P.L. 94–142* definition. According to Bower, "The modifications do serious damage to the integrity of the research and conceptual base from which the definition is drawn" (p. 55). He further concludes: "When one group—in this instance, policy makers—utilizes data and concepts from the other, it should borrow with integrity and consistency. It is clear that the present definitional dilemma emerged out of fiscal and resource limitations to serve this group of handicapped". (p. 60)

The report of a survey conducted by the Council of Administrators of Special Education (CASE, 1983) concluded, "The criteria and procedures most often used in local settings for identifying children who are seriously emotionally disturbed appear appropriate responses for the current federal definition; but current belief would support revision of that definition" (p. 28). Among the revisions suggested are the elimination of the requirement to differentiate socially maladjusted from emotionally disturbed youth and a more precise behavioral and environmental descriptive approach to defining this population.

Historically, the selection of behaviorally disordered students in need of special education programming appears to have been heavily influenced by clinical diagnostic systems commonly used by clinically trained persons such as child psychiatrists (Hocutt, Cox, & Polosi, 1984). The major assumption of such systems is the use of clinical judgment by qualified persons to place children in previously determined categories. While the third revision of the Diagnostic and Statistical Manual by the American Psychiatric Association (APA, 1980) moves in the direction of more precise behavior and environment descriptions suggested by the 1983 CASE report, diagnostic procedures used by mental health professionals remain heavily subjective. "Subjectivity," in this case, means the absence of a predetermined list of instruments of data collection and scoring procedures (Weissenburger, Bielat, Gingrich, & Jensen, 1985). The present federal definition encourages such lack of consistency in assessment and evaluation by its own stress on conditions that cannot be directly observed or described.

Relationship of Labels to Funding

Some scholars assert that labels are only required for funding purposes and outside of such use should be eliminated. Their argument is supported by evidence of the negative consequences of the use of labels in describing any population, which will be reviewed later. Despite these consequences, nearly all states have chosen to label handicapped children according to disability categories. Even those states that consider themselves noncategorical (California, South Dakota, and Massachusetts) are required to convert their noncategorical child counts into categorical child counts in order to receive federal financial support under *P.L. 94–142*.

A comprehensive discussion of noncategorical versus categorical approaches to identifying and serving behaviorally disordered students is beyond the scope of this chapter. Grosenick, Huntze, and Smith (1983) recently edited a volume where the opposing viewpoints are presented. What is important to this analysis is that labeling appears to be the dominant model in use to secure funding and direct programming. Despite the criticism, there is professional support for current practice.

Even Hobbs (1975), who criticized the shortcomings of current labeling practice, concluded:

There is widely expressed sentiment that classification of exceptional children should be done away with. This is a misguided aspiration. Classification and labeling are essential to human communication and problem solving; we do not wish to encourage the belief that abuses can be remedied by not classifying. What we agree to is more precise categories and more discriminant ways of describing children in order to plan appropriate programs for them. (p. 8)

The need is for labeling procedures that are more functional for assessment, evaluation, funding, and placement procedures than many in use at present.

Prevalence

Problems in terminology and definition lead to problems in estimating prevalence, with serious implications for the field. Cullinan, Epstein, and Lloyd (1983) state, "This (prevalence) is the estimate used to determine the amount of federal support for research, demonstration, teacher training, and direct educational services to behaviorally disordered pupils so it is a figure with which many special educators have to reckon" (p. 106). Balow (1979) pointed out that it is not possible to assess the prevalence of any condition without specifying the signs, symptoms and behaviors which define such a condition. This review has shown that there are no commonly accepted criteria for identifying behavioral disorders problems in school-age persons.

As a result, prevalence estimates vary with the source. In 1971 the rates reported by state education offices varied from 0.05% to 15% (Schultz, Hirshoren, Manton, & Henderson, 1971). Balow (1979) points out that, although the empirical base for doing so may be lacking, the federal government has long used a 2% prevalence figure in its reports and publications, in requests to the Congress, and in communication with state school officers. A report recently prepared for Congress (NASDSE, 1985) stated that during the 1982–83 school year the number of behaviorally disordered students served (ages 3–21) averaged 0.89% nationally in the preschool through grade 12 school enrollments. Four states were reported as serving 2% or more of their total enrollment as only behaviorally disordered.

Some investigators have gone directly to teachers to estimate the number of children showing significant behavioral difficulties. Spivack, Swift, and Prewitt (1971) found 16% to 40% of students rated as behavior problems by their teachers. Kelly, Bullock, and Dykes (1977) found 20% of pupils in grades K–12 rated by teachers as behaviorally disordered but only 2.2% rated as severe. Rubin and Balow (1978) reported a high prevalence rate (over 50%) of students who were considered a behavior problem by at least one teacher during their school career. Apparently teacher estimates of student needs are 10–20 times higher than official prevalence estimates.

Within states, the prevalence of identified behaviorally disordered students varies from district to district and is influenced by many noneducational factors. For example, Long (1983) has represented data which she interprets as demonstrating that:

The severity label placed on any given child's condition by district in (her) sample was selected to the level of specialized services available . . . children residing in school districts with above average per capita income, higher school budget expenditures, and a higher proportion of mental health professionals were found to receive more specialized and expensive services. (p. 52)

The services available are associated with district personnel's perceptions of students' needs. Long's data were obtained through telephone interviews with special education providers, however, so we lack an independent determination of the number of students who may have been undetected, overserved, or underserved in the reporting districts.

Long's study is one of the most recent to attempt to cast light on the important issue of potential need for services in this field. The "traditional" estimate of 2% of the school population as seriously emotionally disturbed is based on little more than that: tradition (Wood & Lakin, 1979a). Bower's (1960) estimate of 10% was shown by Salvia, Schultz, and Chapin (1974) to be an artifact of his screening procedures, which directed teachers to nominate the three most behaviorally disordered students from districts where the average class size was 30 students. After reviewing the major studies of prevalence, including the few that presented data on prevalence in the same population followed over time, Wood and Zabel (1978) summarized as follows.

Based on the high range (prevalence) figures, the overall number of students viewed by their classroom teachers as problems at any one time can be estimated as 20–30% of the general school population. Only a small number of this group, probably close to the low (prevalence) figures of 1.5–3%, continue to arouse concern by their behavior throughout their years in school. Adjustment problems of clinical or educational concern persist for varying, shorter periods of time, often only a few months, for the larger group. (p. 49)

None of these estimates differentiates between students who must be served and those who may be served.

Relationship of Behavioral Disorders to Other Conditions

One of the more confusing aspects of specifying the population of students who are behaviorally disordered and "handicapped in obtaining an education" is to differentiate this group from students with other handicapping conditions as well as from those students classified as deviant by other systems such as mental health or corrections. This section will deal with the special education/mental health/correction relationship.

While the behaviorally disordered population may overlap with the youth seen as appropriate clients by mental health and corrections, these populations are not synonymous. Yet, these systems are interrelated. As Apter (1982) concludes, "The great majority of youngsters identified as emotionally disturbed in school have at least some contact (official or unofficial) with at least one of the other major services delivery systems". (p. 35)

Two recent studies have examined the relationship of mental health diagnostic systems to special education placement. Alexson and Sinclair (1986) examined the psychiatric and educational data on 406 outpatient and 185 inpatient students evaluated in a psychiatric facility. The relationship between patient diagnostic status and change in educational placement following hospitalization was investigated. The most salient finding from this record review was that there was a tendency for such youth to be placed in a more restrictive setting following their stay in the hospital.

Sinclair, Forness, and Alexson (1985) examined the diagnostic and statistical manual (American Psychiatric Association, 1980) diagnostic class sections of Axis I (Clinical Psychiatric) and Axis II (Personality and Developmental Disorders) in 350 children referred to psychiatric evaluation. Diagnostic categories were examined in terms of their relationship to age, sex, ethnicity, IQ, achievement, and special education placement. The authors found that psychiatric diagnosis did not specifically translate into specific educational placements.

After considering the relationship of mental illness to behavioral disorders Kerr and Nelson (1983) conclude:

The behavior of some people is determined by model or emotional pathology, and some behaviors can be understood simply by analyzing them in their immediate context. However, both generalizations can lead to inadequate or inappropriate service to problem students by the educational system. (p. 11)

The legal-correctional system also seems to overlap with special education, yet not be synonymous. Eggleston (1984) conducted an open-ended survey sent to correctional educational administrators throughout the country. Among the questions asked was the prevalence of behaviorally disordered youth in such programs. The percentage reported ranged from 0–90%, with a mean of 35.5%. Earlier, Morgan (1979) had surveyed administrators of 204 state correctional facilities on the same issue. He found an estimated prevalence rate of 16.1% for such youth.

An analysis of the complexities of the diagnostic systems used by the mental health and correctional systems and how they may differ from those used by educators is beyond the scope of this chapter. Each of these systems has its own classification system for designating eligible clients. However, many of the clients identified by the other systems are also identified by the educational system as requiring special education because of behavioral disorders.

The Prospects for Change in Terminology and Definition

Currently there is substantial professional and legal debate regarding the most appropriate term to use in describing those students who are educationally handicapped by unacceptable behavioral patterns. This led Congress, in 1983, to commission a special study to determine the implication of replacing the current terminology used in *P.L. 94–142, serious emotional disturbance*, with the term *behavioral disorders*. In a report recently forwarded to Congress by Secretary of Education William Bennett (Tallmadge, Gamel, Munson, & Hanley, 1985) it was recommended that no change be made in the terminology (serious emotional disturbance) or the definition used to describe such students as contained in *P.L. 94–142*. However, we will present some of the reasons given by professionals for desiring the change from seriously emotionally disturbed to behaviorally disordered.

The research literature indicates that the label "emotionally disturbed" has negative associations for teachers, parents, and students (Antonak, 1980; Harasymiw, Horne, & Lewis, 1976; Tringo, 1970). This label and the label "mentally retarded" consistently fall at the bottom of rank orderings of social acceptability.

Recently Wood (1985) reported a survey of 82 graduate students at the University of Minnesota regarding this topic. The respondents included 30 teachers in regular education and 52 teachers providing special education services. These teachers were asked to rate the social acceptability of various handicapping labels on a scale of 1 (low) to 10 (high), first without the label "behaviorally disordered" and later having that label rated separately. The labels "emotionally disturbed" and "mentally retarded" fell at the bottom in terms of acceptability to this group of teachers. When asked which label they preferred for the group of students currently called "seriously emotionally disturbed," 11 (14%) of the teachers who responded preferred keeping "emotionally disturbed" as the label. Thirty-four (43%) preferred to replace that label with "behaviorally disordered" while 35 (44%) preferred some combination of the two labels. Altogether, 87% of the 80 respondents preferred to include "behaviorally disordered" as part of the label for this educational disability.

Tisdale and Fowler (1983) surveyed 390 classroom public school teachers asking them to estimate the number of behaviorally disordered students in their classrooms according to severity. The survey instrument was a modified version of an earlier instrument used by Kelly, Bullock, and Dykes (1974). Approximately one-half of the teachers received questionnaires which used the term "emotional handicap," and one-half received questionnaires which used the term "behavior disorders." It was found that the label used did, in fact, have an effect on teacher's perceptions of the prevalence of such children in the regular classroom. Teachers were more willing to apply the term "behavior disorders." However, this difference was not noted in those cases of students perceived as needing special classes but rather was noted for those students perceived as being mildly involved and requiring assistance while remaining in the regular class. Such a finding challenges the assumptions made by some that terms such as "behavioral disorders" will lead to increased pressure to place children out of regular classrooms into special education options.

Gresham (1984) advocates the adoption of the term "behavioral disorders." In discussing this he states, "This label reflects more than just a semantic change— it recognizes the fact that the major reason these children are referred and placed is primarily related to their disturbing overt *behaviors* rather than their disturbed emotions" (p. 1). In addition, he states that such a change would lead to an increased use of behavioral versus traditional assessments; a move which he believes is a positive direction in assessment practices.

The Council for Children with Behavioral Disorders (CCBD), a division of the Council for Exceptional Children, in 1984 adopted a position paper advocating the term "behavioral disorders" for *P.L. 94–142* (Huntze, 1985). Among the reasons stated for such a stance are:

1. The term *behavioral disorders* has far greater utility for education than does the term *seriously emotionally disturbed*.

2. The behavioral disorders term is not associated exclusively with any particular theory of causation.

3. The behavioral disorders term will lead to a more comprehensive behavioral assessment that will be used in identifying such students.

4. The behavioral disorders term is less stigmatizing.

5. Professional judgment is in favor of the behavioral disorders term, and

6. The behavioral disorders term is representative of a focus on educational responsibility.

This position paper concludes:

> It is the official position of the Council for Children with Behavioral Disorders that the term behaviorally disordered is more descriptive, more accurate, more useful to educators in identifying and planning appropriate educational placements for students, and will be more socially acceptable than the term seriously emotionally disturbed. (p. 3)

This discussion of the choice of terminology for this population of handicapped learners is not balanced in presenting the seriously emotionally disturbed versus behaviorally disordered positions. It appears that most of the written material available represents those professionals advocating a change to the term behavioral disorders. There also appears to be a lack of empirical data addressing this issue of preferred terminology. We will now review the available descriptions of the social and academic behavior of behaviorally disordered students.

Characteristics of Behaviorally Disordered Students

Summaries of Research The best sources for summaries of earlier research on the characteristics of behaviorally disordered students are educationally-oriented texts such as those of Kauffman (1985) and Cullinan, Epstein, and Lloyd (1983). Early research that has had great influence on the field is that of Wickman (1928), which compared teacher and clinician ratings of the seriousness of problem behaviors, and of Bower (1957, 1960), which built on the earlier work of Ullman (1952, 1957) in developing a screening procedure for early identification of behaviorally disordered students needing special attention. The work of Quay and his colleagues on the description of problem behaviors in children also deserves special mention. For a summary, see Quay (1978).

Social and Emotional Behavior

Social behavior, which involves interactions with others, is directly observable in the classroom. Emotional behavior is not directly observable but is inferred from more overt behavior. Most of the available information on the characteristic social and emotional behavior of behaviorally disordered students exists in the form of ratings by teachers and others, although a small number of direct observation studies have been done. There is of course a vast clinical literature on the social and emotional status of normal and behaviorally disordered children and youth, but little of it pertains specifically to school situations.

A recurrent finding in the literature is that the handicapped populations studied overlap with the nonhandicapped. This has been particularly the case in studies of groups labeled learning disabled. For example, Ysseldyke, Algozzine, and Epps (1983) developed an operational definition of learning disabilities and applied it to nonlabeled and learning disabled students. They reported that "88% of the low-achieving sample [low achieving fourth-graders from regular classes] could be identified as learning disabled and 4% of the learning disabled sample did not meet any of the criteria for classification as learning disabled" (p. 160). Cullinan et al. (1984) report considerable overlap in the Behavior

Problem Checklist scores of nonlabeled and behaviorally disordered students at several grade levels when using 90th and 95th percentile cutoff points (p.17) although it is not as extreme as that reported by Ysseldyke et al., 1982. Sherry (1981–82) and Sherry and Algozzine (1981) report the results of related studies in which behaviorally disordered, learning disabled, and educable mentally retarded students were observed in classroom settings. While the observation period for each student was only 20 minutes in each setting, they found no differences in the problem behavior of the different groups. Boucher and Deno (1979) investigated this issue using a different procedure. The 28 teachers in their population matched 106 statements descriptive of pupil behavior with the behaviorally disordered or learning disabled label. The teachers differentiated between the two labels when making eligibility decisions, but there was considerable overlap when program planning was the focus. Perhaps teachers make the differentiation when focusing on classifications of students, but because the pool of interventions is limited, conceptually "regroup" them when thinking about appropriate programming. Whatever the underlying mechanisms, most of the studies to be cited in this review report differences in the mean problem behavior ascribed by teachers and others to groups with differing labels. In all cases the overlap is considerable.

In 1979, Quay published a summary of research by himself and others using the Behavior Problem Checklist (Quay & Peterson, 1979). The populations studied included nonlabeled school children and youth, children in special behaviorally disordered classes, children seen in child guidance clinics, and juvenile delinquents. Four major clusters of interrelated characteristics which Quay labeled Conduct Disorder, Personality Disorder, Inadequacy—Immaturity, and Socialized Delinquency, accounted for nearly all of the variance. It must be emphasized that these are clusters of characteristics, not population groups. More recently, Epstein et al. (1985) reported the clusters factored from Behavior Problem Checklist scores of 727 behaviorally disordered students aged 6–18. Five clusters emerged consistently in the ratings of the four subgroups of their population (Chronological age: 6–11, 12–18; sex: male, female) which they labeled Aggression–Disruption, Social Incompetence, Social Maladjustment, Attention-Deficit, and Anxiety–Inferiority. Some differences in order of importance differentiated between the sex groups, and for girls 12–18, the Social Incompetence factor was replaced by one labeled Depression. The factors obtained by Epstein et al. are similar to the four factors reported by Quay from the Behavior Problem Checklist and the factor structure is also similar to that reported by Edelbrock and Achenbach (1984) who used another rating scale.

In an earlier paper (Cullinan et al., 1984), individual characteristic ratings by teachers of the same 727 behaviorally disordered students making up the population of the factor study were compared with those of 1,116 non-labeled students. Overall, the mean ratings of the behaviorally disordered group were significantly more negative than those of the nonlabeled group for both sexes and at three school-age levels. Few sex differences were found although males seemed characterized by more "acting out" than females. Age differences obtained could largely be predicted by item characteristics: "stays out late" and "delinquent friends" being among the small number of items associated with older students. Cullinan et al. summarize the description of the behaviorally disordered population derived from the ratings as ". . . one of unhappy youngsters who are behavioral misfits at school, likely to cause the consternation of teachers, and almost certain to be avoided or rejected by their peers". (p. 18)

Such a pattern of negative characteristics associated with behaviorally disordered students is the recurrent finding of rating scale research. Sometimes one part of the pattern is the object of more focused study. For example, Ruhl and Hughes (1985) obtained ratings of the frequency and severity of aggressive acts in behavioral disorders classrooms from 178 public school teachers. Ninety-four per cent of these teachers reported instances of extreme aggression toward classroom objects, and 84% had encountered incidents of extreme aggression toward others. Tallies of aggression incidents kept by a subgroup of 75 teachers confirmed the general pattern of the survey responses. Contrary to their expectations, level of aggression was not related to level of placement.

Some investigations have looked at differences between the behavior of subgroups of students with milder or more severe behavioral disorders disabilities. Sherry and Algozzine (1981) did not observe differences in the frequency of problem behavior shown by behaviorally disordered students in the regular classroom and the resource room, although in a related study, Sherry (1981–82) found that while observations of the frequency of problem behavior failed to differentiate between behaviorally disordered, learning disabled, and educable mentally retarded students, the special education students did show more problem behavior in the regular classroom than the resource room and more than shown by nonlabeled students. Earlier research by Paraskevopoulos (1969) had shown that teacher ratings using the Behavior Problem Checklist differentiated between behaviorally disordered, learning disabled, and nonlabeled groups with the behaviorally disordered groups' rating being the most negative. Gajar (1979) and Cullinan, Epstein, and Dembinski (1979) found that behaviorally disordered groups were rated more negatively than learning disabled and nonlabeled groups on some but not all of the subscales of the Behavior Problem Checklist, particularly the one labeled Conduct Disorder. Olson, Algozzine, and Schmid (1980) approached the question whether teachers can reliably differentiate from among mild, moderate, and severe

behaviorally disordered students more directly by asking teachers to check which of 23 characteristics applied to one or more of these groups. The 175 teachers in their sample showed some agreement for the mild and severe labels, agreement being defined as 50% or more assigning a given characteristic to one of the groups, but failed to reach agreement on any characteristics of the moderate labeled group. Sindelar, King, Cortland, Wilson, and Meisel (1985) recently reported the results of a study in which 169 teachers of learning disabled or behaviorally disordered students in resource or special classrooms indicated the number of students in the classes who showed each of five broad patterns of deviant behavior. The interpretation of the results is somewhat complex, but in general it can be said that the behaviorally disordered students rated in their sample differed from the learning disabled students, but the differences were more quantitative than qualitative in nature. Contributing indirectly to the conclusion that there are identifiable differences between behaviorally disordered, educable mentally retarded, and learning disabled students is Carri's (1985) finding that teachers of behaviorally disordered students indicated needs for different skills/competencies than those indicated by teachers of learning disabled and educable mentally retarded students on a self-rating instrument.

Academic Behavior

Kauffman (1985) summarized his review of literature on the achievement of behaviorally disordered students, "Collectively, research leads to the conclusion that most mildly and moderately disturbed children are academically deficient even when their mental ages, which are typically slightly below those of their chronological age mates, are taken into account" (p. 145). This finding is supported by Cullinan, Epstein, and Lloyd (1983). Gajor (1976) reported a pattern of achievement that is typical when behaviorally disordered students are compared with other disability groups: behaviorally disordered students were rated as characterized by more problem behavior than learning disabled and educable mentally retarded groups but had a higher mean reading achievement score.

Epstein and Cullinan (1983) contrasted the academic performance of 16 behaviorally disordered pupils with the same number of learning disabled pupils. Using the Wide Range Achievement Test (WRAT), the Peabody Individual Achievement Test (PIAT), and the Gilmore Oral Reading Test, it was found that in 10 of 12 comparisons significant differences were found between the behaviorally disordered and learning disabled groups. In all cases, behaviorally disordered pupils were functioning at a higher grade level than were learning disabled pupils.

Other studies have not found significant differences between behaviorally disordered students and other handicapping conditions. Schooler, Beebe, and Koepke (1978) compared learning disabled, mentally impaired, and emotionally impaired students on the WISC-R. Overall it was found that the WISC-R was factorially similar for all groups.

Lower than average mean achievement in students labeled behaviorally disordered may be in part only a function of an eligibility criterion requiring that behaviorally disordered student behavior have an adverse effect on educational performance, and the differences from the learning disabled and educable mentally retarded groups, whose academic deficits should be larger, might also be predicted.

The Accuracy of Labelers

Parents, teachers, peers, and researchers: all of these groups are called upon at times to judge and label the social behavior of students. How accurate are their judgments? Evidence supporting the accuracy of their labeling behavior will be presented in this section of the chapter. Evidence of distortion as a result of bias will be presented in the following section.

Parents

Thomson and Bernal (1982) evaluated the appropriateness of parent labeling of their child's behavior as indicating a conduct problem. Their population included 28 sets of parents who had used this label in applying for treatment for their child at a child treatment center. The researchers sought evidence for the inappropriateness of the conduct problem label that indicated (a) that the label was severely discrepant from the child's actual behavior as observed in the home, or (b) that other identifiable (family) factors, which might explain the label, were present. They concluded that the parents perceived the behavior of their children reasonably accurately.

Teachers

How valid are teacher ratings of student behavior? Teachers are directly interacting with their students on a daily basis. Teachers, like other groups studied, appear to show predictable patterns of bias toward "problem students." In what sense can teacher ratings be considered valid descriptions of student behavior?

The most frequently used criterion against which to judge teacher ratings has been an external one, usually the judgment of mental health clinicians. Using this criterion, Wickman (1928) and other psychologists and teacher trainers condemned teachers for placing too much importance on disruptive, acting out behavior while ignoring withdrawn, anxious behavior, which clinicians believed indicative of serious internal conflict. Beilin (1959) and Bower (1960) are representative of the investigators who questioned this interpretation of the ratings differences as unfairly biased against educators and whose research showed that teachers and clinicians had grown closer together over time as they come to share more congruent pictures of the "reality"

of child behavior. Teachers *are* more disturbed by acting out, disruptive behavior than behavior indicative of anxiety or internalized conflict (Algozzine, 1976, 1977, 1979a; Cullinan et al., 1984; Epstein et al., 1985; Herr, Algozzine & Eaves (1976)). However, this fact does not make their ratings invalid. Much depends on the criterion against which teacher ratings are "validated."

Cullinan et al. (1984) have argued recently that teacher ratings are appropriately validated against an internal criterion, citing the results already mentioned in which ratings of labeled behaviorally disordered students were more negative than those of nonlabeled students. They argue that "actual identification of students for special education is an appropriate criterion against which to judge the definition of behavior disorder and procedures intended to discriminate behaviorally disordered from nondisordered students" (p. 10). Their argument is by analogy from the contention of Achenbach and Edelbrock (1981) that referral for mental health services is an appropriate criterion for ratings of child mental health. Far from being subservient to those of other mental health professionals, in Cullinan et al.'s view teachers' ratings are now their own criterion. Internal validity is thus viewed as more relevant than external validity.

Yet another measure of validity can be obtained by comparing teacher ratings with direct observations of the frequency of occurrence of specified student behavior. Nelson (1971) reported relationships between teacher ratings and the observed frequency of several student classroom behaviors. Barr and McDowell (1972) observed differences in vocalizations and negative physical contacts between behaviorally disordered and learning disabled students. The literature of applied behavioral analysis contains many reports of the relatively high frequency of disapproved social behavior observed for individual students who have previously been labeled behaviorally disordered, usually on the basis of teacher ratings. It has been noted elsewhere that Sherry (1981–82) observed differences in the regular classroom and resource room behavior of behaviorally disordered, learning disabled, and educable mentally retarded students, with negative behavior more common in the regular classroom, but found no differences between the behavior of the labeled groups. In a related study, Sherry and Algozzine (1981) found no differences related to either label or level of placement in the observed behavior of behaviorally disordered and educable mentally retarded students. The findings in the latter two studies may have been affected by the relatively short (20 minute) period of observation in each setting. Perhaps the behavior that contributes to differentiation in labeling by influencing teacher ratings is relatively infrequent in occurrence but salient because of its severity and persistence (Bower, 1982). For whatever reason, research support for a relationship between teacher ratings and observed student behavior seems less robust than that between teacher ratings and other criteria.

Teacher ratings of students as "high risk" show limited predictive validity. Glavin (1972) and Chamberlain (1976) have reported that as few as 30% of the students thus identified were given the same label three years later. Cowen, Pederson, Babigian, Izzo, and Trost (1973) reported that peer ratings were better long-term predictors than teacher ratings.

Clearly many factors besides the passage of time affect the validity of teacher ratings of problem behavior. Facts such as the degree of overlap commonly found in ratings of formally labeled and nonlabeled groups have been noted. However, the evidence on balance supports a conclusion that teachers' ratings of student behavior, like those of parents, can be described as "valid," bearing in mind the criteria used to assess validity in each instance.

Peers

Ullman (1952, 1957) and Bower (1960) found peer ratings of student behavior in the form of a sociometric questionnaire to be useful as one of three pooled indicators of behavioral disorders. (The other two are teacher ratings and self-reports.) Cowen et al.'s (1973) study of the predictive validity of ratings showed that young children appeared to identify troubled peers early. In a study of ratings of peers by first, fourth, and seventh graders, Ledingham, Younger, Schwartzman, and Bergeron (1982) found that not only was interrater agreement consistently higher between peer and teacher ratings than between self-ratings and either but that peer ratings provided the best predictor of deviant behavior.

Researchers

While looking critically at the criteria used by various groups in labeling behaviorally disordered students and the accuracy of their labeling practices, it seems appropriate to mention a study by Lakin (Lakin, 1983; Wood & Lakin, 1979a) of the practices of researchers themselves. Lakin took a random sample of articles appearing in frequently cited journals over a 10-year period up to 1978. The analysis showed that ". . . over 80% of the studies reviewed selected subjects by presence in a setting [designated by the primary label of emotionally disturbed or some variant] or by soliciting and accepting nominations of subjects without any attempt to substantiate, quantify, or qualify the cases of those nominations" (pp. 130–131). Researchers do not seem to be setting a good example for the field.

Factors Influencing Labeling Behavior

The literature contains a large number of studies of the influence of labels on other judgments about behavior. The emphasis in this review is on the more recent literature. For assistance in getting to the earlier literature consult the reviews of literature in papers like Foster and Keech (1977), Ysseldyke and Foster (1978), Algozzine and Sherry (1981), and Hannah and Pliner (1983). Persons planning research on this topic will do well to consult the original reports since multifactored designs are common and findings often need more qualification than is well covered in a brief review.

Before reviewing these studies, a comment is in order. Most of this research is interpreted as demonstrating that negatively-valenced labels applied to normal behavior cause the generalization of negative stereotypes to that behavior. Influenced by the label, subjects view normal behavior as disability. It is important to note that the labels are actually applied to the normal behavior by the researchers rather than the subjects. The social prestige of the researcher is behind the false labeling; the subject can view the behavior as normal only by refusing to accept the label of those who present themselves as knowledgeable, trustworthy professional people. While it seems reasonable to believe that labels have the biasing effect hypothesized, the research that demonstrates that bias is thus somewhat confounded.

Biasing Effect of the BD Label when Contrasted with the Label "Normal" or Other Disability Labels

Parents Stevens-Long (1973) showed 60 parents of elementary school children, mostly mothers, videotaped sequences of overactive, underactive, and average-active child behavior. Half of the parents were told the child was "emotionally disturbed." The parents selected a disciplinary practice to manage the child's behavior and rated their affect toward the child at 10 points during the sequence, 5 of which followed an incident of aggression by the child. Few differences in affective responses related to levels of activity, but the overactive child was punished more severely, aggression led to the prescription of more severe disciplinary interventions, and the label "emotionally disturbed" was associated with a lessening of the severity of discipline suggested. With this group of parents, association with a negatively-valenced label seemed to produce a less blaming response.

Peers Young, Algozzine, and Schmid (1979) showed 96 fourth-grade students a videotape of a normal fourth-grade boy. Subjects were randomly assigned to one of eight conditions (boy labeled learning disabled, behaviorally disordered, mentally retarded, or normal and described as having either positive or neutral attributes). No differences in ratings were associated with the categorical labels, which could be related to subjects' lack of familiarity with the differences between the labeled conditions, but an interaction effect was obtained indicating that adding positive information maintained or increased positive ratings but adding neutral material did not affect negative ratings. In a closely related study, Freeman and Algozzine (1980) found similar results although neutral comments were followed by more negative ratings.

Two other studies help to put these findings in context although neither focused on children's responses to the behavioral disorders label. Foley (1979) showed 78 fourth-grade students a tape of a boy demonstrating several academic and social behaviors, both positive and negative. On one tape, a teacher (sex not stated) reacted positively to the child's behavior; on the other, negatively. The boy was labeled learning disabled, mentally retarded, or normal. In this study, the fourth-graders rated the behavior of the "mentally retarded" boy more favorably than the behavior of the boy under the other labels and rated the boy higher when the teacher responded positively to his behavior. These findings conflict with those just mentioned, giving rise to more questions about the ability of younger children to respond differentially to the negative labels. In this regard, it is worth noting that Siperstein, Budoff, and Bak (1980) found that fifth and sixth-graders responded more negatively to the idiomatic label "retard" than to the clinical label "mentally retarded." Perhaps to get a valid sample of children's responses to labels, researchers must use the labels children use in their own conversation. These labels may be more generic than the adult labels from which they are derived.

Psychologists Javel and Greenspan (1983) reported the results of a mail survey of 195 school psychologists who responded from a pool of 600 chosen at random from the National Association of School Psychologists directory. Subjects responded to one of two case studies of an intermediate grade student. In one case study, histograms provided a picture of the student's competence and problems across 12 ability domains. In the other, the competence information was missing. Student information was labeled learning disabled, behaviorally disordered, or not labeled. Deficit-oriented referral information biased the placement decisions of the psychologists in a negative direction, but the labels were not significantly related to differences in decision. Apparently the psychologists in this sample were more responsive to differences in information than differences in labels, a point that will be noted again during the discussion of teacher response to labels.

Teachers When teachers are given a classification task, for example assigning labels to a list of discrete characteristics, they respond differently to different labels. As already noted, Boucher and Deno (1979) found that teachers discriminated when assigning a list of 106 characteristics to the behavioral disorders or learning disability label. They also tend to reverse the processes. When given a case study of a student with

only the label varied (mentally retarded, behaviorally disordered, juvenile delinquent or nonlabeled), teachers tended to ascribe poorer school performance and outcomes to the labeled student although responding somewhat differently to each of the specific labels (Carroll & Reppucci, 1978). These findings suggest that teachers have pre-established attitudes associated with different labels.

Foster and Keech (1977) showed a 12-minute color videotape of a fourth-grade boy of normal intelligence, academic ability, and appearance performing several academic and nonacademic tasks to 50 elementary level teachers. Half of the teachers were randomly assigned to a treatment condition where the child was labeled mentally retarded, the other half were told he was normal. When asked to complete a teacher referral form for the videotape, teachers rated a hypothetical mentally retarded student more negatively than they rated a hypothetically normal child. After being given neutral information about the child's academic performance and shown the videotape, the differences in the ratings still existed, suggesting the bias created by the label persisted in the face of conflicting information. Foster, Algozzine, and Ysseldyke (1980) reported similar results when the behavioral disorders label was used in a study of similar design. Similar findings are consistently reported by other researchers using any of these labels. For example, Jacobs (1978) found that telling the teachers the child was learning disabled tended to bias their observation of a fourth-grade child's behavior.

Herr et al. (1976) found that exposure to behaviorally disordered students in a training program was related to a decrease in rated disturbingness of problem behaviors, further supporting the hypothesis that teachers' ratings are subject to change as a result of experience or change in environmental conditions. The evidence also suggests that teachers' judgments are more influenced by label while those of psychologists are more influenced by information about behavior.

Other researchers have sought more subtle evidence of the biasing effect. Algozzine, Mercer, and Countermine (1977) varied two conditions of label (learning disability or behavioral disorders) with two conditions of case study material (learning disability or behavioral disorders) and found that "disruptive, aggressive behavior was less tolerable when thought to be the behavior of a learning disabled child rather than an emotionally disturbed child" (p. 131), a finding reminiscent of that Stevens-Long (1973) reported for parents.

Biasing Effects of Race, Socioeconomic Status, and Sex. Other labels applied to students may influence teacher decisions about their eligibility or placement in special education programs. Kelly, Bullock, and Dykes (1977) found that identification of students as emotionally disturbed was related to race, with teachers naming black students twice as frequently as white students in grades K-7, but this difference did not occur in the data for the higher grades. They did not investigate any biasing effect this might have on teachers' decision making. However, Zucker and Prieto (1977) found that special education teachers enrolled in graduate classes were more apt to recommend special class placement for a student described in hypothetical case material as functioning somewhat below grade level academically if the student was also labeled "Mexican-American." In a related study (Prieto & Zucker, 1981), teachers were less apt to reject the statement that "placement in special class for emotionally disturbed students would be appropriate for this child" if the student were labeled "Mexican-American."

Kelly, Bullock, and Dykes (1977) also found that males were perceived by teachers as behaviorally disordered twice as frequently as females. Schlosser and Algozzine (1979) reported that the behaviors rated more disturbing were those associated with boys. Cullinan et al. (1984) and Epstein et al. (1985) found that boys predominated in the population of students from behavioral disorders classes and that behavior of girls in those classes tended to resemble that of the boys. A similar suggestion of sex bias discriminating against males is reported by Bernard and Clarizio (1981). Lower socioeconomic status students were also overrepresented in the behavioral disorders classes in their population. They interpret their data as providing no evidence that this is the result of systematic bias in placement decisions, though. However, Touliatos and Lindholm (1980) reported that students of higher socioeconomic status were rated as exhibiting less deviant behavior than their lower socioeconomic class peers.

Lora v. Board of Education: De Facto Evidence of Bias in Decision Making

Lora v. Board of Education of City of New York was a suit filed in June 1975 on behalf of students in the New York City Public Schools who were placed in special programs because of severe emotional disturbance which had resulted in acting out, aggressive behavior in school settings. The plaintiffs argued that their constitutional and statutory rights were violated by the assessment procedures and special education placements provided to them by the public schools. The main facts and findings in the case have recently been reviewed by Wood, Johnson, and Jenkins (1985).

According to information in the court record, the New York City Public Schools provide education for well over a million students. These students come from homes with widely varying life-styles related to ethnic background as well as socioeconomic level where one of more than 60 different languages or dialects may be the first language of the parents. Using the grosser categories of official statistics, the student population was 36% black, 23% Hispanic, and 41% "other" in 1977. In 1977 there were 9 intermediate level special day high schools for behaviorally disordered students. Together they served a total of 2,094 students. The racial composition of the special day schools was 68% black, 27% Hispanic, and 5% other. In addition, disproportionate numbers of white students were placed in private schools with their tuition paid by the public schools. A survey of private schools done at the request of the court showed that in 1977, ". . . the White population ran from a low of 6 percent to a high of 94 percent and averaged 50 percent White. Forty-five percent of the publicly funded children are White—a striking discrepancy from the 5 percent White students in the special day schools" (*Lora*, 1978, p. 1255). Given this striking disproportional assignment to the special day schools and other evidence about referral, assessment, and placement procedures, the plaintiffs argued that the case involved essentially constitutional issues: racial discrimination and the denial of educational rights. This constitutional question was never resolved by the courts since the case was settled by a consent decree which focused on procedures for minimizing bias in identification and placement of behaviorally disordered students. However, the facts in *Lora v. Board of Education* provide an example of the results of apparent bias in decision making regarding identification and placement of such students. That bias affects decision making has been demonstrated in the research; but bias hurts students as shown by *Lora v. Board of Education.*

General Considerations Affecting Decision-Making in Special Education

Regardless of the value attached to the provision of special education, Algozzine and Ysseldyke (1983) observed an accelerating trend in the numbers of identified handicapped students with a substantial increase in costs since the enactment of *PL 94–142*, although the percentage of students assigned the behavioral disorders label has been more stable (Algozzine & Korinek, 1985).

Some special factors affect decision making when behaviorally disordered students are the focus of concern. As has been previously pointed out, there is considerable circularity in procedures for identifying behaviorally disordered students. To recapitulate, after researchers have described previously identified populations of students, their descriptions become the criteria used to identify the next cohort of students, thus preparing the wheel for another turn. The relative social power of participants affects the decision making process (Wood, 1981). It is easier for teachers to have students labeled behaviorally disordered than vice versa, and it is difficult to explain the disproportionate assignment of minority youth to special education classes without reference to conflicting cultural values and differences in socioeconomic status. Thus, it seems important that the study of the decision making process continue so that means can be developed to make it more likely that students will be placed in behavioral

107

disorders programs only when the capacity of the regular program for accommodating them has been stretched to its limit, and that the special education program alternatives be those from which they can reasonably be expected to show greater benefit. (This view seems to the authors to be consistent with the main thrust of *PL 94–142*, but for a dissenting view see Kauffman, McCullough, and Sabornie, 1984). Unfortunately, there is relatively little research available on decision making regarding behavioral disorders labeling and placement decisions. Therefore, the review that follows looks at research on special education decision making and decision making in general.

Multidisciplinary Team Effectiveness

Special education laws mandate the use of multidisciplinary teams (MDT) to make assessment and placement decisions for handicapped children. However, research evidence is inconclusive regarding whether groups of professionals are more effective than individuals in making decisions. There are advocates supporting the use of MDTs (Hogenson, 1973; Pfeiffer, 1981, 1982) and critics who raise serious questions about the effectiveness, efficiency, and benefits from team assessments and decision making (Wallace, 1976; Yoshida, 1980, 1983).

Since present legal mandates prescribe the use of MDTs, the challenge is to ferret out aspects that contribute to effective team functioning from those that detract from it and propose future directions from this information. The remainder of this section will review four aspects of decision making: (a) data, (b) processes, (c) procedures, and (d) alternatives.

Decision Makers' Data

Decisions can only be as sound as the information on which they are based. Consequently information sources are an important element when considering the adequacy of decision making.

Traditional approaches. Traditions are based on histories of past behavior which have become translated into the expected way of confronting future problems. In terms of special education assessments there are two traditions which live on in present practice: creating a generic information base from which differential diagnoses can purportedly be made, and reliance on norm referenced tests for placement and programming decisions.

Often, in an effort to maximize the efficiency of the MDT's work, reduce duplication of effort, and collect data about students' current level of functioning, a common core of data is routinely assembled on all students, including norm referenced tests of intellectual, motor, academic functioning, plus interview and health information. These data sources form a generic pool of information from which special education categorical diagnoses can be made. The difficulty with this generic information base is its limited applicability. It is primarily organized to determine or discount a disability diagnosis. Furthermore, the kind of information gathered in traditional generic assessment procedure does not provide decision makers with information useful for determining a student's educational needs or the teacher's actions necessary to meet those needs.

Traditional assessment approaches have been a mixed blessing and curse in education. For example, intelligence tests, as norm referenced instruments, were designed to assist in the identification of students who would not profit from instruction. Behavior rating scales are normed to permit classification of some students as showing more problem behavior than the general school population. Using this procedure, a student can be compared with others in the normative group and judgments made about the relative standing of the individual in relationship to peers. Such instruments provide a theoretically sound basis for comparing students with others of the same age and background characteristics. This strength is also the weakness of the approach. The technical adequacy of many commonly used norm referenced instruments has been questioned (Salvia & Ysseldyke, 1981), especially for students whose cultural background, language, educational experience, and other factors are sufficiently dissimilar from the normative group to consider comparison with that group inappropriate (Mercer, 1973, 1979). However, Rosenbach and Mowder (1981) argue that tests of academic aptitude, which are designed to predict school performance, are relevant because the validity coefficients for such tests are highly related to school success, which suggests that if bias is operative then it is inherent in the nature of the educational institution not the evaluative instrument.

Sapp, Chissom, and Horton (1984) investigated the ability of the WISC, Key Math, and a teacher rating scale to discriminate between students identified as educable mentally retarded, behaviorally disordered and learning disabled. They found that intelligence quotients differentiated between educable mentally retarded and the behaviorally disordered and learning disabled groups, but these data did not differentiate between behaviorally disordered and learning disabled students. Further, the teacher ratings did not significantly distinguish between behaviorally disordered and learning disabled groups. Thus, traditional data, as the sole source of information, may fail to include data that differentiates among students according to the severity of their behavioral disorders problems.

The solution is not to abandon norm referenced assessments but to consider carefully how the information they provide relates to the questions being asked. Technically adequate instruments are abused when diagnosticians attempt to use normative data for programmatic purposes just as using solely informal and unstandardized data for placement purposes (Reschly,

1980, 1982) is poor practice. MDTs need appropriate data for sound decision making, both norm referenced and informal, and should look for convergence of the information from multiple sources (Gresham, 1983). Sensitivity to client specific variables and availability of suitable measurement devices is essential when designing assessment strategies which yield useful decision making data.

Innovative approaches. The MDT should determine the questions which need to be answered, then tailor the data collection to address those specific questions (Batsche, 1983, 1984; Reschly, 1983; Salvia & Ysseldyke, 1981). Useful assessments are individualized, created to investigate the presenting problems, rather than global factors which would only be helpful to the MDT in considering eligibility and differential diagnosis. It appears that the trinity of meaningful questions, purposeful assessments, and sound decision-making could be a refreshing change from the traditional approach.

Additionally, there are innovative approaches to assessment which hold promise for collecting educationally meaningful information about students' progress useful for instructional and placement decisions. Three illustrations are the Data Based Program Modification (DBPM) discussed by Fuchs, Deno, and Mirkin (1983), AIMSTAR (Hasselbring & Hamlett, 1983), and Developing Models for Special Education (DMSE) reported by Bergquist (1982).

DBPM provides a method of continuous curriculum-based evaluation derived from frequent samples of classroom behavior (Jenkins, Deno, & Mirkin, 1979). This information can be stored on a computer program, available for a progress review and graphic depiction of behaviors across time. Using this system in regular education classrooms has proven a reasonable means of comparing students' progress with other classmates on the same classroom tasks and cues teachers when a referral may be approriate (Marston, Mirkin, & Deno, 1984). Since referral information is a source of data in the decision making process and has been a source of concern (Algozzine & Ysseldyke, 1983), the Marston et al. (1984) research presents a promising possibility for solution of this perplexing problem. Curriculum-based measurements were compared with the teacher referral method in this study with 1,374 students, and curriculum-based measures avoided the problems of teacher bias which were involved in teacher made referrals. Both referral and curriculum-based methods identified approximately the same number, but different students.

AIMSTAR (Hasselbring & Hamlett, 1983) provides a means of managing data about student behavior and plotting improvement trends. Child specific data is plotted on a semilogarithmic chart. Decision rules are incorporated into the computer program to assist educators in selecting appropriate instructional strategies (Haring, Liberty, & White, 1980). The computer program prompts the teachers when their rate of behavior change

strategy is not producing significant results. The decision making process is augmented through the use of computer technology.

The DMSE project reports a study of 37 students considered high-risk candidates for exceptional programs (Bergquist, 1982). While remaining in regular classes period assessments were conducted and, based on trend data, a referral for special education may be initiated. The time series monitoring keeps track of student progress without unwarranted and costly involvement of the MDT. Six of the 37 students were placed in special education programs by the end of the school year.

These three programs illustrate a class of experimental assessment and data management models which are alternatives to the traditional approach. To date, their utility for assessing social and emotional behavior has not been fully developed, but there is enough done to suggest future promise. It is important to note that these innovative methods are not independent of the MDT process, rather they assist professionals in considering data from an alternative perspective, which may lead to more appropriate decision making. Common to these approaches is the assumption that frequent monitoring of behavior in a classroom setting is preferable to global assessments of social behavior, abilities, and achievement.

Decision Makers' Processes

Process refers to how decisions are made. It is analogous to how the digestive system breaks down food to extract nutrition. Likewise, good decisions nourish the educational system.

The MDT, including the parents, are intended to establish agreement on the child's current level of functioning, plan of service, and educational goals for the student. This process, involving people who are forming opinions, may result in varied personal perspective of the same data. Ysseldyke, Algozzine, Richey, and Graden (1982) reviewed 20 videotapes of MDT staffings and concluded that objective data and recognized diagnostic criteria were frequently disregarded and opinions of MDT members dominated the decision making process. This conclusion was supported by Epps, McGue and Ysseldyke (1982) where 18 judges reviewed data from 99 students, 50 of whom had been identified as learning disabled, and generally found a lack of interjudge agreement regarding the diagnosis. Professionals, in groups and individually, reviewing the same data appear to apply different criteria when deciding whether a child is handicapped.

There is substantial research identifying areas where educational decision makers may operate from biased perceptions which affect conclusions, classifications and placement of children in special education. This point is illustrated by Ysseldyke and Algozzine (1981) when they determined that information stated in the referral influenced the classification of students identified as emotionally disturbed (behaviorally disordered). When the referral statement indicated that the student had a behavior problem, according to this study involving 224 school professionals, the classification of behavioral disorders was more influenced by that information than test results indicating average functioning. Demographic or personal characteristics of the student have also been shown to influence teachers' attitudes towards students. Examples are socioeconomic status (Neer, Foster, Jones, & Reynolds, 1973), race (Jackson & Cosca, 1974; Prieto & Zucker, 1981), ethnic background (Zucker & Prieto, 1977), physical appearance (Dion, 1972), opinion of intelligence (Algozzine, Mercer, & Countermine, 1977; Giesbrecht & Routh, 1979), sex (Jackson & Lahaderne, 1967), and information about siblings receiving special education (Sydney & Minner, 1983). Thus, professionals involved in the case decision making process appear to be more influenced by some kinds of information than other kinds.

Yoshida (1980) reviewed a series of interrelated studies identifying barriers to effective team functioning. Fenton, Yoshida, Maxwell, and Kauffman (1979) surveyed 1,535 MDT members in Connecticut and established that team members did not hold uniform perceptions of the goals of the MDT effort, which raises the question: Can teams accomplish their task if individuals within a group do not share a common goal? This study raises concern about that possibility. Perception of roles of MDT members were studied by Yoshida (1980b) who found ambiguity in perceptions within and across professional group members. Can team members function effectively if they do not have a shared understanding of the roles, tasks, and responsibilities of the other team members? Yoshida's conclusions raise concerns on this point. Another investigation (Yoshida, Fenton, Maxwell, & Kauffman, 1978) looked at the extent of participation and satisfaction of team members. They concluded that different professions had varied amounts of perceived participation in team activities and that satisfaction was not simply related to participation. Required attendance with little involvement often resulted in negative attitudes about the process. Can MDTs function as effective decision making teams if members have differential input and satisfaction? In summary, the literature regarding the MDT process indicates there are problems which must be addressed.

The difficulties experienced in establishing an effective decision making group is, in part, a function of insufficient and inadequate preparation for the task. Members of the MDT need appropriate training, skills and knowledge to function effectively (Knoff, 1983a; Pfeiffer, 1981). Yoshida and Abramson (1982) found fewer than 35% of teachers had inservice or preservice preparation for working as part of a decision making team. Poland, Thurlow, Ysseldyke, and Mirkin (1982) reported that out of 100 directors of special education, half indicated information on decision making was provided to decision making MDT members, but only two indicated their staff received training in decision making skills. Numerous inservice training models and concepts

have been proposed for school personnel (Anderlini, 1983; Knoff, 1983a, 1983b; Pfeiffer, 1981).

Decision Makers' Procedures

Present procedure. Complex systems, such as schools, rely on procedures to help order how services are provided. Federal laws, state rules and regulations, and local operational procedures provide the framework in which educational decision making occurs.

State and local educational agencies have developed and disseminated procedural manuals to aid in the assessment, identification and programming for handicapped children (for example, Florida State Department of Education, 1978; Smith & Grimes, 1979; Wood, Smith, & Grimes, 1985). Despite such efforts, marked variability exists in how regulations are implemented by directors of special education (Poland, Thurlow, Ysseldyke, & Mirkin, 1982).

Poland et al. (1982) surveyed 100 directors of special education across the United States regarding major steps in the assessment and decision making activities. There was 63% or higher agreement of some steps, such as child referral, assessment, and development and implementation of individualized education programs. Other steps, including some required by law (for example, parental consent for preplacement evaluation), showed under 50% agreement that these were part of the agencies' procedures. The same variability was found by Perlmutter and Parus (1983) in reviewing 14 school districts. They determined that a lack of uniformity existed in management of initial referrals, testing, and diagnostic criteria utilized in classifying learning disabled students. The concern is that inconsistent and contradictory procedures contribute to different diagnoses of children.

The precision with which identification and eligibility criteria are applied is a source of concern. More than 45% of the students enrolled in Colorado's learning disability programs did not meet the state criteria for placement (Shepard & Smith, 1981). This result is in agreement with Algozzine and Ysseldyke's (1983) finding that 51% of the learning disabled students in their study did not meet placement criteria. Further, Ysseldyke, Algozzine, Shinn, and McGue (1982) found no significant difference between low achievers and identified learning disabled students. Although all of these studies pertain to learning disabled rather than behaviorally disordered students, they suggest the lack of consistency in decisions made by special education MDTs.

Several studies concluded that MDTs do not use a systematic problem solving approach (Fenton, Yoshida, Maxwell, & Kauffman, 1979; Kabler & Genshaft, 1983), which may in part account for the variance in classification decisions and identification rates. There are systematic problem solving models, emphasizing different approaches which MDTs could utilize in refining decision making skills: Essential tasks to complete in arriving at a solution (Fenton, Yoshida, Maxwell, & Kauffman, 1979), decision making activities (Kabler & Carlton, 1982), decision analysis (Maher, 1981, 1983), and improved communication through reducing cognitive dissonance (Spadafore, 1976) have been described.

Administrative philosophy, commonly embedded in district policies and guidelines, affects how MDTs perceive their tasks. Lawler (1984) points out the differential effects on the decision making process if psycho-educational assessments are organized to meet functional in contrast to purposeful goals. Assessment data in the first category serves one primary function: to determine if the student is eligible for special education programs. Functional assessment data, typically the product of traditional assessments, limit the range of considerations of the student's difficulty to the narrow focus of the program eligibility. In contrast, purposeful assessments are designed to address the specific concerns of the school personnel or parents. Such data may not be an adequate basis for eligibility decisions. Once again, it appears that effective MDTs must think carefully about the appropriateness of their procedures in general, and also when applied to each individual case.

Alternative approaches. What alternatives exist, other than having MDTs "try harder"? Computer programs have been developed to assist with educational decisions. Of special note is the use of artificial intelligence applications embodied in expert systems, programs designed to emulate the logic used by experts when arriving at a solution to a specific class of problems. Pioneering efforts to apply expert systems in education have focused on the diagnosis of spelling problems (Hasselbring, 1984; Hasselbring & Crossland, 1982; Hasselbring & Owens, 1983) and reading comprehension difficulties (Colbourn & McLeod, 1983). Duba and Shortliffe (1983) believe that the expert systems approach can be applied whenever a significant body of specialized, empirical, and factual knowledge exists. Thus, educational diagnosis, and perhaps behavioral treatment plans to alleviate the problem behavior, could be a focus of future expert system designs.

More specific to the identification process are systems for diagnosing handicapping conditions. An example is the McDermott Multidimensional Assessment of Children (M.MAC), marketed by Psychological Corporation (1985), which uses student specific descriptions, background, and test data to formulate probability statements useful in establishing a differential diagnosis of a handicapped child. Such procedures may in the future offer a scientifically plausible approach to decision making that will minimize external bias. However, there is also the possibility of error built into the programming "logic" which is not readily apparent to the user, but nonetheless affects probability statements offered to the program user.

Expert systems and artificial intelligence programs can, within limits, offer a new approach to information analysis and problem solving which augments, but cannot effectively replace, the MDT's thoughtful consideration of a student's unique circumstances. No single set of decision making rules can be established to encompass all of the possible combinations of circumstances affecting handicapped children. However, expert systems could be developed to give counsel to the MDT within a prescribed range of problems.

Decision Maker's Alternatives

If it is determined that a student has an educationally significant problem, then the MDT typically considers service alternatives that may be utilized to assist the student. The broader the options the more likely the student will receive the most appropriate needed service, rather than merely the best immediately available service.

Services available in the educational community consist primarily of special education, compensatory education, volunteer programs, and modifications with regular education classes. There are variations within each of these service options.

A concern about general education's overreliance on special education has been noted by the National Task Force on Learning Disabilities (Chalfant, 1985). Support for this position also was documented by Algozzine and Ysseldyke (1983). If special education is viewed as the only option for children with learning and behavioral needs, then costs will continue to rise until funding for special education is legislatively restricted. What seems to be needed is a clearer delineation between roles, responsibilities, and service possibilities of special and regular education, respectively.

Typically the 'cascade of service' models assume that regular educators are passive partners in the problem solving process. Beginning the process in this manner suggests that problems can only be solved with the expertise of special educators. However, Chalfant & Psych (1981) have demonstrated in a study with 200 students with behavioral and academic difficulties that over 66% of these concerns could be resolved through consultation with Teacher Assistance Teams (TAT) composed solely of regular education personnel working together. Further, when referrals for possible placement were needed, the rate of eligibility was 100% in this study. The TAT approach appears to expand effectively the problem solving potential available for teachers while reducing unrealistic reliance on special education personnel to solve all difficulties involving students with unique behavior patterns.

A related concern is the overlap of educational services. Most service agencies, including the public schools, have as a goal the integrating of human services for children and families. However, this goal is easier to express than find in practice (Newman & Simpson, 1983). Special education administrators should encourage related service personnel to assist regular educators in working with problem children. Pryzwansky & Rzepski (1983), are proponents of increased consultation, targeting classrooms and total systems, as a means of bringing about change for individuals and groups.

Guidelines for Decision Making

This section of our research analysis will examine and specifically discuss: (1) traditional versus behavioral approaches to assessing behaviorally disordered students; (2) the types of data used in decision making; (3) the role of various persons in the identification process, and (4) the process of identification.

Traditional versus Behavioral Approaches

The assessment of behavioral deviance has been widely debated in the field of psychological assessment. At the heart of much of this debate has been the question of whether behavior is consistent across settings or whether most behavior can only be defined on the basis of the setting in which it occurs. As Hartmann, Roper, and Bradford (1979) point out, there are varying assumptions, implications, and uses of data, depending on whether one approaches the assessment task from a behavioral (state emphasis) or a traditional (trait emphasis) perspective.

The state theorists (Goldfried & Kent, 1972; Mischel, 1969; Nelson, Hay, & Hay, 1977) tend to view deviant behavior as being under the control of the immediate environment with deviance being highly changeable from one setting to another. Representing the state approach, Nelson, Hay, and Hay (1977) contend that behavior is a dynamic process. According to these researchers, behavioral assessment is not, nor should be, based on generalizability from one setting to another. In contrast to these views of deviance are those of the trait theorists (Alker, 1972; Eysenck, Easting, & Eysenck, 1970; Graham, Rutter, & George, 1973; Watt, Stolorow, Lubensky, & McClelland, 1970). According to this view deviance is a constant variable across settings.

More recently, it appears that both views (state and trait) are regarded as partially correct (Bowers, 1973; Goldfried, 1977; Mischel 1975). Alker (1972) advocates the view that the importance of the state or trait stance may vary according to the population being examined. With hospitalized or severely disturbed individuals the trait or cross-situational assessment may be relevant. A second population, more sensitive to situational variation, may be more appropriately assessed via state or behavioral measures. Thomas (1981) contends that it is important to look at the interaction of these components. His contention, more recently supported by Kagen (1984), is that temperament cannot be expected to show linear continuity over time unless there is total stability in all contributing factors, including environmental influences, motivations, and abilities.

These differing ways of viewing behavioral deviance lead to confusion regarding the means by which students in the school setting are best identified for special education programs. If one approaches childhood behavioral deviance from a purely trait viewpoint, the use of assessment tools such as personality and affective measures, checklists/rating scales would seem appropriate. If, instead, one approaches behavioral deviance from a state viewpoint, such tools as objective observation and setting analysis would seem appropriate.

Types of Data Used

Recently, various scholars (Cowen, 1980; O'Leary & Johnson, 1979; Patten, 1976; Ysseldyke, 1978) have advocated the use of data obtained from multiple sources when making eligibility decisions. This expert opinion is reflected in the regulations implementing P.L. 94–142 which require the use of multiple sources of data to determine if a student is handicapped. These regulations state that "no single procedure shall be the sole criteria for determining an appropriate educational program for a child" (Federal Register, 1977, p. 42497).

In the area of behavioral disorders, several other considerations reinforce the value of making eligibility decisions from multiple data sources: (a) the "deviance" of the behavior may be dependent upon the tolerance level of the person who is making this judgment (Algozzine, 1980; Wood, 1981); (b) references about a child's behavioral difficulties included in referral information may bias the classification outcome (Algozzine, 1979a); (c) students may be viewed more negatively when they are believed to be handicapped (Ysseldyke & Foster, 1978); and (d) factors such as the education program which is available for a youngster may influence the placement decision (Holland, 1980).

Health, academic, and intelligence data. Information relevant in assessing a behaviorally disordered student may include health related, academic, and intellectual assessments as well as information about social and emotional status. Various physical disorders have been shown to be associated with behavioral deviance within the school setting (Feingold, 1975; Hoffer, 1973; Villee & Dethier, 1971). As mentioned earlier, academic deficits have frequently been pointed out as a salient characteristic among behaviorally disordered students (Cullinan, Epstein, & Lloyd, 1983; Kauffman, 1985). Other researchers (Clarizio & Veres, 1983; Hamm & Evans, 1978) have examined the feasibility of using intellectual test information (WISC-R patterns) in diagnosing such students although the use of such cognitive measures as a single source of assessment with behaviorally disordered populations seems not to be promising.

It would appear that comprehensive information such as health, academic, and intellectual assessments are useful in behavioral disorders assessment for the purposes of ruling out factors that may be contributing to the behavioral difficulties. Utility in differential diagnosis beyond this screening function would seem to be limited. Recently, Smith, Frank, and Snider (1984) reported that these three areas of data collection were judged as being of relatively low value in the behavioral disorders identification process by a sample of 120 behavioral disorders teachers and school psychologists.

Social and emotional data. More useful in the behavioral disorders identification process are social functioning data, behavioral rating scales, objective observations, setting analysis data, affective data, and parental perceptions of behavioral patterns.

Each of these types of data tends to focus on viewing deviant behavior from various perspectives. In assessing social functioning, the diagnostic procedures employed focus on the environment, peer and target child rather than only the perceived deviant child. Behavioral rating scales elicit information from significant others (teachers, counselors, principals, parents, etc.) in a child's or adolescent's environment regarding their perceptions of the subject's behavioral normality or deviance. Objective observation involves the tabulation of the actual occurrence or nonoccurrence of deviant behaviors manifested by a targeted pupil. The collection of setting analysis data emphasizes a study of the setting from which a pupil is being referred. Affective data collected in the identification of behaviorally disordered students is used to determine a referred pupil's feelings and attitudes towards school. Home and family data can provide insight into the intensity, duration and consistency of inappropriate behavior observed in the school setting from the parent's perspective. A more detailed description of each of these areas of data collection can be found in Wood, Smith, and Grimes (1985).

Role of Persons Involved in Identification Process

In addition to professional support for the concept (Marcus, Fox, & Brown, 1982), there are requirements under P.L. 94–142 to involve several people in decision making regarding the eligibility of referred students and planning appropriate programs for students deemed to be eligible. Regarding the evaluation component of this process, the regulations state: "The evaluation is made by a multidisciplinary team or groups of persons, including at least one teacher or other specialist with knowledge in the area of suspected disability" (Federal Register 1977, p. 42497).

Although the involvement of several persons in decision making regarding the student's handicap status and programming needs appears to be well founded, this may further complicate the identification of behaviorally deviant school-age pupils. Starting with the classic Wickman study (1928), literature related to perceptions of childhood deviance is filled with discrepant opinions regarding the actual deviance and needs of the students in question. Some of the literature regarding accuracy of labelers and biasing factors has already been reviewed. Discrepancies between the judgments of students and professionals (Adelman, Taylor, Fuller, & Nelson, 1979; Mutimer & Rosemier, 1967), between parents and professionals (Adelman et al., 1979; Auger, 1975; Morris & Arrant, 1978), and between types of professionals (Fremont, Klingsporn & Wilson, 1976; Ullman et al., 1981; Walsh & O'Connor, 1968) have been reported. Such a wide variance in the perceptions of what is deviant behavior clearly suggests the need for intergroup agreement among decision makers in the public schools.

The Process of Identification and Placement

Several recent publications have advocated specific procedures to be followed in the identification of behaviorally disordered students. Gresham (1983) proposes a model to assess such students using direct observations, rating scale, and interview data. He also advocates that diagnosticians must look for the convergence of data to make eligibility decisions. Eaves (1982) advocates a similar model stressing the collection of data from the environment via screening devices and from the child via systematic observation schedules. Wood, Smith, and Grimes (1985) present the Iowa model that requires a look at setting analysis data, pupil behavioral data, and individual trait data. These models are based on pooled experience, and their utility has not been systematically researched. The research literature does provide some evidence of the state of the art in this area, however.

Adelman (1978) attempted to gather information from the original diagnosticians (physicians, psychiatrists, psychologists, etc.) regarding the means by which diagnostic determinations were made for a group of 15 students served in a special school setting. He concluded that only 1 diagnosis out of 15 resulted from a consistent pattern of test findings. Over half of the diagnoses were based primarily on observation, while a third were arrived at despite contradictory evidence. In addition, he found that a large portion of such youngsters were actually "identified" by parents and teachers with merely a verifying diagnosis being provided from outside professionals.

Peterson and Hart (1978) evaluated a state-wide system for the identification of educationally handicapped children through the use of a multiple discriminant function analysis. The assessment information upon which diagnostic specialists based their classification decisions was used concurrently to predict the classification decisions which the diagnosticians made for 477 children representing school districts throughout the state of Utah. The results indicated that the mentally retarded, culturally disadvantaged, and slow learner groups could be differentiated from the no significant problem group, but the distinctions between the labeled handicapped groups were based almost entirely on the variables of full scale IQ and race. Two other classifications, learning disabled and emotionally handicapped, could not be efficiently identified statistically, and the consistency of standards employed for these classifications was questioned.

Waddell (1980) reported on the procedures used to identify behaviorally disordered students in the state of Ohio. The results of a survey mailed directly to persons operating programs described varying levels of assessment of required domains and a heterogeneous methodology regarding types of data gathered.

A series of studies examined the types of data used to identify behaviorally disordered students in the Midwest (McGinnis, Kiraly, & Smith, 1984; Smith, Frank, & Snider, 1984; Zabel, Peterson, Smith, & White, 1981). These studies raise serious concerns regarding the adequacy of information used to identify behaviorally disordered students in the schools. Within these studies it was found that traditional types of information (IQ, achievement, health related) were more likely to be present and to be of higher quality than behaviorally oriented information such as systematic observations, checklist/rating scales or sociometric measures. In addition, with the Smith et al. (1984) study that used files of previously identified students, it was found that the majority of such files were considered to contain inadequate information for the eligibility decision made in the judgment of behavioral disorders teachers and psychologists viewing such files.

Hocutt, Cox, and Polosi (1984) reported findings from site visits to eight local districts in seven states. Among the conclusions related to behavioral disorders identification and programming were: (1) a general confusion was present regarding the differentiation of behaviorally disordered pupils from socially maladjusted pupils; (2) a perception that behavioral disorders identification was more a judgment call than other categories of special education often involving expert opinions of professionals external to the school system; and (3) that behavioral disorders programs had more problems and received more criticism than other types of special education programs.

Wood, Johnson, and Jenkins (1985) recently reviewed the major recommendations regarding assessment and placement procedures intended to eliminate bias in decision making made in the final order in the case of *Lora v. Board of Education* (1984). The standards and procedures for nondiscriminatory assessment and decision making embody several important principles. Important among them are some that are familiar, such as the student's right to placement in the least restrictive setting where an appropriate education is assured and due process guarantees for both students and parents. Because of the facts in *Lora vs. Board of Education*, due process rights related to linguistic, cultural, or ethnic background differences are given detailed attention in the standards and procedures. The court and the parties to the final order accepted the

opinion of experts that no procedures exist that permit objective determination that a student is emotionally disturbed or behaviorally disordered to an extent requiring a special education placement. The fundamental decisions about the existence of disturbance are made subjectively. Experts on best current practice agree that decision making regarding assessment and placement should be done by well-trained professionals, sensitized to watch for bias in their procedures and data, in situations where they have the input of fully informed parents and their chosen advocates. Given the impossibility of avoiding subjectivity in the process, the procedures and standards include requirements that stress professional responsibility. Professionals are required by the final order to leave a "paper trail" describing the activities leading to their decisions as well as the decisions themselves. The individual or team responsible for specific assessment information or decisions must sign off and be prepared to justify those actions publicly should monitoring by supervisors designated by the Board of Education lead to evidence of disproportions in placement such as those which led to this case. In turn, the Board and central administrators have the responsibility to provide staff with the guidance and training needed to make sound decisions.

Conclusion

Gerry (1984) stated that three criteria must be met in the identification of behaviorally disordered students. These are: (1) the determination that there is the presence of a *condition* described as behavioral disorders, (2) that the said condition has an *adverse* effect on education, and (3) that special education and related services are *needed*. The further step toward placement requires attention to additional criteria of appropriateness, minimal restrictiveness, and educational benefit. From this review of the literature on the identification and placement process for such students it appears that there are serious theoretical and applied problems in implementing effective, nonbiased procedures in identification and placement in a consistent manner. There is strong legal and research support for using a multifaceted assessment model but effective implementation of this model has proved difficult. Without continuing checks on procedure, identification and placement teams may easily fall into the patterns of biased decision making which research has shown to be typical of unreflective professional behavior.

Summary and Recommendations
Research

The authors of this chapter have attempted to synthesize the findings of the best of the research available on procedures for identifying and placing behaviorally disordered students. As pointed out in the first few pages, most of this research is characterized by inadequate descriptions of populations and procedures so that any synthesis may appear more solidly based than it is in fact. We have made some progress in measuring the problem, but we have not probed very far beneath its surface. As a result, our summary of findings is brief and overshadowed by recommendations for additional, and hopefully better specified research.

1. The research reflects discrepancies between the estimated prevalence of behavioral disorders problems and numbers of students labeled behaviorally disordered. Prevalence reports may be lowered by noneducational factors such as the legal requirement that identified students be given appropriately labeled service, and parent and student resistance to use of a negatively-valenced label. Some students with mild or moderate behavioral disorders may be receiving appropriate educational service under no label or other labels. Research efforts aimed at screening entire school populations for actual incidence of disturbed and disordered behavior should be undertaken in districts that have been guaranteed temporary protection from penalties for nonlabeling or mislabeling of students. The goal of such screenings would be the collection of data regarding actual rates of occurrence of problem behavior within school-age populations and behavioral and educational needs assessments of the students identified. Students currently placed in correctional facilities should be included in the surveys. The results of such surveys in a systematically selected, representative group of school districts would provide a more adequate base for the discussion of service needs for behavioral disorders type students.

2. A related research issue arises from suggestions by some researchers on decision making that local district or multidisciplinary team factors influence identification and placement in complex interactions with the characteristics of students themselves. Study of decision making where behavioral disorders behavior is of central concern, similar to that undertaken with a focus on learning disability behavior, should lead to a better understanding of this issue.

3. Some research findings suggest that students labeled behaviorally disordered by the schools may be identified as deviant by other social agencies (mental health, corrections, chemical dependency). Research on prevalence should give attention to this issue. Particular attention will need to be given to establishing common nomenclature across such systems to facilitate this effort.

4. The primary source of descriptive information about students labeled behaviorally disordered is teachers' ratings. There is abundant research evidence demonstrating that such ratings are frequently selectively biased, and teachers have been shown to change their ratings as a result of environmental manipulations. Additional research in this area should focus on the issues of "under what conditions" rather than "yes" or "no" and on evaluating the effectiveness of alternative

procedures for minimizing bias related to sex, socioeconomic status, race, culture, and language differences.

5. The research literature indicates that teachers respond strongly to aggressive, acting out behavior. For example, while the social and academic behavior of students labeled behaviorally disordered overlaps with that of students labeled learning disabled or educable mentally retarded, and also that of nonlabeled students, the social behavior of behaviorally disordered students is typically more aggressive and disruptive than that of the other groups of students. What services are provided for less aggressive behaviorally disordered students? Research should be conducted to ascertain whether less aggressive and disruptive disturbed students are not receiving appropriate service, or whether they receive service without labeling or under other labels.

6. Fine tuning of educational practice requires study of the specific needs of subgroups of the behaviorally disordered population. To date, many researchers do not describe the populations that are targets for their interventions in sufficient detail. Some districts group behaviorally disordered students on the basis of differential assessments, but the reasons for such groupings and their relationships to appropriate educational treatments have received little attention. We do not know what interventions work best with different groups of behaviorally disordered students. More attention to subgroup specification and the interaction of subgroup characteristics with interventions is needed.

7. The literature indicates a trend toward gathering data for decision making through more than one procedure and from multiple sources. Multiple source assessment is difficult and costly. Research should continue on the cost/utility of different types of data for educational decision making. Structuring decision making by stages rather than using a predetermined battery of assessment procedures is an approach deserving further study. The ultimate question to be considered is the correlation between quality of assessment information and quality of decision making.

8. Also needed is continuing research on alternative methods for data collection with a view toward reducing cost whenever quality is not compromised. For example, what are the critical features to note and record when observing student-teacher interaction? Is a minimal record sufficient? How does the extensiveness of the record needed interact with the presence or absence of the person doing the observation from the multidisciplinary team meeting?

9. Commonly, in research about decision making, the identification of experts and expertness is inferred from professional certification or current employment. Common sense suggests that all teachers, all psychologists, and all special education directors are not equally capable decision makers. Utilizing the concepts of Gilbert (1978), researchers might focus their study on exemplary decision makers. An exemplar, in this case, would be one whose decisions are valued by others for

their fairness and effectiveness. Similarly, systems might be identified where decision making procedures meet the requirements laid down in *Lora v. Board of Education* (Wood, Johnson, & Jenkins, 1985). Peer nomination supplemented by evidence of parent and student satisfaction would play a role in selection of exemplars.

10. Expert systems, such as those discussed by Hasselbring (1984), could be developed to assist multidisciplinary teams in reviewing decision making options and conclusions. Comparison of alternative process and conclusions reached by different multidisciplinary teams chosen as exemplars when reviewing the same case might help establish the amount of variance to be expected in high quality decision making.

11. The focus of this chapter has been on identification and initial placement. Decisions at this stage of educational intervention are critical. However, other aspects of special education service also need study. Multidisciplinary teams are involved in annual reviews, graduation staffings, exit staffings, and other decision making activities. How do teams decide when a behaviorally disordered student is ready for placement in a less restrictive setting or reintegration into a regular classroom? We need to know.

12. Evaluation of long as well as short-range outcomes of decisions is also important in the validation of exemplary decision making.

Practice

Given the state of research on identification and placement, exemplary practice at present should be viewed as based only in part on soundly demonstrated principles. To a varying degree, this must be supplemented by the judgment of experienced clinicians. The manual on assessment and placement practice recently developed by the Iowa Department of Public Instruction (Wood, Smith, & Grimes, 1985) is an example of an effort to build an approach drawing on the best of research knowledge and clinical skill.

To conceptualize special education practice involving processes as complex as those required for decision making, present models will not be adequate. In a recent article, Pribram (1985) has suggested that psychologists may be ready to move toward a more "holistic" model for conceptualizing their knowledge, as a model which will bring greater rigor to such blendings of research and practice. Such a model might borrow from the perspective of 20th century physicists, who have pointed out "the similarity of their findings with those of the Veda and Upanishads and other spiritual disciplines," so as to allow us to "model psychological processes as diverse as imaging and intuition, as respectable as sensory psychophysics, and as non-sensical (non-sensory) as mystical experience" (p. 6). In the meantime, practice is probably more determined by teacher socialization to a group norm than by research. The recommendations which follow reflect the belief that socialization should

be to a "best practice" model that draws from an experience wider than that of the teachers in a single program or school district.

1. Continuing inservice should be provided to professionals involved in the assessment of students referred because of problem behavior interfering with educational progress. Training should cover data collection procedures, weighing the relative importance of conflicting data collected from different sources or using different procedures, and ways for checking for bias in assessment (Wood, Johnson, & Jenkins, 1985; Ysseldyke, 1978).

2. Multidisciplinary teams should develop and use comprehensive listings of school, community, regional, and state resources when planning for students with behavioral difficulties. Such listings will inform the team of the variety of possible programs and services available for behaviorally disordered students, reducing overdependence on special education placements. Included within the range of options should be alternatives that strengthen the accommodative capacity of the regular education program such as the problem-solving teams suggested by Chalfant and Psych (1979, 1981).

3. Professionals and parents need training in group process and problem-solving. There is need to cultivate understanding of the goals and function of decision making activities in education. Information and training regarding due process rights and effective advocacy behavior is also important. Models for providing such training exist. Such training should be done by coalitions of agencies wherever possible since the goal is consensus among possibly differing viewpoints rather than persuasion of one group by another.

4. Multidisciplinary teams should be trained for efficient formulation of questions to guide purposeful assessment. Focused procedures should make more effective use of time and energy of assessment personnel and contribute to better decisions. The need for continuing research on assessment procedures has already been mentioned, but present knowledge provides an adequate basis for improving present practice (Batsche, 1983, 1984; Salvia & Ysseldyke, 1981; Tucker, 1983).

5. Often members of multidisciplinary teams do not receive feedback on the implementation or outcome of their placement decisions. Feedback could reinforce high quality decision making and focus attention on areas where improvement is required. Supervisory monitoring was a feature of the court order in *Lora v. Board of Education* (Wood, Johnson, & Jenkins, 1985).

Policy Development

Policy development has as its goal the encouragement, or even the mandating, of improved practice. Moving ahead too quickly to reform present policy or make new policy is unwise. Given the weaknesses noted in present systematic study and description of the effects of alternative procedures for the identification and placement of behaviorally disordered students, a conservative position is taken here in recommending policy changes.

1. At present, there appears to be lack of uniformity in terminology, definition, data collecting procedures, and decision making for behaviorally disordered students. Given the absence of solid research on which to base policy, demands for uniformity may be premature. Instead, the goal should be dissemination of information about current best practices and a requirement for accountability regarding present practice from all practitioners.

2. The present national terminology and definition are not regarded as exemplary by the field and should be revised.

3. Arbitrary exclusion of poorly defined subpopulations, such as the "socially maladjusted," from possible special education service is not defensible. The issue to be addressed is the need for an adapted education that permits the student to benefit from school, rather than the label applied to his or her disability. It is to be assumed that this adapted education will be delivered in the least restrictive environment consistent with the learning needs of the student and the peer group.

4. The requirement that decisions be based on data from multiple sources should be a matter of policy. Wood, Smith, and Grimes (1985) have described one possible model based on the practice in Iowa. Policies such as those adopted in Iowa and Louisiana, requiring the documentation of prior attempts to improve the student's educational progress in the present placement before placement in a more restrictive setting is recommended, seem to be particularly needed.

References

Achenbach, T. M., & Edelbrock, C. S. (1981). Behavioral problems and competencies reported by parents of normal and disturbed children aged four through sixteen. *Monographs of the Society for Research in Child Development*, **46** (Serial No. 188).

Adelman, H. S. (1978). Diagnostic classification of learning problems: Some data. *American Journal of Orthopsychiatry*, **48**, 717–726.

Adelman, H. S., Taylor, L., Fuller, W., & Nelson, P. (1979). Discrepancies among student, parent, and teacher ratings of the severity of a student's problems. *American Educational Research Journal*, **16**, 38–41.

Alexson, J., & Sinclair, E. (1986). Psychiatric diagnosis and school placement: A comparison between inpatients and outpatients. *Child Psychiatry and Human Development*, **16**, 194–205.

Algozzine, B. (1976). The disturbing child: What you see is what you get? *Alberta Journal of Educational Research*, **22**, 330–333.

Algozzine, B. (1977). The emotionally disturbed child: Disturbed or disturbing? *Journal of Abnormal Child Psychology*, **5**, 205–211.

Algozzine, B. (1979a). *An analysis of the disturbingness and acceptability of behaviors as a function of a diagnostic label*. Minneapolis: University of Minnesota. (ERIC Document Reproduction Service No. ED 185 748)

Algozzine, B. (1979b). *The disturbing child: A validation report*. (Research Report No. 8). Minneapolis: University of Minnesota, Institute for Research on Learning Disabilities.

Algozzine, B. (1980). The disturbing child: A matter of opinion. *Behavioral Disorders*, **5**, 112–115.

Algozzine, B. (1981). Special education services for normal students: Better safe than sorry. *Exceptional Children*, **48**, 238–243.

Algozzine, B., & Korinek, L. (1985). Where is special education for students with high prevalence handicaps going? *Exceptional Children*, **51**, 388–394.

Algozzine, B., Mercer, C. C., & Countermine, T. (1977). The effects of labels and behavior on teacher expectations. *Exceptional Children*, **44**, 131–132.

Algozzine, B., Richey, L., & Garden, J. (1982). Declaring students eligible for learning disability services: Why bother with the data? *Learning-Disability Quarterly*, **5**, 37–44.

Algozzine, B., Schmid, R., & Connors, B. (1978). Toward an acceptable definition of emotional disturbance. *Behavioral Disorders*, **4**, 48–52.

Algozzine, B., & Sherry, L. (1981). Issues in the education of emotionally disturbed children. *Behavioral Disorders*, **6**, 223–237.

Algozzine, B., & Ysseldyke, J. E. (1983). An analysis of incidence of special class placement: The masses are burgeoning. *The Journal of Special Education*, **17**, 141–147.

Alker, H. A. (1972). Is personality situationally specific or intraphysically consistent? *Journal of Personality*, **40**, 1–16.

American Psychiatric Association (1980). *DSM III: Diagnostic and statistical manual of mental disorders*. Washington, D.C.

Anderlini, L. S. (1983). An inservice program for improving team participation in educational decision-making. *School Psychology Review*, **12**, 160–167.

Antonak, R. F. (1980). A hierarchy of attitudes toward exceptionality. *Journal of Special Education*, **14**, 231–241.

Apter, S. J. (1982). *Troubled children, troubled systems*. New York: Pergamon.

Auger, T. (1975). Differences in child symptom ratings among teachers and parents of emotionally disturbed children. *Psychological Reports*, **36**, 867–873.

Balow, B. (1979). Definitional and prevalence problems in behavior disorders of children. *School Psychology Digest*, **8**, 348–354.

Barr, K. L., & McDowell, R. L. (1972). Comparison of LD and EBD children on three deviant classroom behaviors. *Exceptional Children*, **39**, 60–62.

Batsche, G. M. (1983). The referral oriented, consultative assessment report writing model. In J. Grimes (Ed.), *Communicating psychological information in writing* (pp. 27–43). Des Moines: Iowa Department of Public Instruction.

Batsche, G. M. (1984). Questions oriented referral, consultation, and assessment. Paper presented at conference, *Reevaluation of Psychological Assessment*, Ames, IA.

Beilin, H. (1959). Teachers' and clinicians' attitudes toward the behavior problems of children: A reappraisal. *Child Development*, **30**, 9–25.

Bergquist, C. C. (1982). A methodology for validating placement of children in exceptional child programs. *Exceptional Children*, **48**, 269–270.

Bernard, R., & Clarizio, H. (1981). Socioeconomic bias in special education placement decision. *Psychology in the Schools*, **18**, 178–183.

Boucher, C. R., & Deno, S. L. (1979). Learning disabled and emotionally disturbed: Will the labels affect teacher planning? *Psychology in the Schools*, **16**, 395–402.

Bower, E. M. (1957). A process for identifying disturbed children. *Children*, **4**, 143–147.

Bower, E. M. (1960). *Early identification of emotionally handicapped children in school.* (1st ed.) Springfield, IL: Thomas.

Bower, E. M. (1969). *Early identification of emotionally handicapped children in the schools*, (2nd ed.) Springfield, IL: Thomas.

Bower, E. M. (1982). Defining emotional disturbance: Public policy and research. *Psychology in the Schools*, **19**, 55–60.

Bowers, K. S. (1973). Situationalism in psychology: An analysis and a critique. *Psychological Review*, **80**, 307–336.

Carri, L. (1985). Inservice teachers' assessed needs in behavioral disorders, mental retardation, and learning disabilities: Are they similar? *Exceptional Children*, **51**, 411–416.

Carroll, C. F., & Repucci, N. D. (1978). Meanings that professionals attach to labels for children. *Journal of Consulting Clinical Psychology*, **46**, 372–374.

Chalfant, J. C. (1985). National task force on learning disabilities—referral, assessment, and identification: A summary report. A paper presented at *Innovative Practices in Special Education Conference*, Cedar Rapids, IA.

Chalfant, J. C., & Psych, M. V. (1979). Teacher assistance teams: A model for within building problem solving. *Learning Disabilities Quarterly*, **2**, 85–96.

Chalfant, J. C., & Psych, M. V. (1981). Teacher assistance teams: A model for within building problem solving. *Counterpoint*, **1**, 21.

Chamberlain, R. W. (1976). The use of teacher checklists to identify children at risk for later behavioral and emotional problems. *American Journal of Diseases of Children*, **130**, 141–145.

Chandler, H. N., & Jones, K. (1983a). Learning disabled or emotionally disturbed: Does it make any difference? Part 1. *Journal of Learning Disabilities*, **16**, 432–434.

Chandler, H. N., & Jones, K. (1983b). Learning disabled or emotionally disturbed: Does it make any difference? Part II. *Journal of Learning Disabilities*, **16**, 561–564.

Christenson, S., Ysseldyke, J. E., & Algozzine, B. (1982). Institutional constraints and external pressure influencing referral decision. *Psychology in the Schools*, **19**, 341–345.

Clarizio, H. F., & Veres, V. (1983). WISC-R patterns of emotionally impaired and diagnostic utility. *Psychology in the Schools*, **20**, 409–414.

Colbourn, M., & McLeod, J. (1983). Computer guided educational diagnosis: A prototype expert system. *Journal of Special Education Technology*, **6**, 30–39.

Council of Administrators of Special Education (1983). *A survey of definition and identification of seriously emotionally disturbed youngsters: Local special education administration perspectives and processes.* Council for Exceptional Children, Reston, VA.

Cowen, E. L. (1980). The primary mental health project: Yesterday, today, and tomorrow. *Journal of Special Education*, **14**, 133–154.

Cowen, E. L., Pederson, A., Babigian, H., Izzo, L. D., & Trost, M. A. (1973). Long term followup of early detected vulnerable children. *Journal of Consulting and Clinical Psychology*, **46**, 438–446.

Cullinan, D., & Epstein, M. H. (1979). Administrative definitions of behaviors disorders: Status and directions. In F. Wood & C. Lakin (Eds.), *Disturbing, Disordered, or Disturbed?* (pp. 17–28). Minneapolis: University of Minnesota.

Cullinan, D., Epstein, M. H., & Dembinski, R. (1979). Behavior problems of educationally handicapped and normed pupils, *Journal of Abnormal Child Psychology*, **7**, 495–502.

Cullinan, D., Epstein, M. H., & Kauffman, J. M. (1984). *Behavior disorders of children and adolescents.* Englewood Cliffs, NJ: Prentice-Hall.

Cullinan, D., Epstein, M. H., & Lloyd, J. W. (1983). *Behavioral disorders of children and adolescents.* Englewood Cliffs, NJ: Prentice-Hall.

Dion, K. (1972). Physical attractiveness and evaluations of children's transgressions. *Journal of Personality and Social Psychology*, **24**, 207–214.

Donnellan, A. M. (1984). The criterion of the least dangerous assumption. *Behavioral Disorders*, **9**, 141–150.

Duba, R., & Shortcliffe, E. (1983). Expert systems research. *Science*, **220**, 261–268.

Eaves, R. C. (1982). A proposal for the diagnosis of emotional disturbance. *Journal of Special Education*, **16**, 463–476.

Edelbrock, C. & Achenbach, T. M. (1984). The teacher version of the child behavior profile. I: Boys aged 6–11. *Journal of Consulting and Clinical Psychology*, **52**, 207–217.

Eggelston, C. R. (1984). *Results of a national correctional/special education survey.* Paper presented at Correctional/Special Education Training Project National Conference, Arlington, VA.

Epps, S., McGue, M., & Ysseldyke, J. E. (1982). Interjudge agreement in classifying students as learning disabled. *Psychology in the Schools*, **19**, 209–220.

Epstein, M. H., & Cullinan, D. (1983). Academic performance of behaviorally disordered and learning disabled pupils. *The Journal of Special Education*, **17**, 303–307.

Epstein, M., Cullinan, D., & Sabatino, D. (1977). State definitions of behavior disorders. *Journal of Special Education*, **11**, 417–425.

Epstein, M. H., Kauffman, J. M., & Cullinan, D. (1985). Patterns of maladjustment among the behaviorally disordered. II: Boys aged 6–11, boys ages 12–18, girls aged 6–11, and girls ages 12–18. *Behavioral Disorders*, **10**, 125–135.

Eysenck, H. J., Easting, G., & Eysenck, S. B. G. (1970). Personality measurement in children: A dimensional approach. *Journal of Special Education*, **4**, 261–268.

Federal Register, August 23, 1977. Part II (Rules and regulations for amendments to Part B, *Public Law 94–142*, Education for All Handicapped Children Act of 1975).

Feingold, B. (1975). *Why your child is hyperactive.* New York: Random House.

Fenton, K. S., Yoshida, R. K., Maxwell, J. P., & Kaufman, M. J. (1979). Recognition of team goals: An essential step toward rational decision-making. *Exceptional Children*, **45**, 638–644.

Florida State Department of Education, Bureau of Education for Exceptional Children. (1978). *A resource manual for the development and evaluation of special education programs for exceptional students: Emotionally handicapped.* (ERIC Document Reproduction Service No. ED 161 226; EC 112 364)

Foley, J. M. (1979). Effects of labeling and teacher behavior on children's attitudes. *American Journal of Mental Deficiency*, **83**, 380–384.

Foster, G., Algozzine, B., & Ysseldyke, J. (1980). Classroom teacher and teacher-in training susceptibility to stereotypical bias. *Personnel and Guidance Journal*, **59**, 27–30.

Foster, G., & Keech, V. (1977). Teacher reactions to the label of educable mentally retarded. *Education and training of the mentally retarded*, **12**, 307–311.

Freeman, S., & Algozzine, B. (1980). Social acceptability as a function of labels and assigned attributes. *American Journal of Mental Deficiency*, **84**, 589–595.

Fremont, T. W. S., Klingsporn, M. J., & Wilson, J. H. (1976). Identifying emotional disturbance in children—The professionals differ. *Journal of School Psychology*, **14**, 275–282.

Fuchs, L. S., Deno, S. L., Mirkin, P. K. (1983). Data-based program modification: A continuous evaluation system with computer software to facilitate implementation. *Journal of Special Education Technology*, **6**, 50–57.

Gajor, A. (1976). Educable mentally retarded, learning disabled, emotionally disturbed: Similarities and differences. *Exceptional Children*, **45**, 470–472.

Gerry, M. (1984). Expert witness deposition from *Lavon M. v. Turlington*. Class action lawsuit settled in State of Florida.

Giesbrecht, M. L., & Routh, D. K. (1979). The influence of categories of cumulative folder information on teacher referrals of low-achieving children for special educational service. *American Educational Research Journal*, **16**, 181–187.

Gilbert, T. F. (1978). *Human competence: Engineering worthy performance*. New York: McGraw-Hill.

Gillman, J. E. (1979). Contributions and status rankings of educational planning committee participants. *Exceptional Children*, **45**, 466–468.

Glavin, J. P. (1972). Persistence of behavior disorders in children. *Exceptional Children*, **38**, 367–376.

Glavin, J. P., Quay, H. C., & Werry, J. S. (1971). Behavioral and academic gains of conduct problem children in different classroom settings. *Exceptional Children*, **37**, 441–446.

Goldfried, M. R. (1977). Behavioral assessment in perspective. In J. Cone & R. Hawkins (Eds.), *Behavioral assessment: new directions in clinical psychology*. New York: Brunner/Mazel.

Goldfried, M. R., & Kent, R. N. (1972). Traditional versus behavioral personality assessment: A comparison of methodological and theoretical assumptions. *Psychological Bulletin*, **77**, 409–420.

Graham, P., Rutter, M., & George, S. (1973). Temperamental characteristics as predictors of behavioral disorders in children. *American Journal of Orthopsychiatry*, **43**, 328–339.

Gresham, F. M. (1983). Multirate-multimethod approach to multifactored assessment: Theoretical rationale and practical application. *School Psychology Review*, **7**, 26–34.

Gresham, F. M. (1984). Emotional disturbance or behavior disorders: Semantics or substance? *PAISE Reporter*, **15**, 1–3.

Grosenick, J. K., & Huntze, S. L. (1980). *National needs analysis on behavior disorders: Severe behavioral disorders*. Columbia: University of Missouri.

Grosenick, J. K., Huntze, S. L., & Smith, C. R. (Eds.), (1983). *Non-categorical versus categorical issues in programming for behaviorally disordered children and youth*. National Needs Analysis in Behavior Disorders. Columbia: University of Missouri, Department of Special Education.

Hamm, H. A., & Evans, J. G. (1978). WISC-R subtest patterns of severely emotionally disturbed students. *Psychology in the Schools*, **15**, 188–190.

Hannah, M. E., & Pliner, S. (1983). Teacher attitudes toward handicapped children: A review and synthesis. *School Psychology Review*, **12**, 12–25.

Harasymiw, S. J., Horne, M. D., & Lewis, S. C. (1976). Disability social distance hierarchy for population subgroups. *Scandinavian Journal of Rehabilitation Medicine*, **8**, 33–36.

Haring, N. G., Liberty, K. A., & White (1980). Rules for data-based strategy decision in instructional programs: Current research and instructional implications. In W. Salor, & L. Brown (Eds.), *Methods for instructional improvement for severely handicapped students*. Baltimore, MD: Brookes.

Hartmann, D. P., Roper, B. L., & Bradford, D. C. (1979). Some relationships between behavioral and traditional assessment. *Journal of Behavioral Assessment*, **1**, 3–21.

Hasselbring, T. S. (1984). Computer-based assessment of special-needs students. *Special Services in the Schools*, **1**, 7–19.

Hasselbring, T. S., & Crossland, C. L. (1982). Applications of microcomputer technology to spelling assessment of learning disabled students. *Learning Disability Quarterly*, **5**, 80–82.

Hasselbring, T. S., & Hamlett, C. L., (1983). *AIMSTAR: Charting and graphing individualized student data in the classroom*. Portland, OR: Applied Systems. Instructional Evaluation Publishing.

Hasselbring, T. S., & Owens, S. (1983). Microcomputer-based analysis of spelling errors. *Computer, Reading, and Language Arts*, **1**, 26–31.

Herr, D., Algozzine, B., & Eaves, R. (1976). Modifications of biases held by teacher trainees toward the disturbingness of behavior. *Journal of Educational Research*, **69**, 261–264.

Hobbs, N. (1966). Helping the disturbed child: Psychological and ecological strategies. *American Psychologist*, **21**, 1105–1115.

Hobbs, N. J. (1975). *The future of children: Categories, labels, and their consequences*. San Francisco, CA: Jossey-Bass.

Hocutt, A. M., Cox, J. L., & Polosi, J. (1984). *An exploration of issues regarding the identification and placement of LD, MR, and ED students*. Research Triangle Park, NC Research Triangle Institute #2706-06/01FR.

Hoffer, A. (1973). Mechanisms of action of nicotinic acid and nicotinamide in the treatment of schizophrenia. In D. Haskins & L. Pauling (Eds.), *Orthomolecular psychiatry*. San Francisco, CA: W. H. Freeman.

Hogenson, D. (1973). A multidisciplinary approach to the school management of acutely anxious and depressed students in a large urban senior high school setting. *Pupil Personnel Services Journal*, **3**, 29–31.

Holland, R. P. (1980). An analysis of the decision making process in special education. *Exceptional Children*, **46**, 551–554.

Huntze, S. L. (1985). A position paper of the Council for Children with Behavioral Disorders. *Behavioral Disorders*, **10**, 167–174.

Isaac Lora, et al., v. The Board of Education of the city of New York, et al. (1984). 75 Civ. 917 (E.D. NY, 1984).

Jackson, G., & Cosca, C. (1974). The inequality of educational opportunity of the southwest: An observational study of ethnically mixed classrooms. *American Educational Research Journal*, **11**, 219–229.

119

Jackson, P., & Lahaderne, H. (1967). Inequalities of teacher-pupil contacts. *Psychology in the Schools*, **4**, 204–211.

Jacobs, W. R. (1978). The effect of the learning disability label on classroom teachers' ability objectively to observe and interpret child behaviors. *Learning Disability Quarterly*, **1**, 50–55.

Javel, M. E., & Greenspan, S. (1983). Influence of personal competence profiles on mainstreaming recommendations. *Psychology in the Schools*, **20**, 459–465.

Jenkins, J. R., Deno, S. L., & Mirkin, P. K. (1979). Measuring pupil progress toward the least restrictive alternative. *Learning Disability Quarterly*, **2**, 81–91.

Kabler, M., & Carlton, G. (1982). Educating exceptional students: A comprehensive team approach. *Theory Into Practice*, **21**, 88–96.

Kabler, M. L., & Genshaft, J. L. (1983). Structuring decision-making in multidisciplinary teams. *School Psychology Review*, **12**, 150–159.

Kagen, J. (1984). *The nature of the child*. New York: Basic Books.

Kauffman, J. M. (1979). An historical perspective on disordered behavior and an alternative conceptualization of exceptionality. In F. Wood & C. Lakin (Eds.), *Disturbing, disordered, or disturbed?* (pp. 49–70). Minneapolis: University of Minnesota.

Kauffman, J. M. (1980). Where special education for disturbed children is going: A personal view. *Exceptional Children*, **46**, 522–527.

Kauffman, J. M. (1982). Social policy issues in special education and related services for emotionally disturbed children and youth. In M. M. Noel & N. G. Haring (Eds.), *Progress or change: Issues in educating the emotionally disturbed. Volume I: Identification and program planning* (pp. 1–10). Seattle: University of Washington.

Kauffman, J. M. (1985). *Characteristics of children's behavior disorders*. (3rd ed.). Columbus, OH: Merrill.

Kauffman, J. M., McCullough, L. L., & Sabornie, E. J. (1984). Integrating exceptional students: Special problems involving the emotionally disturbed/behaviorally disordered. *B. C. Journal of Special Education*, **8**, 201–210.

Kelly, T. J., Bullock, L. M., & Dykes, M. K. (1974). Teachers' perceptions of behavioral disorders in children. *Research Bulletin*. Gainesville: Florida Educational Research and Development Council.

Kelly, T. J., Bullock, L. M., & Dykes, M. K. (1977). Behavioral disorders: Teachers' perceptions. *Exceptional Children*, **43**, 316–318.

Kerr, M. M., & Nelson, C. M. (1983). *Strategies for managing behavior problems in the classroom*. Columbus, OH: Merrill.

Knoff, H. M. (1983a). Effect of diagnostic information on special education placement decision. *Exceptional Child*, **49**, 440–444.

Knoff, H. M. (1983b). Investigating disproportionate influence and status in multidisciplinary child study teams. *Exceptional Child*, **49**, 367–370.

Lakin, K. C. (1983). Research-based knowledge and professional practices in special education for emotionally disturbed students. *Behavioral Disorders*, **8**, 128–137.

Lawler, F. (1984). Functional or purposeful assessments: A critical look at assessment procedures and their outcomes. Paper presented at *Reevaluation of Psychological Assessment*, Ames, IA.

Ledingham, J. E., Younger, A., Schwartzman, A., & Bergeron, G. (1982). Agreement among teacher, peer, and self-ratings of children's aggression, withdrawal, and likeability. *Journal of Abnormal Child Psychology*, **10**, 363–372.

Long, K. A. (1983). Emotionally disturbed children as an underdetected and underserved public school population: Reasons and recommendations. *Behavioral Disorders*, **9**, 46–54.

Mack, J. H. (1980). An analysis of state definitions of severely emotionally disturbed. Reston, VA: Council for Exceptional Children. (ERIC Document Reproduction Service No. ED 201 135)

Maher, C. A. (1981). Decision analysis: An approach for multidisciplinary teams in planning special service programs, *Journal of School Psychology*, **19**, 340–349.

Maher, C. A. (1983). Development and implementation of effective individualized education programs (IEPs): Evaluation of two team approaches. *Journal of School Psychology*, **21**, 143–152.

Marcus, S. D., Fox, D., & Brown, D. (1982). Identifying school children with behavior disorders. *Community Mental Health Journal*, **18**, 249–256.

Marston, D., Mirkin, P., & Deno, S. (1984). Curriculum-based measurement: An alternative to traditional screening, referral, and identification. *Journal of Special Education*, **18**, 109–117.

Mash, E. J., & Terdal, L. G. (1976). Observational assessment. In E. J. Mash & L. B. Terdal (Eds.), *Behavior therapy and assessment* (pp. 261–278). New York: Springer.

McCarthy, J. M., & Paraskevolopoulos, J. (1969). Behavior patterns of LD, BD, and average children. *Exceptional Children*, **36**, 69–74.

McGinnis, E., Kiraly, J., & Smith, C. R. (1984). The types of data used in identifying public school students as behaviorally disordered. *Behavioral Disorders*, **9**, 239–246.

Mercer, J. (1973). *Labeling the mentally retarded*. Berkeley, University of California Press.

Mercer, J. (1979). *System of multicultural pluralistic assessment technical manual*. New York: Psychological Corporation.

Mischel, W. (1969). Continuity and change in personality. *American Psychologist*, **24**, 1012–1018.

Mischel, W. (1975). *On the future of personality measurement*. Palo Alto, CA: Stanford University. (ERIC Document Reproduction Service No. ED 116 073)

Morgan, P. I. (1979). Prevalence and types of handicapping conditions found in juvenile correctional institutions: A national survey. *Journal of Special Education*, **13**, 283–295.

Morris, J. D., & Arrant, D. (1978). Behavior ratings of emotionally disturbed children by teachers, parents, and school psychologists. *Psychology in the Schools*, **15**, 450–455.

Mutimer, D. D., & Rosemier, R. A. (1967). Behavior problems of children as viewed by teachers and the children themselves. *Journal of Consulting Psychology*, **31**, 583–587.

National Association of State Directors of Special Education (1978). *Special education programs for emotionally disturbed adolescent: A directory of state education agency services*. Washington, DC: NASDSE.

National Association of State Directors of Special Education (1985). *SED findings: Project forum and decision resources corp*. Washington, DC: NASDSE.

Neel, R. S., & Rutherford R. B. (1981). Exclusion of the socially maladjusted from services under *P.L. 94–142*. In F.

H. Wood (Ed.) *Perspectives for a New Decade* (pp. 79–84). Rosten, VA: Council for Exceptional Children.

Neer, W., Foster, D., Jones, J., & Reynolds, D. (1973). Socioeconomic bias in the diagnosis of mental retardation. *Exceptional Children*, **40**, 38–39.

Nelson, C. M. (1971). Techniques for screening conduct disturbed children. *Exceptional Children*, **37**, 501–507.

Nelson, R. O., Hay, L. R., & Hay, W. M. (1977). Comments on Cone's the relevance of reliability and validity for behavioral assessment. *Behavior Therapy*, **8**, 427–430.

Newman, R. K., & Simpson, R. (1983). Modifying the least restrictive environment to facilitate the integration of severely emotionally disturbed children and youth. *Behavior Disorders*, **8**, 103–112.

O'Leary, D. K., & Johnson, S. B. (1979). Psychological assessment. In H. C. Quay & J. Werry (Eds.), *Psychopathological disorders of childhood*, (pp. 216–246), New York: Wiley.

Olson, J., Algozzine, B., & Schmid, R. E. (1980). Mild, moderate, and severe EH: An empty distinction? *Behavioral Disorders*, **5**, 96–101.

Patten, C. V. (1976). Selecting special students: Who decides? *Teachers College Record*, **78**, 101–124.

Perlmutter, B. F., & Parus, M. V. (1983). Identifying children with learning disabilities: Diagnostic procedures across school districts. *Learning Disabilities Quarterly*, **6**, 321–328.

Peterson, C. R., & Hart, D. H. (1978). Use of multiple discriminant function analysis in evaluation of a state-wide system for identification of educationally handicapped children. *Psychological Reports*, **43**, 743–755.

Pfeiffer, S. I. (1980). The influence of diagnostic labeling on special education placement decision. *Psychology in the Schools*, **17**, 347–350.

Pfeiffer, S. I. (1981). The problems facing multidisciplinary teams: Recurring problems and some possible solutions. *Journal of School Psychology*, **18**, 389–333.

Pfeiffer, S. I. (1982). Special education placement decisions made by teams and individuals: A cross-cultural perspective. *Psychology in the Schools*, **19**, 335–340.

Pfeiffer, S. I. (1983). Utilizing the multidisciplinary team to facilitate a school-family systems orientation. *School Psychology Review*, **12**, 168–173.

Poland, S. F., Thurlow, M. L., Ysseldyke, J. E., & Mirkin, P. K. (1982). Current psychoeducational assessment and decision making practices as reported by directors of special education. *Journal of School Psychology*, **20**, 171–179.

Pool, L. D. (1979). The use of home/family data in the identification of emotionally disabled pupils. In C. R. Smith & J. Grimes (Eds.), *The identification of emotionally disabled pupils: Data decision making* (pp. 197–212). Des Moines: Iowa Department of Public Instruction.

Pribram, K. H. (1985, September). Holism could close cognition era. *APA Monitor*, pp. 6–7.

Prieto, A. G., & Zucker, S. H. (1981). Teacher perception of race as a factor in the placement of behaviorally disordered children. *Behavior Disorders*, **7**, 34–38.

Pryzwansky, Y., & Rzepski, B. (1982). School based teams: An untapped resource for consultation and technical assistance. *School Psychology Review*, **12**, 174–179.

Quay, H. C. (1978). Behavior disorders in the classroom. *Journal of Research and Development in Education*, **11**, 8–17.

Quay, H. C., & Peterson, D. R. (1979). *Manual for the Behavior Problem Checklist*. Available from D. R. Peterson, 39 North Fifth Avenue, Highland Park, NJ 08904.

Reschly, D. J. (1980). School psychologists and assessment in the future. *Professional Psychology*, **11**, 841–848.

Reschly, D. J. (1982). School psychology today: Progress, not impasse. *Professional Psychology*, **13**, 990–998.

Reschly, D. J. (1983). Legal issues in psychoeducational assessment. In G. Hynd (Ed.), *School psychology: Contemporary perspectives* (pp. 67–93). Syracuse, NY: Syracuse University Press.

Rhodes, W. C. (1967). The disturbing child: A problem of ecological management. *Exceptional Children*, **33**, 449–455.

Rhodes, W. C., & Tracy, M. L. (Eds.). (1974). *A study of child variance: Conceptual models*. Ann Arbor: University of Michigan Press.

Roberts, J., & Baird, J. T. (1972). *Behavioral patterns of children in school: United States (Vital and Health Statistics, Series II)*. Rockville, MD: US Department of Health, Education and Welfare, Division of Health Examination Statistics.

Rosenbach, J. H., & Mowder, B. A. (1981). Test bias: The other side of the coin. *Psychology in the Schools*, **18**, 450–454.

Rubin, R. A., & Balow, B. (1978). Prevalence of teacher identified behavior problems: A longitudinal study. *Exceptional Children*, **45**, 102–113.

Ruhl, K. L., & Hughes, C. A. (1985). The nature and extent of aggression in special education settings serving behaviorally disordered students. *Behavioral Disorders*, **10**, 95–104.

Salvia, J., Schultz, E. W., & Chapin, N. S. (1974). Reliability of the Bower Scale for screening of children with emotional handicaps. *Exceptional Children*, **41**, 117–118.

Salvia, J., & Ysseldyke, J. (1981). *Assessment in special and remedial education* (2nd Ed.). Boston: Houghton-Mifflin.

Sapp, G. L., Chissom, B. S., & Horton, W. O. (1984). An investigation of the ability of selected instruments to discriminate areas of exceptional class designation. *Psychology in the Schools*, **21**, 258–263.

Schlosser, L., & Algozzine, B. (1979). The disturbing child: He or she? *Alberta Journal of Educational Research*, **25**, 30–36.

Schooler, D. L., Beebe, M. C., & Koepke, T. (1978). Factor analysis of WISC-R scores for children identified as learning disabled, educable mentally impaired, and emotionally impaired. *Psychology in the Schools*, **15**, 478–485.

Schultz, E. W., & Hirshoren, A., Manton, A. B., & Henderson, R. A. (1971). Special education for the emotionally disturbed. *Exceptional Children*, **38**, 313–319.

Shepard, L. A., & Smith, M. L. (1981). *The identification, assessment, placement, and remediation of perceptual and communicative disordered children in Colorado*. Boulder: Laboratory of Education Research, University of Colorado.

Sherry, L. (1981–82). Non-task oriented behaviors of educable mentally retarded, emotionally handicapped, and learning disabled students. *Educational Research Quarterly*, **6**, 19–29.

Sherry, L., & Algozzine, B. (1981). Commonality of behavioral characteristics of educable mentally retarded and emotionally disturbed children. *Psychological Reports*, **48**, 815–818.

121

Sinclair, E., Forness, S. R., & Alexson, J. (1985). Psychiatric diagnosis: A study of its relationship to school needs. *Journal of Special Education*, **19**, 333–344.

Sindelar, P. T., King, M. C., Cortland, D., Wilson, R. J., & Meisel, C. J. (1985). Deviant behavior in learning disabled and behaviorally disordered students as a function of level and placement. *Behavioral Disorders*, **10**, 105–112.

Siperstein, G. N., Budoff, M., & Bak, J. J. (1980). Effects of the labels "mentally retarded" and "retard" on the social acceptability of mentally retarded children. *American Journal of Mental Deficiency*, **84**, 596–601.

Smith, C. R., Frank, A. R., & Snider, B. F. (1984). School psychologists' and teachers' perceptions of data used in the identification of behaviorally disordered students. *Behavioral Disorders*, **10**, 27–32.

Smith, C., & Grimes, J. (1979). *The identification of emotionally disabled pupils: Data and decision making*. Des Moines: Iowa Department of Public Instruction.

Spadafore, G. (1976). *Cognitive dissonance paradigm: A teaching technique to improve the effectiveness of the team approach*. Pocatello: Idaho State University. (ERIC Document Reproduction Services No. ED 144 263)

Spivack, G., Swift, M., & Prewitt, J. (1971). Syndromes of disturbed classroom behavior: A behavioral diagnostic system for elementary schools. *Journal of Special Education*, **5**, 269–292.

Stevens-Long, J. (1973). The effect of behavioral context on some aspects of adult disciplinary practice and affect. *Child Development*, **44**, 476–484.

Suchar, C. S. (1978). The institutional reaction to child mental illness: Co-dependency labeling. *Journal of Social Issue*, **34**, 76–92.

Sydney, J., & Minner, S. (1983). The influence of sibling information on the placement recommendation of special class teachers. *Behavioral Disorders*, **8**, 43–45.

Tallmadge, G. K., Gamel, N. N., Munson, R. G., & Hanley, T. V. (1985). *Special study on terminology: Comprehensive review and evaluation report*. (Contract No. 300-84-0144). Washington, DC: US Department of Education.

Thomas, A. (1981). Current trends in developmental theory. *American Journal of Orthopsychiatry*, **51**, 580–609.

Thompson, R. J., & Bernal, M. E. (1982). Factors associated with parent labeling of children referred for conduct problems. *Journal of Abnormal Child Psychology*, **10**, 194–202.

Tisdale, P. C., & Fowler, R. E. (1983). The effects of labels on teachers' perceptions of the prevalence of emotionally disturbed children and youth. *Education*, **103**, 278–280.

Touliatos, J., & Lindholm, B. W. (1980). Relationship of children's grade in school, sex, and social class to teachers' ratings on the Behavior Problem Checklist. *Journal of Abnormal Child Psychology*, **3**, 115–126.

Tringo, J. L. (1970). The hierarchy of preference toward disability groups. *Journal of Special Education*, **4**, 295–306.

Tucker, J. (1983). *Non-test based assessment*. University of Minnesota: National School Psychology Network.

Ullman, C. A. (1952). Mental health screening of school children. *Public Health Reports*, **67**, 1219–1223.

Ullman, C. A. (1957). Teachers, peers, and tests as predictors of adjustment. *Journal of Educational Psychology*, **48**, 257–267.

Ullman, D., Doherty, M., Egan, D., Fiedler, N., Jurenec, G., Pliske, R., & Thompson, D. (1981). *The assessment of diagnostic policies for hyperactivity: Comparisons within and across professions*. Paper presented at a meeting of the American Psychological Association, Los Angeles, CA.

Vilee, C. A., & Dethier, V. G. (1971). *Biological principles and processes*. Philadelphia: Saunders.

Waddell, D. D. (1980). *The identification of seriously emotionally disturbed children in the state of Ohio*. Unpublished doctoral dissertation, Ohio State University, Columbus.

Wallace, G. (1976). Interdisciplinary efforts in learning disabilities: Issues and recommendations. *Journal of Learning Disabilities*, **9**, 59–65.

Walsh, J. F., & O'Connor, J. D. (1968). When are children disturbed? *Elementary School Journal*, **68**, 353–356.

Watt, N. F., Stolorow, R. D., Lubensky, A. W., & McClelland, D. C. (1970). School adjustment and behavior of children hospitalized for schizophrenia as adults. *American Journal of Orthopsychiatry*, **40**, 637–757.

Weissenburger, F., Bielat, B., Gingrich, D., & Jensen, B. (1985). Individual trait data. In F. H. Wood, C. R. Smith, & J. Grimes (Eds.). *The Iowa assessment model in behavioral disorders: A training manual*, (pp. 221–261). Des Moines: Iowa Department of Public Instruction.

White, R. Beattie, J., & Rose, T. (1985). A survey of state definitions of behavioral disorders: Implications for adolescent programming. In S. Bratten, R. J. Rutherford, & W. Evans (Eds.) *Programming for Adolescents with Behavioral Disorders: Volume II* (pp. 118–126). Reston, Virginia: CCBD, CEC.

Wickman, E. K. (1928). *Children's behavior and teachers' attitudes*. New York: Commonwealth Fund.

Wood, F. H. (1981). The influence of personal, social, and political factors on the labeling of students. In F. H. Wood (Ed.), *Perspectives for a new decade* (pp. 45–62). Reston, VA: Council for Exceptional Children.

Wood, F. H. (1985). Issues in the identification and placement of behaviorally disordered students. *Behavioral Disorders*, **10**, 219–228.

Wood, F. H., Johnson, J. L., & Jenkins, J. R. (1986). *Isaac Lora, et al.* v. *The Board of Education of the City of New York, et al.*: Nonbiased referral, assessment, and placement procedures. *Exceptional Children*, **52**, 323–331.

Wood, F. H., & Lakin, K. C. (1979a). Defining emotionally disturbed/ behaviorally disordered populations for research purposes. In F. H. Wood & K. C. Lakin (Eds.), *Disturbing, disordered, or disturbed?: Perspectives on the definition of problem behavior in educational settings* (pp. 29–48). Reston, VA: Council for Exceptional Children.

Wood, F. H., & Lakin, K. C. (Eds.). (1979b). *Disturbing, disordered, or disturbed?: Perspectives on the definition of problem behavior in educational settings*. Reston, VA: Council for Exceptional Children.

Wood, F. H., Smith, C. R., & Grimes, J. (Eds.). (1985). *The Iowa assessment model in behavioral disorders: A training manual*. Des Moines: Iowa Department of Public Instruction.

Wood, F. H., & Zabel, R. H. (1978). Making sense of reports on the incidence of behavior disorders/emotional disturbance in school-aged populations. *Psychology in the Schools*, **15**, 45–51.

Yoshida, R. K. (1980). Multidisciplinary decision making in special education: A review of issues. *School Psychology Review*, **9**, 221–226.

Yoshida, R. K. (1983). Are multidisciplinary teams worth the investment? *School Psychology Review*, **12**, 137–143.

Yoshida, R. K., & Abraamson, M. (1982). Effective teacher planning of mainstream programs: Significant development still remains. Paper submitted for publication.

Yoshida, R. K. Fenton, K. S., Maxwell, J. P., & Kaufman, M. J. (1978). Group decision making in the planning team process: Myth or reality? *Journal of School Psychology*, **16**, 237–244.

Young, S., Algozzine, B., & Schmid, R. (1979). The effects of assigned attributes and labels on children's peer acceptance ratings. *Education and Training of the Mentally Retarded*, **14**, 257–261.

Ysseldyke, J. E. (1978). Implementing the "Protection in Evaluation Procedures" provision of *P.L. 94–142. In Developing criteria for evaluation of the protection in evaluation procedures provision of Public Law 94–142*. United States Office of Education, BEH, Division of Innovation and Development, State Program Studies Branch.

Ysseldyke, J. E., & Algozzine, B. (1981). Diagnostic classification decisions as a function of referral information. *Journal of Special Education*, **15**, 429–435.

Ysseldyke, J. E., Algozzine, B., & Epps, S. (1983). A logical and empirical analysis of current practice in classifying students as handicapped. *Exceptional Children*, **50**, 160–166.

Ysseldyke, J. E., Algozzine, B., Richey, L., & Graden, J. (1982). Declaring students eligible for learning disabilities services: Why bother with the data? *Learning Disability Quarterly*, **5**, 37–44.

Ysseldyke, J. E., Algozzine, B., Shinn, M., & McGue, A. (1982). Similarities and differences between low achievers and students classified learning disabled. *Journal of Special Education*, **16**, 73–85.

Ysseldyke, J. E., & Foster, G. G. (1978). Bias in teacher's observations of emotionally disturbed and learning disordered children. *Exceptional Children*, **44**, 613–615.

Zabel, R. H., Peterson, R. L., Smith, C. R., & White, M. A. (1981). Placement and reintegration information for emotionally disabled students. In F. H. Wood (Ed.), *Perspectives for a New Decade*. Reston, VA: Council for Exceptional Children.

Zucker, S. H., & Prieto, A. G. (1977). Ethnicity and teacher bias in educational decisions. *Instructional Psychology*, **4**, 2–5.

Behavioral Interventions with Behaviorally Disordered Students

C. MICHAEL NELSON

University of Kentucky

ROBERT B. RUTHERFORD, Jr.

Arizona State University

Abstract—This chapter reviews the research and practice concerning behavioral interventions with students exhibiting moderate to severe behavioral disorders, regardless of the labels assigned to these pupils for educational classification. The research literature since 1976 is selectively reviewed, and implications, needs, and recommendations are offered for future research, practice, and federal policy-making.

Behavioral interventions with students labeled emotionally disturbed, seriously emotionally disturbed, behaviorally disordered, and the like have a history of over 25 years in special education. The purposes of this chapter are to present an illustrative review of current research with children and youth exhibiting moderate to severe behavior disorders, to discuss the implications the results of this research pose for special education practice, and to provide recommendations for future research and federal policy.

An extensive literature exists regarding behavioral interventions with students manifesting aberrant behavior (Nelson & Polsgrove, 1984). This literature spans a wide range of populations, settings, and interventions. We chose not to restrict our research synthesis to pupils labeled behaviorally disordered for three reasons. First, this label is unreliably applied to a diverse and heterogeneous student population. The range of pupil behaviors and characteristics within this labeled group is quite large, and the label is applied for different reasons by school personnel and researchers (Lakin, 1983). Thus, who is or is not labeled behaviorally disordered for a given educational program or research investigation is likely to depend as much on political and subjective factors as an objective behavioral criteria. The second reason is that behavioral researchers have

not used special education population labels as a basis for organizing or reporting their research. Instead, they typically have provided operational definitions of target behaviors that persons in their subjects' environments have socially validated as undesirable, deviant, or intolerable. The third reason is that aberrant or undesired social behavior is not restricted to students labeled behaviorally disordered by the educational system. As the following synthesis of research will document, social behavior problems requiring intervention occur across a variety of exceptional student populations (our earlier observation that population labels may be applied to pupils for other reasons than, or in addition to, their behavioral characteristics should be kept in mind). Furthermore, the effectiveness of behavioral technology has been demonstrated across the entire range of student populations, from the profoundly retarded to the gifted, preschool to higher education students, from residential school programs to regular classrooms, and for both social and academic behaviors (Nelson & Polsgrove, 1984).

Therefore, our review will include behavioral interventions applied to children and youth exhibiting moderate to severe behavior disorders, disregarding the population labels applied to these students. Moderate to severe behavior disorders are defined here as behaviors occurring with sufficient frequency, intensity, or chronicity across settings so as to be intolerable to educators, parents, or others; that are incompatible with school progress; and/or that threaten the safety or well-being of the student or others. Examples of such behaviors include chronic disruptive behavior, severe tantrums, extreme opposition or negativism, elimination disorders (enuresis, encopresis), severe eating disorders (pica, rumination), helplessness or dependency, ritualistic behaviors, obsessive-compulsive behaviors, social withdrawal or isolation, elective mutism, school phobia and chronic truancy, self-stimulatory behavior (SSB), self-injurious behavior (SIB), other stereotypic or psychotic behaviors (e.g., hair twirling, toe walking, hallucinations, echolalia), verbal or physical aggression, delinquent or criminal behavior, and deviant sexual behavior. In addition, we included as target behaviors appropriate social skills for students with moderate to severe deficits in this area (see Kerr and Nelson, 1983, for illustrative operational definitions of these behaviors).

Scope of the Review

This review is limited by two factors. First, the volume of research used behavioral interventions with moderate to severe behavioral disorders dictated that we restrict our focus chronologically. Therefore, we elected to emphasize studies or reviews that have been published since 1976. Even with this limitation, our review is illustrative of the research published during this period, rather than being exhaustive. A second limitation is imposed by the nature of the research itself; that is, the presence of confounding variables, the failure to assess the generalization and maintenance of intervention effects, the lack of procedural reliability data, and so forth. In addition, our review will not include cognitive behavior modification or procedures based on classical (respondent) conditioning. The first set of procedures is included in the next chapter by Carpenter and Apter on the behavioral disorders topical area, and the second set falls outside the range of interventions usually applied by educators in school settings.

This chapter is concerned with behavioral interventions derived from applied behavior analysis (Baer, Wolf, & Risley, 1968) and from social learning theory (Bandura, 1969). These models emphasize the use of overt, objectively observable behaviors as dependent measures (Nelson & Polsgrove, 1984). Behavioral interventions may be represented on two continua: one depicting behavior enhancement procedures and one depicting behavior reduction procedures. These are illustrated in Figure 1. Both sets of procedures are arranged according to their ease of implementation and their intrusiveness, in terms of teacher time and the degree to which they interrupt ongoing teaching procedures. Thus, those listed nearer the top of the behavior enhancement continuum may be assumed to require greater amounts of teacher time for planning and implementation, and cause a more substantial interruption of direct instruction. Those closer to the bottom of the behavior reduction continuum, on the other hand, are more likely to involve greater amounts of teacher time and to pull both student and teacher away from instructional activities. The latter procedures also are likely to be perceived as more aversive by teachers, an observation that has been supported by research (Norton, Austen, Allen, & Hilton, 1983; Witt & Martens,

FIGURE 1
Behavior and Reduction Procedures

Behavior Enhancement Procedures
Tactile, Sensory Reinforcement
Edible Reinforcement
Tangible Reinforcement
Token Reinforcement
Activity Reinforcement
Contracting
Modeling
Social Reinforcement
Self-Reinforcement

Behavior Reduction Procedures
Differential Reinforcement
Extinction
Verbal Aversives
Response Cost
Timeout
Overcorrection
Physical Aversives

1983). However, it should be pointed out that the position of any given procedure on these continua will vary from practitioner to practitioner and from researcher to researcher. For example, one teacher may spend hours developing contracts with students, while another may find the same edible reinforcer effective and easy to use with all students. Furthermore, researchers have not attempted to determine the relative acceptability of all procedures on these continua. Therefore, our hierarchy should be viewed as arbitrary and relative, not as universal and absolute.

Several issues appeared repeatedly in the course of our review. These include: (1) concern regarding the maintenance and generalization of behavior changes; (2) the selection of target behaviors for modification; (3) the need to analyze behavioral intervention failures; and (4) concern for the potential and real abuse of aversive procedures. These issues will be elaborated upon throughout our discussion.

Review Methodology

The initial context for this review was established by previous reviews of published behavioral research in specific areas, detailed later in the chapter. In addition, we relied upon more general reviews and summaries of behavioral interventions (Gelfand & Hartmann, 1984; Kerr & Nelson, 1983; Nelson & Polsgrove, 1984; Polsgrove & Reith, 1983; Rutherford, 1983; Stainback, Stainback, & Dedrick, 1979). We attempted to update this data base through a comprehensive search of literature pertaining to behavioral interventions with students labeled seriously emotionally disturbed, emotionally handicapped, behaviorally disordered, behaviorally impaired, and the like. Concurrently, we undertook a systematic search of published research since 1976 in the relevant journals. Articles meeting the following research and procedural criteria were selected for inclusion:

1. The subjects' behavior patterns reflected moderate to severe behavior disorder.
2. One or more of the behavioral enhancement or reduction procedures were used.
3. Intervention procedures were school-based, or were applied to behavior occurring in school and/or affecting school performance.
4. A valid single subject experimental design was used; i.e., one in which each subject serves as his/her own control, which includes withdrawal or reversal, multiple baseline, and alternating treatments designs, as well as other designs based on these (Tawney & Gast, 1984).
5. An objective data base (in most cases, direct measures of overt behavior) was employed.
6. Evidence was provided of frequent assessment of reliability of observational data. Interobserver agreements averaged 80% or better.

Finally, articles containing scholarly discussions of ethical and research issues also were reviewed.

The importance of this review rests upon the presentation of a current data base regarding behavioral interventions with children and youth exhibiting moderate to severe behavior disorders. In addition, the findings of this research are compared to practices in the field, from which are derived recommendations for future research, practice, and federal policy.

Research on Behavioral Interventions with Moderate to Severe Behavior Disorders

In this section we will examine the voluminous literature pertaining to behavioral interventions with students exhibiting behavior problems that meet the criteria of being intolerable to others, interfering with the pupil's educational progress, and/or threatening the safety or well-being of the student or others. Over the past two or more decades thousands of studies have demonstrated that behavioral interventions are effective in reducing undesired behaviors and increasing desired behaviors across students of all ages, cultures, and psychological characteristics. There is no evidence that behavioral procedures work differently for pupils labeled behaviorally disordered than for any other group. Researchers and practitioners apply and adjust behavioral interventions as required by the individual characteristics of each pupil. This ability (and demand) to conduct formative evaluations and to adjust intervention procedures while interventions are in progress is a major strength of the behavioral approach (Nelson & Polsgrove, 1984). As we indicated before, the research selected for this review dealt with moderately to severely disordered target behaviors or their desired

prosocial alternatives. The requirement that only research applied to students labeled behaviorally disordered be reviewed would have limited our focus too severely. Furthermore, we believe that so many extraneous factors affect the labeling of pupils as behaviorally disordered as to render this label practically meaningless as a population description.

Our analysis of behavioral interventions begins with a description of behavioral assessment procedures. Next, we briefly review general findings regarding behavior enhancement and reduction procedures. We then present our analysis of a number of recent studies illustrating behavioral interventions. Next, we discuss the maintenance and generalization of intervention effects. This section closes with a description of teacher training in the use of behavioral interventions.

Behavioral Assessment

The purpose of behavioral assessment is to identify target students and behaviors that are the highest priority for intervention, as well as to monitor and evaluate intervention effects (Kerr & Nelson, 1983). Thus, assessment within the behavioral model is an intervention tool rather than a process separate from intervention, as it tends to be in traditional approaches to psychological and educational assessment. Ollendick and Hersen (1984) described three differences between traditional and behavioral child psychological assessment:

1. Underlying assumptions. Traditional assessment assumes the existence of a set of measurable personality traits that drive behavior. Behavioral assessment assumes that behavior is a product of specific learning histories, as well as organismal and situational events.
2. Specifications and selection of test items. In traditional assessment procedures, test items are selected on the basis of a priori theoretical assumptions. Behavioral assessment test items are selected on the basis of the adequacy with which they represent specific stimulus situations associated with the behavior.
3. Level of inference and subsequent interpretation of test responses. Traditional assessment views responses as a sign of underlying personality traits. Behavioral assessment views responses as a low-inferential sample of behavior.

Furthermore, in the behavioral approach, the behaviors sampled must comprise a subset of the actual behaviors targeted for change.

The behavioral model accommodates a wide range of assessment strategies, including behavioral interviews, checklists, rating scales, standardized instruments, self-reports, self-monitoring forms, and behavioral observations (Ollendick & Hersen, 1984). Cone and Hawkins (1977) conceptualized behavioral assessment as a five phase process: screening and general disposition, definition of the problem, pinpointing target behaviors and designing interventions, monitoring progress, and follow-up. Schematically, their model resembles a funnel,

FIGURE 2
The Hourglass Model of Behavioral
Assessment

Parents, teachers, additional related personnel screen the
client for global behavioral excesses and deficits.

Anecdotal recordings of client behavior

Identification of the target behavior

Prioritization and selection of target behaviors
Operational definitions of target
behaviors developed

Determination of antecedent
and controlling variables

Design and intervention
with a treatment plan

Evaluation of the treatment
plan

Ongoing assessment of
maintenance of treatment gains
in therapeutic environment

Ongoing assessment of maintenance of treatment
gains in the extratherapeutic environment

Ongoing assessment of the generalization of the treatment
plan in the extratherapeutic environment

Ongoing assessment of collateral effects

Source: Adapted from M. D. Powers and J. S. Handleman
(1984). *Behavioral assessment of severe developmental
disabilities*. Rockville, MD: Aspen.

in that the process becomes increasingly specific at each
successive phase. Powers and Handleman (1984) elaborated this schema into an hourglass model, which is represented in Figure 2. This model more accurately
illustrates the importance given to follow-up assessment
of maintenance and generalization effects, which of
necessity must be broad-based to evaluate student
behavior over time and in a variety of extratreatment
environments.

The assessment strategies mentioned above can be
used in any phase of the assessment process, and
behaviorists are under the same obligation as other
researchers to demonstrate the reliability and validity of
their measures. In this regard behavioral researchers
have an advantage, in that their primary assessment
tool—direct measures of target behaviors—have at least
face validity. Furthermore, there is a tradition of frequent and rigorous reliability assessment of direct observation data. However, the issue of social validity has
recently been raised (Wolf, 1978). It has been suggested
that researchers may not be identifying behaviors for

intervention that are clinically important rather than
trivial, and that the changes achieved in these behaviors
are not meaningful to students, their caretakers, and
significant others. These problems have been a major
concern of special educators working with severely and
profoundly handicapped students. Brown, Nietupski,
and Hamre-Nietupski (1976) developed an approach to
curriculum design based on the "criterion of ultimate
functioning," which refers to the functional skills
required of adults to participate freely in community-
based environments. In this "top down" approach to
curriculum, instructional goals focus on skill clusters and
natural routines needed for meaningful participation in
the next least restrictive environment, rather than on
isolated target behaviors (Evans & Meyer, 1985).

Bailey and Lessen (1984) addressed the importance
of target behaviors selected by researchers in an analysis
of data-based, applied research articles published in the
1980 and 1981 volume years of two behavioral journals:
Journal of Applied Behavior Analysis and *Education
and Treatment of Children*. Their findings were as follows:

1. Seventy-six percent of the articles specified or
implied a need for the behavior change attempted.

2. Thirty-three percent of the articles specified criterion levels for subjects' terminal behavior, based on
the requirements of the generalization setting.

3. Eighteen percent of the articles evaluated subjects'
target behaviors relative to any other similar population
or a normal group.

4. Fifty-five percent of the articles reported an
empirical determination of how skills for at least one
behavior would be taught.

5. In 27% of the articles, at least some of the subjects'
or target behaviors were assessed in natural settings during either training or probe conditions.

6. In 40% of the articles, the discriminative stimulus
that would occur in a natural setting was presented during training.

7. Forty-seven percent of the studies were training
the terminal behavior for adult competence in that skill
(i.e., were addressing the criterion of ultimate functioning) or were training a behavior that was generalizable
to adult competence (however, on-task was rated as
such as behavior).

8. In 60% of the articles, the skills taught were considered to have utility in adult or "normalized" settings.

Although Bailey and Lessen (1984) saw their results
as indicating that researchers have failed to deal with
important skills having functional utility in subjects'
adult or mainstream environments, their study lacks
baseline data from earlier volume years for comparison.
The emerging techniques of ecological behavioral
assessment (Kerr & Nelson, 1983) and social validation
(Wolf, 1978), as well as the development of normative
rates for targeted social behaviors (Howell, 1981;
Walker & Hops, 1976) are increasing researchers'
awareness of the need to select target behaviors that are
indeed important for modification, and to establish that

persons in students' natural environments see the changes accomplished in these behaviors as significant and helpful. However, in general, practitioners have not attempted to design curricula for less severely handicapped students, including those manifesting behavioral disorders, based on the criterion of ultimate functioning.

In addition, the question of whether students from minority racial or cultural groups are overrepresented in behavioral intervention studies has not been addressed. We presume that this is because behavioral interventions typically are applied to individuals or small groups of students in their natural classroom settings rather than to pupils who have been removed to segregated classes to receive special treatment. Nevertheless, the overrepresentation of such groups in classes for behaviorally disordered students is an issue, and many educational programs for such pupils have a behavioral focus.

Review of Behavioral Enhancement and Reduction Procedures: General Findings

This portion of our review draws upon recent published reviews of specific behavioral intervention procedures, including overcorrection (Axelrod, Brantner, & Meddock, 1978), differential reinforcement (Dietz & Repp, 1983), token economies (Kazdin, 1982; 1983), timeout (Gast & Nelson, 1977; Rutherford & Nelson, 1982), contracting (Rutherford & Polsgrove, 1981), self-control (Polsgrove, 1979), and response cost (Walker, 1983); of a group of related procedures, namely, classroom management strategies (Nelson, 1981) and behavior reduction techniques (Polsgrove & Reith, 1983; Rutherford, 1983); and of procedures used with specific problems: behavior disorders (Kerr & Nelson, 1983) and severe maladaptive behavior (Stainback et al., 1979). The findings will be reported in terms of the continua of behavior enhancement and reduction procedures presented in Figure 1.

Behavioral Enhancement Procedures

Tactile and Sensory Reinforcement. The application of reinforcement involving tactile or sensory stimulation has been used almost exclusively with severely and profoundly handicapped students, and specifically in attempts to control self-stimulatory behaviors (Kerr & Nelson, 1983). The procedure involves identifying sensory consequences that appear to be reinforcing, and arranging for these consequences to be provided contingent upon the emission of desired behavior. With regard to the control of SSB, toys or other devices that appear to provide sensory feedback or stimulation like that the student receives through SSB are made available, and the student is taught to use them. Stainback, et al. (1979) observed that studies using sensory consequences in this manner have reported that SSB has been reduced by

approximately 50%.

Edible Reinforcement. Contrary to testimonies alluding to the "ubiquitous M & M," edible reinforcers have been used infrequently in recent research, except in combination with other behavior change procedures. They appear to be used more with younger and more severely handicapped students, but public school policies tend to restrict their application even in self-contained programs (Kerr & Nelson, 1983). To the extent that an effective edible reinforcer can be identified, a state of deprivation for that reinforcer (or at least a lack of satiation) can be established, and the teacher or researcher can deliver the reinforcer promptly contingent upon the desired behavior, edibles have been highly effective in shaping and maintaining desired behavior.

Tangible Reinforcement. Tangible reinforcers are nonedible items that have reinforcing value for particular students. Although they are frequently used as back-up reinforcers in token economies, they also may be delivered immediately contingent upon desired student behavior; for example, students may be given a smiley face or a sticker. Tangibles tend to be more effective with developmentally younger pupils, and problems involving the identification of effective tangible reinforcers, reinforcer satiation, and immediate contingent delivery affect their usefulness (Kerr & Nelson, 1983).

Activity Reinforcement. The opportunity to engage in desired or high-probability behaviors has proven to be an effective reinforcement procedure with normal students as well as with those exhibiting mild to moderate behavior disorders (Gelfand & Hartmann, 1984). The usefulness of this procedure with more severely disordered students has not been established, although presumably the effectiveness of contingent access to activity reinforcers would be limited only by students' cognitive ability to understand those contingencies. Activity reinforcers are often used as back-up reinforcers in a token system, or as reinforcers for fulfillment of the terms of a behavioral contract (Kerr & Nelson, 1983).

Token Reinforcement. Token economies have been used effectively with an extraordinarily wide range of student populations and age groups, and in numerous educational and treatment settings (Kazdin, 1983). Unlike edible and tangible reinforcers, tokens can be exchanged for a variety of back-up reinforcers, and so are less affected by satiation. Also they may be delivered more quickly and easily (Kerr & Nelson, 1983). However, Kazdin (1982; 1983) noted that not all clients have responded positively to token reinforcement. As Kazdin suggested, the failure of token systems likely reflects deficiencies in the treatment program rather than non-responsive client characteristics. He also observed that long-term maintenance of client gains achieved through token reinforcement is still not entirely predictable. Analysis of the generalization and maintenance effects of token systems is hampered by the fact that they are often only part of a treatment package, and that intervening experiences can obscure the effects of the original program (Kazdin, 1982).

Contracting. A behavioral contract is a formal written agreement negotiated between a student and teacher, parent, peer, or other person. A typical contract specifies the behavior(s) to be increased and/or decreased, the student goal with respect to these behaviors, and the consequences associated with goal attainment or non-attainment (Kerr & Nelson, 1983; Rutherford & Polsgrove, 1981). Contracting has been effective in modifying a variety of desired and undesired behaviors in students of all ages. However, its usefulness with students having moderate to severe learning handicaps is limited by their inability to read or comprehend the terms of the contract. Rutherford and Polsgrove's (1981) review of 35 contracting studies with behaviorally disordered and delinquent children and youth revealed a number of methodological flaws and omissions, in terms of research design, reliability assessment of dependent measures, failure to control for concurrent treatments, and omission of descriptive information, but they concluded that "contracting has contributed to behavioral change in a number of instances with this population" (p. 64).

Modeling. Live adult and peer models have been used successfully to influence the behavior of even severely handicapped students (Kerr & Nelson, 1983; Stainback et al., 1979). Also, vicarious modeling (i.e., films, printed materials) has been effective with students who do not manifest severe developmental delays (Kerr & Nelson, 1983). The chief application of modelling has been in teaching complex behaviors and in reducing the fears of otherwise behaviorally normal individuals (Gelfand & Hartmann, 1984). In the case of behaviorally disordered students, modeling typically is used in conjunction with other procedures, such as prompting, reinforcement, and punishment. Behavioral rehearsal and role-playing interventions involve modeling, as well as direct instruction and massed practice in desired social skills (Kerr & Nelson, 1983).

Social Reinforcement. Social reinforcement includes feedback, attention, and/or approval, delivered contingent upon desired student behavior. Used alone, feedback has had only weak effects, but attention and approval have been found to exert powerful influence on students with moderate to severe behavior disorders,

especially those who are developmentally younger (Nelson, 1981). The effects of differential social reinforcement depend on whether adult attention has been established as a conditioned reinforcer, whether competing reinforcers exist for undesired student behavior, and whether the teacher can be persuaded to use it consistently (Nelson, 1981). With older and more severely disordered pupils, social reinforcement is more effective when used in combination with other behavior enhancement procedures (Kerr & Nelson, 1983).

Self-Reinforcement. Self-reinforcement is actually one of a group of self-management procedures, which also includes self-monitoring and self-evaluation (Polsgrove, 1979). Research involving these procedures with students exhibiting moderate to severe behavior disorders has been relatively limited, although in general, self-management has shown a great deal of promise for changing behavior (Nelson & Polsgrove, 1984). Analyses of the effectiveness of self-management procedures have been confounded by experimenter expectancies and the demand characteristics of the situation, as well as other uncontrolled variables (Nelson, 1981). Polsgrove (1979) suggested that improvement attributed to self-management procedures actually may have been due to students' improved ability to discriminate external stimuli associated with self-regulation conditions. Self-management training prior to allowing students to control reinforcing events appears to be a factor in the success of self-management interventions (Polsgrove, 1979).

Behavioral Reduction Procedures

Differential Reinforcement. There are four strategies for reducing undesired behavior through differential reinforcement. Differential reinforcement of low rates of behavior (DRL) involves providing reinforcement when target behavior occurs no more than a specified amount in a period of time. Differential reinforcement of the omission of behavior (DRO) may be designed to require that target behavior be suppressed for an entire interval of time (whole interval DRO) or only at the end of an interval (momentary DRO). Differential reinforcement of incompatible behavior (DRI) and differential reinforcement of alternate behavior (DRA) involve reinforcing behaviors that are incompatible with, or merely alternatives to, target behavior (Dietz & Repp, 1983). DRL has been used primarily to reduce minor classroom misbehavior. Research is needed regarding appropriate criterion levels, interval lengths, and target behaviors, as are studies of its comparative effectiveness (Polsgrove & Reith, 1983). On the other hand, DRO has been used successfully with a number of severe behavior problems (Dietz & Repp, 1983), although it is usually employed in combination with other procedures (Stainback, et al. 1979). DRI and

DRA have been effective with a variety of populations and target behaviors, but because direct consequences are not provided for target behaviors, these procedures may take longer to work than DRL or DRO (Dietz & Repp, 1983). DRI and DRA also may be ineffective if the target behavior has a long history of reinforcement or when it is maintained by other sources of reinforcement (Polsgrove & Reith, 1983).

Extinction. Withholding reinforcers (e.g., attention) thought to be maintaining undesired behavior contingent on the latter's occurrence has been used successfully with a variety of behaviors and pupils, including, in some cases, the severely handicapped (Polsgrove & Reith, 1983). However, Stainback et al. (1979) concluded that extinction is one of the least effective procedures for controlling severe maladaptive behavior and is an inappropriate choice for behaviors reinforced by consequences other than those controlled by the teacher or researcher (e.g., withdrawal, SSB, aggression, disruptive behavior). Also, the ethics of using extinction with self-injurious behavior (SIB) must be questioned, given the time it takes to work. Sensory extinction involves masking the sensory consequences produced by self-stimulatory behaviors (Kerr & Nelson, 1983). In general, it has been effective in reducing SSB with severely and profoundly handicapped students, but the need for careful monitoring of pupil behavior and for special equipment and procedures tends to limit its usefulness outside of experimental rooms.

Verbal Aversives. Verbal reprimands have been effective in studies with mild and moderate behavior problems (Nelson, 1981; Rutherford, 1983), but by themselves, they are not likely to succeed with more serious forms of maladaptive behavior. However, if they are associated with other punishing consequences, such as response cost, timeout, or overcorrection, they may acquire conditioned aversive properties and subsequently be effective when used alone (Gelfand & Hartmann, 1984).

Response Cost. Research involving the removal of reinforcers contingent on the emission of undesired target behaviors has indicated this to be a powerful, cost-effective procedure for preventing and suppressing the occurrence of a variety of target behaviors across a range of populations (Walker, 1983). However, response cost has not been effective in all studies in which it has been used. Variables critical to its success include the type of behavior, the ratio of fines to reinforcers, and the amount of cost imposed (Polsgrove & Reith, 1983).

Timeout. Timeout from positive reinforcement is a complex intervention, which may be implemented at several different levels, ranging from planned ignoring to seclusion (Nelson & Rutherford, 1983). Research has shown it to be effective with moderate to severe behavior disorders, but many factors appear to influence its success, including the level of timeout used, its duration, whether a warning signal is used, how it is applied, the schedule under which it is administered, and procedures for removing the student from timeout (Gast & Nelson, 1977; Polsgrove & Reith, 1983; Rutherford & Nelson, 1983). Research concerning the situations and target behaviors with which it is most effective, as well as the most appropriate timeout procedures to use, is limited (Polsgrove & Reith, 1983). Stainback, et al. (1979) observed that it has been more effective for reducing severe maladaptive behaviors when combined with other procedures. It is ineffective in cases where the timeout condition may be more reinforcing than the time-in environment, as in withdrawal behavior and SSB, or when timeout results in escape from aversive task demands (Kerr & Nelson, 1983). It should not be used with SIB, when continuation of the behavior may result in physical harm to the student (Stainback et al., 1979).

Overcorrection. Both restitutional and positive practice overcorrection have been effective with a wide variety of behaviors. Like timeout, overcorrection is a complex procedure which involves the components of social punishment, extinction, and timeout (Axelrod, et al., 1978). Positive practice overcorrection has been studied extensively with SSB and SIB exhibited by severely and profoundly handicapped persons (Stainback et al., 1979), as well as with the behavior problems of mildly handicapped and normal students (Nelson, 1981). In general, it has been effective, but neutral and even negative effects have been noted (Axelrod et al., 1978; Polsgrove & Reith, 1983). The effects of restitutional overcorrection have been investigated with aggressive behavior and have been found to be positive (Gelfand & Hartmann, 1984; Stainback et al., 1979). However, as Axelrod, et al. (1978) pointed out, claims that overcorrection is superior to alternative techniques have not been substantiated. Its acceptability by practitioners, and client resistance to overcorrection procedures are also potential obstacles to its effectiveness (Axelrod, et al., 1978).

Physical Aversives. Substances having aversive tastes and odors; electric shock; and slaps, pinches, and spankings comprise the range of physical aversive procedures that have been investigated. In general, punishment procedures have been found to be the most efficient and effective means of weakening severe maladaptive behaviors (Rutherford, 1983; Stainback et al., 1979). However, alternate procedures are required in many public school settings, as parents and community groups frequently object to the use of such extreme interventions as electric shock. On the other hand, many school districts sanction the use of corporal punishment with nonhandicapped and mildly handicapped students, although there are apparently no applied empirical studies that support its use (Rose, 1983).

Each of the intervention procedures described above have been successful with some student populations under some conditions. Although we have discussed these behavioral enhancement and reduction procedures separately, they are frequently used in combination in applied research studies. As the next section will illustrate, the research is showing a trend toward favoring combinations of intervention procedures, including intervention packages of several procedures for teaching complex social skills. In addition, a combination of reinforcement and behavior reduction procedures appears needed to control moderate to severe behavior disorders (Nelson, 1981; Walker, 1979).

Interventions with Moderate to Severe Behavior Disorders: Review of Selected Studies

The following analysis is based on a selective search of journals publishing behavioral research. The criteria mentioned earlier were used to identify studies involving moderate to severe behavior disorders, or prosocial target behaviors in subjects demonstrating moderate to marked behavioral disabilities. A total of 48 studies were analyzed. These could be divided into three groups: those using single-component interventions (20 studies): those using intervention packages (12 studies); and those comparing two or more intervention procedures (16 studies).

Single Component Interventions

Studies evaluating single-component interventions are reported in Table 1. As can be seen, target behaviors ranged from severe stereotypic behaviors to appropriate classroom and verbal performances. Intervention procedures included sensory reinforcement (three studies; note that Rincover et al. used sensory extinction and sensory reinforcement in separate phases), edible reinforcement (one study), tokens (one study), activity reinforcement (contingent home visits: one study), contracting (one study), social reinforcement (one study), self-monitoring and self-reinforcement (one study), differential reinforcement (DRL: two studies, DRO: two studies), sensory extinction (two studies), timeout (two studies), and overcorrection (two studies). Two studies used procedures we would classify as physical punishment: facial screening (Lutzker, 1978) and contingent restraint (Singh et al., 1981). Ten studies were evaluated as successful according to measured changes in target behaviors; 10 were evaluated as partially successful. There appeared to be no common element among either

the successful or the partially successful studies. Maintenance and generalization effects were evaluated in 10 studies, as well as in one experiment in one study. These effects were both assessed and systematically programmed in three studies, including one of two experiments reported by Singh et al. (1981). Maintenance and generalization effects were neither assessed nor programmed in seven studies. No relationship was apparent between the outcome of these studies and the extent to which maintenance and generalization effects were assessed or programmed.

Intervention Packages

Studies using intervention packages, reported in Table 2, involved a similarly wide range of target behaviors, including social skills, disruptive behaviors, and SIB. The greater proportion of prosocial target behaviors in this group probably reflects the current popularity of social skills training packages. Intervention packages contained the following components: sensory reinforcement (one study), edible reinforcement (one study), token reinforcement (one study), activity reinforcement (one study), modeling (one study), social reinforcement (eight studies), differential reinforcement (DRL: one study), timeout (two studies), overcorrection (one study), and physical aversives (lemon juice: one study). In addition, one study used contingent restraint as a reinforcer, four studies used prompting, two studies employed role-playing and rehearsal, three studies included didactic instruction as part of the intervention package, one study used adult proximity, and one study used protective equipment. As this listing suggests, the range of components used in treatment packages is large, even in this limited sample.

Of these 12 studies, 11 were evaluated as successful and one as partially successful. This may reflect the greater power of intervention packages over single component treatments. In three studies maintenance and generalization were neither assessed nor programmed; three studies assessed but did not program for maintenance and generalization; in six studies maintenance and generalization were both assessed and programmed. It would appear that researchers investigating the effects of package interventions have a greater investment in the maintenance and generalization of outcomes. Given the emphasis on social skills training in these studies, this emphasis seems most appropriate.

Comparisons of Interventions

The 16 studies comparing interventions are summarized in Table 3. While these studies tended to focus more on negative and undesired behaviors, two investigations selected appropriate social behaviors as primary targets, and three studies simultaneously monitored undesired and appropriate target behaviors. The variety of procedures used in these interventions was even greater than in the case of treatment packages. One

TABLE 1
Studies Using Single-Component Interventions

Authors, Date	Subjects and Settings	Target Behaviors	Intervention Procedures	Design	Outcome	Maintenance and Generalization
Bierly & Billingsley (1984)	6 year-old autistic male. Special school	Stereotypic object manipulation, appropriate play with toys.	Positive practice overcorrection: functional movement training.	Withdrawal: ABAB	Partially successful: Reduced stereotypic behavior, but no consistent effect on play with toys.	Assessed but not programmed: 5 minute probes at end of each data collection session.
Bizzis & Bradley-Johnson (1981)	17 year-old delinquent female. Public high school.	School attendance.	Contingency contract: 10–15 minute telephone call from Youth Guidance worker contingent on attendance; bonus recreation activity on weekend for 4/5 days attendance for 2 week period. Student gave up smoking for 1 hour on Saturday if latter contingency not met. Self-recording of hourly attendance.	Withdrawal: ABAB	Successful: Attendance rose immediately.	Not assessed or programmed. Student's grades improved from Ds and Fs to Cs.
Calhoun & Lima (1977)	19 year-old moderately retarded female Day training center.	Disruptive behaviors; appropriate social behaviors.	2 minute seclusion timeout in following sequence of schedules: VR8, VR4, CRF, VR8.	Multiple baseline across behaviors; withdrawal phases and sequentially introduced timeout schedules.	Partially successful: VR8 schedule was moderately effective in reducing low-rate behaviors, but was highly effective with high rate behaviors. Inconsistent effects on appropriate social behavior.	Assessed but not programmed. Follow-up observation in setting 2 and 6 weeks after final baseline (timeout not in use); generalization observations in other settings.
Diaddigo & Dickie (1978)	10 year-old emotionally disturbed male. Self-contained class in private residential program.	Appropriate behaviors (number of points earned and % of assignments completed).	Contingent home visits every 2 weeks for average of 28 points daily. No special contingencies for assignment completion.	Withdrawal: ABAB	Successful: Increase in daily point earnings and in assignments completed.	Assessed but not programmed. Increase in assignments completed occurred although no direct contingencies were on this behavior.
Dietz, Slack, Schwarzmueller, Wilander, Weatherly, & Hilliard (1978)	7 year-old learning disabled male. Special class.	Inappropriate behaviors: running, shoving, pushing, hitting, rolling on floor, sliding under desks, pounding on furniture, tapping with pencil or other objects on furniture, throwing objects, dropping objects, destroying objects, sliding furniture, standing on furniture, jumping from furniture, yelling.	Interval DRL: 1 star for each 2 minute period in which 1 or 0 responses occurred. Stars exchanged for time on playground. Intervals increased to 5 minutes.	Changing criterion; withdrawal phase.	Successful: Target behaviors reduced to nearly 0.	Not assessed or programmed.
Epstein, Repp, & Cullinan (1978)	6 behaviorally disordered 6–9 year-olds: 4 males, 2 females. Self-contained special class.	Obscene verbal behavior.	DRL delivered in individual contingencies.	Changing criterion.	Successful: Some pupils slower to respond.	Not assessed or programmed.
Hung (1978)	2 autistic males, 10 and 11 years old. Residential summer camp	Appropriate spontaneous sentences.	Two minutes of self-stimulatory behavior permitted contingent on emission of target behavior.	Withdrawal: ABAB. B = noncontingent SSB.	Successful: SSB can be used as a reinforcer for desired behaviors.	Assessed but not programmed: SSB occurred no more than 30 min. per day when A phase in effect.
Lutzker (1978)	20 year-old mentally retarded male. Residential institution: 3 classrooms.	Self-injurious behaviors: face and head slapping.	Facial screening; "No," putting bib over client's face and head until SIB had stopped for 3 seconds.	Multiple baseline across settings.	Successful: Teachers sometimes couldn't consequate every instance of SIB, but screening was effective.	Assessed and programmed across 3 classrooms and teachers.
Mayhew, Enyart, & Anderson (1978)	18 severely to profoundly retarded 12–20 year-old females. Residential institution.	Proximity, physical contact, and vocalizations.	Verbal and nonverbal social reinforce-ment.	Withdrawal: ABA within students	Partially successful: Social behavior increased and decreased as reinforcement was presented and withdrawn.	Assessed during other time periods, but not programmed. No effects.

TABLE 1 (*Continued*)
Studies Using Single-Component Interventions

Authors, Date	Subjects and Settings	Target Behaviors	Intervention Procedures	Design	Outcome	Maintenance and Generalization
Noland, Arnold, & Clement (1980)	2 behaviorally disordered 11 and 12 year-old females. Regular elementary school.	Academic survival skills: attention, positive talk, inappropriate locale.	Self-monitoring and self-reinforcement: Students recorded target behaviors and self-awarded points if contract contingencies were met.	Multiple baseline across behaviors; withdrawal phases.	Partially successful: Attention and positive talk increased, but inappropriate locale was not affected.	Assessed but not programmed. Rates of attention and positive talk remained at desired levels during final baseline.
Noll & Simpson (1979)	6 year-old autistic-like male. Self-contained special class.	Verbal aggression.	Physical timeout: child held in a basket hold with his eyes covered; released when aggressive behavior had stopped for 30 seconds.	Withdrawal: ABAB	Successful: Dramatic reduction in verbal aggression.	Not assessed or programmed. Narrative states that increase in appropriate social behaviors occurred concomitant to reduced aggression.
Rincover (1978)	3 severely psychotic 7–14 year-olds: 2 male, 1 female. Experimental classroom.	Self-stimulatory behaviors: plate spinning, finger flapping, twirling.	Sensory extinction: sensory feedback masked, depending on student's specific SSB.	Multiple baseline across students with withdrawal phases.	Partially successful: effectiveness depended on behavior. Reduced to nearly 0 in 2 students, by 50% in 1 student.	Not assessed or programmed.
Rincover, Cook, Peoples, & Packard (1979)	4 autistic 8–10 year-olds: 2 male 2 female. Special class.	Self-stimulatory behaviors: hand flapping; object twirling, picking at clothing, finger flapping.	Phase 1: Sensory extinction. Phase 2: Sensory reinforcement – students taught to play with toys providing sensory consequences.	Withdrawal (ABAB) and multiple baseline (Phase 1). Pre-post (Phase 2).	Partially successful: SSB substantially reduced with sensory extinction; sensory reinforcement increased appropriate toy play. One student continued to exhibit fairly high rates of SSB.	Assessed but not programmed: Follow-up probes 1–13 months after Phase 2.
Rose (1979)	9 year-old schizophrenic female. Psychiatric hospital classroom.	Self-injurious behavior: hand biting.	Full session DRO: activity reinforcers for response suppression.	Withdrawal: ABAB	Partially successful: SIB reduced to low level but not eliminated.	Not assessed or programmed.
Rotholz & Luce (1983)	2 autistic 9 and 11 year-old males. Classroom, residential treatment center.	Self-stimulatory behaviors: ceiling gazing, vocalizations.	Access to preferred sensory feedback toy contingent on lower levels of target behaviors.	Withdrawal with DRL changing criterion phases.	Successful: SSB reduced to nearly 0. Levels maintained at 1 year follow-up (student 1) and during spaced post checks (student 2).	Assessed but not programmed (first student). Assessed with reinforcement conditions in effect (second student).
Russo, Cataldo, & Cushing (1981)	3 noncompliant 3–5 year-olds: 1 male, 2 females. Treatment room.	Compliance with commands, specific negative behaviors.	Social and edible reinforcement for compliance, "nagging" condition for one child, tokens exchangable for a penny for one child.	Multiple baseline across therapists; component analysis for individual children.	Successful: Increases in compliance were directly related to reinforcement. Decreases in untreated behaviors occurred when compliance increased.	Assessed during treatment sessions. Some decrease in untreated behaviors. No assessment or programming outside treatment setting.
Russo & Koegel (1977)	5 year-old autistic female Kindergarten and first grade classrooms.	Social behavior; self-stimulatory behavior; verbal response to commands.	Token economy: tokens and praise for social behavior, token removal and verbal reprimand for SSB.	Multiple baseline with 1 withdrawal plus teacher treatment phase.	Successful: All behaviors changed to desired levels. Second experiment established appropriate behaviors in first grade.	Assessed and programmed.
Singh, Dawson, & Manning (1981)	16 year-old profoundly retarded deaf-blind female. Institutional residential unit.	Self-injurious behaviors: face slapping, face punching.	Exp. 1: Contingent restraint in a soft jacket for 1 or 3 minutes. Exp. 2: Client's hands restrained at sides for 1 or 3 mins. by regular ward staff.	Exp. 1: ABACAC Exp. 2: Alternating treatments (1 or 3 min. restraint).	Partially Successful: 1 minute restraint significantly reduced SIB: 3 min. restraint increased it (Exp. 1). 1 min. restraint more effective than 3, but not as much as in Experiment 1 (Exp. 2).	Exp. 1: Assessed, but not programmed. Exp. 2: Assessed and programmed.
Woodward, Maginn, & Johnston (1983)	4 hearing and/or visually impaired 7–10 year-olds; 3 males, 1 female. Residential school.	Self-stimulatory behavior: hand jerking, head banging, hyperventilation, finger tapping, body rocking or spinning, chin banging.	Interval DRO: ice cream and "smarties" as reinforcers for non-emission of target behaviors.	Multiple baseline across behaviors.	Partially successful: 4 of 6 target behaviors showed a statistically significant reduction in frequency. One student sent home for unrelated reasons.	Assessed, but not programmed. Anecdotal report 12, 18, and 24 months after intervention on each subject. respectively. SSB present, but at lower rates, except in one subject.
Zehr & Theobald (1978)	2 profoundly retarded 19 and 24 year-old females. Residential institution.	Self-injurious behaviors: head hitting, face scratching.	Positive practice overcorrection (manual guidance).	Withdrawal: ABAB	Successful: Manual guidance was an effective punishment procedure.	Not assessed or programmed.

TABLE 2
Studies Using Intervention Packages

Authors, Date	Subjects and Settings	Target Behaviors	Intervention Procedures	Design	Outcome	Maintenance and Generalization
Bryant & Budd (1984)	6 behaviorally disordered 4–5 year-olds; 5 males, 1 female. Special class.	Sharing behaviors	Training package for appropriate sharing: training, promoting, and reinforcement; modeling, behavioral rehearsal; contingent observation timeout for aggressive behavior.	Multiple baseline across 3 pairs of students.	Successful: Sharing increased and negative interactions decreased for all students.	Assessed but not programmed. Behavior assessment rating items related to sharing showed improvement 1 year later.
Dorsey, Iwata, Reid & Davis (1982)	3 severely to profoundly retarded 14–16 year-olds: 1 male, 2 females. Residential institution.	Self-injurious behaviors: head hitting, hand biting, eye gouging.	Continuous and contingent wearing of protective equipment, with timeout and contingent access to sensory stimulating toys.	Multiple baseline across time and settings.	Successful: Contingent protection equipment and access to sensory stimulating toys may support maintenance.	Assessed and programmed.
Favell, McGimsey, & Jones (1978)	Exp. 1: 15 year-old profoundly retarded female. Exp. 2: 8 year-old and 27 year-old profoundly retarded female. Exp. 3: 27 year-old profoundly retarded female. Residential institution (all experiments).	Exp. 1 & 2: Self-injurious behaviors: eye poking, head banging, hair pulling. Exp. 3: Marble in the hole.	Exp. 1; Lemon juice; lemon juice plus restraint for non-SIB and "distraction." Exp. 2: Restraints contingent on non-SIB. Exp. 3: 30 second restraint contingent on correct response (control condition).	Exp. 1: Withdrawal: ABCACBC. Exp. 2: Multiple baseline across clients. Exp. 3: Withdrawal: ABABCB.	Exp. 1: Successful: package more effective than lemon juice alone. Exp. 2: Successful: restraints contingent on non-SIB reduced SIB to near 0. Exp. 3: Successful: use of contingent restraint increased correct responses.	Assessed and programmed.
Ford, Evans, & Dworkin (1982)	10 year-old emotionally disturbed male. Group home treatment program.	Social skills: greeting guest at door, answering telephone, departure skills.	Didactic instruction (instruction cards; instruction cards plus proximity of staff; teaching interaction (9 step package).	Multiple baseline across behaviors.	Successful: Teaching interaction package increased percent of correct use of social skills components. Instruction cards and proximity of staff had variable effect.	Not assessed or programmed.
Foxx (1977)	8 year-old autistic male, 8 year-old severely retarded female, 6 year-old retarded male. Training room in daycare center.	Eye contact following prompt, "Look at me."	Overcorrection: functional movement training (head positioning) if eye contact not maintained for 5 sec. following prompt. Food and praise for eye contact during baseline and intervention.	Simultaneous treatment and changing criterion.	Successful: Avoidance of functional movement training, plus praise and edibles increased eye contact to nearly 90% in all 3 students. Edibles and praise alone increased it to only 55% of trials.	Assessed and programmed following completion of formal study.
Gaylord-Ross, Haring, Breen, & Pitts-Conway (1984)	Exp. 1: 17 and 20 year-old autistic males. Special class and outdoor courtyard (public high school). Exp. 2: 18 year-old autistic male. Same setting.	Social initiation toward non-handicapped peers, duration of social interactions (both experiments).	Social skills and object-use training. Students were taught to use objects (PacMan, Walkman, chewing gum), then to use them in social interactions (both experiments).	Multiple baseline across objects with generalization probes.	Successful: Students initiated and maintained social interactions with non-handicapped peers in courtyard. Generalization occurred across persons and time, except for one student.	Assessed and programmed. Multiple exemplars used in Experiment 1.
Hendrickson, Strain, Tremblay, & Shores (1982)	Exp. 1: 3 behaviorally handicapped 4 year-old males. Special preschool. Exp. 2: 2 behaviorally handicapped 6–7 year-olds: 2 male, 1 female. Special school.	Positive and negative social behaviors.	Peer confederate taught to emit social initiation behaviors, was prompted and reinforced for social initiations with target students. Exp. 2 replicated these procedures with a behaviorally handicapped peer confederate.	Withdrawal: ABAB (both experiments).	Successful: Confederate social initiations and student responses increased during intervention. Generalization did not occur without structured confederate initiations. Handicapped confederate required twice as much training.	Assessed and programmed in another setting.

TABLE 2 (*Continued*)
Studies Using Intervention Packages

Authors, Date	Subjects and Settings	Target Behaviors	Intervention Procedures	Design	Outcome	Maintenance and Generalization
Jackson, Salzberg, Pacholl, & Dorsey (1981)	10 year-old behaviorally disordered male. Special class (Exp.1); bus (Exp. 2).	Exp. 1: On-task, mild disruptive behavior, severe disruptive behavior. Exp. 2: Inappropriate bus riding: yelling, name-calling, out of seat, grabbing and throwing objects, spitting, hitting, pinching, and pushing.	Exp. 1: Contingent teacher attention to appropriate behavior; timeout for severe disruptive behavior. Exp. 2: DRL contingent afternoon privileges at home (TV and playing outside).	Withdrawal: ABAB (both experiments).	Successful: Loss of privileges occurred only twice in Experiment 2.	Assessed but not programmed: post checks with contingencies still in effect.
Lebsock & Salzberg (1981)	14 year-old behaviorally disordered female, 15 year-old behaviorally disordered male. Special class and experimental room.	Inappropriate verbalizations: talking back, denial, verbal reactions.	Role-playing and corrective feedback plus praise. Four sequential stages.	Multiple baseline across behaviors with subsequent withdrawal and reinstatement phases.	Successful: Target behaviors reduced in both students, low rates maintained during follow-up.	Assessed and programmed in classroom.
Ragland, Kerr, & Strain (1978)	3 autistic 8–9 year-olds: 2 males, 1 female.	Positive and negative social behaviors.	Peer confederate taught to emit positive social initiations and to respond positively to students' social initiations.	Multiple baseline across students with withdrawal phases.	Successful: Students' positive behaviors increased and negative behaviors decreased dramatically.	Not assessed or programmed.
Strain, Kerr, & Ragland (1979)	4 autistic 9–10 year-olds: 3 males, 1 female. Special school.	Positive motor-gestural and vocal-verbal behavior.	Peer trainer social initiations, prompting and reinforcement of social play.	Withdrawal: ABAB, ABAC.	Successful, but no generalization when peer trainer wasn't present.	Assessed but not programmed.
Walker, Greenwood, Hops, & Todd (1979)	18 mildly to moderately behaviorally disordered 6–12 year-olds: 9 males and 9 females (6 in each of 3 experiments). Experimental classroom.	Verbal, non-verbal, and/or physical social interactions: rate, quality, initiation, duration, number of peers interacted with.	Token system paired with teacher praise. Package intervention used in Experiment 3.	Withdrawal, with DRO; different components of social interaction were reinforced in different phases.	Partially successful: Reinforcement of continued social interactions was more effective than reinforcement of initiations or responses alone.	Not assessed or programmed.

TABLE 3
Studies Comparing Interventions

Authors, Date	Subjects and Settings	Target Behaviors	Intervention Procedures	Design	Outcome	Maintenance and Generalization
Carden-Smith & Fowler (1984)	Exp. 1: 3 remedial kindergarten students (ages & sexes not given). Exp. 2: 3 remedial kindergarten students, 6 years old. Preschool class for behavior problem students.	Disruptive behavior: participation during transition (both experiments).	Exp. 1: Teacher monitoring of student behavior, teacher awarded points; peer team captain monitored behavior and awarded points. Exp. 2: Peer monitoring with corrective teacher feedback; peer monitoring with no corrective feedback.	Exp. 1: withdrawal (ABAC) Exp. 2: Multiple baseline across students.	Exp. 1: Successful: Both teacher and peer conditions substantially reduced disruptive behavior and increased participation. Exp 2: Partially successful: One male student was disruptive during bathroom transitions when female peer was monitoring during no teacher feedback condition.	Not assessed or programmed (either experiment).
Cavalier & Ferretti (1980)	5 year-old profoundly retarded female. Special school.	Stereotypic behaviors: finger dragging, tongue protrusion, skin sucking, object manipulation.	Mild slap on forearm proceeded by "No"; DRA; overcorrection plus DRA; slap plus DRA.	Withdrawal: ABACADAE, replicated across behaviors.	Partially successful: Slap plus DRA most effective, except for object manipulation. Slap alone also effective, but didn't strengthen alternative behavior. Overcorrection and DRA relatively ineffective.	Assessed and programmed. Some generalization across settings, times, and trainers.
deCatanzaro & Baldwin (1978)	2 profoundly retarded 8 and 12 year-old males. Institution day room.	Self-injurious behavior: head hitting.	Overcorrection: forced arm exercise; DRO; overcorrection and DRO; generalization training.	Withdrawal: ABACDE, ABADE.	Successful: SIB reduced to nearly 0. Arm exercice and reinforcement more effective than reinforcement alone.	Assessed and programmed. Gradual removal of restraints.
Dorsey, Iwata, Ong, & McSween (1980)	Exp. 1: 7 profoundly retarded 5–37 year-olds; 1 male, 6 females. Exp. 2: 2 profoundly retarded 21 and 26 year-old males. Private nursing home (both experiments).	Self-injurious behaviors (both experiments): mouthing, hand biting, skin biting, skin tearing, head banging.	Exp. 1: Water mist sprayed toward clients' faces. Exp 2: Verbal "no"; DRO, water mist, and "no"; "no" plus DRO; DRO alone (one client in one setting.)	Exp. 1: withdrawal: ABAB (AB with 1 client). Exp. 2: Modified multiple baseline across clients.	Exp. 1: Successful: SIB reduced an average of 51.5% in first intervention, 60.1% in second. Exp. 2: Successful: Neither "no" nor DRO alone reduced SIB. When water mist was paired with "no" behavior was suppressed.	Assessed and programmed across settings and experimenters. "No" acquired stimulus control over SIB after pairing with water mist.
Gamble & Strain (1979)	2 behaviorally disordered classes, 8 pupils each. One class for 7–10 year-olds one for 9–11 year-olds.	Appropriate verbal and non-verbal social behavior.	Dependent and inter-dependent group contingencies.	Withdrawal: ABAC (group 1), ACAB (Group 2).	Both group contingencies were successful.	Not assessed or programmed.
Harris & Wolchik (1979)	4 autistic-like 5–7 year-old males. Special day school.	Self-stimulatory behaviors: repetitive hand movements, stroking, or tapping, turning objects, crumbling, stroking, tapping fingers, touching body parts.	DRO, timeout, and overcorrection applied separately in treatment phases counterbalanced across students.	Withdrawal: ABACADAD; ADACABACAC; ADABACAC.	Successful: Overcorrection reduced SSB for all students in training setting; timeout effects were variable. DRO had no to minimal effects. Little generalization to other settings.	Assessed across settings for one student. No generalized suppressive effect. Not programmed.
Luce & Hall (1981)	Exp. 1: 6 year-old seriously emotionally disturbed male. Exp. 2: 12 year-old autistic male. Exp. 3: 6 year-old schizophrenic male. Special classroom (all experiments).	Inappropriate and bizarre verbalizations (all experiments).	Exp. 1: Contingent exercise (running in play area) plus DRO. Exp. 2: Contingent exercise plus DRO; DRO alone. Exp. 3: DRO (during baseline); Contingent exercise plus DRO.	Exp 1: Withdrawal; ABAB. Exp. 2: Withdrawal; ABCAB. Exp. 3: Multiple baseline across sessions.	Successful (all 3 experiments): Target behaviors were quickly reduced to 0 or near 0. Contingent exercise was more powerful than DRO, but DRO should be used with it.	Assessed but not programmed. 3 post checks at 2, 4, and 6 week intervals in Experiment 2. Contingencies remained in effect.
Miles & Cuvo (1980)	9 year-old severely retarded female. Special school.	13 disruptive behaviors; task completion.	2 minute seclusion timeout for disruptive behaviors, plus physical and social reinforcement for appropriate behavior; extinction plus ignoring.	Withdrawal: A-BC-A-BC-A-CD-A-CD-BC.	Successful: Immediate 70% decrease in disruptive behavior following timeout and positive reinforcement; 10% increase following extinction and positive reinforcement.	Not assessed or programmed.

137

TABLE 3 (*continued*)
Studies Comparing Interventions

Authors, Date	Subjects and Settings	Target Behaviors	Intervention Procedures	Design	Outcome	Maintenance and Generalization
Murphy, Ruprecht, & Nunes (1979)	17 year-old profoundly retarded male. Public school: special class, gym, household area.	Self-injurious behavior: self-slapping.	2 minute timeout in restraints (VR2 for self-slapping); 2 min. timeout with no restraints; 2 min. timeout in restraints (VR6 for self-slapping); 2 min. timeout in restraints (VR2 for self-slapping) plus blindfold. Alternate behaviors verbally reinforced.	Withdrawal: ABABCBDBEA.	Successful: 99% reduction in SIB with VR2 timeout in restraints. Verbal control and VR6 timeout schedule were not as effective.	Assessed but not programmed. Follow-up for 2 years at 3 month intervals.
Ollendick, Shapiro, & Barrett (1981)	3 mentally retarded and emotionally disturbed 7–8 year-olds; 2 males, 1 female. Psychiatric hospital classroom.	Stereotypic behaviors (hair twirling, hand posturing); accurate task performance.	Physical restraint (verbal warning and 30 sec. manual restraint); positive practice overcorrection; verbal warning and 30 sec. manual guidance through task manipulations; no-treatment control condition.	Alternating treatments, followed by phase involving most effective intervention for each student.	Successful: Physical restraint superior with one student; positive practice superior with 2. Overcorrection did not improve task performance, although procedure involved functional movements.	Not assessed or programmed.
Pease & Tyler (1979)	15 learning disabled/behaviorally disordered 7–14 year-olds; 11 males, 4 females. Special class.	15 disruptive behaviors.	Teacher-determined timeout durations; self-determined timeout duration.	Repeated measures: B-A-B-C-BC.	Successful: Self-determined timeout duration was as effective as teacher-determined timeout duration.	Not assessed or programmed.
Plummer, Baer, & LeBlanc (1977)	5 year old autistic female. Preschool special class.	Disruptive behaviors.	1 minute planned ignoring timeout; paced instructions, and DRO; paced instructions.	Multiple baseline across 2 teachers; sequential intervention within teachers (2 experiments).	Unsuccessful: Procedural timeout increased disruptive behaviors; paced instructions more effective.	Not assessed or programmed.
Rapoff, Altman, Christopherson (1980)	5 year-old deaf-blind non-ambulatory male. "Preschool-like" therapy room; student's home.	Self-injurious behaviors.	DRO (primary reinforcers); Overcorrection (functional movement training); contingent lemon juice squirted in mouth; aromatic ammonia capsule placed under student's nose.	Multiple baseline across locations; withdrawal phases.	Successful; Ammonia produced greatest suppression, lemon juice next best. DRO and overcorrection were ineffective.	Not assessed or programmed.
Trice & Parker (1983)	2 disruptive 16 year-old males. Resource room.	Swearing.	DRL and public graphing (praise if frequency of use was below average of previous baseline); response cost and public graphing (5 minutes after school detention if over 3 occurrences per day).	Withdrawal: ABACA, ACABA (counter-balanced across students).	Successful: Both DRL and response cost decreased swearing to low levels. Response cost had a more immediate effect.	Not assessed or programmed.
Warrenfeltz, Kelly, Salzberg, Beegle, Levy, Adams, & Crouse (1981)	4 behaviorally disordered 15–16 year-olds: 3 males, 1 female. Residential treatment center.	Appropriate responses to direct commands and to supervisor's critical feedback.	Didactic classroom instruction, role-playing and self-monitoring.	Multiple baseline across pairs of students.	Partially successful: Didactic sessions didn't generalize: role-playing and self-monitoring did, but effects for 1 student were weak.	Assessed and programmed. Daily generalization sessions.
Wells, Forehand, Hickey, & Green (1977)	4 autistic-like 5–7 year-old males. Special day school.	Self-stimulatory behaviors: object manipulation mouthing, hand movement.	DRO, timeout and overcorrection applied separately in treatment phases counterbalanced across students.	Withdrawal: ABACADAD; ADACABACAC; ACABACAC	Partially successful: Overcorrection reduced SSB for all students in training setting; timeout effects were variable. DRO had no to minimal effects. Little generalization to other settings.	Assessed across settings for one student. No generalized suppressive effect. Not programmed.

comparison involved social reinforcement procedures, one included self-monitoring, one compared self- to teacher-determined timeout duration, one contrasted teacher and peer monitoring procedures, and the following procedures were used in one study each: instructions, paced instructions, and role-playing. Eight studies compared a differential reinforcement procedure to other interventions, one used extinction, two employed verbal aversives, and one used response cost. Five comparisons involved timeout, six involved overcorrection, one used contingent exercise, three employed physical aversives, two used restraint, and one involved blindfolding. In addition, two group contingencies were compared in one study. Eleven studies and one of two experiments in one study were rated as successful in changing target behaviors; three studies and one experiment in another study were evaluated as partially successful, and one study was evaluated as unsuccessful, in that timeout failed to control the target behavior (although paced instructions did). Four studies assessed and programmed for maintenance and generalization, four studies assessed but did not program maintenance and generalization, and eight studies did not assess or program these effects.

However, these evaluations should be viewed in the light of the purpose of these investigations, which was to compare interventions. Given this research focus, it is not surprising that investigators paid relatively less attention to generalization and maintenance. It is interesting to note that studies comparing behavior reduction procedures consistently found the more intense or aversive procedure, or procedures involving multiple components (e.g., DRO plus water mist, timeout plus restraints) more effective than less severe or complex interventions.

To summarize the research involving behavioral interventions, the following observations seem warranted.

1. Tactile, sensory, edible, and tangible reinforcers have been used mainly with younger and more severely handicapped pupils. All have been effective, although they are impractical in some settings.

2. Token and activity reinforcement, as well as modeling and contracting, have wide applicability across students of all ages. They appear to be used more often with higher functioning pupils.

3. Social reinforcement is a robust procedure, especially with younger pupils or when combined with other intervention strategies.

4. Self-monitoring, self-evaluation, and self-reinforcement procedures have not been as well researched, but promise to be useful in promoting maintenance and generalization, especially in more mature students.

5. Milder aversive procedures are most effective with less serious behavior disorders. In combination with behavior enhancement or other reductive procedures, they are effective in controlling moderate to severe problem behaviors.

6. The effects of timeout and overcorrection are variable, depending on a number of student and procedural factors. Situations in which they are to be used should be assessed carefully.

7. Physical aversives are the most effective means of controlling severe maladaptive behaviors, but there are a number of ethical and practical limitations on their use outside of institutional programs. The use of corporal punishment with mildly to moderately behaviorally disordered pupils is not recommended.

8. Package interventions seem to exert more powerful control over behavior, especially in teaching social skills, than single component interventions, and researchers appear to have attended more carefully to the maintenance and generalization of their effects.

The Maintenance and Generalization of Behavioral Intervention Effects

Our analysis of the results of the studies described above suggests that enduring and generalized outcomes of behavioral interventions are by no means assured, even when such effects are specifically programmed. Nearly a decade ago, Stokes and Baer (1977) advocated the development of a technology of generalization, and programmatic suggestions for achieving such effects are found throughout the practitioner literature (see Gelfand & Hartmann, 1984; Kerr & Nelson, 1983). Stokes and Baer (1977) reviewed 270 applied behavior analysis studies related to generalization and observed that in over half of these studies, generalization was assessed, but not actually pursued or programmed.

Rutherford and Nelson (1988) reviewed 103 behavioral studies in education published since 1977, plus 53 secondary sources reporting maintenance and generalization research. They noted that although more researchers were addressing this area, the technology of maintenance and generalization is still insufficient and scattered. Our selective review of the research summarized above indicates that maintenance and generalization effects continue to be ignored or are assessed but not programmed. Other reviews of behavioral interventions (e.g., Burchard & Lane, 1982; Kazdin, 1983; Lane & Burchard, 1983) have documented that the "albatross of generalization" continues to hang around the necks of behaviorists; that is, behavior can be changed, but often the changes accomplished in treatment settings do not extend over time or into students' natural environments. This criticism may be made of interventions based on any model, as the failure of treatment gains to last outside of the immediate therapeutic environment is a problem common to all intervention models, whatever their theoretical or practical basis.

The fact is, the development of effective maintenance and generalization procedures is a hard task for any treatment program. Behavioral researchers are working toward a technology of generalization on two fronts. One approach focuses on procedures to influence the client's behavior during treatment so that it will maintain in the natural environment. Strategies in this area include: (1) selecting and training target behaviors that will increase the likelihood of their being reinforced in natural environments; (2) loosening experimental control over stimuli and responses in the treatment setting so that differences between discriminative stimuli in treatment and natural settings are more difficult to discriminate; (3) using stimuli in the training setting likely to be found in the natural environment; (4) making the limits of training contingencies unclear by manipulating the schedule and timing of reinforcement; and (5) teaching subjects to self-monitor, self-evaluate, and self-reinforce their behavior. The other approach is to prepare the environment to support subjects' new behaviors. Strategies in this area include: (1) assessing natural environments to identify stimuli that can be incorporated into treatment programs; (2) identifying significant persons in the natural environment and training them to model, prompt, and consequate behaviors; and (3) training subjects to recruit reinforcement (Kerr & Nelson, 1983; Nelson, 1981). The developing technology of behavioral-ecological analysis is helping researchers to identify and program such variables (Nelson & Polsgrove, 1984), but examination of exemplary studies, such as Gaylord-Ross et al. (1984) and Jackson et al. (1981) illustrate the complexity and difficulty of this task.

Level systems are a fairly recent curriculum innovation in programs for students with behavioral disorders that have potential for improving the maintenance and generalization of adaptive behavior changes (Kerr & Nelson, 1983). Level systems are based upon graduated increases in behavioral and academic expectations, as well as increasingly powerful and naturalistic reinforcement associated with student improvements. For example, at the lowest level students may be expected to demonstrate knowledge of classroom rules, attempt academic tasks, and work for immediate tangible or social reinforcers. They are also likely to be allowed less choice in matters involving their movement in the classroom and building, and to require more structure and supervision. Expectations and privileges at higher levels are likely to include demonstration of self-regulation skills, independent completion of academic work, access to mainstream classes and activities, and greater freedom of choice and movement. Students enter a level system at their current functional level, based on criterion-referenced evaluation, and progress through the levels is determined by continuous assessment (Kerr & Nelson, 1983).

Ideally, level systems represent a "top down" approach to curriculum design, in that each level represents an approximation to the skills required for successful participation in less restrictive educational environments. The terminal behaviors, then, are those exhibited by behaviorally normal students in regular school settings. For example, one such system is the Madison Plan (Taylor and Soloway, 1973). Because the terminal behaviors are those likely to be required and reinforced in the natural environment, the probability of maintenance and generalization of these desired behaviors is enhanced.

Teacher Training in Behavioral Interventions

Despite the widespread use of behavioral interventions in special education programs for students exhibiting moderate to severe behavior disorders, there is a dearth of research concerning teacher training in this area. Studies of preservice training have occurred primarily in undergraduate psychology classes, where instructional systems based on behavioral principles, such as Keller's (1968) Personalized System of Instruction (PSI) have been used to teach standard course content. The objectives of such programs have been similar to those of behavioral methods of instruction in public schools: that is, to maximize students' acquisition of content, as measured by criterion-referenced tests and performance measures. Malott (1984) critiqued these efforts, and concluded that, "in the past 19 years, behavior modification in higher education has not accomplished what we had hoped for, but it has accomplished more than other approaches" (p. 218).

Renne and Blackhurst (1977) compared a programmed instruction approach based on PSI in an undergraduate introduction to special education course to a traditional lecture approach and a self-paced instruction approach, and found that competency-based instruction was superior, based on student performance on content examinations. Nelson, Berdine, and Moyer (1978) evaluated a competency-based cross-categorical special education methods course, but the relative efficacy of this method of instruction could not be determined, as their evaluation lacked a control group. In any case, these studies did not evaluate preservice teacher's acquisition and use of behavioral interventions. Tawney's (1972) Practice What You Preach model, in which teachers were observed in their classrooms subsequent to training, and receipt of special education certification was contingent upon their demonstrated competence in using the methods they had been taught, constitutes a direct evaluation of teacher training in behavioral methods, but his model also was not compared to other forms of instruction.

An analysis by Cooke (1984) of the content of preservice textbooks presenting information about the behavioral model provides some disturbing news about the way behavioral psychology may be represented in teacher education. He reviewed four preservice teacher textbooks, written by nonbehavioral scholars but presenting behavioral viewpoints on major issues, and found numerous misrepresentations of the behavioral model. These included: (1) errors in terminology; (2) use of nonexistent technical terms; (3) incorrect use or definition of technical terms; (4) inappropriate choice of representatives (e.g., Pavlov and Watson; association of behavior modification with aversive control only); (5)

incorrectly stated principles; (6) inappropriate application of principles; and (7) incorrect interpretations of the philosophical implications of behaviorism. Again, this is not an evaluation of special education preservice teachers or their use of behavioral interventions, but it does suggest that the context in which such training occurs is not conducive to an accurate interpretation of the behavior model.

An indication of the context in which inservice special education teachers and students work is provided by White's (1975) and Thomas, Presland, Grant, and Glynn's (1978) studies of teachers' use of approval and disapproval in regular classrooms. White (1975) measured the rates of approval and disapproval of 104 teachers in grades 1–12. A steady increase in disapproval rates was associated with increasing grade levels, and disapproval rates were higher than rates of teacher approval from the second grade on. Thomas et al. (1978) replicated White's study in 10 seventh-grade classrooms in New Zealand, and found that the majority of teachers in their sample emitted more disapprovals than approvals. Walker, Hops, and Fiegenbaum (1976) studied differential teacher attention toward acting-out children. They followed five disruptive students from an experimental classroom back into separate regular classrooms. The regular classroom teachers praised these students an average of 2.4 times per day, while emitting disapprovals toward them an average of 36 times per day. Moreover, the five teachers spent an average of 14% of their time with the disruptive pupil, which indicates that negative behavior on the part of these students resulted in disproportionate teacher attention, compared to that provided other students.

These data suggest that one of the major problems involving social reinforcement as an intervention is getting teachers to use it (Nelson, 1981). Breyer and Allen (1975) were unable to train a teacher with 23 years of teaching experience to praise desired behavior and ignore undesired behavior. McNamara (1971) compared the effects of feedback, response cost (point losses for attending to undesired pupil behavior, with points redeemable for beer), and positive reinforcement to the teacher on increasing appropriate attending and ignoring of three special education teachers. All three procedures were effective, but rates of pupils' disruptive behavior remained high until response cost contingencies were imposed on the latter.

Direct consultation with, and supervision of, teachers probably has been the surest way to train inservice practitioners in the use of behavioral interventions. However, this strategy lacks the efficiency of group instruction. The latter approach continues to be the predominant mode of inservice teacher education, although certainly not the most effective. Nelson (1978) observed that appropriate follow-up procedures, including contingencies on desired teacher performances, are necessary to ensure that teachers maintain skills acquired in pre- or inservice training. Reitz, Barbetta, Sestili, Hawkins, and Dickie (1984) developed a supervisory model based on the concept of the Individualized Education Program. Personal teacher objectives were developed, worked on, and evaluated throughout the year. However, Reitz et al. (1984) pointed out that their model is incompatible with the work loads and priorities of most public school supervisors, and that by continuing to burden supervisors with administrative responsibilities, schools will ensure ". . . that future generations of teachers will view the process of supervision as nothing more than a necessary evil associated with their profession" (p. 264).

Joyce and Showers (1982) introduced the coaching model for training regular classroom inservice teachers. This model is based on strategies used for coaching athletics: learning the theory and principles associated with instructional and behavior management procedures; observation of an expert performing these procedures; practicing these procedures with immediate feedback under controlled conditions; and coaching one another in the procedures at work. Joyce and Showers (1982) recommended strategies for enhancing the transfer of skills from training to classroom settings. These include forecasting the transfer process throughout training (i.e., training teachers to generalize their performances); attaining the highest possible level of skill development during training; and developing "executive control," that is, a meta-understanding of the strategies involved.

The introduction of computer technology into teacher education presents exciting possibilities that are just beginning to be explored. Kauffman, Strang, and Loper (in press) developed a program in which teacher trainees interact with microcomputer-simulated students. Technological innovations such as this substantially increase trainees' opportunity to practice and obtain systematic feedback in instructional and behavior management skills early in their professional training.

Implications of Research for Practice

In this section we attempt to address the translation of behavioral research into practice. There are areas in which the technology developed through research has been applied effectively by practitioners, as well as areas in which discrepancies exist. Our discussion focuses on three topics: the use of behavioral interventions, ethical and legal issues involving behavioral interventions, and suggestions for improving the use of behavioral research.

The Use of Behavioral Interventions

There is no question that behavioral technology has had a major impact on special education instructional methods and behavior management procedures, especially in the treatment of behavior disorders exhibited by severely and profoundly handicapped students. In fact, behavioral interventions are the only strategies that have demonstrated any degree of efficacy with SIB,

SSB, other stereotypic behaviors, and extreme aggression (Kerr & Nelson, 1983). In addition, classroom management systems based on behavioral principles are widely used in educational programs for the mildly and moderately handicapped, as well as in regular classrooms with educationally "normal" students (Kazdin, 1982; Nelson, 1981). The volume of behavioral research published annually in the professional literature also indicates that behavioral interventions are becoming part of the repertoire of many practitioners. Four areas in which this technology has recently been making a substantial contribution include the development of functional assessment procedures, data-based decision making, social skills training, and intervention strategies addressing the issue of maintenance and generalization.

Functional Assessment Procedures

Earlier we mentioned that a technology for establishing normative rates of target behaviors is being developed through behavioral assessment research (Howell, 1981; Ollendick & Hersen, 1984). These normative data may be used as criteria for determining a student's eligibility for special education, for deciding whether a given behavior requires intervention, and for evaluating the outcome of an intervention strategy. In addition to these applications, functional assessment includes criterion-referenced and continuous daily measures of student performances related to both academic and social instructional objectives (Howell, Kaplan, & O'Connell, 1979; Nelson, Gast, & Trout, 1979; White & Haring, 1980). These assessment procedures are functional because they measure student behaviors that are directly related to the curriculum, and because they are continuous, they permit teachers formatively to evaluate and adjust individual educational programs.

In addition, behavioral assessment procedures are potentially useful for determining if and when students may be decertified for special education purposes. For example, school personnel could take data on normative rates of critical "school survival" behaviors of nonhandicapped students in mainstream educational settings. These data would provide a basis for comparison with similar data collected on handicapped students (i.e., those labeled behaviorally disordered) in mainstream settings. Such assessments would allow educators to make empirical decisions about removing students from special education caseloads. The lack of such criteria in the past may be at least partly responsible for the tendency to retain students in programs for behaviorally disordered pupils until they move out of the district or become too old for available programs.

Data-Based Decision Making

The technology of data-based decision making (Deno & Mirkin, 1978; White & Haring, 1980) is another assessment tool that has proven useful in formatively evaluating students and instructional programs. This approach enables teachers visually to analyze trends in student performance data, apply criterion-referenced decision rules, and adjust interventions frequently, thus potentially reducing the time students spend in nonproductive instructional programs. Haring, Liberty, and White (1980) reported studies indicating that mildly handicapped pupils whose teachers used data-based decision rules made greater academic progress than did students of teachers who did not. This technology is also being applied to social behavior interventions (Kerr & Nelson, 1983).

Social Skills Training

Some of the research described in the previous section has focused on developing intervention packages to increase the academic and social skills of handicapped children and youth. Examples of programs that have been more thoroughly researched include PASS: the Program for Academic Survival Skills (Greenwood, Hops, & Walker, 1977), ASSET: A Social Skills Program for Adolescents (Hazel, Schumaker, Sherman, & Sheldon-Wildgen, 1981), the Social Competence Intervention Project (Day, Lindeman, Powell, Fox, Stowitschek, & Shores, 1984), CLASS: Contingencies for Learning Academic and Social Skills (Hops, Fleischman, & Hutton, 1974), and the ACCEPTS Program: the Walker Social Skills Curriculum (Walker, McConnell, Holmes, Todis, Walker, & Golden, 1983). These curricula include a variety of instructional and reinforcement procedures, materials, and assessment strategies for social skill domains. Horton, Walker, and Rankin (1983) are developing social behavior skills assessment procedures for determining the standards and expectations of regular classroom teachers and pupils with regard to student behaviors. These standards and expectations may then provide a basis for developing objectives and content of social skills training for pupils who teachers wish to mainstream. Social skills training programs illustrate the progress that has been made in: (1) developing strategies for identifying functional target behaviors; (2) including social skills instruction in curricula for behaviorally disordered students; and (3) socially validating the outcomes of this instruction in less restrictive environments.

Maintenance and Generalization Strategies

Social skills curricula designed to facilitate mainstreaming also address the issue of maintenance and generalization to the extent that they focus on instruction in functional social skills and on assessing the behavioral expectations of less restrictive environments. Anderson-Inman, Walker, and Purcell (1984) described the strategy of transenvironmental programming, which consists of four components: (1) assessing the behavioral expectations of the target environments; (2) competency training in the special education environment; (3)

selection and use of techniques for promoting the transfer of skills across settings; and (d) monitoring and evaluating student performance in the target environment. The researchers described how generalization strategies were incorporated into the ACCEPTS curriculum, but they also pointed out that, "we actually have very little data demonstrating that application of the suggested procedures might have any real effect on the performance of handicapped students in regular classes" (p. 28).

This comment reflects the current state of practice with regard to programming for changes in social behavior that persist when students are returned to natural or less restrictive environments. Bailey and Lessen (1984) criticized the failure of researchers to deal with important skills that have functional utility in subjects' adult or mainstream environments. While the current emphasis on social skills training in special education programs is an indication that practitioners are concerned about the social validity and generalizability of their curricula, these efforts comprise a relatively small part of the instructional program in most special education classrooms. Whether attempting to improve the reading skills of a 17-year-old delinquent youth by a fraction of a grade level constitutes a functional curricular objective should be evaluated in the light of what skills such a person would need to succeed in the adult world without resorting to criminal behavior. By the same token, implementing treatment programs in restrictive environments that attempt to develop or restore normalized social functioning must be seriously questioned. Lane and Burchard (1983) conducted an exteensive review of behavior modification programs for delinquent youth and observed an apparent relationship between recidivism and the restrictiveness of the treatment environment. Their conclusion should be considered by all practitioners who intervene on behalf of children and youth in restrictive or segregated environments: "To the extent that delinquents and criminals are locked up in institutions, the rationale for doing so should be to punish and/or to temporarily protect the community, not to rehabilitate. Very restrictive environments make rehabilitation less likely to happen" (p. 273).

We believe that social skills assessment and transenvironmental programming should become a fundamental part of special education programs for behaviorally disordered pupils. Assessment of social skills and deficits, against local normative rates of such behaviors in nonhandicapped students, would provide a criterion for certifying pupils as eligible for special education as well as for decertifying them following intervention. Progressively higher expectations for desired social behaviors should also be incorporated into level systems, as should systematically increased access to less restrictive educational settings. In order for transenvironmental programming to be maximally effective, regular education personnel must be included as key members of students' child study teams, and trained to implement the specific components of Individualized Education Programs dealing with the acquisition and maintenance of appropriate social behaviors in regular classrooms. Until this happens, the direct teaching of desired social skills to handicapped students will continue to occur primarily in self-contained special classes, and the maintenance of improved levels of these skills will be left largely to chance. Both of these conditions increase the likelihood that students identified as behaviorally disordered and placed in special education settings will continue to require such placements throughout their school years.

Another impediment to the effective transition of students with moderate to severe behavior disorders to less restrictive settings is the lack of training of, and support for, regular education personnel with regard to procedures for monitoring and managing behavior. Anderson-Inman et al. (1984) noted that the most difficult component of transenvironmental programming to implement has been that involving the monitoring and evaluation of student behavior in the target environment, because regular teachers are not trained to collect data, and support personnel and systems for data collection are not widely available. Even those special education teachers who are trained at the preservice level systematically to observe and record behavior often fail to practice these skills once they enter the field. Tawney (1984) observed that the tradition of data collection has not existed in special education. Kerr and Nelson (1983) noted that data collecting behaviors in special educators are not differeentially reinforced, because awareness of the value of thhese skills is lacking in their supervisors and administrators.

Ethical and Legal Issues

The excessive and inappropriate use of aversive procedurees constitutes one of the more sensitive areas of special education practice. The extent to which abuses occur in special education is difficult to determine, but Rose's (1983) survey of randomly selected school districts in 18 states regarding the use of corporal punishment by principals indicated that such practices with the mildly handicapped are widespread. Furthermore, Rose noted that while the short- and long-term effects of corporal punishment are virtually unknown, there is an apparent reluctance to investigate these effects. He urged that in cases where corporal punishment is to be used parental permission should be obtained, its effects on the pupil's behavior should be documented, it should be included in the students' Individualized Education Program, and its use should be justified.

Barton, Brulle, and Repp (1983) reviewed judicial rulings with regard to the use of aversive techniques. They found that except for *Morales v Turman* (1973), which allowed slaps in extreme circumstances, all rulings have expressly forbidden corporal punishment with handicapped persons. The use of electric shock was upheld in *Wyatt v Stickney* (1971), but only under carefully defined conditions. Similarly, restraint has not been sanctioned as a treatment procedure except under qualified supervision and after the failure of other techniques has been documented. The use of aversive oral and olfactory substances has not been reviewed judicially; neither have overcorrection procedures. Seclusion timeout has been litigated a number of times, but whether these decisions establish precedent for other levels of timeout is unclear. Response cost also has not been judicially reviewed. Because extinction and differential reinforcement do not involve the application of aversive stimuli, it is doubtful that they will be subject to legal scrutiny. Barton, Brulle & Repp (1983) cautioned that, "any person who provides aversive behavioral therapies for handicapped persons without knowledge of the current legislative and litigative mandates governing such provision and concern for the rights of the individual invites both professional and personal disaster" (p. 5). Information regarding such legal and ethical issues should be an integral part of teacher training in the use of behavior reduction procedures. Pre- and inservice teachers also should learn how to evaluate the acceptability of their interventions by other educational staff, parents, and the students themselves. Another target for training is strategies for socially validating the outcome of special education interventions. The determination of which social behaviors critically affect student survival in local mainstream classrooms and the collection of data on normative rates of these behaviors are two important social validation strategies.

Returning to our earlier observation, it is difficult to determine the extent to which aversive behavior control techniques are abused in special education. Wood and Braaten (1983) pointed out that punishment is assumed to be seductive for those who use it, because the punishing individual is reinforced by the immediate desired affect on the punished individual's behavior. They suggested that students may be protected from abusive punishment either by abolishing it altogether, or by restricting and carefully supervising those who use it. They concluded that the need for strong control measures for highly disruptive and aggressive pupils dictates that the latter option be chosen, but advocated that until the effects of punishment can be established empirically, its use is justified only in combination with procedures for teaching desired replacement behaviors. With regard to corporal punishment, their stance is clear: it "has no place in a special education program" (p. 71).

Selection of the most appropriate treatment alternative constitutes another ethical and legal concern for special education practitioners (Barton et al., 1983). This involves using more restrictive or aversive procedures only after less intensive interventions have been tried and have failed. Determining when a procedure has been ineffective, and selecting an appropriate alternative, can be difficult, given the variety of strategies available and their many potential interactions with student and setting variables. In this regard, Gaylord-Ross (1980) provided a useful decision model to guide practitioners in the selection of procedures for managing

deviant behavior. His model consists of five components: (1) *assessment*, to identify and validate the behavior as a problem and to rule out medical explanations; (2) *reinforcement*, which suggests alternate reinforcement procedures depending on whether the behavior is maintained by positive reinforcement, negative reinforcement, or a low density of reinforcement; (3) *ecology*, which includes a set of interventions to eliminate crowding, to increase engaging objects in the environment, or to remove pollutants that could be maintaining the behavior; (4) *curriculum*, which addresses potential covariance between instructional tasks and undesired behavior; and (5) *punishment*, which is the final choice after response-building alternatives have proven unfeasible.

The issue of a student's right to treatment has been legally tested in the case of institutionalized persons (e.g., *Morales v Turman*, 1973; *Wyatt v Stickney*, 1971). The question of whether a public school student's special education program is the most effective and appropriate alternative has not been considered, to our knowledge. However, given current public concern regarding the status of education in the United States, we believe that litigation on this matter is a distinct possibility. It is becoming clear that special education is no longer being accorded the laissez faire status it enjoyed a decade ago. Whether watered-down academic curricula or training in classroom compliance behaviors contribute to adult independence and social competence are ethical issues that should be widely discussed within the profession, and may soon be tested by the courts. Behavioral technology is a tool that can be made to serve any master. It is gratifying that behavioral researchers and practitioners are showing a strong interest in using the criterion of ultimate functioning to evaluate the relevance and efficacy of their programs and interventions. Adult competence in the skills required for independent, productive living should be the outcome of special education programs. Particularly at the secondary level, special educators should adopt the "top down" approach to curriculum design. If independent adult living skills were the terminal behaviors in the curriculum, and students' acquisition and maintenance of these skills were structured through progressive level systems, secondary curricula for pupils who are handicapped by their social behavior would be far more relevant and functional than at present.

Improving the Use of Behavioral Research

Progress in the translation of behavioral research findings into practice with students exhibiting moderate to severe behavior disorders has been accelerating. Fifteen years ago, behavioral interventions were almost non-existent in the repertoires of special education practitioners; now they constitute the dominant set of intervention procedures. Nevertheless, the failure of teachers to use these tools appropriately, even after receiving intensive preservice training, suggests the need for maintenance and generalization training, as well as new strategies for inservice training. Neither pre-service nor inservice training will have sufficient impact on nonconsumers of behavioral technology unless reinforcement contingencies in the field are altered so as differentially to reinforce teachers who use accountable procedures, and who evaluate these through direct and continuous measures of their pupils' behavior. Tawney (1984) suggested a new professional role: namely, that of the teacher-researcher, who would receive support services from a center for excellence, whose goal would be to create an environment in which it is possible to document that students benefit from instruction. Without adequate support systems for model teaching procedures, there is a danger that today's Zeitgeist of accountability will become tomorrow's poltergeist. The concluding section addresses recommendations for preventing such an occurrence.

Needs and Recommendations

The foregoing review of research procedures and outcomes, and of the implementation of research findings in behavioral interventions with moderate to severe behavior disorders, suggests both that much is possible and that much remains to be done. In this section we discuss these needs in terms of the implications of our findings in four areas: personnel training; future research; educational practice; and federal policies, regulations, and funding practices. We offer specific recommendations in each of these areas. However, these recommendations should be evaluated in the light of existing obstacles to the application of research using behavioral interventions, which we discuss first.

Impediments in the Application of Behavioral Research

Of all the categorical special education areas, that of behaviorally disordered students perhaps has been most affected by divergent theories and philosophies. The issue of whether the field should be conceptualized around a student population having disordered emotions or disordered behavior is one area in which professional opinions are polarized (Huntze, 1985). Behaviorists clearly are aligned with the latter position, inasmuch as they view environmental antecedents and consequences as far better predictors of behavior than internal states and population labels (Nelson & Polsgrove, 1984). Rhodes and Tracy (1972a, 1972b) identified several theoretical models of deviant behavior that have had considerable impact on research and practice with behaviorally disordered pupils. The nonbehavioral models are not necessarily antagonistic to behavioral interventions, but neither do they encourage the systematic manipulation of environmental variables while carefully measuring effects on specific target behaviors.

The attitudes of regular education teacher trainers and practitioners toward behavioral psychology range from open hostility to skepticism to advocacy, with most leaning toward the negative side of this continuum. We have noted the misrepresentation of the behavioral model in introductory college texts (Cook, 1984). Erroneous information may lead to negative attitudes and misuse of behavioral procedures; these are problems many behaviorists have encountered in their work in schools. Even practitioners who have received adequate training in behavioral principles and procedures fail to use or to keep up their skills once they leave settings where they receive appropriate supervision and are expected to be accountable. Sloppy practice generates poor intervention effects, which influences the attitudes of both those who engage in such practices and those who observe these noneffects: namely, supervisors, other teachers, and parents. The following sets of recommendations address the broad issues we identified at the outset of this paper: maintenance and generalization, the selection of target behaviors and establishing the social validity of behavioral changes, the abuse of aversive procedures, and the analysis of intervention failures.

Implications for Personnel Preparation Programs

The often-observed failure of behavioral interventions to achieve lasting impact on students exhibiting disordered behavior is both discouraging to practitioners and a disincentive to putting forth the time and effort required to implement long-range behavior change programs. Program supervisors and administrators who observe these noneffects also are more likely to develop negative attitudes and to discourage the use of behavioral procedures. We believe that two training strategies can potentially impact on the development of more effective long-term behavioral interventions. The first strategy consists of more thorough training in maintenance and generalization procedures in preservice special education teacher preparation programs. It may seem premature to suggest such an addition to training curricula, given the current limitations of this technology. However, as we attempted to show in our review, generalization training does work, although it requires great effort and skill. The techniques Stokes and Baer (1977) articulated for enhancing the generalization and maintenance of student behavior also could be applied to teachers in preservice and inservice training programs. These procedures could be incorporated into Joyce and Showers (1982) coaching model for inservice teacher training in behavior management.

Furthermore, behavioral research is an applied science, and many of those who collaborate on field research are classroom teachers. The compatibility between research and practice in behavioral technology means that teachers can be generators of new knowledge, not merely passive recipients of research information (Nelson & Polsgrove, 1984). More practitioners doing generalization training and research means more progress in this vital area.

The second strategy for improving the use of effective and enduring behavioral intervention procedures consists of training administrators in behavioral technology. Such training, which for practical reasons would need to focus on the inservice level, would have two important potential effects. First, it would make program administrators and supervisors more aware of the complexity of behavioral interventions, and their increased knowledge and skill might increase their support of maintenance and generalization programming. This support would be especially helpful to teachers attempting to implement generalization training strategies outside of primary treatment settings, for example, in regular classrooms as well as students' communities and homes. Educators who implement such programs need the support and encouragement of knowledgeable administrators, not to mention released time, the authorization to work in other settings, and assistance in planning, evaluating, and revising generalization programs. The second possible effect would be to increase the maintenance and generalization of teachers' use of behavioral procedures in the field. Administrators who systematically monitor, differentially reinforce, and provide consultation in behavioral procedures to their staffs will find that their teachers use these procedures more consistently and more accountably.

Areas for Future Research and Development

Although behavior interventions reported in the literature may be somewhat limited in scope: that is, in terms of the target behaviors selected for modification, the extent to which behavior changes generalize across time and into other environments, and the clinical importance of these changes to caretakers and other significant persons, they have been generally successful. Their allegiance to empiricism has led behavioral researchers to a greater acceptance of negative evidence than perhaps is characteristic of proponents of other intervention models. However, the growing status of behavioral psychology creates the risk of it becoming as politically self-defensive as the rest of the field (Graziano & Bythell, 1983). Thus, it is important for researchers to address the questions of where behavioral interventions fail, and why (E. Edgar, personal communication, February, 1985). Graziano and Bythell (1983) identified two categories of failure: contextual failures and technical failures.

Contextual failures occur when nontherapeutic control is exerted by some aspect of the surrounding context, and include conflicts between the researcher/practitioner's values and those of the social environment: parents, teachers, administrators, communities, etc. For example, teachers and pupils both

may become bored, upset, lose control, and behave irrationally and disruptively, but only the pupil's behavior is corrected (Graziano & Bythell, 1983). The service of behavior analysts toward such goals has been criticized in the past (Winett & Winkler, 1972). More recently, Bailey and Lessen (1984) documented the failure of researchers to select important target behaviors that have functional utility in subjects' mainstream or adult environments. In an analysis of the failures of behavior modification programs with delinquents, Lane and Burchard (1983) suggested that instead of focusing on compliance as target behaviors, intervention programs should undertake to shape decision making, self-control, and problem solving, as well as how to develop day to day objectives and to self-reinforce behaviors, as these skills have a higher probability of being useful in subjects' natural environments. Bailey and Lessen (1984) recommended that educational research that is not designed to advance subject independence should not be accepted for publication.

Another example of contextual failure occurs when the applied researcher does not assess whether the environment can provide needed support, as in the failure to teach parents new responses to their children's behavior (Graziano & Bythell, 1983). The impact of sociopolitical and ecological variables has been a concern of behavioral researchers and practitioners for a number of years (e.g., Klinger, 1975; Reppucci, 1977; Repucci & Saunders, 1974), but studies addressing these factors are still not plentiful (see Nelson & Polsgrove, 1984). Researchers and practitioners working with pupils manifesting severe developmental delays have developed ecological assessment procedures for determining the contribution of environmental factors such as lighting, temperature, ventilation, and task characteristics to desired and undesired student behavior (Evans & Meyer, 1985; Gaylord-Ross 1980). The contribution of such environmental variables to the performance of less severely handicapped students has not been adequately investigated.

The failure of practitioners to implement intervention procedures appropriately constitutes another contextual area that needs investigation. For example, Kazdin (1982) observed that too little attention has been directed toward how token systems are monitored and evaluated, as well as the identification of administrative and organizational obstacles to the initiation and implementation of token economies. Similarly, Lane and Burchard (1983) pointed out that community correctional workers are not monitored to determine the extent to which they implement behavior modification programs consistently.

Technical failures are independent of the social context and include the lack of demonstrated long-term behavior changes across settings (Graziano & Bythell, 1983). Keeley, Shemberg, and Carbonell (1976) found objective follow-up data at least six months after treatment in only eight of 146 operant studies. Stokes and

Baer's (1977) analysis of generalization in applied studies revealed that over half of the 270 studies they evaluated fell in the "train and hope" category, where generalization was assessed but not programmed. Our selective review of the literature since 1976 suggests that maintenance and generalization training procedures still occur in the minority of studies: in 35% of our sample of 48 studies maintenance and generalization were neither assessed nor programmed; 41% of the studies assessed these effects informally or through objective data collection, while maintenance and generalization were both assessed and programmed in only 24% of these studies. Epstein and Cullinan (1984) asked 54 nationally recognized authorities in the education of students exhibiting behavior disorders to identify the three most important current research issues in the field. The 42 respondents rated generalization of intervention effects across settings and long-term maintenance as the first and second most important issues, respectively.

Other technical failures include the use of inappropriate or insufficiently powerful reinforcers, less than optimal reinforcer delivery, the failure to establish that reinforced responses exist in subjects' repertoires, subjects' failure to understand reinforcement contingencies, and other subject characteristics that may affect responsiveness (Kazdin, 1983). Unfortunately, such failures are seldom reported in the professional literature, as journal review boards have been conditioned to differentially reinforce (i.e., accept for publication) only studies reporting success. However, the tradition in behavioral research of conducting ongoing formative assessments of intervention procedures and adjusting these until an effective procedure is found is a model for all types of client-centered intervention. As the research literature base grows, so too does our knowledge regarding what behavioral interventions work, for whom, and under what circumstances. Delineation of these factors is crucial to establishing a technology of maintenance and generalization.

Every major review of behavioral interventions we analyzed listed specific recommendations for future research. In general, these suggestions closely followed the points we have just discussed; that is, the need to conduct follow-up and generalization studies, to collect procedural reliability data, to analyze the contributions of situational variables to program effects, and to determine the relative effectiveness of various procedures on different target behaviors and on pupils having different characteristics. The compilation and analysis of these variables is particularly important in the case of aversive behavior reduction procedures. Such analysis should also include interactions between the perceived aversiveness of a punishment procedure, the effort required to implement it, and its effectiveness with given pupils in given settings. For example, overcorrection appears to be an effective alternative to physical punishment for reducing stereotypic behaviors in severely and profoundly handicapped students. However, its implementation clearly involves greater teacher effort. Its

usefulness with less severely handicapped subjects in less intensive educational programs has not been as thoroughly investigated, yet teacher trainers are prone glibly to present overcorrection as a viable intervention alternative. Similarly, differential reinforcement procedures are highly touted as effective in reducing undesired behaviors through increasing desired alternate behaviors, yet the research suggests that differential reinforcement may be ineffective with some clients or target behaviors.

There is a need to assemble research findings concerning the interactions of intervention procedures with client and setting characteristics into a coherent literature for teacher trainers and practitioners to use as guidlines. The willingness and ability of practitioners to use complex interventions involving equipment and technical procedures (e.g., overcorrection, contingent restraint, sensory extinction) also should be thoroughly investigated, and those procedures found impractical should be revised or discarded in favor of more usable alternatives. Researchers should continue to study the effects of social skills training packages and to refine such curricula accordingly.

Our final recommendation for research concerns the extent to which racial and ethnic minority groups are targeted for behavioral intervention. Because the subjects of behavioral research studies are not necessarily selected from school populations where racial or ethnic biases have been demonstrated (e.g., classes for mildly retarded or behaviorally disordered students), there is no basis for inferring that minority students are singled out for behavioral intervention more often than are nonminority pupils. However, the racial and ethnic status of subjects in behavioral research is infrequently reported. Analysis of such data would indicate whether any biases exist with regard to the identification of minority groups for behavior modifications.

Suggestions for Improving Educational Practice Involving Behavioral Interventions

In our discussion of implications for training we recommended strategies for improving the appropriate use of behavioral intervention technology. For obvious reasons, much of this training should occur at the inservice level. We suggest that regular and special education supervisors and administrators be targeted for such training, as they control the reinforcement contingencies most likely to impact on teachers' performance. Furthermore, as we suggested earlier, the development of effective maintenance and generalization strategies is likely to require administrative input and approval.

In conjunction with inservice training of leadership personnel, we recommend that a shift in reinforcement contingencies for professionals be encouraged. Specifically, incentives should be made available for administrators and supervisors who visit teachers' classrooms and provide systematic feedback, reinforcement, and consultation. One such incentive is a dramatic reduction in the supervisory caseloads and administrative duties of program supervising staff. A change in the behavior of leadership personnel would be likely to occasion a change in the behavior of classroom staff. With regard to the latter, behaviorists have discussed the possibility of making such reinforcers as special recognition and promotion contingent upon desired changes in pupil behavior. However, unless the assignment of students to teachers were carefully monitored, there is the risk that the "best" teachers would consistently be given the "worst" students. Perhaps a better strategy would be to provide reinforcers such as continuing education units to teachers upon their demonstrated appropriate use of behavioral interventions over time.

We believe that systematic inservice training directed at strategic personnel and altered contingencies of reinforcement for professional staff would have a further beneficial effect, which is that practitioners would discard the erroneous perception of behavioral interventions as mechanical and simplistic. Instead, they would view them as complex and dynamic strategies, requiring constant evaluation and adjustment. Such a view would encourage collaborative planning, implementation, and evaluation of behavioral interventions, with administrators and supervisors as partners in this enterprise. The change toward support for a student-centered educational system would be dramatic, in that educational staff would be working toward the same specific objectives (i.e., those involving students' educational progress) instead of toward the compartmentalized and incompatible goals occasioned by the practitioner versus administrator dichotomy.

Our final recommendation for educational practice is for the adoption of guidelines regulating the use of behavioral interventions. These are available in the professional literature for specific interventions such as timeout (e.g., Gast & Nelson, 1977; Nelson & Rutherford, 1983), for aversive procedures (e.g., Wood & Braaten, 1983), and for the continuum of behavioral interventions (e.g., Woods, 1982). In addition, guidelines for selecting from among behavior reduction procedures those which are most appropriate for given pupils and circumstances are available (e.g., Gaylord-Ross, 1980; Gelfand & Hartmann, 1984), although practitioners must be adequately trained to use such decision-making strategies effectively. Some professional and parental organizations, such as the National Association for Retarded Citizens, have adopted guidelines for behavioral interventions (Sajwaj, 1977), and so have a number of state departments and many school districts. However, much disparity exists among sets of guidelines, and within a school district regulations may be quite specific for some procedures (e.g., timeout) but nonexistent for others (e.g., overcorrection). Efforts should be made to review and evaluate these guidelines to ensure their fidelity to behavioral principles as well as to best professional practices.

Barton, Brulle and Repp (1983) pointed out that "inadequate or inappropriate treatment of handicapped persons violates the due process clause" (p. 1), and suggested the following procedural steps prior to treatment: (1) seeking and obtaining informed consent; (2) assuring that the student's due process rights are observed; and (3) selecting treatments in accordance with the doctrine of the least restrictive alternative. Witt and Martens (1983) recommended that practitioners ask five questions regarding the acceptability of an intervention before implementing it: (1) Is it suitable for mainstream classrooms? (2) Does it present unnecessary risks to students? (3) Does it require too much teacher time? (4) Does it have negative side effects on other students? (5) Does the teacher have the skill to implement it? Until program supervisors and administrators have the information and skill to evaluate such questions, it is doubtful that procedural guidelines will have the desired impact on day to day decision making regarding behavioral interventions.

Suggestions for Changing Policies, Regulations and Funding Practices

The implications of the recommendations we offered in the preceding discussion for federal policy are obvious. This section addresses suggestions for research and training priorities derived from the needs described above.

First, in terms of training, we recommend that the inservice training of school administrative personnel in behavioral principles and technology be encouraged. In addition to content and procedures, proposals in this area should address meaningful incentives to make such training attractive, as well as to promote the maintenance and generalization of supervisory procedures. This training also should address the effective implementation of procedural guidelines.

Second, intervention program proposals aimed at developing model maintenance and generalization procedures should be solicited. The current requests for proposal (RFPs) for model transition projects address this issue to some extent, but the explicit use of behavioral procedures should be encouraged. Another area in which model programs should be encouraged is the adoption of procedures for monitoring, evaluating, and making data-based decisions regarding the use of behavioral interventions. Procedures have been developed for monitoring timeout (e.g., Braaten, 1983), but these need to be refined and elaborated into systems for objectively assessing the use and effectiveness of all behavioral interventions. The ultimate goal of this priority would be to establish empirical decision-making strategies for matching interventions to pupil, teacher, and setting characteristics. As we mentioned earlier, another important area for study is the possible over-representation of minority groups in behavioral interventions.

We also believe that the promotion of a large-scale analysis of behavioral intervention failures is an important area for future research. Such an analysis would assemble data that could be used by practitioners to assess the feasibility of intervention procedures for given students and settings, and reduce the time pupils spend in noneffective programs.

Finally, we recommend that a set of criteria, somewhat like those we used in this review, be adopted to use in evaluating behavioral interventions with students exhibiting all degrees of behavior disorders. To go even further, we suggest that the behavioral model would be useful for evaluating all interventions based on any theoretical model. This would require that researchers and practitioners specify (1) what pupil behaviors or characteristics they propose to change and the criteria for selecting these; (2) how these changes will be monitored, including how the reliability of the dependent measures will be established; (3) the intervention procedures to be employed and why these were selected; (4) the research design to be used; and (5) procedures for assessing and promoting the maintenance and generalization of the behavior changes accomplished. We also urge that studies proposing to increase self-concept, self-esteem, or other personological characteristics be required to show how changes in these variables affect subjects' daily functioning and social competence, based on subjects' and caretakers' evaluations of the social validity of the procedures and outcomes.

References

Anderson-Inman, L., Walker, H., & Purcell, J. (1984). Promoting the transfer of skills across settings: Transenvironmental programming for handicapped students in the mainstream. In W. R. Heward, T. E. Heron, D. S. Hill, and J. Trap-Porter (Eds.), *Focus on behavior analysis in education* (pp. 17–39). Columbus, OH: Merrill.

Axelrod, S., Brantner, J. P., & Meddock, T. D. (1978). Overcorrection: A review and critical analysis. *Journal of Special Education, 12*, 367–391.

Baer, D. M., Wolf, M. M., & Risley, T. R. (1968). Some current dimensions of applied behavior analysis. *Journal of Applied Behavior Analysis, 1*, 91–97.

Bailey, S. L., & Lessen, E. I. (1984). An analysis of target behaviors in education: Applied, but how useful? In W. L. Heward, T. E. Heron, D. S. Hill, and J. Trap-Porter (Eds.), *Focus on behavior analysis in education* (pp. 162–176). Columbus, OH: Merrill.

Bandura, A. E. (1969). *Principles of behavior modification*. New York: Holt, Rinehart, & Winston.

Barton, L. E., Brulle, A. R., & Repp, A. C. (1983). Aversive techniques and the doctrine of least restrictive alternative. *Exceptional Education Quarterly, 3*, 1–8.

Bierly, C., & Billingsley, F. F. (1984). An investigation of the educative effects of overcorrection on the behavior of an autistic child. *Behavioral Disorders, 9*, 11–21.

Bizzis, J., & Bradley-Johnson, S. (1981). Increasing the school attendance of a truant adolescent. *Education and Treatment of Children, 4*, 149–155.

Braaten, S. (1983). *A computer-based system for monitoring timeout interventions*. Presentation at the Seventh Annual Conference on Severe Behavior Disorders of Children and Youth, Arizona State University, Tempe, AZ.

Breyer, N. L., & Allen, G. T. (1975). Effects of implementing a token economy on teacher attending behavior. *Journal of Applied Behavior Analysis, 8*, 373–380.

Brown, L., Nietupski, J., & Hamre-Nietupski, S. (1976). The criterion of ultimate functioning. In A. Thomas (Ed.), *Hey, don't forget about me!* (pp. 2–15). Reston, VA: Council for Exceptional Children.

Bryant, L. E., & Budd, K. S. (1984). Teaching behaviorally handicapped preschool children to share. *Journal of Applied Behavior Analysis, 17*, 45–56.

Burchard, J. D., & Lane, T. W. (1982). Crime and delinquency. In A. S. Bellack, M. Hersen, & A. E. Kazdin (Eds.), *International handbook of behavior modification and therapy* (pp. 613–652). New York: Plenum.

Calhoun, K. S., & Lima, P. P. (1977). Effects of varying schedules of timeout on high- and low-rate behaviors. *Journal of Behavior Therapy and Experimental Psychiatry, 8*, 189–194.

Carden Smith, L. K., & Fowler, S. A. (1984). Positive peer pressure: The effects of peer monitoring on children's disruptive behavior. *Journal of Applied Behavior Analysis, 17*, 213–227.

Cavalier, A. R., & Ferretti, R. P. (1980). Stereotyped behavior, alternative behavior and collateral effects: A comparison of four intervention procedures. *Journal of Mental Deficiency Research, 24*, 219–230.

Cone, J. D., & Hawkins, R. P. (1977). *Behavioral assessment: New directions in clinical psychology*. New York: Brunner/Mazel.

Cooke, N. L. (1984). Misrepresentation of the behavioral model in preservice teacher education textbooks. In W. L. Heward, T. E. Heron, D. S. Hill, & J. Trap-Porter (Eds.), *Focus on behavior analysis in education* (pp. 197–217). Columbus, OH: Merrill.

Day, R. M., Lindeman, D. P., Powell, T. H., Fox, J. J., Stowitschek, J. J., & Shores, R. E. (1984). Empirically-derived teaching package for socially withdrawn handicapped and nonhandicapped children. *Teacher Education and Special Education, 7*, 46–55.

deCatanzaro, D. A., & Baldwin, G. (1978). Effective treatment of self-injurious behavior through a forced arm exercise. *American Journal of Mental Deficiency, 82*, 433–439.

Deno, S. L., & Mirkin, P. K. (1978). *Data-based program modification; A manual*. Reston, VA: The Council for Exceptional Children.

Diaddigo, M., & Dickie, R. F., (1978). The use of contingency contracting in eliminating inappropriate classroom behaviors. *Education and Treatment of Children, 1*, 17–23.

Dietz, D. E., & Repp, A. C. (1983). Reducing behavior through reinforcement. *Exceptional Education Quarterly, 3*, 34–46.

Dietz, S. M., Slack, D. J., Schwarzmueller, E. B., Wilander, A. P., Weatherly, T. J., & Hilliard, G. (1978). Reducing inappropriate behavior in special classrooms by reinforcing average interresponse times: Interval DRL. *Behavior Therapy, 9*, 37–46.

Dorsey, M. F., Iwata, B. A., Ong, P., & McSween, T. E. (1980). Treatment of self-injurious behavior using a water mist: Initial response suppression and generalization. *Journal of Applied Behavior Analysis, 13*, 343–353.

Dorsey, M. F., Iwata, B. A., Reid, D. H., & Davis, P. A. (1982). Protective equipment: Continuous and contingent application in the treatment of self-injurious behavior.

Journal of Applied Behavior Analysis, **15**, 217–230.

Epstein, M. H., & Cullinan, D. (1984). Research issues in behavior disorders: A national survey. *Behavioral Disorders*, **10**, 56–59.

Epstein, M. H., Repp, A. C., & Cullinan, D. (1978). Decreasing "obscene" language of behaviorally disordered children through the use of a DRL schedule. *Psychology in the Schools*, **15**, 419–423.

Evans, I. M., & Meyer, L. H. (1985). *An educative approach to behavior problems: A practical decision model for interventions with severely handicapped learners.* Baltimore, MD: Brooks.

Favell, J. E., McGimsey, J. F., & Jones, M. L. (1978). The use of physical restraint in the treatment of self-injury and as positive reinforcement. *Journal of Applied Behavior Analysis*, **11**, 225–241.

Ford, D., Evans, J. H., & Dworkin, L. K. (1982). Teaching interaction procedures: Effects upon the learning of social skills by an emotionally disturbed child. *Education and Treatment of Children*, **5**, 1–11.

Foxx, R. M. (1977). Attention training: The use of overcorrection avoidance to increase the eye contact of autistic and retarded children. *Journal of Applied Behavior Analaysis*, **10**, 489–499.

Gamble, A., & Strain, P. S. (1979). The effect of dependent and interdependent group contingencies on socially appropriate responses in classes for emotionally handicapped children. *Psychology in the Schools*, **16**, 253–260.

Gast, D. L., & Nelson, C. M. (1977). Legal and ethical considerations for the use of timeout in special education settings. *Journal of Special Education*, **11**, 457–467.

Gaylord-Ross, R. (1980). A decision model for the treatment of aberrant behavior in applied settings. In W. Sailor, B. Wilcox, & L. Brown (Eds.). *Methods of instruction for severely handicapped students* (pp. 135–155). Baltimore, MD: Brooks.

Gaylord-Ross, R. J., Haring, T. G., Breen, C., & Pitts-Conway, V. (1984). The training and generalization of social interaction skills with autistic youth. *Journal of Applied Behavior Analysis*, **17**, 229–247.

Gelfand, D. M., & Hartmann, D. P. (1984). *Child behavior analysis and therapy* (2nd ed.). New York: Pergamon.

Graziano, A. M., & Bythell, D. L. (1983). Failures in child behavior therapy. In E. B. Foa & P. M. G. Emmelkamp (Eds.), *Failures in behavior therapy* (pp. 406–424). New York: Wiley.

Greenwood, C. R., Hops, H., Walker, H. M., Guild, J. J., Stokes, J., & Young, K. R. (1977). Standardized classroom management program: Social validation and replication studies in Utah and Oregon. *Journal of Applied Behavior Analysis*, **12**, 236–253.

Haring, N. G., Liberty, K. A., & White, O. R. (1980). Rules for data-based strategy decisions in instructional programs: Current research and instructional implications. In W. Sailor, B. Wilcox, & L. Brown (Eds.). *Methods of instruction for severely handicapped students* (pp. 159–192). Baltimore, MD: Brooks.

Harris, S. L., & Wolchik, S. A. (1979). Suppression of self-stimulation: Three alternative strategies. *Journal of Applied Behavior Analysis*, **12**, 185–198.

Hazel, J. S., Schumaker, J. B., Sherman, J. A., & Sheldon-Wildgen, J. (1981). *ASSET: A social skills program for adolescents.* Champaign, IL: Research Press.

Hendrickson, J. M., Strain, P. S., Tremblay, A., & Shores, R. E. (1982). Interactions of behaviorally handicapped children. *Behavior Modification*, **6**, 323–353.

Hops, H., Fleischman, P. H. & Hutton, S. B. (1974). *CLASS: Contingencies for learning academics and social skills.* Eugene, OR: Center at Oregon for Research in the Behavioral Education of the Handicapped.

Horton, G. O., Walker, H. M., & Rankin, R. (1983). *Psychometric characteristics of the SBS student inventory of social behavior standards—Expectations and the SBS correlates checklist.* Unpublished manuscript, Center at Oregon for Research in the Behavioral Education of the Handicapped, Eugene, OR.

Howell, K. W. (1981). Establishing criteria for social behaviors. In R. B. Rutherford, Jr., A. G. Preito, & J. E. McGlothlin (Eds.), *Severe behavior disorders of children and youth* (Vol. 4), (pp. 34–39). Reston, VA: Council for Children with Behavioral Disorders.

Howell, K. W., Kaplan, J. S., & O'Connell, C. Y. (1979). *Evaluating exceptional children: A task analytic approach.* Columbus, OH: Merrill.

Hung, D. W. (1978). Using self-stimulation as reinforcement for retarded children. *Journal of Autism and Childhood Schizophrenia*, **8**, 355–363.

Huntze, S. L. (1985). A position paper of the Council for Children with Behavioral Disorders. *Behavioral Disorders*, **10**, 167–174.

Jackson, A. T., Salzberg, C. L., Pacholl, B., & Dorsey, D. S. (1981). The comprehensive rehabilitation of a behavior problem child in his home and community. *Education and Treatment of Children*, **4**, 195–215.

Joyce, B., & Showers, B. (1982). The coaching of teaching. *Educational Leadership*, **40**, 4–8.

Kauffman, J. M., Strang, H. R., & Loper, A. B. (1985). Using microcomputers to train teachers of the handicapped. *Remedial and Special Education*, **6** (5)m 13–17.

Kazdin. A. E. (1982). The token economy: A decade later. *Journal of Applied Behavior Analysis*, **15**, 431–445.

Kazdin. A. E. (1983). Failure of persons to respond to the token economy. In E. B. Foa & P. M. G. Emmelkamp (Eds.), *Failures in behavior therapy* (pp. 335–354). New York: Wiley.

Keeley, S. M., Shemberg, K. M., & Carbonell, J. (1976). Operant clinical intervention: Behavior management or beyond? Where are the data? *Behavior Therapy*, **7**, 292–305.

Keller, F. S. (1969). "Goodbye teacher". *Journal of Applied Behavior Analysis*, **1**, 79–89.

Kerr, M. M., & Nelson, C. M. (1983). *Strategies for managing behavior problems in the classroom.* Columbus, OH: Merrill.

Klinger, R. (1975). Epilog: After the fall. In C. A. Parker (Ed.), *Psychological consultation: Helping teachers meet special needs* (pp. 94–102). Minneapolis: Leadership Training Institute/Department of Special Education, University of Minnesota.

Lakin, K. C. (1983). Research-based knowledge and professional practices in special education for emotionally disturbed students. *Behavioral Disorders*, **8**, 128–137.

Lane, T. W., & Burchard, J. D. (1983). Failure to modify delinquent behavior: A constructive analysis. In E. B. Foa & P. M. G. Emmelkamp (Eds.), *Failures in behavior therapy* (pp. 355–377). New York: Wiley.

Lebsock, M. S., & Salzberg, C. L. (1981). The use of role play and reinforcement procedures in the development of generalized interpersonal behavior with emotionally disturbed-behavior disordered adolescents in a special education classroom. *Behavioral Disorders*, **6**, 150–163.

Luce, S. C., & Hall, R. V. (1981). Contingent exercise: A procedure used with differential reinforcement to reduce bizarre verbal behavior. *Education and Treatment of Children*, **4**, 309–327.

Lutzker, J. R. (1978). Reducing self-injurious behavior by facial screening. *American Journal of Mental Deficiency*, **82**, 510–513.

McNamara, J. R. (1971). Teachers and students as sources for behavior modification in the classroom. *Behavior Therapy*, **2**, 206–213.

Malott, R. W. (1984). In search of human perfectability: A behavioral approach to higher education. In W. R. Heward, T. E. Heron, D. S. Hill, & J. Trap-Porter (Eds.), *Focus on behavior analysis in education*, (pp. 218–245). Columbus, OH: Merrill.

Mayhew, G. L., Enyart, P., & Anderson, J. (1978). Social reinforcement and the naturally occurring social responses of severely and profoundly retarded adolescents. *American Journal of Mental Deficiency*, **83**, 164–170.

Miles, C. L., & Cuvo, A. J. (1980). Modification of the disruptive and productive classroom behavior of a severely retarded child: A comparison of two procedures. *Education and Treatment of Children*, **3**, 113–121.

Morales v. Turman. (1973). 364 F. Supp, 166.

Murphy, R. J., Ruprecht, M., & Nunes, D. L. (1979). Elimination of self-injurious behavior in a profoundly retarded adolescent using intermittent time-out, restraint, and blindfold procedures. *AAESPH Review*, **4**, 334–345.

Nelson, C. M. (1978). Field-based teacher training and the university: Mismatch or match made in heaven? In C. M. Nelson (Ed.), *Field-based teacher training: Applications in special education* (pp. 3–25). Minneapolis: Department of Psychoeducational Studies, University of Minnesota.

Nelson, C. M. (1981). Classroom management. In J. M. Kauffman & D. P. Hallhan (Eds.), *Handbook of special education* (pp. 663–687). Englewood Cliffs, NJ: Prentice-Hall.

Nelson, C. M., Berdine, W. H., & Moyer, J. (1978). The evolution of a non-categorical competency-based special education methods course. *Journal of Special Education Technology*, **2**, 37–46.

Nelson, C. M., Gast, D. L., & Trout, D. D. (1979). A charting system for monitoring student progress in instructional programs. *Journal of Special Education Technology*, **3**, 43–49.

Nelson, C. M., & Polsgrove, L. (1984). Behavior analysis in special education: White rabbit or white elephant? *Remedial and Special Education*, **5**, 6–17.

Nelson, C. M., & Rutherford, W. B. (1983). Timeout revisited: Guidelines for its use in special education. *Exceptional Educational Quarterly*, **3**, 56–67.

Noland, S. A., Arnold, J., & Clement, P. W. (1980). Self-reinforcement by under-achieving, under-control girls. *Psychological Reports*, **47**, 671–678.

Noll, M. B., & Simpson, R. L. (1979). The effects of physical time-out on the aggressive behaviors of a severely emotionally disturbed child in a public setting. *AAESPH Review*, **2**, 399–406.

Norton, G. R., Austen, S., Allen, G. E., & Hilton, J. (1983). Acceptability of time out from reinforcement procedures for disruptive child behavior: A further analysis. *Child and Family Behavior Therapy*, **5**, 31–41.

Ollendick, T. H., & Hersen, M. (1984). An overview of child behavior assessment. In T. H. Ollendick & M. Hersen (Eds.)., *Child behavioral assessment* (pp. 3–19). New York: Pergamon.

Ollendick, T. H., Shapiro, E. S., & Barrett, R. P. (1981). Reducing stereotypic behaviors: An analysis of treatment procedures utilizing an alternating treatments design. *Behavior Therapy*, **12**, 570–577.

Pease, G. A., & Tyler, V. O. (1979). Self regulation of timeout duration in the modification of disruptive classroom behavior. *Psychology in the Schools*, **16**, 101–105.

Plummer, S., Baer, D. M., & LeBlanc, J. M. (1977). Functional considerations in the use of procedural timeout and an effective alternative. *Journal of Applied Behavior Analysis*, **10**, 689–705.

Polsgrove, L. (1979). Self-control: Methods for child training. *Behavioral Disorders*, **4**, 116–130.

Polsgrove, L., & Nelson, C. M. (1982). Curriculum interventions according to the behavioral model. In G. Brown, R. L. McDowell, & J. Smith (Eds.). *Educating adolescents with behavior disorders* (pp. 30–59). Columbus, OH: Merrill.

Polsgrove, L., & Reith, H. J. (1983). Procedures for reducing children's inappropriate behavior in special education settings. *Exceptional Education Quarterly*, **3**, 20–33.

Powers, M. D., & Handleman, J. S. (1984). *Behavioral assessment of severe developmental disabilities*. Rockville, MD: Aspen.

Ragland, E. U., Kerr, M. M., & Strain, P. S. (1978). Behavior of withdrawn autistic children: Effects of peer social initiations. *Behavior Modification*, **2**, 565–578.

Rapoff, M. A., Altman, K., & Christopherson, E. R. (1980). Suppression of self-injurious behavior: Determining the least restrictive alternative. *Journal of Mental Deficiency Research*, **24**, 37–46.

Reitz, A. L., Barbetta, P. M., Sestili, D. J., Hawkins, R. P., & Dickie, R. F. (1984). IEPs for teachers: Supervision as a skill development process. In W. R. Heward, T. E. Heron, D. S. Hill, & J. Trap-Porter (Eds.). *Focus on behavior analysis in education*. Columbus, OH: Merrill.

Renne, D. J., & Blackhurst, A. E. (1977). Adjunct autoinstruction in an introductory special education course. *Exceptional Children*, **43**, 224–225.

Reppucci, N. D. (1977). Implementation issues for the behavior modifiers as institutional change agent. *Behavior Therapy*, **8**, 597–605.

Reppucci, N. D., & Saunders, J. T. (1974). Social psychology of behavior modification: Problems of implementation in natural settings. *American Psychologist*, **29**, 649–660.

Rhodes, W. C., & Tracy, M. L. (1972a). *A study of child variance*, Ann Arbor: Institute for the Study of Mental Retardation and Related Disabilities, University of Michigan.

Rhodes, W. C., & Tracy, M. L. (1972b). *A study of child variance: Vol. 2: Intervention*. Ann Arbor: Institute for the Study of Mental Retardation and Related Disabilities, University of Michigan.

Rincover, A. (1978). Sensory extinction: A procedure for eliminating self-stimulatory behavior in developmentally disabled children. *Journal of Abnormal Child Psychology*, **6**, 299–310.

Rincover, A., Cook, R., Peoples, A., & Packard, D. (1979). Sensory extinction and sensory reinforcement principles for programming multiple adaptive behavior change. *Journal of Applied Behavior Analysis*, **12**, 221–233.

Rose, T. L. (1979). Reducing self-injurious behavior by differentially reinforcing other behaviors. *AAESPH Review*, 4, 179–186.

Rose, T. L. (1983). A survey of corporal punishment of mildly handicapped students. *Exceptional Education Quarterly*, 3, 9–19.

Rotholz, D. A., & Luce, S. C. (1983). Alternative reinforcement strategies for the reduction of self-stimulatory behavior in autistic youth. *Education and Treatment of Children*, 6, 363–377.

Russo, D. C., Cataldo, M. F., & Cushing, P. J. (1981). Compliance training and behavioral covariation in the treatment of multiple behavior problems. *Journal of Applied Behavior Analysis*, 14, 209–222.

Russo, D. C., & Koegel, R. L. (1977). A method for integrating an autistic child in to a normal public-school classroom. *Journal of Applied Behavior Analysis*, 10, 579–590.

Rutherford, R. B. (1983). Theory and research on the use of aversive procedures in the education of moderately behaviorally disordered and emotionally disturbed children and youth. In F. H. Wood & K. C. Lakin (Eds.). *Punishment and aversive stimulation in special education* (pp. 41–64). Reston, VA: Council for Exceptional Children.

Rutherford, R. B., & Nelson, C. M. (1982). Analysis of the response contingent time-out literature with behaviorally disordered students in classroom settings. In R. B. Rutherford, Jr. (Ed.). *Severe behavior disorders of children and youth* (Vol. 5), (pp. 79–105). Reston, VA: Council for Children with Behavioral Disorders.

Rutherford, R. B., & Nelson, C. M. (1988). Decentralization and maintenance of treatment effects. In J. C. Witt, S. N. Elliott, & F. M. Gresham (Eds.). *Handbook of behavior therapy in education* (pp. 227–324). New York: Plenum.

Rutherford, R. B., & Polsgrove, L. J. (1981). Behavioral contracting with behaviorally disordered and delinquent children and youth: An analysis of the clinical and experimental literature. In R. B. Rutherford, A. G. Prieto, & J. E. McGlothlin (Eds.). *Severe behavior disorders of children and youth*, (Vol. 4), (pp. 49–69). Reston, VA: Council for Children with Behavioral Disorders.

Sajwaj, T. (1977). Issues and implications of establishing guidelines for the use of behavioral techniques. *Journal of Applied Behavior Analysis*, 10, 531–540.

Singh, N. N., Dawson, M. J., & Manning, P. J. (1981). The effects of physical restraint on self-injurious behavior. *Journal of Mental Deficiency Research*, 25, 207–216.

Stainback, W., Stainback, S., & Dedrick, C. (1979). Controlling severe maladaptive behaviors. *Behavioral Disorders*, 4, 99–115.

Stokes, T. F., & Baer, D. M. (1977). An implicit technology of generalization. *Journal of Applied Behavior Analysis*, 10, 349–367.

Strain, P. S., Kerr, M. M., & Ragland, E. U. (1979). Effects of peer-mediated social initiations and prompting/reinforcement procedures on the social behavior of autistic children. *Journal of Autism and Developmental Disorders*, 9, 41–54.

Tawney, J. W. (1972). *Practice what you preach: A project to develop a contingency-managed methods course and to measure the effects of this course by in-field evaluation.* Lexington: University of Kentucky.

Tawney, J. W. (1984). Empirical verification of instruction: A realistic goal? In W. R. Heward, T. E. Heron, D. S. Hill, & J. Trap-Porter (Eds.), *Focus on behavior analysis in education* (pp. 246–253). Columbus, OH: Merrill.

Tawney, J. M., & Gast, D. L. (1984). *Single subject research in special education*. Columbus, OH: Merrill.

Taylor, F. D., & Soloway, M. M. (1973). The Madison School Plan: A functional model for merging the regular and special classrooms. In E. N. Deno (Ed.), *Instructional alternatives for exceptional children* (pp. 145–155). Reston, VA: Council for Exceptional Children.

Thomas, J. D., Presland, I. E., Grant, M. D., & Glynn, T. L. (1978). Natural rates of teacher approval and disapproval in grade-7 classrooms. *Journal of Applied Behavior Analysis*, 11, 91–94.

Trice, A. D., & Parker, F. C. (1983). Decreasing adolescent swearing in an instructional setting. *Education and Treatment of Children*, 6, 29–35.

Walker, H. M. (1979). *The acting-out child: Coping with classroom disruption*. Boston: Allyn & Bacon.

Walker, H. M. (1983). Applications of response cost in school settings: Outcomes, issues, and recommendations. *Exceptional Education Quarterly*, 3, 47–55.

Walker, H. M., Greenwood, C. R., Hops, H., & Todd, N. M. (1979). Differential effects of reinforcing topographic components of social interaction: Analysis and direct replication. *Behavior Modification*, 3, 291–321.

Walker, H. M., & Hops, H. (1976). Use of normative peer data as a standard for evaluating classroom treatment effects. *Journal of Applied Behavior Analysis*, 9, 159–168.

Walker, H. M., Hops, H., & Fiegenbaum, E. (1976). Deviant classroom behavior as a function of combinations of social and token reinforcement and cost contingency. *Behavior Therapy*, 7, 76–88.

Walker, H. M., McConnell, S., Holmes, D., Todis, B., Walker, J., & Golden, N. (1983). *The Walker social skills curriculum: The ACCEPTS program*. Austin, TX: Pro-Ed.

Warrenfeltz, R. B., Kelly, W. J., Salzberg, C. C., Beegle, C. P., Levy, S. M., Adams, T. A., & Crouse, T. R. (1981). Social skills training of behavior disordered adolescents with self-monitoring to promote generalization to a vocational setting. *Behavioral Disorders*, 7, 18–27.

Wells, K. C., Forehand, R., Hickey, K., & Green, K. D. (1977). Effects of a procedure derived from the overcorrection principle on manipulated and nonmanipulated behaviors. *Journal of Applied Behavior Analysis*, 10, 679–687.

White, M. A. (1975). Natural rates of teacher approval and disapproval in the classroom. *Journal of Applied Behavior Analysis*, 8, 367–372.

White, O. R., & Haring, N. G. (1980). *Exceptional teaching* (2nd ed.). Columbus, OH: Merrill.

Winett, R. A., & Winkler, R. C. (1972). Current behavior modification in the classroom: Be still, be quiet, be docile. *Journal of Applied Behavior Analysis*, 5, 499–504.

Witt, J. C., & Martens, B. K. (1983). Assessing the acceptability of behavioral interventions used in classrooms. *Psychology in the Schools*, 20, 510–517.

Wolf, M. M. (1978). Social validity: The case for subjective measurement or how applied behavior analysis is finding its heart. *Journal of Applied Behavior Analysis*, 11, 203–214.

Wood, F. H., & Braaten, S. (1983). Developing guidelines for the use of punishing interventions in the schools. *Exceptional Education Quarterly*, 3, 68–75.

Woods, T. S. (1978). Procedures and policies for regulating

field-based behavioral technology. *Behavioral Disorders*, **8**, 32–40.

Woodward, R. J., Maginn, C., & Johnston, W. A. (1983). The reduction of self-stimulating behaviors using a differential reinforcement of other behavior (D.R.O.) schedule. *The British Journal of Mental Subnormality*, **29**, 65–73.

Wyatt V. Stickney, 325, F. Supp. 781 (1971); 334 F. Supp. 1341 (1971); 344 F. Supp. 373 (1972); 344 F. Supp, 387 (1972).

Zehr, M. D., & Theobald, D. E. (1978). Manual guidance used in a punishment procedure: The active ingredient in overcorrection. *Journal of Mental Deficiency Research*, **22**, 263–272.

Research Integration of Cognitive-Emotional Interventions for Behaviorally Disordered Children and Youth

ROBERT L. CARPENTER

State University of New York at Binghamton

STEVEN J. APTER

Syracuse University

Abstract—This paper reviews and integrates research on a variety of interventions, termed *cognitive-emotional interventions*, that are typically associated with a psychoeducational orientation to behavioral disorders. Current research is summarized on the following interventions (or families of interventions): cognitive-behavorial interventions, social-cognitive interventions, social skills training, ecological interventions, life space interviewing, cooperative learning, and affective education. This is preceded by an integration of research on two elements of assessment important to cognitive-emotional interventions: ecological assessment and the assessment of social competence. The paper concludes with a discussion of possible implications for future research, teacher training, and policy development.

With the possible exception of the behavioral perspective, no single orientation has emerged from Rhodes and Tracy's (1972) conceptual project as a satisfactory conceptual model for explaining behavioral disorders. No straightforward definitions are viewed as adequate, no single theory is sufficiently elegant to encompass this elusive phenomenon. Further, unlike more hygienic academic disciplines where ideas can compete in a pure intellectual reality, applied disciplines are grounded in the reality of day-to-day work with children and youth. Research on cognitive-emotional interventions, for example, is not strictly research in the service of theoretical explication but more often includes evaluations of planful action designed to effect a positive change in some aspect of a person's life. It is important to understand that research on cognitive emotional interventions in behavioral disorders is less theory-driven than effect-driven. Although certain research questions may address narrow increments in the development of a more general theory, the overarching concerns in most cognitive-emotional intervention research are whether or not an intervention works. Moreover, these interventions are commonly pragmatic hybrids, borrowing, for instance, from developmental theory, social psychology, and applied behavioral analysis.

Under such conditions, a rigid and well-recognized vocabulary has not developed, nor at this point can such interventions always be neatly circumscribed as of one distinct family representing one clear, conceptual model. *Cognitive-emotional intervention* is a term coined specifically for this research integration in order to embrace the broad array of approaches that have emerged from developmental and social perspectives and that are described in the literature on interventions for emotional disturbance and behavioral disorders of school-age children and youth. Thus, although this chapter examines interventions that might typically be employed in a program espousing a psychoeducational orientation, only the interventions themselves are addressed, not the contexts (psychoeducational or otherwise) in which they are employed.

The integration begins with a section reviewing the state of assessment strategies currently employed that are relevant to the cognitive-emotional model. The integration then proceeds with a discussion of behavioral interventions that assume and utilize cognitive processes as a component of the intervention procedure. These interventions are subdivided under two headings: cognitive-behavioral interventions and social-cognitive interventions. Interventions in three other domains are then addressed: social skills training, ecological interventions, and affective education. These domains are

155

not mutually exclusive, nor are they inclusive of every approach addressed or endorsed in the literature. Thus, additional sections on life space interviewing and co-operative learning review research in areas not readily included in the aforementioned domains. The chapter concludes with a section addressing the implications of the research integration in three areas: directions for future research, teacher preparation and renewal, and considerations for public policy and funding.

By agreement with the other authors of this section, we acknowledge the position adopted by the Executive Committee of the Council for Children with Behavioral Disorders (Huntze, 1985) and use the term *behavorial disorders* as a descriptor for children and youth who are handicapped by their behavior and eligible for services under PL 94–142.

The research integrated in this document variously used the terms *emotionally disturbed*, *seriously emotionally disturbed*, *behaviorally disordered*, and *behaviorally handicapped*. As Smith, Wood, and Grimes discuss in another chapter of this volume, definitional and identification issues for the population of concern confound the perimeters of this review. When research with populations other than as described above is cited, it is so noted.

In the chapter, we have also chosen not to attempt to distinguish between what might be termed, the *state of the art* and the *state of practice*. This is because, with the exception of the cognitive behavioral subcategory, research in cognitive emotional interventions is typically not conducted with a view to theory development or intervention refinement. Cognitive emotional interventions are embedded in the complexity of setting variables and, further, are rarely used in isolation from other interventions. Survey data are simply not available about what happens in actual classroom practice, nor are there even descriptive narratives from randomly selected classrooms. From what is available, it may be inferred that teachers use a variety and combination of different theoretical models and interventions (Carpenter, 1985; Schmid, Algozzine, Maher, Wells, 1984). The state of practice might well be described as a state of essential pragmatism, where teachers learn to employ whatever seems to work for them in their particular situations with their particular students.

Sources of information for this integration work were initially identified through a computerized search utilizing the Educational Research Information Center data base. This was supplemented with a review of journals judged most pertinent to the subject (*Behavioral Disorders*, *Exceptional Children*, *Journal of Special Education*, and *Psychology in the Schools*) for the years 1978 through 1985. A review of the series, *Monograph in Behavioral Disorders*, 1978–1984, was also conducted, as was a review of pertinent publications from the National Needs Analysis in Behavior Disorders Project at the University of Missouri and the Advanced Institute

for Trainers of Teachers for Seriously Emotionally Disturbed Children and Youth at the University of Minnesota.

Integration of Research

Assessment

This section addresses two important areas of assessment relevant to cognitive emotional interventions: ecological assessment and assessment of social competence. These are currently the most active and promising directions for the assessment of behaviorally disordered children.

Ecological Assessment

Ecological assessment attempts to develop data from the several environments in which a child lives. These data include descriptions of the various environments and the expectations for the child in each of the environments, the interactions and skills of the people involved in each of the situations, and the situations that are successful or unsuccessful for the child. The data gathered are then summarized, and an intervention plan is devised (Laten & Katz, 1975, in Wallace & Larsen, 1978). The specific assessment tools used to carry out this plan range from systematic behavioral observation, to a variety of rating scales and sociometric devices, to student teacher interaction analyses. A variety of self-report devices are also available to obtain information from the student's perspective (Prillaman & Abbott, 1983). An assessment package developed by Wahler, House, and Stambaugh (1976) has systematized this approach for the collection of data on interactions of an individual child in a variety of settings, while such data are time-consuming to collect, interventions flow directly from the assessment data. Interventions may then be tailored by the school and community personnel serving the child, together with the child's parents. Using naturalistic data collected in this manner, the process of determining services may become more of a group problem-solving exercise than an assignment of a child to a setting and a curriculum.

Although promising, ecological assessment is still in its infancy. Research is needed to carefully describe critical variables in school and community settings, as well as critical student behaviors and how they interact, so that a committee on handicapped students may design a better ecological fit (Apter, 1982).

Assessment of Social Competence

An alternative (and essentially educational) perspective for viewing the assessment of behavioral disorders is in terms of social competence and social skills. Dodge and Murphy (1984) broadly considered social competence assessment to be "(1) measurements of specific behaviors considered to be competent by researchers;

(2) judgments of an individual's competence by external raters; and (3) measurements of internal structures such as cognitive skills that may be related to behavior judged to be competent" (p. 64). Ratings of an individual's status are commonly used in school settings. The Behavior Problem Checklist (Quay & Peterson, 1967) and the Problem Behavior Identification Checklist (Walker, 1970) are but two examples. However, these are not judged as particularly useful except as screening devices since they do not specify particular skills on which to intervene.

The Developmental Therapy Objectives Rating Form (DTORF) (Wood, 1975) enumerates 144 behaviorally stated goals for students. The goals are sequenced developmentally in four curriculum areas: behavior, communication, socialization, and (pre)academics. A child's proficiency in each area may be rated by observers using the DTORF, and an educational plan may then be developed for the skill levels at which the child is determined to be functioning. Although there does not appear to be any social validation of its goal statements (Kazdin, 1977; Wolf, 1978), the DTORF stands as the most comprehensive social competence assessment device for younger behaviorally disordered children.

Another approach to social competence assessment is to rate the performance of an individual when he or she is asked to role-play specific hypothetical situations. This analogue approach has been modified for practical reasons in that situations are presented to individuals and they are asked to describe how they would respond (Freedman, Rosenthal, Donahoe, Schlundt, & McFall, 1978; Gaffney & McFall, 1981). Problems such as stimuli selection and limitations of verbal responses limit the utility of this approach (Dodge & Murphy, 1984).

The most promising approach to the assessment of social competence appears to be the objective measurement of an individual's response to a stimulus or a situation. Asking children for their judgment of different facial expressions (Camras, 1980), for instance, allows one to measure a subskill judged to be a prerequisite to social competence. Decision skills may be measured in much the same fashion (Spivack, Platt, & Shure, 1976).

Future research on the assessment of social competence should center on identifying specific social tasks necessary for competence in particular problematic settings (Dodge & Murphy, 1984). Van Hasselt, Hersen, Whitehill, and Bellack (1979) cited research suggesting particular generalized social skills for possible training with children (e.g., dispensing positive social reinforcers, role-taking).

Cognitive-Behavioral Interventions

This section reviews research on interventions that, though behavioral in nature, actively employ the cognitive processes of the student in the intervention procedure. The principal goal of the interventions discussed is the self-control of the student's own behavior as opposed to the external control of behavior exemplified by conventional behavioral interventions. As noted by Rueda, Rutherford, and Howell (1980), clarification of terms and concepts in self-control research has not yet emerged. Typically, cognitive-behavioral interventions consist of three stages: self-monitoring, self-evaluation, and self-reinforcement. Each of these stages is discussed below.

Self-Monitoring. Self-monitoring involves requiring the student to attend to his or her own specific behavior or class of behaviors in a conscious and systematic fashion. In this way, the student is made aware of a behavior that may later be targeted for more formal intervention. For example, students may be asked to set standards based on their observations. Self-monitoring is systematically conducted using standard observational procedures of applied behavioral analysis. Self-monitoring has only rarely been evaluated except as part of a larger scheme involving additional procedures such as self-evaluation and self-reinforcement (McLaughlin, 1976). Broden, Hall, and Mitts (1971) used self-recording to increase study behavior but obtained mixed results. Gottman and McFall (1972) found similarly confounding results using self-monitoring of contributions to classroom discussions.

Self-monitoring is a procedure incorporated with other strategies to teach social and metacognitive skills. The Model Affective Resource Curriculum (MARC) (1983), Think Aloud (Camp & Bash, 1981), and the cognitive training program of Douglas, Parry, Marton, and Garson (1976) all employ self-monitoring as an initial strategy. Self-monitoring is also used in conjunction with certain counseling procedures such as rational-emotive therapy (Ellis, 1962) and cognitive therapy (Beck, 1976).

Taken alone, however, self-monitoring might not necessarily be dismissed simply as a preliminary activity, only occasionally useful by itself. It seems possible that, in the case of well-motivated students, simply providing a systematic procedure by which they may become clearly aware of their own behavior may be sufficient for them to modify the topology of that behavior. There is an intriguing simplicity to the technique if research can establish which behaviors are most amenable to change by which students and under what circumstances.

Self-Evaluation. In the self-evaluation stage, the student compares his or her observations during the self-monitoring stage against some preestablished standard. This standard may be established as a result of data collected during the monitoring (in which case the self-monitoring data become the baseline), or the standard may be predetermined. The standard may be determined by the student or by the teacher, or it may be negotiated by both. If the student is asked to evaluate his or her performance against some standard, they may presumably engage in covert self-reinforcement/punish-ment. In this way, the student learns to maintain his or her behavior without external control (Polsgrove, 1979).

Rueda, Rutherford, and Howell (1980) explicated the essential steps of self-regulation, citing research with both normal and disruptive children and adolescents who were successfully taught self-monitoring, self-evaluation, and self-reinforcement/punishment in class-room settings (Bolstad & Johnson, 1972; Broden, Hall, & Mitts, 1971; Glynn, Thomas, & Shee, 1973; Gottman & McFall, 1972; Lovitt & Curtiss, 1969).

Self-Reinforcement. A more recent study (Ruther-ford, Howell, & Rueda, 1982) confirms that self-reinforcement, the final stage of self-regulation, is poss-ible with behaviorally disordered students. Self-reinforcement may be as effective as external teacher reinforcement when the transition from one condition to another is made gradually and systematically (Drab-man, Spitalnik, & O'Leary, 1973). However, more rapid transition with adolescent behaviorally disordered subjects resulted in a breakdown of the previously estab-lished external controls on the target behavior (Santo-grossi, O'Leary, Romanczyk, & Kaufman, 1973).

Wilson (1984), in a thorough review of self-control research related to the management of aggressive behaviors, concluded that, although self-reinforce-ment's effectiveness may be established for adaptive classroom behaviors, it does not appear to be effective for managing aggressive behavior—except possibly as a technique for maintaining nonaggression after non-aggressive behaviors have been learned through exter-nally directed procedures.

Implementation problems exist regarding the general-ization of self-regulative behaviors to different settings and their maintenance over time. In general, self-regu-lation is most effective when students are motivated to change or where natural contingencies support the tar-get behavior (Polsgrove, 1979). O'Leary and Dubey (1979) concluded that self-control procedures with self-reinforcement are as effective as externally controlled procedures and also compare favorably in terms of maintenance.

Social-Cognitive Interventions

Social-cognitive interventions refer to the group of techniques designed to teach the student better to com-prehend and deal with social and interpersonal events (Greenspan, 1979). The following discussion of social-cognitive interventions is organized around research investigating the efficacy of two principle elements of such interventions: self-instruction and social problem solving. Typically, these elements are used in combi-nation and may be preceded, if necessary, by cognitive-behavioral or strictly behavioral procedures.

The MARC Curriculum (1983) is an example of a comprehensive, social-cognitive curriculum that com-bines these elements. A self-instructional element employing private speech is taught to increase self-con-trol. The student is then taught a general, several-step, problem-solving procedure. Communication skills are also taught, as a supplement to problem solving. Modeling and rehearsal are specific teaching techniques employed throughout the curriculum.

Self-Instruction

Self-instruction is the process by which a student pro-vides verbal prompts to himself or herself in order to direct or maintain a particular behavior (Alberto & Troutman, 1982). Meichenbaum and Goodman (1971) demonstrated that private speech can be used as a mediator of overt behavior. In a sequential process, they moved children from adult instruction in verbal mediation, to overt self-verbalization of mediation, to cover self-instruction in order to improve behaviors such as attention to tasks and test performance. Encouraged by Meichenbaum's (1977) findings, self-instructional strategies have become a component of more complex interventions for purposes of teaching self-control. The Turtle Technique (Schneider & Robin, 1974) for instance, involves a self-instruction to withdraw to a "turtle position" when faced with threatening situ-ations. The child is them taught relaxation techniques and problem-solving procedures. With primary-age stu-dents, the program has been effective in significantly reducing aggressive behavior (Robin, Schneider, & Dol-nick, 1976). The specific effect of the self-instructional component alone has not been investigated.

Camp, Blom, Hebert, and vanDoorninck (1977) found mixed results with their Think Aloud program. Prosocial behaviors were improved in the experimental group, but control of aggressive behaviors did not occur. Mixed results were also found in a set of studies examin-ing the effect of self-instructional procedures on task attention and impulsive behavior in upper elementary-age children (Kendall & Finch, 1978; Kendall & Wilcox, 1980; Kendall & Zupan, 1981).

Wilson (1984) concluded that, although the effective-ness of self-instructional programs to change test and task performance has been demonstrated, extensions to self-control of social behaviors has not. Self-instruction appears to be a useful component of multiple-compon-ent interventions.

Garrison and Stolberg (1983) took a somewhat differ-ent tack from the verbal mediation strategies reviewed above. Hypothesizing that overt, angry behaviors in children might well be a function of preexisting, angry, cognitive structures, upper elementary-age boys ident-ified as preponderantly angry were presented with an imagery training program designed to sensitize them to internal cues for differentiating between various feelings (and for reducing the mislabeling of emotions). Signifi-cant changes for the experimental group were measured by follow-up testing, but the intervention was short, and the 2-week follow-up indicated an erosion of treatment effects.

Social Problem Solving

The goal in problem-solving interventions is to teach the child a cognitive process for decision making. The assumption is that the child lacks (or possesses faulty) metacognitive processess that would allow him or her to react flexibly and in his or her own best interest when facing ordinary social problems (Glenn, Rueda, & Rutherford, 1984).

Initially, Spivack and Shure (1974) trained disruptive preschoolers to generate alternative solutions to their social problems and found that the training improved social adjustment in school. Elias (1983) showed that problem-solving skills could be effectively taught to behaviorally disordered boys by combining the guided viewing of short videotapes depicting children involved in working through real life, common problems such as teasing, coping with peer pressure, and expressing feelings (*Inside/Out*, 1973). Viewings were followed by guided discussions with teachers. In the 5 weeks of the Elias study, children receiving the treatment showed significant gains in a variety of social behaviors related to interpersonal problem solving. Gains were still apparent after a 2-month follow-up.

A carefully constructed curriculum for teaching problem-solving skills involving role-playing, videotape modeling, cartoon workbooks, and class discussions was reported by Weissberg, Gesten, Carnrike, et al. (1981) as being effective in teaching several problem-solving skills. However, these skills did not relate to adjustment gains. The authors indicated that similar effects were reported in previous studies with elementary-age children. This is in contrast to Spivack and Shure's (1974) results with preschool children. In an evaluation of their entire training program, Weissberg et al. (1981a) reiterated that problem-solving skills such as alternative solution thinking, development of discrete, step-by-step plans, and anticipating consequences can be taught to elementary-age children in suburban and urban schools through carefully constructed curricula with motivated teachers. That feeling-identication skills were not acquired was probably a function of weak teaching materials (Weissberg et al., 1981). It is discouraging that these learned skills were not reflected in adjustment gains.

Goldstein, Apter, and Harootunian (1984) reviewed the specific skills typically addressed in social problem-solving approaches and raised the question as to which skills were most potent in realizing behavioral changes in students. They reported that research is too thin to make conclusions regarding skill-student matching. In this regard, researchers might also look to the broad array of cognitive problem-solving programs available. If skills such as generating alternative solutions, for instance, are related to improved social adjustment, a teacher might supplement the social problem-solving approach with curricula designed to teach the intellectual skill of alternative solution generation, such as in Creative Problem Solving (Parnes, 1967) or the Productive Thinking Program (Covington, Crutchfield, & Davies, 1972).

The social problem-solving approach is attractive to teachers because it involves conventional teaching techniques and assumes that the aberrant behavior is really the student's failure to learn. Research with the approach is as yet inconclusive. Variables such as the content of the curriculum, the way the curriculum is presented to the students (teacher/teaching variables), and the age and other demographic features of the students certainly affect outcomes (Weissberg, Gesten, Rapkin, et al., 1981), but in ways not yet predictable.

Social Skills Training

Some overlap between social skills training and self-instruction and problem solving is inevitable: Some degree of self-instruction is necessary to select and initiate appropriate social skills, and problem solving may be thought of as a particular and sequential set of social skills. Ths social skills training approach to intervention with behaviorally disordered students is an essentially educational approach to maladaptive behavior. Students are assessed for behavioral deficits in various social skills areas, such as skills related to the environment, interpersonal skills, self-related behaviors, and task-related behaviors (Stephens, 1978). These skills are then actively and directly taught to the student. The following discussion focuses on research related to the assessment, methods of teaching, and generalization and maintenance of social skills.

Assessment. Assessment of social skills is ideally a multifactored assessment using naturalistic observation, sociometric measures, and teacher ratings. Agreement or convergence of these various sources dictates the particular skills or areas of skills to be taught (Gresham, 1983). Naturalistic observations should be across a variety of settings and conditions; rating scales may be completed by teachers and parents. Goldstein, Sprakin, Gershaw, and Klein (1980) suggested an emphasis on grouping rather than specific selection of skills. They suggested a checklist, or menu, of skills, which can be completed by someone who knows a student well—perhaps even by the student. Goldstein et al.'s approach stresses group composition as well as addressing skill assessment. Since social skills training is typically conducted in groups, there may, in practice, be significant, individual variance in the mastery of any particular skill within the group.

In another social skills curriculum, the MARC Curriculum (1983), the particular skills to be addressed are considered so necessary and so universally absent in the adolescent behaviorally disordered population for whom the curriculum is intended that no special arrangements are made for individual assessment. This represents an unresolved issue for social skills training: How thorough should skill assessment be if the student is then going to be grouped for training on the basis of group therapeutic compatability rather than (or, perhaps, in addition to) skill deficits? Perhaps the rigor recommended for skill assessment in academic areas where the teaching is individualized might be relaxed for social skills training when the instruction is conducted in groups, since individual skills in the group will presumably vary.

Another incompletely resolved issue involves the ethical decisions regarding which social skills should be taught. Who determines what is to be taught/changed? Also, by what process is it decided that the new skill to be taught is proper in light of cultural differences that may exist between the school personnel and the student? Gresham's (1983) multifactorial assessment plan is a response to these issues, but questions remain as to whether such thorough assessment can or will be conducted in practice.

The opportunity to address the issue of cultural differences and social validity of a particular skill often exists in the teaching process. Since social skills instruction typically occurs in groups, there exists the potential for feedback from the peer group regarding the practicality of a particular skill. An alert teacher can then modify the skill in question to accommodate the response of the student and/or the peer group. As is noted later, skills that possess high social validity are more likely to transfer to natural settings.

Methods of Teaching

Training in social skills is based on Bandura's (1977) social-learning theory model. This involves a paradigm that consists of instruction, modeling, rehearsing or guided practice, and performance feedback. Provisions to enhance generalization and maintenance are ideally built into this instructional procedure. A variety of training programs have been developed in recent years to teach interpersonal social skills (see Elardo & Cooper, 1977; Goldstein, Sprafkin, Gershaw, & Klein, 1980, as examples of more popular programs).

Research on the effectiveness of Skillstreaming, a comprehensive social skills curriculum for use with adolescents in groups (Goldstein, Sprafkin et al., 1980), is extensive. Consistently positive support has been found for the suggested instructional procedures as a means of teaching a variety of social skills to aggressive adolescents and preadolescents in public and residential school settings. The considerable body of research on modeling, role-playing, and performance feedback has resulted in a reliable instructional approach.

Stephens (1977) advocated modeling, contracting, and social reinforcement as instructional approaches for teaching social skills. A study by La Nunziata, Hill, and

Krause (1981) reported that social behaviors were readily learned using these approaches and were maintained at a 2-week follow-up.

The modeling, prompting, and praising sequence for teaching social skills is appropriate for preschool-age children as well. Day, Fox, Shores, Lindeman, and Stowitschek (1983) reported successfully teaching social behaviors to obtain positive responses from peers. The children were severely handicapped preschoolers.

A self-controlled curriculum developed by Fagen, Long, and Stevens (1975) is a less structured or directed approach to teaching a set of cognitive and social skills that "seem to determine an individual's capacity to maintain free control over his own behavior" (p. v). Empirical data on the effectiveness of the curriculum are too limited to warrant conclusions, and, as Fagen and Long (1979) noted, "without a long-term programmatic effort, research activity (on the viability of the curriculum) will continue to be largely piecemeal and uncoordinated" (p. 80).

The Fagen, Long, and Stevens curriculum allows the teacher maximal flexibility regarding the presentation of the social skills material and, as such, is roughly representative of a broader body of work referred to as a psychoeducational approach to behavioral disorders. In a psychoeducational approach, the teacher-child relationship is seen as central to the learning environment and the intervention process (Knoblock, 1983). Psychoeducational programs thus tend to be idiosyncratic and not readily replicable for research purposes. As such, the psychoeducational approach does not lend itself well to conventional empirical research. This issue is addressed in the implications section of this chapter; it is mentioned here as a possible explanation for the lack of published research on psychoeducational interventions such as those developed by Fagen, Long, and Stevens.

Generalization and Maintenance

The major problem with social skills training is that the skills learned in one training situation do not readily transfer to another setting. Cartledge and Milburn (1978) reviewed numerous early studies of classroom social skills training with a variety of student populations and concluded that the transfer of skills across conditions constituted the major problem with this approach. Goldstein, Apter, and Harootunian (1984) suggested social skills training using several different co-role players, maximizing the probability that newly learned skills will be reinforced outside the training site, and using imaginative self-reward procedures as ways of enhancing transfer.

Classroom behaviors such as attending and asking and answering questions can be readily reinforced in the classroom since opportunities for performance are frequent and the teacher has direct control over many contingencies. This is one probable reason for the successful maintenance described by La Nunziata, Hill, and

Krause (1981). First, the social behaviors were taught in the site where they were to be performed. Second, the teachers who taught the new social skills were present at times when the newly learned skills were to be performed and could reinforce performance. Third, the skills taught were typical classroom social behaviors (e.g., containing talk-outs, ignoring distractions, on-task behavior, and initiating "thank-you" statements). Lebsock and Salzberg's (1981) study of maladaptive behavior reduction and social skills training through the use of reinforcement and in-class role-playing is illustrative of the intervention complexity necessary to obtain generalization and maintenance.

Warrenfeltz et al. (1981) were able to demonstrate generalization of two social skills of a slightly more sophisticated nature ("appropriate responses to instruction" and "appropriate responses to critical feedback and conversation") through the use of didactic teaching, role-playing, and self-monitoring. The separate effects of the self-monitoring and role-playing could not be isolated in their design, but maintenance in a simulated work site was noted one month after the intervention ended.

Social skills such as negotiation, avoiding trouble, or dealing with group pressure are required less frequently in the classroom, so there is less opportunity to manipulate contingencies that would reinforce performance. These skills are typically used on an occasional basis in out-of-school situations, where natural reinforcement is much more problematic. Friedman, Quick, Mayo, and Palmer (1983) reported how social skills can be learned in a structured setting and when combined with other therapeutic interventions available through day treatment programs. The day treatment program they described merges the efforts of the special education program with group and individual counseling and family interventions. This integrated program maintained infrequently required social skills in out-of-school environments. As there are many features to the program, attribution of effects to interventions is difficult.

Another approach to enhancing the likelihood of transfer across conditions and setting was described by Filipczak, Archer, Winett, and Fennell (1978). Combining an ecological perspective with social skills training, they described a procedure for validating social skills objectives in the settings where the behaviors are to occur. For instance, a rather deferential, only mildly assertive, interview behavior was modified in the direction of more active assertion based on data from the community suggesting that this would be a more successful strategy. Filipczak et al. (1978) suggested that contingencies may be more rewarding if the skills better match the settings where they are to be used.

Ecological Interventions

Our discussion of interventions based on an ecological perspective of behavioral disorders begins with a brief overview of Project Re-Education, the most prominent and fully developed model program incorporating this unique and still-emerging perspective. Recent research and speculation on the expansion of the Re-Education model (frequently referred to as the *Re-Ed* model) is considered together with related work that might suggest directions for social policy, personnel training, and service delivery.

Project Re-Ed began as a residential treatment program that focused on the child and the child's relationship to the important components in his or her "ecosystem." *Re-education* involved helping the child's family, the referring school, and the child's local community to provide better support to the individual child while simultaneously improving the adaptive behavior of the child. The distinctive features of this program were an essentially educational, as opposed to a psychiatric, approach; the liberal use of teacher-counselors in an expanded child care role; and a liaison-teacher counselor to coordinate and nurture transactions between the school, the home, and the community (Hobbs, 1966, 1978, 1983).

Reflecting on Project Re-Education, Hobbs (1983) stated:

"Perhaps the single most important idea to emerge from Project Re-Ed is the conceptualization of the problem of the troubled and troubling child or adolescent in ecological terms. The problem is to be discovered not in the child but in the transactions between the child and the people who play crucial roles in his life." (p. 17)

Project Re-Ed received model demonstration project status in 1973 (Project Re-Education, 1973) in confirmation of the approach's significant positive impact on the lives of the children served. Montgomery and Van Fleet (1978) reported significant positive changes in children's academic progress, social behavior, peer and adult interactions, and neighborhood and home interactions following the children's enrollment in a Re-Ed program where the length of stay ranged from 9 to 48 weeks. No follow-up data were available. The model's demonstration status and concurrent positive reports of ability to effect positive change in students is reflected in the propagation of the model: In 1981, there were 23 functioning Re-Ed programs preponderantly located in southeastern states (Hobbs, 1983).

Certain changes and modifications were necessitated as the model was adopted in new locations. Originally developed for children aged 6 to 12, the age limits for some of the newer sites well extended upward and downward to serve children and their ecosystems from preschool age through adolescence (Hobbs, 1983).

However, Lewis (1980) noted that certain Re-Ed centers are not necessarily true to the original model. In Tennessee, for instance, the Re-Ed model has been adopted for nearly all the adolescent service units of that state's mental health system. Services provided by the Department of Mental Health are supervised by physicians more familiar with the traditional medical model and are subject to the Department of Mental Health's certification criteria. Children's services must meet those criteria if the hospital is to maintain accreditation. Project Re-Ed was originally developed as a radical alternative to the more traditional psychiatric services enshrined in the accreditation criteria. Further, the original model utilized some exclusion criteria for children entering the Re-Ed program. This is not a luxury available to state psychiatric centers. The result is that Re-Ed programs in some locations are now serving more disturbed children, who function at lower academic levels and who are from more disorganized family situations. In Lewis's words:

"The Re-Ed model did not change the basic character of the programs, but the possibility of institutional inertia may also leave a friendly skeptic wondering whether we are employing the best possible procedures available to us now in 1980. The last, and only large scale, systematic program evaluation was done in the late 1960's and limited to children from one program . . ." (p. 13)

The ecological perspective argues for a more holistic approach to behavioral disorders in children as opposed to the piecemeal strategies historically employed. Lewis (1982) reviewed follow-up studies of children and adolescents discharged from residential treatment centers where the focus of intervention was intrapsychic and child centered. Improvement during treatment was found to be unrelated to adjustment on follow-up; rather, Lewis showed that adjustment following treatment was directly related to the amount of social support a child received from family members and community agencies while he or she was enrolled in the residential program. Why some families and agencies were able to be supportive while their children were in residence and other families and agencies were not remains an open question. Lewis suggested that ecosystem factors outside the family also influence the adjustment.

Unfortunately, there is a paucity of research on the effects of ecological interventions on the adjustment of behaviorally disordered children and youth. Swap's (1978) model for conceptualizing the ecological network of a child remains a "proposed synthesis." The complexity of a child's ecology resists the quantitative methodologies favored in contemporary research journals. Cohen (1980) noted that, with the press to show accountability in human services, there is a tendency to utilize simplistic quantifiable objectives and outcomes such as units of service and eligible target populations served. Data on ecological factors are not routinely maintained.

Yet, social support is a phenomenon that has been investigated in research. Cauce, Felner, and Primavera (1982) reported three distinct dimensions of social support—family; formal support (e.g., guidance counselors, state employment service officers), and informal support (peers, adults other than relatives—and noted

that the perceived helpfulness of each of these dimensions varied by sex, grade, and ethnic background. The population in this study was made up of adolescents from high-stress, low-socioeconomic status, inner-city backgrounds. Asp and Garbarino (1983) reviewed informal and formal intraschool support systems and models of organized support between schools and their communities but without particular attention to special education populations. Similarly, Barth (1983) scrutinized the variety of social support networks for families in crisis. Further work in the area of social support mechanisms for high-risk, school-age children is undoubtedly available, but it is beyond the purview of this research integration.

Affective Education

Affective education is concerned with assisting the student to develop a positive self-concept and high self-esteem. Concurrent with this personal dimension is a social dimension emphasizing the development of a student's prosocial behavior (Morse, Ardizzone, Macdonald, & Pasick 1980). As may be inferred from this condensation of Morse et al.'s explanation, specifying outcomes and clearly measurable goals for affective education programs is difficult and highly personal. Wood (1982) distinguished between affective education, which stresses thoughts, feelings, and interpersonal relationships, and social skills training, which focuses on teaching explicit behaviors to elicit positive responses from the environment. This distinction is observed in this chapter.

There exist several reviews of affective programs and curricula in the literature (i.e., Baskin & Hess, 1980; Elardo & Elardo, 1976; Hughes, 1977; Lockwood, 1978; Medway & Smith, 1978). The conclusions of these reviews are synthesized below.

1. Underlying conceptual principles for affective programs and curricula are either missing or vaguely addressed. What theoretical base is provided is judged as insufficient to explicate goals such as interpersonal understanding or self-awareness (Elardo & Elardo, 1976; Hughes, 1977; Medway & Smith, 1978).

2. Related to the absence of defined conceptual principles is a poorly articulated developmental perspective: The curricula reviewed are generally not well-integrated into current child development research and theory (Elardo & Elardo, 1976; Lockwood, 1978). Research by Day and Griffin (1980) noted differential responses by age/grade to a particular affective program, suggesting that future investigations might attempt a better student-to-program match.

3. Existing research suggests the confounding effects of the affective educator/teacher (Baskin & Hess, 1980; Day & Griffin, 1980; Hughes, 1977; Medway & Smith, 1978). Affective behavior is

especially likely to be influenced by teacher personality/familiarity/behavior. Further, some programs stress teacher training, while others clearly indicate that no special inservice training is required.

4. The research evaluating affective education programs faces the usual methodological criticisms leveled at most educational research for factors such as control groups, random assignment, instrumentation that is reliable and possesses content validity, and blind evaluation (Baskin & Hess, 1980; Lockwood, 1978). Coupled with some of the aforementioned problems, definitive statements about affective program effectiveness are difficult.

5. Several of the programs reviewed had some value if used on a consistent and long-term basis (Medway & Smith, 1978). Baskin and Hess (1980) considered that affective education programs deserved an opportunity to mature theoretically and operationally. Elardo and Elardo (1976) stressed the importance of continuing process-oriented research to improve social and emotional curricula.

Life Space Interviewing

Of several crisis counseling approaches utilized by educators in schools, the approach known as life space interviewing (Redl, 1959) was developed directly from work with emotionally disturbed children. Certainly other counseling approaches, such as rational behavior training (Goodman & Maultsby, 1974), reality therapy (Glasser, 1975), or the social discipline approach of Dreikurs and Cassel (1972), are used frequently with emotionally disturbed children, but these basic approaches were generated with other populations.

Life space interviewing is intended to be utilized while a child is in an aroused state—usually following some sort of emotional incident. The adult is to draw from the child his or her perception of what happened, the sequence of events that transpired, and his or her feelings about those events. Part of this exploration with the child might go beyond the immediate incident to similar situations or feelings generated in other parts of the child's "life space." Taking care to avoid value judgements, the adult helps the child to associate how his or her perceptions and feelings are related to his or her behaviors and to the actions of others in the environment (Fagen and Guedalia, 1977).

The primary goals of this approach are to maintain and strengthen the adult-child relationship and to provide emotional first aid when the child is confused, frightened, angry, or a victim of his or her intense emotional state. In addition, the use of this technique sometimes allows the adult to seize this often particularly "teachable moment" to help the child to discover carefully hidden, positive values or to realize the need to try new behaviors in his or her own best interest.

Sufficient descriptions of this counseling approach exist in the literature (Apter and Conoley, 1984; Brendtro & Ness, 1983; Fagen & Guedalia, 1977; Fagen &

Hill, 1977), and some anecdotal support for the approach has been presented (Fagen & Long, 1981). Empirical support is limited but encouraging. Reilly, Imber, and Cremins (1978) reported the effective use of life space interviewing within a resource room setting in a junior high school. The intervention itself proved practicable, and target behaviors were significantly reduced.

DeMagistris and Imber (1980) demonstrated the effectiveness of life space interviewing using a multiple baseline design with a control group over a 9-week period. The study was conducted with eight adolescent boys in a residential treatment center for emotionally disturbed youth. There were some noted limitations to the study in terms of the reliability of the behavior observations and some apparent contamination between the two experimental groups, but the effectiveness of the life space interviewing procedure was demonstrated.

Cooperative Learning

Research in cooperative learning methodology began in the early 1970s, partially in response to acute racial tensions in schools but also as an approach to reducing the isolation and hostility perceived to exist in many highly competitive classrooms. Under this methodology, teachers assign students to four-to-five-member learning groups, each containing a mix of low, average, and high-achieving students. Other variables, such as race and sex, are typically considered so as to reflect the major demographic elements of the class as a whole. Learning then proceeds under a variety of configurations using individual and group activities in which students support and contribute to the learning of other members of the group to which they are assigned. Since individuals can attain their goals only if other group members also attain their goals, an attitude of positive interdependence is attained and sustained (Knight, Peterson & McGuire, 1982). A variety of cooperative learning models have been developed and tested (see Johnson & Johnson, 1975; Slavin, 1981). This section reviews research on cooperative learning as an intervention with behaviorally disordered students.

Research on cooperative learning has typically measured the effect of the approach on the academic achievement and intergroup relations of typical students. Slavin (1980) reviewed results comparing cooperative learning and traditional classroom arrangements and noted significant positive effects favoring cooperative learning for academic achievement in the majority of 27 studies reviewed. Research on the effects of certain types of cooperative learning designs on improving intergroup relations has also been significantly positive (Slavin, 1981).

Cooperative learning studies with typical students have also positively influenced other variables more directly related to emotional disturbance. Internal locus of control appears to be influenced through the use of these methods (Slavin, 1983), as do other motivation-related attitudes. Other evidence cited by Slavin (1983) supports the conclusion that cooperative learning improved positive relationships between students, who acted more altruistically and were better able to understand someone else's perspective. Although contamination between experimental groups weakened the study, Slavin, Madden, and Leavey (1984) found some indications that cooperative learning could positively affect the sociometric status of mildly handicapped, elementary-age children in mainstreamed situations.

Johnson and Johnson (1983) compared cooperative, competitive, and individualistic learning conditions for 59 fourth-grade students, 12 of whom were diagnosed as having severe learning and behavioral problems. Handicapped and nonhandicapped students interacted significantly more frequently in the cooperative condition and during free time following the learning activities. The nonhandicapped students also were better able to take the social perspective of their handicapped peers in the cooperative condition than in the competitive condition. Self-esteem was elevated for both groups under cooperative conditions.

Slavin (1977) conducted one study of cooperative learning methods with behaviorally disordered students. Teams-Games-Tournament (TGT), a particular type of cooperative learning, was compared with individualized instructional procedures in a special day school for adolescent students identified as behaviorally disordered. Pre- and post-measures of experimental and control groups after 12 weeks showed higher levels of peer mutual attraction and on-task behavior in the TGT group than in the control group. A 5-month follow-up after all the students had been reassigned to new classes indicated that higher peer interaction was maintained.

Cooperative learning methods directly contradict present trends toward increased homogeneous grouping in special class programs. Also, although there exists ample support for individualized instruction for cognitive learning, the essential isolation in which special education students work may do nothing to address deficiencies in interpersonal adjustment. Such problems may even be exacerbated. Some mix of cooperative learning with individualized instructional time may be especially appropriate for behaviorally disordered students.

Implications for Future Research and Policy Development

Within the perimeters of this review are some subjects for which there is considerable current research and theoretical activity and other subjects for which little or no publication activity exists. There is, for instance, an abundance of recently published work on cognitive-behavioral interventions, while investigation in the use of affective education as an intervention is relatively moribund. To some extent, this unevenness of activity

is reflected in the following discussion of the three areas: future research, teacher training, and implications this integration work holds for policy development.

Future Research

1. Several recent literature reviews attest to the heavy research activity on cognitive-behavioral interventions (Albion, 1983: Kazdin, 1982; O'Leary & Dubey, 1979; Rosenbaum & Drabman, 1979; Rueda, 1981). Psychologists have found this area of study particularly exciting, as it represents a confluence of behavioral, developmental, and clinical psychology (Kazdin, 1982). And, as indicated earlier, this family of interventions is especially promising for children and youth with behavioral disorders.

One of the problems with evaluating the efficacy of cognitively based procedures is that they are often used in natural settings in combination with other cognitive procedures. Self-monitoring and evaluation might be combined with modeling or relaxation activities, for instance, making it difficult to determine the effects of individual interventions. Future research could be designed to measure the effect of each component procedure.

Trainee variables might also be fruitfully explored. What personality variables interact with self-control training? Is there a population for whom cognitive interventions would be more (or less) efficacious? Does lower cognitive ability, for instance, influence self-control training? Are cognitive-behavioral interventions useful with children diagnosed as autistic?

But the overriding research issues remain maintenance of a behavior and generalization across settings and situations. How does one learn to value self-control in the absence of rewarding contingencies? Since contingencies can be manipulated in settings such as classrooms or other institutional milieu, cognitively-based procedures do promise to relieve teachers from immediate control issues and free them to teach academic skills. But if the generalization problem cannot be resolved, cognitive-behavioral interventions will be limited to use only in such highly controllable settings such as self-contained classrooms.

2. Social skills training research is subject to the same problems discussed regarding cognitive-behavioral interventions. Social skills training is typically conducted in combination with other behavioral or cognitive-behavioral procedures, maintenance and generalization of training is problematic but infrequently addressed in available research, and the interaction of these interventions with trainee variables is lacking.

In addition, there are unresolved issues regarding the content of the training curriculum and how this variable interacts with teacher, teaching method, and student variables. All of these variables may be assumed to affect outcomes, but in ways that are not yet predictable.

Cultural differences between teachers and students also raise potentially serious issues about the content of social skills curricula. Educators involved in social skills curricula development must be alert to variations in social behavior across cultures and must incorporate mechanisms for cultural adaptation into curricula as they are developed.

3. Although considerable effort has been spent devising rigorous assessment regimes for determining specific social skills to be taught to individual students, group instruction appears to be the preferable mode of instruction. Group instruction suggests a focus on more general than more specific skills instruction. Applied research is needed to suggest ways of resolving this apparent paradox.

4. The research on ecological interventions available in traditional special education sources is sparse. This perspective has been emerging for over a decade, and it is disappointing that there has not been more research activity. But the complexity of a child's ecology resists typical quantitative methodologies. Case studies, ethnographic methodologies, and careful explications of existing programs must be undertaken in order to reveal salient ecological variables and how they interact. There is potentially useful material in the fields of sociology and human development that is simply not well-integrated with special education literature.

5. Not since 1964 (Morse, Cutler, & Fink) have professionals in the field of behavioral disorders had the opportunity to view the state of practice through a national survey. No one knows, for instance, how much social skills training actually occurs in programs for behaviorally disordered children. We have no idea as to what degree teachers utilize any cognitive-behavioral interventions. Are affective education programs widely used in elementary school programs? A major national survey focusing on current practice is necessary to inform researchers and teacher educators of what exists beyond their limited local school programs.

Teaching Training

1. This research integration suggests that the diversity and complexity of promising cognitive-emotional interventions require a sophisticated teacher training program possible only at the graduate level. It is difficult to comprehend how a fledgling teacher just completing an undergraduate program could become competent in the myriad of skills necessary for teaching content areas, and then reach an application level of competence in skills such as those suggested in this chapter as necessary for working with behaviorally handicapped children. Yet, many states award provisional or temporary certification to teachers completing bachelor degree programs with a proviso that they complete graduate training—usually within 5 years. That both the teachers and their students should endure those 5 years without benefit of good training in the application of cognitive-emotional interventions is unwise.

2. This synthesis confirms considerable research activity in the area of cognitive-behavioral interventions. Although recent texts in behavior modification have incorporated this research, there may be some problem in reaching practicing teachers who are no longer taking formal course work. In-service education should be concerned with translating research for teachers. Because the quality, or even the existence, of in-service education varies from school district to school district, how new, promising, and readily adaptable practices reach teachers is a problem that should be addressed.

3. This integration also suggests that special education teacher educators should remain vigilant of developments in general education. Cooperative learning research, for instance, is not a subject addressed in any contemporary behavioral disorders texts, yet the implications for teaching behaviorally disordered students are important. Thus, further investigation is needed to address questions such as: Are there other bodies of research, especially those examining the interface between child behavior and the school/teaching structure, of which special educators are generally unaware; and, Has special education teacher training become too parochial to be sensitive to research in general education?

4. Finally, ecological interventions are possible only if school personnel are aware of other community agencies and the services they provide to school-age students and their parents. Teacher education programs need to address how teachers can gain access to community programs for their students and their students' parents if ecological interventions are ever to be incorporated into programming for behaviorally disordered students.

Policy Development

1. This research synthesis indicates that research on various cognitive-emotional interventions should be stimulated, that cognitive-behavioral research in natural settings should be a high priority, and curricula and materials development for social-cognitive interventions should be encouraged.

One obvious method for stimulating quality research is through focused research and curriculum development grants from appropriate federal and state governmental agencies. Invited converences drawing together researchers from the areas of psychology and special education should also be considered. Such conferences might be organized by appropriate professional organizations, such as the Council for Exceptional Children or the American Psychological Association, with sponsorship from a federal agency or a private foundation.

2. Advances in cognitive-emotional interventions must be made available to practicing teachers. Preservice programs should be of sufficient length and depth that new teachers are competent to apply various cognitive-emotional interventions before they receive certification to teach behaviorally disordered students.

To this end, state education departments should review their sponsored inservice programming for the inclusion of content regarding the basis for and practice of cognitive-emotional interventions. Requirements for federal "flow-through" money could stipulate such a review. Colleges and universities with graduate programs in special education need to provide summer course-work in cognitive-emotional interventions as a service to teachers seeking to continue their professional education. Finally, the Council for Exceptional Children might consider a method for voluntary certification of special education teacher preparation programs as a means of monitoring recency of content.

3. Administrators, teachers, and support personnel working in school and residential programs for behaviorally disordered students must be encouraged to reach beyond their traditional boundaries and seek to develop ecologically broader intervention approaches.

Such encouragement could be in the form of collaborative interagency funding from state or federal sources to service providers, with inducements for observation and replication of successful programs. These activities should be carefully documented with a view to development of a broader knowledge base regarding ecological interventions. (The topic of cooperative interface between school and other child care agencies is discussed at length in this volume's chapter by Huntze.)

References

Alberto, P. A., & Troutman, A. C. (1982). *Applied behavior analysis for teachers.* Columbus, OH: Merrill.

Albion, F. (1983). A methodological analysis of self-control in applied settings. *Behavioral Disorders, 8,* 87–102.

Apter, S. J. (1982). *Troubled children, troubled systems.* Elmsford, NY: Pergamon.

Apter, S. J., & Conoley, J. C. (1984). *Childhood behavior disorders and emotional disturbance.* Englewood Cliffs, NJ: Prentice-Hall.

Asp, E., & Garbarino, J. (1983). Social support networks and the schools. In J. K. Whittaker & Garbarino (Eds.), *Social support networks: Informal helping in the human services* (pp. 251–297). New York: Aldine.

Bandura, A. (1977). *Social learning theory.* Englewood Cliffs, NJ: Prentice-Hall.

Barth, R. (1983). Social support networks in services for adolescents and their families. In J. K. Whittaker & J. Garbarino (Eds.), *Social support networks: Informal helping in the human services* (pp. 299–352). New York: Aldine.

Baskin, E. J., & Hess, R. D. (1980). Does affective education work? A review of seven programs. *Journal of School Psychology, 18,* 40–50.

Beck, A. T. (1976). *Cognitive therapy and the emotional disorders.* New York: International Universities.

Bolstad, O. D., & Johnson, S. M. (1972). Self-regulation in the modification of disruptive classroom behavior. *Journal of Applied Behavior Analysis, 5,* 443–454.

Brendtro, L. K., & Ness, A. E. (1983). The life-space interview: A re-examination. In L. K. Brendtro & A. E. Ness (Eds.), *Re-educating troubled youth* (pp. 177–201). New York: Aldine.

Broden, N., Hall, R. V., & Mitts, B. (1971). The effect of self-recording on the behavior of two eighth-grade students. *Journal of Applied Behavior Analysis, 4,* 191–199.

Camp, B. W., & Bash, M. A. (1981). *Think Aloud: Increasing social and cognitive skills, a problem solving program for children.* Champaign, IL: Research Press.

Camp, B. W., Blom, G. E., Hebert, F., & vanDoorninck, W. J. (1977). "Think Aloud": A program for developing self-control in young aggressive boys. *Journal of Abnormal Child Psychology, 5,* 157–169.

Camras, L. A. (1980). Children's understanding of facial expressions used during conflict encounters. *Child Development, 51,* 879–885.

Carpenter, R. L. (1985). Curricula and instruction for emotionally handicapped students. **The Forum,** *11* (3), 11–13.

Cartledge, G., & Milburn, J. F. (1978). The case for teaching social skills in the classroom: A review. *Review of Educational Research, 48,* 133–156.

Cauce, A. M., Felner, R. D., & Primavera, J. (1982). Social support in high risk adolescents: Structural components and adaptive impact. *American Journal of Community Psychology, 10,* 417–428.

Cohen, R. (1980 September). *Serving troubled children: Program and policy planning for the future.* Paper presented at the 88th American Psychological Association Convention, Montreal, Canada. (ERIC Document Reproduction Service No. ED 206 992).

Covington, M. V., Crutchfield, R. S., & Davies, L. B. (1972). *The Productive Thinking Program.* Berkeley, CA: Pragellen.

Day, R. W., Fox, J. J., Shores, R. E., Lindeman, D. P., & Stowitschek, J. J. (1983). The social competence intervention project: Developing educational procedures for teaching social interaction skills to handicapped children. *Behavioral Disorders, 8,* 120–127.

Day, R. W., & Griffin, R. E. (1980). Children's attitudes toward the magic circle. *Elementary School Guidance and Counseling, 15,* 136–146.

DeMagistris, R. J., & Imber, S. C. (1980). The effects of life space interviewing on academic and social performance of behaviorally disordered children. *Behavioral Disorders, 6,* 12–25.

Dodge, K. A., & Murphy, R. R. (1984). The assessment of social competence in adolescents. In P. Karoly & J. J. Steffan (Eds.), *Adolescent behavior disorders: Foundations and contemporary concerns in child behavioral analysis and therapy.* (Vol. 3, pp. 61–96). Lexington, MA: Lexington Books.

Douglas, V., Parry, P., Marton, P., & Garson C. (1976). Assessment of a cognitive training program for hyperactive children. *Journal of Abnormal Child Psychology, 4,* 389–410.

Drabman, R. S., Spitalnik, R., & O'Leary, D. D. (1973). Effects of reinforcement on children's academic behavior as a function of self-determined and externally imposed contingencies. *Journal of Applied Behavior Analysis, 6,* 241–250.

Dreikurs, R., & Cassel, P. (1972). *Discipline without tears* (2nd ed.). New York: Hawthorn.

Elardo, P., & Cooper, M. (1977). *AWARE: Activities for social development.* Reading, MA: Addison-Wesley.

Elardo, P., & Elardo, R. (1976). A critical analysis of social development programs in elementary education. *Journal of School Psychology, 14,* 118–130.

Elias, M. J. (1983). Improving coping skills of emotionally disturbed boys through television-based social problem solving. *American Journal of Orthopsychiatry*, **53**, 61–72.

Ellis, A., (1962). *Reason and emotion in psychotherapy*. New York: Lyle Stuart.

Fagen, S. A., & Guedalia, L. J. (1977). *Individual and group counseling*. Washington, DC: Psychoeducational Resources.

Fagen, S.A., & Hill, J. M. (1977). *Behavior management*. Washington, D.C.: Psychoeducational Resources.

Fagen, S. A., & Long, N. J. (1979). A psychoeducational curriculum approach to teaching self-control. *Behavioral Disorders*, **4**, 68–82.

Fagen, S. A., & Long, N. J. (Eds.). (1981). Life space interviewing [Special issue]. *The Pointer*, **25**(2).

Fagen, S. A., Long, N. J., & Stevens, D. J. (1975). *Teaching children self-control*. Columbus, OH: Merrill.

Filipczak, J., Archer, M., Winett, R., & Fennell, S. (1978, August). *Social skills training in the community with behaviorally disruptive youth*. Paper presented at the annual convention of the American Psychological Association, Toronto, Canada. (ERIC Document Reproduction Service No. ED 170 632).

Freedman, B. J., Rosenthal, L., Donahoe, C. P., Schlundt, D. G., & McFall, R. M. (1978). A social-behavioral analysis of skill deficits in delinquent and nondelinquent boys. *Journal of Consulting and Clinical Psychology*, **46**, 1448–1462.

Friedman, R. M., Quick, J., Mayo, J., & Palmer, J. (1983). Social skills training within a day treatment program for emotionally disturbed adolescents. In C. W. LeCroy (Ed.), *Social skills training for children and youth* (pp. 139–152). New York: Haworth.

Gaffney, L. R., & McFall, R. M. (1981). A comparison of social skills in delinquent and nondelinquent girls using a behavioral role-playing inventory. *Journal of Consulting and Clinical Psychology*, **49**, 959–967.

Garrison, S. R., & Stolberg, A. L. (1983). Modification of anger in children by affective imagery training. *Journal of Abnormal Child Psychology*, **11**, 115–130.

Glasser, W. (1975). *Reality therapy*. New York: Harper & Row.

Glenn, D. S., Rueda, R., & Rutherford, R. B. (1984). Cognitive approaches to social competence with behaviorally disordered youth. In J. K. Grosenick, S. L. Huntze, E. McGinnis, & C. R. Smith (Eds.), *Social/affective interventions in behavioral disorders* (pp. 25–42). Columbia: The National Needs Analysis in Behavioral Disorders Project, University of Missouri.

Glynn, E. L., Thomas, J. D., & Shee, S. M. (1973). Behavioral self-control of on task behavior in an elementary classroom. *Journal of Applied Behavior Analysis*, **6**, 105–113.

Goldstein, A. P., Apter, S. J., & Harootunian, B. (1984). *School violence*. Englewood Cliffs, NJ: Prentice-Hall.

Goldstein, A. P., Sprafkin, R. P., Gershaw, N. J., & Klein, P. (1980). *Skillstreaming the adolescent: A structural learning approach to teaching prosocial behavior*. Champaign, IL: Research Press.

Goodman, D. S. & Maultsby, M. C. (1974). *Emotional well-being through rational behavior training*. Springfield, IL: C. C. Thomas.

Gottman, J., & McFall, R. (1972). Self-monitoring effects in a program for potential high school dropouts. *Journal of Consulting and Clinical Psychology*, **39**, 273–281.

Greenspan, S. (1979). Social intelligence in the retarded. In N. R. Ellis (Ed.), *Handbook of mental deficiency: Theory and research* (2nd ed.). Hillsdale, NJ: Erlbaum.

Gresham, F. M. (1983). Social skills assessment as a component of mainstreaming placement decisions. *Exceptional Children*, **49**, 331–336.

Hobbs, N. (1966). Helping disturbed children: Psychological and ecological strategies. *American Psychologist*, **21**, 1105–1115.

Hobbs, N. (1978). Perspectives on Re-Education. *Behavioral Disorders*, **3**, 65–66.

Hobbs, N. (1983). Project Re-Ed: From demonstration project to national program. *Peabody Journal of Education*, **60**(3), 8–24.

Hughes, C. (1977). Affective education. In R. E. Schmid & L. M. Nagata (Eds.), *Contemporary issues in special education* (pp. 150–160). New York: McGraw-Hill.

Huntze, S. L. (1985). CCBD Subcommittee on Terminology. A position paper of the Council for Children with Behavioral Disorders. *Behavioral Disorders*, **10**, 167–174.

Inside/Out: A guide for teachers. (1973). Bloomington, IN: Agency for Instructional Television.

Johnson, D. W. & Johnson, R. T. (1975). *Learning together and alone: Cooperation, competition and individualization*. Englewood Cliffs, NJ: Prentice-Hall.

Johnson, R. T. & Johnson, D. W. (1983). Effects of cooperative, competitive, and individualistic learning experiences on social development. *Exceptional Children*, **49**, 323–329.

Kazdin, A. E. (1977). Assessing the clinical or applied importance of behavior change through social validation. *Behavior Modification*, **1**, 427–452.

Kazdin, A. E. (1982). Current developments and research issues in cognitive behavioral interventions: A commentary. *School Psychology Review*, **11**, 75–82.

Kendall, P., & Finch, A. (1978). A cognitive-behavioral treatment for impulsivity: A group comparison study. *Journal of Consulting and Clinical Psychology*, **46**, 110–118.

Kendall, P., & Wilcox, L. (1980). Cognitive behavioral treatment for impulsivity: Concrete versus conceptual training in non-self-controlled problem children. *Journal of Consulting and Clinical Psychology*, **48**, 80–91.

Kendall, P., & Zupan, B. (1981). Individual versus group application of cognitive behavioral self-control procedures with children. *Behavior Therapy*, **12**, 344–359.

Knight, C. J., Peterson, R. L., & McGuire, B. (1982). Cooperative learning: A new approach to an old idea. *Teaching Exceptional Children*, **14**, 233–238.

Knoblock, P. (1983). *Teaching emotionally disturbed children*. Boston MA: Houghton Mifflin.

La Nunziata, L. J., Hill, D. S., & Krause, L. A. (1981). Teaching social skills in classrooms for behaviorally disordered students. *Behavioral Disorders*, **6**, 238–246.

Laten, S. & Katz, G. (1975). *A theoretical model for assessment of adolescents*: The ecological/behavioral approach Madison, WI: Madison Public Schools.

Lebsock, M. S., & Salzberg, C. L. (1981). The use of role-play and reinforcement procedures in the development of generalized interpersonal behavior with emotionally disturbed-behavior disordered adolescents in a special education classroom. *Behavioral Disorders*, **6**, 150–163.

Lewis, W. W. (1982). Ecological factors in successful residential treatment. *Behavioral Disorders*, **7**, 149–156.

Lewis, W. W. (1980, August). *Tennessee Re-Ed: From innovation to establishment*. Paper presented at a topical conference of the Council for Exceptional Children, Minneapolis, MN.

Lockwood, A. L. (1978). The effects of values clarification and moral development curricula on school-age subjects: A critical review of recent research. *Review of Educational Research*, **48**, 325–364.

Lovitt, T. C., & Curtiss, K. (1969). Academic response rate as a function of teacher and self-imposed contingencies. *Journal of Applied Behavioral Analysis*, **2**, 49–53.

MARC Curriculum (1983, June). A resource manual for the development and evaluation of special programs for exceptional students. Tallahassee, FL: Department of Education.

McLaughlin, T. F. (1976). Self-control in the classroom. *Review of Educational Research*, **46**, 631–663.

Medway, F. J., & Smith, R. C. (1978). An examination of contemporary elementary school affective education programs. *Psychology in the Schools*, **15**(2), 260–268.

Meichenbaum, D. (1977). *Cognitive-behavior modification*. New York: Plenum.

Meichenbaum, D., & Goodman, J. (1971). Training impulsive children to talk to themselves: A means of developing self-control. *Journal of Abnormal Psychology*, **77**, 115–126.

Model Affective Resource Curriculum for Secondary Emotionally Handicapped Students (1983, June). Tallahassee, FL: Department of Education.

Montgomery, P. A., & Van Fleet, D. S. (1978). Evaluation of behavioral and academic changes through the Re-Ed process. *Behavioral Disorders*, **3**, 136–146.

Morse, W. C., Ardizzone, J., Macdonald, C., & Pasick, P. (1980). *Affective education for special children and youth*. Reston, VA: Council for Exceptional Children.

Morse, W. C., Cutler, R. L., & Fink, A. H. (1964). *Public school classes for the emotionally disturbed: A research analysis*. Washington, DC: Council for Exceptional Children.

O'Leary, S. G., & Dubey, D. R. (1979). Application of self-control procedures by children: A review. *Journal of Applied Behavioral Analysis*, **12**, 449–465.

Parnes, S. J. (1967). *Creative behavior guidebook*. New York: Scribner.

Polsgrove, L. (1979). Self-control: Methods for child training. *Behavioral Disorders*, **4**, 116–130.

Prillaman, D., & Abbott, J. C. (1983). *Educational diagnosis and prescriptive teaching*. Belmont, CA: Pitman Learning.

Project Re-Education for Emotionally Disturbed Children, Validation Report (1973, February), Elementary and Secondary Education Act, United States Department of Education Title III, Validation Team, John W. Schaerer, Chair.

Quay, H. C., & Peterson, D. R. (1967). *Manual for the Behavior Problem Checklist*. Champaign: University of Illinois, Children's Research Center.

Redl, F. (1959). The concept of the life space interview. *American Journal of Orthopsychiatry*, **29**, 1–18.

Reilly, M. J., Imber, S. C., & Cremins, J. (1978, April). *The effects of life space interviews on social behaviors of junior high school special needs students*. Paper presented at the 56th International Conference of the Council for Exceptional Children, Kansas City, MO.

Rhodes, W. C., & Tracy, M. L. (1972). *A study of child variance: Conceptual models* (Vol. 1). Ann Arbor: University of Michigan, Institute for the Study of Mental Retardation and Related Disabilities.

Robin, A., Schneider, M., & Dolnick, M. (1976). The Turtle Technique: An extended case of self-control in the classroom. *Psychology in the Schools*, **13**, 449–453.

Rosenbaum, M. S., & Drabman, R. S. (1979). Self-control training in the classroom: A review and critique. *Journal of Applied Behavioral Analysis*, **12**, 467–485.

Rueda, R. (1981). Future directions in self-control research. In R. B. Rutherford, A. G. Prieto, & J. E. McGlothlin (Eds.), *Severe behavior disorders of children and youth* (Vol. 4, pp. 16–21). Reston, VA: Council for Children with Behavioral Disorders.

Rueda, R., Rutherford, R. B., & Howell, K. W. (1981). Review of self-control research with behaviorally disordered and mentally retarded children. In R. B. Rutherford, A. G. Prieto, & J. E. McGlothlin (Eds.), *Severe behavior disorders of children and youth* (Vol. 3, pp. 188–197). Reston, VA: Council for Children with Behavioral Disorders.

Rutherford, R. B., Howell, K. W., & Rueda, R. (1982). Self-control instruction for behavior disordered students: Design and implementation. *Instructional Psychology*, **9**, 91–99.

Santogrossi, D. A., O'Leary, K. D., Romanczyk, R. G., & Kaufman, K. F. (1973). Self-evaluation by adolescents in a psychiatric hospital school token program. *Journal of Applied Behavior Analysis*, **6**, 277–287.

Schmid, R., Algozzine, B., Maher, M., & Wells, D. (1984). Teaching emotionally disturbed adolescents: A study of related teacher and teaching characteristics. *Behavioral Disorders*, **9**, 105–112.

Schneider, M., & Robin, A. (1974). *Turtle manual*. Washington DC: U.S. Office of Education. (ERIC Document Reproduction Service No. ED 128 680).

Slavin, R. E. (1977). A student team approach to teaching adolescents with special emotional and behavioral needs. *Psychology in the Schools*, **14**, 77–84.

Slavin, R. E. (1980). Cooperative learning. *Review of Educational Research*, **50**, 315–342.

Slavin, R. E. (1981). Synthesis of research on cooperative learning. *Educational Leadership*, **38**, 655–659.

Slavin, R. E. (1983). *Cooperative learning*. New York: Longman.

Slavin, R. E., Madden, M. A., & Leavey, M. (1984). Effects of cooperative learning and individualized instruction on mainstreamed students. *Exceptional Children*, **50**, 434–443.

Spivack, G., Platt, J. J., & Shure, M. B. (1976). *The problem-solving approach to adjustment*. San Francisco, CA: Jossey-Bass.

Spivack, G., & Shure, M. (1974). *Social adjustment of young children: A cognitive approach to solving real life problems*. San Francisco: Jossey-Bass.

Stephens, T. M. (1977). *Teaching skills to children with learning and behavior disorders*. Columbus, OH: Merrill.

Stephens, T. M. (1978). *Social skills in the classroom*. Columbus, OH: Cedars.

Swap, S. W. (1978). The ecological model of emotional disturbance in children: A status report and proposed synthesis. *Behavioral Disorders*, **3**, 186–196.

Van Hasselt, V. B., Hersen, M., Whitehill, M. B., & Bellack, A. S. (1979). Social skill assessment and training for children: A review. *Behavior Research and Therapy*, **17**, 413–437.

Wahler, R. G., House, A. E., & Stambaugh, E. E. (1976). *Ecological assessment of child problem behavior*. Elmsford, NY: Pergamon.

Walker, H. (1970). *Problem Behavior Identification Checklist*. Los Angeles, CA: Western Psychological Services.

Wallace, G., & Larsen, S. C. (1978). *Educational assessment of learning problems: Testing for teaching*. Boston, MA: Allyn & Bacon.

Warrenfeltz, R. B., Kelly, W. J., Salzberg, C. L., Beegle, C. P., Levy, S. M., Adams, T. A., & Crouse, T. R. (1981). Social skills training of behavior disordered adolescents with self-monitoring to promote generalization to a vocational setting. *Behavioral Disorders*, *7*, 18–27.

Weissberg, R. P., Gesten, E. L., Rapkin, B. D., Cowen, E. L., Davidson, E., Flores de Apodaca, R., & McKim, B. J. (1981). Evaluation of a social-problem for suburban and inner-city third-grade children. *Journal of Consulting and Clinical Psychology*, *49*, 251–261.

Weissberg, R. P., Gesten, E. L., Carnrike, C. L., Toro, P. A., Rapkin, B. D., Davidson, E., & Cowen, E. L. (1981). Social problem-solving skills training: A competence-building intervention with second-to-fourth grade children. *American Journal of Community Psychology*, *9*, 411–423.

Wilson, R. (1984). A review of self-control treatments for aggressive behavior. *Behavioral Disorders*, *9*, 131–141.

Wolf, M. M. (1978). Social validity: The case for subjective measurement or how applied behavior analysis is finding its heart. *Journal of Applied Behavior Analysis*, *11*, 203–214.

Wood, F. H. (1982). Affective education and social skills training: A consumer's guide. *Teaching Exceptional Children*, *14*, 212–216.

Wood, M. M. (Ed.). (1975). *Developmental therapy*. Baltimore, MD: University Park Press.

Preparation of Teachers for Behaviorally Disordered Students: A Review of Literature

Robert H. Zabel

Department of Administration & Foundations
College of Education
Kansas State University

Abstract—The state of the art and practice in preparation of teachers for behaviorally disordered students encompasses several interrelated topics. These include preparation of regular classroom teachers, identified competencies for BD teachers, and model preparation programs. On-going controversies over competency-based teacher education and categorical training are discussed, and relationships between personal and professional characteristics of teachers and their preparation programs are examined. A final section attempts to synthesize the literature, identify as yet unanswered questions and challenges, and suggest policy implications.

How are teachers of behaviorally disordered students prepared for their professions? What kinds of personal traits and skills are viewed as contributing to the success of these teachers? Are there identifiable important or necessary competencies for this profession? How do they compare with those for other special educators and regular classroom teachers? What kinds of teacher preparation are currently being provided? What kinds of training should be provided to best insure the success of those teachers? What are the personnel needs of the field and the characteristics of those presently teaching? Who provides the training?

Questions such as these concerning preparation of teachers for seriously behaviorally disordered students are not readily answered. To address them it is necessary to examine a number of issues involved in teacher preparation in the field. The purpose of this chapter is to review literature that may help provide answers to the above questions and suggest how the as yet unanswered questions concerning preparation of teachers of behaviorally disordered students might be approached.

Boundaries of the Review

The scope of this review and synthesis is limited to issues surrounding preparation of special education teachers for emotionally disturbed and/or behaviorally disordered students. Definitional issues and labeling concerns in the field are considerable and as yet unresolved (Wood & Lakin, 1979), frequently making it difficult to know what is meant by either of these terms. *Emotionally disturbed* and *behaviorally disordered* will be treated as nearly synonomous terms for purposes of this review. Questions persist over whether these categories should include children diagnosed as *autistic* or those considered *socially maladjusted*, since both diagnoses have been technically, if not always as a matter of practice, removed from the federal definition of *seriously emotionally disturbed* (*Federal Register*, 1977). The author's decision has been to include literature concerning such populations when they are subsumed under the emotional disturbance or behavioral disorders labels and definitions, but to exclude literature when restrictive labels and definitions separate these groups from the larger emotional disturbance/behavioral disorders population. In this paper the behavioral disorder designation will be used.

Methods of Search and Selection

An attempt has been made to provide a comprehensive review of published literature on the topic. The initial step in this process was to identify relevant subtopics. These were used to generate key word descriptors for a computerized literature search, covering the years 1974–1983.

In addition, a number of other potential sources of literature were searched. These included examination of several major journals, for the years 1979–1985, as well as various additional potential sources. Finally, references in reviewed literature and communication with experts in the field led to some additional relevant publications on the topic.

From this combination of approaches to searching the literature, there was considerable redundancy, with some references located in a number of venues. Still, some useful information undoubtedly has been overlooked due to limitations of bibliographic sources, lack of inclusion of some sources into accessible data banks, nonpublication and dissemination of some worthwhile information, and the creative limitations of the author. Throughout the search and review process, the author made decisions regarding quality and usefulness that excluded some literature due to factors such as poor presentation of information. Generally, nonpublished sources of information were not included in the review.

Subtopics

A topic like teacher preparation in behavioral disorders consists of a number of interrelated facets. There are a number of subtopics and angles at which these can be examined. Although dividing the topic into discrete subtopics is artificial and tends to present a fragmented picture, there are some issues that can best be addressed separately.

This review begins with an examination of some literature concerning regular teacher education: the context within or beside which the preparation of teachers for behaviorally disordered children occurs. It includes attention to teacher competencies, preparation programs, and major issues in the preparation of regular classroom teachers. This is followed by reviews of literature concerned with the special competencies for teachers of behaviorally disordered students. There follows a review of literature concerning programs for teaching some of these competencies. A related topic is categorical versus noncategorical or generic special education teacher preparation and the controversies surrounding this issue. In addition, literature on characteristics of teachers, including certification issues, teacher supply and demand, attrition and burnout will be examined. Finally, characteristics and training of those engaged in teacher training are reviewed.

It should be noted at the outset of the review that research on this topic is limited. Most existing literature consists of opinion, critiques of the state of the art, descriptions of practice, and/or proposals for improvement of practice. Empirical data are scarce and the boundaries between state of the art and state of practice are indistinct.

Following the review, its implications for the preparation of teachers for behaviorally disordered students will be discussed. It is hoped that from this review a clearer understanding of the needs of the field will emerge: needs that include some means of reducing the discrepancies between best practice and current practice, identifying necessary areas of research and development, and highlighting the direction of policies, regulations, and funding practices.

Preparation of Regular Teachers

In recent years, there has been a renewed attention to the state of United States education. Several major reports, such as those prepared by the National Commission for Excellence in Teacher Education, the Twentieth Century Fund, the Education Commission of the States, the Carnegie Foundation for the Advancement of Teaching, the Holmes Group, and most recently, the National Commission for the Excellence of Teacher Education, have critically examined American education. Some have called for reforms that would affect the content and structure of teacher preparation. Although it is beyond the scope of this review to examine in depth the preparation of regular elementary and secondary teachers, this topic cannot be excluded from consideration here for a number of reasons. Perhaps first among these is that most special educators are drawn from the pool of regular education personnel. Most teacher training in behavioral disorders is contingent upon prior or concurrent training in regular education. Also, the professional skills or competencies of regular and special education teachers overlap. Thus, it is necessary to examine the larger context of teacher preparation to understand preparation of teachers of behaviorally disordered children.

Several recent comprehensive reviews on this topic are available (e.g., Clark, in press; Evertson, Hawley, & Zlotnick, 1984; Imig, 1982; Kerr, 1983; Nemser, 1983; Rice, 1984). These reviews address the current status of teacher education, respond to the various commission reports, raise additional concerns, and propose solutions.

Status of Regular Teacher Preparation

Imig (1982), for example, has provided an overview of the structure and form of teacher education. He pointed out that most institutions of higher education (more than 1,300) provide preservice preparation of educators. Of these, all offer undergraduate programs, approximately two thirds offer master's level programs, and one fifth offer doctorates. Programs range in size from those with one student and one faculty member to those with 7,000 full-time equivalent students and 480 faculty. Approximately 85% of the faculty hold doctorates and more than 90% have had significant experience in elementary and secondary schools. Like their students, teacher education faculty tend to have relatively humble social class origins. Clark (in press), Kerr (1983), National Commission for the Excellence in Teacher Education (1985) and others have noted that teacher education students, faculty, and programs are generally held in relatively low esteem on college campuses.

Imig (1982) documented a precipitous drop in teacher education enrollment since the early 1970s and predicted continued decreases. Based upon birthrate data, it has been predicted that by 1990 the pool from which teacher education draws its students will continue to shrink, while there will be an increase in the number of preschool and elementary students (National Commission for Excellence in Teacher Education, 1985). Reasons for the decrease in teacher education enrollments have been ascribed to few job opportunities for regular elementary and secondary teachers over the past 15 years, less competitive salaries for teachers, and expanded job opportunities for women (Kerr, 1983). Kerr also cited studies indicating that the more capable teachers are less likely to be hired initially and most likely to leave the profession. At present, shortages exist in some subject matter areas such as the sciences and math at the secondary level. Shortages of teachers in several areas of special education, including behavioral disorders, have existed for several years.

Content of Regular Preservice Programs

There is considerable similarity in the content and structure of most preservice teacher preparation programs. The typical teacher preparation program consists of four components: general education or liberal studies, advanced study of one or more academic areas, professional studies in foundations and methods of teaching, and student teaching experience. Only about one third of the elementary and one fourth of the secondary teacher preparation programs involve professional studies in education (Smith & Street, 1980). A conclusion of a recent conference on the topic of teacher preparation was that, "the liberal arts sectors of colleges and universities are more deeply involved in the education of individual teachers than are the schools of education" (Rice, 1984, p. 4).

Clark characterized the commonality of teacher education as its fatal weakness, saying:

> "It is easily accessible in every sense of that term: geographically proximate to the consumer, easy to enter, short in duration, optimally convenient to the remainder of the college student's academic program, easy to complete, inexpensive, non-exclusive (i.e., does not rule out other career options), and, until recently almost certain to result in placement in a secure, respectable professional situation . . . the parts fit together in an harmoniously ineffective fashion. (Clark, in press, p. 17)

Within institutions of higher education, teacher education is a revenue producing program, generating approximately 11% of student credits, while receiving less than 3% of the resources (Imig, 1982). Some have criticized this underfunding of teacher education (e.g. Kerr, 1983, National Commission for Excellence in Teacher Education, 1985; Rice, 1984) and the undergraduate context in which it occurs (Clark, in press) as the major impediments to more sophisticated development of teacher education.

Nemser (1983) has reviewed research on how teachers actually learn to teach. Although teacher training is usually meant to refer to professional preservice training in colleges and universities, she believes the process actually involves four phases: pretraining, preservice, induction, and inservice. The research of Lortie (1975) and others has emphasized the role of pretraining or early influences on learning how to teach. It is not so much specific skills but traits such as warmth, patience, and empathy that elementary education majors cite as qualities that will make them effective teachers. The research on preservice preparation indicates that "most preservice students want recipes" and consider their professional coursework "too theoretical." (Nemser, 1983, p. 155) Although the student teaching experience is one of the most studied aspects of formal training, some research implies that it is not necessarily a beneficial one. "Research suggests that student teaching leaves future teachers with a utilitarian perspective in which getting through the day, keeping children busy, maintaining order are the main priorities." (Nemser, 1983, p. 157) The first year of teaching, or the induction phase, is another critical phase of teacher preparation. Its recurrent theme is the teacher's attempt to establish a level of control. According to Nemser, first year floundering "reinforces a belief that learning to teach is a matter of individual trial and error," (p. 167) and habits may be learned that are actually not good teaching. In sum, Nemser concludes that only a small proportion of teacher training occurs in our present teacher preparation programs. "Learning to teach is a bigger job than universities, schools, experience or personal disposition alone can accomplish." (Nemser, 1983, p. 168)

Inservice Preparation in Regular Education

In addition to preservice undergraduate teacher preparation, additional teacher training occurs in inservice programs, some in collegiate residential and/or extension programs resulting in academic credit and graduate degrees; some provided through public schools, state agencies, and other institutions. Approximately half of all teachers hold advanced degrees, although such a degree is required in only a handful of states. Critics, such as Clark and Kerr, believe that the graduate level, inservice programs suffer from the same weaknesses as those in undergraduate programs that result, at least in part, from underfunding. Actually, according to Nemser (1983, p. 151), "existing research tells us very little about the actual conduct of teacher preparation and inservice."

Elements of Effective Preparation of Regular Teachers

The reports on the status of United States education have generally charged that it is wanting, could/should be improved, and point to deficiencies in teacher education. However, few attempts have been made to address qualitative, as opposed to structural, issues in teacher preparation. An exception to that is a review of Evertson, Hawley, and Zlotnick (1984). Evertson et al. raise several questions concerning characteristics of effective preservice teacher preparation programs for enhancing the teacher's capability to contribute to student learning of traditional academic subjects. They claim that despite a "mountain of words written about teacher education" most of these words are "criticism, description, prescription, and exhortation . . . Not only is the body of research small, it is methodologically and theoretically anemic" (pp. 2–3).

Evertson, Hawley, and Zlotnick (1984) reviewed several aspects of regular teacher preparation, including the efficacy of teacher preparation against no preparation, standards of admission to teacher preparation programs and entry to the profession, content of teacher preparation programs, subject matter expertise and effectiveness, pedagogy of teaching to teach, and the induction phase of training. They concluded that, despite criticism of teacher preparation, the available research does suggest that teachers who complete formal preservice preparation programs are likely to be more effective teachers than those who have not. This is the case even though teacher preparation programs (in foundations, curriculum and methods, and field practicum) typically constitute only about one fourth to one third of the teacher's preservice preparation program. Furthermore, according to the Evertson et al. review, most efforts to teach students specific knowledge and skills in these programs seem to succeed, at least in the short run.

As far as evidence supporting the importance of higher admission standards to teacher education, Evertson et al. (1984) conclude that, with the exception of a correlation between teacher candidates' verbal ability and their students' performance, available research does not support a link between teacher's performance on conventional measures of academic aptitude such as the American College Testing (ACT) examination, the Scholastic Aptitude Test (SAT), the Miller Analogies Test (MAT), and their students' performance on standardized achievement tests. Likewise, relationships between teachers' scores on the National Teacher Exam (NTE) and their students' achievement are also limited and mixed. Even studies relating teachers' preservice attitudes and personality to their behavior and perceived effectiveness as teachers show no consistent relationships.

These reviewers advocated drawing content for teacher preparation programs from research based conclusions about teaching and learning. They identified five core teaching skills that can be adapted to variations in content, learning objectives, and student needs. These are:

—Maximizing academic learning time by providing students with sufficient opportunities to learn and to cover academic content.

—Managing and organizing the classroom, including arrangement of the physical space, planning rules and procedures and teaching these to students, making clear the consequences and rewards for appropriate and inappropriate behavior, monitoring student work and behavior, keeping students accountable for academic work, providing time for explanation, rehearsal, and feedback, planning lessons and providing for alternate ways of grouping students.

—Utilizing interactive teaching strategies which place emphasis on frequent lessons in which the teacher presents information, develops concepts through lecture and demonstration, and elaborates with feedback to students.

—Communicating high expectations for student performance in which teachers maximize opportunities for both high and low achievers to participate in ways that facilitate their learning. This includes providing lows with ample opportunities to respond, answer questions and participate appropriately in lessons.

—Rewarding student performance so as to reinforce appropriate student behavior that is related to academic achievement and to provide students with feedback and knowledge of the result of their efforts. (Evertson et al., 1984, pp. 27–27)

The reviewers caution that, while it may be reasonable that preservice programs which provide prospective teachers with these core teaching skills will produce effective teachers, there is currently no research to demonstrate this assumption. It should also be noted that we presently know little about which of these skills are being taught in preservice regular education programs or how they are taught.

Another perhaps surprising conclusion of Evertson et al. (1984) concerns the relationship between subject matter expertise and teacher effectiveness. Several studies were cited which have found only "educationally insignificant" or no relationship between knowledge of teachers, as measured by grade point average and standardized test performance, and student achievement.

One approach to preparation of teachers that received considerable attention particularly in the late 1970s was competency-based teacher education (CBTE). However, Kerr (1983) stated that "it is unclear just how CBTE enthusiasts would distinguish a CBTE program from any other program of teacher preparation that is operating under the same constraints and that might be deemed reasonably relevant to teaching" (p. 134). Additional criticism has been leveled at CBTE as too technical and leading to a proliferation of skills that may have no compelling link to student learning. In any event, Kerr noted that the CBTE movement has faded, with full-scale programs currently provided by only about 13% of the institutions in the American Association of Colleges for Teacher Education (ACTE).

Summary

The literature concerning preparation of regular classroom teachers includes a number of topics relevant to preparation of special educators, since regular teacher preparation provides the context within which the special preparation occurs. Recent critiques of American education and teacher preparation, analyses of financial support for programs, teacher supply and demand, status of the profession, important competencies and their relationship to training, can contribute to understanding the state of the art and practice in preparation of behavioral disorders/B.D. teachers. The following sections focus on issues directly related to preparation of these teachers. Topics include teacher competencies, preparation programs, competency based teacher education and critiques, categorical versus noncategorical training, and characteristics of behavioral disorders teachers and teacher educators.

Teacher Competencies

The issue of important competencies, skills, and characteristics for teachers of children with emotional and behavioral disorders has received considerable attention in the professional literature for at least the past 30 years. Several reports have defined competencies by categorical or generic populations served, while others use delivery model or age level for identifying specific skills.

The topic of teacher competencies is central to teacher preparation, since delineation of necessary skills and traits could be expected to provide the basis both for content and structure of teacher preparation programs. In most literature on this topic, the determination of important teacher competencies has been a matter of opinion of individual "experts," groups of teachers and other practitioners, teacher educators, or some combination of sources. Sometimes, there is no attempt empirically to validate competencies; they are drawn from experience or "logically" derived. In other instances, knowledgeable groups have been asked to evaluate the importance of specific competencies. In a few cases, there have been attempts empirically to evaluate their use by teachers and their effect upon students. The number of competencies identified in the literature varies from fewer than 10 to well over 100. Polsgrove and Reith (1979) provided a review of prior literature on the topic of competencies for teachers of behaviorally disordered students together with the results of their own study. Several of the reports reviewed by Polsgrove and Reith, as well as some others, are included in the following discussion.

An early, often cited study that has served as the basis for several subsequent studies was conducted by Mackie, Kvaraceus, and Williams (1957). Mackie et al.

reported their data and analyses from a major, multifaceted study of the qualifications and preparation of teachers of children who are "socially and emotionally maladjusted." Seventy-five "superior teachers" nominated by state departments of education and working in a variety of geographical areas and educational environments rated the importance of 88 competencies that had been previously compiled by a special study group. The competencies consisted of "knowledges, understandings, and concepts" and "skills and techniques." Of the 88, 20 received the highest rating of "very important" and fell into the following categories:

1. Knowledge and ability for establishing and operating stimulating, flexible, tension free classrooms capable of meeting a child's individual needs (five competencies).
2. Ability to use differential diagnosis and to interpret psychological tests, reports, and case histories (four competencies).
3. Ability to counsel students with regard to their attitudes and problems (two competencies).
4. Ability to manage child's individual social behavior and develop self control (four competencies).
5. Knowledge of the causes of behavior problems and of students' psychological needs (four competencies).
6. Ability to work with other professional groups (one competency). (Mackie et al., 1957, p. 21)

Mackie et al. (1957) noted "outstanding agreement" on several items indicating that, "Above all, the teacher should have knowledge of teaching techniques which help the child in his personal adjustment, by providing a flexible school program to permit individual adjustment and development and by providing experiences in which pupils can be successful" (p. 26). When teachers in this study were asked about important personal characteristics that differ from those of regular classroom teachers, over two thirds indicated necessary special characteristics. "The teacher, all agree, should be a well-adjusted, warm, and accepting person . . . objective and supporting. He must have achieved a high degree of maturity himself. In addition, he must be able to 'take it' " (p. 33).

The teachers were also asked to rate the importance of 18 professional preparatory experiences for teaching maladjusted children. None of these were rated as "very important," but all 18 were rated "important." Supervised student teaching of maladjusted children at the elementary level received the highest rating; followed by experiences in interpreting psychological reports; experiences developing case reports; planned observations of placement, curriculum development, and child study conferences; experiences in developing and interpreting individual educational records; and observation of multiprofessional case conferences. In addition, both the teachers and surveyed state and local directors and supervisors expressed strong support for prior regular classroom teaching experience together with substantial special student teaching experiences. For example, even for experienced teachers, the "ideal" length of student teaching in this area was 183–227 clock hours.

A few years following the Mackie et al. (1957) study, one of the participants from the original study group proposed a model training program for teachers of emotionally disturbed and socially maladjusted children (Rabinow, 1960). The proposed content of the program was derived from a set of competencies which emphasized the role of the teacher as a member of a treatment team and included the following areas of education:

1. Psychiatric understanding of psychological growth and development.
2. Psychological understanding of the nature of intelligence, learning disabilities, diagnosis and remediation techniques.
3. Sociological understanding of culture conflict and class differences, and the problems of group living in tension areas.
4. Knowledge of community organizations and resources.
5. Knowledge of competencies and roles of related professions.
6. Knowledge of group work.
7. Mastery of skills in practical arts and media. (Rabinow, 1960, p. 292)

Rabinow advocated a full year of preparation including practica, one half with emotionally disturbed pupils; the other with socially maladjusted. One half of the year would be in an institutional setting; the other in a school setting.

Hewett (1967b) provided a somewhat different dimension to teacher competencies and added a more behavioral orientation. He suggested a hierarchy of teacher competencies based upon his experiences directing the Neuropsychiatric Institute School at UCLA. Although Hewett acknowledged that all of his competencies were collectively important, he placed them in the following order of importance from higher to lower; objectivity, flexibility, structure, resourcefulness, social reinforcement, curriculum expertise, and intellectual model. Hewett believed that a background in regular education should be a prerequisite to special training and that programs should be full-time and graduate level.

Schwartz (1967) described competencies for the "clinical teacher." These were the ability to 1) identify medical, psychological and social aspects in growth and development; 2) locate available resources in community agencies; 3) utilize expertise in various disciplines and services; 4) plan, design, and conduct remedial programs; 5) select and employ appropriate educational activities, techniques, equipment, and materials; and 6) evaluate student programs, report on programs and referral.

A decidedly more behavioral and educational (as opposed to clinical) orientation to behavioral disorders teacher competencies was proposed by Haring and Fargo (1969). They identified eight important competencies: 1) observation and behavioral analysis; 2) use of academic, verbal, social, physical and behavioral assessment information for program planning; 3) selection of appropriate instructional materials; 4) identifying motivational requirements of the child; 5) use of contingency management procedures; 6) procedures for establishing and maintaining learning activities; 7) continuous monitoring of student progress; and 8) application of teaching skills to individuals and groups.

Some subsequent research served to support the Haring and Fargo (1969) orientation. Using the Mackie et al. (1957) list of 88 competencies, Bullock and Whelan (1971) asked 47 teachers of emotionally disturbed children to rate the importance of each. The results were compared to those in the earlier study. On the whole, these teachers did not rate the competencies as being as important as did the original group, although they did tend to view the relative importance of the competencies similarly to the original group. Based upon their data, Bullock and Whelan (1971) called for a renewed emphasis on individualized and sequential programming techniques, knowledge of regular and special curriculum and materials, and knowledge of the education and psychology of various types of exceptional children.

Kerr, Shores, and Stowitschek (1978) continued the more behavioral perspective by emphasizing the measurement of change in student behavior. After asking graduates of their program to identify the most useful competencies for teachers of behaviorally disordered students, they attempted to validate them by observing the frequency of teacher use of several "assessment and planning" and "direct training and evaluation" competencies in field-based training programs. They determined that task analysis was used most frequently, followed by criterion referenced testing, instructional programming, concept analysis, and observation. Prompting, modeling, shaping, direction giving and questioning were the major competencies employed in applied settings.

Feinberg and Wood (1978) analyzed actual field procedures in a training program to arrive at 13 "goals" for teachers. These were:

1. Employ assessment techniques in the classroom
2. Assist students in describing their goals and preferred behavior objectives
3. Work constructively with parents
4. Write an IEP for a student described as emotionally disturbed/behavior disordered
5. Demonstrate effective and positive interpersonal skills with students
6. Work cooperatively with team members
7. Develop and implement plans for systematic teaching of social behavior

8. Conduct interpersonal communication/problem solving interviews and group discussions

9. Develop and implement contracts with individual students

10. Develop and implement group reinforcement plans

11. Use a variety of preventive procedures

12. Use a variety of crisis management procedures to control/contain problem behavior and redirect pupils in desired direction

13. Use time-out and isolation procedures appropriately. (p. 21)

From the earlier cited review of literature on competencies, examination of texts in the field, and contacts with practicing teachers, Polsgrove and Reith (1979) prepared a list of 138 competencies in seven categories. They considered these competency statements as relevant for field-based application and written in such a way that they could be measured. The statements were submitted to a panel of experts: 23 teacher educators from across the country who were participating in a working conference sponsored by the Advanced Training Institute for Trainers of Teachers for Seriously Emotionally Disturbed Children and Youth. Each teacher trainer independently rated each competency statement in terms of its importance along a five point scale. "Importance" was based upon frequency of use of the competency by teachers. Although many of the competencies were viewed as important, some were rated "greatly needed." In Table 1 are the categories used in the study, with the number of constituent competencies in parentheses, and the competencies rated as "greatly needed" (i.e. mean rating of 4.5 or above):

Assessment Competencies (16)

TABLE 1

1. Correctly selects, administers, and interprets various informal and standardized instruments for assessing students' social performance (e.g., behavioral checklists, sociograms, anecdotal records).

2. Correctly administers and interprets various informal measures of students' academic performances (e.g., criterion-referenced measures, teacher-made tests, permanent-product information).

3. Uses appropriate informal and formal observation systems/techniques for collecting data on students' academic and social behavior.

4. Selects appropriate academic and social behaviors for intervention programs with students.

5. Uses assessment information to place students in appropriate instructional sequences.

6. Realistically appraises influence of situational variables that may affect an intervention program.

Behavioral Management Competencies (12)

1. Arranges antecedent and consequent stimuli to change behavior in desirable directions.

2. Can establish and maintain a structured learning environment for students.

3. Uses various strategies for developing students' self-control.

4. Designs, implements, and evaluates effective behavior management programs for students.

5. Selects and successfully employs appropriate management strategies in various situations.

6. Arranges physical environment to facilitate management possibilities.

7. Selects appropriate reinforcers for use in motivating students.

8. Designs management programs to facilitate generalization and maintenance of acquired behaviors.

Communication/Consultation Competencies (11)

1. Establishes and maintains open communication with students, other teachers, administrators, and parents.

2. Follows proper legal procedures regarding assessment, placement, programming, and consultation with parents and other professionals.

Personal Competencies (14)

1. Remains calm in crisis, inflammatory, or provocative situations.

2. Provides an acceptable model of self-control for students.

3. Maintains flexibility in managing students' behavior and in administering their academic programs.

4. Objectively evaluates students' behavior.

5. Expresses joy and enthusiasm under appropriate circumstances.

Instructional Competencies (29)

1. Accurately analyzes students' strengths and weaknesses in given areas for planning an instructional sequence.

2. Adapts instructional materials for meeting long- and short-term objectives.

3. Provides effective individual and small group instruction.

4. Uses various strategies (e.g., modeling, imitation, rehearsal, inquiry, prompting, cueing, feedback, consequation, discussion, lecture) in isolation or in combination for providing appropriate instruction for students.

5. Selects and writes appropriate long- and short-term academic and social goals based on assessment information.

6. Selects appropriate placement for students in instructional sequences based on assessment information.

7. Uses continuous assessment to modify instructional activities for meeting students' instructional needs.

8. Teaches personal development skills such as: self-control, self-help, communication, responsibility-taking, self-confidence, problem solving, aesthetics.

Administrative Competencies (12)

1. Establishes and maintains a resource room, self-contained classroom or residential school classroom and itinerant class for students.

2. Develops and implements appropriate IEPs for students.

3. Keeps appropriate records on students.

4. Functions as a member of a team for planning social and educational interventions with students.

Cognitive Competencies (45)

1. Demonstrates knowledge of general child development. (Polsgrove & Reith, 1979, pp. 34–44

It is evident from these ratings that the teacher educators placed more emphasis on the importance of behavior management, instructional, and some personal competencies than on the cognitive competencies. Only 1 out of the 45 "understandings" received a mean rating of "greatly needed." Some competencies in this category received notably low ratings (e.g., "Outlines the history of the field of behavior disorders"). According to these teacher educators, the competencies viewed as relevant to intervention were deemed more important than those relevant to understanding disturbed/disordered behavior. This appears to represent a major shift in emphasis from early reports such as Mackie et al. (1957) and Rabinow (1960). Polsgrove and Reith (1979) also noted some trends in the literature on teacher competencies: competency lists have moved toward analysis of specific training programs and field-based requirements, there has been movement away from emphasis on diagnosis using standardized measures toward use of direct observation and functional analysis of behavior, competencies are increasingly stated in terms of measurable outcomes, competency lists are more concerned with actual teaching skills for changing student behavior rather than developing a knowledge base, and there has been increased emphasis on individualized instruction and the uses of behavioral methodology (p. 32).

Based upon their review of several of the above studies and their own study of the competencies. Polsgrove and Reith (1979) concluded that four major skill areas are necessary for teachers of emotionally disturbed/ behaviorally disordered children. These are 1) skill in establishing a structured classroom environment, providing clear-cut expectations and limits, yet with flexibility in meeting the needs of students; 2) ability to work with other professions in the treatment process; 3) ability effectively to manage children's behavior; and 4) objectivity, warmth, tolerance, and emotional stability (p. 32).

At the same conference (Wood, 1979), the teacher educators studied the issue of competencies particularly important for working with secondary age pupils. Four working groups attempted to identify critical areas of teacher skill for this population. On the whole, these did not differ in kind from those competencies viewed as important for teachers of all ages of behaviorally disordered students. The groups emphasized understanding of adolescent growth and development and its special challenges. They stressed the importance of providing relevant and motivating curricular modifications, especially in career/vocational education and practical living skills, and awareness of other systems outside of school in which adolescents are involved. One group addressed special secondary level competencies by designing a model teacher training program. It included "foundations" courses in typical and abnormal adolescent development, assessment (especially informal techniques), and the law; and "content" courses in at least one subject matter area, special reading, behavior management and interactions systems.

Rutherford, Nelson and Wolford (1985) have called for special education training for teachers in juvenile corrections facilities. According to survey data collected by the Correctional/Special Education Training Project in 1984, an estimated 81% of juvenile, handicapped offenders are receiving special education, but only 28% of teachers in those programs are certified special educators. The authors report on the development and field

testing of inservice curricula for use by state departments of corrections. Although they do not specify compentencies needed by correctional special educators, they do suggest components of effective programs, including the following:

(1) procedures for conducting functional assessments of the skills and learning needs of handicapped offenders;

(2) the existence of a curriculum that teaches functional academic and daily living skills;

(3) the inclusion of vocational special education in the curriculum;

(4) the existence of transitional programs and procedures between correctional programs and the community;

(5) the presence of a comprehensive system for providing institutional and community services to handicapped offenders. (Rutherford, Nelson, & Wolford, 1985, pp. 8–9)

Each of these has implications for the kinds of competencies required for teachers in such settings.

A recent study (Ruhl & Hughes, 1985) focuses on a specific area of competence for teachers of emotionally handicapped students: coping with aggressive behavior. Based upon a survey of a sample of such teachers in Florida, teachers reported frequent encounters with verbal and physical aggression directed at themselves, students, and objects. Most teachers reported confidence in their ability to handle student aggression and that they had received some training in dealing with aggression. However, only about one third reported having received such training in preservice preparation, while about two thirds had received inservice training sponsored by a school system. More than 80% of the teachers expressed a desire for additional training in methods for coping with student aggression. Ruhl and Hughes conclude that preservice training in both preventative strategies and physical intervention are necessary.

In most of these proposed competency lists, certain personality traits have been deemed important. Some attention has been given to determination of specific, important affective or personality characteristics of behavioral disorders teachers. Although no definitive delineation of the effective teacher's personality has been provided, one trait that appears to be important is empathic understanding (Morgan, 1977; Scheuer, 1971). While the measurement of personality traits is troublesome and attempts at teaching them are elusive, descriptions of training efforts involving affective competencies have been reported (e.g., Pattavina & Ramirez, 1980).

Model Preparation Programs

Over the years some descriptions of model programs for preparing teachers of behaviorally disordered students have appeared in the literature. These have tended to emphasize unique features such as preservice preparation, competency based training, preparation for particular delivery models, or field-based training. Only a few have actually offered evaluative data.

Morse, Bruno, and Morgan (1973) attempted to provide an overview of the training of teachers for behaviorally disordered students. They identified "critical program elements" that could be used to analyze preparation programs. These elements could be placed on a grid depicting a program's "goals," "processes," and "evaluation" techniques. The researchers reported limitations in using this procedure, however, due to incomplete available information on programs and the necessity for extensive interpretation that might misrepresent the intent and accomplishments of given programs. However, Morse, Bruno, and Morgan (1973) defended the heuristic value of their model as a way of examining critical features of programs. They also included such analyses prepared by faculty members from teacher training programs reflecting "educational-remedial," "humanistic," "therapeutic," and "eclectic" approaches.

Earlier, Balow (1966) had reported some evaluative data on a training program at the University of Minnesota. He described the development, content, operation and outcomes of a graduate level program which included coursework, extensive and varied field practices, and a group process seminar emphasizing self-understanding. Outcome measures of job placement, evaluation of the program by graduates, and evaluations of graduates' performance on the job by their supervisors are described.

Spence (1978) described a field-based program for training "clinical educators" at the Child Center, a residential and day treatment center for seriously emotionally disturbed children. In this program, teacher competencies are determined by what are viewed as the general treatment goals for the children: development of an adequate "inner" life or self-concept, interpersonal relations skills, and competencies for living. Necessary teaching skills in this program are 1) nurturing and being a parent model, active caring for and about the child; 2) teaching skills: task analysis, academic assessment, direct teaching, appropriate curriculum; 3) child management and group care (limit setting, stimulus arrangement, consequation, observation systems, data collection, record keeping, and behavioral analysis); and 4) parent training and family therapy (teaching behavioral management to others, home visits and behavioral observation, analyzing family systems and patterns, emotionally supporting the parents) (p. 36). However, in this description, no procedures or criteria were outlined for evaluating acquisition of these competencies.

Fagen (1978) provided a model for school-based training provided in the Mark Twain Teacher Internship Program of Montgomery County (Maryland) Schools. It is a graduate level, full-time training program for experienced teachers. Coursework, extensive practicum experiences, individual projects, a human relations group, and orientation and review sequences are used to achieve student competence in five areas: psycho-educational assessment and programming, human relations and counseling, curriculum development and implementation, behavior management, school resources, and consultation skills. Students provide self-evaluations of their performance on these competencies, as do practicum supervisors and program management staff. Achievement of the competencies is based upon ratings of skill proficiency.

Competency-Based Teacher Education

There is a sizable amount of literature on the topic of Competency-Based Teacher Education (CBTE) in special education. Some of this has included the training of teachers of behaviorally disordered children. Much of this literature appeared during the 1970s when the topic was widely discussed in general teacher education. Most CBTE literature has been presented as noncategorical or generic in nature. A major proponent of CBTE stated that such a program "stresses systematic application of learned skills in work settings which approximate and, in some cases, match exactly the posttraining occupational situation." (Lilly, 1979, p. 20) Semmel and Semmel (1976) refer to the same salient feature of CBTE programs, in which the trainee is ". . . required to (a) demonstrate behaviors known to promote desirable learning and/or (b) demonstrate that (s)he can bring about learning in pupils" (p. 69).

There have been some reports of attempts to evaluate CBTE training. Edgar and Neel (1976), for example, reported the results of a CBTE program at the University of Washington to train teachers for emotionally disturbed and learning disabled students. Although their findings were qualified by a number of acknowledged limitations in research design, Edgar and Neel proposed that measurement of competency acquisition must be undertaken at three points: acquisition (e.g., coursework), proficiency (student teaching), and maintenance (follow-up questionnaires from trainees and supervisors) on the desired behaviors.

Shores, Cegelka, and Nelson (1973), had taken CBTE evaluation a step further by calling for actual measurement of effect of trainee use of competencies on their pupils' performance. They reviewed the "voluminous" literature on the topic and surveyed "prominent" teacher training programs to derive and validate special education teacher competencies. Much of their review was relevant to training in the area of behavioral disorders. They noted that competency statements were mostly grounded in expert opinion and sometimes verified by practitioners' judgment, but little research had been conducted which directly measured the effects of teacher skills on students. Further, they found little evidence of relationships between personality variables of teachers and their competence as teachers. What evidence did exist was based upon pencil and paper tests and was largely correlational. Consequently, Shores, Cegelka, and Nelson recommended that competency statements be derived from experimental procedures including direct observation of both teachers and their students.

Shores, together with various colleagues (Kerr, Shores, & Stowitschek, 1978; Shores, 1979; Shores, Roberts, & Nelson, 1976), later proposed procedures developed at Peabody College, Nashville, for the empirical validation of special education teacher competencies. That model included determination of competencies through review of literature and of program graduates' views of important competencies, followed by development of courses to include training in those competencies. Students were evaluated to determine if they reached mastery criteria on those skills, and field experiences were later monitored to determine how students used the skills to change their own students' performance.

At the time of publication of this series of papers, Shores and his colleagues considered the Peabody CBTE program to be successful. Teacher trainees were reported to acquire the competencies in courses; use them in their field work across categories of handicapping conditions, across curricular areas, and in different educational systems; and were shown, using data-based monitoring procedures, to have positive effects on pupil performance of specified objectives. However, the writers of the report focusing on competencies for teachers of children with behavior disorders (Shores, Roberts, & Nelson, 1976) urged caution regarding their results, noting that input came from a single teacher preparation program emphasizing applied behavior management. They also state that, "Undoubtedly, the time and expense involved in researching teacher competencies through this model is prohibitive for most training institutions" (p. 131).

Blackhurst, McLoughlin, and Price (1977) proposed generic competencies for teachers of children with learning and behavior problems. They acknowledged that trainee competencies and the nature of the individual training program are ". . . based upon professional judgment, logic, opinion, speculation, hunches, and/or faith" (p. 168), since little research exists to support the assumption that teachers should be prepared to teach both learning disabled and behaviorally disordered students or that their preparation should be competency-based. However, they presented 66 generic competencies in the following 10 categories: assessment of learner behavior (5); design and implementation of instructional programs (11); selection and utilization of instructional materials (8); management of the learning environment (7); providing for the unique needs of children with sensory and physical impairments (9); implementing resource teacher programs (8); implementing due process safeguards (3); working effectively with parents (6); maintaining student records (4); and demonstrating appropriate professional characteristics (5).

The researchers advocated the writing of specific objectives for each competency, yet acknowledged that precise measures are lacking for many of these.

Another approach to noncategorical competency-based training has involved training in specific service delivery roles. Walker, Hops, and Greenwood (1976) reported on the development of behavior management packages used in training of teachers that included some CBTE features. For example, the use of contingencies for teaching academic and social behavior is taught using a highly structured set of procedures, materials, and schedules to produce changes in child behavior. The skills are first mastered by teacher consultants who then train classroom teachers in their use. Walker et al. proposed that effectiveness could be determined by changes in both teacher and student behavior.

Idol-Maestas (1981) outlined the data- and field-based program at the University of Illinois for Resource/Consulting teachers. Included in the evaluation of trainee performance are specific projects requiring the application of skills. These include direct observation, formal evaluation, monitoring of progress, and completion of permanent products. Data-based criteria for performance are established and evaluations of student performance are obtained from the students themselves, supervising teachers, university supervisors, and program coordinators.

The field-based program at the University of Vermont for inservice training of cross-categorical consulting teachers has also stressed the evaluation of trainee acquisition of specific competencies (e.g., Knight, 1978). Competency areas include foundations of special education, identification and diagnosis, development and implementation of individual education programs, evaluation of individual education programs, classroom management, professionalism, reporting, and dissemination. Lectures, on-the-job practica, and mentor-style advisement are the means of training, with periodic evaluation of task completion by trainees (Knight, 1978).

The development, field testing, and revision of a CBTE program with an "interactive evaluation" system for preservice training of teachers for emotionally disturbed and mentally retarded students was recently described (Wheeler, Tuchman, Miller, and Wambold, 1985). The STEM (Systematic Teacher Evaluation Manual) was developed to coordinate university course work and field experiences at the University of Wisconsin. Evaluations of student performance on predetermined competencies in four major areas (professionalism, assessment and program development, instructional teaching techniques, and behavioral teaching techniques) consists of periodic "grading" by cooperating teacher, university supervisors, and the trainees themselves. The authors reported that follow-up surveys of students and cooperating teachers indicate their satisfaction with the STEM system.

Gable and Strain (1979) addressed the issue of staff training in residential programs for behaviorally disordered children by outlining a model based on behavioral technologies. Their proposal included three critical components: goal statements regarding anticipated training outcomes, a training cycle including appropriate practice with ongoing feedback, and monitoring and evaluation of progress. Although Gable and Strain did not provide evidence of application of the model, they suggested that research establishing the effectiveness of techniques such as modeling of desired behavior, perhaps employing video or audio tape simulations, with feedback from trainers appears to hold promise for these staff training procedures.

More recently, Englert and Sugai (1983) studied the effects of peer observation for providing feedback to preservice special education teachers on their behavior management skills, instructional management, and feedback strategies. Using a structured, continuous recording procedure, peer students observed both trainee and pupil behavior. When compared to control group teachers whose observers developed their own recording systems, the researchers found that trainees given specific teacher-pupil feedback data were better able to monitor and manage pupils' achievement, maintained a "brisker" presentation and correct response rate, and offered fewer prompts for correct responses and fewer correct responses to pupils following incorrect responses.

It appears that in CBTE programs, even those that are field-based, traditional course-type instruction has usually been used to teach the understandings and skills (competencies) that are viewed as important (Blackhurst, 1981; Bullock, Dykes, & Kelly, 1974). The thrust of CBTE programs, however, is in the actual demonstration of the competencies in field-based settings. Some innovative research on teaching trainees to modify their behavior to effect changes in their pupils has been reported (e.g., Fink & Brownsmith, 1977; Semmel, 1976). In his early work on using computerized feedback to trainees on the effectiveness of their teaching techniques, Semmel stated:

> There exists little or no empirical support of specific teaching competencies which are related to pupil growth . . . Nor does there exist empirical validation of current teacher education programs in special or regular education in terms of trainee growth in teaching competencies and the relationships of those competencies to learner growth. (1976, p. 141)

Since then, relatively few efforts have been reported that provide such empirical support.

Teachers' Perceptions of Training

Even with the discussion of model training programs and procedures for evaluating trainee competencies that have been presented in the literature, it is difficult to assess the degree to which these models have been put into practice. One method for addressing the adequacy of teacher preparation has been to survey practicing teachers on their perceptions of competence and the nature and value of their training. In an early study of practicing teachers' perceptions of their skills and training, Gersh and Nagle (1969) surveyed 225 Michigan teachers. Among their conclusions were inadequacy in educational diagnosis and remedial teaching, difficulties in applying behavioral controls, and inadequate field experiences for practicing methods and techniques.

Kavale and Hirshoren (1980) believe that incongruities in theoretical orientation exist between teacher preparation programs and practicing teachers. They surveyed public school special education administrators to determine the theoretical orientations of their programs for behaviorally disordered students. They found a lack of theoretical purity, with behavioral disorders teachers using eclectic approaches. Kavale and Hirshoren conclude that there is a mismatch between the predominately behavioral orientation of teacher preparation programs that had earlier been reported by Fink, Glass, and Guskin (1975) and the orientations of practitioners.

Lutkemeir (1983) surveyed practicing teachers of emotionally handicapped children about the adequacy of their preservice preparation. The respondents indicated their support for training focused on pragmatic, day-to-day concerns of teaching as opposed to theory. Most supported the expansion in number and scope of methods courses. Just over half of the public school behavioral disorders teachers rated their preparation programs as "adequate," while fewer teachers in residential and institutional facilities thought their preparation was "adequate." Interestingly, although fewer than 20% of the teachers were currently teaching in categorical emotionally handicapped programs, about two thirds believed that the most effective format for teaching methods courses is a categorical treatment.

Critiques of Competencies

Several writers have expressed their skepticism of the emphasis placed on teacher competencies and competency-based teacher education. Morse, Bruno, and Morgan (1973) commented on the relationship of specific competencies to the process of teaching behaviorally disordered students. They said:

> The more competencies become isolated specifics, the more unreal they become as indicators of performance in the teaching gestalt unless one ignores the multiple phasing when a teacher deals with a group or various groups of children. It is easier to settle for a bit of the mosaic than the whole display. (p. 59)

Later, Morse (1976) expressed his concern that competency-based training had grown out of the teacher accountability movement which places the onus of responsibility primarily on the teacher's shoulders. He said:

> There are those who argue the school is impotent to do for the normal pupil the things for which it is granted its shares of societies' resources. When it comes to the socially and emotionally impaired pupils, expecting the special education teacher to counteract all of the forces acting on the child is a scene from the theater of the absurd. The way out is to set up goals which are minute and specific whether they are related to anything or not. (p. 83)

Blatt (1976) strongly expressed several biases about CBTE, charging that "CBTE is either a very large umbrella or a very fragile idea" (p. 90). He noted that the CBTE literature explains very little, that there are enormous catalogs on competencies available, but there is little substantive discussion or empirical validation of these. He, too, expressed concern over the implications of CBTE for teacher responsibility, and charged that CBTE would strengthen the movement toward national standardization, control, and certification of teachers. Blatt also disputed the CBTE implication that "learning is more efficiently and effectively promoted when it is supervised in the context of small definable operations and tasks as on a factory assembly line, with order of difficulty increasing in some lawful manner" (p. 94).

Bloom (1979) commented on the dilemma of a "proliferation and trivialization of instructional competencies" on the one hand, while avoiding the trap of "foggy bottomed generalizations which can not guide instructional activity" (p. 67) on the other. Bloom went on to observe, "The very best that can be said of the competencies we enumerate is that they are the set of propositions or statements by which we reduce the complexity of teaching to manageable proportions" (p. 68–69).

Categorical versus Noncategorical Training

A major issue in design of teacher preparation programs in the behavioral disorders is that of categorical versus noncategorical (or cross-categorical) training. Most published perspectives on this issue have advocated noncategorical programming for mildly/moderately handicapped students (e.g., Reynolds, 1979), usually meant to include learning disabled, educable mentally retarded, and emotionally disturbed children. At present nearly equal numbers of states have categorical and noncategorical special education certification standards (Smith-Davis, Burke, & Noel, 1984).

The central arguments against categorical programming are that the categories are diagnostically indistinct, are educationally irrelevant, perpetuate detrimental labelling, and result in artificially fragmented and inefficient service delivery (Blackhurst, 1981; Brady, Conroy, & Langford, 1984; Heward, Cooper, Heron, et al., 1981; Idol-Maestas, Lloyd, & Lilly, 1981.

Consequently, these advocates argue that teacher training should also be noncategorical. Some have proposed competency-based, noncategorical or generic preparation which can meet certification requirements even in states with categorical certification (Blackhurst, 1981; Heward et al., 1981). Others subscribe to a similar view, but conceptualize it somewhat differently. Schworm (1982), for example, has described a "repertoire orientation" to teacher preparation which includes cross-categorical application of teaching techniques and principles, with performance and field-based preparation. Some have outlined noncategorical training for particular service delivery models such as the resource/consulting teacher (Idol-Maestas et al., 1981). According to Brady et al. (1984), most noncategorical CBTE programs include "instruction in applied behavior analysis, curriculum and content, field experiences, assessment, instructional procedures, parent intervention, a special education professional seminar, and a nature/needs course covering mildly, moderately, or severely handicapped conditions" (p. 23).

An innovative approach to addressing the categorical-noncategorical training issue used a debate format (Greenough, Huntze, Nelson, & Simpson, 1983). Despite considerable literature to support each position, the debaters acknowledged that "arguments on both sides of the issue lean toward an emphasis on rhetoric, as opposed to empiricism" (p. 5).

An argument against categorical programming of students (and thus training of teachers) was that such programs have been perpetuated largely due to historical precedent, namely, categorical certification patterns, federal and state funding formulas, and teacher training programs (Heller, McCoy, & McIntire, 1979). In addition, proponents of noncategorical training argued that neither instructional materials nor methods are category specific, but should be determined by a student's specific functional strengths and weaknesses. Advantages of noncategorical teacher preparation are that teachers are better prepared to teach students with a variety of educational characteristics, school officials have greater flexibility in using special education staff, and revisions in teacher training curricula have improved the range and depth of teachers' skills. Competency based teacher education, with its emphasis upon necessary teaching skills, such as those for training resource and/or consulting teachers (e.g., McKenzie, Egner, Knight, Perelman, Schneider, & Garvin, 1970), was cited as consistent with a more generic approach.

Advocates in favor of the categorical training, on the other hand, charged that noncategorical programs may provide flexibility for use of teachers at the expense of behaviorally disordered students. Categorical training, they argued, provides greater focus on the skills and issues relative to teaching behaviorally disordered students. Despite an acknowledged overlap of skills needed for teaching mildly/moderately handicapped children, they cited the large body of category specific literature, research, and skills. In addition, they argued that teacher trainer expertise is primarily categorical and that there are a number of category specific competencies. Even proponents of noncategorical preparation concurred that "noncategorical teacher training programs have tended to neglect the preparation of teachers to effectively deal with problem behavior" (Greenough et al., 1983, pp. 57–58).

There is as yet no resolution to the debate over the efficacy of categorical versus noncategorical training. According to Blackhurst (1981), the trend has been away from categorical preparation. However, it is unclear how many preparation programs currently could be considered noncategorical, nor is it clear if such a trend will continue.

In addition, there may be as much variation in content and organization of noncategorical programs as there is in categorical programs. In their analysis of teacher preparation programs for behaviorally disordered children, Morse, Bruno, and Morgan (1973) concluded, "Programs are to a considerable extent built around people and diversity is the name of the intellectual game" (p. 242). This observation could likely be applied to the categorical/noncategorical issue. There are probably few pure programs. Most "categorical" behavioral disorders teacher preparation programs include considerable generic introductory and supporting coursework, and many "noncategorical" training programs might be better characterized as "multicategorical" with "categorical" coursework and even field practice. According to some proponents of noncategorical teacher preparation, "Unfortunately, common guidelines for noncategorical teacher preparation programs have not been developed" (Brady, Conroy, & Langford, 1984).

Characteristics of Teachers

Some data and analyses of the supply, demand, and quality of teachers and other personnel involved in the education of behaviorally disordered students have been provided by several sources (e.g., Huntze & Grosenick, 1980; Smith-Davis, Burke, & Noel, 1984; US Department of Education, 1984). These reports have been based upon data provided by state education agencies, surveys, and in the case of the Huntze and Grosenick monograph, informal discussions with knowledgeable sources.

Huntze and Grosenick (1980) pointed out that the need for teachers is determined partly by the number of students identified as needing services, but also by factors such as available supply of personnel to provide the services and the kinds of service delivery models utilized.

The number of seriously emotionally disturbed students has been a matter of some discussion (Wood & Zabel, 1978). The official US Department of Education estimate of 2% of the school-age population is generally considered conservative. Yet, at the time of the Huntze and Grosenick review (1980), only 0.56% of the United States school-age population were formally identified as seriously emotionally disturbed. This number has increased to 0.89% over the past few years according to the latest figures (US Department of Education, 1984). Despite a general decline in the school-age population, the number of seriously emotionally disturbed students reported by the states increased in number by about 25% between 1976–77 and 1982–83. While some other categories have decreased in number and proportion of handicapped students during this period, the serious emotional disturbance category has grown, although not nearly as dramatically as the learning disabilities population. Explanations for this growth include greater efforts by state and local education agencies to serve this underserved population and the increased provision of services in school settings. Still, despite the increase in the size of the serious emotional disturbance category, less than half of the conservatively estimated population is currently receiving special education services.

According to the 1984 government report, the number of serious emotional disturbance teachers increased from 21,700 in 1976–77 to 29,100 in 1981–82, even though the number actually declined slightly between the last 2 years covered by the report. This phenomenon is interpreted as largely attributable to movement toward noncategorical programming particularly for "mildly" handicapped students. In an analysis of the percentages of students served in different delivery models in a sample state, the figures were as follows: consultant (5.1), itinerant (21.4), resource (37.1), self-contained (33.6), work study (0.7), and home/hospital (2.1) (US Department of Education, 1984).

In their earlier report, Huntze and Grosenick (1980) stated. "While there are concerns relative to numbers and quality of various types of personnel in the area, teachers are clearly the most critical problem and must represent a 'first line of attack' " (p. 124). They pointed to actual shortages of certified teachers for behaviorally disordered students in most states ranging between 25–40%. They projected that through 1983, the number of new teachers needed to serve a growing population, combined with attrition, would increase and shortages would become more severe. According to the National Association of Placement Personnel, the demand for teachers of behaviorally disordered children increased each year between 1976 and 1980. By 1984, the rated demand for behavioral disorders teachers was not considered as great, although it still ranked highest among special education categories (Akin, 1985). According to the recent Smith-Davis et al. survey (1984), 33 states reported shortages of teachers in this area, with 12 reporting "extremely serious" shortages. They said,

"When coupled with shortages in severe emotional disturbance . . . the findings suggest that mild to severe emotional disturbance is the single most vulnerable program area in special education where manpower is concerned" (p. 52).

Temporary Certification

In 1980, Huntze and Grosenick expressed concern over the frequent practice of filling behavioral disorders teaching positions with less than fully certified teachers, by providing temporary, provisional, or emergency certificates. In some states, temporary certificates have been issued to persons without even regular teacher certification. In their sampling of several states, they found a range of 0–80% of the teachers in this categorical area were temporarily certified, with the practice most common in rural areas and in mental health and youth corrections facilities. Huntze and Grosenick estimated that state training institutions combined are providing only one fifth or less of the needed teachers each year. Smith-Davis et al. (1984) point to continued insufficient production of teachers by preservice programs. The result of this inadequate supply of teachers, they believe, is a lowering of the quality of services to behaviorally disordered children and the creation of credibility problems with regular education and parents.

Attrition and Burnout

Teacher attrition has been viewed as both a contributor to and consequence of inadequately trained personnel. Citing evidence from a study conducted in the late 1970s, Huntze and Grosenick (1980) reported that 53% of personnel in behavioral disorders leave the profession over a 5 year period, with the largest proportion leaving within the 1st year. This is higher than most other areas of special education. According to the previously cited DOE report (1984), the average annual attrition rate of special education teachers is about 6%. If these figures are accurate, it would appear that teachers of behaviorally disordered students are leaving their jobs at a higher rate than other teachers of exceptional children.

There are a number of possible interpretations (e.g., other opportunities), but attrition due to teacher burnout is one contributor. Smith-Davis et al. (1984) estimated that attrition due to burnout among behavioral disorders teachers accounts for attrition rates as high as 30% every 3–4 years. Some research on this topic has been reported in the literature (Lawrenson & McKinnon, 1982; Zabel & Zabel, 1981, 1983). These studies indicate that working with difficult kids on a day-to-day basis is one contributing factor, but burnout is also related to teachers' perceptions of support from administrators, colleagues, and students' parents. In addition, certain individual factors such as age, experience, and amount of training appear to be critical, with younger, less experienced, and less trained teachers at higher risk (Zabel & Zabel, 1983).

When the growth in the field over the past few years is combined with shortages of trained, experienced teachers, and the temporary certification situation, burnout and other factors involved in attrition become critical issues in teacher preparation. Many teachers may simply have inadequate preparation and unrealistic expectations for their jobs. The role demands and identification with their students may further separate them from potential sources of support. With relatively little investment in professional preparation in the field, many teachers may be likely to leave. A model of the cyclical nature of burnout with teachers of behaviorally disordered children was recently provided by Zabel, Boomer, and King (1984). Some suggestions for ameliorating the stresses encountered by teachers, such as those working with aggressive adolescents (Schloss, Sedlak, Wiggens, & Ramsey, 1983), have appeared in the literature, but little attention has been given to larger issues such as types of preparation to minimize burnout and the kinds of support systems that might reduce attrition.

Age Level Preparation

Another issue discussed by Huntze and Grosenick (1980) concerns training for specific age levels. Their analysis indicated that teachers are unlikely to be trained to work with a single age level, although there is a trend toward preparation geared to programs for adolescents and preschool special education. According to Smith-Davis et al. (1984), most states continue to offer K-12 special education certification, although nine require regular secondary certification for special education teachers at that level.

Preservice Preparation

It appears that most preservice preparation leading to certification and/or a degree, whether competency-based or not, requires student completion of a sequence of courses. These typically include the following: 1) coursework in regular education; 2) an introductory course in behavior disorders; 3) methods courses (methods, programming, diagnosis and curriculum, behavior management); 4) general and child or adolescent psychology; 5) theory of behavior disorders; and 6) student teaching (practicum) (Huntze & Grosenick, 1980). This report included overviews of 22 preservice training programs funded by Bureau for Education of the Handicapped in 1979–80.

It is difficult at times to distinguish between preservice and inservice preparation. Smith-Davis et al. (1984) stated, "It would appear that problems of supply, demand, and deployment are blurring certain distinctions between inservice and preservice." Partly due to the temporary certification situation discussed earlier, many "preservice" certification programs also operate as "inservice" programs for teachers completing certification requirements. Little has appeared in the literature concerning the number of teachers involved in such preparation, the sequencing of coursework and experiences, or the relative efficacy of such training. Practicum may be a particular concern, when it is required for temporary endorsement, prior to introductory and supporting coursework.

Preparation for Delivery Models

Huntze and Grosenick (1980) also pointed to the absence of preservice preparation of behavioral disorders teachers for work in specific service delivery models stating, ". . . there appears to be virtually no systematic effort to train teachers differentially at the pre-service level" (p. 82), other than the practicum experience. Further, practicum in one type of setting (e.g., resource room) does not preclude the certified teacher from teaching in another (e.g., institution).

Categorical/Noncategorical Preparation

The movement toward more generic teacher preparation, at least for mildly/moderately handicapped students, has been discussed above. The recent DOE report confirms a trend toward noncategorical delivery of services, and some training programs now prepare teachers for generic roles such as noncategorical resource teachers or consulting teachers. However, there has been concern with this trend. Huntze and Grosenick, again, noted strong sentiment "that non-categorical or cross-categorical teacher training and service delivery models actually hurt the development of a cadre of professionals dedicated to teaching behavior disordered students" (1980, p. 84).

Inservice Preparation

Inservice, or continuing education, of behavior disorders teachers is another topic about which little has been systematically researched. In special education as a whole, inservice programs have been criticized as frequently ineffective, irrelevant, and a waste of time and money (Wood & Thompson, 1980). Cline (1984), Grosenick and Huntze (1982), and Huntze and Grosenick (1980) have examined some of the problems with inservice training and have offered suggestions for improvement. According to Grosenick and Huntze (1982), most existing inservice related to education of behaviorally disordered students is conducted by local school districts using their own staff, state department or area education agency personnel, or university faculty. They concluded that inservice efforts have paid little attention to the specific needs of teachers of behaviorally disordered students. What has occurred has focused on behavior management, mainstreaming, and identification.

Grosenick and Huntze (1982) charged that existing inservice is frequently poorly conceived and delivered,

and it does not contribute to changes of teacher behavior. They suggested that effective inservice must be reconceptualized as an integrated, ongoing process requiring commitments of recipients' time and money. Essential features are needs assessment, consciousness raising, models for change, guided change, follow-up, and evaluation (1982, p. 93). In an appendix to their earlier analysis, Huntze and Grosenick (1980) included descriptions of 33 inservice and combined preservice/inservice training programs in behavior disorders funded by the Bureau for Education of the Handicapped in 1979–80.

Other Inservice Experiences

There are other types of inservice experiences that effect the preparation of teachers and others working with behaviorally disordered students that have been scarcely addressed in the literature. For example, over the past few years, the Council for Children with Behavioral Disorders (CCBD) of the Council for Exceptional Children (CEC) has actively supported development of activities at the state and regional levels. There are now 22 CCBD state federations and at least two local affiliates (Guetzloe, 1984). These professional organizations sponsor retreats, conferences, and newsletters for membership. CEC and its CCBD division have also provided some direct financial support for several conferences, including a National Topical Conference in Minneapolis in 1980, annual conferences in Tempe, Arizona, regional conferences in New England and the midwest, and national conferences focusing on secondary level programs. Imber (1981) provided guidelines for the development of such conferences.

Each of these conferences has attracted sizable numbers of participants. The Midwest Symposium for Leadership in Behavior Disorders, for example, has grown each year with approximately 800 registrants, a majority of whom were teachers, in 1985. In addition to the conferences themselves, conference summaries and proceedings have in some cases been prepared and disseminated to participants and other interested persons (e.g. Grosenick, Huntze, Peterson, & Zabel, 1984). Each of these conferences has been jointly planned by personnel representing institutions of higher education, local and state educational agencies. In addition, state level professional organizations, such as in New York and Iowa, have sponsored conferences, newsletters, etc.

While the extent and impact of these kinds of opportunities for continuing education are unclear, they do appear to be meeting a preparation need judging by their popularity with teachers. It is interesting to note that as teacher preparation and service delivery tend to become less categorically oriented, these experiences focusing on more categorically relevant issues appear to be growing in popularity. The Midwest Symposium, for example, has grown dramatically over the past 3 years from a Kansas Symposium to one which attracts participants from a four state region and beyond. This has occurred at a time when interest, as measured by attendance, at the multicategorical state and national CEC conferences has dwindled.

Demographic Characteristics

Relatively little is known about the demographic and personal characteristics of teachers of behaviorally disordered students. What data exist generally have been collected as parts of projects with other primary purposes.

In a 1980 study of reintegration practices, for example, information was gathered from 389 behavioral disorders and resource teachers working with behavior disordered students in Iowa, Kansas, and Nebraska (Peterson, Smith, White, & Zabel, 1983) Peterson, Zabel, Smith, & White, 1983). Of these, about 43% were at the elementary, 38% at the secondary, and 18% at "other" (mostly multi-age) levels. These teachers were nearly evenly represented by those in resource and self-contained settings (about 40% in each), with 5.9% working in residential facilities, and 14% reporting "other" types of delivery roles.

It is difficult to determine how similar the demographic characteristics of behavioral disorders teachers are to those of other special education teachers, but more information is available for the latter group. In a large sample (N=601) of Kansas special education teachers (Zabel & Zabel, 1981), slightly more than 20% considered themselves teachers of behaviorally disordered students. Of the total sample, 86.9% were females, 96% were white, and 64.7% were married. The sample was relatively young with nearly 45% under 30 years of age and less than 12% over 40. About 58% had master's degrees, with an average of 16 additional hours of credit. The special education teachers had a mean of 3.7 years of regular classroom teaching experience and 5.3 years of experience in special education. However, the modal number of years of regular teaching experience was 0 and the mode for special education experience was only 2 years. Of this sample, only about 40% reported they had been fully certified in special education when they began to teach.

It is not known how these demographic characteristics compare with those for other states. Some comparisons among teachers according to the categorical labels of their students indicated that behavioral disorders teachers were similar in age distribution and amount of experience to other special education teachers, but there were also some differences. There was a higher proportion of male behavioral disorders teachers (about 20%) than was found in most other categories. For example, fewer than 10% of learning disability teachers were males. Behavioral disorders teachers also had had more professional preparation than teachers of mentally retarded students, although they presented patterns of

preparation similar to those of most other exceptionalities.

Schmid, Algozzine, Maher, and Wells (1984) recently reported some demographic information for a national sample of 222 teachers of emotionally disturbed adolescents that tends to confirm the above findings. Their data compared junior and senior high teachers. At the junior high level, approximately two thirds were female, 92% were under 36 years of age, and 56% were taking additional training beyond a bachelor's degree. At the high school level, 59% were female, 84% were less than 36 years old, and 60% pursuing preparation beyond a bachelor's degree. For these secondary level teachers, about 60% were assigned to resource and about 25% to self-contained programs. This emphasis on resource type service delivery at the secondary level is noted as a shift from the emphasis on self-contained programs at the secondary level a few years earlier (Nelson & Kauffman, 1977).

Characteristics of Teacher Educators

As with teachers of behaviorally disordered students, relatively little has been reported in the literature about those who provide for their formal preparation, although there has recently been some attention to characteristics of special education teacher educators that may shed some light on this topic.

In a study involving members of the Teacher Education Division (TED) of CEC, for example, 622 teacher educators from across the United States provided some information about themselves and their professional satisfaction (Smith, White, & Zabel, 1984; White, Zabel, & Smith, 1983; Zabel, Smith, & White, 1984). The mean age of these teacher educators was 43.2 years, they had an average of 3 years of regular and 5 years of special education experience, and 2½ years of nonteaching special education experience. The subjects also averaged nearly 9 years in higher education, with only half beginning in higher education more than 10 years earlier. Nearly three fourths of those with doctorates had received them in special education, the rest in educational psychology, curriculum and instruction, and other areas. The calculated mean annual salary for this sample (in 1981–82) was $24,400.

Some comparisons were made between male and female teacher educators. Females accounted for more than half of the sample. Males were much more likely to have tenure, to be at higher academic ranks, and to earn higher salaries than females (by about 30%). The patterns of salary discrepancies between males and females were similar to those found for other disciplines in higher education (*Chronicle of Higher Education*, 1983). However, the mean salaries for both males and females in special education were lower than those in most other disciplines. Males were more likely to hold doctorates than females (92% and 71%, respectively), were about 2 years older, and had been in higher education somewhat longer. More than 42% of the total sample fell into the single, divorced/single, or divorced/remarried categories, although the proportion of unmarried females was about 3 times that of males.

Nearly one half of this sample worked at colleges and universities with fewer than 10,000 students. More than one half were in departments of special education, with the others in various subdivisions of larger departments or colleges. Most of their programs provided training at both bachelor's and master's levels, with only 15% exclusively undergraduate and 10% exclusively graduate level programs.

Respondents were nearly equally divided between those in categorical and in noncategorical or generic teacher preparation programs. Most teaching was done on campus, and nearly 80% considered "teaching," as opposed to research, administration, or service to be their major responsibility.

The professional satisfaction of these teacher educators was determined by their ratings on a 29 item questionnaire comprising five statistically derived factors (social/community conditions, advancement opportunities, program quality, financial conditions, and departmental resources). Among the most highly rated individual items were the teacher educator's own qualifications, recreational activities, housing, and quality of special education program. The lowest satisfaction ratings were provided for financial resources, time to pursue professional interests, clerical support, and financial support for professional development (White, Zabel, & Smith, 1983).

Based upon the researchers' analyses of relationships between several job-related and personal characteristics and the ratings of satisfaction for the five factors, there were several conclusions. Overall, faculty from larger institutions, offering advanced degrees, noncategorical in orientation, and located in urban and suburban areas were more satisfied with their professional lives than were those from smaller institutions, in rural areas, offering undergraduate, categorically oriented programs (Smith, White, & Zabel, 1984). The analysis of relationships between job satisfaction and personal characteristics led to the following profiles of the most and least satisfied special education teacher educators.

> The former would be a married, male, full professor with tenure, over 40 years of age, earning more than $40,000, who has been in higher education and in his present position for more than 20 years. The least professionally satisfied individual . . . would be an unmarried, female, nontenured, assistant professor, under 40 years of age, earning less than $25,000, with less than 6 years in higher education and in her present position (Zabel, Smith, & White, 1984).

Because so many special education teacher educators fall into this category, this situation may be a major cause for concern.

Preparation of Teacher Educators

Little attention has been given to the kinds of preparation teacher educators in the area of behavioral disorders have had or should have. If the above data for special education teacher educators generally reflect the situation for this population, it appears that most have had considerable experience in teaching and other related professional roles outside of higher education and most have completed doctorates in special education. However, little is known about the nature of those experiences or their professional preparation, particularly at the doctoral level.

Schofer and Chalfant (1979) addressed this concern in a collection of papers from a conference on doctoral programs in special education. Among their recommendations was the need to develop a balance between scholarship and pragmatism in doctoral program content. Based upon this proposition, Grosenick and McCarney (1984) presented a model for preparation of teacher educators in the area of behavioral disorders that was developed at the University of Missouri-Columbia. Emphasizing the importance of the teaching role, they analyzed the skills required of doctoral level personnel in the field. The resulting model includes course/practicum experiences in the following areas: course design; design and supervision of field experiences; design of inservice; preparation of grant proposals, development, administration, and evaluation; research and writing; understanding related services; and related professional opportunities, all with emphasis on behavioral disorders. Grosenick and McCarney noted informal evaluations from participating students to be encouraging.

Prehm (1984) recently discussed leadership preparation in special education pointing out problems due to declines in enrollment in doctoral programs, "minimal" prior preparation of students in related disciplines, lack of doctoral level focus and content, lack of monitoring student practica, and lack of agreement on what constitutes quality practice. He called for an emphasis on scholarship, a clear mission, generic doctoral preparation, and location of programs at a limited number of institutions in which "there is a significant amount of inquiry occurring and in which there is a core of leadership personnel who can serve as role models and mentors for the future teacher educators" (Prehm, 1984, p. 63). A similar analysis has been presented by Tymitz-Wolf (1984) who said that internal and external influences on higher education generally, and special education specifically, indicate a need for well-conceived faculty development efforts. She cited factors that contribute to the failure of special education faculty development programs and suggested some that contribute to their success (e.g., faculty autonomy, systematic planning and programming, career development patterns, and appropriate institutional support).

Discussion and Recommendations

The above review of the preparation of teachers for behaviorally disordered students has required examination of literature on several relevant subtopics: preparation of regular education teachers, special competencies of behavioral disorders teachers, model training programs, categorical versus noncategorical preparation, and characteristics of behavioral disorders teachers and teacher trainers.

This literature does not provide a comprehensive, complete picture of the topic. It is rather like a puzzle with pieces missing. Still, several conclusions can be drawn. One of the most striking is the paucity of what could be characterized as research. Most literature on this topic consists of opinion, and what research does exist is largely descriptive. Little empirical data exist to evaluate either the state of the art or the state of practice. In fact, in the literature they may be nearly one and the same. State of the art literature consists largely of descriptions of teacher training efforts or proposals for improvement. Given some information presented in the literature, one suspects that the state of practice may lag behind. We know, for example, that there has been rapid growth of behavioral disorders training programs over the past 10 years to meet personnel needs. There has been tremendous pressure to produce sufficient numbers of teachers. Programs have undoubtedly been developed by persons unqualified to do so, and "trainees" certified who should not have been. The research available on teacher burnout and attrition in this area is indicative of some inadequacies in the ways we select, prepare, and endorse teachers. Of course, description and documentation of this state of practice is rarely included in the professional literature.

This does not mean that the literature has nothing to say on the topic of preparation of teachers for behaviorally disordered students, but that empirically validated conclusions are largely unavailable. Perhaps a better way of characterizing some of the literature is that which deals with qualitative issues (such as important teacher competencies) and that which is concerned with quantitative issues (such as personnel needs). However, even such a distinction is not clean, since a quantitative issue such as determination of the need for personnel is directly affected by qualitative issues such as categorical or noncategorical nature of training.

Relationship with Regular Education

The relationship of teacher preparation in behavioral disorders to regular teacher preparation is an area that begs for additional attention. Certainly, the quality of preparation of regular classroom teachers is a concern for special educators, most of whom have received such preparation. Also, regular educators are the colleagues of special educators. Most behaviorally disordered students participate, at least part of the time, in regular educational programs. Indeed, a widely accepted principle of special education programming has been education in the least restrictive environment possible for meeting a child's needs. The regular classroom is generally viewed as the least restrictive, or more normal, educational environment, although in some cases it may actually constitute a more restrictive environment for behaviorally disordered students. For all of these reasons, quality of preparation of regular classroom teachers is a major concern to special educators.

Relatively little attention has been given to special education in the recent commission reports and reactions on the status of American education. It may be that the focus on *excellence*, meaning academic excellence, has effectively excluded consideration of excellence in education for exceptional children.

Regular teacher preparation, however, has been soundly criticized in a number of commission reports and self-examinations within the profession. Criticism has been leveled at the proliferation of substandard programs producing substandard teachers. Some of the criticism has been aimed directly at teacher training programs and faculty, even though they control only a relatively small amount of preservice preparation of teachers. As several reviews have pointed out, multiple factors, including declining fiscal support for higher education, inequitable allocation of resources within institutions of higher education, a smaller pool from which to draw teacher trainees, inadequate salaries and decreasing status in the teaching profession, and greater employment opportunities for women have contributed to the current state of affairs.

Proposed solutions for these ills have included higher academic standards for admission to teacher education programs and for teacher certification, and the extension of preservice training to 5 years to allow for 4 full years of general education followed by a year of professional training (Jacobson, 1985; National Commission for Excellence in Teacher Education, 1985).

While these proposals may provide partial solutions to the quality issue, there are unresolved problems. One is a quantity issue. If implemented, what will be the effects on what is already projected to be a shortage of classroom teachers in coming years? In addition, how will they affect the recruitment and training of minority teachers? Another unresolved issue is the determination of critical competencies for regular classroom teachers. If the conclusions of Evertson, Hawley and Zlotnick (1984) are correct, increasing the academic achievement level of teachers may not be the only, or even the key, factor in determining academic achievement of students. None of the core teaching competencies they identified in their review are directly related to teachers' academic achievement. However, some of those important skills are strikingly similar to those deemed important in the literature for teachers of behaviorally disordered students. A needed area of research concerns relationships of recent research on effective teaching with the literature on important competencies for behavioral disorders teachers. These two bodies of literature have been generated differently, but each may be able to provide some important contributions to the other.

A challenge for those advocating improvement of teacher education is the provision of adequate resources to accomplish the proposed reforms. Will sufficient federal, state, and local funding be provided to do the job? Will institutions of higher education reallocate resources to provide additional support for teacher education to attract more able students to professional education and to attract, reward, and retain top flight teacher educators? Will public support of education provide sufficient financial and status rewards, administrative and community support, and professional opportunities to attract and retain talented persons to careers in education?

At present, despite calls for improvement of American education and the quality of teachers, the availability of resources has not matched the availability of words. This situation appears to be directly influencing professional satisfaction of both teachers and teacher educators and, perhaps, is indirectly affecting their job performance. As Smith-Davis, Burke, and Noel (1984) observed:

> Although the improvement of public education is currently a popular cause, and much concern is centered on the quality of teachers and teaching, state and federal policy makers are not uniformly assuming the responsibility for changing the status quo. Clearly, however, we are not going to get educational excellence on the cheap." (p. 218)

Regular teacher educators' reactions to the various commission reports have also failed to address the relationship of special education to teacher education. However, some special educators have recently called for a unified system of regular and special education, asserting that special education has met its major goal: the right to a free and appropriate education for all students (Stainback & Stainback, 1984). However, this position has been met with skepticism by some special educators. Mesinger (1985), for example, pointed to the existing underidentification and lack of educational services provided for behaviorally disordered students. He identified the critical impediment to a unification as "teacher qualities," citing the reports on the declining quality of regular teacher preparation programs, faculty, and students. Mesinger also questioned the competence of many regular teachers to work with exceptional children, saying:

> Clinical observation indicates that one educational problem relating to the diversity of human behavior is that adults, including teachers, vary in their abilities to cope with, manage, and teach groups of differing ranges and intensity of diversity. Some adults can cope well with large numbers of youths behaving

in more divergent ways than others can. (1985, p. 511)

It is just such critical "coping" abilities that are expressed in the behavioral disorders teacher competency lists reviewed earlier. A policy implication would include targeting of federal personnel preparation funds for programs that attempt to integrate state of the art training for regular and special education teachers of behaviorally disordered students. Best practice from each field could be used to enhance training in the other.

Teacher preparation in special education, including teachers for behaviorally disordered students, is directly affected in both quantitative and qualitative ways by regular teacher preparation. If the number of students enrolled in regular preservice teacher education continues to fall and there are increased teaching opportunites for regular classroom teachers, this may directly affect the numbers who participate in behavioral disorders teacher preparation. If the quality (by whatever measures) of preservice and inservice teachers continues to decline, this would also likely affect the quality of behavioral disorders teachers.

Competencies for Behavioral Disorders Teachers

Despite the evolution of perceptions of important competencies for teachers of behaviorally disordered students, there has actually been a good deal of agreement in the literature. The evolution has been in the direction of increasing specification of constituent skills that are measureable. In some cases, as critics have pointed out, this movement has resulted in a proliferation of subskills, that may be measured but may also result in a fragmented picture of teacher competence. In addition, there are some personal and affective competencies that cannot be quantitatively measured. Demonstrated performance of numerous individual skills, as in competency-based teacher education, does not necessarily add up to successful teaching. Of course, the absence of demonstrated application of skills and reliance on subjective judgments of students' competence is an even more precarious position. At least, delineation of competencies provides direction to teacher preparation.

Judging from published program descriptions and those provided in personnel preparation grant applications, many behavioral disorders teacher preparation programs are systematically identifying important competencies and incorporating them in both preservice and inservice programs. In only a few instances has documentation based upon performance by trainees and their students in applied settings been provided. In these cases, measurement has focused on competencies that are most amenable to direct observation.

Some unanswered questions related to the teaching of specific competencies include the degree to which they are actually taught in preparation programs, the relative emphasis placed upon the teaching of different understandings and skills in coursework and field experiences, and the continued use of the competencies by teachers in the field. In regard to the last of these questions, research on the skills that teachers actually use and how they correspond with their training could provide helpful information to teacher educators. It may be that even training programs that have carefully monitored the demonstration of specified skills by their trainees, have a limited long-range influence on actual teacher behavior. This is an area that could be examined in a variety of ways, including surveys of practicing teachers' training in and actual use of interventions and naturalistic case studies of teacher behavior.

Categorical/Noncategorical Training

The relationship of preparation of behavioral disorders teachers with training of other special education teachers is another major issue unresolved in the literature. As indicated earlier, the trend appears to be in the direction of noncategorical programming, and thus noncategorical teacher training, at least for mildly/moderately handicapped students. Despite this trend, some of the arguments of categorical advocates may be valid, particularly the assertion that behaviorally disordered students may be short-changed in the noncategorical programs.

There may be some important differences between teachers who choose to teach behaviorally disordered students and those who choose to teach other exceptional children. Some of the necessary competencies may differ. In a report on a national survey of competencies for professionals in the field of learning disability (Newcomer, 1982), for example, there are some dramatic differences when compared with the studies of competencies for behavioral disorders teachers. Teachers working in the learning disability area rated competencies in teaching academic subjects, particularly reading, as most important and also rated their skills as highest in these areas. The ratings for behavior management skills, however, ranked at about the middle level for both importance and skill. In one area, "behavior management instruction," the ratings of importance and skill were "relatively low." As was apparent in the review of the behavioral disorders teacher competency literature, behavior management skills have been consistently viewed as critically important for behavioral disorders teachers.

Certainly, there are competencies that cut across traditional categorical lines: competencies generic to teaching in programs for various exceptionalities. Perhaps the most prudent approach to the preparation of teachers is multicategorical, with generic introductory and supporting coursework in areas such as assessment, behavior management, individual educational programming, and working with parents, together with more categorically oriented preparation in several areas dealing with characteristics and methods more specific to special populations.

Attrition and Burnout

Although there are some signs that some behavioral disorders teachers are staying longer in the profession and that a larger percentage of behaviorally disordered students are being educated in cross-categorical programs, the supply of behavioral disorders teachers remains seriously inadequate. This appears to be the result of underproduction of new teachers and high attrition rates, much of the latter due to burnout. Preservice and inservice training must deliberately attend to factors involved in burnout by informing prospective teachers of the kinds of challenges they will face in their jobs, providing challenging, yet supportive, practica, and helping students develop effective personal coping strategies. School systems too, must attempt to provide individual and programmatic support for behavioral disorders teachers if they wish to help them survive. Ongoing support and assistance from special and regular education administrators and from specially trained and experienced consultants and mutual support teams would appear to be beneficial. Factors involved in burnout are now well established, but additional research is required to examine the efficacy of various strategies to ameliorate burnout.

Preparation of Teacher Educators

Teacher educators appear to have had relevant professional experience for their roles. However, little is known about the kinds of "academic" preparation that will best prepare them for their teacher educator roles or what kinds of continuing professional development will best equip them to provide leadership in a still rapidly evolving field. The previously cited model behavioral disorders doctoral program described by Grosenick and McCarney (1984) and the suggestions of Prehm (1984) regarding special education leadership preparation offer some worthwhile direction for preparation of teacher educators. However, this is an area that demands additional attention from researchers and program developers.

References

Akin, J. N. (1985). *Teacher supply/demand 1985: A report based upon an opinion survey of teacher placement officers.* Madison, WI: Association for School, College and University Staffing.

Balow, B. (1966). A program of preparation for teachers of disturbed children. *Exceptional Children, 32*, 455–461.

Blackhurst, A. E. (1981). Noncategorical teacher preparation: Problems and promises. *Exceptional Children, 48*, 197–205.

Blackhurst, A. E., McLoughlin, J. A., & Price, L. M. (1977). Issues in the development of programs to prepare teachers of children with learning and behavior disorders.

Behavioral Disorders, 2, 157–168.

Blatt, B. (1976). On competencies and incompetencies, instruction and destruction, individualization and depersonalization: Reflections on the now-movement. *Behavioral Disorders, 1*, 89–96.

Bloom, R. B. (1979). Why That One? Some thoughts about instructional competencies for teachers of emotionally disturbed adolescents. In F. H. Wood (Ed.), *Teachers for secondary school students with serious emotional disturbance: Content for programs* (pp. 65–72). Minneapolis: Department of Psychoeducational Studies, University of Minnesota.

Brady, M. P., Conroy, M., & Langford, C. A. (1984). Current issues and practices affecting the development of noncategorical programs for students and teachers. *Teacher Education and Special Education, 1*, 20–26

Bullock, L. M., Dykes, M. K., & Kelly, T. J. (1974). Competency based teacher preparation in behavioral disorders. *Exceptional Children, 41*, 192–194.

Bullock, L. M., & Whelan, R. J. (1971). Competencies needed by teachers of the emotionally disturbed and socially maladjusted: A comparison. *Exceptional Children, 37*, 485–489.

Chronicle of Higher Education. (1983). Men's and women's 1982–83 salaries compared. Survey by John Minter Associates, **26** (1), 26.

Clark, D. L. (in press). Transforming the contexture for the professional preparation of teachers. In L. G. Katz & J. D. Raths (Eds.), *Advances in teacher education.*

Cline, D. (1984). Achieving quality and relevance in inservice teacher education. *Teacher Education and Special Education, 7*, 199–208.

Edgar, E., & Neel, R. S. (1976). Results of a competency based teacher training program. *Exceptional Children, 42*, 33–35.

Englert, C. S., & Sugai, G. (1983). Teacher training: improving trainee performance through peer observation and observation system technology. *Teacher Education and Special Education, 6*, 7–17.

Evertson, C., Hawley, W., & Zlotnick, M. (1984). *The characteristics of effective teacher preparation programs: A review of research*. Nashville, TN: Peabody Center for Effective Teaching, Vanderbilt University.

Fagen, S. A. (1978). Sustaining our teaching resources: A public school-based internship in special education. In C. M. Nelson (Ed.). *Field-based teacher training: Applications in special education* (pp. 83–112). Minneapolis: Department of Psychoeducational Studies, University of Minnesota.

Federal Register (1977). *42*, 42, 474 as amended in *Federal Register*, 1981, **46**, 3866.

Feinberg, F. C., & Wood, F. H. (1978). Goals for teachers of seriously emotionally disturbed children. In F. H. Wood (Ed.), *Preparing teachers to develop and maintain therapeutic educational environments* (pp. 19–34). Minneapolis: Department of Psychoeducational Studies, University of Minnesota.

Fink, A. H., & Brownsmith, K. (1977). Project INSTEP: A model inservice training program for teachers of the behaviorally disordered. *Behavioral Disorders, 2*, 223–224.

Fink, A. H., Glass, R. M., & Guskin, S. L. (1975). An analysis of teacher education programs in behavior disorders. *Exceptional Children, 42*, 47–48.

Gable, R. A., & Strain, P. S. (1979). Staff training issues within residential programs for behavioral disordered children.

Behavioral Disorders, 4, 201–207.

Gersh, M., & Nagle, R. (1969). Preparation of teachers for the emotionally disturbed. *Exceptional Children, 35*, 633–639.

Greenough, K. N., Huntze, S. L., Nelson, C. M., & Simpson, R. L. (1983). *Noncategorical versus categorical issues in programming for behaviorally disordered children and youth*. Columbia: National Needs Analysis/Leadership Training Project, Department of Special Education, University of Missouri.

Grosenick, J. K., & Huntze, S. L. (1982). An inservice model for leadership personnel in behavior disorders. *Teacher Education and Special Education, 5*, 59–66.

Grosenick, J. K., Huntze, S. L., Peterson, R. L., & Zabel, R. H. (Eds.) (1984) *Reflections on deviance in 1984: Proceedings of the Midwest Symposium for Leadership in Behavioral Disorders*. Columbia: National Needs Analysis/Leadership Training Project, Department of Special Education, University of Missouri.

Grosenick, J. K., & McCarney, S. B. (1984). Preparation of teacher educators in behavior disorders. *Teacher Education and Special Education, 7*, 101–106.

Guetzloe, E. (1984). CCBD Newsletter. *Behavioral Disorders*, **10**, 75–78.

Haring, N. G., & Fargo, G. A. (1969). Evaluating programs for preparing teachers of emotionally disturbed children. *Exceptional Children, 36*, 157–162.

Heller, H. W., McCoy, K., & McIntire, B. (1979). Group summary. *Teacher Education and Special Education, 2*, 8–10.

Heward, W. L., Cooper, J. O., Heron, T. E., Hill, D. S., McCormick, S., Porter, J. T., Stephens, T. M., & Sutherland, H. A. (1981). Noncategorical teacher training in a state with categorical certification requirements. *Exceptional Children, 48*, 206–212.

Hewett, F. M. (1967a). Educational engineering with emotionally disturbed children. *Exceptional Children, 33*, 459–467.

Hewett, F. M. (1967b). A hierarchy of competencies for teachers of emotionally handicapped children. *Exceptional Children, 33*, 66–67.

Huntze, S. L., & Grosenick, J. K. (1980). *National needs analysis in behavior disorders: Human resource issues in behavior disorders*. Columbia: Department of Special Education, University of Missouri.

Idol-Maestas, L. (1981). A teacher training model: The resource/consulting teacher. *Behavioral Disorders, 6*, 108–121.

Idol-Maestas, L., Lloyd, S., & Lilly, M. S. (1981). A noncategorical approach to direct service and teacher education. *Exceptional Children, 48*, 213–221.

Imber, S. C. (1981). Organizing regional conferences: Practice and philosophy. *Behavioral Disorders, 6*, 65–67.

Imig, D. G. (1982). *An examination of the teacher education scope: An overview of the structure and form of teacher education*. Washington, DC: American Association of Colleges of Teacher Education.

Jacobson, R. L. (1985). University education deans seek elite corps of schoolteachers. *The Chronicle of Higher Education, 30*, 16–17.

Kavale, K., & Hirshoren, A. (1980). Public school and university teacher training programs for behaviorally disordered children? Are they compatible? *Behavioral Disorders, 5*, 151–155.

Kerr, D. H. (1983). Teacher competence and teacher education in the United States. In L. S. Shulman & G. Sykes (Eds.), *Handbook of teaching and policy* (pp. 126–149).

New York: Longman.

Kerr, M. M., Shores, R. E., & Stowitschek, J. J. (1978). Peabody's field-based special teacher education program: A model for evaluating competency-based training. In C. M. Nelson (Ed.), *Field-based teacher training: Application in special education* (pp. 67–82). Minneapolis: Department of Psychoeducational Studies, University of Minnesota.

Knight, M. F. (1978). Vermont's consulting teacher model for inservice training of educational personnel. In C. M. Nelson (Ed.), *Field-based teacher training: Application in special education* (pp. 113–127), Minneapolis: Department of Psychoeducational Studies, University of Minnesota.

Lawrenson, G. M., & McKinnon, A. J. (1982). A survey of classroom teachers of the emotionally disturbed: Attrition and burnout factors. *Behavioral Disorders, 8*, 41–49.

Lilly, M. S. (1979). Competency-based training. *Teacher Education and Special Education, 2*, 20–28.

Lortie, D. C. (1975). *Schoolteacher: A sociological study.* Chicago: University of Chicago Press.

Lutkemeir, D. M. (1983). Training teachers of emotionally handicapped children: Priorities identified by school practitioners. In R. B. Rutherford (Ed.), *Severe behavioral disorders of children and youth* (Vol. 6), (pp. 35–39). Reston, VA: Council for Children with Behavioral Disorders.

Mackie, R. P., Kvaraceus, W. C., & Williams, H. M. (1957). *Teachers of children who are socially and emotionally maladjusted.* Washington, DC: US Government Printing Office.

McKenzie, H. S., Egner, A. N., Knight, M. F., Perelman, P. E., Schneider, D. M., & Garvin, J. S. (1970). Training consulting teachers to assist elementary teachers in the management of handicapped children. *Exceptional Children, 37*, 137–143.

Mesinger, J. F. (1985). Commentary on "A rationale for the merger of special and regular education" or, Is it now time for the lamb to lie down with the lion? *Exceptional Children, 51*, 510–512.

Morgan, S. R. (1977). Personality variables as predictors of empathy. *Behavioral Disorders, 2*, 89–94.

Morse, W. C. (1976). Competency in teaching socio-emotional impaired. *Behavioral Disorders, 1*, 83–88.

Morse, W. C., Bruno, F., & Morgan, S. (1973). *Training teachers for the emotionally disturbed: An analysis of programs.* Ann Arbor: School of Education, University of Michigan.

National Commission for Excellence in Teacher Education (1985). A call for change in teacher education. *The Chronicle of Higher Education, 30*, 13–20.

Nelson, C. M., & Kauffman, J. M. (1977). Educational programming for secondary age delinquent and maladjusted pupils. *Behavioral Disorders, 2*, 102–113.

Nemser, S. F. (1983). Learning to teach. In L. S. Shulman and G. Sykes (Eds.), *Handbook of teaching and policy* (pp. 150–170). New York: Longman.

Newcomer, P. L. (1982). Competencies for professionals in learning disabilities. *Learning Disability Quarterly, 5*, 241–252.

Pattavina, P., & Ramirez, R. R. (1980). Generic affective competencies: A common bond between regular and special educators. Paper presented at The 58th International Council for Exceptional Children Convention, Philadelphia, PA.

Peterson, R., Smith, C., White, M., & Zabel, R. (1983). *Reintegration practices for behavior disordered children in three midwestern states: A preliminary report.* Paper presented at the International Convention of The 61st International Council for Exceptional Children Convention, Philadelphia, Pennsylvania.

Peterson, R. L., Zabel, R. H. Smith, C. R., & White, M. A. (1983). Cascade of services model and emotionally disabled students. *Exceptional Children, 49*, 404–408.

Polsgrove, L., & Reith. H. J. (1979). A new look at competencies required by teachers of emotionally disturbed and behaviorally disordered children and youth. In F. H. Wood (Ed.), *Teachers for secondary school students with serious emotional disturbance: Content of programs* (pp. 25–46). Minneapolis: Department of Psychoeducational Studies, University of Minnesota.

Prehm, H. (1984). Preparation for leadership in personnel preparation. *Teacher Education and Special Education, 7*, 59–65.

Rabinow, B. (1960). A proposal for a training program for teachers. *Exceptional Children, 26*, 59–60.

Reynolds, M. C. (1979). Categorical vs. noncategorical teacher training. *Teacher Education and Special Education, 2*, 5–11.

Rice, R. E. (1984). *Toward reform in teacher education: Strategies for change.* Reflections on a Conference at Wingspread sponsored by The Johnson Foundation and The Fund for the Improvement of Postsecondary Education.

Ruhl, K. L., & Hughes, C. A. (1985). Coping with student aggression: A need for special education teacher preparation. *Teacher Education and Special Education, 8*, 41–47.

Rutherford, R. B., Nelson, C. M., & Wolford, B. I. (1985). Special education in the most restrictive environment: Correctional/special education. *Journal of Special Education, 19*, 59–71.

Scheuer, A. L. (1971). The relationship between personal attributes and effectiveness in teachers of the emotionally disturbed. *Exceptional Children, 38*, 723–731.

Schloss, P. J., Sedlak, R. A., Wiggins, E. D., & Ramsey, D. (1983). Stress reduction for professionals working with aggressive adolescents. *Exceptional Children, 49*, 349–354.

Schmid, R., Algozzine, B., Maher, M., & Wells, D. (1984). Teaching emotionally disturbed adolescents: A study of selected teacher and teaching characteristics. *Behavioral Disorders, 9*, 105–112.

Schofer, R. C., & Chalfant, J. C. (1979). *The Missouri Symposium on doctoral programming in special education: Considerations for the 1980s.* Columbia: Department of Special Education, University of Missouri.

Schwartz, L. (1967). Preparation of the clinical teacher for special education: 1866–1966. *Exceptional Children, 34*, 117–124.

Semmel, M. I. (1976). Assessing performance of teachers through direct observation and computer processing. *Behavioral Disorders, 1*, 133–143.

Semmel, M. I., & Semmel, D. S. (1976). Competency-based teacher education: An overview. *Behavioral Disorders, 1*, 69–82.

Shores, R. E. (1979). Evaluation and research. *Teacher Education and Special Education, 2*, 68–73.

Shores, R. E., Cegelka, P. T., & Nelson, C. M. (1973). Competency based special education teacher training. *Exceptional Children, 40*, 192–197.

Shores, R. E., Roberts, M., & Nelson, C. M. (1976). An empirical model for the development of competencies for teachers of children with behavior disorders. *Behavioral Disorders, 1*, 123–132.

Smith, D. C., & Street, S. (1980). The professional component in selected professions. *Phi Delta Kappa, 62*, 103–107.

Smith, M. L. White, W. J., & Zabel, R. H. (1984). College/University program variables and their relationship to the job satisfaction of special education teacher educators. *Teacher Education and Special Education, 7*, 39–45.

Smith–Davis, J., Burke, P. J., & Noel, M. M. (1984). *Personnel to educate the handicapped in America: Supply and demand from a programmatic viewpoint.* College Park: Institute for the Study of Children and Youth, Department of Special Education, University of Maryland.

Spence, J. (1978). Clinical educator: A direction in training for seriously emotionally disturbed children. In C. M. Nelson (Ed.), *Field-based teacher training: Applications in Special Education* (pp. 27–39). Minneapolis: Department of Psychoeducational Studies, University of Minnesota.

Stainback, W., & Stainback, S. (1984). A rationale for the merger of special and regular education. *Exceptional Children, 51*, 102–111.

Tymitz-Wolf, B. (1984). Faculty development: Concerns and considerations for effective programming. *Teacher Education and Special Education, 7*, 119–131.

US Department of Education. (1984). Implementation of Public Law 94–142: The Education for All Handicapped Children Act. Sixth annual report to Congress. Washington, D.C.: Special Education Programs (ED/OSERS), Division of Educational Services.

Walker, H. M., Hops, H., & Greenwood, C. R. (1976). Competency-based training issues in the development of behavior management packages for specific classroom behavior disorders. *Behavioral Disorders, 1*, 112–122.

Wells, D., Schmid, R., Algozzine, B., & Maher, M. (1983). Teaching LD adolescents: A study of selected teacher and teaching characteristics. *Teacher Education and Special Education, 6*, 227–234.

Wheeler, M. A., Tuchman, L., Miller, D., & Wambold, C. (1985). STEM: An interactive approach for training and evaluating teacher trainees in special education. *Teacher Education and Special Education, 8*, 33–40.

White, W. J., Zabel, R. H., & Smith, M. (1983). Job satisfaction among special education teacher educators. *Counterpoint*, (May/June), 17–18.

Wood, F. H. (1979). Issues in training teachers for the seriously emotionally disturbed. In R. B. Rutherford & A. G. Prieto (Eds.), *Severe behavior disorders of children and youth* (Vol. 2), (pp. 1–13). Reston, VA: Council for Children with Behavioral Disorders.

Wood, F. H., & Lakin, K. C. (Eds.) (1979). *Disturbing, disordered or disturbed?* Minneapolis: Department of Psychoeducational Studies, University of Minnesota.

Wood, F. H., & Thompson, S. R. (1980). Guidelines for better staff development. *Educational Leadership, 37*, 374–378.

Wood, F. H., & Zabel, R. H. (1978) Making sense of reports on the incidence of behavior disorders/emotional disturbance in school-age populations. *Psychology in the schools, 15*, 45–51.

Zabel, R. H., Boomer, L. W., & King, T. R. (1984). A model of stress and burnout among teachers of behaviorally disordered students. *Behavioral Disorders, 9*, 215–221.

Zabel, R. H., Smith, M. L., & White, W. J. (1984). Relationships between selected personal characteristics of special education teacher educators and their job satisfaction. *Teacher Education and Special Education, 7*, 132–141.

Zabel, M. K., & Zabel, R. H. (1983). Burnout among special education teachers: The role of age, experience, and training. *Teacher Education and Special Education, 6*, 255–259.

Zabel, R. H., & Zabel, M. K. (1981). *Factors involved in burnout among teachers of emotionally disturbed and other types of exceptional children.* Paper presented at 59th Annual International Council for Exceptional Children Convention, New York. (ERIC Document Reproduction Service No. ED 204 943)

Cooperative Interface of Schools and other Child Care Systems for Behaviorally Disordered Students

SHARON L. HUNTZE

University of Missouri-Columbia

Abstract—Cooperative interface, interagency cooperation, and interagency collaboration are terms used interchangeably to describe the coordination that needs to occur between and among the agencies that are potential service providers for students who are handicapped by their behavior. The chapter reviews the reasons for cooperative interface and the models currently used and proposed and examines the examples of state-of-the-art cooperative interface that have met the challenge of coordinated service delivery. Also presented is a review of the current state of practice and a discussion of the concerns that have kept and are keeping viable cooperation from existing. Finally, the chapter explores the implications of the previous information by discussing needs and recommendations for federal, state, local, and training agencies and research.

Definitions

The following statements describe three very different situations. There is, however, a common thread.

1. A 9-year-old girl has been placed in a public school self-contained classroom for behaviorally disordered students. The school faculty and the child's parents agree that a short-term, residential, diagnostic period at a nearby community mental health center would be useful.
2. A 14-year-old boy is receiving resource room services from the junior high teacher of behaviorally disordered students. The teacher is very concerned that the home environment is neglectful and abusive and has determined to contact the local social service agency that provides family support, assistance, and counseling.
3. An 18-year-old has spent 6 of the last 12 school years identified as behaviorally disordered and receiving various types of services (i.e., itinerant, self-contained classroom, resource room) at different times. It appears that he will not receive a standard high school diploma

at year's end. An Individualized Education Program review staffing has been called to determine how best to proceed during the remainder of the school year and what are the programs and/or services into which he might be transitioned.

The common thread in these situations is that they each will require cooperative interface between the public school and other service agencies if the behaviorally disordered student is to remain or become able to benefit from school or to function in a postschool environment.

Cooperative interface of schools and other child care systems; *Interagency cooperation*; *interagency collaboration*: In one sense, these phrases are well understood. There is little disagreement about what cooperative interface, cooperation, or collaboration means. A task force for the Midwest Regional Resource Center Task Force (1979) used the following definition of interagency collaboration, but the definition is equally viable for the phrases cooperative interface and interagency cooperation. They state that interagency collaboration is:

> A process which: encourages and facilitates an open and honest exchange of ideas, plans, approaches, and resources across disciplines, programs and agencies; enables all participants jointly to define their separate interests and mutually identify needed changes in order to best achieve common purposes; and utilizes formal procedures to help clarify issues, define problems and make decisions. (Midwest Regional Resource Center Task Force, 1979, p. 1)

The terms interagency collaboration and interagency cooperation are the ones most often encountered in the literature. As a result of early problems and false starts in the pursuit of interagency collaboration, the terms are often greeted with some deserved cynicism (McCormick, 1982; Rogers & Farrow, 1983). For that reason, the term cooperative interface sounds a bit fresher and may, as a result, encourage a more open mind toward the entire concept it describes. Regardless of that fact, its usage amounts to label swapping, a familiar phenomenon in our field. However, any assistance in approaching the concept in a fresh, open, enthusiastic manner may prove beneficial to the behaviorally disordered children and youth whose programming often depends upon it. In this chapter, the three terms are used interchangeably, the selection based primarily on the source of the ideas being shared.

In another sense, the three terms are not well understood. As is often the case with names selected for concepts, the terms suggest both outcomes and processes. Cooperative interface is a dynamic process suggesting how professionals conduct themselves. The ongoing process produces ongoing results or products that accrue to children and youth in the form of appropriate services. Although the terms technically refer to processes, they often conjure up the services, programs, and people that function in the process.

The agencies with which a public school might need to engage in cooperative interface are too numerous to list exhaustively, and, of course, exact names are idiosyncratic to each state's administrative organization. However, the types of agencies most often involved in interagency collaboration for behaviorally disordered children include public schools; mental health agencies (including local and county community mental health centers, residential facilities, and in-community living arrangements); correctional facilities for juveniles (including attention centers, detention centers, training schools, and group homes); vocational education programs; and social service agencies.

Parameters

An intergrative review focused solely on cooperative interface in relation to behaviorally disordered children and youth would be a brief exercise indeed, limited primarily to the review of paper agreements at the state level and to specific descriptions of independent cooperative interface efforts in isolated local areas. Although that information is included herein and the product descriptions are the most exciting of the information, a broader framework is required. Thus, the information used in this review concerns interagency collaboration in a broad sense as well as the manner in which the specifics of interface for behaviorally disordered persons fit into the framework.

Several avenues of information were pursued: Educational Resources Information Center, government publications, reports, projects, symposium proceedings, and journals. The literature is primarily descriptive narrative. Statistical data are primarily of the descriptive type. Interestingly, the most useful source of information came not from journals but from symposium proceedings and final reports.

Finally, this author uses the term *behaviorally disordered* to describe those children and youth who are

handicapped by their behavior. Behaviorally disordered is the term used in statute in the author's home state and is also the author's personal preference. It is used within this chapter to refer to those children and youth who are handicapped by their behavior and as a result are eligible for services under the regulations of Public Law 94–142 as well as the various social service statutes and regulations that allow or mandate services to individuals with handicapping behavior. In the literature these individuals are referred to as behaviorally disordered, emotionally disturbed, seriously emotionally disturbed, behaviorally handicapped, autistic, socially maladjusted, and so forth. In this chapter the term behaviorally disordered is used inclusively to refer to children identified by all these terms.

Need

The last 8 years have seen a resurgence of interest in the cooperative interface concept as it relates to special education generally. A combination of reasons including statutory mandates, diminishing fiscal resources, and public opinion were primarily responsible for this resurgence. While it is obvious why the focus of this renewed attention is on special education, generally, the result has been a lack of focus on the specific problems of serving the behaviorally disordered population, problems that lend themselves to improvement as a result of interagency collaboration. There is great utility in drawing together information on what has been done and what remains to be done in order to ensure that the behaviorally disordered population receives appropriate, unduplicated services across services agencies.

State of the Art

The first two sections of this discussion deal with cooperative interface in a general fashion. The reasons for supporting cooperative interface and the models for effective cooperative interface are not specific to the behaviorally disordered population. Rather, the rationale for and the delineation of model approaches cut across all categories. The third section looks at the specific types of interface that would be valuable to the behaviorally disordered population. This delineation of valuable interface is drawn primarily from examples that relate specifically to the behaviorally disordered population.

Reasons for Cooperative Interface

It is a common misconception that a variety of federal and state mandates resulted in the attention to interagency collaboration that has arisen and persisted over the past 8 years. In fact, a host of other reasons actually gave rise to this attention to interagency collaboration. The mandates, however, gave a strong impetus to the intensity of the attention which came to be focused on the issue. The following discussions examine many of the initial concerns that gave rise to the interagency collaboration issue in special education and also examine the mandates that spurred the investigation of interagency collaboration.

Initial impetus. While there is no attempt to arrange these reasons for interagency collaboration chronologically, there is some logic to discussing them from broad to narrow philosophical points of view. Services to all handicapped children are organized by function, category, and various eligibility factors (Audette, 1980). Since functions (e.g., education, mental health services, social services) and categories (e.g., behaviorally disordered, mentally retarded) and eligibility criteria (e.g., age, income, severity) overlap, so do services. Thus, it is possible and probable that a given person (for example, a low-income bracket, 11-year-old, behaviorally disordered child who is out of school and neglected) will qualify for assistance from several service providers. The ensuing duplication of services is worse than wasteful in light of the fact that virtually all service providers cite waiting lists, too-large case loads, overworked staff and unserved clients. The justification for this duplication has historically been related to the differing philosophical orientations and regulatory mandates of the various service providers. However, the clear failure rate of all providers with some of their populations would not tend to support the singular correctness of any given philosophy or mandate. Many, probably most, professionals concur with Willner (1972) that "no one discipline is the panacea for troubled children" (p. 13).

Boss (1982) cites "the inevitability of shrinking resources" as a major impetus for cooperative interface (p. 90). Economic constraints are forcing a search for alternatives that allow the maintenance or expansion or services with the same or fewer dollars. Interagency collaboration is a primary vehicle for meeting this goal (Baxter, 1982; Johnson, McLaughlin, & Christensen, 1982). The fact of shrinking resources, coupled with the evidence that many state agencies have interpreted the single line of responsibility concept in *Public Law 94–142* (to be discussed later) to mean that state and local education agencies have sole financial responsibility for all services to children, have put public schools in a particularly difficult position (Joe & Farrow, 1983). The necessity for state and local education agencies to pursue interagency collaboration that delegates cost is an important objective.

Another impetus for interagency collaboration is related to the fiscal issue but is a separate concern. The current political climate continues to advocate an "abandonment of federal responsibilities" (Boss, 1982, p. 90). Boss feels that the block grants are a tangible example of the philosophy of withdrawing federal involvement from services to children and youth. Although the block grant monies have fiscal implications, they are essentially a statement concerning the direction of federal

responsibilities in meeting the needs of children and youth.

Finally, an impetus also related to fiscal concerns involves the "shifting value structure in American society" (Boss, 1982, p. 2). The American taxpayer is increasingly concerned about all tax dollars and will no longer allow tax dollars inefficiently to fund duplicated services (Audette, 1980). While this is a fiscal concern, it is also a concern that represents a perspective that demands closer accountability for the conceptualization of services delivered.

Thus, concerns for duplicated services in the face of unserved clients, retracting fiscal resources, political climate, and value shifts in the tax-paying public have all combined to create a demand for cooperative interface between public schools and other child care systems.

The mandates.. The various legal mandates that support the cooperative interface process are, as is often the case with laws, a reflection of existing concerns as cited above and a spur for additional change of thought and action. The term *mandate* is actually a misnomer. While mandate refers to *requiring* certain behaviors, many forms of legal support to interagency collaboration come in the form of language that *allows* collaborative assessment, shared resources, and so forth. Common usage has conferred the meanings of both obligatory and allowed action to the word mandate.

Since 1970, 35 federal laws have been passed that relate to handicapped persons. Most of these laws were in response to a given crisis or outcry. As a result, the legislation is most often piecemeal, not reflecting a larger plan but, rather, reflecting services created "in direct proportion to the effectiveness of its advocates" (Audette, 1980, p. 26). Audette (1980) suggests that the terms often used to describe some handicaps "(nonadaptive, noncommunicative, perseverative) could more aptly be used to describe the array of organizations and agencies" strengthened or created by that plethora of legislation (p. 27). Given the number of laws and the perception of the unique function of each, it is clear that a role exists for interagency cooperation.

Although there are many forms of legal mandates in additional to federal legislation, few have had greater philosophical and practical impact on interagency cooperation than some sections of Public Law 94–142. Rogers and Farrow (1983) state:

> Several of P.L. 94–142's provisions have led to increased contacts and stronger working relationships between state education agencies (SEAs) and other state human resource agencies. First, the requirement that the SEA act as the single state agency responsible for assuring the provision of special education and related services to all handicapped children in the state changed many SEAs' roles with regard to other state agencies (see 20 U.S.C. 1412 (6)). For example, this provision

197

required SEAs to ensure that educational programs in state institutions complied with federal law — thereby forcing SEAs to exercise new authority over other state agency programs. Second, P.L. 94–142's mandate that education agencies assure the availability of related services led many SEAs to negotiate access to services offered by other human service systems. (p. v)

Many authors have focused on the related services provisions of Public Law 94–142 as being the ones that gave the most impetus to interagency collaboration (Grub & Thompson, 1982; Johnson, McLaughlin, & Christensen, 1982). Perhaps that is because those services, rarely provided within classrooms in 1978, were the most alien to state and local educational personnel who suddenly faced the mandate of assuring the provision of related services to handicapped children. However, the assurance of provision of special education services provided at least as much impetus, particularly for the severely handicapped populations whose ongoing educational programs were often occurring outside of public schools. Additionally, the required team concept written into Public Law 94–142 at the evaluation and program planning stages has generally highlighted the tendency to think in a cooperative interagency mode (Grub & Thompson, 1982).

Another major service of mandated federal support for cooperative interface occurred in 1980 when the US Department of Health, Education and Welfare Education Division General Administrative Regulations (EDGAR) published specific guidelines for educational personnel regarding coordination with other activities (100a580 & 100b580) and methods of coordination (100a581 & 100b581) (Johnson, McLaughlin, & Christensen, 1982; McCormick, 1982). EDGAR states that the agency should to the extent possible, coordinate its project with other activities that are in the same geographic area served by the project and that serve similar purposes and target groups" (pp. 22512–24).

Audette (1980) lists 40 federal programs and/or laws for handicapped children that require or allow services that are part of or should be coordinated with the mandates of Public Law 94–142. These include Crippled Children's Services, Educationally Disadvantaged Children-Handicapped (Public Law 89–313), Handicapped Early Childhood Assistance, and Social Services for Low Income and Public Assistance Recipients (Title XX, Social Security Act). Most recently, 1984 amendments to the Public Health Services Act designed to provide assistance to alcohol, drug abuse, and mental health services set aside a specific percentage of these monies to assist children and adolescents.

Clearly, the requirements of or allowance for a wealth of interagency collaborative efforts has overwhelming support at the federal level. Further, federal agencies themselves are taking a leadership role. Johnson, McLaughlin and Christensen (1982) Point out:

In [an] event of significance to the interagency collaboration movement the Office of Special Education and the Office of Civil Rights have joined in a "Memorandum of Understanding" to coordinate activities in four areas: enforcement, data collection, policy development, and technical assistance in coordinating services to states in the implementation of P.L. 94–142 and P.L. 93–112, Section 504. This memorandum reinforces an ongoing commitment by the Office of Special Education to seek coordinated activities with other agencies as a way of providing services to states to assist in the most efficient provision of services to their handicapped populations. Precursors to this particular memorandum can be found in other agreements, letters of transmittal, and memorandums jointly and separately written by the Office of Special Education and other related federal agencies, for example, Joint Policy Statement/Bureau of Education for the Handicapped and the Bureau of Community Health Services; Cooperative Agreement Between the Office of Child Health Medicaid Bureau and the Bureau of Education for the Handicapped; Cooperative Agreement Between the Education and Vocational Rehabilitation Agencies; Development of Formal Cooperative Agreements Between Special Education, Vocational Rehabilitation, and Vocational Education Programs to Maximize Services to Handicapped Individuals. (p. 396)

Some states have also found it useful to follow the legislative path to ensure interagency cooperation on the part of state and local agencies. An example of this occurred in California where the legislature has passed two laws which required (1) the development of written interagency agreements to assign fiscal responsibilities for providing special education and related services, and (2) a plan to identify and waive, as necessary, all legislative obstacles to interagency collaboration (Rogers & Farrow, 1983).

State agencies, responding to federal or state mandates, have been actively involved in pursuing interagency agreements. As early as 1979, one year after Public Law 94–142 was in full implementation, 44 state education agencies indicated in their annual program plans that they had one or more interagency agreements in place (Hockenberry, 1979). It is, however, these early paper agreements to which McCormick (1982) and Rogers and Farrow (1983) referred when they discussed the disenchantment with early interagency efforts. Nonetheless, it is currently the case that virtually every state education agency now has cooperative agreements of some nature with a range of other child care systems.

The courts have also had some limited opportunity to mandate cooperative interface. In Hawaii, the resulting consent agreement in *Silva et al. v. Board of Education, State of Hawaii* (C.A. #41768) requires that the state education agency has the sole responsibility for the education of handicapped children and orders interagency agreements to be developed. In Tennessee, the *Doe v. Henderson* (C.A. #7980-I) case proceedings resulted in the undertaking of several interagency agreements between state education agencies and other child care systems (Hockenberg, 1979).

Thus, it is apparent that there currently exists a wealth of federal, state, and judicial mandates that require or encourage the development of cooperative interface between state education agencies and other child care systems responsible for handicapped children.

Models for Cooperative Interface

Considering the generally accepted complexity of interagency collaboration, or, perhaps, because of it, there is a surprising dearth of original research and/or thought on the topic. The writings of a few persons (Audette, Magrab, Elder, Johnson, McLaughlin, Martinson) and the Midwest Regional Resource Center Task Force appear to serve as the basis for most material on the analyses and processes of interagency collaboration in special education. The following discussion on the ideal processes for pursuing interagency collaboration draws heavily on their work as well as that of others who have added ideas to the core effort. The limited amount of published information on the topic, provides an unusual opportunity for this review to cover virtually all of the information available in the literature. Thus, although overlap of information in the following sections is generally avoided, it is occasionally allowed as a result of the uncommon opportunity to present original information with all of the subtlety that is occasionally lost in the summary process.

The section begins with some definitions of interagency collaboration, which expand upon the introductory discussion presented earlier. The definitions are followed by a discussion of the need for collaboration as perceived by various authors. The *purposes* of cooperative interface are then discussed, many of which relate to the earlier "impetus" section. The next subtopic reviews some general considerations that must precede the initiation of collaborative planning. Foundations for specific processes are presented. These models are somewhat obscure in their condensed form, but relay some interesting mind-set variables, which precede engaging in the collaborative process. Specific steps in the collaborative process are then delineated. Some of these steps are presented as models for the process, others delineate the steps conceptually. The next discussion is of barriers that may hamper the specific steps, and finally, there is a discussion concerning evaluation of the collaborative process.

Definition. This chapter began with a definition of interagency collaboration written by the Midwest Regional Resource Center Task Force. It stated that interagency collaboration is a process which:

• Encourages and facilitates an open and honest exchange of ideas, plans, approaches, and resources across disciplines, programs, and agencies.

• Enables all participants jointly to define their separate interests in mutually identified needed changes in order to best achieve common purposes.

• Utilizes formal procedures to help clarify issues, define problems, and make decisions relative to solutions (Vol. 1, p. 1).

Johnson, McLaughlin, and Christensen (1982) state:

In its simplest sense an interagency collaborative effort can be viewed as a process through which two or more agencies work together to articulate their separate programs for the purpose of providing special educational and related services to handicapped learners and their families (p. 396).

And Elder and Magrab (1980) define interagency collaboration as '—coordination efforts made by professionals and administrators across different agencies or organizations to ensure that the client is provided appropriate, nonduplicated services (p. 1). The definitions are similar, though not identical. The main threads in these definitions are:

1. Coordination across agencies exists.

2. Coordination is for the purpose of providing services to handicapped individuals.

3. Agencies should be able to pursue their separate purposes within the definition of the common purpose of appropriate services to handicapped children.

This coordination may occur at the systems level, meaning that heads of agencies enter into agreements and practices that commit their entire agencies to certain behaviors. This is certainly the most common perception of interagency collaboration and two of the three terms utilized in this chapter are particularly associated with this perception: interagency collaboration and interagency coordination. This coordination may also occur at a local or personal level, meaning that local level directors may enter into agreements and practices that bind their local agencies to certain behaviors, or that individuals may agree to certain procedures and practices, which they pursue in the course of carrying out their individual responsibilities. Although the terms interagency collaboration and interagency coordination do apply to this set of circumstances, the more common perspective of agency-wide change has been associated with them. The term cooperative interface may be more descriptive of local and/or personal cooperation simply because it does not include the word agency. Despite these differences in usage, the three terms remain synonymous and equally appropriate for all levels of collaboration.

The need for collaboration. Martinson (1982) states that "interorganizational dependency is a logical corollary of organizational autonomy and specialization" (p. 387). If that is so, then the need to collaborate must be great. The child service agencies (e.g., special education, mental health, youth corrections, social services) all specialize not only in certain types of children but also in certain aspects of children. Such specialization does seem to have created the need to coordinate. The literature suggests a wealth of reasons for collaborative measures. McLaughlin and Christensen (1980) refer to many of these reasons as the "driving forces" behind the interagency collaboration movement. Others have concurred with and/or expanded this list of reasons:

1. Pressures from clients, parents, and advocates. As the number and specialization of agencies has grown, clients, their parents, and their advocates have become increasingly disturbed by the difficulty in obtaining a full spectrum of appropriate, unduplicated services.

2. Federal initiatives. The mandates discussed earlier provided both requirements and possibilities for collaboration. State education agencies, suddenly faced with the sole responsibility for assuring provision of services, found themselves to be in organizational structures that did not allow them the authority to control those things for which they were legally responsible.

3. Economic pressures.

4. The need to reduce and/or eliminate duplication of services.

5. The continuing development of new and improved treatment strategies.

6. The need for additional comprehensive services and/or the redistribution of existing services.

7. Inter/intraprofessional pressures, based on the need for continuing education.

8. Fragmented service delivery systems.

9. Overlap in service definitions.

10. Multiple funding bases.

11. Multiple planning bodies.

12. Varying models for service delivery. (McLaughlin & Christensen, 1980; Rogers & Farrow, 1983; Baxter, 1982; Oversight Hearing on Interagency Cooperation, 1985; Greenan & Phelps, 1982).

The list of reasons for pursuing coordinated interface is thorough. Surely every agency lists one or more of those concerns among their own.

Purpose. In one sense, the purpose of cooperative interface is to address the previously listed needs. However, those concerns can be discussed and expanded upon in a positive fashion giving us a set of positive striving goals as opposed to a purpose that reflects running away from concerns. There are six major goals:

1. To pool or maximize resources (Baxter, 1982).

2. To improve the delivery system (Baxter, 1982).

3. To act cooperatively to insure all necessary services to handicapped children and youth (Joe & Farrow, 1983).

4. "To coordinate the therapeutic efforts of groups of people without rejecting their potential contributions to behavior change based on their preferred intervention procedures" (Wood, 1982, p. 117).

5. To focus coordination on agencies that most often serve children (e.g., education, social welfare, legal/judicial/correctional, and medical/mental health (McCormick, 1982).

6. Specifically, to improve the areas of "individualized service planning, organization and delivery of services, program monitoring and reporting and program planning and budgeting" (Regional Resource Centres Task Force, 1979).

Although some of the above purposes overlap, each clearly states a separate component of purposeful interagency collaboration. With purposes in mind, it is possible to take a look at the general considerations that precede a discussion of the specific processes in the task of interagency cooperation. The next two discussions, on general considerations and process specifics, grapple with the question: "How do we facilitate role and rule changes within these organizations to make possible the collaboration that a comprehensive service delivery system requires?" (Wood, 1982, p. 119).

General Considerations. Wood (1982) states that "comprehensive service delivery requires intelligent planning for dealing with a complex group of organizations, each with its own rules for its members, its own environmental constraints, and its own rules for the interactions of its members with the larger environment" (p. 119). This would indicate that the process of interagency collaboration must be a complex and detailed one. Generally speaking, this is true, although alternatives will be discussed later in the chapter.

Prior to delineating specific steps in the interagency process, there are some general considerations to bear in mind that help to keep in focus the issues mentioned in the preceding quote. Although each consideration could be discussed at great length, each is also clear in a simpler statement form. General considerations that persons pursuing cooperative interface should be aware of include:

1. Most successful cooperative arrangements require the commitment of resources: funds or personnel (Wood, 1982);

2. Financial support is the strongest reinforcer of service delivery change and also the least flexible variable (Wood, 1982; Rogers & Farrow, 1983);

3. There should be a focus on changing the behaviors of the systems involved, not the structure of the systems. This will help reduce concerns about "intrusions on turf" (Regional Resource Centres Task Force, 1979; Rogers & Farrow, 1983);

4. The process specifics should begin with "a plan; start small; proceed with order and method; approach each step in a timely persistent fashion and above all, communicate" (Midwest Regional Task Force, 1979);

5. Facilitators with assigned responsibility to pursue cooperative agreement must be utilized. They may or may not be disinterested third parties, but must have skills in group processes and an interest in handicapped persons. Inclusion of higher state government units may help (Regional Resource Center Task Force, 1979; Rogers & Farrow, 1983);

6. There should be a plan to follow an ongoing collaborative process rather than a one-shot experience. (Rogers & Farrow, 1983);

7. "Any number of agencies may become involved in collaborative efforts, depending on the service needs of the population. Typically, one or more of the following have been involved: education, rehabilitation, crippled children services, social services, mental health/mental retardation, and corrections" (Johnson, McLaughlin & Christensen, 1982, p. 396);

8. The collaborative process requires an ecological perspective so that various agencies can intervene in various parts of the handicapped child's environment (Wood, 1982);

9. Since education, mental health, and correction agencies are social organizations, they exhibit norms and values *as organizations*. Therefore, the organization must support the collaboration (Wood, 1982);

10. Schools, parents, and other child care systems must accept joint responsibility for the problem (Wood, 1982);

11. The process must be approached with knowledge of five basic areas in order to select the best basis for various decisions. The areas are: constitutional law, legislation, administrative regulation, legal interpretations, and case law (Martinson, 1982; McLaughlin & Christensen, 1980);

12. It is useful to remember that "disciplines do not exist in their own right" but to meet the needs of handicapped persons (Magrab & Schmidt, 1980).

These general considerations should be viewed as indicating two requisites: (a) a general "mind set" that is helpful to the interagency collaboration process, and (b) sets of information that are necessary to proceed with the interagency collaborative process. Some of these considerations overlap the initial steps of the actual process of interagency collaboration.

Foundations of the Interagency Collaboration Process. Martinson (1982) describes four general models that may form the foundation for the interagency process. This description draws heavily from the work of Levine & White (1961), Benson (1975), and Zeitz (1980).

Interorganizational models may provide a basis for conceptualizing processes necessary for negotiating interagency agreements. Though such agreements may vary in regard to levels of formality and extensiveness of the collaborative efforts, the basic dynamics of interorganization relationships appear helpful in developing effective planning and implementation processes.

The exchange model (Levine & White, 1961) assumes voluntary relationships motivated by the expectation that unique and common goals will be more effectively achieved via collaborative activities. This model further assumes an economic base in that organizations lacking in resources will be more likely to develop interactive service arrangements. The lack of resources leads to exchange in accessing program components essential to an organization but not available within it. The perceived or designated domains for the respective organizations provide the basis for identifying internally available or externally needed program elements. This voluntary, mutual problem-solving model has generally characterized much of the collaborative program development over the past several decades.

The political economy model (Benson, 1975), focuses more straight-forwardly on interrelationships motivated by intended acquisition of authority and financial support. This model suggests that interagency development relates to the use of authority to accrue resources within the context of political economics and more general conditions affecting the related organizations.

The dialectical model (Zeitz, 1980) proposes interorganizational relationships as a process of constant renegotiation based on "antagonistic cooperation,": i.e., resolution of immediate conflicts leading to new points of issue. This model assumes that organizations are concerned with production of resources to establish their domains and stresses control of interaction networks. Interorganizational conflict is both system integrative and system disintegrative; e.g., conflict resolution leads to new conflicts. Internal status and external interactions are both constrained by resource structures and relationship networks. The dialectical model departs significantly from the assumptions of consensus and mutuality common to the historically accepted exchange model (p. 390–91).

Any of these models may be used depending upon the specific situations which exist in a given state or local area. The general model orientation may affect the amount of emphasis given to any particular step in the processes discussed below, but it will not affect the need to give some consideration to each step.

FIGURE 1
A Process Outline for Interagency Planning—State

Establishing the Need	*Document* needs, rationale and plans for initiation of inter-program collaboration project 1.0	*Define* service delivery population(s) of interest 2.0
Establishing the Data Base	*Identify* agencies and programs serving or authorized to serve the target population(s) 3.0	*Define* current program policies and services responsibilities of identified programs 4.0
Identifying the Planning Targets	*Compare* the analyzed programs to identify program modifications which would enable satisfaction of the needs and rationale for improved collaboration and specify the desired modifications 5.0	*Specify* the funding decisions necessary for the specified program modifications, and determine funding options and constraints affecting those decisions 6.0
Establishing Interagency Provisions	*Establish* the organizational capacity and authority base for interagency decision-making 7.0	*Negotiate* specific agreements between or among agencies/programs as necessary to satisfy needs and rationale for improved interagency collaboration 8.0
Assuring Collaboration in Service Delivery	*Determine* appropriate strategies for implementing necessary program modifications 9.0	*Enable* implementation of program modifications at the service delivery level 10.0

Reproduced from the Midwest Regional Resource Center

Specific Steps in the Interagency Collaborative Process. The most heavily drawn on work in regard to the interagency process is that of the Midwest Regional Resource Center Task Force. Figure 1 shows the "Process Outline for Interagency Planning" suggested for state level efforts. Figure 2 is the process for local level efforts. These two processes are articulated in detail in two lengthy volumes which delineate numerous strategies and tasks for each major step on the outline.

Martinson (1982) suggests a slightly different process, but one which has many steps common with the Task Force (1979) outline:

1. Identification of the statutory mandates, state and federal, which specify agency responsibilities and service requirements. A summary matrix organizing these data is very helpful. This exercise makes

basic information regarding needs and requirements visible for mutual review and negotiation.

2. Translation of the mandates responsibilities and authorities into statements of objective(s) for each agency, permitting review by individual agencies and identification of interagency gaps or overlaps.

3. Planning to consider the specific program functions and operations projected by each agency. This step is essential for organization of data for interagency agreements and management of related program units.

4. The identification of necessary resources (fiscal, human, and physical) to specify the minimum of support necessary to implement program operations. Negotiation of these resource requirements

on an interagency basis is difficult due to the inherent competitive nature of the process.

5. Negotiation of the procedures for administering jointly shared responsibilities. This step is essential but complicated by the common requirement to designate one agency as having final program authority, particularly since the underlying legislative mandates usually establish the basis for single agency primacy. The evolution of the Department of Human Resources illustrates the difficulties involved as well as providing a model for review.

6. Integration of individual agencies' specific evaluation and accountability needs with those of related agencies. Specific reciprocal procedures must be developed to minimize duplicative or conflicting data bases. Many agencies are becoming increasingly resistant to random uncoordinated requests for data.

7. Establishing procedures to assure processing of planning, management, monitoring, and evaluation data among participating agencies.

8. Procedures for use of program monitoring and evaluation data for negotiation of program revision(s) among the participating agencies. This component provides the basis for ongoing program adaptation and improvement. (pp. 391–392)

The Midwest Regional Resource Center Task Force (1979) outlines suggest the need for slightly different processes by virtue of delineating one for state level and one for local level collaboration. Martinson (1982) expands that concept to indicate that the planning process should consider client program and systems level collaboration:

FIGURE 2

A Process Outline for Interagency Planning—Local

Establishing the Need	*Determine* needs and rationale for initiation of interprogram collaboration project 1.0	*Define* service delivery population of interest 2.0
Establishing the Data Base	*Identify* agencies and programs serving or authorized to serve the target population(s) and contact agency administrator 3.0	*Define* current program policies and services responsibilities of identified programs 4.0
Identifying the Planning Targets	*Compare* local programs and procedures across agencies to identify gaps, overlaps, constraints, and other linkages 5.0	*Identify* local policy and procedures wherein modifications would enable satisfaction of need and rationale for collaboration and *specify* the needed modifications 6.0
Establishing Interagency Provisions	*Determine* which modifications can be made on the local level and incorporate these modifications in a local interprogram agreement 7.0	
Assuring Collaboration in Service Delivery	*Enable* implementation of interprogram modifications 8.0	*Implement* local evaluation functions 9.0

Reproduced from the Midwest Regional Resource Center

Client level coordination is illustrated by integration of separate services for an individual to eliminate service gaps or duplication. Program level interagency collaboration involves integration of administrative structures or functions to facilitate operational coordination. Systems level planning focuses on broader systems of services beyond the administrative constraints of particular agencies (Magrab & Elder, 1979). The relationship between programmatic planning and policy development must also be considered. (p. 392)

A final example of a model for the development of interagency collaboration is suggested by McNulty & Soper (1982). They outline both dynamic issues and discrete components.

Dynamic Issues:	(1) communication
	(2) group dynamics and behavior
	(3) conflict resolution strategies
	(4) management of transition
	(5) commitment
Discrete Components	(1) determine shared needs, common goals
	(2) definition of roles and responsibility
	(3) determine leadership roles
	(4) commitment of time and resources
	(5) knowledge of external forces
	(6) identification of and focus on target populations
	(7) utilization of procedural guidelines
	(8) planning for benefit/cost analysis
	(9) determination of evaluation procedures

Some elements of these models for the interagency process have been emphasized by other writers. Audette (1980) emphasizes that interagency agreements must recognize the "constraints, requirements and discretionary authority of each agency" (p. 36) and that there must be a listing of the methods for cooperatively allocating resources, while Wood (1982) states that specific program ownership (in the case of local collaboration) should be determined "up front." McCormick (1982) suggests that in addition to looking for common goals, participants should seek consensus on alternatives for some individual goals. The Regional Resource Center Task Force (1979) also suggests that agreed-upon changes should result in "specific roles and responsibilities be(ing) assigned to positions rather than persons in each agency" (p. 7).

Consideration of individual needs, attention to the general considerations, regard for the assumptions of a model, and selection of some form of a delineated pro-

cess should put agencies on the road to effective interagency collaboration.

Barriers. Several authors have cited common problems that hamper the interagency collaborative process, either at its onset or as the collaborative efforts proceeds. Advance knowledge of these is helpful to participants interested in avoiding problems. The following list of barriers is summarized and condensed from the work of several individuals.

1. Fragmented fiscal support, including the failure to coordinate budgets with the service mandates and a lack of clarity on "first dollar responsibility" (Johnson, McLaughlin & Christensen, 1982; LaCour, 1982);

2. Variability of or disagreement on target populations and client eligibility (Johnson, McLaughlin & Christensen, 1982);

3. Differing views on the necessary confidentiality of information and transference of records (Johnson, McLaughlin & Christensen, 1982; LaCourt, 1982);

4. Lack of sustained availability of key people to facilitate planning and pursue activities. This may result from the pressures of ongoing commitments or staff turnover (Johnson, McLaughlin & Christensen, 1982);

5. Competitiveness of long-established institutions/agencies and their boards and staffs (Elder & Magrab, 1980; Johnson, McLaughlin & Christensen, 1982);

6. Poor communication as evidenced by not including staff in planning efforts, awkwardness in sharing information in a "foreign" vocabulary, no centralized information base, and disparate procedures for information dissemination (Elder & Magrab, 1980; Johnson, McLaughlin & Christensen, 1982);

7. Resistant personnel as a result of poor definition of agency responsibility and authority, variability of roles and responsibilities across and within agencies, difficulty in defining decision-making rules among developers neglecting the cultivation of *direct* provider acceptance/understanding, and varying priorities (Johnson, McLaughlin & Christensen, 1982; Elder & Magrab, 1980; LaCour, 1982).

8. Lack of organizational structure to bring agencies together around mutual interests and parochial interests of agencies that make them myopic to the needs of the broader community (Elder & Magrab, 1980);

9. The temptation of system delivery designers to become preoccupied and fixated on the system design rather than the functional role of the system (Elder & Magrab, 1980).

Martinson (1982) groups the concepts in these various barriers into a provocative set of "syndromes that can plague the interagency collaborative process":

1. The "Competition/Cooperation Paradox" Syndrome. History suggests that cooperation is basically "coordinated competition." Agencies will commonly cooperate to more effectively compete with other groups for program and resources. This

syndrome is particularly acute during austerity periods.

2. The "Poker Chip" Syndrome. This behavior is based on the assumption that a finite number of chips (status, power, or funds) exist. Practitioners believe that no one will voluntarily lose "chips" and cooperation must be arranged to force "winning." Conversely, some people assume an infinite number of chips and everyone can win by generating more chips to be shared. Only the very optimistic adhere to this latter view.

3. The "Inability to Escape the Penalties of Preliminary Success" Syndrome. Such an attitude is based on immediate pain reduction, e.g., "I don't need you any more now that my immediate problem is solved!" The result is a series of sporadic relationships based on the notion that "Now that I have improved my position in cooperation with you, I can compete on my own."

4. The "Tower of Babel" Syndrome. This condition relates to compulsive efforts of each agency or discipline to develop a unique language of terms and acronyms to describe who they are and what they do. Ready communication is precluded by the need for translation of these diverse languages.

5. The "Professional Preservation" Syndrome. These symptomatologies relate to the hazard to individuals of generating new, innovative program objectives supported by a reordering of functions designed for other purposes. Simplistically, innovative program functions may produce innovative results. Descriptions of innovative program goals based on reordering old functions will not.

6. The "Agency Incest" Syndrome. The notion of territorial imperatives provides a basis for a high level of agency partisanship. The need for professional separateness and identity is augmented by an interagency or intradisciplinary caste system. This condition affects interagency "trust relationships" and the capacity to engage in individual or collective risk behavior.

7. The "Divide and Defeat Ourselves" Syndrome. This is an immediate stage of the preceding syndrome, evidenced by the position that "Unless I get what I want, no one is going to get anything." The condition has basis in the excessive, overly rigid attempts to achieve visibility and status for particular agencies.

8. The "Snatching Defeat from the Jaws of Victory" Syndrome. Such a syndrome represents the most advanced state of the "Agency Incest" and the "Divide and Defeat Ourselves" Syndromes. It occurs when subgroups or units of the enterprise take action to compromise general program objectives to achieve specific, individual advantages. The lack of cohesiveness and the level of inter-unit competition become evident to external control agencies. The problems become acute when legislative and associated resource control bodies are involved.

This syndrome tends to generate autonomous but fragmented program support and negates the potential for continuity in comprehensive, long-term planning. Common responses to the absence of self-initiated regulations are: (1) "Since you can't regulate yourselves, we'll do it for you" and (2) "When those of you having specific program responsibilities can coherently define and document your needs, we will consider priorities for support." (pp. 392–393.

Despite the lengthy, almost overwhelming list of barriers, there are two which are cited most often as the greatest barriers to interagency collaboration: lack of resources as reflected in both money and personnel; and communication (Gedo, 1978; Johnson, McLaughlin, Christensen, 1982; Wood, 1982).

Evaluation. The idea of evaluating interagency collaboration is not well articulated in the literature. However, as in most service endeavors it is not only useful but essential to evaluate efforts that require the great amount of work and personnel time that goes into interagency collaboration. McLaughlin & Elder (1982) describe several types of evaluation questions that may be pursued: (a) has the service population been accurately described? (b) is the agreement technically and politically sound? (c) is the implementation according to agreement? (d) are the services accessible? (e) have conflicts been resolved or managed? (f) are service goals met? (g) what are the driving and restraining forces for the given plan? Clearly, one can evaluate any or all parts of collaborative agreements. Each question may be evaluated in a different manner, although Flaherty, Barry & Swift (1978) suggest that the perusal of written records is least obtrusive. Good evaluation is essential because "the very complexity of the system, not to mention human factors and other barriers, will defeat anything less than a very well-planned, systematic effort" (Midurst Regional Resource Center Task Force, 1979, p. 7).

Interface Needed with Direct Care Systems

Public schools have been given the responsibility to assure that a handicapped child receives all necessary special education and related services. At this point in the chapter, attention becomes focused specifically on behaviorally disordered individuals and the child care systems which most often serve those children and youth: public schools; mental health, corrections and social services. If interagency collaboration, as described in the previous section, were to exist on a large scale, what would the interface between public schools and other child care systems serving behaviorally disordered students look like? Probably the best answer to that question is to look at some examples of promising cooperative interface that have operated on behalf of behaviorally disordered students. From those examples it is possible to draw some conclusions what co-operative interface, in its "state of the art" form, consists of.

Promising Cooperative Interface Between Public Schools and Other Child Care Agencies. In this discussion *public schools* may be represented by a State Department of Education, a local school district, or even a few schools within a district. The same is true for *other child care agencies*, that is, the examples may be those of a state level agency or an individual institution/program. By far the largest percentage of cooperative interface efforts on behalf of behaviorally disordered children and youth occur between public schools and mental health services. Some of those efforts are mandated or encouraged at a state agency level. Many occur within a more limited geographical context: counties or local school districts.

An early collaborative effort in Memphis, Tennessee was reported by Willner (1972) and Garret et al (1979). The City Board of Education and the Department of Mental Health as well as a private social service agency which provided foster care for emotionally disturbed children participated in the much written about Project TREAT. Rotating meeting sites and meeting chairs in order to create joint decision making on a paper and affective level, Project TREAT staff determined that the City Board of Education would pay the salaries of teaching staff while the mental health center paid the salaries of the therapeutic recreation staff who served emotionally disturbed children. Screening and selection as well as service was coordinated between agencies. Since the staff was well aware of general methodological differences, they determined to map out a unified system, agreeing in advance on philosophy, goals, intake procedures, responsibilities, and general operating procedures. They "found that once [they] can agree on [their] *basic* objectives and goals in working with the child and his family, [then] other differences become relatively minor" (p. 14). While the Project TREAT experience was a successful one on this scale, both Willner and Garret recommend that a larger program (one expanded within district or without) would require a central administration as opposed to the shared administration by current staff.

Sheare & Larson (1978) write of cooperative interface between the Fairfax County-Falls Church (VA) Community Center for Mental Health and the Fairfax County Public Schools. This highly populous area has a very large school district. These two agencies jointly operate four programs for seriously emotionally disturbed students which include three elementary day schools and one adolescent residential center for males. Their arrangement for financial support determines that all teaching staff and materials are the responsibility of the public schools, the psychological, psychiatric and social work staff are supported by the mental health budget, and the physical operations are supported by

the budget of the agency which owns the facility (two each). These programs have joint administrators whose responsibility it is to coordinate the educational and clinical staff as they carry out the educational/therapy plan.

A key element in the successful implementation and operation of the joint programs is cooperative planning. The single most destructive obstacle to hurdle is program control. Program ownership, if not clearly delineated, invariably leads to power struggles between agencies and results in disjointed staff relationships. Initial planning efforts were aimed at establishing program ownership and control issues, with the realization that failure to do so would result in hidden agendas and program failure (Sheare & Larson, 1978, p. 543).

Sheare & Larson go on to delineate the need for the various agency personnel to agree on basic assumptions of the services. Those assumptions might be: (a) an educational service/program with mental health support; (b) a mental health program with educational support; (c) an equal thrust program with different staff working on different goals; (d) various others. The selection of assumption is probably less critical to program success than agreement on an assumption. This particular cooperative effort selected different assumptions concerning the staff and their rules for each of the four programs. Just as the principal's style sets the tone for a school building, Sheare and Larson suggest that success of cooperative interface of this nature is dependent upon the interaction of the joint administrators. Further, "in those cases where program difficulties are severe and repetitive, the most functional solution may be to replace one or both of the managers" (p. 544).

In 1980 Barr and Delfava reported on a day treatment program for preschoolers, many with behavioral problems, which was jointly served by the public school district and the community mental health center. Administered by a team consisting of an educator, a mental health specialist and a team coordinator, the public schools agreed to provide the educational staff and instructional materials. The mental health budget supports the mental health staff and the therapeutic materials. While this program selected developmental therapy as its framework, Barr and Delfava state that the specific framework is not as important as the agreement on *one* set of assumptions/goals so that everyone is not "doing their own thing." Their joint sequential referral-planning process results in a I.E.T.P. (individualized educational and treatment plan).

The School Mental Health Cooperative for Seriously Emotionally Disturbed is a federally funded project reported by Mirkes (1981) in which the public schools, the Community Mental Health of South Dade County, Florida program, and the Children's Psychiatric Center entered into a "contractual cooperative arrangement." Among them, these agencies provide a comprehensive

FIGURE 3

Factors leading to the development of special education/vocational rehabilitation cooperative agreements

	Special Education	Vocational Rehabilitation
Problem	No experience with vocational or work training programs.	No experience working with the retarded.
	No model for preparing the retarded for employment.	No source of appropriate referrals.
	No resources to purchase medical evaluation or sheltered workshop services.	Lack of staff with training to provide counseling, job placement, and followup service for the retarded.
Need	Funds to purchase services.	Retarded clients ready to benefit from rehabilitation services.
	A model for work training.	Training for vocational counselors to work with retarded clients.
	Training for staff in vocational counseling, placement, and followup techniques.	More staff time to identify and supervise on-the-job training.
Available Resources	Special education teachers, educable mentally impaired students, and diagnostic staff.	Funds to purchase service and rehabilitation counselors.
Cooperative Agreement	School gets use of Vocational Rehabilitation funds.	School diagnoses and refers appropriate clients to Vocational Rehabilitation
	Vocational Rehabilitation counselor helps school staff set up on-the-job training program.	School staff provides intensive counselling and supervises on-the-job training.
Results	Special Education students get jobs and graduate at no additional cost to the school.	The number and percent of retarded clients rehabilitated increases and the cost per rehabilitation is reduced because of diagnosis, counseling and other services provided by the school.

Reproduced from Baxter, J. M. (1982). Solving problems through cooperation. *Exceptional Children, 48,* 400–407.

range of services: diagnostic and educational classrooms, individual education and treatment plans, parent training, support therapy, individual and group therapy, tracking between schools and mental health services and consultation to teachers and counselors.

In Rhode Island the state education agency:
Used part of its *P.L. 94–142* set-aside funds to issue an RFP soliciting joint proposals between LEAs and Community Mental Health Centers (CMHC's) for services to severely handicapped students with behavioral disorders. The SEA funded three localities in which services were expanded and a plan for treating severely handicapped children was subsequently advanced (Rogers & Farrow, 1983, p. vi).

Some cooperative interface arrangements are fairly informal by comparison to the above examples. They can be, nonetheless, effective. One situation that occurs entails space and personal sharing between schools and mental health programs. The public schools may provide a teacher for a classroom housed in a mental health center or vice versa. This arrangement constitutes cooperative interface in some cases. In other cases it does not. This will be discussed later.

Cooperative interface between public schools and various agencies serving the delinquent population is

the focus of other agreements. Although critical, there appear to be few such promising efforts. The ones outlined below are dated and at a state level.

The 1973 agreement between the Pennsylvania Departments of Education and Welfare was spurred by concerns about the effects of institutionalization on delinquents. Initial directions focused on the improvement of educational services to the committed juvenile population including: "assessment of student needs, professional staff development, program development, and program evaluation" (Pittinger, 1976, p. 39). The parties then focused on the financial issues and the efficient flow of money for services to the educational program of the young people concerned (Pittinger, 1976).

In an effort to "treat symptoms of delinquency early" (Powell, 1972, p. 19), the Oklahoma Department of Institutions and Social Services funded an interagency demonstration project in cooperation with the State Department of Public Schools and the State Department of Mental Health (Powell, 1972). This project assigned four social workers to four elementary schools in order to accept referrals for any type of problem. The focus was on grades K-3. The prevention concept resulted in social workers trying to match referred children and their families to an appropriate community service.

Other types of cooperative interface include efforts to ensure educational continuity from hospital situations to school (Mirkes, 1981), and a cooperative arrangement between the San Diego Public Schools and the San Diego Children's Home (a private facility). In the latter partnership, the children's home supports physical facilities for five classes of emotionally disturbed children. Three of the classes are for residentially placed children and is these classes treatment and education are autonomous units. Two of the classes are day treatment programs operated on a team concept. The public schools are responsible for the teachers, aides and 95% of the instructional materials.

Vocational education for behaviorally disordered students has been another area in need of collaborative interface. While not limited to the behaviorally disordered population, Rogers and Farrow (1983) discuss two examples of promising interface at a state level:

> The Special Education Division of Michigan's Department of Education, working with the Vocational Education Division of the same Department and the State Division of Rehabilitation Services, has developed policies to facilitate and stimulate improved secondary level vocational services. An interagency agreement developed at the state level outlines a general delivery system which LEAs can adapt to local conditions. After resolving the major impediments to collaboration at the state level, staff of the three agencies provided intensive technical assistance to LEAs, as well as conducting joint inservice training to staff of all the agencies.
>
> The Massachusetts SEA issued an RFP soliciting joint Special Education/Vocational Education programs from LEAs. After competitive proposals were submitted, forty-six awards were made. Local agencies accepting the funds agreed that local special education and vocational education monies would be used in addition to state seed money, and that local support eventually would replace start-up funds (p. x).

Baxter (1982) presents a "summary of how the special educational/vocational rehabilitation cooperative agreement process was used to meet the needs of both agencies to improve services" (p. 492). (See Figure 3.) In this case the population in question was mentally retarded students. But parallels are obvious to the behaviorally disordered population.

Finally, there are some collaborative efforts that are multiagency in focus. Randall (1975) outlines a coordinated service delivery system for disturbed adolescents. Thirteen agencies each have representatives along with lay persons on a board of representatives which operates an entry center. The funding is centralized and presumably follows the adolescent to their recommended service(s). Unfortunately, Randall does not address what role, if any, the public schools play. Similarly, the Direction Service, on a case-by-case basis, refers individuals

to appropriate services and serves as case managers (Elder & Magrab, 1980).

Personnel: speech and language clinicians, physical therapists, physicians, nurses, dental hygienists, nurse midwives, and dieticians are the focus of inservice aimed at encouraging coordination and cooperation among the various agencies' services (Del Polito, 1983). Despite funding and "turf" problems, the focus is on interdisciplinary training to increase alliances in health education.

Gromanda (1975) describes a neighborhood advocacy system for emotionally disturbed children in which health services, day care, the ministerial services, counseling and day and residential treatment are available options.

Summary of State of Art Practices. Clearly, there are some examples of cooperative interface that, if not state of the art, are certainly promising. The common threads of these cooperative efforts begin to be apparent as enough examples are reviewed. While each cooperative effort is unique in many ways, some patterns emerge. Thus, state of the art practices in cooperative interface for the behaviorally disordered include:

1. Financial sharing. Each agency, at whatever level, bears some responsibilities for physical, staff, or consumable assets.

2. Agreement on a single assumption or philosophy that accepts the value of the perspectives of separate parties.

3. Joint administration, not just in appearance, but in practice.

4. Development of vocabulary which incorporates perspectives of all parties (i.e., individualized education/treatment plan).

5. State support via facilitating agreements, REPs, etc.

Clearly some agencies have "taken to heart" the previously discussed models for interagency collaboration.

State of Practice

What should be, what can be, and actual examples of good practice are sometimes at variance with the existing situation. That is unfortunately the case with cooperative interface between public schools and other child care systems for behaviorally disordered students. In a general sense the reality could be described by a review of the restraining forces listed in an earlier section. However, specific examples may give more meaning to those barriers. Prior to a discussion of what we're doing wrong it might be useful to consider a thought forwarded by the Regional Resource Center Task Force (1979):

> There are no villains in the play, and these problems are not due to lack of skill, expertise, commitment, or concern on the part of professionals and agencies. Rather the problem is one of complexity and resulting inertia. It has taken many years, hundreds of

laws and thousands of regulations to achieve the current state of affairs. The complexities are not likely to change in the foreseeable future regardless of efforts to reorganize, control, redirect, or curtail the system. Collaboration among agencies seems to be the only practical way to deal with the problems and confusions (p. 2).

Interface as it Exists

Some of the restraining forces which impact cooperative interface appear to have most relevance to the concerns of the behaviorally disordered population. These will be addressed below.

Effect of Federal and State Agreements. Despite the various federal and state interagency agreements that were designed to enforce or encourage similar moves at the local level, there is little evidence to support a belief that those agreements have been effective in fostering real cooperative interface at the local level. They have often fostered similar paperwork but have seldom resulted in effective interface (Hershberger, 1981). Even in states where the state level agreements have combined resources to expand services, there is a breakdown at the local level. McCormick (1982) feels that this may be a function of inexperience in "teaming" with professionals rather than resistance to the concept. Hershberger (1981), in a study of effectiveness and cost of state level agreements in California, found that there was little local impact from state level agreements. Reasons for this appeared to be that: (a) local education agencies saw little benefit from the agreements; (b) rural areas saw even less value accruing from agreements; (c) agreements were not written specifically enough to be of value; (d) agreements merely committed to writing the current practices; and (e) most agreements did not specify fiscal issues. Whatever the combination of problems, state level examples have rarely, of themselves, produced cooperative interface at the local level.

Agency Organization. Human service agencies at a state or local level are usually organized on a pyramidal model. This model utilizes a vertical responsibility and decision-making chain. "The pathology of the pyramidal model used by most human service agencies" (p. 55) is that this vertical authority results in: (a) a reduction of personalized relationships; (b) an internalization of roles; and (c) a decreased search for alternatives (McNulty & Soper, 1982). These problems result in "predictable behavior" on the part of employees, i.e., "rigid" behavior. The ridigity and decrease of searches for alternatives does not bode well for cooperative interface. As we have already discussed, effective interface requires the ability to accept altered assumptions and creative ways to meet new goals. Since interagency

agreements must have the support of local staff who have the least latitude in the pyramidal structure, it is not surprising that local staff resistance often prevails (Hershberger, 1981).

Fiscal Specificity. Local service delivery systems for behaviorally disordered students have a tendency to view cooperative interface as something less than that if fiscal matters are not shared. Local education agencies often see only funding, not agreements, as the issue (Hershberger, 1981). That element is, in fact, present in virtually all of the "model" state and local practices discussed previously. Wood (1982) states:

> As emotional disturbance is often generalized across several situations, both in and out of the school, an IEP drawing on outside resources outside of the school would be very desirable. For the present, however, the school remains the only system delegated by law to provide free services to emotionally disturbed children and youth (p. 122).

Given that, it is understandable that local education agencies are suspicious of cooperative interface that does not delineate fiscal responsibilities.

"Turf". The term "turf issues" is often listed among the reasons for intractable behavior by persons and agencies who desire power or a disproportionate share of resources and has often come to connote greedy bullheadness. In fact, turf issues arise not only from drives for power and resources, but also from legitimate philosophical and methodological issues. For that reason, this author would prefer to see the word "turf" eliminated from discussions of agency differences which extend beyond power and resources. No doubt there are instances of turf problems. More often, however, the issues are concerned with legitimate differences in service approaches. Sheare (1978) states:

> Although logic may dictate that the best approach for dealing with children with severe emotional problems is through the combined efforts of both educators and mental health professionals, these programs often experience systems difficulties or conflicts prohibiting their operations. There has been a mutual lack of awareness or understanding of the goals, motivations and operating procedures of the other (p. 542).

Thus control and power struggles ensue, based upon a belief in the correctness of one's own perspective (supported, of course, by the pyramidal structure).

Severity. Sheare & Larson (1978), in the preceding quote, specifically refers to the logic of cooperative interface for severely disturbed children. Wood (1982) indicates that most cooperative efforts for behaviorally disordered students occur for those most severely disordered. Based on data collection from states' annual program plans and from personal interviews with state and local level people in five states. Huntze and Grosenick (1980) concur that most cooperative interface occurs on behalf of seriously behaviorally disordered students. While this is necessary, and a good starting point, there remain two problems: (a) even for seriously behaviorally disordered students the interface is inadequate; and (b) many mildly behaviorally disordered children and youth would also benefit from extensive cooperative interface.

Duplication and Tracking. Two additional, often cited concerns are those of duplication of service and the difficulty of tracking individuals among services. In recent Oversight Hearings on Interagency Cooperation (1985) a repeated concern was that of duplicating services, especially evaluation. A child initially seen by one agency and evaluated may experience another complete evaluation at an agency to which he or she is referred. Each agency, often under mandate, prefers its own evaluative procedure. The nonduplicative alternatives might include: (a) an agency accepting all or part of another agency's recent evaluation, or (b) each agency being responsible for part of a total evaluation.

In regard to tracking problems, agencies often find that they are unaware of previous services received by a behaviorally disordered student. When a child leaves an agency, files may be closed and no follow-up exists. Often, an agency is aware of a previous service but is unable to secure records from that agency in order to facilitate the current service. Reasons for that may include: (a) records are not sent in a timely fashion; (b) records are not sent at all as a result of poor planning or follow-through by the sending agency, or (c) confidentiality of records rules may preclude all or part of the information being forwarded (Grosenick & Huntze, 1980; Nichol, 1974). Whatever the reason, children and youth are, at the very least, inconvenienced and, at the worst, inappropriately served when services are duplicated and information is not communicated between agencies.

Cooperative Interface Which Isn't. There are many examples in which two or more agencies provide services to the same child or population but no real interface occurs. Some examples of these situations are discussed below. Despite the fact that these activities are often "billed" as cooperative interface, they qualify only as interface. Purnell (1972) and Gatti and Coleman (1976) both describe one-way interaction, that is, one agency offers assistance to another in the form of coming on-site and suggesting to the "receiving" agency how they might better solve their problems. Gatti and Coleman

(1976) describe a weekly consultation to school personnel by mental health personnel. On a case-by-case basis the mental health staff made suggestions to school staff concerning how to handle a child and indicate when family therapy is indicated (which the school must request). The entire process was unconnected with special education (perhaps as a function of the year) and suggests a one-way flow of information. Similarly, Purnell (1972) describes an interface in which a volunteer agency offered group counseling services to schools that were receptive, that is, the principal was supportive, and the schools allowed sessions during the school day. Again, the value of the service is not suspect, but the amount of cooperative interface is. A variation on the one-way interface occurs when an agency provides liaison services to the public schools only when the agency determines that the child can benefit from the school setting. The placement decision and recommendations are unilateral (Broten, 1972). While interface occurs, it is not cooperative.

Yet another variation on the one-way flow of assistance can occur when an agency employs a liaison to assist in transitions from one placement to another. In this case the receiving agency is willing to accept assistance from the liaison but has no mechanism for proactive involvement. Thus, if the local education agency or local mental health center employs a liaison to assist in transitions then information is shared; if not, then the agency makes no attempt to gather the information. Further, the "receiving agency" may or may not have useful mechanisms for absorbing and utilizing the shared data (Huntze and Grosenick, 1980). The success of the liaison concept is greatly increased when two or more agencies jointly employ the liaison, as occurs in a program described by Wood (1982).

Another form of interface that has great and often met potential, but which is sometimes hollow in the cooperative sense is that of public schools and mental health centers conducting services in the other's facilities (Noel, 1982; Huntze and Grosenick, 1980). If the staff who provide the "outside" service integrate themselves (or are allowed to do so) into the environment, then cooperative interface occurs. If the service provider remains an isolated individual providing a service not coordinated with the home environment, then limited interface exists and there is no cooperation beyond the sharing of physical space.

Finally, interdisciplinary efforts are often confused with interagency ones. Such practices as including persons from various disciplines on the evaluation team (McCormick, 1982) or when an agency employs a consultant (McCormick, 1982) or full-time staff person from another discipline (Wood, 1982) do not constitute interagency collaboration. Once again, this is not to negate the value of such endeavors. It is only to point out that interagency cooperation is different from simply employing other perspectives within one's own agency.

While "cooperative interface which isn't" may not represent the goal of cooperative interface, it may represent a starting point. To the extent that it represents a more open way of thinking on the part of any agency, it has the potential to serve as a foundation for full cooperative interface.

Exclusion/Extrusion

Despite the number of human services available from numerous agencies, it is still possible, and in the case of the behaviorally disordered adolescent, likely, that a child can be excluded or extruded from the system. Exclusion connotes a deliberate process by which individuals are removed from services. Extrusion connotes a deliberate or nondeliberate series of events that pushes individuals out of services. In some cases, behaviorally disordered children do not respond as hoped to the selected services and the agency cannot or does not pursue other agencies as an option. Grosenick and Huntze (1980) delineate several common ways for removing these individuals from the school system. Sometimes individuals simply "fall between the regulatory cracks," not fitting exactly into any agency's population description (Oversight Hearings, 1985). In either event, behaviorally disordered children do not receive necessary services.

Needs and Recommendations

The following suggestions are offered with the greatest humility. The complexity of interagency cooperation generally and as it affects behaviorally disordered students appears overwhelming to those who have made no study of the topic, and worse to those who have. Drawing on patterns that appear in the literature as well as specific suggestions offered by some researchers, the following needs and recommendations are organized within the following topics: federal and state level, local level, training, research.

Federal and State Level

There are several areas in which federal and state education agencies can make improvements. In addition to discussing what improvements can be made, one section deals with some ideas for how those improvements might be facilitated.

Agreements. Initially, it is important for federal and state level agencies to continue pursuing the development of interagency agreements despite the difficulty or concerns about the outcome (Grosenick & Huntze, 1980). Conceptually, it is easier to improve an existing agreement than to embark on activity that has had no "ground broken." Also, there is some evidence that there is benefit from being involved in the process regardless of the eventual judgment on the product

(Hershberger, 1981). If problematic or "paper only" agreements exist then it is imperative to pursue alteration in those agreements. It may require monitoring (to be discussed later) to determine the utility of existing agreements. LaCour (1982) indicates that useful agreements at the state level need not be vague or rigid. He delineates these points as characteristic of a useful state agreement:

1. The language is simple and clear. Anyone who reads it should understand what has been agreed to and who will implement the activities.
2. It is systematically written and has sections that (a) describe the reason for writing the agreement; (b) identify the responsibilities of each agency and the method for performing those responsibilities; (c) identify the standards each agency must meet when performing an activity; (d) describe the process for exchanging information on common clients; and (e) describe the method for modifying the agreement.
3. It is flexibly written, focusing on the desired outcome, not the process for getting there.
4. It does not jeopardize an agency's funding or turf. An agreement should serve to clarify each of these issues.
5. The mutual benefit is evident. This will enhance the opportunity for future agreement as well as the full implementation of current agreement (p. 266).

After reviewing examples of state agreements, some apparently effective, some not, it appears that the above guidelines serve as a useful recommendation to both types of agreements.

Understanding Components of Interagency Cooperation. In one respect, this comes under the heading of training recommendations, which are addressed later. In another, however, it represents a portion of a job description and a set of competencies that must be part of the expertise of federal and state level agency professionals. "First, the political alliances of special education must be broader than they have been in the past" (Joe & Farrow, 1983, p. 253). Interagency collaboration requires some forms of expertise in the political arena that have not traditionally been required. Further, Rogers and Farrow (1983) suggest that federal and state level people must become knowledgeable concerning sources of financing across agencies, professional identification issues, problems with definition and classification across agencies, the role of constituency groups, and the separate administrative structure of agencies. An agency administrator who attempts to participate in the development of an interagency cooperative agreement without the above set of skills has little chance of facilitating an effective agreement.

Methods. The mechanisms for pursuing interagency cooperation are varied, limited only by a lack of openness to alternatives. Some of the methods which have shown promise are discussed here.

The earlier section concerning mandates enumerates examples of legislation which engendered interagency cooperation. While all such legislation was not successful in sparking meaningful interagency collaboration, those states whose legislation allowed for monitoring of programs were most successful.

The request for proposal (RFP) strategy has been very successful in some states. Its benefits include: (a) it recognizes and allows for local variations; (b) it does not create resistance by forcing interagency cooperation where it is not sought, and (c) it is an effective use of state education agency discretionary funds (Rogers & Farrow, 1983).

Another vehicle for collaboration that has been successful is the interagency committee created by legislation or appointed by high level government offices. It is most useful for initial communication, problem-solving and information sharing as opposed to establishing process or monitoring activity (Rogers & Farrow, 1983).

The willingness to monitor and a mechanism for monitoring appear to be important components of most meaningful agreements (Whitted, Cohen & Katz, 1983). A first step in the ability to monitor is the creation of an "on-going information base with dissemination capabilities as a means for collecting, storing, and sharing information related to collaborative interagency planning implementation" (McLaughlin & Christensen, 1980). The best use for such a data base is to assist state and local agencies in improving their interagency collaboration by pinpointing specific areas of need. It can, however, be used as a source of information to assist in the determination of resource allocation. There is, of course, a threat component to that, namely that more dollars are available to agencies with meaningful interagency agreements. However, this form of monitoring does have some limited usefulness as an incentive to establish meaningful interagency collaboration (Wood, 1982; Whitted, Cohen, & Katz, 1983).

There are several other suggestions that appear useful to states pursuing interagency agreements:

1. It is useful to have all *residential* placements and the concomitant funding handled by one agency without regard to reason for placement (e.g., educational, medical, etc.) (Whitted, Cohen, & Katz, 1983).

2. Positive incentives are needed to promote interagency collaboration (McLaughlin & Christensen, 1980). Positive incentives create a far different "mind set" than the incentive which comes from fear of punishment, that is, loss of resources.

3. A cost benefit analysis is a critical element to include in the interagency collaborative process. Not only are existing resources better utilized, but carefully planned collaboration can assist a state in using federal funds whenever possible and thus direct previously used state funds into service expansion in needed areas.

General Guidelines. Rogers & Farrow (1983) summarize the following general factors which are the "most important" for a state education agency achieving effective interagency collaboration:

- *Involvement of a higher unit of state government* in order to reduce and resolve policy disputes.
- *Use of an on-going process of collaboration* rather than a one-time action or agreement.
- *Allocation and continued commitment of agency resources* to the process of interagency collaboration in order to assure follow-through at the state and local level.
- *Provision of strong leadership*, either by the SEA or another unit of state government, with clear enunciation of goals and a plan for achieving them.
- *Matching of the interagency mechanism to desired goals.* Interagency committees seem best suited for communication, problem solving, and information sharing. Interagency agreements (with follow-through and enforcement) seem particularly effective in assigning service delivery and financial responsibilities.
- *Appreciation of the informal dimensions* of interagency collaboration.
- *Attention to local follow-through* so that counterpoint local agencies understand and can implement state-level agreements (p. xiv).

Local Level

The following ideas offer some manageable activity and real hope for the goal of cooperative interface efforts at the local level.

Local Level Collaboration is Best. Elder and Magrab (1980) state that the best place for interagency collaboration is at the local level. After reviewing the literature for this chapter, this author concurs. The most appealing ideas, the most tangible examples of method, the most functional collaborative arrangements generally occur at the local level, whether or not the state level agencies had functional collaborative agreements. While this does not negate the value of meaningful state level collaboration as both a model and a means of sharing resources, it may indicate that good state level agreements do not automatically engender good local collaboration.

In 1980, Grosenick & Huntze examined interagency collaboration in relation to the behaviorally disordered population. They found that individuals first begin most collaborative efforts. It appears that doing "what we can" does make a difference. It may be that a great deal of energy is wasted on plans for system-wide change that have little effect on complex and inert organizations. Wood (1982) concurs. In regard to the "unmanageable complexity" of human service agencies, he writes:

> Rather than being overawed by what actually exists, practitioners should approach such systems with the intention of working on whatever part of it can be improved through the application of the resources and skills at their disposal, confident that if the functioning of a part is improved, the total system will benefit (p. 132).

Perhaps this is the critical information to impart: that total systems may be nearly hopeless, but parts of it aren't. In fact, going beyond the local level to the individual level it can be said that "I, alone, can start some type of interagency collaboration." By committing some of one's own resources, it is possible to make a difference.

It is important to make a couple of additional statements regarding the potential of local level collaboration. First, this recommendation, in no way, suggests that federal and state level efforts should not be systematically pursued. As indicated in the previous section, the advantages of such agreements are numerous, including the fact that good federal and state agreements facilitate local efforts and set good models for local efforts, and almost any state and federal interagency cooperative effort, regardless of outcome, continues the development of mutual understanding.

Secondly, it is critical to reiterate that while statements about the value of local and individual collaboration may sound naive, the literature indicates otherwise. Virtually without exception, the promising practices discussed in an earlier part of this chapter were initiated at local/individual levels. Although it is possible that a state level agreement served as an impetus for some, none cite that reason in their discussions. If demonstrated impact reflected in the literature is the measure, then local level collaborative/interface is the most viable route. The question then becomes one of how to get the right information in the hands of those local level agencies and persons who are most likely to create and facilitate cooperative interface. Edgar and Maddox's (1982) "cookbook model" discussed later in this chapter may offer some direction.

Case Manager Role. One element present in many promising local cooperative situations is the case manager role. Sometimes called a case manager (Grub & Thompson, 1982; Whitted, Cohen, & Katz, 1983), sometimes called a liaison (Huntze & Grosenick, 1980), a person in the case management role is invaluable in effecting the cooperative interface set forth in agreements. A single person responsible for individual cases

and specific procedures appears to do the best job of coordinating interagency services. Behaviorally disordered children and youth are more likely to have records follow them, avoid duplicative evaluation, experience consistency between environments, make behavioral progress, and generally avoid falling "between agency cracks" when their case is assigned to one individual to manage, regardless of the number of agencies which may assist the child.

Value of Process. It has been indicated previously that the value of the effort to create interagency interface may lie not only in the product, but also in the process (Hershberger, 1981). That process goes a long way toward creating a common mindset. In that sense the process itself is tantamount to inservice (Whitted, Cohen, & Katz, 1983). Thus, almost any attempt at cooperative interface should be pursued, regardless of suspected outcome. The dialogue that occurs, even in "unsuccessful" attempts at collaboration, may eventually be the building blocks of another collaborative effort.

Discovering Existing Interface. It is this author's opinion, based on past experience with interagency planning and confirmed by chapter reviewers, that there is, in fact, much promising interface going on that is not finding its way into the literature base. A major need exists to find ways to disseminate information concerning successful cooperative interface that is occurring. Because of the conviction that local interface works best, the vehicle for such dissemination may be state level efforts to describe/analyze viable cooperative efforts occurring across their state.

Enabling Financial Sharing. The necessity of financial sharing has been repeatedly stressed. State statute and regulations must create or allow sufficient flexibility to allow local agencies/providers the ability to utilize funds in interagency endeavors.

Utilization of Computer Technology. This need/recommendation could be discussed under any of the broad divisions of this section. "Local Level" was selected because most of the information input is at this level. The ready availability of computer technology is both an enhancer and an inhibitor of cooperative interface. Its existence greatly simplifies the process of conveying information between agencies. This very case, however, intensifies existing concerns of the separate agencies in regard to confidentiality issues. It would seem clear that while this technology must be used to facilitate the cooperative sharing of data, the exact parameters of that usage will and should become a larger issue in the cooperative planning stages.

Interface that Isn't. In a previous discussion some time was spent on types of interface that were not truly cooperative, although they are often billed as such. While it is true that they are not really cooperative interface, these activities still hold promise for the improvement of services to the behaviorally disordered population. The activities referred to are ones characterized by the term *interdisciplinary*, not interagency. In these instances an agency, usually a public school, which is in need of a type of service not usually provided by that agency, employs someone who represents a perspective typical of a different service agency. The most common form of this is a public school that employs psychologists, psychiatrists, social workers, and so forth (Marrone, 1970; Myers, 1972; Wood, 1982). This process certainly does not solve any of the agency level concerns of shared resources, nonduplicative services, and so forth. It does, however open the system to different perspectives. Having such experiences increases the likelihood that public schools will pursue and be comfortable in more extended cooperative interface.

Training

Interagency collaboration has three characteristics: it is complex, idiosyncratic within parameters, and amenable to the instruction process. While no one can teach anyone else exactly how to develop interagency collaboration, either in general or for a specific instance, it is possible to expose people to attitudes and ideas that increase the likelihood of future interagency collaboration. There are training opportunities at both the inservice and preservice levels.

Inservice. McLaughlin and Christensen (1980) summarized the population for and nature of training in the collaboration process. The recipients fall into four categories: the implementers, and the three categories listed below:

The "intended audience" or recipients of future training fall into three general categories: 1) *influencers* (those individuals, who because of position, power and/or personal interests, have a significant impact on the delivery of services to handicapped individuals); 2) *planners* (those who may be directly or indirectly involved in planning future collaborative interagency efforts); and 33) *evaluators* (those persons with the responsibilitty for monitoring and evaluating the effectiveness of collaborative interagency programs). Individuals and agency representatives who might be listed under each category include:

Influencers
- Parents, consumers, advocates
- Agency heads

- Program administrators/managers
- Professional service providers (public/private)
- Fiscal (budget) analysts
- Local elected policy makers
- Legislators

Planners
- Agency representatives (with planning responsibility)
- Independent consultants
- Parents, consumers

Evaluators
- Parents, consumers, advocates
- Political, civic, and organization leaders
- Agency heads
- Program administrators/managers
- Professional service providers (public/private)
- Fiscal (budget) analysts
- Local elected policy makers
- Legislators
- Independent consultants (pp. 29–30)

These people represent individuals from all agencies/ disciplines that will be involved in the collaboration. The training needs of each population are summarized by McLaughlin and Christensen (1980) as follows:

Influencers
- Principles of collaborative interagency programming (i.e., cost benefits, inherent problems, long range effects, . . .)
- Resources (current, future needs, duplication, accountability, etc.)
- Client needs
- Legal bases (e.g., state/federal legislation, rules, regulations, and policies)
- Peripheral knowledge of political networking
- Existing model programs
- Broad-based awareness of existing programs and services offered by public and private agencies.

Planners
- The training needs for planners were seen as being basically the same as those specified for influencers, except that *the specificity of information increases directly proportional to the extent of each individual's involvement in the planning process.*

Evaluators
- Evaluation techniques and methodology at various levels of sophistication.
- All previous information, the *specificity* of which *increases in direct proportion to the extent of each individuals involvement in the evaluation process*

Finally in addition to the above, particular attention must be given to the training needs of a fourth group of individuals—the *implementers*, those who have specific responsibility for both the provision of services, as well as for the "grass roots," "day-to-day" coordination of collaborative interagency program efforts.

Though they, too, have the need for training in all of the areas previously listed, additional training must be considered in the following areas to enhance the chances of success of collaborative interagency program efforts:

- Human awareness
- Interpersonal relations and communications
- The dynamics of organizational behavior
- Time management for self and others (pp. 30–31)

Of course, the initial problem is that few of the participants listed above are trained at all (McLaughlin & Christensen, 1980). Thus the foregoing delineations of trainees and content are useless without a recommendation which suggests that federal and state level agencies must support inservice training in interagency collaboration. And, as with the collaboration itself, the participating agencies must combine funds for such endeavors. Additionally, there is a need for: (a) development of comprehensive training packages, and (b) a trained pool of consultants to serve as collaboration facilitators (McLaughlin & Christensen, 1980).

Others have suggested inservice activities, although not on the scale implied above. Elder (1982) suggests papers and workshops as a form of technical assistance. Gedo (1982) and LaCour (1982) both recommend that education and mental health personnel should receive training in the basic concepts of both agencies, including each agency's mandate. A unique idea is presented by Edgar and Maddox (1982). The Single Portal Intake Project suggests that the local education agency serves as the single initial referral site. From that "single portal," determinations can be made concerning the range of human services required to meet any student's needs. This concept is thwarted by the concerns of many for education's involvement in a "too broad" spectrum of services. On the other hand, the single line of responsibility mandate suggests that there is some feasibility in this idea. The concept would require local education agencies to enter into collaborative agreement with other services. The researchers suggest a "cookbook model" in which numerous "recipes" are offered which address methods of collaboration for various types of services and special problems. Local education agencies then have models or ideas of how to pursue agreements that meet their needs. Even if the "single portal" concept proves unworkable, a range of delineated methods for collaboration with other agencies may be a useful concept.

Preservice. Many researchers in this field see the need for preservice education to address the interagency collaboration issue. At this level, the primary focus should be on attitudes. An open attitude is probably best achieved by ensuring that students trained in the area of behavior disorders are given more than cursory exposure to various theoretical perspectives. Singular training creates a narrow focus which eventually limits communication and therefore cooperation (Garret et al., 1979). In addition to a variety of theoretical perspectives, practicum experiences can be useful. Educators who have had the opportunity to do observation, aiding or teaching in mental health facilities, correctional facilities, Head Start, and so forth are in a better position to approach those agencies and their personnel in an open and trusting fashion (Olasov, Bruno, & Olasov, 1983).

Joe and Farrow, (1983) recommend that the training of special education teachers should provide "a systematic understanding of how special education fits into the broader constellation of services" (p. 219).

Some authors recommend even more specific training components. McLaughlin and Christensen (1980) recommend:

> Core curriculum additions to existing programs within professional schools (colleges/universities), as a basis for the eventual establishment of certification/licensure requirements for interagency program facilitators.
>
> - Examples of existing higher education programs where curriculum changes may be initiated include: special education, nursing, medicine, social services, public administration, etc.

The development and implementation of preservice degree or endorsement programs for facilitators of collaborative interagency programs (p. 28).

In a more detailed program such as that suggested above, coursework/training might be in group processes, consultation and collaboration models, problem solving and conflict resolution. Clearly both attitudes and instructional content should be addressed at the preservice level.

Reseach

The majority of literature that addresses the interagency collaboration issue is conceptual and descriptive in nature. This author does not see that as particularly problematic. While data-based research on the evaluation of specific agreements makes sense and is a logical next step, data-based research on the evaluation of interagency collaboration, generally, may be unmanageable. Except for a few specific components (accrued cost benefits, for example) the complexity and idiosyncracy of interagency collaboration, generally, may make it nonamenable to traditional forms of data collection. That is not to suggest that systematic inquiry should not be pursued. Interagency collaboration may be more amenable to naturalistic research methods or some creative alternative approach.

What does appear to be a useful next step is research into the specific cooperative interface efforts that have been successful. Public schools, mental health facilities and correctional facilities are the primary contact points for behaviorally disordered students. Cooperative efforts among these agencies and by these agencies with yet others should be examined. The purpose should not be to describe "model efforts" but rather to discern patterns or components that appear in most successful cooperative ventures. The term "model" suggests that a given procedure or practice can be transplanted and duplicated. Track records for that type of duplication are not good. Given the amazing number of variables present when agencies collaborate, the chances of duplication elsewhere are slight. Each situation will demand its own solutions. For that reason discernment of successful patterns and components can be useful to a new endeavor, but not suffocating. Specific questions to be pursued might include: Who are the instigators and decision makers? How do students enter and move among the systems? Where does entry/movement break down and why? Exactly how are funds co-mingled? If this type of work is being done, it is not reflected on a large, or even modest, scale in the literature. The current literature is still reflective of the early idea and planning stages of a concept. The next set of information needed is that described above.

References

Amendments to Title XIV of the Public Health Service Act, (1984). Washington, DC: Congressional Record, Vol. 130 (1984). [Public Law 98–509].

Audette, R. H. (1980). Interagency collaboration: The bottom line. In J. O. Elder and P. R. Magrab, (Eds.). *Coordinating services to handicapped children: A handbook for interagency collaboration*. Baltimore, MD: Brookes.

Barr, W., & Delfava, C. (1980). *Public school and community mental health interagency cooperation for treatment of the child with special educational needs*. Tacoma, WA: Pierce County Health Department. (ERIC Document Reproduction Service No. ED 201 077).

Baxter, J. M. (1982). Solving problems through cooperation. *Exceptional Children, 48*, 400–407.

Benson, J. K. (1975). The interorganizational network as a political economy. *Administrative Science Quarterly, 20*, 229–249.

Boss, G. (1982, June). *Social shock: The revolution of human services*. Paper presented at the National Invitational Symposium on Interagency Collaboration, Denver, CO. (ERIC Documents Reproduction Service No. ED 235 669).

Broten, A. (1972). The joining of group home care and counseling offers a variety of services to emotionally disturbed girls in Chicago. In Building education into youth services. *Human Needs, 1*, 16–18.

Del Polito, C. M. (1983, Febuary). *Personnel preparation: Alliances in health education*. Paper presented at the Annual Convention of the Eastern Educational Research Association, Baltimore, MD. (ERIC Document Reproduction Service No. 232 389).

Edgar, E. B., & Maddox, M. (1982 June). *The cookbook model: An approach to interagency collaboration*. Paper presented at the National Invitational Symposium on Interagency Collaboration. (ERIC Document Reproduction Service No. 235 669).

Elder, J. O., & Magrab, P. R. (Eds.) (1980). *Coordinating services to handicapped children: A handbook for interagency collaboration*. Baltimore MD: Brookes.

Flaherty, E. W., Barry, E., & Swift, M. (1978). Use of an unobtrusive measure for the evaluation of interagency coordination. *Evaluation Quarterly, 2*, 261–273.

Garret, G., Rehm, T., Montague, E., McDaniel, W. C., Paavola, J., Rich, H. L., Randalls, C., & Dean, G. H. (1979, April). *Project TREAT: An interagency approach to serving severely emotionally disturbed children in a public school setting and Sequoyah Mental Health Center*. Paper presented at the Annual International Convention, The Council for Exceptional Children, Dallas, TX. (ERIC Document Reproduction Service No. ED 171 037).

Gatti, F., & Coleman, C. (1976). Community network therapy: An approach to aiding families with troubled children. *American Journal of Orthopsychiatry, 46*, 608–617.

Gedo, D. G. (1978). Providing technical assistance and advocacy: A liaison program between a mental health unit and the schools. In F. H. Wood (Ed.), *Preparing teachers to develop and maintain therapeutic educational environments*. Minneapolis: Special Education Programs, University of Minnesota.

Greenan, J. P., & Phelps, L. A. (1982). Delivering vocational education to handicapped learners. *Exceptional Children, 48*, 408–411.

Gromanda, H. T. (1975). *Working together for children: A neighborhood advocacy system*, Final Report. Upper Marlboro, MD: Prince Georges County Board of Education. (ERIC Document Reproduction Service No. ED 1116 433).

Grosenick, J. K., & Huntze, S. L. (1980). *National needs analysis in behavior disorders: Adolescent behavior disorders*. Columbia: Department of Special Education, University of Missouri-Columbia.

Grub, R. D., & Thompson, M. D. (1982). Delivering related services to the emotionally disturbed: A field based perspective. In M. M. Noel & N. G. Haring (Eds.), *Progress or change: Issues in educating the emotionally disturbed* (pp. 85–95). Seattle: University of Washington.

Hershberger, A. M. (1981). *A study to determine the effectiveness of local interagency agreements and identify their costs*. Final report. Menlo Park, CA: SRI International.

Hockenberry, C. M. (1979). *Policy issues and implications on the education of adjudicated handicapped youth*. Reston, VA: The Council for Exceptional Children.

Huntze, S. L., & Grosenick, J. K. (1980). *National needs analysis in behavior disorders: Human resource issues*. Columbia: Department of Special Education, University of Missouri-Columbia.

Joe, T., & Farrow, F. (1983). Guides for future special education policy. *Policy Studies Review, 2*, 213–225.

Johnson, H. W., McLaughlin, J. A., & Christensen, M. (1982) Interagency collaboration: Driving and restraining forces. *Exceptional Children, 49*, 265–267.

LaCour, J. A. (1982). Interagency agreement: A national response to an irrational system. *Exceptional Children*, **49**, 265–267.

Levine, S., & White, P. (1961). Exchange as a conceptual framework for the study of interorganizational relationships. *Administrative Science Quarterly*, **5**, 583–601.

Magrab, P. R., & Schmidt, L. M. (1980). Interdisciplinary collaboration: A prelude to coordinated service delivery. In J. O. Elder, & P. R. Magrab (Eds.). *Coordinating services to handicapped children: A handbook for interagency collaboration* (pp. 13–24). Baltimore, MD: Brooks.

Marrone, R. T. (1970). Innovative public school programming for emotionally disturbed children. *American Journal of Orthopsychiatry*, **40**, 694–701.

Martinson, M. C. (1982). Interagency services: A new era for an old idea. *Exceptional Children*, **48**, 389–394.

McCormick, L. (1982). Service delivery teams: Definition, process, and accountability. In N. G. Haring & M. M. Noel (Eds.). *Progress or change: Isssues in educating the emotionally disturbed* (pp. 59–83). Seattle: University of Washington.

McLaughlin, J. A., & Christensen, M. (1980). *A study of interagency collaborative agreements to discover training needs for special education administrators*. Washington, DC: Bureau of Education for the Handicapped (Grant No. C00790093).

McLaughlin, J. A., & Elder, J. O. (1982, June). *Notes on the evaluation of interagency collaborations*. Paper presented at the National Invitational Symposium on Interagency Collaboration, Denver, CO. (ERIC Document Reproduction Service No. 235 669).

McNulty, B., & Soper, E. (1982, June). *Critical elements of successful interagency practice*. Paper presented at the National Invitational Symposium on Interagency Collaboration, Denver, CO. (ERIC Document Reproduction Service No. 235 669).

Midwest Regional Resource Center Task Force. (1979). *Interagency collaboration on full services for handicapped children and youth. Vol. I: A guide to state planning and development*. Washington, DC: Office of Special Education Learning Resource Branch.

Mirkes, D. Z. (Ed.) (1981). *Overview Directory & Product Guide, 1980–81*. Seattle: Program Development Assistance System, College of Education, University of Washington.

Myers, R. M. (1972). School children with behavioral problems are aided by guidance experts under contract to Northampton, Massachusetts, Schools. In Building education into youth services. *Human Needs*, **1**, 5–7.

Nichol, H. (1974). Children with learning disabilities referred to psychiatrists: A follow-up study. *Journal of Learning Disabilities*, **7**, 118–722.

Noel, M. M. (1982). Public school programs for the emotionally disturbed: An overview. In N. G. Haring & M. M. Noel (Eds). *Progress or change: Issues In educating the emotionally disturbed* (pp. 1–28). Seattle: University of Washington.

Olasov, L., Bruno, R., & Olasov, J. (1983). Using a psychiatric facility as a field for future classroom teachers. *Education*, **104**(1), 23–28.

Oversight hearings on interagency cooperation (1985). Washington, DC: US Government Printing Office (39-533-0).

Pittinger, J. (1976). A Philosophy of commitment. *Behavioral Disorders*, **2**, 39–40.

Powell, H. (1972). An Oklahoma project attempts to alleviate behavioral problems in school children which lead to future delinquency. In Building education into youth services. *Human Needs*, **1**, 10–25.

Purnell, J. C. (1972). Richmond, VA., agencies have pooled their resources to offer more comprehensive service delivery for public school children. In Building education into youth services. *Human Needs*, **1**, 11–12.

Randall, D. (1975, March). The four-phase system: A multiagency coordinated service for very disturbed adolescents. A paper presented at the Alberta Health and Social Development Integration Conference, Alberta. (ERIC Document Reproduction Service No. ED 116 065).

Rogers, C., & Farrow, F. (1983). Effective state strategies to promote interagency collaboration. *The handicapped public policy analysis project*. Washington, DC: The Center for the Study of Social Policy.

Sheare, J. B., & Larson, C. C. (1978). Odd couple: Effective public schools/mental health joint programming to provide educational therapeutic services to emotionally disturbed students and their families. *Psychology in the Schools*, **15**, 541–544.

U.S. Department of Health, Education and Welfare, Office of Education, Education Division General Administrative Regulations (EDGAR) Washington, DC: Author, Federal Register, April 3, 1980.

Whitted, B. R., Cohen, M. D., Katz, L. (1983). *Interagency cooperation: Miracle or mirage: A study of interagency cooperation in the delivery of special education and related sources*. Skokie, IL: Educational Information Planning Association. (ERIC Document Reproduction Service No. ED 229 997).

Willner, M. (1972). Three Memphis agencies have pooled their facilities and personnel to offer a variety of services to emotionally disturbed children. In Building education into youth services. *Human Needs*, **1**, 13–15.

Wood, F. H. (1982). Cooperative full-service delivery to emotionally disturbed students. In M. M. Noel & N. G. Haring (Eds.). *Progress or change: Issues in educating the emotionally disturbed* (pp. 115–132). Seattle: University of Washington.

Zeitz, G. (1980). Interorganizational dialectics. *Administrative Science Quarterly*, **25**, 72–88.

SECTION 3

Learning Disability

Learning Disability: Introduction

BARBARA K. KEOGH

University of California, Los Angeles

Few areas of program development have generated as much interest and controversy as the topic of learning disability, and few topics are as conceptually and operationally confused. Some of the ambiguities about learning disability have to do with its relationship to other boundary conditions, with the blurring of causes and correlates, and with the impact of the social-political context in which policies governing learning disability services are developed and implemented. Thus, despite an increasingly large body of published literature and an abundance of treatment and intervention programs, understanding of learning disability and of what to do about it continues to be limited, even controversial. As a consequence, there are wide disparities in numbers and types of individuals served, broad differences in program orientations and effectiveness, and a professional literature often characterized more by rhetoric than by evidence. The goal of the set of chapters in this section is to synthesize the research literature in five related aspects of learning disability. Each chapter stands alone as a comprehensive analysis of a particular topic in the area, with implications for research and practice. Importantly, however, when taken as a whole, the chapters identify common themes, content, problems, and needs, and point to important directions for policy, practice, and research.

In the chapter entitled, "Learning Disability: Diversity in Search of Order," Keogh relates issues of conceptualization, definition, and classification to empirical findings on incidence and prevalence, and she discusses as a major point the need for a taxonomy for ordering the many facets of learning disability. Influences on identification and selection that lead to wide differences in prevalence according to service delivery systems or geographic area are reviewed. A shared attribute approach to definition is proposed.

The second chapter in this section, by McKinney, is on the topic, "Research on Conceptually and Empirically Derived Subtypes of Specific Learning Disabilities." McKinney provides a comprehensive and critical review of the theoretical and empirical work

on the identification of subtypes of learning disabilities, including the educational relevance of subtype definitions. Research on learning disability subtypes is organized and evaluated according to the major approaches used to classify children: clinical-inferential, empirically derived, or rationally defined. McKinney concludes that, although it is feasible to use empirical classification techniques to create homogeneous subtypes of relevance for special education, additional work is needed before subtype work can have a direct impact on practice.

Gresham's chapter, entitled, "Social Competence and Motivational Characteristics of Learning Disabled Students," provides a conceptualization and discussion of components of social competence of importance in both identification and remediation. Social skills and peer acceptance, two components of social competence, are emphasized. Self-concept and social-perceptual abilities of learning disabled individuals are discussed and evaluated, and intervention approaches are described.

Kavale's chapter on, "The Long-Term Consequences of Learning Disabilities" is based on a comprehensive review of longitudinal studies of both normally developing and atypical subjects. Methodological problems in longitudinal research, including problems related to design, sampling, measurement, and statistical analyses, are considered. Kavale identifies common generalizations across studies, making an important point of the imprecision in predictions about individual learning disabled children.

In the final chapter of this section, entitled, "Direct Academic Interventions in Learning Disabilities," Lloyd provides an analysis of evidence testing the effectiveness of various treatments or interventions. The primary groups of programs discussed by Lloyd are those that represent medical, indirect, or direct approaches. Illustrative programs are described in each category, and the trend toward interventions that focus directly on instruction is noted. A final section contains discussion of issues in intervention: generality of effects, mediating variables, student roles, and the adaptation of instruction to individual differences.

Taken as a whole, these five chapters cover conceptual, definitional, social, developmental, and treatment aspects of learning disability. All of the chapters have in common an emphasis on empirical findings, critical concern for the adequacy of research and program methods, and recognition of the limits of the present data base for decision making. Each of the five authors exhibits a guarded optimism that our understanding of learning disability can be increased through changes in policy and research and that interventions can be grounded in solid theory and evidence.

A number of generalizations about the state of the art can be extracted from the chapters in this section and translated into recommendations for action. First, there is an overwhelming consensus that identified learning disabled individuals differ widely in academic, cognitive, social, motivational, and other personal attributes. There is no single prototype of a learning disabled child. The learning disability rubric is so broad and unspecified that is subsumes a range of individuals. In one sense, this is advantageous, as it allows services to be provided for many individuals who might not otherwise receive special help. On the other hand, such broad subject variability confounds both research and practice and sorely limits inferences about the nature of learning disabilities and about program impact. It is thus recommended that continued research be directed at the specification of conceptually and empirically sound subgroups within the broad learning disability and category.

Second, the authors agree that learning disability must be understood relative to other problem conditions, especially general low achievement, mild mental retardation, social and behavioral disorders, and mild emotional disturbance. This point is closely tied to the need for identification of subgroups within learning disability, but it also addresses a fundamental definitional question of what constitutes learning disability. Clearly, it is essential to put learning disability in alignment with other similar, but presumably different, conditions. Research on learning disability and evauation of programs for learning disabled students should be conducted within cross-categorical designs, thus allowing for delineation of similarities and differences within the large group of mildly impaired students.

Third, recognition of the diversity within the learning disability classification and of the overlap among special education categories has led to a common concern about policy that directs practice. It is reasonable that some of the inconsistencies in incidence and prevalence within and among related special education categories have to do with regulations governing the implementation of *P.L. 94–142*, especially the regulations concerned with identification and selection. It is recommended that *P.L. 94–142* regulations and guidelines that direct practices related to learning disability be reviewed and evauated by an appropriate group, such as a group including consumers of services; professionals involved in research and services; and local, state, and federal officials who are responsible for policy.

Fourth, a common point in all of the chapters in this section is an awareness that learning disability is embedded in a developmental framework and that the expression of learning disability varies over time. However, the natural course of learning disability has not been comprehensively described, nor have the influences on development been well documented. The research literature is provocative but fragmented, often based on short-term and/or retrospective designs with preselected samples. Issues of when and how to identify learning disabled individuals, the kinds of primary and secondary support systems needed, and the long-term consequences of learning disability are still uncertain. Yet, from both practical and theoretical perspectives, understanding the course of learning disability over time and identifying the factors that influence it are essential. A major effort should thus be directed toward prospective, comprehensive, longitudinal studies of learning disability, taking into account both individual and extra-individual influences.

Fifth, from somewhat different perspectives, the authors address links between the learning disability condition(s) and treatments or interventions, and they also raise questions of the comparative effectiveness of programs. Which interventions are most effective for which individuals is, for the most part, unknown, but it is an important practical question. The answer is related to subtypes of learning disability, but it also implicates the range and diversity among program practices. Services differ in orientation, content, intensity, timing, and emphasis. Such variation, taken together with the diversity of subject attributes has confounded tests of program effectiveness, too often making the choice of intervention a matter of belief rather than evidence. Systematic evaluation of major programs or treatment approaches should be carried out to test hypothesized subject-intervention links and to determine the relative effectiveness of major program models.

Sixth, there is a consensus about the importance of policy for the future of the field. Given the importance of the issues that affect both practice and research in learning disability, it is essential that a coherent policy for research and program development be formulated and implemented at the federal level. At the least, such policy must meet several requirements: Expertise from a number of relevant disciplines should be included; opportunities for both short-term, limited-focus studies and long-term, programmatic work should be provided; and rigorous review and monitoring procedures should be included to ensure quality and relevance. A point emphasized by all five authors in this section is the need for support for programs of research over time, thus allowing coordination, continuity, and development of research and educational efforts. It is recommended, therefore, that a long-range plan for research and program development in learning disability be conceptualized at the federal level, giving emphasis to programmatic research that cuts across categorical and disciplinary boundaries.

Learning Disability: Diversity in Search of Order[1,2]

BARBARA K. KEOGH, PH.D

University of California, Los Angeles

Abstract—Issues of conceptualization, definition, and classification in the area of learning disability are related to empirical findings on incidence and prevalence. Influences which account for disparities in numbers of identified individuals with learning disabilities (professional perspectives, formulae for operationalizing aptitude-achievement discrepancies, measurement limitations, and institutional constraints) are reviewed. A shared attribute approach to definition is proposed and an argument is made for development of a taxonomy of learning disability. Recommendations include study of individual and social system characteristics and their interactions, evaluation studies to determine comparative program effectiveness, separation of research on the learning disability condition from service delivery needs, and the formulation of coherent national policy to ensure resources for continuity of research and evaluation.

Introduction

This chapter is focused on issues and problems in (a) the scientific study of learning disabilities, and (b) the provision of services for learning disabled individuals. Lack of a consensual conceptualization of learning disabilities has had consequences for the equitable distribution of educational services, and has muddied research directed at understanding the condition(s) of learning disability. Identification and selection criteria and practices differ geographically and according to date, and there is often a confounding of learning disability and other handicapping conditions. There is little argument that a substantial number of individual have serious and unexpected problems in achieving at a normative level. Yet the specifics of who they are, why they have problems, and what to do about the problems remain unanswered, even controversial.

The uncertainties which characterize learning disability are in part related to the lack of clear differentiation of learning disability from other boundary conditions such as mild mental retardation, mild emotional disturbance, or general underachievement. The understanding of learning disability is further limited by possible confounds of social, economic, or cultural influences on achievement, and by a multitude of pedagogical or treatment practices. Closely related, professional and disciplinary perspectives have logically resulted in selected research approaches and techniques and to sometimes parochial interpretations and inferences. Finally, the state of the art in the field of learning disability is also greatly influenced by social-political factors. The interactions among parents, professional advocates, and governmental decision makers has contributed to the remarkable growth of the learning disability field. At the same time, the social-political realities have resulted in policy decisions which, while often expedient, were not necessarily based on scientific evidence. This is not to impugn the efforts nor integrity of advocates of government decision makers, but rather to note that too frequently the scientific evidence on which to make rational decisions has not been available. The result, then, is an increasingly large but for the most part uninterpretable research literature focused on learning disability and complex but inconsistent service systems which are based more on advocacy and political influence than on solid data.

The present chapter is organized to consider both research and applications in the field of learning disability. The context or frame of reference for selection and discussion of content is educational, although content included covers the range from preschool to adulthood. Material which forms the basis of this review was selected from publications in education, psychology, medicine, and related fields, as well as from government reports and in some cases as yet unpublished documents. Both computer and hand searchers were used. In order to keep the volume of information manageable and interpretable, only information with direct ties to the area of learning disability was included. This necessarily meant sometimes excluding related and likely pertinent information, for example, reports on mental retardation, underachievement, and so forth. As will be seen in the bulk of this review, the so-called "boundaries" are particularly difficult to establish in the area of learning disability.

In the first major section of the chapter (Overview of the Problem) issues of incidence and prevalence are discussed, with special emphasis given to two points: the disparities in numbers of students identified as having learning disabilities in different service systems and in different geographic areas; and the increase in numbers of individuals identified and classified as having learning disabilities. Also included in the Overview section is discussion of the confounds between learning disability and other classes of poor achievement. The second section (Influences on Classification Decisions) contains a review of research on identification and selection which may provide insight into the already noted disparities in numbers of students with learning disabilities. These influences include professional and disciplinary perspectives, techniques for operationalizing ability-achievement discrepancies, measurement, and institutional and organizational constraints.

A third major section of the chapter (The Need for Classification) deals with the importance of a conceptually sound and workable classification system for study of clinical conditions. Following discussion of monothetic and polythetic approaches to classification, criteria for evaluating the adequacy of classification systems are described. These criteria are not specific to the area of learning disability but rather identify aspects of classification to be considered in any clinical grouping system. A final subsection deals with the distinction between classification and identification.

The fourth section of the review (Classification in the Area of Learning Disability) is focused specifically on classification issues in this area, and deals with two primary questions. What are the necessary and sufficient characteristics which define classes and sub-classes of learning disability? How accurately and reliably can we identify individuals to fit these classes? Subtyping approaches to classification and identification are discussed briefly. The fifth and final section of this chapter (Discussion and Recommendations) contains a synthesis and discussion of the major findings in the review, and sets out proposed implications for practice, research, and policy.

Overview of the Problem

A major change in American education over the past 10 years has been the growing importance of special services to handicapped learners. The impact is evident at both state and local levels, in allocation of financial and human resources, and in programmatic and instructional modifications. What had been relatively limited services to a few have become mandated full services for many. In the 3 years immediately following the passage of *PL 94–142* there was an increase of over 328,000 identified handicapped children receiving special education services; the regular education public school population declined by over 6% during the same time period. In the 1982 year over 3.8 million pupils, almost 10% of

the school population as a whole, were eligible for special services. Financial resources for special education rose at a rate of 14% a year, a figure twice as great as that for regular education budgets (Stark, 1982). According to the *Sixth Annual Report to Congress* (prepared by the Office of Special Education Programs, 1984), during the 1982–83 school year 4,298,427 handicapped children were served, an increase of 65,000 over the previous year. From 1976–77 (when the first child count was taken) to 1982–83, the number of identified handicapped children increased by more than 500,000, a 16% change. Clearly, special educational services to handicapped children have become a significant and important part of the general education scene. Clearly, too, mandated services to handicapped children have necessitated important reconsiderations and adjustments in policy and resources. Major issues relate to prevalence, as a number of practical accommodations and changes are tied to numbers of pupils to be served. The question of prevalence is particularly troubling in the learning disability category, where definitional inconsistencies and controversies abound.

Prevalence of Learning Disability

Determination of incidence and prevalence of a condition within a population is an important step in understanding a problem. Stein (1981) notes that study of incidence and prevalence allows development of "rational policies," improves planning of appropriate services, aids in the search for causes, and contributes to planning for prevention. For the sake of clarity, both terms require definition. Following the World Health Organization (WHO) definition, incidence refers to "the number of instances of an illness commencing . . . during a given period. More generally, the number of new events, e.g., new cases of a disease in a defined population, within a specified time period" (Last, 1983, p. 49). Prevalence, according to Last, is "the number of instances of a given disease or other condition in a given population at a given time" (p. 52). Prevalence, thus, includes the number of new cases in any given time period (incidence) plus cases already identified as exemplars of the condition. Most reports describing the numbers of individuals identified as having learning disabilities (e.g., the *Sixth Annual Report to Congress*, 1984) are based on prevalence figures. Incidence figures are less frequently reported, yet may be important in understanding changes in prevalence, a point to be discussed somewhat later in this paper.

Considering prevalence, under federal guidelines developed to implement *PL 94–142*, it was estimated that approximately 2% of the school-age population would be learning disabled. At that time (1975–77) 2% represented 17% of the population of handicapped children. According to the report from the Government Accounting Office (1981), in 1980 12 states reported that students with learning disabilities represented 40% of their total population of handicapped children; 6 other states reported a 50% figure. Figures contained in the 1984 *Sixth Annual Report to Congress* on the Implementation of Public Law 94–142 confirm the high number of children identified as having learning disabilities. Table 1, taken in part from the *Sixth Annual Report* (1984), lists number and percent of identified learning disabled and mentally retarded individuals (ages 3–21) by state and by category. In 1982–83 the total number of handicapped individuals ages 3–21 (aggregated across states and territories) was 4,298,327; of that number, 1,745,871 or 40.6% were classified as having learning disabilities. This is in contrast to 1976–77 when 757,213 individuals were identified as having learning disabilities. The 1983 figure represents over 3% of school children nationally.

Two points about prevalence deserve particular attention. The first has to do with the variation in prevalence by states, the second with the dramatic change in prevalence rates over time. Referring to Table 1, it may be seen that for the 1982–83 year Hawaii (64%) and Rhode Island (63%) had the highest percent of children identified as having learning disabilities; Alabama (26%), Indiana (27%), and Kentucky (27%) had the lowest. Among the territories prevalence ranged from a high of 26% in Guam to a low of 0.4% in American Samoa. The District of Columbia identified 28% of all handicapped children as having learning disabilities; the Bureau of Indian Affairs so identified 52%. Looking at the states with high numbers of handicapped children (operationally defined in this analysis as 200,000 or greater), it is clear that variation is still the rule. On the average the five states with over 200,000 identified handicapped children classified 46% of them as having learning disabilities. The percentages by states were: California 55%, Illinois 37%, New York 44%, Ohio 36%, and Texas 52%. Comparable learning disability figures for the 21 states with fewer than 50,000 identified handicapped children varied from 58% (New Hampshire) to 30% (South Dakota). On the average, these 21 states identified 42% of all handicapped children as having learning disabilities. As the average percentage of pupils with learning disabilities was similar for the over-200,000 and the under-50,000 handicapped children states (46% and 42%, respectively), it seems reasonable to conclude that identification as learning disabled is not a function of total number of children identified. However, given the disparities in percentage of children with learning disabilities by states, it does seem fair to conclude that identification as learning disabled is strongly influenced by local policies and procedures.

The second point of interest and, for service providers, of concern, relates to changes in prevalence figures. Citing figures from the *Liaison Bulletin*, Edgar and Hayden (1984–85) note that the numbers of individuals in all handicapping conditions has increased 16% since 1976–77, but learning disability has increased 119%. Figures from the *Sixth Annual Report* (1984) reflect the pattern of change. In 1976–77, the four major categories of handicapping conditions (in rank order of numbers

served) were speech impaired (1,302,066), mentally retarded (969,547), learning disabled (757,213), and emotionally disturbed (283,072). In 1982–83, by contrast, rank order and numbers were: learning disabled (1,745,871), speech impaired (1,134,197), mentally retarded (780,831), and emotionally disturbed (353,431). Both speech impairment and mentally retardation categories dropped in number and there was a modest increase in the number of individuals identified as emotionally disturbed. The major increase was in the learning disability category where the number of pupils more than doubled (797,213 to 1,745,871).

According to the *Sixth Annual Report to Congress* (1984) the rate of increase so dramatic during the first years of the learning disability category has slowed. Ten states reported that numbers of students with learning disabilities decreased, nine reported moderate increases. However, in an analysis of the *Annual Report*, Gerber (1984) suggests that these figures are misleading, as only four states reported lower percentages of children served. One of these states was New Mexico which does not provide services under *PL 94–142*. Gerber estimates that 16 states had no change or less than 1% change in service rates, concluding that "most of the decrease in number of students identified as learning disabled is simply an artifact of overall enrollment declines. Actually, most states are continuing to identify the same or an increasing percentage of students as learning disabled despite declining enrollment" (p. 214).

Returning to the distinction between incidence and prevalence, it should not surprise us that prevalence increases annually. As reflected in incidence figures, each year newly identified pupils are provided services as learning disabled. At the same time, many already identified pupils continue to be served as learning disabled. Put directly, the numbers entering programs are not balanced by the numbers leaving programs. As a consequence, the total number of those identified as having learning disabilities (prevalence) increases. Further, it is likely that incidence numbers will increase. The notion of learning disability has been extended to younger and older age groups (preschool and adult populations), thereby enlarging the pool of possible cases; assessment techniques and screening programs are more widely used; and advocacy programs for services are stronger. At the same time, interventions are only partly effective, and many pupils with learning disabilities continue to need services for several years, some for their whole school careers. In sum, both incidence and prevalence of learning disability will probably continue to increase, but will vary by state, given lack of agreed-upon operational criteria for identification, and given the still tenuous links between condition and intervention.

TABLE 1
Number and Percent of Identified LD and MR Individuals (CA 3–21) According to State or Territory

State	Total # Handi-capped	LD N	LD %	MR N	MR %	State	Total # Handi-capped	LD N	LD %	MR N	MR %
Alabama	81,609	20,899	26	34,986	43	New Hampshire	14,143	8,220	58	1,419	10
Alaska	12,017	6,826	57	665	6	New Jersey	161,481	62,736	39	12,463	8
Arizona	51,862	25,710	50	6,002	12	New Mexico	26,334	12,237	46	2,782	11
Arkansas	49,004	19,436	40	16,013	33	New York	264,835	116,753	44	37,810	14
California	364,318	198,696	55	28,580	8	North Carolina	120,586	49,019	41	33,240	28
Colorado	45,126	19,654	44	5,795	13	North Dakota	10,802	4,340	40	1,920	8
Connecticut	66,010	29,352	44	6,208	9	Ohio	202,234	72,031	36	56,802	28
Delaware	14,405	6,670	46	2,115	15	Oklahoma	65,819	28,625	43	12,582	19
Florida	155,609	58,105	37	27,537	18	Oregon	46,201	23,459	51	4,781	10
Georgia	112,555	35,722	32	28,214	25	Pennsylvania	196,277	63,413	32	46,402	24
Hawaii	12,876	8,189	64	1,514	12	Rhode Island	18,589	11,729	63	1,498	8
Idaho	17,673	8,233	47	2,948	17	South Carolina	71,705	20,830	29	22,404	31
Illinois	261,769	96,805	37	44,546	17	South Dakota	11,841	3,563	30	1,481	13
Indiana	100,228	27,434	27	24,189	24	Tennessee	106,091	42,804	40	20,245	19
Iowa	56,109	21,340	38	12,228	22	Texas	289,343	150,768	52	30,769	11
Kansas	44,159	16,190	37	6,779	15	Utah	38,968	13,611	35	3,159	8
Kentucky	73,170	20,064	27	21,741	30	Vermont	9,309	2,973	32	2,563	28
Louisiana	86,009	39,707	46	15,742	18	Virginia	100,713	38,614	38	16,878	17
Maine	26,485	8,974	34	5,167	20	Washington	64,295	31,286	49	9,400	15
Maryland	90,879	48,366	53	7,943	9	West Virginia	42,418	14,719	35	11,066	26
Massachusetts	138,480	48,884	35	29,357	21	Wisconsin	72,219	27,224	38	13,234	18
Michigan	155,771	55,467	36	26,971	17	Wyoming	11,144	5,095	46	943	8
Minnesota	77,658	34,748	45	13,789	18	*Territories*					
Mississippi	50,883	16,788	33	15,381	30	D.C.	5,809	1,629	28	1,237	21
Missouri	99,984	36,224	36	19,530	20	Puerto Rico	35,173	1,852	5	21,159	60
Montana	15,215	7,208	47	1,515	10	American Samoa	244	1	.4	161	66
Nebraska	30,448	12,227	40	5,669	19	Guam	2,031	530	26	913	45
Nevada	13,326	7,041	53	1,047	8	Virgin Islands	1,237	220	18	626	51
						Bur. of Indian Aff.	4,849	2,531	52	723	15

Modified from the *Sixth Annual Report to Congress* prepared by the Division of Educational Services, Special Education Programs, 1984.

Learning Disabilities and Low Achievement

The disparities in prevalence by state or geographic area suggest differences in the characteristics of individuals served, thus posing serious threats to generalizability of research findings and to determination of efficacy of clinical services. The heterogeneity of subjects subsumed by the learning disability classification has been well documented (Kavale & Nye, 1981; Keogh, Major-Kingsley, Omori-Gordon, & Reid, 1982; Kirk & Elkins, 1975; Norman & Zigmond, 1980; Torgesen & Dice, 1980). In a series of studies Ysseldyke and his associates (Algozzine & Ysseldyke, 1983; Ysseldyke, Algozzine, Richey, & Graden, 1982; Ysseldyke, Algozzine, Shinn, & McGue, 1982) have questioned the validity of many classification decisions, finding that school district-classified learning disabled and non-classified children were virtually indistinguishable. Support for their work has been provided by Shepard and her colleagues (Shepard, Smith, & Vojir, 1983; Smith, 1982) in a detailed study of learning disability in the State of Colorado. In a quantitative analysis of 1,000 "representative" learning disability cases (school district-identified), Shepard and Smith (1983) found that 28% met strict learning disability criteria and that an additional 15% showed "weak signs of the handicap." Fifty-seven percent of the 100 did not meet Colorado learning disability criteria: 10.6% were normal; 11.4% were slow learners; and 6.6% had some specific language interference problems. A qualitative analysis of an additional 200 cases yielded similar, if anything, more powerful results, leading the authors to conclude that while 60% of the cases needed special educational help, 22% needed other than "LD-type" interventions, for example, psychotherapy or intensive English training.

The confounding of learning disability and other achievement-related problems is also addressed in the work of the Kansas Learning Disabilities Institute investigators (Schumaker, Deshler, Alley, & Warner, 1980, 1983; Warner, Schumaker, Alley, & Deshler, 1980).

These investigators studied 246 school-identified learning disabled students grades 7–12 and a comparison group of 229 low achieving students of comparable grades. The Kansas group found that the major difference between learning disability and low achievement groups was degree of disability. The learning disabled students' performance in reading, math, and written language was significantly below that of the low achieving students at both junior and senior high school levels, and the groups also differed on estimated ability at the senior high school level. However, the average intellectual ability score for the learning disability groups was "substantially below" the norm of 100, a finding consistent with the analyses of learning disability research samples carried out by Keogh et al. (1982). Based on their sample, the Kansas investigators suggest that "for many of the LD students, the traditional label of 'slow learner' would be more appropriate" (Warner et al., 1980, p. 31). Further, there were significant school district effects such that mean IQs for low achieving students and students with learning disabilities differed in some districts, but not in others. Apparently in some districts the defining criterion for selection as learning disabled was low achievement, rather than a significant discrepancy between ability and achievement. Thus, district selection criteria may further confound the already murky learning disability/low achievement question. The Kansas researchers documented considerable overlap between school-identified learning disabled and low achieving pupils, finding that many students identified as having learning disabilities were characterized by "generalized rather than specific learning deficits" which made it difficult to separate them from other low achieving students. In essence, the learning disabled students represented a more extreme position on the achievement deficiency continuum. Often "LD-ness" was a matter of degree, not of kind or pattern of deficits. In this regard Zigmond (1983) suggests a definition of learning disability based on an "easy-to-teach" to "very-hard-to-teach" continuum. In her view students with learning disabilities are those who, despite aptitude, are "nonresponders" to educational treatments. In contrast, the underachievers are more responsive to instruction.

Similar problems in differentiating students with learning disabilities from other low achieving students is seen at the college and adult levels. In an ongoing project conducted by the Consortium for the Study of Learning Disabilities in California Community Colleges (1983), researchers attempted to identify educationally relevant attributes or characteristics and technically adequate instruments which distinguished those with learning disabilities from other low achievers. Using literature searches and surveys of professionals, a list of 116 attributes was compiled; 55 of these distinguished those with learning disabilities from other low achievers. Ten discriminating items related to reading, eight to written communication, and eight to items in medical histories; seven were found to be professional-specific.

Based on pilot work involving assessment of students with learning disabilities and randomly selected comparison students, Consortium investigators applied several different eligibility models, setting a 10% prevalence criterion. Thirty-five percent of students identified as having learning disabilities were found to qualify on the basis of reading scores, 46% were eligible according to measures of written communication, and 26% qualified in arithmetic. Using the same formulae and cut-off level, 14%, 17%, and 23% of randomly selected non-learning disabled students were identified as eligible for learning disability designation on the three achievement dimensions, respectively. The mean IQ of the non-learning disability group was 108 (14.4); the mean for the learning disability group was 83 (9.3). Consortium investigators concluded on the basis of this pilot work that, "The profile of the LD population appears to be that of the low achieving student who is achieving at his/her expected achievement level" (p. 17).

Taken as a whole, then, across the range elementary school through community college, it is difficult to distinguish between individuals with learning disabilities and those who are more properly viewed as low achievers. Indeed, Edgar and Hayden (1984–85) suggest that "the early quantifiable aspect of the LD definition is low achievement" (p. 533). As noted by Turner and Wade (1982), issues of definition and identification as learning disabled are "even more acute in the birth to 3-year-old range" (p. 83). Given the escalating numbers of individuals identified as eligible for learning disability services, and given the overlap of those identified as having learning disabilities with normally developing and underachieving groups, it is clear that, to date at least, there are no agreed upon conceptual or operational criteria for classification. It is not surprising that prevalence figures vary dramatically from state to state, school district to school district, and clinician to clinician. It becomes necessary, then, to consider a variety of influences on classification decisions, and thus, upon incidence and prevalence.

Influences on Classification Decisions

The definitional problem at both conceptual and operational levels has plagued the field since its inception, and the published literature contains many perspectives, sometimes arguments, about what learning disability "really" is. (See *The Annual Review of Learning Disabilities*, 1983; Berk, 1984; Clements, 1966; Cruickshank, 1981, 1984; Friedrich, Fuller, & Davis, 1984; Kirk, 1962; Hallahan & Cruickshank, 1983; Hammill, Leigh, McNutt, & Larsen, 1981; National Advisory Committee on Handicapped Children, 1968; Shepard & Smith, 1983.) Rather than review the arguments presented in these sources, it may be more useful to identify and analyze the factors or influences which result in such inconsistencies. These include: professional and/or disciplinary perspectives; operational

TABLE 2
Disciplinary Perspectives on Learning Disabilities

	Medical/Neurological	Process	Behavioral	Educational
Focus and Etiology	Organic, in child	Psychological, in child	Setting/child inter-interaction	Child/instructional program interaction
When Identify	Infancy, preschool	Preschool	Preschool, school	School
Symptoms	Physical, neurological anomalies, soft signs	Visual, auditory, motoric processing problems	Disturbed behavior and achievement problems	Low achievement, behavior problems
How Identify	Neurological examination, EEG, psychoneurological tests	Process measures: ITPA, Bender Gestalt, psychoneurological tests	Behavior observation, task analysis	Educational and ability tests
Treatment Emphasis	Medication, diet	Process training	Behavior modification, situational change	Pedagogy, remedial intervention
Major Professional	M.D.	Psychologist	Psychologist/Teacher	Teacher

criteria used in identification, such as discrepancy formulae; measurement; other special education services; and system constraints. These are not mutually exclusive but have somewhat different emphases.

Professional and Disciplinary Perspectives

In contrast to some problem areas in which disciplinary or professional lines and responsibilities are clearly drawn (e.g., diagnosis and treatment of physical illness), the area of learning disabilitity is viewed as a reasonable and legitimate problem for professionals from many different disciplinary backgrounds. Learning disabilities and what to do about them are discussed in diverse literatures: neurology, psychiatry, opthalmology, optometry, psychology, education, occupational therapy, physical therapy, speech and language, social work, to name but a few. Professionals in these fields bring somewhat different views of what constitutes learning disability, how it should be assessed and diagnosed, and what should be done about it (Hocutt, Cox, & Pelosi, 1984; Keogh et al., 1982). There are also differences of opinion about who should be the professional in charge, and what constitutes muiltidisciplinary collaboration. For purposes of illustration, four somewhat different perspectives are summarized in Table 2. Particular techniques or approaches which characterize particular disciplines are provided as examples, not as comprehensive description.

Obviously, these approaches are not mutually exclusive; there is overlap and some consistency across perspectives. Yet, it is apparent that there are differences on a number of dimensions: focus and etiology, time of identification, symptoms, identification techniques, treatment, and professional responsibility. While some children will likely be identified as having learning disabilities by all approaches, specifics of perspectives and practices will lead to differences in numbers identified and in ways in which individuals are identified. The

diversity of perspectives and techniques was well illustrated in the UCLA Marker Variable Project (Keogh et al., 1982), which included a detailed review of 408 published research articles focused on the area of learning disability. Disciplines represented included medicine, education/psychology, and related fields (e.g., speech and hearing, optometry, etc.). More than 1,400 techniques and tests, including 38 different ability tests and 78 achievement measures, were reported used in diagnosis and identification of learning disability. The array of symptoms was also diverse (e.g., hyperactivity, hypotonia, sleep problems, vision inefficiencies), as well as general school failure and specific and limited disabilities. The range of attributes thought to characterize learning disability is probably in part related to differences in professional or disciplinary training and perspective (the eye of the beholder), as well as reflecting the complexity of the condition itself. Some of the inconsistencies and disparities in prevalence likely relate to who does the identification, and what data are used in diagnostic decisions.

Ability-Achievement Discrepancy Formula

Whatever the disciplinary perspectives and techniques, the notion of descrepancy is implicit in learning disability diagnosis (Keogh & Hall, 1984; Shepard, 1980). Indeed, a discrepancy between actual development or performance and expected development or performance is widely accepted "red flag" for learning disability even at preschool ages. What is often unclear, however, is how discrepant and discrepant from what? As the focus in this chapter is on learning disability within an educational context, the discrepancy between ability and achievement, including its operational implementation, will be emphasized. It is interesting to note that most definitions (Kirk, 1962; National Advisory Committee on Handicapped Children, 1968; National Joint Committee on Learning Disabilities, 1981; *PL 94–142*,

1975) do not operationally define discrepancy; rather, the discrepancy is inferred. The regulations developed to implement *PL 94–142*, for example, include a "definition" to be used by multidisciplinary teams in diagnosing learning disability. According to the statement, determination as learning disabled:

> is made based on (1) whether a child does not achieve commensurate with his age or her age and ability when provided with appropriate educational experience, and (2) whether the child has a severe discrepancy between achievement and intellectual ability in one or more of seven areas relating to communication skills and mathematical abilities. (*Federal Register*, 1977, 42, p. 655082)

Relatively early on in the development of operational regulations (*Federal Register*, 1976) the then Bureau of Education for the Handicapped proposed the following formula for determining a severe discrepancy: $SD = CA(IQ/300 + 0.17) = 2.5$. Following discussion and review by professional and advocacy groups (see Danielson & Bauer, 1978; Senf, 1978), this formula was subsequently rejected, and the final rules and regulations did not contain a specific formula for determining severe discrepancy. Rather, states were allowed to develop their own criteria within the broadly stated federal regulations. As particular states have adopted somewhat different formulae, it should not surprise us that prevalence figures vary so widely. Berk (1984), Boodoo (1984–85), Chalfont (1984), Cone and Wilson (1981), Friedrich et al. (1984), Loper and Reeve (unpublished), McLeod (1979), Page (1980), Reynolds (1984–85), Reynolds et al. (1984–85), Shepard (1980), Short and McKinney (1983), Willson and Reynolds (1984–85), and Wilson and Cone (1984) have provided critical analyses of various approaches to quantifying discrepancy. Cone and Wilson (1981) group the techniques into 4 major categories: grade level deviation, expectancy formula, standard score comparison, and regression analysis. The adequacy of these approaches relative to eight criteria (e.g., ease of implementation, error of measurement, regression to the mean, etc.) are shown in Table 3, taken from Cone and Wilson (1981, p. 369). Examination of the content of Table 3 shows clearly that the grade level deviation method (either constant deviation or graduated deviation) and the expectancy formulae have many flaws.

It should be emphasized, however, that none of the methods is without limitations. The years below grade level discrepancy, the simplest and widely used technique, has the most serious problems. As noted by Reynolds et al. (1984–85), from a mathematical perspective age and grade equivalents are inadequate; they are imprecise and easily misinterpreted. When used in a discrepancy formula they over-identify slow learners and under-identify bright children; they also over-identify children at the upper grades, not necessarily because

of real changes in ability, but because the standard deviation in grade equivalent units increases with grade level.

Expectancy formulae (see Algozzine, Forgnone, Mercer, & Trifiletti, 1979; Bond & Tinker, 1973; Harris, 1970; Johnson & Myklebust, 1967; Kaluger & Kolson, 1969), while somewhat more adequate than the grade level discrepancy in that they take into account ability and sometimes grade level, also have flaws. Shepard (1980) suggests that normative expectations for children with very high and very low mental ages at various chronological ages are uncertain; regression effects result in proportionally more bright than dull pupils identified; and, because the size of discrepancy is unspecified, small normal fluctuations in ability and achievement may be misinterpreted as expressing a real discrepancy. Despite these problems and limitations, Cone and Wilson (1981) report that at the time their article was published the expectancy formula proposed by Harris (1970), with slight modifications by the U.S. Office of Education, was the method most frequently used by states to quantify a discrepancy.

There is considerable agreement that both standard score comparisons and regression approaches are preferred alternatives to the techniques already described (Reynolds et al., 1984–1985; Shepard, 1980). Both are more defensible technically and both allow comparability of norms across tests, ages, and grades. A number of specific standard score formulae have been proposed (e.g., Erickson, 1975; Hanna, Dyck, & Holen, 1979). In essence, each involves computing standard scores on both ability and achievement measures. In the case of the standard score approach, the discrepancy is a direct comparison of ability and achievement scores; in the case of regression the scores are entered into a regression formula.

Standard scores provide a common scale for making comparisons between individuals or between tests. The unit of comparison is distance from the mean expressed in standard deviation units. The advantage of standard scores is that both ability and grade level are considered on comparable metrics. Where ability and achievement are similar (as in the case of normal learners or slow learners), the standard score (or deviation from the means) would be similar. In the case of children with learning disabilities the ability and achievement standard scores should differ. How different the scores must be or how large the discrepancy must be is uncertain. Erickson (1975) considered the 10% of pupils with the greatest discrepancy between IQ and achievement as those having learning disabilities. This method of determining discrepancy does not take into account regression effects, however; thus, brighter children will more likely be identified as having a significant discrepancy between ability and achievement than will duller children. Shepard (1980) proposes that one solution to the problem is to identify 10% of children with the largest discrepancies at each IQ level, thus ensuring

TABLE 3
Responsiveness of Criteria Types to Critical Variables

	Deviation from Grade Level	Expectancy Formula	Standard-Score Comparison	Regression Analysis
Ease of Implementation	Yes	Questionable	Yes, if values are tabled	Yes, if values are tabled
Years in school	No	Some	No	No
Increasing Range and Variability of Scores at Upper Grades	Yes, if a graduated procedure	Questionable	Yes	Yes
Systematic and Consistent Treatment of IQ/Achievement Interrelationship	No	Questionable	Yes	Yes
Error of Measurement	No	No	Yes	Yes
Regression toward Mean	No	No	Partially, if estimated true score procedures are used	Yes
A Priori Approximation of Incidence	No	No	No	Yes
Comparability of Norms	N/A	No	Yes, certain group tests; possibly certain individual tests	Yes, certain group tests; possibly certain individual tests

From T. Cone & L. R. Wilson, Quantifying a severe discrepancy: A critical analysis. *Learning Disability Quarterly*, *4*(4), p. 369.

sampling across the full performance continuum. Unfortunately, from a practical perspective this solution requires large sample sizes and is often not feasible to implement in many school districts.

The regression-discrepancy approach has received considerable support from a number of investigators (Horn & O'Donnell, 1984; Reynolds, 1984–85; Reynolds et al., 1984–85; Shepard, 1980; Willson & Reynolds, 1984–85; Wilson & Cone, 1984). Summarizing the strengths and weaknesses of the regression discrepancy method, Shepard (1980) suggests that advantages include: students with learning disabilities and slow learners are distinguished, as expected performance is predicted from ability across a full range of ability scores; grade level is taken into account, thus accounting for opportunity to learn; the 10% discrepancy based on standard scores at each grade level ensures comparability of numbers across grade; the multiple regression technique is based on actual relationship between ability and achievement; when used with similarly normed tests, sampling differences are minimized. The regression-discrepancy technique, like others, however, is vulnerable to two types of error: false identification of normal children as having learning disabilities (false positive); and false identification of children with learning disabilities as normal (false negative). Errors in classification are related to measurement errors, to

unreliability of instruments, and to use of tests which are normed on different populations. Further, an identified discrepancy may be due to a number of factors such as opportunity for schooling, motivation, and the like. These are not necessarily independent of learning disability, and may yield a higher number of pupils with discrepancies between ability and achievement who by other criteria would not be learning disabled. Finally, it should be noted that children with learning disabilities may be missed because the reasons for their poor performance on achievement tests (e.g., poor perceptual skills) may influence performance on ability tests, thus making them appear more like slow learners than like those with learning disabilities.

The consequences of the use of different discrepancy formulae is well illustrated by the work of several investigators. Horn and O'Donnell (1984) applied two discrepancy formulae to identify learning disabled and low-achieving first-graders. They found that different numbers of children were identified as having learning disabilities when unadjusted raw scores or regression–discrepancy criteria were used. Forness, Sinclair, and Guthrie (1983) applied eight different discrepancy formulae to a sample of 92 hospital inpatient children, ages 7–13 (CA mean = 10.1, $SD = 1.6$). All subjects were given the WISC-R and the Peabody Individual Achievement Test (PIAT); the reading recognition subtest was used in the discrepancy analysis. The eight discrepancy formulae applied were those proposed by U.S. Office of Education (1976), Bond and Tinker (1973), Harris (1982), Algozzine et al. (1979), Kaluger and Kolson (1969), Erickson (1975), Johnson and Myklebust (1967), and a simple "years behind" notion. Numbers of children identified as having learning disabilities varied from 10.9 to 37% of the sample. The fewest numbers were identified by the Johnson and Myklebust formulae (10.9%), the most by the Erickson formula (37%). The "years behind" formula, while the simplest, also identified a large number of children (32%). Only seven children (7.6%) were identified by all formulae. Most agreement was found between the Harris and the USOE formula, these identifying 17% and 25%, respectively. The Forness et al. (1983) findings are consistent with those of Epps, Ysseldyke, and Algozzine (1983), who applied 14 different learning disability definitions to a sample of 145 elementary-age children, 48 of whom were school-identified as having learning disabilities. Percentages of sample pupils identified as having learning disabilities ranged from 5.3 to 69.6 according to particular formulae. No formulae identified all the children with learning disabilities (range = 7.3% to 80.6%) All formulae identified some non-learning disabled children as learning disabled (range = 3.3% to 64.6%). Complete psychometric findings were available for 34 pupils with learning disabilities. Two of these were not identified as having learning disabilities with any of the formulae used; 17.6% were not identified by more than one. The investigators concluded that "identification as LD is a function not only of pupil characteristics but also of the formulae used as well as the specific tests used to derive the scores that are put into the formulae" (p. 349).

It should be noted that differences in numbers of children identified as having learning disabilities is not just a matter of differences in formulae applied. Danielson and Bauer (1978) applied the proposed federal (then Bureau of Education for the Handicapped) formula to 14 different school-generated data bases. Sizes of learning disability samples varied from 30 to 2,428. Across districts the percentage of already-identified pupils with learning disabilities qualifying according to the BEH formula varied from 38–95%; the mean percentage was 58%. The same formula classified 8–12% of non-learning disabled pupils as learning disabled. Clearly the discrepancy notion, while appealing on an intuitive level, has many problems in quantification and application. Some formulae are better than others, but all have weaknesses. Cone and Wilson (1981) stress that the various discrepancy methods require empirical validation. They note further that this means taking into account factors which affect the number of children evaluated. Many of these factors may be subsumed by Mehan, Meihls, Hertweck, and Crowdes' (1981) institutional constraints, a point discussed in a subsequent section of this chapter. Others relate to measurement. Shepard's (1983) advice is sound: "It is a good general rule when dealing with fallible measures never to trust a diagnosis unless it is independently confirmed by other measures" (p. 89).

Before a more detailed discussion of measurement issues and problems, it is important to underscore a major point about use of a discrepancy formula for identifying pupils with learning disabilities. Reynolds et al. (1984–1985), in the report of the Work Group on Assessment, emphasize that the presence of a severe discrepancy does not identify a child as having learning disabilities. Rather, the use of mathematically sound and appropriate formulae establish "a pool of children eligible for the diagnosis of learning disabled" (p. 32). Not all children in the pool will subsequently be determined to have learning disabilities, as the discrepancy may be caused by a number of factors. However, "The establishment of a severe discrepancy is a necessary but not sufficient condition for the diagnosis of a learning disability" (Reynolds et al., 1984–1985, p. 32). The discrepancy only provides a common "starting point" for more refined diagnostic efforts, a point to be elaborated in a later section of this chapter.

Measurement

The adequacy of any operational definition or quantitative formula is inherently tied to the adequacy of the data which provide the basis for the mathematical operations. As noted by Reynolds et al. (1984–1985), "Tests with less than the desirable psychometric characteristics can be misleading or lack adequate power to detect a severe discrepancy . . . The mathematical manipulations recommended . . . cannot transform the quality of the initial data" (p. 35). Unfortunately, in the identification of learning disability the quality of assessment is too often poor, a finding decried by many (Berk, 1984; Coles, 1978; Shepard, 1982, 1983; Shepard & Smith, 1983; Somwaru, 1979).

The issue of technical adequacy of tests used in learning disability decision-making has been addressed extensively by Ysseldyke and his colleagues. Thurlow and Ysseldyke (1979) documented which tests were most frequently used in learning disability "model" programs, finding many commonly used tests to be psychometrically inadequate. In this and in other work by the Minnesota group, technical adequacy was defined in terms of norms, reliability, and validity; these dimensions are consistent with the American Psychological Association 1974 test standards and with the criteria elaborated by Salvia and Ysseldyke (1981). Thurlow and Ysseldyke (1979) found that the various learning disability model centers used a range of tests, but that only 9 of the 30 most commonly used instruments (23%) met the three criteria (norms, reliability, validity). In a subsequent study Ysseldyke, Algozzine, Regan, and Potter (1980) found that the choice of technically adequate tests varied during the decision process, the earlier choices more adequate than later choices. LaGrow and

233

Prochnow-LaGrow (1982) applied the same three criteria to the 11 tests most commonly used by school psychologists in the state of Illinois, finding that only 2—the revised Wechser Intelligence Scale for Children (WISC-R) and the Peabody Picture Vocabulary Test (PPVT)—met all three requirements. A number of the most commonly used tests were inadequate on all three criteria. As part of the Consortium for the Study of Learning Disabilities in California Community Colleges (1983), the nine most commonly used tests for evaluating adult students were reviewed by three experts. Three tests of aptitude and two tests of achievement met the requirements of technical adequacy which made them appropriate for inclusion in discrepancy formulae.

These findings are supported by Davis and Shepard's (1983) study of Colorado specialists' use of tests. Their sample was made of learning disability teachers ($N=542$), school psychologists ($N=130$), and speech and language teachers ($N=179$). Overall they found that professionals "preferred" technically better tests, but frequently used those whose reliability and validity were inadequate. Tests were overrated by all three groups, and in general there was a notable lack of understanding of psychometric limitations. Interpretation was also problematic. Over one-third of the professionals sampled could not correctly identify a significant discrepancy presented in percentiles, many overestimating the significance of lesser discrepancies. Davis and Shepard essentially concur with Ysseldyke and his colleagues when they note that "the findings of this study suggest that the validity of the identification process for learning disabled students is reduced by a lack of technical knowledge on the part of professionals involved" (p. 137). In this regard, McDermott (1981) suggests that errors of diagnostic decision making include inconsistent decision rules, inconsistent theoretical orientations, inconsistent weighting of diagnostic cues, and inconsistency of diagnostic style.

Clearly there are problems on two levels: the actual psychometric properties of the tests, and the level of knowledge of the practitioners who use them. Both are likely contributors to the inconsistencies in learning disability prevalence rates. Further, as noted by Shepard (1983), an additional problem in learning disability identification relates to specialists' limited understanding of normal variability. Because of the focus on referred pupils, many professionals do not have a frame of reference grounded in normal development. There is, thus, a tendency to interpret particular behaviors as deviant when in fact they fall well within the range of individual differences expected in normal variation. This may be an additional factor which contributes to the high number of pupils identified as having learning disabilities.

In sum, then, measurement limitations, tied to inconsistencies in operationalizing discrepancies, contribute to the variation in learning disability prevalence figures. The measurement issue is particularly troubling, as measurement is a topic which has received excruciatingly detailed analysis by psychologists and psychometricians over the years. Yet, practice does not match the level of knowledge available. The APA has provided an explicit set of guidelines to govern testing. Salvia and Ysseldyke (1981) are among the many who have proposed reasonable and feasible criteria for test selection and use. In a recent analysis of learning disability identification practices, Reynolds et al. (1984–1985) proposed 11 guidelines for those involved in diagnosis. The points are mostly self-explanatory, so are merely listed. More detailed discussion and rationale may be found in the report of the Work Group (see Reynolds et al., 1984–1985), who suggest that input data in decisions about LD status should meet the following criteria: Tests should meet all requirements stated for assessment devices in the rules and regulations implementing *PL 94-142*; normative data should meet contemporary standards of practice and be provided for a sufficiently large, nationally stratified random sample of children; standardization samples for tests whose scores are being compared must be the same or highly comparable; for the purpose of arriving at a diagnosis, individually administered tests should be used; age-based standard scores should be used for all measures and all should be scaled to a common metric; the measures employed should demonstrate a high level of reliability and have appropriate studies for this determination in the technical manual accompanying the test; the validity coefficient, r_{xy}, representing the relationships between the measures of aptitude and achievement should be based on an appropriate sample; validity of test score interpretations should be clearly established; special technical considerations should be addressed when using performance-based measures of achievement (e.g., writing skill); bias studies on the instruments in use should have been conducted and reported. Adherence to these points would at least minimize one major source of error in identifying pupils with learning disabilities.

Finally, even when the psychometric properties of tests and the expertise of testers are adequate, a number of influences may lead to inappropriate conclusions or invalid inferences. Salvia and Ysseldyke (1981) emphasize that several conditions must be met before it is possible to draw inferences about traits or abilities from tests or other data collection techniques. These are especially relevant when attempting to measure abilities and characteristics of mildly handicapped children. First, there must have been opportunity for the individual to acquire the skill or behavior. Second, there must be motivation to perform. Third, the behavior-construct relationships must be similar in the child's culture/environment and in the validating situation. As Salvia and Hunt (1984) note, "If the student has not had the opportunity to acquire the skills, we are measuring the extent of disadvantage and not the constructs. Given unmotivated performance, we measure apathy, not the construct" (p. 34). Clearly, all of these influences are threats to the validity of identification of pupils with learning disabilities.

Institutional and Organizational Constraints

A number of recent analyses of special education programs (see Algozzine, Christenson, & Ysseldyke, 1982; Chalfont, 1984; Christenson, Ysseldyke, & Algozzine, 1982; Guiton, 1984a,b; Hocutt et al., 1984; Mehan et al., 1981; Shepard & Smith, 1981) suggest that referral, identification, and placement of pupils are influenced, even determined in part, by "institutional constraints," that is, by federal and state legislation, by school district policy, and by organizational arrangements within school districts. Mehan et al. (1981) base their argument on theories of organizational behavior which consider that school districts, like other public organizations, face competing demands or imperatives in the conduct of their business. In the case of special education, district personnel may be faced with demands of professional performance which may or may not be consistent with administrative requirements determined by extradistrict legislation or policy; for example, legal limits on numbers of pupils identified, or assessment procedures and time-lines. Hocutt et al., (1984) found that funding was the "major factor" which influenced programming policies and decisions. Pope (1982) has discussed statutory influences on pupil placement. Within the US, states use different guidelines for identifying mildly impaired pupils (Frankenberger, 1984; Hocutt et al., 1984; Norman & Zigmond, 1980). Further, changes in definition, legislation, and availability of resources lead to selection of somewhat different individuals as representatives of a given special education category or classification (Keogh & MacMillan, 1983; MacMillan, Meyers, & Morrison, 1980; MacMillan, Keogh, & Jones, 1986). The case is well illustrated by changes in the population served as mildly retarded (Algozzine & Korinek, 1985; Polloway & Smith, 1983). As will be discussed later, changes in one category have implications for changes in others, thus affecting prevalence. Some institutional influences on classification decisions deserve brief discussion.

Based on a microethnographic study of one public school district in California, Mehan et al. (1981) identified powerful institutional constraints which affected the referral and placement process and, thus, the nature of educational decisions about individual pupils. These institutional constraints also determined in part the number of pupils identified as having learning disabilities. In the district studied, 141 new referrals (5% of the total 2,781 pupils enrolled) were processed in a given calendar year. Thirty-six (25.7%) of those referred were placed in learning disability programs; 28 pupils (20%) were reviewed by the school appraisal team but were retained in regular classes; another 29 pupils (20%) remained in regular classes because of interruptions in the review process: in a sense, a placement by default. As Mehan et al. point out, pupils' progress through the

process was not necessarily a function of pupil characteristics, but rather reflected a number of decisions related directly to institutional constraints. Such constraints deserve brief discussion.

As noted by a number of observers, differences in definitions of learning disability and in formal and informal screening practices across schools lead to differences in formal referral rates. Mercer, Forgnone, and Wolking (1976) found 75 different educational components represented in the formal definitions of learning disability in 42 different states. Robbins, Mercer, and Meyers (1967) noted that there was variability in referral rates according to schools within one school district, some principals encouraging referrals, other principals discouraging them. In the school district studied by Mehan et al. (1981), formal referral varied because some building principals were actively involved in school level informal screening and review. One consequence was that cases were expedited through the system, leading to faster placement decisions and to higher placement rates. Administrative procedures and changes in administrative procedures for referral and review have also been found to influence rates of placement, as more complicated and formal referral procedures reduce the number of referrals. In contrast, inservice about learning disability may increase teachers' sensitivity to children's needs and lead to a larger number of referrals. In the Mehan et al. (1981) study, time of year was also an influence on referral rates, few referrals occurring in the last months of the school year (May and June), the highest referral rates in the midfall (October) and midwinter (February and March). These peaks and valleys in referral likely reflected in part teachers' awareness of children's problems and their feelings that referral would lead to services. They also may have reflected school psychologists' case loads, the backlog of accumulated cases in the spring, and/or the availability of space in particular programs. This interpretation is consistent with the findings of Robbins et al. (1967) that referral rates were related to psychologists' time allocations. As noted by Mehan et al. (1981), "it is not possible to be a 'special student' in the absence of institutionalized practices for their recognition and treatment . . . these [special educators] designations are influenced by the calendar and work load, which are institutionalized arrangements" (p. 396).

From material already reviewed, it is apparent that referral and placement decisions are influenced by legislatively designated limits or ceilings on numbers of pupils allowed, by the operational formula chosen to operationalize learning disability, and by the availability and training of professional personnel. Further, the economics of programs and space may be influences on selection. To illustrate, some school districts may seek more eligible pupils in order to fill empty quotas; other districts may deny learning disability status to pupils because of lack of space in programs. Funding resources thus becomes an influence on eligibility criteria and on numbers of pupils identified (Hocutt et al., 1984; Murai,

Barbara K. Keogh

1982).

Classification and placement are also related, in part, to the availability of other services, such as special reading programs. Where there are many services available, the need for extensive learning disability programs is reduced. Competition among special programs may also affect designation for special services. This problem is particularly relevant in the case of ethnic minority bilingual pupils. School district personnel are often reluctant to identify ethnic minority pupils as educable mentally retarded or as having learning disabilities, especially if the pupils may be receiving services in bilingual programs or in other compensatory programs. The long history of litigation concerning assessment and placement of minority children has not necessarily resulted in lower prevalence rates for minority children in special education (Lambert, 1981). However, it may have made school psychologists and administrators more sensitive to the implications of referral, placement, and labeling (see volumes edited by Hobbs, 1975). Thus, it might be argued that ethnic minority children may be underrepresented in learning disability programs, and that institutional and legal influences have resulted in denial of services to minority children with learning disabilities. It is possible, too, as suggested by Mehan et al. (1981), that in efforts to maintain ethnic parity in bilingual programs, school district personnel may be reluctant to remove nonminority children from such classes. In this case majority pupils may be denied opportunities for learning disability services.

The impact of legislative and political influences on institutional practices is seen in changes in classification of ethnic minority pupils as mentally retarded (see MacMillan, 1982; MacMillan et al., 1986; MacMillan et al., 1980). In California during the 1960s and 1970s the state mandated programs for educable mentally retarded and supported programs for educationally handicapped pupils, the latter now viewed as having learning disabilities. Differences in ethnic representation within the two classifications, coupled with the challenge of the identification and placement procedures for diagnosing ethnic minority pupils as educable mentally retarded, led to several pieces of legislation having major impact on program operation. Specifically, admission and continuance procedures for educable mentally retarded pupils were revised as were procedures for assessment and classification (California Education Code, 1970, Section 6902.10). Further, pupils already identified and placed in educable mental retardation programs were to be re-evaluated, and inappropriately placed pupils were to be moved to compensatory or supplementary educational programs, primarily within the regular education system (California Education Code 6902.08 and 6902.09, 1970). One immediate consequence of the legislation was that numbers of pupils in the educable mentally retarded and educationally handicapped categories changed dramatically. Whereas the prevalence figures for educable mental retardation had been stable over the 5-year period 1965–70 (mean number of educable mentally retarded

pupils approximately 53,000), following the legislation there was a sharp reduction in numbers so that in 1971–72 there were 38,200 pupils so classified. At the same time the number of educationally handicapped pupils increased to 58,000. It should be noted that the total number of pupils identified remained essentially the same. It was estimated that between 11,000 and 14,000 California pupils classified as educable mentally retarded changed status as a result of the 1970 legislation (Keogh, Becker, Kukic, & Kukic, 1972).

Similar findings are reported by Tucker (1980) in an analysis of a representative sample of 50 school districts in the southwest United States. The districts served over 40,000 pupils, the primary ethnic groups Anglo, black, and Mexican-American. Tucker's data show that the districts served 4.1% of the school population in special education in 1970, 11.8% in 1977. Of particular interest were changes in the percentages of pupils identified as having learning disabilities or as being educable mentally retarded: the former increased from 0.2% in 1971 to 5.2% in 1977; the latter declined from 1.5% to 1.2% over the same period of time. In 1973 the two prevalence curves crossed, learning disability and educable mental retardation classifications each serving 1.7% of the school population. Broken down by ethnic groups, Tucker found that blacks were overrepresented in educable mental retardation classes and that the numbers increased until 1973 when the percentage in the educable mentally retarded category leveled off and the percentage in the learning disability category climbed dramatically. As Tucker noted, "It does not take much imagination to infer that there is at least the possibility that when it was no longer socially desirable to place black students in EMR classes, it became convenient to place them in the newly provided LD category" (p. 103–104). Clearly the complexities associated with both learning disability and educable mental retardation definitions complicate the interpretation of "child counts" for either category and make it nearly impossible to estimate accurately prevalence of either condition. This point is argued by Guiton (1984b), who suggests that "the distribution of racial, ethnic and social groups may be a result of emphasis on proportional representation rather than the actual prevalence within the various groups . . . the exclusion of cultural and economic causes of disabilities . . . influences identification of minorities" (p. 15).

A similar effect of policy on prevalence may be seen in the adoption of a 50% discrepancy formula as a criterion for identification of students as having learning disabilities in New York. As noted by Stark (1982), in the 12 months following adoption of the 50% discrepancy criterion, the numbers of pupils identified as having learning disabilities dropped from 28,000 to 12,167. In essence, the 50% discrepancy made the learning disability category available primarily to severely impaired pupils. This policy was challenged by 18 pupils with learning disabilities and their parents on the basis that it exclusively affected one disability group, and that it disfavored children with mild handicaps, the Court ruling in their favor. By this decision the "unclassified" pupils still had learning disabilities and were eligible for services. However, the decision by the U.S. District Court was reversed by the U.S. Court of Appeals. In arriving at this decision, the Court acknowledged that the 50% discrepancy rule might deny special education opportunities to children, but noted that according to the Compliance Officer for *PL 94–142* from the Bureau of Education for the Handicapped, the federal regulations did not prohibit such a formula. Apparently, then, the number of children identified as having learning disabilities in New York may vary as a function of particular court decisions.

Finally, Christenson et al., (1982) studied the influences on teachers' decisions to refer children for evaluation and possible placement. These investigators suggest that barriers to and factors facilitating referral could be grouped into two categories. The first, institutional constraints, included three influences already discussed: organizational factors (e.g., district procedures, etc.), availability of services, and "hassle" (e.g., amount of paperwork, scheduling of meetings, etc.). The second, external pressures, included: external agencies (advocacy groups, etc.), federal and state guidelines and regulations, parents, and the socio-political climate. The institutional and external pressures as perceived by teachers were consistent with the findings of other investigators using different data sources and techniques, and thus lend support to the importance of system variables in decision making. It is likely that a range of system-related variables also influence decision of placement teams, as it has been shown that team decisions are often not data-based (Ysseldyke, Algozzine, Richey, & Graden, 1982).

Considerable evidence, thus, supports Mehan et al.'s (1981) argument that most special education decisions are "rarely developed in the manner implied by law" (p. 417), as the force of the many institutional constraints almost negates this possibility. This is not to question the integrity or competence of school district personnel, but rather to emphasize that decisions about special education classification are not only functions of child characteristics but also involve powerful organizational influences. Number of programs, availability of space, incentives for identification, range and kind of competing programs and services, number of professionals, and federal, state, and community pressures all affect classification decisions. Given the many influences and the lack of a clear consensus on what constitutes and characterizes learning disability, it should not surprise us that we face a serious and continuing definitional problem.

The Need for Classification

It is increasingly clear that the field is in need of a reasonable classification system, whether it is to provide programs and services or for the study of learning disability. To date, efforts at systematic description and classification have been driven by our search for a single definition. As a consequence, the definitional problem in the area of learning disability has been argued for years and still appears far from resolution, despite the efforts and opinions of many individuals and the position statements of professional groups. In 1971 Applebee suggested that, "The sine qua non of systematic investigation would seem to be a good operational definition of the phenomenon under study, one which is unambiguous, in some sense meaningful, and capable of being used by independent investigators" (p. 91). With the possible exception of meaningfulness, most definitions of learning disability fail to meet Applebee's criteria. Given the history of theory and research on the topic, it is reasonable to suggest that the definitional argument will go on so long as we seek a single class or category which presumably captures the parameters of a single condition. Rather, what is needed is a classification system or taxonomy which encompasses and organizes logically the diversity contained in learning disability. Fleishman (1982, p. 824), based on Sokal's (1974) work, notes that "the *subject matter* of taxonomy arises from questions regarding the matter of similarity." Bailey (1973) defines classification as "the ordering of concepts into groups (or sets) on the basis of their relationships, that is, of their associations by contiguity, similarity, or both (adapted from Sokal and Sneath, 1963:3)" (p. 19).

The need for a workable taxonomy is not unique to the field of learning disability, of course. Questions of classification confront all scientific fields. From a broad clinical perspective Shaywitz and Shaywitz (1984) suggest "that fundamental to diagnosis is the necessity to precisely and systematically define the clinical entity in question. Central to such a definition is the establishment of a nosology, a generally accepted classification system that would be useful and relevant to both clinicians and investigators" (p. 429). Typologies and taxonomies provide the basis for organization of content, determine group membership, order attributes, and direct research and program efforts. Typologies bring order to a field by identifying classes or groups which have certain characteristics, attributes, and properties. A class is defined in terms of the necessary and sufficient properties for membership. As noted by Bailey (1973), some classes are *monothetic*: possession of a certain characteristic(s) assures class membership as the attribute is both necessary and sufficient. Other classes are *polythetic*: no single characteristic is necessary or sufficient for membership, but groups are defined by the number of shared attributes. It might be noted that the natural sciences (e.g., botany) tend to use monothetic taxonomic approaches, while polythetic groupings are more common in the social sciences.

Monothetic classification systems may be defined from a conceptual level exclusively, but most polythetic typologies are empirically derived. That is, they emerge from empirical description of individuals, and are often

237

defined on the basis of statistically determined probabilities. Polythetic categories are not as conceptually clean as monothetic ones, but from a clinical perspective they may reflect the complexity of the symptom array. For example, clinical syndromes (i.e., a set of symptoms which covary) have usually been identified on the basis of clinical observations and tests. Any one individual within the syndrome may not have all of the symptoms which define the syndrome but all will share some of the characteristics.

Applying this to learning disabilities, it is clear that not all children called learning disabled exhibit all symptoms. Not all are hyperactive or have reading problems or evidence reversals or are hypotonic; not all have perceptual or memory or auditory sequencing problems. However, many share *some* of these characteristics. Except for "normal ability" and some achievement or performance deficit(s)—Reynolds et al.'s (1984–1985) criteria for membership in the learning disability eligibility pool—there are no specific symptoms or characteristics which are necessary or sufficient to ensure that a child will be called learning disabled. Learning disability is clearly a polythetic grouping system which allows considerable heterogeneity. A whole variety of subgroups are subsumed under this broad rubric. Following this line of reasoning, we should anticipate that few groups of learning disabled children would be similar on all characteristics. A learning disability classification system, then, might best be viewed as a polythetic system in which subgroups are defined in terms of the frequency and the salience of particular characteristics. This is a "shared attribute" notion which gets away from monothetic typologies or single syndrome classes.

It should be emphasized that in applied fields such as special education in general and learning disability specifically, classifications or groupings are almost exclusively empirically derived. Rather than being conceptually based, classification systems are developed to meet particular needs. Fleishman's (1982) argument that the first priority in a classification effort is to determine purpose is relevant. "Once the purpose for classification has been established, the attributes of the organism or relationships to be classified can be specified" (p. 825). Unfortunately, in the field of learning disability the purposes are often unspecified or overlapping. In earlier work Keogh (1983) suggested that learning disability classification serves several purposes: as a focus for advocacy, for the delivery of services, and for the scientific study of the condition. The purposes determine the operational definitions and selection practices. Importantly, the definitions and procedures may differ according to purpose. Specifically, if the purpose of classification is to determine eligibility for services for children with learning/achievement problems, then a precise definition may not be necessary; services should be provided to all who need them. If the purpose of classification is to study a specific type of learning disability (e.g., a learning disability associated with a known neurological condition, a specific mathematics

disability, or short-term memory problems), then precise and limiting definitions are imperative. Confusions and inconsistencies occur when inferences are drawn from one definitional category to another, or when individuals identified under one definition are assumed to represent another. The implications of this point for research and program evaluation are discussed in detail in a later section of this chapter. At this point it is sufficient to reiterate that given the multipurposes of learning disability classification, and because the classification approach is polythetic rather than monothetic, we should expect heterogeneity, not homogeneity, within groups.

What seems increasingly clear is that we have perpetuated our misunderstanding of learning disability by attempting to relate theory, research, practice, advocacy, and policy to a single definition. Rather than a single classification of learning disability, we need a multidefinitional approach which encompasses a series of learning disabilities. It would be expected that such a set of learning disabilities would have reliably specifiable characteristics and relationships. Indeed, some classes would probably be subsumed to logical superordinates. What is needed, then, is a taxonomy of learning disabilities. The purpose of a taxonomy is not to do away with the heterogeneous array now gathered under the term learning disability, but rather to describe and order the array in a logical and useful definitional system.

A Lesson from Psychiatry?

In a classic article, Zigler and Phillips (1961) addressed some of the vagaries and complexities in diagnostic classification in psychiatry, stating, "Reduced to its essential, diagnostic classification involves the establishment of categories to which phenomena can be ordered . . . Class membership conveys information ranging from the descriptive similarity of two phenomena to a knowledge of the common operational processes underlying the phenomena" (p. 608). At issue, of course, is the degree to which a classification system yields homogeneous, reliable, and meaningful categories or subgroups. Blashfield and Draguns (1976) suggest four empirical criteria for evaluating classification in psychiatry: reliability, coverage, descriptive validity, and predictive validity. These deserve brief review.

Reliability refers to the degree of agreement with which individuals are assigned to a category. Do different classifiers agree that Child A is learning disabled, mildly retarded, emotionally disturbed, or none of these? Or that learning disabled Child B is dyseidetic or disphonetic, or a global language disability subtype rather than a specific language and auditory perceptual subtype? Reliability or extent of diagnostic agreement may be influenced by a number of factors not directly related to the child, for example, the specificity and precision of the definition of the classification or category, the training of the diagnostician, the nature and amount of information used by the diagnostician, and the consistency of the diagnostician (Blashfield & Draguns, 1976). Given the imprecision of definition which characterizes learning disability, the many professions and disciplines involved in the field, and the array of tests and diagnostic techniques used in identification, it should come as no surprise that diagnosis and classification is unreliable. One consequence of unreliability of diagnosis, well documented by different investigators, is that identification as having or not having learning disabilities varies by school district, state, and diagnostician, a point already covered in some detail.

A second criterion for a classification system is *coverage*, defined by Blashfield and Draguns (1976) as "the applicability of a classification to the domain of patients for which it was intended" (p. 114). Put directly, does the classification system account for all of the individuals who represent the condition? The point is particularly relevant in the study of learning disability, as the exclusionary emphasis in many definitions may lead to limited coverage. For example, it is possible that there are a number of children with learning disabilities who are visually impaired, but who are not diagnosed as having learning disabilities because of their sensory impairment. It is likely that there are pupils from culturally different or disadvantaged socioeconomic homes who are denied services because of their ethnic or economic status. Blashfield and Draguns point out that reliability and coverage are inversely related. The more precise the definitional criteria, the better the reliability but the more limited the coverage. Blashfield (1973) suggests that this paradox might be addressed through the use of diagnostic categories which represent homogeneous clusters of individuals. (See discussion of the use of clustering techniques for the delineation of subtypes of learning disability by McKinney, 1984, 1988.) The point to be emphasized here is the importance of coverage in a classification system.

A third criterion for evaluating classification systems proposed by Blashfield and Draguns (1976) is *descriptive validity*, "the degree of homogeneity of the category of behaviors, symptoms, personality characteristics, social history data, and other kinds of information which are used to make a diagnosis" (p. 115). These criteria were suggested in regard to psychiatric diagnosis. In the case of learning disability types and subtypes, the criteria might include instead (or in addition) individual characteristics of ability, achievement in various subject matter areas, associated behavioral and motivational attributes, and the like. While theoretically the notion of homogeneity is an attractive one, it is obviously difficult to achieve, especially when identification is polythetic, that is, is based on many variables. The more precise and detailed the definitional parameters, the more homogeneous the group, but the fewer individuals who fit. However, Zigler and Phillips (1961) suggest that the inclusion of a heterogeneous array within a category does not negate the value of a classification system, as homogeneity is a function of the classification principle

employed. Given the number of different classification criteria employed in the area of learning disability, it should not surprise us that any learning disability classification would contain a wide range of subject attributes. What is lacking to date is the specification and organization of relationships among these attributes. If a taxonomy of learning disability were to be developed it would likely be composed of some broad superordinate categories containing a relatively heterogeneous array of individuals; the broad array, however, would necessarily include a number of smaller but tighter subgroups. What is important, of course, is similarity on the classification principle(s).

Finally, Blashfield and Draguns (1976) argue that *predictive validity* must be considered a primary criterion in developing a classification system, as membership in a class presumably has implications for treatment: "a classification is important to clinicians if it helps them treat their patients more adequately" (p. 116). From an educational perspective, Torgesen (1985) also argues that the importance and validity of a classification system is its usefulness in predicting response to treatment, that is, to educational intervention. This point is particularly important in the area of learning disability where the primary purpose for identification of individuals is to provide services. Thus, the issue of predictive validity, for example, how is identification as learning disabled linked to treatment or intervention, is especially troublesome. As discussed earlier, in the field of learning disability there are many advocates for a variety of treatment approaches. This in part is a reflection of the multidisciplinary nature of the field. Professionals bring different orientations to the same learning disability problem. Unfortunately, the efficacy of many programs is often unknown, even untested, and possible aptitude-treatment interactions are ignored. The identification and test of links between diagnostic category and treatment are essential considerations in learning disability classification efforts.

Classification and Identification

The monothetic-polythetic classification distinction has already been noted. It is also important to recognize differences between classification and identification. As pointed out by Bailey (1973), classification is measurement-free. It is conceptual. Identification is measurement-based, and involves the assignment of individuals to given classes. The distinction is important, as in some clinical typologies or classification systems there often appears to be a confounding of classification and identification. That is, the operationally identified groups are presumed to have conceptual credibility and to represent theoretically sound classification criteria. Such an inference is clearly suspect in the area of learning disability, in that many definitions of learning disability were not developed from theoretical or conceptual perspectives, but rather emerged from the characteristics of subjects already identified. The circularity of such classification is obvious and has been discussed in detail by MacMillan et al. (1980, 1986) and by Keogh and MacMillan (1983); implications for both research and practice are elaborated in a subsequent section of this chapter.

The quality of measurement poses an additional threat to the validity of identification and thus to empirically defined classification. That is, a class or category may be conceptually sound but the defining criteria may not be measured with precision. Referring specifically to the field of learning disability, Shepard (1983) noted that troublesome measurement problems include: the technical adequacy (inadequacy) of tests; lack of awareness of technical inadequacy by clinicians; inappropriate selection of measures, that is, selection based on traditional, disciplinary-linked tests; the continued application of inaccurate "conventional wisdom" in regard to learning disability. Additional problems of measurement and identification relate to limited understanding of normal variations, leading to inaccurate and invalid interpretations of particular behaviors or signs and the continued and usually inappropriate use of discrepancy formulae for indentification and selection.

Classification in the Area of Learning Disability

Given the distinction, then, between classification and identification and the realization that most learning disability classifications have been derived from preselected samples using inadequate measures, major questions become: Can we identify necessary and sufficient characteristics which constitute membership in a class or subclasses of learning disability? Can we accurately and reliably identify individuals to fit these classes or categories?

In their 1976 *Introduction to Learning Disabilities*, Hallahan and Kauffman noted that most definitions of learning disability rely on three general factors as signalling learning disabilities within a school context: achievement discrepant from presumed ability, uneven academic and/or ability patterns, and behaviors suggestive of some underlying neurological problem. These three factors continue to appear in more recent definitions of learning disability (e.g., National Joint Committee on Learning Disabilities, 1981), the ability-achievement discrepancy being the single most widely accepted index of learning disability (see Keogh & Hall, 1984, for discussion). What is important to emphasize is that none of these factors is itself definitive, but rather identifies a pool of potential individuals with learning disabilities (Reynolds et al., 1984–1985). Whether a child with an ability-achievement discrepancy will be identified as having learning disabilities depends upon a number of factors, including child characteristics and system variables.

The system influences on identification and selection of children as having learning disabilities have already

been discussed. Examination of descriptive studies of individuals with learning disabilities suggests that a wide range of personal attributes are also characteristic. Yet, not every individual identified as having learning disabilities will evidence all of the characteristics; some may be characterized by only one or two, others by a long list. Some children with learning disabilities may have a number of mild symptoms which lead to identification, others may have only a few extreme indicators. Both number of learning disability characteristics and their salience are probable influences on identification. The Reynolds et al. (1984–1985) notion of a "pool" of possible pupils with learning disabilities based on the ability-achievement discrepancy criterion suggests that the discrepancy is a necessary but not a sufficient condition for identification as learning disabled. It also acknowledges that there are many child and extrachild variables which may in combination lead to identification. What is proposed, then, is a shared attribute approach to defining learning disability.

Nichols and Chen's (1981) follow-up of the large sample of children included in the National Collaborative Perinatal Project (NCPP) of the National Institute of Neurological and Communication Disorders and Stroke is instructive in regard to the shared attribute notion. The NCPP study was carried out prospectively in 12 university hospitals in various parts of the country and included pre-, peri-, and postnatal data on over 44,000 women and their offspring. The women were registered in the study between 1955 and 1959. The follow-up study of offspring was carried out when the children were 7 years old. Following exclusion for lack of complete information (or because the IQ was below 80 or the child had been diagnosed as having cerebral palsy, etc.), 29,889 children were studied for possible manifestation of minimal brain dysfunction (MBD), a condition often associated with and sometimes considered the same as learning disability. Four sets of symptoms were assessed: behavioral, cognitive and perceptual-motor, academic, and neurological. No single MBD factor emerged from statistical analyses. Rather, four factors were identified: hyperkinetic-impulsive behavior (HI), learning difficulties (LD), neurological soft signs (NS), and social immaturity. Each child was assigned a factor score on each factor, and the extreme (lowest 8%) on each factor were considered representative of the condition. For purposes of this paper only the findings for the first three factors will be considered.

The Learning Difficulties group was made up of children whose achievement test scores were "considerably lower" than their performance predicted from IQ, a criterion consistent with traditional definitions of learning disability. The Hyperkinetic Impulsive and Neurological Soft Signs groups evidenced symptom patterns consistent with accepted clinical interpretation. Table 4, taken from Nichols and Chen (1981, p. 43), provides a description of the pattern of conditions across sex and ethnic groups. What is especially to be noted, is that almost 79% of the total sample had no abnormal scores;

TABLE 4
MBD SYMPTOMS AMONG NCPP CHILDREN

Percentages of Children in the MBD Cohort with Abnormal
MBD Factor Scores

Abnormal Scores	White Boys	White Girls	Black Boys	Black Girls	Total
LD only	6.89	3.51	10.81	5.27	6.54
HI only	6.96	5.07	5.83	5.47	5.85
NS only	9.66	6.05	5.41	3.14	6.15
LD + HI	1.27	0.61	1.38	0.67	0.98
LD + NS	1.13	0.40	0.84	0.26	0.66
HI + NS	1.74	0.64	0.77	0.33	0.89
LD + HI + NS	0.37	0.08	0.19	0.08	0.18
LD (Total)	9.66	4.60	13.22	6.28	8.36
HI (Total)	10.33	6.40	8.17	6.56	7.90
NS (Total)	12.90	7.17	7.21	3.81	7.88
No Abnormal Scores	71.99	83.64	74.77	84.78	78.76

From P. L. Nichols & T. C. Chen (1981). *Minimal Brain
Dysfunction: A Prospective Study*. Hillsdale, New Jersey:
Erlbaum. p. 43.

TABLE 5
Percentages of NCPP Followup Sample (CA 7 Years)
Showing MBD Symptoms, by Subgroups and Total

Symptom	Hyper-kinetic Impulsive N=2356	Neuro-logical Soft Signs N=2358	Learning Diffi-culties N=2358	Total Sample N=29,889
Hyperactivity	80.4	15.9	16.2	9.3
Hypoactivity	1.5	14.7	11.9	13.2
Impulsivity	50.4	7.2	6.9	4.0
Short attention span	60.3	20.2	25.3	12.5
Emotional lability	28.7	8.0	6.6	4.6
Withdrawal	2.9	9.0	8.4	5.9
Socioemotional immaturity	19.0	19.4	13.6	14.3
Low verbal IQ	8.0	7.5	12.3	9.1
Low performance IQ	13.2	13.7	7.0	10.0
Poor condition	14.0	73.9	9.9	8.1
Abnormal gait	6.9	38.4	4.3	3.5
Impaired position sense	1.7	8.5	1.8	1.1
Nystagmus	1.1	4.3	1.0	0.8
Strabismus	10.1	18.5	9.5	8.1
Astereognosis	1.1	3.5	1.3	0.8
Abnormal reflexes	17.1	43.9	15.8	14.2
Mirror movements	2.8	14.1	2.0	2.1
Other abnormal movements	4.0	16.9	1.8	1.9
Abnormal tactile finger recognition	20.7	16.6	22.6	12.9

Adapted from Nichols and Chen, 1981.

fewer than 1% of the children had abnormal scores in
all three problem areas. Yet, approximately 8% had
abnormal scores in one of the three (Learning Difficulties 8.36%, Hyperkinetic-Impulsive 7.90%, and Neurological Soft Signs 7.88%).

Table 5, adapted from Nichols and Chen (1981), provides a summary of symptoms or problems represented
in the three groups under consideration. There are obvious differences in patterns of problems across the
groups, providing further support for some association
of symptoms within grouping, at the same time under-
scoring the variability of symptom patterns within conditions. Within the Learning Difficulties group, for
example, percentages of children showing symptoms
varied from 25.3% (short attention span) to 7% (poor
coordination) and 2% (mirror movements), all frequently suggested as learning disability characteristics.
It is interesting, too, that the values for hyperactivity
and hypoactivity were 16.2% and 11.9%, respectively.
More children with learning difficulties were withdrawn
(8.4%) than were impulsive (6.9%). Taken as a whole,
the Nichols and Chen findings underscore the variability
of within-group characteristics.

If child attributes are viewed as "symptoms," it seems
likely that it is number, salience or intensity, and chronicity of attributes which determine which individuals in
the eligibility pool are identified as having learning disabilities. The idea of shared attributes rather than specific criterial attributes may provide a way to organize
the broad array of subject variables into conceptually
coherent and empirically consistent categories of learning disability. That is, certain characteristics may appear
together with regularity (e.g., attention deficits and
hyperactivity); other characteristics may have underlying process links (e.g., various kinds of memory
problems). Some attributes may be age-linked, while
others are independent of developmental level. Still
other attribute-symptoms may be relatively stable and
be elicited across many situations. Covariation among
attributes or symptoms may allow identification of useful empirically derived subclasses within the broad
learning disability category. Such subclasses may also
provide a direction for conceptual clarity.

A number of empirical or statistical approaches to
definition and classification have included learning disability or learning disability-relevant variables and provide a background for definitional efforts. Examples of
such approaches include Achenbach and Edelbrock's
(1978) work on child psychopathology (Achenbach,
1978), DeRuiter, Ferrell, and Kass' (1975) Bayesian
aggregation approach, Gajar's (1979, 1980) discriminant function studies, McDermott's systems-actuarial
method (1980 a, 1980 b, 1981; Hale & McDermott,
1984; McDermott & Hale, 1982); and Quay's (1972)
factor analytic efforts. In addition, a number of inferential or consensus classification systems (e.g., the 1980
Diagnostic and Statistical Manual [DSM-111] of the
American Psychiatric Association) have attempted to
bring order to a complex array of problems. Currently

there is considerable interest in efforts to identify, through various empirical techniques, useful and stable subtypes of learning disability. Detailed review of such work may be found in papers by McKinney (1984, 1988).

Subtype Studies

As argued by McKinney (1984), subtyping efforts are based on the view that a "single syndrome" theory cannot account for the substantial heterogeneity within samples of children with learning disabilities drawn under the present definition used in PL 94–142. McKinney supports the direction taken by Doehring (Doehring, 1978; Doehring & Hoshko, 1977; Doehring, Hoshko, & Bryans, 1979) and Satz (Satz & Fletcher, 1980; Satz & Morris, 1981) in the study of reading problems. Doehring and his colleagues proposed a "multiple syndrome paradigm" in which the broad reading problem rubric is viewed as including a number of distinct but relatively homogeneous subgroups. The identification of consistent and reasonable subgroups within the learning disability category would be helpful both theoretically and practically. Further, the specification of similarities and differences within the learning disability category might also sort out some of the overlap with other diagnostic groupings, such as mild mental retardation, slow learners, etc. Despite the appeal of the notion of reasonable and stable learning disability subgroups, their specification and test is not without problems (see Fisk & Rourke, 1984; Lyon, 1985; Morris, Blashfield & Satz, 1981; Rourke, 1976). One of the most obvious problems in integrating the work to date is that different researchers using different measures and different statistical techniques sometimes identify qualitatively and quantitatively different subtypes. (See Boder, 1973; Doehring & Hoshko, 1977; Lyon, Stewart & Freedman, 1982; Lyon & Watson, 1981; Lyon, Watson, Reitta, Porch & Rhodes, 1981; Mattis, 1978; Mattis, French & Rapin, 1975; Petrauskas & Rourke, 1979; Satz & Morris, 1981; Speece, McKinney & Appelbaum, 1985.)

While it is clear that there are some similarities across subtypes, it is also clear that the number and precise definitions of 100 subgroups vary by investigator. These differences in part may reflect the many disciplines and professions involved in the study and treatment of learning disabilities. Medical, psychological, and educational investigators rely on somewhat different signs and symptoms and may respond to different expressions of the condition. It is not surprising, then, that investigators from different disciplines identify somewhat different subgroups of learning disability. As already noted, sampling practices may affect the number and nature of subgroups, so we should expect that research with system-identified samples will yield some inconsistencies in subtypes. To add further to the problems, subtyping methods may influence the number and content of categories. For example, Riley (1980) found 13 clusters when using a qualitative analysis, 8 when using a statistical clustering technique. Based on his own work as well as the findings of others, Lyon (1983, 1985) suggests that multivariate classification procedures are promising, but are still being tested within the context of learning disability subtyping. Despite the substantive and methodological problems in subtype delineation, however, it represents one empirically-based approach to the development of a system or taxonomy within the learning disability field. Given the lack of conceptual clarity to direct our definitional and classification efforts, it seems likely that an empirical approach is necessary.

From an educational perspective Torgesen (1985) posed three questions to guide such work: (1) What specific processing disabilities are responsible for the patterns of scores used to identify groups? (2) How do those processing disabilities affect performance on important school tasks? and (3) Are there treatment procedures that are uniquely effective or ineffective with particular subgroups? Torgesen's questions provide a frame of reference in which both the internal adequacy of a classification system and its relevance for services to pupils with learning disabilities can be considered.

Discussion and Recommendations
The Definitional Problem

Up to this point in this chapter no attempt has been made to define learning disability. This has not been oversight, but rather was a purposeful omission. The history of the field of learning disability has been characterized by controversy about "the definition." Based on the material contained in this review, it seems unlikely that a single theoretically sound and empirically verifiable definition is possible, at least at this time in our history. Rather, it seems more reasonable and more productive to direct our efforts toward a comprehensive descriptive system which can encompass the many facets in the field and which will be useful to clinician/practitioners, researchers, and policy makers. The search for a single definition to drive the various forces in the field has proved fruitless in the past; somewhat pessimistically, one may conclude that it will probably continue to be so in the future.

While acceptance of a single definition of learning disability is improbable, it is instructive to consider some of the reasons for the continuing definitional arguments. A number of these reasons are contained in previous sections of this chapter, for example, disciplinary and professional points of view, institutional constraints, measurement limitations, and so forth. More fundamental, however, is the point that definitions serve different purposes, have meaning for different constituencies, carry diverse operational and conceptual implications. The researcher who attempts to test particular components of memory or attention must define learning disability in certain conceptually and operationally concise ways; only a few individuals from a large learning disability pool may meet the specific definitional criteria.

In constrast, a school district arguing for more support to increase the number and the scope of services may apply a broader definition. Such a definition would likely subsume a number of researcher-defined groups and would ensure services to the largest number of pupils possible. Definitions are linked to purposes, and thus the reasons for definition and classification require specification and clarity. Recognition of the multiple purposes for defining learning disability is a first and necessary step in reducing the present confusion and controversy.

Another step towards resolving the definitional problem is to acknowledge that there are few, if any, specific criterial attributes of learning disability. Rather, within the school context, at least, we have a substantial number of individuals whose low performance, relative to their presumed aptitude, makes them eligible for further consideration as possibly having learning disabilities. This point has already been discussed in this chapter and by Reynolds et al. (1984–1985). In addition to a pool of individuals, we also have a pool of attributes or symptoms which appear in varying combinations and in different degrees of severity, intensity, and chronicity. Thus, one pupil identified as having learning disabilities, in addition to a performance-aptitude difference, may have mild signs of impulsivity, inattention, social withdrawal, poor fine motor coordination, and clumsiness. The combination of these mildly expressed problems may be enough to lead to identification as learning disabled. In contrast, a second pupil with learning disabilities in the same group may have excellent fine and gross motor coordination and be socially adequate, but be extremely hyperactive and inattentive. Although few in number, the severity of symptoms or attributes may also lead to identification as learning disabled. In short, learning disability definitions must necessarily take into account both number and severity of attributes. Here is where the shared attributes notion is relevant. Part of the research task is to delineate and describe the probabilities of various associations or relationships of attributes within the symptom pool. A related task is to determine the impact of these combinations of attributes on the probability of identification as learning disabled, taking into account the purposes of identification and the nature of the constraints of the system within which the identification occurs.

Solving the definitional problem, then, is not just a matter of reliable specification of child or subject characteristics. Its resolution involves consideration of the social and institutional context in which identification occurs, thus necessitating inclusion of program as well as subject variables. This broader perspective on defining learning disability carries a number of implications for those providing services and for those conducting research. It also brings current limitations on research and practice into sharp focus.

Limitations on Research and Practice

The need for a closer liaison between research and practice has been a continuing call in education in general and in special education in particular. The notion has intuitive appeal as it conjures up such terms as relevant, meaningful, and useful, and makes the clinician-practitioner and the researcher partners in a worthwhile effort. However, review of the state of the art of both research and practice suggests that the combined efforts to date have not worked well. It might be argued that the research literature is weakened by efforts to be relevant, and that practice is carried out in ignorance of or in actual rejection of research findings. The literature on learning disability is replete with examples (e.g., issues surrounding process training for reading disabilities). Where there is conflict it is not possible to say whether the clinician or the researcher is correct. In essence, they ask different questions: What do we know about the nature of this condition? What services should be provided? The first is a "scientific" question; the second is a systems or organizational question. Unfortunately, in our efforts to respond to each, we may have confounded both. Research directed at understanding learning disability has too often been limited by its programmatic context. That is, we have attempted to generalize about the nature of learning disability from study of individuals and programs classified as learning disabled. This is clearly circular.

Kavale (1983) has discussed sources of variability in special education research, including differences in theoretical frameworks, design, data analytic methods, and so forth. He has also implicated sampling differences and program labels, a point to be stressed in the present discussion. In this regard Gallagher (1984) noted that the "key element in populations of learning disabled children is not their commonality but their diversity" (p. 571), a point seconded by many researchers and clinicians. What is important to emphasize is that subject diversity has different implications for program practices and for research.

At the level of services, pupil diversity can be tolerated and responded to, as individualization of instruction is possible, even desirable, if we take seriously the idea of the Individual Education Program (IEP). In any group of pupils with learning disabilities there may need to be as many different instructional programs as there are pupils; pupils will differ from each other on a range of personal abilities and attributes, and may respond to somewhat different instructional and treatment programs. Further, groups of pupils with learning disabilities will likely differ by school, school district, and by state. The consequence of different system influences is diversity or heterogeneity of individuals selected. Thus, the effectiveness of a given program may be different in various geographic areas. From a clinical perspective this is probably to be valued as it reflects local needs.

From a research perspective, it raises serious and continuing problems which limit inferences and generalizations about the nature of learning disability.

Several points are illustrative. Considering first the selection of research samples, it should be noted that the majority of research studies of learning disability draw subjects from pools of individuals already identified as having learning disabilities, for example, from public school learning disability programs, from clinic rosters, from rolls of special private schools or services, and so forth. System effects on identification and selection have already been reviewed. MacMillan et al. (1980) have described the problems of research on mental retardation using "system-identified" subjects. Similar problems are apparent in the study of learning disability (Keogh & MacMillan, 1983; MacMillan et al., 1986). The use of system-identified subjects for research may tell us a good deal about differences in selection practices but limits drastically generalizations about the learning disability condition(s). Given variability across systems, it should come as no surprise that the findings in the learning disability research and program evaluation literature are inconsistent and discrepant. In part, at least, these differences are a function of sample differences.

Carrying the subject variability notion further, it is also likely that within-sample variance confounds results of many studies carried out within the experimental tradition. The principles of that method are of necessity routinely violated or ignored in research on learning disability: random assignment of subjects to treatment is usually not possible for both ethical and practical reasons; homogeneity of subgroups on a number of individual attributes is suspect; control or comparison groups may contain unknown exemplars of learning disability. Given the vagaries of selection and identification documented by Shepard and Ysseldyke and their associates (Shepard, 1983; Shepard & Smith, 1981, 1983; Ysseldyke et al., 1982), we have good reason to believe that a number of unidentified "learning disability" pupils are in regular classes, and thus may be selected as normal controls in research studies. In short, the use of system-identified subjects in most cases challenges the assumptions of the experimental paradigm, confounds findings, limits interpretations, and threatens external validity.

The impact of sample variance is no less important for the program evaluator who attempts to document instructional effects or who seeks to delineate program-pupil interactions. Specification of links between instructional approaches and learning disability is clearly of high priority for both clinicians and policy makers. A variety of evaluation models are available to further efforts at documenting program effects, and many of these, including the single subject designs (Repp & Brusca, 1983; Strain, McConnell & Cordisco, 1983; White, 1984) are extraordinarily powerful. Yet, review of the instructional effects literature with learning disability yields inconsistent and often conflicting findings. Just as sample variance is a threat to the validity of research directed at understanding learning disability, so it is a threat to the delineation of instructional effects. A given program may work well in one state but not in others, in one school but not another, in one time period but not another. Program practices may be similar, but the children served may differ, thus leading to different findings and to different judgments about efficacy. What is important to emphasize is that at the clinical level, school or other professionals who provide direct services to children with learning disabilities are not necessarily concerned about program generalization. They are concerned about whether their program works with their children, that is, children selected by their particular criteria. The problems arise when we attempt to generalize across settings, when we assume that system-designated categorical labels identify individuals who are representative of something beyond specific and possibly idiosyncratic criteria. We may be at a point where we must consider program development and study of the learning disability conditions as important but separate enterprises. This somewhat cynical view is proposed not in criticism of researchers or practitioners, but rather to emphasize that it may be necessary to adopt different stategies if we are to understand learning disability and to work effectively with individuals with learning disabilities.

Recommendations

Whether directed at the study of a condition or at the delivery of services, broad-based recommendations too easily become platitudes or caveats which are noncontroversial but which contain little power. We would all agree that we should conduct "better" studies, provide "more effective" instruction, employ "highly quailied" professionals. These are worthwhile and easily agreed upon goals. Yet they do not direct action, do not move us from established ways. The major recommendations proposed in this chapter are derived from the assumptions that the overall long-term goal in the field of learning disability is improved services, and that improved services require the commitment and expertise of professionals involved in research as well as those providing services. The recommendations are also posed with the awareness that both the study of learning disability and the delivery of services to individuals with learning disabilities are influenced by policy at local, state, and national levels. Thus, those who make policy and those who influence policy makers are integral to this effort. The recommendations are not presented in order of importance. Ideally, all would be implemented concurrently, following somewhat paralleling but converging paths.

Recommendation One. Programs of service, both preventive and remedial, should be directed at a broadly-defined poor achiever population. Specifically, it is recommended that at the program level the emphasis on differential diagnosis and classification be shifted to a focus on instructional services for all mildly learning impaired individuals.

This recommendation is made with the recognition that it challenges the traditional mental health model in which problems are viewed as having their locus in the individual. It also challenges the notion of categorical special education services. The recommendation is based on evidence from several primary areas covered in this chapter: documented inconsistencies in classification and placement decisions; the unreliability and questionable validity of many psychometric practices for identification of students with learning disabilities; the lack of consistent criteria to differentiate among mildly handicapped groups (e.g., educable mentally retarded, learning disabled, emotionally disturbed); the increasingly large numbers of individuals whose academic performance does not reach normative expectancy. Support for a broad-based approach to services is not new (e.g., Hallahan & Kauffman, 1977) but deserves reconsideration given the current state of the art. Professional time and energy as well as the financial resources now spent on assessment for differential placement of mildly handicapped pupils have not necessarily led to educationally or psychologically defensible subgroups within an increasingly large. low achiever population. This is not to suggest that such subgroups do not exist, nor that they cannot be identified. However, to date the boundaries delineating learning disabled, emotionally disturbed, educable mentally retarded and slow learners remain murky. Further, the preoccupation with differential diagnosis has not resulted in well-documented and effective interventions for particular subgroups of pupils. Within the educational context the concern for diagnosis appears more important for compliance to legal and legislated mandates than for educational programming. Until the research evidence allows reliable delineation of reasonable and coherent subtypes of learning and achievement problems, and until there is clear evidence linking diagnosis and intervention (aptitude treatment interactions), the emphasis upon extensive, fine-grained assessment is questionable. In contrast, an expanding instructional effects literature argues for emphasis on improved pedagogy.

Recommendation Two. Support should be provided for systematic and comprehensive documentation and evaluation of program practices and intervention effects. Specifically, it is recommended that a program of evaluation research be implemented to test the comparative effectiveness of different program orientations, and to identify the relative importance of particular program components or practices.

The learning disability field is characterized by broad variance on demographics, individual subject variables, and program content. Number and types of programs increase yearly. To date, however, there has been little systematic widescale effort to assess practice; and there are few studies which compare programs, making determination of relative effectiveness difficult if not impossible. The burgeoning and increasingly sophisticated field of evaluation offers powerful models and techniques for assessing program impact. Their application may clarify some of the ambiguities in learning disability programs and practices, and may provide more definitive evidence on which to assess program decisions. Inherent in this recommendation is the assumption that more adequate evaluation will lead to delineation of links between program characteristics and individual attributes. Such efforts will require the collaborative interactions of a number of applied researchers and program professionals, but will also necessitate the commitment of financial resources at local, state, and national levels.

Recommendation Three. Applied research should be carried out to document the social system variables which affect services for individuals with learning disabilities. Specifically, it is recommended that social system analyses be applied to both special and general educational programs across a range of units or levels, for example, individual classrooms to governmental agencies.

This recommendation is made to underscore the need for systematic and comprehensive documentation of institutional decision-making and program practices. Social system approaches allow understanding of programs within their institutional contexts. Because of the many ambiguities and controversies surrounding the area of learning disability, services for individuals with learning disabilities are provided in many settings and involve both special and general educators. What happens in one system affects the other. Information included in this review has documented that referral, identification, and instructional decisions are influenced by a variety of conditions within both educational systems and governmental agencies, as well as by broad sociopolitical considerations. Thus, it is essential that program analyses be broad-based and include sources of influence on many levels. A reasonable product of a systems approach is development and test of models of service delivery taking into account characteristics of special and general educational systems and the contextual variables which affect them.

Recommendation Four. The study of learning disability conditions should be separated from concerns for the delivery of services to identified individuals. Specially, it is recommended that support be available for research on basic processes which are implicated in learning disability, such support to allow both cross-sectional and longitudinal efforts, and to involve investigators from diverse professional backgrounds.

This recommendation is directed at funding policy and has direct implications for both research and practice. It is based on materials contained in the present chapter which suggest that the confounding of scientific and service issues has diluted the state of the knowledge about both. The confusion of subject attributes and system influences makes it difficult, if not impossible, to draw generalizations across studies and programs, and makes test and evaluation of interventions suspect. Inconsistencies in current practices threaten both internal and external generalizability of results, and sorely limit the interpretability and applicability of research findings. The importance of support for research without direct and immediate applicability has been demonstrated in related fields such as medicine. A similar commitment to long-term and more basic research in the field of learning disability is also necessary. Current research in neuropsychology, genetics, information processing, and learning are examples of promising efforts which may provide insight into learning disability. However, their immediate impact on learning disability services is limited. Questions about these topics will not be easily nor quickly answered. Their resolution will likely require cooperation and collaboration of investigators from a number of different disciplines. Their resolution will also require substantial financial support over time. As with other more basic research, a number of approaches will fail and others may not lead to immediate improvement in practices. Yet our understanding of learning disability is dependent upon developing a scientifically solid conceptual foundation upon which to base programmatic decisions. Initially at least this may require separating basic and applied questions. This is not to imply that basic and program-related research would remain forever separate. Rather, it is based on the belief that clearer understanding of learning disability conditions will further our understanding of both.

Recommendation Five. Support should be provided for the development and test of a comprehensive classification system or taxonomy of learning disability. Specifically, it is recommended that support be provided for a multiyear project with the exclusive and primary goal the development of a conceptual framework for organizing the field.

This recommendation is based on the materials included in the present review which demonstrate the diversity and inconsistency within the learning disability enterprise, and which argue for a multidefinitional approach. At present learning disability professionals are known more for their differences than for their agreements. Both agreements and disagreements are to be valued and respected, but both need to make sense within a larger context. Thus far in the history of learning disability the context or conceptual framework has been lacking. Thus, the development of a comprehensive and reasonable classification system or taxonomy is a prime need in the field. It is not something which will

be accomplished easily, however. First, the task is a complex one which requires both conceptual and empirical efforts. Because of the multiple perspectives involved this will take time and resources. Second, efforts to bring organization and clarity to the field of learning disability may force us to acknowledge diversity not yet recognized. The very process of clarification may lead to troubling new inconsistencies and ambiguities. Third, a coherent classification system may threaten long-held beliefs and advocacy positions, may force us to relinquish old views and to question accepted practices. Such a restructuring of perspectives is often anxiety-provoking and sometimes even solidifies personal beliefs and prejudices. Finally, the effort is a risky one as there is a real possibility of failure. Put directly, a taxonomy may not be realistic given the nature of the field. Yet, the very process of analysis will yield insights of fundamental importance in understanding the nature of learning disability.

Recommendation Six. A comprehensive and coherent long-term plan for research and evaluation in learning disability, including support and review mechanisms, should be developed at the federal level. Specially, it is recommended that support be provided for the conceptualization and implementation of major programmatic efforts.

Materials covered in this review suggest that the field of learning disability is still plagued with disagreements and uncertainties which limit understanding of the condition and dilute the effectiveness of services. Given the fundamental nature of many of these disagreements, it is unlikely that their resolution will come from single short-term studies or limited evaluation projects. Rather, major questions (e.g., delineation of subtypes, program-pupil interactions, the relative impact of interventions or treatments) require consistent study over time; they also require the perspectives and expertise of different disciplines. Such efforts are not possible when support for research and evaluation is uncertain and/or short-term. Thus, there is need for policies and support mechanisms which allow time and opportunity for systematic and thoughtful approaches to these problems. This recommendation is made with the recognition that commitment of major resources to long-term programmatic work is not without risk. It is essential, therefore, that any comprehensive plan contain acceptable procedures for decision making and review so that quality can be assured. It is also essential that the continuing need for individual investigator projects be recognized, as such projects have proved a rich source of information for the field.

The future of research and evaluation in the field of learning disability is a high priority and requires both professional and governmental attention. The time is right for implementing research and evaluation efforts which will lead to a clearer conceptualization of learning disability and which will provide empirical support for program practices. The diversity of policies, practices, and procedures governing learning disability programs in different states makes leadership at the federal level critical. The substantive nature of the disagreements in the field mandates strong professional involvement in the development of learning disability policy.

Some Personal Comments

Considering the six major recommendations in light of the pressing practical needs in the field makes the author keenly aware of their limitations. Many readers will find these recommendations unsatisfactory because they do not address specific problems and because they do not provide clearly spelled out operational directions for change. Yet, many specific and immediately implementable recommendations are inherent in the material covered in the review: school psychologists need better training to understand both normative and psychometric aspects of the tests they use; school principals need to be more aware of their influence on placement practices and consequences; placement teams need to understand how the decision-making process operates to determine child classifications; researchers need to be sensitive to sample selection influences in their studies; and policy makers need to recognize that prevalence figures are a function of many influences (including the discrepancy formula applied), not just of child attributes. Those interested in recommendations for changes in particular areas of practice will find a rich source of information in the rapidly enlarging published literature on learning disability. We do know more now than we knew 10 years ago. Careful interpretation of this information can lead to immediate improvements in practice.

More pessimistically, however, it is clear that we are still a goodly distance away from understanding learning disability. The history of the field suggests that the search for a single and unitary condition known as learning disability is a fruitless one. Instead, we deal with multiple conditions, multiple causes, and multiple expressions of learning disability. There is a broad range in number, kind, intensity, and chronicity of individual attributes which characterize the individuals placed in a potential learning disability pool. These attributes are shared with varying degrees of commonality, some clusters appearing together with regularity. Other attributes have a low likelihood of commonality, but may be particularly salient in directing recognition and classification. Our task is to make sense of these many variously shared attributes in order to identify and describe the nature of learning disabilities.

In a recent article, Scarr (1985) suggested that, "Each of us has our reality of which we try to persuade others. Facts do not have an independent existence. Rather, facts are created within theoretical systems that guide selection of observations and the invention of reality" (p. 499). Acceptance of the constructionist perspective may help us understand why there are so many continuing ambiguities, inconsistencies, and controversies about learning disability. Our history has been one of blatant empiricism, but the search for "facts" has been conducted from widely diverse and usually unrecognized sets of beliefs. These "constructions" or "invented realities" need analysis and organization according to their scientific merit and according to their practical relevance for services for individuals with learning disabilities. The result of such analysis could be development of a reasonable and coherent conceptualization which can organize and order the many learning disabilities within the learning disability field.

References

Achenbach, T. M. (1978–79). The Child Behavior Profile: An empirically based system for assessing children's behavioral problems and competencies. *International Journal of Mental Health*, 7(3–4), 24–42.

Achenbach, T. M., & Edelbrock, C. S. (1978). The classification of child psychopathology: A review and analysis of empirical effects. *Psychological Bulletin*, **85**(6), 1275–1301.

Algozzine, B., Christenson, S., & Ysseldyke, J. (1982). Probabilities associated with the referral to placement process. *Teacher Education and Special Education*, 5(3), 19–23.

Algozzine, B., Forgnone, C., Mercer, C., & Trifiletti, J. (1979). Toward defining discrepancies for specific learning disabilities: An analysis and alternatives. *Learning Disability Quarterly*, 2(4), 25–31.

Algozzine, B., & Korinek, L. (1985). Where is special education for students with high prevalence handicaps going? *Exceptional Children*, **51**(5), 388–394.

Algozzine, B., & Ysseldyke, J. (1983). Learning disabilities as a subset of school failure: The oversophistication of a concept. *Exceptional Children*, **50**(3), 242–246.

American Psychiatric Association (1980). *Diagnostic and statistical manual of disorders* (3rd ed.), Washington, DC: Author.

Annual Review of Learning Disabilities, 1983. New York: Professional Press.

Applebee, A. N. (1971). Research in reading retardation: Two critical problems. *Journal of Child Psychology and Psychiatry*, 12(2), 91–113.

Bailey, K. D. (1973). Monothetic and polythetic typologies and their relation to conceptualization, measurement, and scaling. *American Sociological Review*, 38(1), 18–33.

Berk, R. A. (1984). An evaluation of procedures for computing an ability-achievement discrepancy score. *Journal of Learning Disabilities*, 17(5), 262–266.

Blashfield, R. (1973). An evaluation of the DSM-11 classification of schizophrenia as a nomenclature. *Journal of Abnormal Psychology*, 82(3), 382–389.

Blashfield, R. K., & Draguns, J. G. (1976). Evaluative criteria for psychiatric classification. *Journal of Abnormal Psychology*, 85(2), 140–150.

Boder, E. (1973). Developmental dyslexia: A diagnostic approach based on three atypical reading-spelling patterns. *Developmental Medicine and Child Neurology*, 15(5), 663–687.

Bond, G. L., & Tinker, M. A. (1973). *Reading difficulties: Their diagnosis and correction* (3rd ed.). New York: Appleton-Century-Crofts.

Boodoo, G. M. (1984–85). A multivariate perspective for aptitude-achievement discrepancy in learning disability assessment. *The Journal of Special Education*, **18**(4), 489–494.

California Education Code (1970). Sections 6902.08, 6902.09, & 6902.10. Sacramento, California.

Chalfant, J. C. (1984). *Identifying learning disabled students: Guidelines for decision making.* Burlington, VT: The Northeast Regional Resource Center.

Christenson, S., Ysseldyke, J., & Algozzine, B. (1982). Institutional constraints and external pressures influencing referral decisions. *Psychology in the Schools*, **19**(3), 341–345.

Clements, S. D. (1966). *Minimal brain dysfunction in children* (NINDS Monograph No. 3, US Public Health Service Publication No. 1415). Washington, D.C.: US Government Printing Office.

Coles, G. S. (1978). The learning-disabilities test battery: Empirical and social issues. *Harvard Educational Review*, **48**(3), 313–340.

Cone, T. E., & Wilson, L. R. (1981). Quantifying a severe discrepancy: A critical analysis. *Learning Disability Quarterly*, **4**(4), 359–371.

Consortium for the Study of Learning Disabilities in California Community Colleges (1983). *Summary of Final Report.* Research prepared for the Office of the Chancellor, California Community Colleges.

Cruickshank, W. M. (1981). Learning disabilities: A definitional statement in W. M. Cruickshank (Ed.), *Selected writings* (Vol. 2). Syracuse, N.Y: Syracuse University Press.

Cruickshank, W. M. (1984). Comments regarding the IARLD research monograph series. *Thalamus*, **4**(1), 53–57.

Danielson, L. C., & Bauer, J. N. (1978). A formula-based classification of learning disabled children: An examination of the issues. *Journal of Learning Disabilities*, **11**(3), 163–176.

Davis, W. A., & Shepard, L. A. (1983). Specialists' use of tests and clinical judgment in the diagnosis of learning disabilities. *Learning Disability Quarterly*, **6**(2), 128–138.

DeRuiter, J. A., Ferrell, W. R., & Kass, C. E. (1975). Learning disability classification by Bayesian aggregation of test results. *Journal of Learning Disabilities*, **8**(6), 365–372.

Doehring, D. G. (1976). The tangled web of behavioral research on developmental dyslexia in A. L. Benton & D. Pearl (Eds.), *Dyslexia: An appraisal of current knowledge.* New York: Oxford University Press.

Doehring, D. G., & Hoshko, I. M. (1977). Classification of reading problems by the Q-technique of factor analysis. *Cortex*, **13**(3), 281–294.

Doehring, D. G., Hoshko, I. M., & Bryans, B. N. (1979). Statistical classification of children with reading problems. *Journal of Clinical Neuropsychology*, **1**(1), 6–16.

Edgar, E., & Hayden, A. H. (1984–85). Who are the children special education should serve and how many children are there? *The Journal of Special Education*, **18**(4), 523–539.

Epps, S., Ysseldyke, J. E., & Algozzine, B. (1983). Impact of different definitions of learning disabilities on the number of students identified. *Journal of Psychoeducational Assessment*, **1**(4), 341–352.

Erickson, M. T. (1975). The Z-score discrepancy method for identifying reading disabled children. *Journal of Learning Disabilities*, **8**(5), 308–312.

Federal Register (1976). 41, 52404–52407.

Federal Register (1977). 42, 65082–65085.

Fisk, J. L., & Rourke, B. P. (1984). Neuropsychological subtypes of learning disabled children: History, methods, implications. In J. K. Torgesen & G. M. Senf (Eds.), *Annual Review of Learning Disabilities*, **2**, 46–48.

Fleishman, E. A. (1982). Systems for describing human tasks. *American Psychologist*, **37**(7), 821–834.

Forness, S. R., Sinclair, E., & Guthrie, D. (1983). Learning disability discrepancy formulas: Their use in actual practice. *Learning Disability Quarterly*, **6**(2), 107–114.

Frankenberger, W. (1984). A survey of state guidelines for identification of mental retardation. *Mental Retardation*, **22**(1), 17–20.

Friedrich, D., Fuller, G. B., & Davis, D. (1984). Learning disability: Fact and fiction. *Journal of Learning Disabilities*, **17**(4), 205–209.

Gajar, A. H. (1979). Educable mentally retarded, learning disabled, emotionally disturbed: Similarities and differences. *Exceptional Children*, **45**(6), 470–472.

Gajar, A. H. (1980). Characteristics across exceptional categories: EMR, LD, and ED. *The Journal of Special Education*, **14**(2), 165–173.

Gallagher, J. J. (1984). Learning disabilities and the near future. *Journal of Learning Disabilities*, **17**(9), 571–572.

Gerber, M. M. (1964). The Department of Education's sixth annual report to Congress on *P.L. 94-142*: Is Congress getting the full story? *Exceptional Children*, **51**(3), 209–224.

Government Accounting Office (1981). *Report to the Chairman, Subcommittee on Select Education, Committee on Educational Costs, House of Representatives: Disparities still exist in who gets special education.* Washington, DC.

Guiton, G. W. (1984a). *Overidentification of students as learning disabled: Recommendations for practitioners in the schools.* Unpublished paper, Los Angeles, CA: UCLA.

Guiton, G. (1984b). LD working paper. Unpublished, Los Angeles, CA: UCLA.

Hale, R. L., & McDermott, P. A. (1984). Pattern analysis of an actuarial strategy for computerized diagnosis of childhood exceptionality. *Journal of Learning Disabilities*, **17**(1), 30–37.

Hallahan, D. P., & Cruickshank, W. M. (1963). *Psychoeducational foundations of learning disabilities.* Englewood Cliffs, N.J: Prentice-Hall.

Hallahan, D. P. & Kauffman, J. M. (1976). *Introduction to Learning Disabilities. A Psycho-Behavioral Approach.* Englewood Cliffs, N.J.: Prentice-Hall.

Hallahan, D. P., & Kauffman, J. M. (1977). Labels, categories, behaviors: ED, LD, and EMR reconsidered. *The Journal of Special Education*, **11**(2), 139–149.

Hammill, D. D., Leigh, J. E., McNutt, G., & Larsen, S. C. (1981). A new definition of learning disabilities. *Learning Disability Quarterly*, **4**(4), 336–342.

Hanna, G. S., Dyck, N. J., & Holen, M. C. (1979). Objective analysis of achievement-aptitude discrepancies in LD classification. *Learning Disability Quarterly*, **2**(4), 32–38.

Harris, A. (1970). *How to increase reading abilities: A guide to developmental and remedial methods* (5th ed.). New York: David McKay.

Harris, A. J. (1982). How many kinds of reading disability are there? *Journal of Learning Disabilities*, **15**(8), 456–460.

Hobbs, N. (1975). *Issues in the classification of children* (Vols. 1 & 2). San Francisco: Jossey-Bass.

Hocutt, A. M., Cox, J. L., & Pelosi, J. (1984). *An exploration of issues regarding the identification and placement of LD, MR, and ED students.* A policy-oriented study of special education's service delivery system. (RTI Report No. RT1/2706-06/01ES). Washington, DC: Department of Education.

Horn, W. F., & O'Donnell, J. P. (1984). Early identification of learning disabilities: A comparison of two methods. *Journal of Educational Psychology*, **76**(6), 1106–1118.

Johnson, D. J., & Myklebust, H. S. (1967). *Learning disabilities: Educational principles and practices*. New York: Grune and Stratton.

Kaluger, G., & Kolson, C. J. (1969). *Reading and learning disabilities*. Columbus, OH: Charles E. Merrill.

Kavale, K. A. (1983). Fragile findings, complex conclusions, and meta-analysis in special education. *Exceptional Education Quarterly*, **4**(3), 97–106.

Kavale, K., & Nye, C. (1981). Identification criteria for learning disabilities: A survey of the research literature. *Learning Disability Quarterly*, **4**(4), 383–388.

Keogh, B. K. (1983). Classification, compliance, and confusion. *Journal of Learning Disabilities*, **16**(1), 25.

Keogh, B. K., Becker, L., Kukic, M. B., & Kukic, S. J. (1972). *Programs for educationally handicapped and educable mentally retarded pupils: Review and recommendations*. Technical report. University of California, Los Angeles, Graduate School of Education.

Keogh, B. K., & Hall, R. J. (1984). Cognitive training with learning-disabled pupils. In A. W. Meyers & W. E. Craighead (Eds.), *Cognitive behavior therapy with children*. New York: Plenum Press.

Keogh, B. K., & MacMillan, D. L. (1983). The logic of sample selection: Who represents what? *Exceptional Education Quarterly*, **4**(3), 84–96.

Keogh, B. K., Major-Kingsley, S., Omori-Gordon, H., & Reid, H. P. (1982). *A system of marker variables for the field of learning disabilities*. Syracuse, NY: Syracuse University Press.

Kirk, S. A. (1962). *Educating exceptional children*. Boston: Houghton-Mifflin.

Kirk, S. A., & Elkins, J. (1975). Characteristics of children enrolled in the Child Service Demonstration Centers. *Journal of Learning Disabilities*, **8**(10), 630–637.

LaGrow, S. J., & Prochnow-LaGrow, J. E. (1982). Technical adequacy of the most popular tests selected by responding school psychologists in Illinois. *Psychology in the Schools*, **19**(2), 186–189.

Lambert, N. M. (1981). Psychological evidence in Larry P. v. Wilson Riles: An education by a witness for the defense. *American Psychologist*, **36**(9), 937–952.

Last, J. M. (Ed.) (1983). *A dictionary of epidemiology*. New York: Oxford University Press.

Loper, A. B., & Reeve, R. E. (unpublished). *Quantitative procedures to estimate underachievement*. Charlottesville, VA: The University of Virginia.

Lyon, G. R. (1983). Learning-disabled readers: Identification of subgroups. In H. R. Myklebust (Ed.), *Progress in learning disabilities* (Vol. 5). New York: Grune and Stratton.

Lyon, G. R. (1985). Educational validation studies of learning disability subtypes. In B. Rourke (Ed.), *Learning disabilities in children: Advances in subtype analysis*. New York: Guilford Press.

Lyon, R., Stewart, N., & Freedman, D. (1982). Neuropsychological characteristics of empirically derived subgroups of learning disabled readers. *Journal of Clinical Neuropsychology*, **4**(4), 343–365.

Lyon, R., & Watson, B. (1981). Empirically derived subgroups of learning disabled readers. Diagnostic characteristics. *Journal of Learning Disabilities*, **14**(5), 256–261.

Lyon, R., Watson, B., Reitta, S., Porch, B., & Rhodes, J. (1981). Selected linguistic and perceptual abilities of empirically derived subgroups of learning disabled readers. *Journal of School Psychology*, **19**(2), 152–166.

MacMillan, D. L. (1982). *Mental retardation in school and society* (2nd ed.). Boston: Little, Brown.

MacMillan, D. L., Keogh, B. K., & Jones, R. (1986). Special education research on mildly handicapped learners. In M. C. Wittrock (Ed.), *Handbook of research on teaching* (3rd ed.). New York: MacMillan.

MacMillan, D. L., Meyers, C. E., & Morrison, G. M. (1980). System-identification of mildly mentally retarded children: Implications for interpreting and conducting research. *American Journal of Mental Deficiency*, **85**(2), 108–115.

Mattis, S. (1978). Critical reviews of dyslexia-prevalence and types. In A. L. Benton & D. Pearl (Eds.), *Dyslexia: An appraisal of current knowledge*. New York: Oxford University Press.

Mattis, S., French, J. H., & Rapin, I. (1975). Dyslexia in children and young adults: Three independent neuropsychological syndromes. *Developmental Medicine and Child Neurology*, **17**(2), 150–163.

McDermott, P. A. (1980a). A systems-actuarial method for the differential diagnosis of handicapped children. *The Journal of Special Education*, **14**(1), 7–22.

McDermott, P. A. (1980b). Congruence and typology of diagnoses in school psychology: An empirical study. *Psychology in the Schools*, **17**(1), 12–24.

McDermott, P. A. (1981). Sources of error in the psychoeducational diagnosis of children. *The Journal of School Psychology*, **19**, 31–44.

McDermott, P. A. (1982). Actuarial assessment systems for the grouping and classification of school children. In C. R. Reynolds & T. B. Gutkin (Eds.), *The handbook of school psychology*. New York: Wiley.

McDermott, P. A., & Hale, R. L. (1982). Validation of a systems-actuarial computer process for multidimensional classification of child psychopathology. *Journal of Clinical Psychology*, **38**(3), 477–486.

McKinney, J. D. (1984). The search for subtypes of specific learning disability. *Annual Review of Learning Disabilities*, **2**, 19–26.

McKinney, J. D. (1988). Research in conceptually and empirically derived subtypes of specific learning disabilities. In M. Wang, M. Reynolds, & H. Walberg (Eds.) *The handbook of special education: Research and practice*. Oxford, England: Pergamon.

McLeod, J. (1979). Educational underachievement: Toward a defensible psychometric definition. *Journal of Learning Disabilities*, **12**(5), 322–330.

Mehan, H., Meihls, J. L., Hertweck, A., & Crowdes, M. S. (1981). Identifying handicapped students. In S. B. Bacharach (Ed.), *Organizational behavior in schools and school districts*. New York: Praeger.

Mercer, L. D., Forgnone, C., & Wolking, W. D. (1976). Definitions of learning disabilities used in the United States. *Journal of Learning Disabilities*, **9**(6), 376–386.

Morris, R., Blashfield, R., & Satz, P. (1981). Neuropsychology and cluster analysis. Potentials and problems. *Journal of Clinical Neuropsychology*, **3**(1), 79–99.

Murai, H. M. (1982). Eligibility criteria for learning disabilities programs: institutionalized discrimination. *Journal of Learning Disabilities*, **15**(5), 267.

National Advisory Committee on Handicapped Children (1968). *Special education for handicapped children: First annual report*. Washington, DC: Department of Health, Education, and Welfare.

National Joint Committee on Learning Disabilities (1981). A new definition of learning disabilities. *Learning Disabilities Quarterly*, 4(4), 336–342.

Nichols, P. L., & Chen, T. C. (1981). *Minimal brain dysfunction: A prospective study*. Hillsdale, NJ: Lawrence Erlbaum.

Norman, C. A., Jr., & Zigmond, N. (1980). Characteristics of children labeled and served as learning disabled in school systems affiliated with Child Service Demonstration Centers. *Journal of Learning Disabilities*, 13(9), 542–547.

Page, E. B. (1980). Tests and decisions for the handicapped: A guide to evaluation under the new laws. *The Journal of Special Education*, 14(4), 423–483.

Petrauskas, R. J., & Rourke, B. P. (1979). Identification of subtypes of retarded readers: A neuropsychological multivariate approach. *Journal of Clinical Neuropsychology*, 1(1), 17–37.

Polloway, C. A., & Smith, J. D. (1983). Changes in mild mental retardation: Population, programs, and perspectives. *Exceptional Children*, 50, 149–159.

Pope, L. M. (1982). State statutory and administrative regulation of pupil placement in public schools. In R. L. Sprague (Ed.), *Advances in law and child development* (Vol. 1). Greenwich, CT: JAI Press.

Public Law 94–142: The Education of All Handicapped Children Act of 1975.

Quay, H. S. (1972). Patterns of aggression, withdrawal, and immaturity. In H. C. Quay & J. S. Werry (Eds.), *Psychopathological disorders of childhood*. New York: Wiley.

Repp, A. C., & Brusca, R. M. (1983). Single-subject research: Basic designs for research in special education. *Exceptional Education Quarterly*, 4(3), 27–39.

Reynolds, C. R. (1984–1985). Critical measurement issues in learning disabilities. *The Journal of Special Education*, 18(4), 451–476.

Reynolds, C. R., Berk, R. A., Boodoo, G. M., Cox, J., Gutkin, T. B., Mann, L., Page, E. B., & Willson, V. C. (1984–85). *Critical measurement issues in learning disabilities*. Report of the Work Group of Measurement issues in the Assessment of Learning Disabilities. Washington, D.C.: U.S. Department of Education, Program in Special Education.

Riley, A. M. (1980). *A study to identify homogeneous subgroups of children with perceptual-communication disorders*. Unpublished doctoral dissertation, University of Illinois, Chicago Circle.

Robbins, R. C., Mercer, J. R., & Meyers, C. E. (1967). The school as a selecting-labeling system. *Journal of School Psychology*, 5(4), 270–279.

Rourke, B. P. (1976). Issues in the neuropsychological assessment of children with learning disabilities. *Canadian Psychological Review*, 17(2), 89–102.

Salvia, J., & Hunt, F. M. (1984). Measurement considerations in program evaluation. In B. K. Keogh (Ed.), *Advances in special education: Vol. 4. Documenting program impact*. Greenwich, CT: JAI Press.

Salvia, J., & Ysseldyke, J. E. (1981). *Assessment in special and remedial education* (2nd ed.). Boston: Houghton Mifflin.

Satz, P., & Fletcher, J. (1980). Minimal brain dysfunctions: An appraisal of research concepts and methods. In H. E. Rie

& E. D. Rie (Eds.), *Handbook of minimal brain dysfunctions: A critical review*. New York: Wiley.

Satz, P., & Morris, R. (1981). Learning disability subtypes: A review. In F. J. Pirozzola & M. C. Wittrock (Eds.), *Neuropsychological and cognitive processes in reading*. New York: Academic Press.

Scarr, S. (1985). Constructing psychology: Making facts and fables for our times. *American Psychologist*, 40(5), 499–512.

Schumaker, J. B., Deshler, D. D., Alley, G. R., & Warner, M. M. (1980). *An epidemiological study of learning disabled adolescents in secondary schools. Details of the methodology* (Research Report No. 12). Lawrence, KS: The University of Kansas Institute for Research in Learning Disabilities.

Schumaker, J. B., Deshler, D. D., Alley, G. R., & Warner, M. M. (1983). Toward the development of an interaction model for learning disabled adolescents: The University of Kansas Institute. *Exceptional Education Quarterly*, 4(1), 45–74.

Senf, G. (1976). Implications of the final procedures for evaluating specific learning disabilities. *Journal of Learning Disabilities*, 11(3), 124–126.

Shaywitz, S. E., & Shaywitz, B. A. (1984). Diagnosis and management of attention deficit disorder: A pediatric perspective. *Pediatric Clinics of North America*, 31(2), 429–457.

Shepard, L. (1980). An evaluation of the regression discrepancy method for identifying children with learning disabilities. *The Journal of Special Education*, 14(1), 79–91.

Shepard, L. A. (1982). *Assessment of learning disabilities* (ERIC/TM Report 64). Princeton, NJ: Educational Testing Service.

Shepard, L. A. (1983). The role of measurement in educational policy: Lessons from the identification of learning disabilities. *Educational Measurement Issues and Practice*, 2 (3), 4–8.

Shepard, L. A., & Smith, M. L. (1981). *The identification assessment, placement, and remediation of perceptual communication disordered children in Colorado*. Boulder, CO: Laboratory of Educational Research, University of Colorado.

Shepard, L. A., & Smith, M. L. (1983). An evaluation of the identification of learning disabled students in Colorado. *Learning Disability Quarterly*, 6(2), 115–127.

Shepard, L. A., Smith, M. L., & Vojir, C. P. (1983). Characteristics of pupils identified as learning disabled. *American Educational Research Journal*, 20 (3), 309–331.

Short, E. J., & McKinney, J. D. (1983, October). *A two fold classification system based on discrepancy formulas: Simultaneous consideration of age and IQ among disabled learners*. Paper presented at the annual meeting of the Council for Learning Disorders, San Francisco.

Sixth Annual Report to Congress on the implementation of Public Law 94–142: The Education for All Handicapped Children Act. (1984). Office of Special Education, US Department of Education.

Smith, M. L. (1982). *How educators decide who is learning disabled: Challenge to psychology and public policy in the schools*. Springfield, IL: C. C. Thomas.

Somwaru, J. P. (1979). *A new approach to the assessment of learning disabilities*. Monograph No. 9 of the Institute for Research on Learning Disabilities. Minneapolis: University of Minnesota.

Speece, D. L., McKinney, J. D., & Appelbaum, M. I. (1985). Classification and validation of behavioral subtypes of learning disabled children. *Journal of Educational Psychology*, **77**(1), 67–77.

Stark, J. H. (1982). Tragic choices in special education: The effects of scarce resources on the implementation of *P.L. 94–142. Connecticut Law Review*, **14**(47), 477–493.

Stein, Z. (1981). Why is it useful to measure incidence and prevalence? *International Journal of Mental Health*, **10**(1), 14–22.

Strain, P. S., McConnell, S., & Cordisco, L. (1983). Special educators as single-subject researchers. *Exceptional Education Quarterly*, **4**(3), 40–51.

Thurlow, M. L., & Ysseldyke, J. E. (1979). Current assessment and decision-making practices in models LD programs. *Learning Disability Quarterly*, **2**(4), 15–24.

Torgesen, J. K. (1985, April). *Comments on learning disabilities subtypes*. Paper presented at The Council for Exceptional Children Annual Meeting, Anaheim, CA.

Torgesen, J. K., & Dice, C. (1980). Characteristics of research on learning disabilities. *Journal of Learning Disabilities*, **13**(9), 531–535.

Tucker, J. A. (1980). Ethnic proportions in classes for the learning disabled. Issues in nonbiased assessment. *The Journal of Special Education*, **14**(1), 93–105.

Turner, K., & Wade, G. C. (1982). Learning disabled, birth to three: Fact or artifact. *Journal of the Division for Early Childhood*, **5**, 79–85.

United States Office of Education (1976). *Definition of learning disabilities*.

Warner, M. M., Schumaker, J. R., Alley, G. R., & Deshler, D. D. (1980). Learning disabled adolescents in the public school: Are they different from other low achievers? *Exceptional Education Quarterly*, **1**(2), 27–36.

White, O. (1984). Selected issued in program evaluation: Arguments for the individual. In B. K. Keogh (Ed.), *Advances in special education: Volume 4. Documenting program impact*. Greenwich, CT: JAI Press.

Willson, V. L., & Reynolds, C. R. (1984–85). Another look at evaluating aptitude-achievement discrepancies in the diagnosis of learning disabilities. *The Journal of Special Education*, **18**(4), 477–487.

Wilson, L. R., & Cone, T. (1984). The regression equation method of determining academic discrepancy. *Journal of School Psychology*, **22**(1), 95–110.

Ysseldyke, J. E., Algozzine, B., Regan, R., & Potter, M. (1980). Technical adequacy of tests used by professionals in simulated decision making. *Psychology in the Schools*, **17**(2), 202–209.

Ysseldyke, J. E., Algozzine, B., Richey, L., & Graden, J. (1982). Declaring students eligible for learning disability services: Why bother with the date? *Learning Disability Quarterly*, **5**(1), 37–43.

Ysseldyke, J. E., Algozzine, B., Shinn, M. R., & McGue, M. (1982). Similarities and differences between low achievers and students classified learning disabled. *The Journal of Special Education*, **16**(1), 73–85.

Zigler, E., & Phillips, L. (1961). Psychiatric diagnosis: A critique. *Journal of Abnormal and Social Psychology*, **63**(3), 607–618.

Zigmond, N. (1983, April). *Toward a new definition of learning disabilities*. Paper presented at the annual meeting of the American Educational Research Association, Montreal, Canada.

Acknowledgements

1) This paper was prepared for the University of Pittsburgh project: Research Integration of Selected Issues in the Education of Handicapped Children.

2) I wish to thank Dr. Antionette Krupski, my colleague at UCLA, for her careful review and helpful comments about this paper. I also thank the reviewers in the Pittsburgh Research Integration project for their insightful suggestions.

Research on Conceptually and Empirically Derived Subtypes of Specific Learning Disabilities

JAMES D. McKINNEY

Frank Porter Graham Child Development Center
University of North Carolina at Chapel Hill

Abstract—This review summarizes and evaluates the educational relevance of research that has attempted to identify more discrete subgroups of learning disabled children. The initial sections of the paper provide an overview of the significance and theoretical background for research on learning disabilities subtypes, and describe other approaches to classification based on etiology, the assessment of ability profiles, and IQ-achievement discrepancy. Research on learning disabilities subtypes is organized and evaluated according to the major approach used to classify children: clinical-inferential subtypes, empirically derived subtypes, and rationally defined subtypes. Also, a section is included on intervention with learning disabilities subtypes. It is concluded that while this research has significant implications for theory, practice and policy in the field, a great deal of additional work is needed before knowledge in this area will impact practice directly. Research priorities are recommended in six areas to facilitate the future application of work on learning disabilities subtypes and to help resolve substantive policy issues involved in the appropriate classification of students with learning disabilities.

Introduction

Although considerable progress has been made as the result of research on learning disability, the field still lacks an empirically sound theoretical focus to guide educational practice and policy. A major factor that continues to inhibit progress is the great diversity among students who are eligible for special education according to the present definition of learning disabilities. The problem of heterogeneity among students with learning disabilities has not only frustrated efforts to build a generalizable body of knowledge, but also has contributed greatly to the present controversy over misclassification and what constitutes appropriate special education for students with learning disabilities.

The purpose of the present review is to summarize and evaluate that body of research that has addressed the question of whether there are conceptually and empirically discrete subgroups of children among those who are identified as learning disabled. This review will also address the issue of the educational relevance of research on learning disabilities. Finally, recommendations will be offered concerning future directions for research and development, along with a discussion of implications for research policy and current issues in the identification of students with learning disabilities.

Significance for Special Education

The term *specific learning disability* was first used in the 1960s to describe a broad collection of disorders related to school failure which could not be attributed to other known forms of exceptionality or to environmental disadvantage. The advent of this category of exceptionality reflected the belief by scientists, educators and parents that some children had learning handicaps which did not fit existing categories, but it also reflected a general lack of consensus about the principal manifestations of learning disability, and its prevalence, etiology and appropriate treatment. Subsequently, the federal definition of learning disability which was incorporated into *P.L. 94–142* included children who did not achieve at a level commensurate with their age and ability, and eligibility for special education services was established when other categorical forms of exceptionality and environmental disadvantage could be excluded.

Over the past decade the field of learning disability has grown to the point where it now represents over one fourth of the handicapped students receiving special education nationally. At the same time, it is one of the least understood of the various handicapping conditions that affects school-age children. Although much of the confusion in the field could be attributed to its newness. It is also the case that existing practice has often been based on fragmentary evidence and largely speculative theories that provide little understanding about what processes might be involved in the development of learning disabilities.

Since the definition of learning disability allows students to be placed in special education programs without determining the exact nature of their learning handicap, it is possible to include students who fail to achieve because of social, motivational, or pedagogical factors rather than because of some inherent defect in development. Some authorities have estimated that if all such students were classified as learning disabled, the prevalence figure for learning disability would be as high as 20% of the school population (Gallagher, 1982). Although school failure for whatever reason is a source of grave concern, it is important to differentiate those students who can benefit from support services that are available as part of mainstream education from those who require special education as the most appropriate treatment of choice.

Overview of Background Research

Since all known forms of exceptionality were excluded from the present definition of learning disability, researchers in the field have had the arduous task of trying to specify exactly how children with learning disabilities are handicapped apart from their failure to profit from regular class instruction. As a result, an extensive literature has evolved over the past 15 years cataloguing the various deficits displayed by such children (Bryan & Bryan, 1978, Hallahan & Kauffman, 1976; Keogh, Major-Kingsley, Omori-Gordon, & Reid, 1982; McKinney & Feagans, 1984; Ramey & McKinney, 1981; Torgesen, 1975). One major limitation of previous research on child characteristics is that it has been unsatisfactory conceptually, which has led to empirically unwarranted speculations about the underlying processes that explain poor performance. For example, much of the early work in the field attempted to link learning disabilities to a variety of specific ability deficits under the assumption that subtle neurological factors produced an uneven pattern of development, as opposed to a general deficit (Feagans & McKinney, 1981; Gallagher, 1966; Ross, 1976; Torgesen, 1975; Wong, 1979).

One of the early hypotheses in this regard (Orton, 1937) was that learning disabilities result from deficits in visual-perceptual processes (Benton, 1975; Hallahan & Cruickshank, 1973; Torgesen, 1975). The most popular rival hypothesis to the perceptual deficit position has been that learning disabilities result from deficits in linguistic processes (Satz & Van Nostrand, 1973; Shankweiler & Liberman, 1976; Vellutino, 1978). Still other investigators have provided evidence in favor of an attention-deficit hypothesis (Hallahan & Reeve, 1980; Ross, 1976), and/or deficiencies in memory processes (Torgesen & Kail, 1980).

Although research can be cited which implicates one particular single deficit hypothesis at the expense of another (Satz & Fletcher, 1980; Torgesen, 1975; Vellutino, 1978), it has become increasingly clear that a "single syndrome" theory cannot account for the substantial heterogeneity within samples of children with learning disabilities which are drawn under the present definition. Accordingly, several authors have recommended that the search for a single syndrome of learning disability be abandoned in favor of a *multiple syndrome paradigm* which can accommodate the range of disorders within heterogeneous samples of children with learning disabilities (Doehring, 1978; Satz & Fletcher, 1980). At present, the most compelling evidence for the multiple syndrome view comes from studies which have successfully subdivided heterogeneous samples into three or more homogeneous groups based on the pattern of performance across multivariate data sets (McKinney, 1984; Satz & Morris, 1981).

Scope and Methods of Review

The present chapter is organized into four major sections. The initial section provides an overview of the theoretical background for research on learning disabilities subtypes. The second section describes alternative approaches to classification based on etiological factors, the assessment of ability profiles, and IQ-achievement discrepancy. The bulk of the chapter is contained in the third section which describes and evaluates the research on learning disabilities subtypes. This section is organized according to the major approach used to classify children, including clinical-inferential classification, empirical classification, and rationally defined subgroups. This section also contains the relevant research on intervention with learning disabilities subtypes. The research within this section is further organized according to the major projects or laboratories that produced it, as well as the specific methodologies that were employed. The final section of the chapters discusses the implications of this body of research for special education, and delineates six priority areas for further research on learning disabilities subtypes.

In preparing this review, I sought to include all studies that could be located that presented minimal standards of scientific quality. The latter decision was made in an attempt to provide a comprehensive review of a relatively new and emerging area of research. Accordingly, a number of dissertations, paper presentations, and papers in review or in press are cited. Also, a number of articles in foreign journals are cited. As the reader will observe, the quality of research in this area varies greatly across individual studies and particular approaches to the problem of subtyping. Rather than exclude all marginal studies, I chose to report some that were flawed when in my opinion they provided a unique perspective and/or relevant information about an underresearched topic. In order to assist readers who may be unfamiliar with the methods used in many of these studies, I discuss the methods used in each set of studies that were reviewed, and evaluate their merit and limitations collectively at the end of each section.

The studies which form the basis for this review were obtained from publications in psychology, medicine, and public health, as well as general and special education. It was the case that the bulk of this research was conducted outside the field of special education, and tended to concentrate in fields of reading research, neuropsychology, school and clinical psychology, and developmental pediatrics. Both computer and hand searches were used to collect material. In addition, a personal appeal for relevant literature was made to six leading investigators who had published in the area. Although significant work on subtyping emotional problems and other conditions exists, the review was limited to studies of children with learning disabilities and those with related conditions. Accordingly, studies of children who were labeled as reading disabled (RD) or dyslexic, and as having minimal brain dysfunction (MBD), were included.

Significant Previous Reviews

Since the topic of subtyping of children with learning disabilities is relatively recent, significant previous reviews have appeared only since 1981. The first comprehensive review was made by Satz and Morris (1981) who described studies of reading disabled children completed through 1979. In the same year Doehring, Triter, Patel, and Fiedorowicz (1981) published a review of previous research along with early clinical approaches to classification. In 1983, Fisk and Rourke reviewed the literature on neuropsychological classification; more recently Rourke (1985) has edited a book that provides reviews based on the same perspective. The special education literature contains two recent reviews; the first by Harris (1982) and the second by McKinney (1984).

Apart from recency, the present review differs substantially from previous reviews in both focus and scope. As noted above, an attempt was made to include research on all aspects of the subtypes problem, including rationally defined subgroups as well as clinical-inferential and empirical classification, and other approaches to psychoeducational classification such as the analysis of ability patterns and IQ-achievement discrepancy. Also, an attempt was made to focus this review specifically on issues in theory and practice relevant to special education. Accordingly, the background for the subtype research problem was presented in terms of theories of learning disability as viewed from a psychoeducational perspective, and the available research on intervention as well as classification was reviewed. In the same vein, the conclusions, implications, and recommendations were focused on issues relevant to special education.

Other Related Research

As defined in this paper, learning disabilities subtype research represents an attempt to subdivide heterogeneous samples of children into more homogeneous subgroups that reflect different patterns of specific disabilities. The research question in subtype studies is typically addressed by either clinical-inferential methods or empirical classification techniques such as Q-factor analysis and cluster analysis. Another approach that is similar in some ways to clinical-inferential classification has been to select out rationally defined subsets of children with learning disabilities who have a common characteristic (e.g., memory deficits) in order to study them experimentally. However, some investigators have addressed the problem of heterogeneity among children with learning disabilities from different perspectives. For example, some studies related learning disabilities as an outcome variable to etiological classifications or factors. Also, a number of psychoeducational classifications have been devised based on the analysis subtest scatter in an attempt to distinguish children with learning disabilities from normal children. Finally, several authors have proposed IQ-achievement discrepancy criteria for distinguishing students with learning disabilities from slow learners and for defining what constitutes a "severe learning disability" with respect to eligibility criteria for special education services.

Since the goals and procedures for the classification of children in these studies differ from those of subtype studies, as defined above, they will be reviewed only briefly under the topic of related research.

Classification by Etiology

Throughout the history of the field, an underlying assumption on the part of many investigators has been that while there are many environmental causes of school failure, learning disability was due to some form of neurological dysfunction that was intrinsic to the individual (Hammill, Leigh, McNutt, & Larsen, 1981; Kavale & Forness, 1985; Satz & Fletcher, 1980). The concept of neurological dysfunction has a long and controversial history in the field. A thorough review of the literature linking neurological and constitutional factors to learning disability is beyond the scope of this chapter (see Kavale & Forness, 1985; Nichols & Chen, 1981; Rie & Rie, 1980; Rourke, Bakker, Fisk, & Strang, 1983; and Whalen & Henker, 1980 for reviews). However, since a number of clinical classifications have been proposed, it is appropriate to consider briefly several recent studies that have examined the utility of these diagnostic categories as they relate to research on specific learning disabilities.

The neurological bases for learning problems was first postulated by Berlin in 1887 and was later related to educational processes by Orton in 1937. Subsequently, Strauss and Lehtinen (1947) drew a distinction between exogenous (brain damage) and endogenous (cultural-familiar) mental retardation and described the behavioral characteristics of the two groups. Strauss and Kephart (1955) then extended the concept of exogenous mental retardation to children of normal intelligence who had learning problems, thereby distinguishing intrinsic forms of learning disability from school failure due to factors that were extrinsic to the child. Although considerable debate centered on the validity of this distinction in the field of mental retardation (Sarason, 1949), the behavioral differences proposed by Strauss and Werner between exogenous and endogenous children were widely accepted in the early history of the field of learning disability and were slowly transformed into what is currently classified as minimal brain dysfunction (Clements, 1966; Nichols & Chen, 1981).

At the same time, correlational and factor analytic studies of the various signs and symptoms of MBD have not been successful in isolating a single syndrome of learning disabilities associated with suspected neurological dysfunction (Paine, Werry, & Quay, 1968; Routh & Roberts, 1972; Werry, 1968). Similarly, attempts to distinguish between specific developmental dyslexia, which is presumably of constitutional origin (Critchley, 1964), and poor reading due to extrinsic environmental factors have not been successful (Taylor, Satz, & Friel, 1979).

The most recent comprehensive evidence on the phenomenon of MBD and learning disabilities was reported by Nichols and Chen (1981) based on an unselected sample of 29,889 7-year-olds from the Collaborative Perinatal Project. This project was begun in 1957 by the National Institute of Neurological and Communicative Disorders and Stroke to study perinatal risk factors associated with a variety of handicapping conditions. The original sample was based on over 53,000 pregnancies in women treated by 12 national medical centers. At the 7-year follow-up of the children, data were collected on child behavior, academic achievement, ability, neurological status, and a variety of perceptual and cognitive measures.

In the initial analysis Nichols and Chen (1981) intercorrelated 26 signs and symptoms of MBD and found only slight associations, thereby confirming earlier evidence against a single MBD syndrome. Based on factor analysis of these data, they selected three clinical groups for further study; a learning difficulties (LD) group that represented 8.36% of the sample, a hyperkinetic-impulsive (HI) behavior group (5.85%), and a neurological soft signs (NS) group (6.15%). Approximately 79% of the sample showed no abnormal signs or symptoms. The LD group was defined by achievement lower than that predicted by IQ; the HI group was defined by ratings of hyperactivity, impulsivity, poor attention span and emotional lability; and the NS group was defined by cutoff scores that represented the number of neurological symptoms presented.

Of particular interest in this study was the number of learning difficulties cases that also presented hyperactive behavior and/or clinically significant neurological signs. Behaviorally suspicious ratings were given by clinicians to 8.0% of the MBD cohort and to 16% of the learning difficulties children; 9% of the cohort presented neurological signs and 18% of the children with learning difficulties were given suspicious neurological signs.

Thus, indications of hyperactivity and neurological factors were associated with learning disability (as defined by ability-achievement discrepancy) about twice as often as found in the total sample, but the vast majority of children with learning difficulties did not present these symptoms. Similarly, relatively few perinatal risk factors were related to learning difficulties. On the other hand socioeconomic and demographic variables such as family size were strongly related to learning difficulties.

Collectively, these results from the Collaborative Perinatal Project, as well as those from other studies cited above, do not support the utility of clinical classifications such as MBD or developmental dyslexia in differentiating an intrinsic or primary form of learning disability from school failure due to environmental determinants. Moreover, diagnostic classifications that presume a neurological or constitutional basis for learning disability have not been shown to produce subgroups that present fundamentally different learning characteristics that would differentiate those children who need special education from those who are likely to respond to conventional instruction (Taylor et al., 1979).

Classification of Ability Profiles

One common characteristic associated with learning disabilities is an uneven pattern of abilities (Feagans & McKinney, 1981; Hallahan & Kauffman, 1976). An uneven ability profile was first proposed by Gallagher (1966) in his concept of "developmental imbalances" to distinguish between learning disability and mental retardation. He noted that while mentally retarded children displayed low ability across most measures of intellectual functioning, children with learning disabilities displayed strengths in some areas and deficits in others. Again while research on test scatter does not pertain to the classification of learning disabilities subtypes per se, it is relevant to the subtypes research question because it is an attempt to isolate test patterns that are characteristic of children with learning disabilities as a group.

The most popular application of this concept has been in the clinical interpretation of the Wechsler Intelligence Scales, and a variety of classification schemes have been devised to index learning disabilities (Bannatyne, 1968, 1974; Bush & Waugh, 1976; Kaufman, 1981; Keogh & Hall, 1974; Vance & Singer, 1979). For example, Bannatyne (1974) grouped the WISC subtests in four categories, verbal conceptual (similarities, vocabulary, comprehension), spatial (picture completion, block design, object assembly), sequential (arithmetic, digit span, coding), and acquired knowledge (information, arithmetic, vocabulary). In Bannatyne's system learning disability would be indicated by a spatial–conceptual–sequential pattern. On the other hand, Kaufman (1979) proposed the so called "ACID" pattern in which strengths on most subtests were seen relative to deficits on arithmetic, coding, information, and digit span. In addition to the analysis of subtest patterns and subtest recategorization, large verbal-performance IQ discrepancies in favor of performance IQ have been taken as a sign of learning disability (Kaufman, 1981).

Although the interpretation of Wechsler subtest pattern as an index of learning disability enjoys wide acceptance in the field, the bulk of research conducted over the past 10 years does not support the practice. Recently, Kaufman (1981) reviewed the literature on the WISC-R with respect to factor analytic studies, subtest recategorization, and scatter analysis, and concluded that there was little evidence for a stereotypical pattern that could define learning disability. More recently, Kavale and Forness (1984) conducted a meta-analysis of 94 studies of the validity of Wechsler scatter analysis and recategorization and reached the same conclusion. Although Kaufman (1981) notes that these negative findings may be distressing to some, they do serve to redirect research on classification and diagnosis in the field, perhaps in ways that are more relevant to special education.

Classification by IQ-Achievement Discrepancy

Most definitions of learning disability attribute the disorder to deficiencies in the "basic psychological processes" that underlie school learning. However, as noted in the introduction to this chapter, although attempts have been made to identify the key marker variables that might index learning disability (Keogh, Major-Kingsley, Omori-Gordon, & Reid 1982), research has yet to produce consensus on exactly what psychological processes define the condition or how they should be measured. Basically, this is the essential research question addressed by subtype studies; in the language of the Keogh et al. (1982) classification system, it is the search of the "topical markers" for the condition.

Lack of consensus on the major topical markers of learning disability and the failure of psychometric and etiological classification procedures to provide useful indexes have led to an increased reliance upon IQ achievement discrepancy as the principal index of learning disability. In order to delimit the number of children who are identified as having learning disabilities and serve more severely handicapped children, most states have either revised their rules and regulations to require discrepancy criteria or are in the process of doing so. In general, most of the proposed revisions involve specifying a particular method for calculating the discrepancy and setting more stringent cut-offs for service eligibility. Although the use of discrepancy criteria has the advantage of providing a more objective index of underachievement, this approach to classification also presents a host of methodological, conceptual, and practical problems that deserve brief consideration here.

To date most of the research on the use of IQ-achievement discrepancies to identify children with learning disabilities has been methodological in nature and has involved the comparison of various formulas and assessment of the effects of different cut-off criteria (Cone & Wilson, 1981; Forness, Sinclair, & Guthrie, 1983; Shepard, 1980). In general, none of the available methods for calculating discrepancy scores is without serious methodological limitations. Most researchers favor the regression method because it is the most robust statistically; however, it is the most difficult to implement practically. Nevertheless, the choice of methods has been shown to be critical since different methods identify different children (Alberg, 1985) as well as different numbers of children. Moreover, different children are identified by different methods at different levels of ability, as well as when different cut-off criteria are applied.

For example, Alberg (1985) recently compared the effects of proposed changes in the North Carolina criteria that use a standard score difference method and regression analysis. She found that the standard score method identified fewer children, but overidentified bright children compared to regression analysis. The extent to which the same children were identified by the two methods was related to IQ level such that there was more agreement in the average range and less agreement at the extremes of the IQ distribution.

Perhaps the most basic issue in the use of discrepancy criteria is whether discrepancy scores actually indicate the presence of learning disabilities. In this regard, it is interesting to note that the concept of ability-achievement discrepancy is not included in most definitions of learning disability, but rather is inferred as a consequence of disorders in specific psychological processes. Because children with learning disabilities are impaired specifically as opposed to generally (i.e., mental retardation), they display poor achievement in spite of average or above average ability. Thus, it is possible theoretically for a child (particularly a young child) to present a pattern of signs and symptoms traditionally associated with learning disability (e.g., in attention, deficits in perception or language) and not display a significant discrepancy between ability and achievement. For example, recently this author examined WISC-R-reading achievement discrepancies for school-identified children with learning disabilities who had been subtyped in the Carolina Longitudinal Project (Speece, McKinney, & Appelbaum, 1985) and found that only 35% of those classified as having attention deficits were discrepant. Moreover, only 40% of those with narrative language disabilities in this first and second grade sample (Feagans & Appelbaum, in press) were discrepant.

Conversely, a child can present an IQ-achievement discrepancy because of motivational, emotional, social, and/or pedagogical reasons as well as learning disability. In sum, the presence of an IQ-achievement discrepancy is an index of underachievement which may or may not reflect the presence of learning disability defined theoretically. Clearly, additional research is needed on the validity of discrepancy criteria, and in particular on the characteristics of children who do and do not meet these criteria for special education services.

Research on Learning Disabilities Subtypes

The literature on learning disabilities subtypes can be organized into two broad categories according to how investigators classified their subjects. Clinical-inferential studies result in conceptually based typologies that reflect the investigators' a priori theoretical orientation and/or clinical impressions. In these studies, children are usually matched by visually comparing their performance on psychoeducational or neuropsychological tests. In some clinical-inferential studies children are classified according to their profile pattern and in others according to within-test discrepancies (i.e., scatter) in their level of performance. The majority of the early studies on learning disabilities subtypes in the 1960s and 1970s used this approach.

More recently a growing number of investigators have used multivariate classification techniques that result in empirically-based typologies. These studies fall into two groups that reflect the statistical method employed, either Q-factor analysis or cluster analysis. Since the application of these techniques to educational research is relatively recent they will be described in some detail below by way of introduction to this literature on learning disabilities subtypes.

In addition to the general approach taken in classifying children, the methods for grouping children, and variables employed, individual studies also vary in the samples that were used. Most of the early studies used clinical samples of children who had been seen or were under referral for learning and/or behavior problems. Other studies used school-based samples of underachievers who were selected for the study sample purposively. Relatively few subtype studies have been made of school-identified children with learning disabilities who met the *P.L. 94–142* federal definition; however, there is a growing body of evidence on such children that deserves special attention in this review.

Clinical-Inferential Classification

During the 1960s a number of subtypes were proposed based on the theory that reading disorders could be attributed to deficient visual and auditory processes. Subsequent research on the classification of reading disorders in children tended to follow two lines. Some investigations focused on the reading process itself and classified children according to their performance deficits on academic tasks, while others focused on the neuropsychological correlates of poor performance. Also, a great deal of work during the 1970s was devoted to the validity of various classification schemes for assessing subtest scatter on psychometric measures of intelligence such as the Wechsler scales. However, since the research question in studies of profile scatter pertains more to the identification of students with learning

disabilities as different from normal students rather than to the subdivision of students with learning disabilities as a heterogeneous group, this topic will be covered in a later section on related research.

Early Clinical Classification

The first attempts to classify different subtypes of reading disorders were rooted primarily in the clinical experience of the investigators. Nevertheless, three early clinical reports are noteworthy for their heuristic value in stimulating the more rigorous classification studies that followed.

For example, in 1969 Ingram proposed that three different types of reading disabilities could be distinguished according to the pattern of deficits in visuospatial and auditory-linguistic skills. Subsequently, Ingram, Mann, and Blackburn (1970) examined patterns of children's reading errors retrospectively and sorted the sample into three subgroups which they described as auditory dyslexia, visuospatial dyslexia, and mixed. Similarly, Johnson and Myklebust (1967) initially proposed two subtypes of reading disability: visual and auditory dyslexia. Later Myklebust (1978) added several other subtypes that involved different combinations of mixed visual and auditory deficits (e.g., cross-modal dyslexia).

In addition to Ingram (1969) and Johnson and Myklebust (1967) several conceptually similar classifications were proposed based on the clinical interpretation of various psychoeducational tests. For example, Bateman (1968) suggested that different visual and auditory subtypes could be distinguished on the Illinois Test of Psycholinguistic Ability (ITPA). Also, Kinsbourne and Warrington (1963) described two subgroups of reading disabled children based on verbal-performance IQ discrepancies on the Wechsler Intelligence Scale for Children (WISC). Children with a 20-point discrepancy in favor of their performance IQ (language retardation group) had delayed speech and verbal-production problems, whereas those with greater verbal than performance IQs had perceptual-motor impairments.

Classification of Academic Performance

One of the first attempts to subdivide a large sample of children using clinical-inferential methods was made by Boder (1971, 1973). Boder (1973) examined the reading and spelling errors of 107 reading disabled children who ranged in age from 8 to 16 years. Although little detail was reported concerning the exact method of classification, she emphasized a qualitative clinical approach that assessed children's learning styles in performing the task as well as their level of performance. Based on her clinical impressions of error patterns, she classified 93% of the sample into three subtypes.

The largest subtype (67%) was classified as dysphonetic. This subgroup had particular difficulty analyzing words phonetically and tended to use a visual approach in which they read words globally rather than analytically. A much smaller subtype (10%) was classified as dyseidetic. Unlike the first subtype, these children were described as "word-blind." Although dyseidetic children approached words phonetically, they read very laboriously: "as if he is seeing each word for the first time" (Boder, 1973, p. 670). Boder (1973) classified the third subtype (23%) as alexic (mixed dysphonetic-dyseidetic) because they had a pattern of performance that was consistent with both syndromes. The latter group was the most severely impaired group in terms of overall reading achievement.

Although Boder's (1973) subtypes were generally consistent with those described in other clinical reports at the time (e.g., Ingram, 1969; Johnson & Myklebust, 1967), she offered no evidence with respect to the reliability of the classification procedure or the external validity of the subtypes. However, three more recent studies have provided supplementary information of these questions.

Camp and Dolcourt (1977) administered Boder's reading and spelling tests to a sample of 34 average to above average fifth graders and a group of 18 fourth-to-sixth grade retarded readers who were placed in special programs. They devised a priori decision rules and a diagnostic flow chart for classifying Boder's subtypes more objectively. The sample was first divided into high, average, and low reading groups and then classified as either normal, dyseidetic, dysphonetic, or alexic. Only one child in the high reading group showed an atypical performance pattern. The average reading group contained 4 normals, 5 dyseidetics, and 1 dysphonetic/alexic child; the low reading group contained 11 normals, 4 dyseidetics, and 9 dysphonetic/alexics. Although Camp and Dolcourt's (1977) diagnostic classification was fairly reliable (76%–91% agreement), the proportional membership in each subtype did not replicate Boder (1973). Also, the low reading group contained approximately as many normal children as those in atypical subtypes, although the latter findings could be attributed to differences in samples.

In a second study based on Boder's subtypes, Obrzut (1979) used the classification procedure developed by Camp and Dolcourt (1977) to subdivide a sample of 144 second and fourth grade boys into subgroups of 45 (34%) normal readers, 18 (13%) nonspecific poor readers, and 80 (56%) dyslexic readers. The dyslexic group was further classified as dysphonetic (54%), dyseidetic (31%) and, alexic (15%). Nonspecific readers were those who read below grade level but did not show an atypical pattern of errors on Boder's reading and spelling tests. Obrzut also administered dichotic listening tasks (pairs of digits were presented as auditory stimuli) and bisensory memory tasks (visual and auditory stimuli presented simultaneously). Results showed that normal and dyseidetic readers performed better than dysphonetic and alexic readers, thereby suggesting that Boder's subtypes were related to performance on tasks other than those that were used to classify children diagnostically. Obrzut (1979) speculated that the performance of alexic and dysphonetic children may reflect difficulties in processing linguistic information in the left hemisphere.

Finally, Bayliss and Liversey (1985) used the Camp and Dolcourt classification procedure to study visual memory strategies in dysphonetic ($n=8$), dyseidetic ($n=11$), and normal ($n=11$) readers. In the first experiment in this study, no differences were obtained between combined dyslexic and normal readers on both easy to label and hard to label items. However, when broken out by subtypes, dyseidetic children performed better than dysphonetics on hard to label items but not easy to label items; presumably because they used different memory strategies. This hypothesis was confirmed in a second experiment which showed that dysphonetics tended to remember items spatially, whereas dyseidetics preferred a serial recall strategy. When tested for recall under spatial and serial conditions, dysphonetic readers performed better in the spatial condition whereas dyseidetics performed better in the serial condition. However, this study suggested that normal readers were as heterogeneous in their learning styles as dyslexics, for again when the two subtypes were combined they did not differ from normal readers.

Neuropsychological Classification

Several investigators have used clinical-inferential methods to subtype reading disabled children on measures that were thought to reflect various aspects of neurological development and functioning. The conceptual framework for this research is based on the literature on the psychometric characteristics of children and adults with brain injuries and soft neurological signs (minimal brain dysfunction); and related research on the behavioral correlates of brain function as assessed by neurological evaluation and methods such as electroencephalograms. Although the neuropsychological tradition has a long and controversial history in the study of learning disabilities, a review of the theoretical bases and validity of this research is beyond the scope of this chapter. However, two recent books by Filskov and Boll (1981) and Rie and Rie (1980) provide excellent overviews of this area. Also, a series of articles reprinted by Torgesen and Senf (1984) and a book by Rourke et al. (1983) discuss the application of neuropsychological concepts to the assessment of learning disabilities.

Mattis, French, and Rapin (1975) studied 113 children between the ages of 8 and 18 who were diagnosed as brain-damaged dyslexics ($n=53$), brain-damaged readers ($n=31$), and nonbrain-damaged dyslexics ($n=29$) by pediatric neurologists, electroencephalograms, and educational assessment. Children were given a battery of neuropsychological tests that indexed general ability (WISC), visual-spatial abilities, perceptual-motor performance, and language. A priori decision rules were developed to classify a language disorder subtype

(39%), an articulation-graphomotor dyscoordination subtype (37%), and a visual-perceptual disorder subtype (16%). The characteristics associated with each of the Mattis et al. (1975) subtypes were as follows:

(1) Language disorder subtype—deficiencies in naming, listening comprehension, oral recitation, and speech sound discrimination;

(2) Articulation-graphomotor dyscoordination subtype—poor performance on ITPA sound blending and on copying and drawing tests with normal receptive language abilities;

(3) Visual-perceptual disorder subtype—lower performance IQ than verbal IQ, poor spatial ability (Raven's Matrices) and visual memory (Benton).

Within the various diagnostic groups selected by Mattis et al. (1975), language disorders were more common among brain-damaged dyslexics (43%), while articulation and graphomotor disorders were more frequent among developmental dyslexics (48%). Disorders of visual perception were less common and spread evenly across diagnostic groups.

Mattis (1978) attempted to replicate the earlier study with a sample of 163 minority children who were diagnosed as dyslexic, and identified the same subtypes in 78% of the sample. Unlike the first study, 63% of the minority children were classified as language disordered; only 10% presented articulation-graphomotor problems and 5% had visual-perceptual impairments. Unfortunately, neither study reported data on the reliability of the classification procedure nor on the external validity of the subtypes. Also, according to Mattis et al. (1975), children were classified into mutually exclusive homogeneous subtypes that had no overlapping features. As Satz and Morris (1981) note, this degree of homogeneity in classification does not conform to other clinical and empirical studies that typically find subtypes with a mixed pattern of deficits.

For example, Denckla (1972) described three clinical syndromes that were similar to those reported by Mattis et al.: a language disorder subtype, a visual-spatial disorder subtype and a dyscontrol subtype. However, she noted that 70% of her clinic sample of disabled readers either did not fit subtypes described elsewhere in the literature or presented mixed patterns of deficits. Later Denckla (1977, 1978) proposed six subtypes with the following characteristics:

(1) Global-mixed language disorder—generally low language abilities,

(2) Articulation-graphomotor disorder—poor articulation and fine motor skills,

(3) Anomic-repetition disorder—poor naming, digit span and sentence repetition,

(4) Dysphonemic sequencing disorder—similar to subtype 3 but characterized by phonetic errors and problems with syntax,

(5) Verbal learning disorder—general low verbal ability, and

(6) Correlational disorder—absence of atypical reading patterns but reading below that expected from IQ scores.

Although a number of Denckla's subtypes resemble those reported in the clinical literature of the time, they appear to be based primarily on clinical impressions and evidence was not offered concerning external validity (Doehring, Triter, Patel, & Fiedorowicz, 1981; Satz & Morris, 1981).

Finally, Pirozzolo (1979) and Pirozzolo and Rayner (1978) described two subtypes of reading disabled children using clinical-inferential classification. The first subtype (auditory-linguistic) had lower verbal than performance IQs, poor phonetic reading skills and other language deficits. The second subtype (visual-spatial) showed relatively lower performance than verbal IQs, a high number of visual discrimination errors in reading, and poor spatial abilities. Subsequently, Rayner (1981) reported that children in the visual-spatial subtype made more inaccurate eye movements in word recognition tasks; however, since oculator-motor training did not improve reading in such children, Pirozzolo (1979) argued that difficulties in eye movement were secondary to deficiencies in processing visual-spatial information.

Evaluation of Clinical-Inferential Classification

The various subtypes described in this section have a great deal of intuitive appeal because they tend to confirm expectations based on prevailing clinical impressions and practices. On the other hand, much of the research on clinical-inferential subtypes is seriously flawed, both methodologically and conceptually, and should be approached with the upmost caution in drawing implications for current research and practice in special education.

In evaluating the utility of these studies, the first problem encountered is the nature of the research samples themselves. As Satz and Morris (1981) point out, most of the clinical-inferential studies did not include appropriate comparison groups of normal readers to determine whether clinical subtypes were indeed devient or idiosyncratic of learning disabled children. As noted in the next section, it is common to find "normally appearing" subtypes in empirical studies of learning disabled samples. A related problem is that in most studies, the sample was preselected and subject to referral and diagnostic bias. Perhaps more importantly, clinic-based samples may not represent the range of child and sociodemographic characteristics in more typical school-identified samples.

Also, attention to the issues of reliability and validity was notably absent from reports reviewed in this section. This criticism pertains to both the reliability and validity of the measures used, as well as to the reliability and validity of the subtype classification procedures. The specific criteria used to classify individuals was obscure in many of these studies. Although decision rules were developed in some studies to sort children into categories, the clinical-inferential method still relies solely on the visual inspection of complex multivariate profiles. Although it should be recognized that such procedures conform to what usually occurs in clinical practice when diagnostic decisions are made about individual children, they still suffer from a serious lack of objectivity.

Finally, a critical issue in evaluating the utility of this work for special education is the lack of evidence concerning external validity. For example, it would be important to know whether the subtypes described in this section differed according to age, sex, race, IQ, and school performance. In sum, the value of the literature on the clinical-inferential classification of learning disabilities subtypes for special education seems to rest primarily on its heuristic merit in stimulating more objective research and assisting in the clinical interpretation of results from more rigorous studies.

Empirical Classification

Each of the studies reviewed in this section used multivariate statistical classification techniques to subdivide heterogeneous learning disabled samples into more homogeneous subtypes based on their performance across an array of variables. Although these methods of taxonomic analysis have firm historic roots in the biological sciences, they are relatively new and have been little used in the educational and behavioral sciences. Accordingly this section of the review will begin with a brief overview of these classification methods in order to set the stage for evaluating the individual and collective merit of an empirical classification research.

Methodological Considerations

The basic problem addressed by empirical subtype research is the following. Given a heterogeneous sample of individuals who vary both across and within a given set of attributes, is it possible to group individuals into subsets that are highly similar to one another and relatively different from those assigned to other subsets? Generally, there are two basic empirical techniques for accomplishing this task: Q-factor analysis and cluster analysis. The Q-factor technique is conceptually similar to traditional factor analysis (sometimes called the R technique). However, the Q technique involves the factor analysis of correlations among subjects, as opposed to correlations among tests which is the usual practice in R-factor studies. Thus, the Q technique results in factors that describe groups of similar children rather than groups of similar tests. Cluster analysis, on the other hand, is an iterative technique which successively matches children who display either a similar level of response or a similar patter of response across an array of variables. Although the definition of similarity and the rules for joining subjects may vary, the basic technique operates in such a fashion as to increase the homogeneity within subsets of children while decreasing the overlap among subsets. Thus, over successive iterations, the variance within subsets becomes small in relation to

variance among subsets.

With respect to the interpretation of the results of these subtype studies, it is important to note that although these techniques are empirical, the investigator has no a priori knowledge concerning the number of factors or clusters that may be obtained. Therefore, the choice of variables and the selection of the sample are critical in determining whether the results yield educationally and psychologically meaningful subgroups. Accordingly, some theoretical perspective should guide the selection of variables and samples to ensure interpretable results.

Also, it is important to note that although these techniques are multivariate, they are not based on probabilistic models. Rather, these techniques are more accurately described as descriptive. Thus, the investigator does not have a specified alpha level (e.g., $p < 0.05$) to determine what is a "significant" number of clusters or to determine the reliability of the classification of individual cases. Therefore, since there is no "one best solution" to the classification problem, the outcomes of these studies are heavily dependent upon the wise judgment of the investigator. Fortunately, however, the investigator is aided by a number of very good guidance functions. If followed, these guidance procedures will produce reliable and interpretable results, but they are only guidance functions as opposed to strict probabilistic statistics.

In the application of empirical classification techniques to the problem of learning disabilities subtyping, a number of important decisions need to be made that can potentially influence the study outcome. One of the most fundamental decisions concerns the definition of similarity, that is, how the individuals in a given subtype are alike. Generally, in learning disabilities subtyping, one is primarily interested in identifying specific syndromes of learning disabilities as revealed by children's patterns of strengths and weaknesses across a set of measures. However, in some instances the investigator may wish to form subtypes that reflect different levels of severity as well as patterns of specific disabilities.

In choosing an index of similarity, the investigator must consider the relative importance of response elevation, profile shape, and scatter (within profile variance) in terms of the research question and the particular set of variables that are used (Lorr, 1983: Skinner, 1978). A distance metric considers all three pieces of information in determining similarity whereas a correlational measure considers only profile shape. Most of the cluster analytic studies with children with learning disabilities have used distance measures; however, it is important to note that the interpretation of the subtypes in these studies is complicated by the confounding of elevation, shape and scatter. Thus, whereas some subtypes may reflect similarities in level of severity across the measures (i.e., response elevation), others may reflect similar patterns of response (i.e., profile shape and/or scatter). Studies that use correlational measures typically control elevation and scatter in order to focus on profile shape as the defining feature of subtypes (Speece, 1985; Speece et al., 1985). However, correlational measures may result in subtypes of children who show markedly different levels of severity with respect to the same pattern of performance and this may obscure clinical interpretation.

In general, support can be found for either approach in defining similarity; however, it is often the case that investigators have failed to provide a clear rationale for the approach taken in previous studies and/or have not discussed the consequences of their choice with respect to the interpretation of their subtypes.

A second important decision in carrying out subtype studies is the choice of an algorithm. Some algorithms are more sensitive to certain aspects of the data (e.g., profile elevation) than others. Also, the choice of a particular algorithm influences the degree of homogeneity or compactness of the resulting clusters. In general, good practice would involve the use of more than one algorithm to determine the extent to which the results were method specific (Morris, Blashfield, & Satz, 1981).

In addition to decisions concerning the definition of similarity and basic method of combining subjects, the investigator must be concerned with both the internal and external validity of the solution. After the investigator establishes that the resulting subgroups "make sense" theoretically, the internal consistency of the solution must be checked. There are a variety of techniques available for checking internal consistency including using a different algorithm to join subjects, split sample replication, forecasting a separate sample into the classification sample, and so forth. However, in each case one is interested in the stability or replicability of the solution with alternative methods and samples.

Finally, a critically important issue in evaluating the applied significance of these studies is external validation. It is the case that empirical classification techniques will cluster random data. The presence of reliable subtypes that appear to be theoretically meaningful does not ensure that they index relevant domains of behavior or that they have any practical value. Generally, external validation is established by relating subtype membership to variation on relevant subject variables (e.g., IQ, sex, socioeconomic status), independent measures of the processes that define the subtype, and measures of academic performance. For example, if a given subtype were defined by deficits in attention and hostility as rated by teachers, it would be important to know whether these children were actually off-task more often in the classroom and were aggressive in their interactions with classmates. Similarly, it would be important to know if children with these characteristics differed from those in other subtypes intellectually or academically.

A more complete discussion of empirical classification methods can be found in Aldenderfer and Blashfield (1984), Anderberg (1973), Everitt (1980), and Lorr (1983), and its application to subtyping learning disabled students has been discussed by Fisk and Rourke (1983),

Morris, Blashfield, and Satz (1981), Rourke (1985), and Lessig, Williams, and Gil (1982).

Q-Factor Research

Two major programatic research efforts have used *Q*-factor analysis as the primary classification strategy. The first set of studies was carried out by Doehring and his colleagues at McGill University, and the second by Rourke and his colleagues at Windsor University, Canada. The general approach taken in the McGill studies was to first classify subjects according to their reading deficits and then to assess linguistic and neuropsychological correlates. The Windsor studies classified on neuropsychological measures and then sought neurological and educational correlates.

The McGill Studies

The first study in this series involved a sample of 34 reading disabled children in a summer program who ranged in age from 8 to 16 years (Doehring & Hoshko, 1977). Children were given a battery of 31 reading-related measures (letters, words, syllables and sentences), that assessed visual and auditory-visual matching, oral reading, and visual scanning. *Q*-factor analysis of this sample yielded the following three subtypes. Three children were unclassified:

> *Type O* (*n* = 12, 35%)—Oral reading problems; poor word, phrase and sentence reading with near normal silent reading as assessed by matching tasks.
> *Type A* (*n* = 11, 32%)—Intermodal association problems: poor in matching spoken and printed letters, words and syllables.
> *Type S* (*n* = 8, 23%)—Sequential relation problems: poor in visual and visual-auditory matching of words and syllables compared to letters.

Doehring and Hoshko verified these three subtypes in a sample of 31 children with mixed handicaps including mental retardation. Also, they found a fourth subtype that reflected visual-perceptual problems that was not represented in the original reading disabled sample. Three (8%) reading disabled children and 5 (16%) children with mixed problems were unclassified.

Although Doehring and Hoshko (1977) did not report comparisons among their subtypes on external measures, they did collect information on teacher-recommended remediation strategies. Teachers recommended comprehension training for children in subtype O. Comprehension training plus work in visual-auditory association and oral expression was recommended for subtype A. Training in phonetic analysis, sound blending, oral expression and written sequencing was recommended for subtype S. Unfortunately, Doehring and Hoshko did not report the degree of convergence between teacher recommendations and subtype membership.

The second study in this series compared the Doehring and Hoshko (1977) samples to a sample of normal readers in grades 1–11 who had been given the same classification measures (Doehring, Hoshko & Bryans, 1979). Unlike the children in the reading disabled sample who were classified into three distinct subtypes, normal readers were not classified into discrete subtypes, and represented as many as six different performance patterns that were distributed evenly across the range of individual differences in the sample.

In order to evaluate the overlap among the reading disabled and normal children, Doehring et al. (1979) matched 31 normal readers to 31 disabled readers on age and sex. *Q*-factor classification of the combined sample revealed little overlap. As in the previous separate analyses, reading disabled children were classified in the same three subtypes, whereas normal readers were either unclassified (23%) or evenly distributed across the four major factors that resulted. Doehring et al. (1979) concluded that subtypes of reading disabled children did not simply represent exaggerated patterns of normal individual differences. Moreover, it appeared that the patterns of skill deficits among disabled readers were not characteristic of young beginning readers in the normal sample.

In the latest study by the McGill group, Doehring et al. (1981) explored the characteristics of their subtypes more fully and related reading skill subtypes to those formed by linguistic and neuropsychological measures. The sample for this study was composed of 88 children and adults aged 8–27 who had been referred to the Ottawa Hospital Neuropsychology Clinic for difficulties in school. In the first analysis Doehring et al. replicated the same three subtypes they found previously with the same 31 reading skill measures; however, a larger than expected number of subjects was left unclassified (18%). No clear trend in subtype membership was found with respect to sex; however, subjects in Subtype O were older than those in Subtype A who in turn were older than those in Subtype S.

In order to assess the relationship between language and reading disability, Doehring et al. (1981) administered 22 language measures that assessed phonemic segmentation, naming, oral repetition, following instructions, and semantics-syntactic usage. Initial analysis showed a general language deficiency in the reading disordered sample compared to 70 normal achievers; however, their measures of language failed to discriminate the three subtypes of reading disability. Doehring et al. next attempted to classify language subtypes but found only two stable factors which differed mainly on oral repetition tests (subtype 1) and naming and following instructions (subtype 2). Only 51 (58%) subjects were classified on the language measures, and rather weak associations were found between joint classifications of language and reading subtypes.

Finally, Doehring et al. (1981) assessed the relationship between neuropsychological deficits and reading disability subtypes with a battery of 22 measures of perceptual, verbal, motor, and tactile tests. Contrary to other evidence reviewed below, *Q*-factor analysis did not produce any characteristic neuropsychological profiles for the reading disabled sample. However, neuropsychological measures did discriminate the three reading disability subtypes such that Subtype O was least impaired and Subtype A was more impaired.

In sum, the McGill studies were successful in isolating three relatively stable subtypes of reading disability that appeared to have implications for differential treatment (Doehring, 1983, 1984); however, the practical value of this approach to subtyping remains to be demonstrated. Also, the theoretical implications of this work are obscured by the failure to demonstrate clear relationships between patterns of reading skills deficits and more basic psychological and linguistic processes. On the other hand, the potential practical merit of subtyping based on reading skills is considerable and certainly warrants further investigation.

The Windsor Studies

Research conducted by the Windsor group stemmed from their earlier work which related a number of neuropsychological variables to learning disabilities (Rourke, 1975, 1978; Rourke & Finlayson, 1978). The first studies in the series used the *Q*-factor technique to classify children on neuropsychological tests. Later studies involved the selection of a priori subgroups based on patterns of achievement. Since the latter research concerned comparisons among conceptually-based rather than empirically-derived subtypes, it will be reviewed under the topic of related research below.

Petrauskas and Rourke (1979) classified a sample of 133 clinic-referred reading disabled 8 and 9-year olds who were compared to 27 normal readers. Their neuropsychological test battery included 44 measures in 6 categories: tactile, sequencing, motoric, visual-spatial, auditory-verbal, and abstract-conceptual. In order to assess the reliability of classification, the total sample was randomly subdivided for separate and combined analyses. Although six factors were found, reliable classification was obtained for only three that represented 50% of the sample; another 30% were unclassified. The three major subtypes were described as follows:

Subtype 1 (*n* = 40, 25%)—Language disorder: poor auditory-verbal and language-related skills relative to good visual-perceptual and visual-spatial skills.
Subtype 2 (*n* = 26, 16%)—Mixed linguistic/sequencing deficits: impaired memory for sentences, visual-spatial memory and verbal fluency relative to adequate kinesthetic, psychomotor, semantic, and reasoning abilities.
Subtype 3 (*n* = 13, 8%)—Expressive language/psychomotor deficits: poor verbal fluency, sentence memory and eye-hand coordination with adequate

visual matching, kinesthetic, sound blending and semantic skills.

The fourth subtype was composed mainly of normal readers, but it was not replicated across separate analyses. Subtype 1 showed a 3 to 1 sex ratio and much lower verbal IQs relative to performance IQs on the WISC. Subtype 2 was predominately male and showed a minimal verbal IQ-performance IQ descrepancy. The third subtype showed a moderate discrepancy in favor of performance IQs and a 2 to 1 sex ratio.

The follow-up study in this series involved 264 clinic-referred children who ranged in age from 9 to 13 years (Fisk & Rourke, 1979). *Q*-factor analysis with the same 44 measures yielded three reliable subtypes that accounted for 54% of the sample; 20% was unclassified and 26% was classified unreliably. Two of the major subtypes described above were found at all age levels; the third subtype was found for older children but not at the 9–10 year level. In this study sample, the language and sequencing subtypes appeared with comparable frequency (approximately 19%). The third subtype was better represented in this sample (15%) than in the Petrauskas and Rourke (1979) sample, probably due to age variation.

Although the subtypes reported in these studies resemble some of these reported previously based on neuropsychological tests (e.g., Mattis et al., 1975), they suffer from a lack of external validation which precludes drawing definite implications about their practical or theoretical significance for special education based on the evidence presented.

Cluster Analytic Research

Review of literature on the application of cluster methods to the problem of learning disabilities subtypes revealed four major programatic research efforts, although there have been a number of individual studies as well. The first studies in this group were carried out as part of the Florida Longitudinal Project on underachievement (Satz & Morris, 1981; Satz, Taylor, Friel & Fletcher, 1978). The second set was conducted at Northwestern University by Lyon (1983) and his associates, and the third was conducted at the Boys Town Institute Indianna, for Communication Disorders by Watson, Goldgar and Ryschon (1983). The fourth programatic effort is the Carolina Longitudinal Project (McKinney & Feagans, 1984) at the Frank Porter Graham Children Development Center, University of North Carolina.

The Florida Study

The Florida study reported by Satz and Morris (1981) and Morris, Blashfield and Satz (1981) followed an initial classification study by Darby (1978). This study was unique in that cluster analysis was first used to identify children with learning disabilities within a large

($n = 236$) sample of typical fifth graders who were assessed at the endpoint of a 6-year longitudinal study. In order to select a learning disabled sample, Wide Range of Achievement Test (WRAT) grade level discrepancy scores were used to classify nine subgroups which differed on IQ, socioeconomic stakes and neuropsychological measures. Two subgroups ($n = 89$) that had average or better IQ scores and were two or more years behind in achievement were classified as learning disabled and retained for further analysis. Also these two subgroups contained children with a larger number of "soft" neurological signs compared to the other five clusters.

Children in the two learning disabilities subgroups were then clustered on a battery of neuropsychological measures including perceptual, perceptual-motor, reasoning, and linguistic tasks (see Fletcher & Satz, 1979, 1980). Four different clustering solutions were used to test for convergence and the following five subtypes were identified:

Subtype 1 (N = 27, 30%)—Global language impairment.
Subtype 2 (n = 14, 16%)—Specific language impairment in fluency.
Subtype 3 (n = 10, 11%)—Mixed global language and perceptual impairment.
Subtype 4 (n = 23, 26%)—Visual and perceptual-motor impairment.
Subtype 5 (n = 12, 13%)—No neuropsychological impairment.

Satz and Morris (1981) then compared the five subtypes on external measures of socioeconomic status, neurological status, and parent reading levels. Subtypes 1 (global language), 3 (language and perceptual), and 4 (perceptual-motor) showed a higher proportion of children with soft neurological signs compared to Subtypes 2 (specific language) and 5 (no neuropsychological problems). Also, the parents of children in Subtypes 2 and 5 scored higher on the WRAT reading subtest than those of children in the other three subtypes. Significant socioeconomic status differences were not found. Satz and Morris (1981) speculated that Subtype 5 (no impairment) might be explained by motivational or emotional factors, but were unable to find evidence for this hypothesis with personality tests.

Most recently, Satz, Morris, and Fletcher (1985) reported a retrospective analysis in which children in the Florida Project in grades 5, 2, and K were clustered separately on the same cognitive measures. Although details of this analysis were not given, Satz et al. reported that the global language, mixed deficit, and visual-perceptual subtypes found in the earlier fifth grade study were also found essentially unchanged among young children. However, the specific language and normal profile subtypes showed an improvement from grades K to 5 in cognitive perfomance. It was noted previously (Satz & Morris, 1981) that the latter two subtypes had fewer soft neurological signs and tended to come from higher educational and socioeconomic status homes. Satz et al. suggested that subtype membership may signal predictive changes in cognitive status over part time which are prognostic of later outcomes, but cautioned that prospective longitudinal research would be required to address the issue of developmental change and prognosis.

The Northwestern Studies

With the exception of Satz and Morris (1981) who used an empirically-derived sample, most subtype studies have used either clinic-referred samples or samples of poor readers defined solely by achievement tests. In contrast, the work of Lyon and his colleagues was based on school-identified samples of children with learning disabilities who met *P.L. 94–142* criteria and who were receiving special education services.

In the first study in this series Lyon and Watson (1981) administered a battery of 8 diagnostic measures to a sample of 100 learning disabled and 50 normal 11- and 12-year-olds in the public schools. The battery included two measures of receptive language, three measures of expressive language, a measure of visual-spatial ability, one measure of perceptual-motor ability, and one measure of visual memory. Cluster analysis yielded six subtypes.

Subtype 1 (11%)—Combined auditory and visual deficits: deficits in receptive language, auditory memory, sound blending, perceptual and perceptual-motor skills.
Subtype 2 (13%)—Combined linguistic and perceptual-motor deficits: poor language comprehension, auditory memory, and visual-motor integration skills.
Subtype 3 (13%)—Expressive language deficits: poor phonetic skills and receptive language ability.
Subtype 4 (34%)—Visual perceptual deficits: specific impairment in perceptual motor performance relative to adequate language.
Subtype 5 (13%)—Auditory sequencing deficits: impairment in syntactical, phonetic, and expressive language.
Subtype 6 (17%)—Normal diagnostic profile.

Lyon and Watson (1981) found that subtypes 1 and 5 scored lower on both the reading recognition and comprehension subtests of the Peabody Individual Achievement Test (PIAT) compared to subtypes 2, 3, and 4. As expected subtype 6 scored higher than all other subtypes on achievement measures. Like Satz and Morris (1981), they speculated that subtype 6 may represent children who perform poorly in school because of social or emotional factors but could not offer evidence to that effect.

Subsequently, Lyon, Watson, Reitter, Porch, and Rhodes (1981) compared the Lyon and Watson (1981) subtypes on four measures of spelling skills as well as measures of family characteristics and parent reports of developmental milestones. Subtypes 1, 3, and 5 made more errors on the function, names, and dictation subtests of Porch Index of Communicative Ability than subtypes 2, 4, and 6. Subtypes 1 and 3 performed more poorly than other subtypes on the graphic spelling subtest of the Porch. Sociodemographic and historical variables did not distinguish the subtypes.

More recently, Lyon, Steward, and Freeman (1982) expanded their 8 test battery to 10 measures of linguistic and visual perceptual skills which they administered to 75 learning disabled readers and 42 normal readers between 6 and 9 years of age. The results of cluster analysis with this younger sample and additional measures were substantially different from those reported by Lyon and Watson (1981) and Lyon et al. (1981). This study yielded five rather than six subtypes.

Subtype 1 (n = 18, 24%)—Visual perceptual deficit: uniformly poor performance in visual perception, visual-motor integration, and spatial skills relative to adequate linguistic skills.
Subtype 2 (n = 10, 13%)—Auditory linguistic deficit: general poor performance in syntax, sound blending, language comprehension, auditory memory and discrimination, and naming with corresponding strengths in all perceptual skills.
Subtype 3 (n = 12, 16%)—Normal diagnostic profile.
Subtype 4 (n = 15, 20%)—Auditory sequencing—Visual/spatial deficit: severe deficiency in language comprehension, with mild deficits in sound blending, naming, and visual perception.
Subtype 5 (n = 9, 12%)—Mixed phonetic and perceptual deficits: poor performance in sound blending, grammatic closure, and perceptual-spatial skills with adequate receptive and expressive language.

Analysis of Woodcock reading tests showed that subtypes 4 and 5 scored lower on the word attack subtest than all other subtypes, while subtypes 2 and 4 obtained lower word comprehension scores. Also, children in subtypes 2 and 4 showed the lowest scores on the passage comprehension subtest. Children in subtype 1 were younger than those in subtypes 2 and 4, and those in subtypes 5 were younger than those in subtype 4. Thus, it appeared visual perceptual and auditory-verbal deficits were associated with younger children with learning disabilities, while language comprehension and conceptual deficits were characteristic of older children with learning disabilities.

The Boys Town Study

Recently Watson, Goldgar, and Ryschon (1983) cluster analyzed 65 children with learning disabilities, ranging in age from 7 to 14 years, who had been referred to the Boys Town Institute for Communication Disorders. A unique feature of this study was the use of multiple measures of achievement, psychological processes, and behavior within the same large classification battery. Included were 8 measures of reading and spelling, 6 language measures, 3 measures of visual perception, 4 memory measures, and one each to tap perceptional organization and visual motor integration. Watson et al. (1983) factor analyzed their data initially revealing an achievement test factor, a language factor, a visual factor, and a memory factor. Accordingly, their clusters appeared to represent different combinations of deficit performance across the various factors or combinations of variables that were assessed.

Cluster 1 ($n = 20$, 30%) showed a general visual-perceptual deficit compared to average performance on all language measures with uniformly poor reading achievement. Cluster 2 ($n = 17$, 26%), in contrast to cluster 1, displayed a general language disorder but average performance on visual perceptual tasks. This cluster also showed a deficit on memory tasks and uniformly poor achievement. Cluster 3 ($n = 28$, 43%) was interpreted as a "minimal deficit" subgroup with subaverage performance on four of the 23 measures. Since many of the children in this subgroup had only very mild reading problems, Watson et al. argued that they may represent the lower end of the reading distribution without any outstanding deficits in underlying abilities.

The Carolina Longitudinal Project

The Carolina Longitudinal Project began in 1978 and is still under way at present (McKinney & Feagans, 1982, 1984). The learning disabled students in the sample were 63 newly-identified first and second graders who were placed in special education resource settings in public schools. When each learning disabled child was identified, he or she was matched by sex and race to a randomly selected normally achieving child (NLD) from the same mainstream classroom. In order to determine the developmental processes that distinguish LD and NLD children, and to isolate distinct subtypes of learning disabilities, both groups were followed longitudinally over a 3 year period with multiple measures of linguistic, cognitive, and behavioral competence. In addition to school achievement, data were also obtained on health and educational histories of the children and a variety of descriptive family variables.

Apart from the prospective longitudinal design, a unique feature of this project with respect to research on subtypes was the multivariate, multiple domain approach to assessment. This feature is important

because it provided the capability for the external validation of learning disabilities subtypes on sets of independent measures that assessed the same processes measured by the classification variables. For example, behavioral data on the same instrument were collected from both classroom teachers and special educators as well as from independent classroom observations. Similarly each task selected for the cognitive and language batteries had another conceptually similar task that could be used for validation purposes. Also, given the longitudinal focus, the opportunity exists to assess the stability of subtypes over time as well as their prognostic value with respect to academic outcomes.

In addition to these features, another unique feature of these studies was the way the normal sample was used. In addition to providing a benchmark for interpretation, normal children were forecasted into the clusters formed by children with learning disabilities in order to assess overlap and facilitate interpretation. As noted above, a number of cluster studies have reported "normal-appearing" subtypes. The forecasting technique assessed the "normality" of learning disabilities subtypes more directly based on the characteristics of a randomly selected sample of average achievers.

Each set of studies will be reviewed for each domain of measurement (behavioral, linguistic, cognitive).

Behavioral Subtypes. Since theory in the field of learning disabilities has been influenced greatly by the concept of specific ability deficits (Satz & Fletcher, 1980; Torgesen, 1975), most of the work on learning disabilities subtypes has focused on neuropsychological and psychoeducational test batteries. However, earlier studies in the Carolina Learning Disabilities Project showed that children with learning disabilities, as a heterogeneous group, displayed maladaptive behavior patterns in the classroom that predicted academic failure over the elementary grades (McKinney & Feagans, 1983, 1984; McKinney & Speece, 1983).

The first study by Speece, McKinney, and Appelbaum (1985) involved the classification and validation of behavioral subtypes in the Carolina Longitudinal sample based on classroom teacher ratings of independence, dependence, task-orientation / distractibility, extroversion / introversion, and considerateness / hostility. The resulting subtypes were interpreted as follows:

Cluster 1. Attention Deficit (28.6%)—This subtype was characterized by deficiencies in task-oriented behavior and independence but displayed normal personal/social behavior.

Cluster 2. Normal Behavior (25.4%)—Although this subtype showed slightly elevated ratings on considerateness and introversion, all profile points were within ±1 *SD* of the normal sample means.

Cluster 3. Conduct Problems (14.3%)—These children displayed mild attention deficits combined with elevated hostility and distractibility.

Cluster 4. Withdrawn Behavior (11%)—This cluster was composed primarily of LD girls and was rated as overly dependent and introverted.

Cluster 5. Normal Behavior (9.5%)—Like cluster 2 all the profile points for this subtype were in the normal range, but with slight elevated ratings on hostility.

Cluster 6. Low Positive Behavior (6.3%)—Children in this small subgroup showed uniformly low ratings on all positive behaviors but no corresponding elevation on negative behaviors.

Cluster 7. Global Behavior Problems (4.8%)—This very small subgroup of 3 boys was rated as significantly impaired on all classroom behaviors.

The interpretation of subtypes 2 and 5 as normal patterns of behavior was supported by the fact that 85% of the NLD children were classified into these two subtypes by the forecasting technique. Contrasts among the subtypes on the Schedule for Classroom Activity Norms observational system (McKinney, Mason, Perkerson, & Clifford, 1975) generally confirmed hypotheses about classroom behavior generated from the cluster descriptions of classroom teachers. For example, subtypes 3, 7, and 6 (problem behavior types) differed from all others with respect to gross motor inappropriate behavior and aggression. Similarly, the frequency of observed off-task behavior differentiated the normal clusters from the other five as well as subtypes 4, 6, and 7 from the others. Comparable ratings from learning disability resource teachers also differentiated the subtypes; however, more importantly, the cluster profiles generated from the learning disability teachers showed the same shape as those obtained from classroom teachers with some minor differences in elevation.

Generally, the seven subtypes conformed to expectation based on contemporary theories of adaptive classroom behavior (McKinney & Feagans, 1983; Schaefer, 1981; Von Isser, Quay, & Love, 1980). Nevertheless, it was interesting that the seven subtypes did not differ in academic achievement the first year the children with learning disabilities were placed in special education (Speece, McKinney, & Appelbaum, 1985). However, in a previous study, McKinney and Feagans (1984) reported that children in the same longitudinal sample, as a heterogeneous group, declined over a 3 year period compared to average achievers.

In order to assess the longitudinal stability and academic consequences of subtype membership, McKinney and Speece (1986) reclassified the learning disabled sample over the next 3 years of elementary school and assessed academic progress longitudinally. This analysis showed that although children in the various subtypes did not differ in achievement in the first and second grades, they were differentiated over the next two years such that (a) those in normal behavior subtypes and those in the withdrawn subtype showed linear progress on the PIAT, while (b) those in the attention deficit subtype and those exhibiting problem behaviors (subtypes 3, 6, and 7) showed a declining pattern of progress.

Also, McKinney and Speece (1986) report evidence for the longitudinal stability of behavioral subtypes as assessed two distinctly different ways. The first approach was the use of a forecasting technique to reclassify children in subsequent years based on their original subtype membership. When viewed in terms of clinically significant variations (i.e., normal, attention deficit, withdrawn, and conduct problems), it was more likely for a child to be classified as maladaptive at both year 1 and year 3 (55%) than to move from a maladaptive subtype to an adaptive one (11%). One of the most notable trends was for children in the attention deficit cluster to shift toward problem behavior clusters. In addition to this evidence with respect to subtype stability, McKinney and Speece (1986) showed that classroom teachers in subsequent years produced the same profile patterns that defined each subtype the first year of the study. In the same vein, external validation was also obtained longitudinally with respect to the ratings of learning disability teachers who produced essentially the same profiles as classroom teachers each year of the study.

Since all of the children with learning disabilities received special education for at least 2 years, and since the nature of special education services were documented, it was possible to speculate about the factors that produced differential responsiveness to treatment as a function of behavioral subtype. In general, children with learning disabilities in this longitudinal study received very similar treatment with respect to form, intensity, and content of services; on the average they were seen in resource rooms 1 hour per day, 4 days per week, and received instruction aimed at assisting them with basic skills work in the regular classroom (McKinney & Feagans, 1984). The longitudinal findings for the various behavioral subtypes suggest that while this pattern of service might be appropriate for some subtypes of students with learning disabilities, those with severe attention and behavior problems may require a more intense, behaviorally oriented pattern of service. Unfortunately, behavioral assessment is not typically included as part of the classification procedure and program planning for students with learning disabilities (McKinney & Feagans, 1983).

Language Subtypes. Feagans and Appelbaum (1986) used the same cluster procedures described above to subtype the Carolina Longitudinal sample on six measures of syntax, semantics, and discourse (narrative) skills. This study used an experimental task to assess both the comprehension and production of narrative language (Feagans & Farran, 1981). In this task, children were shown a toy grocery store with dolls and various props. They were read a story about the store and people and then were asked to act out the story with the props provided. After comprehension was assured, the children were asked to tell the story in their own words. The comprehension measure was the number of trials required to act out the story correctly while the production measures were the number of words used to paraphrase the story, the number of information units communicated, and the complexity of the child's language (number of subordinate clauses). Additional measures were a syntax text (Feagans, 1980) and vocabulary test. Feagans and Appelbaum (1986) identified the following six language subtypes:

Cluster 1. Narrative Deficit (*n* = 9, 16%)—This subtype showed poor comprehension and accuracy of communication relative to adequate syntax and semantics with marginal verbal output.

Cluster 2. Production Deficit (*n* = 9, 16%)—Although this subtype had superior vocabulary, they showed subaverage verbal output and language complexity with marginal narrative performance.

Cluster 3. Hyperverbal (*n* = 8, 14%)—This subtype displayed a great amount of output (words) and a high amount of complexity in relation to much lower (but average) comprehension, vocabulary, and syntax.

Cluster 4. Structural Deficit (*n* = 15, 27%)—These children displayed lower semantics and syntax scores compared to better than average narrative scores.

Cluster 5. Normal-Structural (*n* = 9, 16%)—Normal profile with better narrative and production scores than vocabulary and syntax scores.

Cluster 6. Normal-Narrative (*n* = 5, 9%)—Normal appearing profile but with low narrative and production scores relative to semantics and syntax scores.

As in the Speece et al. (1985) study, the interpretation of normal subtypes in this study was supported by forecasting procedures which classified 71% of the NLD sample into normal appearing LD cluster. The six clusters did not differ in nonverbal IQ; however, consistent with expectation from studies of high-risk children (Feagans & Farran, 1981), the structural deficit subtype contained a higher number of lower socioeconomic status children. Based on previous studies (Feagans, 1983; Feagans & Short, 1984), Feagans and Appelbaum (1986) hypothesized that children with narrative language deficits would score lower on reading tests intitially and make less progress longitudinally compared to those with better narrative skills relative to poorer structural skills and/or to those without language deficits.

Clusters 1, 2, and 6 had lower achievement scores than clusters 4 and 5 when the children were classified in the first and second grades. Similarly, longitudinal analyses showed that learning disabled children with narrative language deficits progressed at a slower rate over the 3 years of the study compared to those with structural language deficits, hyperverbal children, and those without apparent language deficits. The latter finding is particularly interesting given the concentration of lower socioeconomic status children in the structural deficit subtype.

Perceptual/Cognitive Subtypes. To date two separate studies have been completed in this domain within the Carolina Longitudinal Project. The first used the longitudinal school-identified sample and a battery of perceptual and linguistic problem-solving measures (McKinney, Short, & Feagans, 1985). The second study used a purposive sample of reading disabled third and fourth graders and a theoretically-based battery of information-processing measures (Speece, 1987).

The McKinney et al. study used six measures to index the following processes: visual recognition (match-to-sample), sequential problem-solving (information units), perceptual-motor skills (WISC-R coding) linguistic comprehension (trials to criterion in an instructional problem), linguistic production (information communicated), and semantics (WISC-R vocabulary). Children in the Carolina Longitudinal sample were clustered by using the same procedures as other studies in this section. The following subtypes were identified:

Cluster 1. *Normal* (*n* = 6, 11%). This subgroup of learning disabled children had profile points within ± *ISD* of the means of the average achieving comparison sample with one exception: their performance in sequential problem-solving (pattern including bits) was above average.

Cluster 2. *Severe Perceptual Deficit* (*n* = 4, 7%). All of the learning disabled children in Cluster 2 showed deviations of −3.0 *SD* or to greater on the matching-to-sample task as well as slightly subaverage linguistic comprehension and production. Sequential, perceptual-motor, and semantic skills were within the normal range.

Cluster 3. *Severe Comprehension Deficit* (*n* = 15, 27%). This subgroup showed a marked deficiency in language comprehension as assessed by the instructional task, as well as subaverage language production. Semantic and perceptual-motor skills were marginal relative to adequate visual recognition and sequential skills.

Cluster 4. *Normal* (*n* = 12, 22%). Although 3 children in this cluster showed significant deviations on the matching-to-sample task, the general pattern of profile points for the group as a whole was within the average range with a tendency toward marginal performance on WISC-R coding.

Cluster 5. *Mixed Perceptual-Linguistic Deficits* (*n* = 8, 14%). This subgroup showed mixed pattern of deficits and was the least homogeneous of the six subtypes. Generally these children showed a combination of mild deficits in visual matching, language comprehension and language production compared to relatively good semantic and perceptual-motor skills. However, three children showed severe perceptual deficits combined with either severe comprehension or production deficits.

Cluster 6. *Marginal Perceptual—Semantic Problems* (*n* = 10, 18%). Unlike Clusters 1 and 4, all children in this subgroup showed strengths in perceptual-motor skills with generally adequate sequential and language comprehension skills. Six out of ten of these children showed mild deficits in visual matching and four out of ten showed marginal vocabulary and communications skills.

The results of this study were similar to others in this section which reported distinct perceptual, linguistic, and mixed perceptual-linguistic subtypes (e.g., Lyon & Watson, 1981; Satz & Morris, 1981). However, the low prevalence of severe perceptual deficits (7%) compared to language deficits (27%) was unexpected. In this regard, it was interesting that 29% of the average achieving sample was forecasted into Cluster 2 (perceptual deficit), while 63% were classified into normal-appearing learning disabilities clusters. The six clusters did not differ in reading achievement initially in the first and second grades; however, Clusters 2, 3, and 5 scored lower on math than Clusters 1, 4, and 6. As with the other longitudinal studies described above, the various perceptual-linguistic subtypes showed different patterns of academic progress. Clusters 2, 3, and 5 showed a declining pattern of progress in reading compared to Clusters 1 and 4. Interestingly, Cluster 6 maintained its relative superiority in math but fell behind in reading.

In the second study in the cognitive domain, Speece (1987) sought to identify theoretically-based subtypes by using experimental measures of information processing that were related to various single deficit hypotheses of reading disability. The seven measures were selected to index sustained attention, phonetic and semantic encoding, speeding of recoding, short-term memory capacity and strategic organization in memory. The study sample contained 59 third and fourth grade school-identified learning disabled children who were 1.5 years or more behind on the Gray Oral Reading Test and were

average or better in Verbal IQ. Also data were collected on 21 average achievers for comparison purposes. Six clusters were identified.

Cluster 1. *Short-term Memory Deficit* (*n* = 9, 15%)—Children in this subtype showed subaverage performance on memory for digits and speed of recoding (naming) compared to average encoding and memory skills.

Cluster 2. *Speed of Recoding Deficit* (*n* = 12, 20%)—This subtype had severe deficits in their ability to recode (name) both digits and words; also they were weak in short-term memory, but displayed good memory organization and adequate encoding.

Cluster 3. *Mild Recoding/Attention Deficit* (*n* = 10, 17%)—Although this subtype showed strengths in phonetic encoding, performance was subaverage for both recoding tasks and marginal for sustained attention.

Cluster 4. *Mild Encoding/Severe Recoding Deficit* (*n* = 10, 17%)—The most salient feature of this subtype was strength in sustained attention relative to weakness in both phonetic and semantic encoding and recoding of words.

Cluster 5 *Marginal Performance* (*n* = 9, 15%)—The profile for this subtype was the "flattest" of the six. Although these children showed adequate memory, the general impression was one of borderline performance.

Cluster 6. *Mild Memory/Recoding Deficit* (*n* = 9, 15%)—This subtype showed strength in semantic encoding with marginal performance on both short-term memory and memory organization with deficits on both recoding tasks.

With respect to external validation, Speece (1987) found no differences among her information-processing subtypes on the WISC-R or reading subtests of the Woodcock-Johnson Achievement Battery. Similarly, sociodemographic characteristics did not differentiate the clusters. Nevertheless, Speece's study does provide important information on the relative frequency of various information-processing deficits that have been reported in the experimental literature, but studied from a univariate as opposed to a multivariate perspective. Her categorization of the sample as a whole indicated that most readers with learning disabilities exhibited a speed deficit (76%) which supports previous research in this area (e.g., Denckla & Rudel, 1976; Stanovich, 1981). Short-term memory capacity was the next most frequent problem (51%), followed by semantic encoding (29%), and sustained attention (24%) (e.g., Hallahan & Reeve, 1980; Swanson, 1984; Torgesen & Licht, 1983; Vellutino, 1978). Memory organization and phonetic encoding were the most infrequent deficits (15 and 9%, respectively).

Evaluation if Empirical Classification

In sum, the research on empirical classification demonstrates the feasibility of creating more homogeneous subtypes of specific learning disability which may have important theoretical and practical implications for special education. At the same time, this research effort is still at a very embryonic stage, and a great deal of additional work is needed before its potential benefits are realized in practice.

Since different investigators have taken different approaches with respect to classification procedures and have used different types of measures, it is not possible to draw firm conclusions at this time about the existence of particular subtypes, the number of subtypes that characterize the learning disability population, or the number of children they represent. Nevertheless, several common patterns have emerged from this diverse set of studies that are worthy of comment. In general, these findings illustrate the limitations of traditional group differences research in the field which ignores the problem of sample heterogeneity and are instructive with respect to the continuing controversy over what specific psychological processes are implicated in the school performance of children with learning disabilities.

Visual Perceptual/Perceptual-Motor Processes.. Most of the empirical classification studies that have used both perceptual and linguistic measures have reported specific visual-perceptual and/or perceptual-motor subtypes that display average to above average language abilities. The prevalance of this pattern ranged from 24% to 34% of the samples in the majority of studies, although McKinney et al. (1985) and Mattis et al. (1975) reported low prevalence figures of 7% and 8%. The rather consistent evidence for specific perceptual subtypes provides some support for early single deficit theories that emphasized perceptual processes in reading (Benton, 1975; Hallahan & Cruickshank, 1973). On the other hand, the theoretical basis and practical importance of perceptual subtypes is difficult to determine given other evidence on the low correlation between visual-perceptual measures and reading (Kavale, 1982), as well as evidence on the efficacy of perceptual training (Kavale & Mattson, 1983). However, the same difficulties are also presented in the case of linguistic subtypes (Kavale & Forness, 1985).

Linguistic and Auditory Processes.. As with the general domain of perceptual processing, the majority of studies that classified children with measures from both domains reported subtypes with specific auditory and linguistic deficits combined with intact perceptual and/or perceptual-motor skills. The prevalance of linguistic and/or auditory processing subtypes varied from 13% to 41% of the samples studied. Also, as with the perceptual hypothesis, these findings lend some support to single deficit theories that emphasize the importance of linguistic processes. However, the bulk of the empirical classification studies that used both perceptual and linguistic measures also found evidence for mixed deficit subtypes.

Mixed Perceptual/Linguistic Deficits.. Although less prevalent than specific deficit patterns across either perceptual or linguistic measures, all but one of the empirical studies with appropriate measures reported mixed deficit subtypes that comprised from 8% to 23% of the sample. The presence of mixed deficit subtypes as well as specific deficit subtypes in one domain but not another suggests that the performance of all children with learning disabilities (or even most of the population) cannot be explained by a single syndrome theory, and that all children with learning disabilities do not subdivide neatly within the larger domains of perceptual and linguistic processes.

Normal Appearing Subtypes.. All but two of the empirical classification studies found one or more subtypes that did not present deficits on the measures that were used. Also many of the *Q*-factor studies left substantial numbers of children unclassified. The most frequent explanation offered for the presence of these subtypes is that they may represent underachievement due to motivational or pedagogical factors. However, an equally plausible explanation is that previous studies have not adequately sampled all of the domains of psychological processes that are relevant to learning disabilities. As noted in the introduction to this section, most investigators have selected measures that sample auditory and visual perception and receptive and expressive language. Although the selection of measures in these areas can be justified theoretically, it should be noted that they represent only one half of the domains designated as topical markers in the Keogh et al. (1982) Marker Variable System for indexing learning disabilities. In particular, measures of attention, activity level, memory, and narrative (pragmatic) language appear to have been unsampled or undersampled in the definition of subtypes.

At the same time, evidence has been found for the existence of subtypes that reflect attentional disorders (Speece et al., 1985) and memory deficits (Speece, 1987; Torgesen, 1982), as well as those defined by perceptual and linguistic measures on more traditional psychoeducational and neuropsychological test batteries. Also, the data from at least two studies indicate that specific subtypes can be found within domains of psychological processes such as language (Feagans & Appelbaum, 1986) and information processing (Speece, 1987). Accordingly, although it is clear from several studies (e.g., see Feagans & Appelbaum, 1986 and Speece et al., 1985) that children with learning disabilities share some characteristics with normal children, it would not be appropriate at this time to conclude that children in normal appearing subtypes were misclassified as having learning disabilities because of the limited range of variables that have been studied thus far.

Apart from the fact that different investigators have taken different approaches with respect to classification procedures and have used different types of measures, there are a number of methodological and conceptual limitations of previous studies that restrict the application of current knowledge about learning disabilities subtypes.

The first major limitation, like that of the clinical-inferential studies, results from the nature of the samples that were studied. Many of the studies on empirical subtypes used clinic-referred samples of convenience. In some studies reading disabled children were preselected based on assumptions about etiology (e.g., developmental dyslexia). Since it is reasonable to assume that school-defined learning samples would be more heterogeneous than clinic-referred samples, one could question the generality of these studies for issues related to the classification and appropriate treatment of students with learning disabilities defined by *P.L. 94–142*. Also, many of the studies that used samples of convenience included children who differed greatly in age and sociodemographic characteristics, and the effects of these factors were often not reported or assessed by the study design. In the same vein, many of the studies reviewed in this section failed to include normal samples. In such studies cannot be determined whether the subtypes were idiosyncratic to learning disabilities, or represented normal individual differences among children. Moreover, since children with learning disabilities are not incompetent in all areas of functioning, some subtypes can be expected to have some attributes in common with average achievers.

A second major limitation concerns the issue of external validation. Approximately half of the studies reviewed provide no evidence for the external validity of the subtypes that were identified, and the majority of those that did present sparse evidence. As noted earlier in the section on methodology, empirical classification techniques are simply designed to group individuals together who share some attributes in common; they do not ensure that the derived subtypes are meaningful, generalize to other behaviors or settings, or that they have any practical value. Accordingly, although there are notable exceptions to this criticism, the problem of external validity alone seriously limits the potential

application of much of this work.

In this regard, it should be noted that the educational relevance of this body of research has not been firmly established. This is particularly the case with many of the neuropsychological studies that did not link subtypes to acaemic performance directly. Although the search for etiological factors is important theoretically, speculation about neurological processes seems to be questionable in the absence of evidence to validate hypotheses about neurological correlates. Although the possibility of neurological factors should not be discounted, the educational importance of subtypes defined by neuropsychological criteria must still be established if they are to have practical value for diagnosis and treatment in school settings.

Thirdly, with the exception of the Carolina Longitudinal Project and the Florida Project, little information is available at this time on the stability of subtype membership or the relationship between subtypes and long-term academic outcomes. It would be important in terms of future application to know how different subtypes emerge and change over time as well as how the characteristics of different subtypes contribute to academic performance specifically.

Finally, the theoretical potential of this body of research has yet to be realized due in part to its embryonic stage of development, and in part to a lack of well-developed theories in the field as a whole. Nevertheless, the application of empirical classification techniques to the issue of learning disabilities subtypes has provided the means for describing research samples more adequately which many ultimately produce a more generalizable body of knowledge to guide research and practice.

Intervention with Learning Disabilities Subtypes

One of the major questions to be addressed by subtype research is whether children with different types of specific learning disabilities respond differently to alternative instructional strategies. The answer to this question not only concerns the issue of external validity of the subtypes themselves, but also will ultimately determine the practical value of this research for special education programs. Unfortunately, evidence is sparse on the differential responsiveness of children in various subtypes to treatment, and the work completed to date might best be regarded as pilot research.

The first study of this nature was conducted by Lyon (1983) as a follow-up to his initial classification studies (Lyon & Watson, 1981). Because of the limited number of children in each of the various subtypes, Lyon selected 5 subjects from each of the original 6 subtypes (see page 265 for a description) who were matched on age, IQ, race, sex, and reading scores. All 30 children were given a synthetic phonics program developed by Traub and Bloom (1975) for 1 hour per week for 26 weeks.

Post-tests on the PIAT Reading Recognition subtest indicated that gains were a function of subtype membership such that (a) children with significant auditory and phonetic language problems responded least, (b) those with moderate problems in these areas responded moderately, and (c) those without significant problems on the measures used and those with problems in other areas (e.g., visual-perceptual processing) responded best. Lyon (1983) suggested that weaknesses in auditory processes and sound blending displayed by the language impaired subtypes may have reduced their ability to profit from phonics instruction. Accordingly, the results of Lyon's (1983) study would support teaching practices and methods that take advantage of the child's strengths as determined by subtype characteristics, as opposed to those which attempt to strengthen their weaknesses.

This implication was also suggested in two other pilot studies that compared different instructional strategies. Recently Lyon (1985) compared the response of a small number of children in language impaired subtypes who were given either the synthetic phonics program described above or an analytic reading program that emphasized content and structure. Those who received the analytic program responded favourably to instruction while those who received the phonics program failed to benefit from treatment. In the same vein, Aaron, Grantham, and Campbell (1982) compared phonics and look-say reading methods with children who were classified as either dysphonetic or dyseidetic by Boder's (1973) methods (see page 258 of this chapter for a description). Although the number of subjects for this study was quite small, the data suggested a treatment of X subtype interaction such that dysphonetic children seemed to benefit more from the look-say method while dyseidetic children profited more from the phonics method.

Although the results of these preliminary studies are very encouraging with respect to the implications of subtype membership for instruction, they require replication with larger samples of children. Also, it is clear that a great deal of additional research on instructional methods with a variety of different subtypes is required. However, at present there are a number of impediments to future research on instruction with learning disabilities subtypes that need to be overcome.

As noted by Lyon (1985), one reason for the paucity of instructional studies with learning disabilities subtypes concerns the methodological requirements for appropriate research designs in this area. The cost of such designs in terms of subjects and personnel to implement a programatic series of instructional studies is considerable. Ideally research in this area could take two basic approaches: either a trait X treatment approach or a single subject replication approach based on the a priori classification on individual children. Research using the former approach would require the classification of a very large number of subjects initially in order to ensure a sufficient number of subjects in each subtype for random assignment to various treatment

groups in a factorial design. Thus, for example, while sample sizes of 100 children would be more than adequate for initial subtyping, the resulting numbers of subjects for the various subtypes can be expected to vary considerably and many would produce too few subjects for further subdivision into treatment groups. Similarly, even if a priori subtype classification were possible, a very large pool of potential subjects would still be required to ensure adequate replication with single subject designs if several different subtypes were studied.

In short, the commitment of resources to instructional research with learning disabilities subtypes is likely to be substantial. However, preliminary evidence from available pilot studies certainly suggests that greater effort along these lines is warranted in order to (a) understand more fully why some children with learning disabilities do not benefit from special education, and (b) devise more appropriate interventions to meet their individual pattern of strengths and weaknesses.

Rationally Defined Subgroups

An alternative approach to subtyping an entire sample in order to delimit heterogeneity among children with learning disabilities is to select a subgroup of children who have one salient charactistic in common. This technique is well suited for experimental studies in which the investigator wishes to determine the effects of a specific type of learning problem on performance and/or how performance varies under different task demands or treatments. As such this technique could be considered as a variation of an aptitude X treatment design (Cronbach, 1967) in which child characteristics are varied along a single variable, as opposed to the multiple variable strategy used in most subtypes studies.

One of the best examples of research in this vein can be found in a series of studies by Torgesen and his colleagues on memory processes (Torgeson, 1982). Another recent example can be found in the work of Bradley and Bryant (1982) who studied backward readers and normal readers as a function of whether they could both read and spell words that varied in difficulty. Also, Rourke (1982) used this approach to subtype children who showed different patterns of deficits on reading, spelling, and arithmetic subtests.

Short Term Memory Subgroup. The experiments by Torgesen (1982) and his colleagues compared the performance of three groups. The target group was composed of children with learning disabilities who showed severe deficits in short-term memory (STM) capacity as measured by a digit span task. This group was compared to two control groups composed of (a) children with learning disabilities who did not show memory deficits and (b) average achievers. In an initial series of 13 experiments, it was demonstrated that the performance deficits of the target group were stable across tasks and materials, and were unaffected by incentives or the use of mnemonic strategies (see Torgesen, 1982). Having demonstrated that children with STM deficits formed a relatively homogeneous subgroup who exhibited stable performance on experimental tasks, Torgesen then attempted to show a relationship between STM group membership and academic problems.

In the first study in this series Torgesen and Houck (1980) asked children in the three subgroups to follow directions that varied in complexity. The two control groups (learning disabled-normal STM and normal) did not differ on criterion tasks and were superior to the STM deficit group. In a second study, Torgesen and Rashotte (1980) tested for retention of surface features and comprehension of prose and found again that while the learning disabled normal STM and average achievers did not differ, learning disabled-STM deficit children showed poorer retention. However, in this study learning disabled-STM deficit children did not differ from controls in comprehension, suggesting that STM deficits may affect academic performance selectively.

Subsequently, Foster and Torgesen (1980) demonstrated differences between the learning disabled-STM deficit learning disabled and normal STM group as a function of study methods. Learning disabled-STM deficit children had great difficulty learning to spell new words in both free study and structured study conditions, whereas difficulty for the learning disabled-STM normal group was apparent only in the free study condition. Finally, the sound blending performance of the learning disabled-STM deficit group was shown to diminish as the number of phonemes in words increased in relation to that shown by learning disabled-STM normal and average achieving children (Torgesen, 1982).

Achievement Subtypes. Rourke (1975, 1982) and his colleagues studied three rationally defined subgroups of children who showed different combinations of deficits on the Wide Range Achievement Test (WRAT). The first subgroup had reading, spelling and arithmetic scores below the 19th percentile on all three subtests. Subgroup 2 (reading and spelling disabled) displayed good arithmetic scores relative to poor reading and spelling scores. Subgroup 3 (arithmetic disabled) showed good reading and spelling combined with lower arithmetic scores.

Rourke and Finlayson (1978) and Rourke and Strang (1978) compared the three subgroups on neuropsychological tests and found that subgroup 3 children had adequate verbal skills, but poorer visual-perceptual and tactile skills. Subgroup 2 children displayed better visual-spatial skills but poorer linguistic skills. Children who were deficient in all three achievement areas showed severe verbal deficits. Recently, Fletcher (1985) and Siegel and Linder (1984) reported differences between Rourke's achievement subgroups on memory tasks.

Evaluation of Rationally Defined Subgroup. In sum, the series of studies cited above illustrate two approaches to creating more homogeneous subgroups of children with learning disabilities that do not involve multivariate empirical classification techniques. Also, they demonstrate the importance of controlling sample heterogeneity in experimental studies as opposed to simply comparing heterogeneous groups of learning disabled and normal children. However, as noted by Torgesen (1982), this approach is not without its limitation, the major one being that although children within a subgroup may have a given characteristic in common, they are likely to vary greatly with respect to other characteristics which are not controlled in selecting the target group. Thus, heterogeneity on uncontrolled variables may influence performance in ways that cannot be explained by the research design. Also, since children are selected according to a priori criteria, it is difficult to estimate the number of children who present a given characteristic in relation to those who show other types of problems or no problems in the domain of variables that are sampled. This is not the case in most subtype studies in which an entire sample is subdivided and the proportional membership in various subgroups can be determined. Nevertheless, the rationally defined subgroups approach represents an important advance over heterogeneous group comparisons because it (a) facilities experimental replication, (b) provides an excellent paradigm for theory testing, and (c) allows the investigator to explore more subtle and complex relationships between processing deficits and performance because of reduced within-group heterogeneity.

Conclusion and Recommendations

Collectively, research on conceptually-based and empirically-based subtypes of specific learning disabilities does demonstrate the feasibility of subdividing heterogeneous samples of children with learning disabilities into more homogeneous subgroups. Moreover, sufficient evidence is available to suggest that this type of research, in particular the use of empirical multivariate classification techniques, has significant implications for theory, practice and policy development in the field. However, it does not appear that the knowledge base provided by this research to date is sufficient to permit the direct application of specific findings to special education practice. This is the case because significant gaps exist in our knowledge about the nature and development of various learning disabilities subtypes, and their relationship to academic performance and instructional outcomes.

Therefore, although subtype research holds considerable promise for resolving many of the complex issues associated with the classification and appropriate education of learning disabled students, most of the important questions to be addressed by this research remain unanswered. In this regard, I would recommend the following as potentially useful directions for future research:

Theoretically Based Research

Although research on learning disabilities subtypes has provided a useful paradigm for addressing the problem of heterogeneity among children with learning disabilities, the existing literature on subtypes suffers from a similar problem with respect to variance among investigators in the use of different methods and measures. Although several common trends in the findings from these studies were noted, the generality and potential for application of this body of research is severely limited by its diversity. Some investigators have sought more homogeneous subgroups of children within a particular domain of functioning such as language or academic performance, while others have used clinically-based psychoeducational and neuropsychological test batteries. Rarely, however, have various investigators given a clear theoretical rationale for the use of a particular method or the selection of a particular set of measures.

The issue of diversity among methods and measures is difficult to deal with scientifically because traditionally the individual investigator has the prerogative to choose those methods and measures which in his or her professional judgment best address the research question of interest. On the other hand, as Kavale (1985a) noted recently in a symposium on learning disabilities subtypes, there is the real danger with any relatively new and promising approach that the method will drive the science. The history of science, and indeed that of learning disability research in particular, shows that when this is the case the larger goal of applied research which is to build a theoretically sound, generalizable body of knowledge to guide practice is compromised.

Developmental Research

Although some cross-sectional age comparisons can be found in the literature, research in the field as a whole lacks a developmental perspective. Similarly, with the exception of the Carolina and Florida projects, little is known about how specific learning disabilities subtypes emerge and change over time and contribute to our understanding of school failure. As noted elsewhere in this chapter, the classification procedures used to subtype children with learning disabilities are merely descriptive. Although an adequate description of the population is essential at this stage of the science, it is difficult to see how the discovery of learning disabilities subtypes per se will contribute to practice unless they help us understand the development of learning disabilities and can be shown to predict significant academic outcomes.

In this regard, longitudinal research on LD subtypes is essential to future progress because it:

1. describes exceptional patterns of growth with respect to basic developmental competencies;
2. examines the cumulative effect of processes affecting school performance;
3. predicts developmental outcomes and estimates the prognosis associated with specific learning disabilities;
4. determines changes in the relationship among variables, particularly as the result of intervention; and
5. assesses the long-term effects of intervention.

Cross-Categorical Research

Comparative studies of different handicapped groups and underachievers are rare in the literature but appear to be particularly critical at the present time. This is the case because of persistent concerns about the misclassification of slow learners, mildly retarded and problem behavior children as learning disabled. Evidence presented in this chapter suggests that empirical classification techniques can be applied to determine the similarities and distinguishing features of different diagnostic categories of children. This methodology could provide more direct evidence on the overlapping features of different handicaps than more traditional group comparisons research because classification is based on patterns of within-group variance rather than between-group variance.

In addition to the issue of appropriate classification, this research would have direct implications for the emerging practice of cross-categorical placement. The utility of labeling children as learning disabled, educable mentally retarded, or emotionally handicapped is based in part on the assumption that different categories of handicapped children present fundamentally different characteristics that require different types of special education. Although some evidence is available on this point (Finn & Resnick, 1984; Gajar, 1980; McKinney & Forman, 1982), the need for differential placement and treatment is increasingly being questioned, and many special educators recommend cross-categorial placement for mildly handicapping conditions (Hallahan & Kauffman, 1982; Lerner, 1985).

Finally, cross-categorical research is important theoretically. It is unfortunate that the history of research in the field of learning disability suggests little theoretical relationship to that in other fields of exceptionality, as well as to child development in general (Kavale & Forness, 1985; Keogh, 1982; Torgesen, 1975). As noted by McKinney (1982), many recent advances in the treatment of learning disability were based on concepts that produced similar advances in the field of mental retardation. Accordingly, cross-categorical research based on subtype methodology may offer the potential for developing more general theories of exceptionality to guide practice.

Intervention Research

The literature on intervention with children with learning disabilities indicates that many different types of treatment strategies have been tried, including process and behavioral approaches, direct instruction, and biomedical approaches (see Loyd, 1988 for a research integration paper on intervention). Although many of these approaches have been evaluated favorably for some children under some conditions (usually experimental conditions), it is fair to conclude that many children have not benefited or have had limited benefits based on follow-up studies (see Kavale, 1988 for a research integration paper on the long-term consequences of learning disability). This is particularly the case in typical public school settings where it is difficult to document and monitor the specific nature of the treatment (McKinney & Feagans, 1980).

Guided by the philosophy of individualized instruction, most special educators continue to believe that different children learn better when given one kind of instruction than if they were given another (Lloyd, 1984). On the other hand, research conducted within an aptitude X treatment paradigm has failed to produce convincing evidence for interactions between learner characteristics and types of instruction in either general education (Cronbach & Snow, 1977) or special education (Lloyd, 1984). Although many undetermined factors could account for these negative results, a very plausible hypothesis, based on evidence from subtype studies, is that the major independent variable (i.e., students' aptitudes or traits) was not specified adequately. As observed several times in this chapter, subtype research demonstrates the limitations of single deficit theories and shows that classification based on a single attribute does not account for the majority of the variance in learning disability samples, nor does it in any way deal with the different patterns of strengths and weaknesses displayed by children with learning disabilities.

Since the philosophy of individualized instruction is based on the assessment of patterns of strengths and weaknesses across several domains of functioning, it may be argued that the hypothesis of differential responsiveness to different treatments has not been tested adequately. However, research on learning disabilities subtypes appears to offer an alternative paradigm for conducting this type of instructional research. Indeed, subtype studies were reviewed that offered preliminary evidence to suggest an interaction between instructional methods and subtype membership.

Clearly additional research along these lines is warranted. However, the potential application and impact of such research on practice will depend on our ability consistently to identify valid subtypes that have demonstrated educational importance.

Process-Oriented Research

This style of research is particularly timely now because the existing literature on learning disabilities subtypes is chiefly descriptive. Process-oriented research would focus on *how* children in various learning disabilities subtypes process information and adapt to the demands of their environment rather than on the *what* (description of deficits) or *why* (etiology) of the performance deficits. The practical value of this type of research is that it bridges the gap between classification and intervention by explaining how child characteristics are translated into school performance. The example, a central concept that is emerging from recent research on information-processing is that students with learning disabilities often do not use their intact abilities to generate task-appropriate learning strategies, but that they are capable of doing so with appropriate instruction (Hallahan, Kneedler, & Lloyd, 1983; Torgesen & Licht, 1983).

Process-oriented learning strategies research with learning disabilities subtypes may have considerable potential for application for the following reasons. First, it may provide a parsimonious explanation for a wide range of problems experienced by students with learning disabilities at different age levels on different types of academic tasks. Second, recent research has illustrated its practical application by devising instructional methods and materials for a broad array of academic problems, as well as for problems in adaptive behavior and social skills development. Finally, the application of knowledge about information-processing strategies to the problems of students with learning disabilities has the benefit of substantial developmental research with normal children and is based on contemporary theories of information processing.

Policy Research

The numerous issues and practical problems surrounding the identification of students with learning disabilities and in determining eligibility for special education services have been reviewed by Keogh (1988) in her research integration paper on this topic and will not be reiterated here. However, it is important to note that state and federal policies pertaining to the definition and identification of students with learning disabilities are being revised with the general policy objectives of serving fewer children and those who present the most severe disabilities. As noted earlier, the principal means for achieving these objectives is to require the calculation of IQ-achievement discrepancies and to set more stringent cut-off scores for service eligibility. In spite of the many methodological problems involved with discrepancy scores (Cone & Wilson, 1981; Shepard, 1980), there remains the very substantive question of whether these changes in identification practice actually result in the selection of students who are more deserving of special education than those identified in the past.

It is clear from preliminary evidence (e.g., Alberg, 1985) that different formulas identify different children as well as different numbers of children. Moreover, since a discrepancy between ability and achievement can be due to many factors other than specific learning disability, and since there are probably more children who underachieve for reasons other than learning disability (Horn & O'Donnell, 1984), the use of discrepancy criteria runs the risk of increasing rather than decreasing heterogeneity in the population served. For example, a study (Alberg, 1985) that estimated discrepancies from group tests for the entire third grade ($N = 1,445$) in a large North Carolina city found that 13.4% met state criteria based on 15 point standard score discrepancy and that regression analysis identified 18.2%. During the same school year, the schools served 4.7% as learning disabled. Thus, it is likely that if IQ-achievement discrepancy were the sole criterion for eligibility in this school district, many more children would show "a severe discrepancy" than are presently being served or that would be eligible theoretically. At present, I know of no research that has studied specifically the relationship between IQ-achievement discrepancy and theoretically defined learning disabilities subtypes.

In any event, additional research is needed to determine more precisely the characteristics of children who underachieve as defined by alternative criteria. In this regard, subtype methodology could be used to differentiate students with learning disabilities from other types of underachievers theoretically, as well as to determine the similarities and differences among students who met new criteria from those who were previously classified as having learning disabilities who do not. In this fashion, subtype methodology may contribute to an evaulation of the impact of changes in school identification practices, although other types of research such as epidemiological studies are needed also.

Role of Federal Agencies

Although research on learning disabilities subtypes holds considerable promise for resolving many of the complex issues involved in the classification and appropriate treatment of children with learning disabilities, it is evident that this promise will not be realized easily in the near future without a substantial commitment of resources. However, I do not believe that the allocation of additional resources per se, or merely setting research priorities along the lines suggested above, is sufficient to ensure that this exciting new paradigm for learning disability research will have a significant impact on practice.

Practitioners and decision makers are often frustrated by the slow pace of research and development. This frustration is justified since it can take up to 20 years for new knowledge to have a practical impact on services for children (Gallagher, 1979). As a result there has been an increasing tendency for agencies to support research centers and institutes that assemble the collective resources of a number of different investigators to work on a common problem of national significance. It is assumed that stable funding for a period of time will allow a team of investigators, often in different parts of the country, to pursue a complex problem in a programmatic fashion to the point at which practical and generalizable conclusions can be drawn and, thereby, accelerate the development of new products and innovative practices.

Although it is the case that research on learning disabilities subtypes is a relatively new development in the field it is also the case that this type of research has not been (a) pursued in a very programmatic fashion, (b) marked by extensive collaboration among investigators, or (c) tied in any significant way to program planning, technical assistance and dissemination efforts in special education. Accordingly, while this research demonstrates the feasibility of these methods for better classifying students with learning disabilities and, thereby, demonstrates some promise with respect to improvement in practice, it has yet to be applied to most of the substantive problems in the field in a fashion that enhances the likelihood of practical application in the near future.

Accordingly, it is recommended that the agency pursue a more concentrated strategy of support for the subtype research area that encourages cross-instituational as well as cross-disciplinary collaboration aimed at achieving the research priorities outlined above in a programmatic fashion over an extended period of time. Also, it is recommended that it ensure that this research effort is tied in a meaningful fashion to demonstration and technical assistance programs in the field.

The recommendation for programmatic support in the context of research centers and/or institutes is made with the realization that such programs are not without limitations and present a unique set of problems in their own right with respect to resource allocation and research administration (Gallagher, 1979; Keogh, 1983). However, this strategy was tried before in the case of the five learning disability institutes funded by the Office of Special Education Programs, Department of Education in 1977. At that time, many of the issues involved in the classification of learning disability were not foreseen and the research priorities addressed were primarily in the area of intervention (McKinney, 1983). As a result, the learning disability institute program was successful in advancing the state-of-the-art in treatment strategies, but left many issues concerning identification and appropriate treatment unresolved (Keogh, 1983; McKinney, 1983).

Although the agency runs considerable risk in tying up resources in a few large-scale programs, perhaps at the expense of individual research studies, the potential benefits of a center-based research program appear to off-set these risks given the history of advances produced this way in the past. Also, it may be argued that this strategy is the most efficient and economical means for supporting long-term programmatic research efforts of the kind outlined above. In sum, the critical nature and complexity of the issues in the field of learning disabilities demand a response from the research community that adequately addresses the complexity of these problems in the shortest time possible.

References

Aaron, P. G., Grantham, S. L., & Campbell. (1982). Differential treatment of reading disability of diverse etiologies. In R. N. Malatesha and P. G. Aaron (Eds.), *Reading disorders: Varieties and treatments*. New York: Academic Press.

Alberg, J. (1985). Evaluation of alternative procedures for identifying learning disabled students. Unpublished doctoral dissertation, University of North Carolina, Chapel Hill.

Aldenderfer, M. S., & Blashfield, R. K. (1984). *Cluster analysis*. Beverly Hills, CA: Sage Publications.

Anderberg, M. R. (1973). *Cluster analysis for applications*. New York: Academic Press.

Bannatyne, A. (1968). Diagnosing learning disabilities and writing remedial prescriptions. *Journal of Learning Disabilities*, 1, 242–249.

Bannatyne, A. (1974). Diagnosis: A note on recategorization of the WISC scaled scores. *Journal of Learning Disabilities*, 7, 272–274.

Bateman, B. D. (1968). *Interpretation of the 1961 Illinois Test of Psycholinguistic Abilities*. Seattle, WA: Special Child Publications.

Bayliss, J., & Liversey, P. J. (1985). Cognitive strategies of children with reading disabilities and normal readers in visual sequential memory. *Journal of Learning Disabilities*, 18(6). 326–332.

Benton, A. L. (1975). Developmental dyslexia. Neurological aspects. *Advances in Neurology*, 7, 1–41.

Boder, E. (1971). Developmental dyslexia: A diagnostic screening procedure based on three characteristic patterns of reading and spelling. In B. Bateman (Ed.), *Learning disorders* (Vol. 4). Seattle, WA: Special Child Publications.

Boder, E. (1973). Developmental dyslexia: A diagnostic approach based on three atypical reading-spelling patterns. *Developmental Medicine and Child Neurology*, 15, 663–687.

Bradley, L., & Bryant, P. (1982). Reading and Spelling Difficulties. In J. P. Das, R. F. Mulcahy and A. E. Wall (Eds.), *Theory and research in learning disabilities*. New York: Plenum Press.

Bryan, T. S., & Bryan, J. H. (1978). *Understanding learning disabilities* (2nd ed.). Sherman Oaks, CA: Alfred Publishing Co.

Bush, W. J., & Waugh, K. W. (1976). *Diagnosing learning disabilities* (2nd ed.). Columbus, OH: Charles E. Merrill.

Camp, B. W., & Dolcourt, J. L. (1977). Reading and spelling in good and poor readers. *Journal of Learning Disabilities*, 10(5), 46–53.

Clements, S. D. (1966). *Minimal Brain Dysfunction in Children*, *NINDS Monograph No. 3*. Washington, DC: Government Printing Office.

Cone, T. E., & Wilson, L. R. (1981). Quantifying a severe discrepancy: A critical analysis. *Learning Disability Quarterly*, 4, 359–371.

Critchley, M. (1964). *Developmental dyslexia*. London: Heinemann.

Cronbach, L. J. (1967). How can instruction be adapted to individual differences. In R. M. Gagne (Ed.), *Learning and individual differences*. Columbus, OH: Charles E. Merrill.

Cronbach, L. J., & Gleser, G. C. (1953). Assessing similarity between profiles. *Psychological Bulletin*, 50, 456–473.

Cronbach, L. J., & Snow, R. E. (1977). *Aptitudes and instructional methods*. New York: Irvington.

Darby, R. O. (1978). Learning disabilities: A multivariate search for subtypes. Unpublished doctoral dissertation, University of Florida, Gainesville.

Denckla, M. B. (1972). Clinical syndromes in learning disabilities: The case for "splitting" vs. "lumping." *Journal of Learning Disabilities*, 5, 401–406.

Denckla, M. B. (1977). Minimal brain dysfunction and dyslexia: Beyond diagnosis by exclusion. In M. E. Blaw, J. Rapin, & M. Kinsbourne (Eds.), *Child neurology*. New York: Spectrum.

Denckla, M. B. (1978). Critical review of "Electroencephalographic and neurophysiological studies in dyslexia." In A. L. Benton & D. Pearl (Eds.), *Dyslexia: An appraisal of current knowledge*. New York: Oxford University Press.

Denckla, M. B., & Rudel, R. G. (1976). Rapid "automized" naming (R.A.N.): Dyslexia differentiated from other learning disabilities. *Neuropsychologia*, 14, 471–479.

Doehring, D. G. (1978). The tangled web of behavioral research on developmental dyslexia. In A. L. Benton & D. Pearl (Eds.), *Dyslexia: An appraisal of current knowledge*. New York: Oxford University Press.

Doehring, D. G. (1983). What do we know about reading disabilities? Closing the gap between research and practice. *Annals of Dyslexia*, Vol. 33, 175–183.

Doehring, D. G. (1984). Subtyping of reading disorders: Implications for remediation. *Annals of Dyslexia*, Vol. 34, 205–216.

Doehring, D. G., & Hoshko, I. M. (1977). Classification of reading problems by the Q-technique of factor analysis. *Cortex*, 13, 281–294.

Doehring, D. G., Hoshko, I. M., & Bryans B. N. (1979). Statistical classification of children with reading problems. *Journal of Clinical Neuropsychology*, 1, 5–16.

Doehring, D. G., Triter, R. L., Patel, P. G., & Fiedorowicz, C. A. M. (1981). *Reading disabilities: The interaction of reading, language and neuropsychological deficits*. New York: Academic Press.

Everitt, B. (1980). *Cluster analysis*. 2nd edition. New York: Halsted Press.

Feagans, L. (1980). Children's understanding of some temporal tells denoting order, duration and simultaneity. *Journal of Psycholinguistic Research*, 9,(1), 41–57.

Feagans, L. (1983). Discourse processes in learning disabled children. In J. D. McKinney, & L. Feagans (Eds.). *Current topics in learning disabilities*, Vol. 1 (pp. 87–115). Norwood, NJ: Ablex.

Feagans, L., & Appelbaum, M. I. (1986). Language subtypes and their validation in learning disabled children. *Journal of Educational Psychology*, 78(5), 373–481.

Feagans, L., & Farran, D. (1981). How demonstrated comprehension can get muddled in production. *Developmental Psychology*, 17, 718–727.

Feagans, L., & McKinney, J. D. (1981). Pattern of exceptionality across domains in learning disabled children. *Journal of Applied Developmental Psychology*, **1**(4), 313–328.

Feagans, L., & Short, E. J. (1984). Developmental differences in the comprehension and production of narratives by reading disabled and normally achieving children. *Child Development*, 1727–1736.

Filskov, S. B., & Boll, T. J. (1981). *Handbook of clinical neuropsychology*. New York: Wiley.

Finn, J. D., & Resnick, L. B. (1984). Issues in the instruction of mildly mentally retarded children. *Educational Researcher*, **13**, 9–11.

Fisk, J. L., & Rourke, B. P. (1979). Identification of subtypes of learning disabled children at three age levels: A neuropsychological, multivariate approach. *Journal of Clinical Neuropsychology*, **1**, 289–310.

Fisk, J. L., & Rourke, B. P. (1983). Neuropsychological subtyping of learning-disabled children: History, methods, implications. *Journal of Learning Disabilities*, **16**(9), 529–531.

Fletcher, J. M. (1985). External validation of learning disability typologies. In B. P. Rourke (Ed.), *Neuropsychology of learning disabilities*. New York: The Guilford Press.

Fletcher, J., & Satz, P. (1979). Unitary deficit hypotheses of reading disabilities: Has Vellutino led us astray? *Journal of Learning Disabilities*, **12**, 155–159.

Fletcher, J. M., & Satz, P. (1980). Developmental changes in the neuropsychological correlates of reading achievement: A six-year longitudinal followup. *Journal of Clinical Neuropsychology*, (1), 23–37.

Forness, S. R., Sinclair, E., & Guthrie, D. (1983). Learning disability discrepancy formulas: Their use in actual practice. *Learning Disability Quarterly*, **6**, 107–114.

Foster, K., & Torgesen, J. K. (1980). Learning to spell under two study conditions by learning disabled children. Unpublished manuscript, Florida State University.

Gajar, A. H. (1980). Characteristics across exceptional categories: EMR, LD, and ED. *Journal of Special Education*, **14**, 166–173.

Gajar, A. H., Hale, R. L., Kuzovich, C., & Saxe, J. (1984). Profile analysis of a referral sample. *The Journal of Psychology*, **116**, 207–214.

Gallagher, J. J. (1966). Children with developmental imbalances: A psycho-educational definition. In W. M. Cruickshank (Ed.), *The teacher of brain-injured children*. Syracuse, NY: Syracuse University Press.

Gallagher, J. J. (1979). The trend to contract research: Problems and opportunities. *Educational Evaluation and Policy Analysis*, **1**(5), 29–38.

Gallagher, J. J. (March, 1982). *Learning disabilities: Where are we headed?* Paper presented at the International Academy for Research in Learning Disabilities, Winnipeg, Canada.

Hallahan, D. P., & Cruickshank, W. M. (1973). *Psycho-educational foundations of learning disabilities*. Englewood Cliffs, N.J.: Prentice-Hall.

Hallahan, D. P., & Kauffman, J. M. (1976) *Introduction to learning disabilities: A psycho-behavioral approach*. p. 1045. Englewood Cliffs, NJ: Prentice-Hall.

Hallahan, D. P., & Kauffman, J. (1982). *Exceptional children*. Englewood Cliffs, NJ: Prentice-Hall.

Hallahan, D. P., Kneedler, R. D., Lloyd, J. W. (1983). Cognitive behavior modification techniques for learning disabled children: Self-instruction and self monitoring. In J. D. McKinney & L. Feagans (Eds.), *Current Topics in Learning Disabilities Vol. 1*. Norwood, NJ: Ablex Publishing.

Hallahan, D. P., & Reeve, R. C. (1980). Selective attention and distractibility. In B. K. Keogh (Ed.), *Advances in special education* (Vol. 1). Greenwich, CT: JAI Press.

Hammill, D. D., Leigh, J. E., McNutt, G., & Larsen, S. C. (1981). A new definition of learning disabilities. *Learning Disability Quarterly*, **4**, 336–342.

Harris, A. J. (1982). How many kinds of reading disability are there? *Journal of Learning Disabilities*, **15**, 456–460.

Horn, W. F., & O'Donnell, J. P. (1984). Early identification of learning disabilities: A comparison of two methods. *Journal of Educational Psychology*, **76**(6). 1106–1118.

Ingram, T. T. S. (1969). Developmental disorders of speech. In P. J. Vinken & G. W. Bruyn (Eds.), *Handbook of clinical neurology* (Vol. 4). Amsterdam: North Holland.

Ingram, T. T. S., Mann, A. W., & Blackburn, I. (1970). A retrospective study of 82 children with reading disability. *Developmental Medicine and Child Neurology*, **12**, 271–282.

Johnson, D. J., & Myklebust, H. R. (1967). *Learning disabilities*. New York: Grune & Stratton.

Kaufman, A. S. (1979). *Intelligent Testing with the WISC-R*. New York: Wiley Interscience.

Kaufman, A. S. (1981). The Wechsler Scales and learning disabilities. *Journal of Learning Disabilities*, **14**(7), 397–398.

Kavale, K. A. (1982). Meta-analysis of the relationship between visual perceptual skills and reading achievement. *Journal of Learning Disabilities*, **15**, 280–289.

Kavale, K. A. (1985a). The far side of heterogeneity. Paper presented at the DLD Symposium of LD Subtyping Research, Council for Exceptional Children, Anaheim, CA, April.

Kavale, K. A. (1988). The long-term consequences of learning disabilities. In M. C. Wang, H. J. Walburg, and M. C. Reynolds (Eds.). *The Handbook of Special Education: Research and practice*. Oxford, Pergamon Press (this volume).

Kavale, K. A., & Forness, S. R. (1984). A meta-analysis of the validity of Wechsler Scale profiles and recategorizations: Patterns of parodies? *Learning Disability Quarterly*, **7**, 136–156.

Kavale, K. A., & Forness, S. R. (1985). *The science of learning disabilities*. San Diego, LA: College Hill Press.

Kavale, K. A., & Mattson, P. D. (1983). Meta-analysis of perceptual-motor training. *Journal of Learning Disabilities*, **16**, 165–173.

Keogh, B. K. (1982) Research in learning disabilities: A view of status and need. In J. P. Das, R. F. Melcahy, & A. E. Wall (Eds.). *Theory and Research in Learning Disabilities*, New York: Plenum.

Keogh, B. K. (1983). A lesson from Gestalt psychology. *Exceptional Education Quarterly*, **4**(1). 115–128.

Keogh, B. K. (1988). Learning disabilities: Diversity in search of order. In M. C. Wang, H. J. Walburg and M. C. Reynolds (Eds.). *The Handbook of Special Education: Research and practice*. Oxford, Pergamon Press (this volume).

Keogh, B. K., & Hall, R. J. (1974). WISC subtest patterns of educationally handicapped and educable mentally retarded pupils. *Psychology in the Schools*, **11**, 296–300.

Keogh, B., Major-Kingsley, S., Omori-Gordon, H. & Reid, H. P. (1982). *A system of marker variables for the field of learning disabilities.* Syracuse, NY: Syracuse University Press.

Kinsbourne, M., & Warrington, E. K. (1963). Developmental factors in reading and writing backwardness. *British Journal of Psychology*, **54**, 145–156.

Lerner, J. (1985). *Learning disabilities: Theories, diagnosis, and teaching strategies* (4th Ed.). Boston: Houghton Mifflin.

Lessig, E. E., Williams, V., & Gil, E. (1982). A cluster-analytically derived typology: Feasible alternative to clinical diagnostic classification of children? *Journal of Abnormal Child Psychology*, **10**, 451–482.

Lloyd, T. W. (1984). How shall we individualize instruction—or should we? *Remedial and Special Education*, **5**, 7–15.

Lloyd, J. W. (1988). Learning disabilities intervention. In M. C. Wang, H. J. Walburg, and M. C. Reynolds (Eds.). *The Handbook of Special Education: Research and Practice.* Pergamon, Oxford, England (this volume).

Lorr, M. (1983). *Cluster analysis for social scientists.* San Francisco: Jossey-Bass Inc.

Lyon, G. R. (1983). Subgroups of learning disabled readers: Clinical and empirical identification. In H. Myklebust (Ed.), *Progress in Learning Disabilities* (Vol. V). New York: Grune and Stratton.

Lyon, G. R. (1985). Identification and remediation of learning disability subtypes: Progress and pitfalls. *Learning Disability Focus*, **I**.

Lyon, R., Stewart, N., & Freeman, D. (1982). Neuropsychological characteristics of empirically derived subgroups of learning disabled readers. *Journal of Clinical Neuropsychology*, **4**, 343–365.

Lyon, R., & Watson, B. (1981). Empirically derived subgroups of learning disabled readers: Diagnostic characteristics. *Journal of Learning Disabilities*, **14**(5), 256–261.

Lyon, R., Watson, B., Reitta, S., Porch, B., & Rhodes, J. (1981). Selected linguistic and perceptual abilities of empirically derived subgroups of learning disabled readers. *Journal of School Psychology*, 1981, **19**(2), 152–166.

Mattis, S. (1978). Dyslexia syndromes: A working hypothesis that works. In A. L. Benton & D. Pearl (Eds.), *Dyslexia: An appraisal of current knowledge.* New York and London: Oxford University Press.

Mattis, S., French, J. H., & Rapin, I. (1975). Dyslexia in children and adults: Three independent neuropsychological syndromes. *Developmental Medicine and Child Neurology*, **17**, 150–163.

McKinney, J. D. (1983). Contributions of the institutes for research on learning disabilities. *Exceptional Education Quarterly*, **4**(1), 129–144.

McKinney, J. D. (1984). The search for subtypes of specific learning disability. *Journal of Learning Disabilities*, **17**, 43–50.

McKinney, J. D., & Feagans, L. (July, 1980). *Learning disabilities in the classroom.* Final report: Bureau of Education for the Handicapped. U.S. Department of Health, Education, and Welfare, Grant No. G00-76-0-5224, Washington, D.C.

McKinney, J. D., & Feagans, L. (March, 1982). *Longitudinal research on learning disabilities.* Paper presented at the Association for Children and Adults with Learning Disabilities. Chicago.

McKinney, J. D., & Feagans, L. (1983). (Eds.). *Current*

topics in learning disabilities. (Vol. 1) Norwood, NJ: Ablex Corp.

McKinney, J. D., & Feagans, L. (1984). Academic and behavioral characteristics: Longitudinal studies of learning disabled children and average achievers. *Learning Disability Quarterly*, **7**(3), 251–265.

McKinney, J. D., & Forman, S. G. (1982). Classroom behavior patterns of EMH, LD and EH students. *Journal of School Psychology*, **20**(4), 271–289.

McKinney, J. D., Mason, J., Perkerson, K., & Clifford, M. (1975). Relationship between classroom behavior and academic achievement. *Journal of Educational Psychology*, **67**, 198–203.

McKinney, J. D., Short, E. J., & Feagans, L. (1985). Academic consequences of perceptual-linguistic subtypes of learning disabled children. *Learning Disabilities Research*, **I**.

McKinney, J. D., & Speece, D. L. (1983). Classroom behavior and the academic progress of learning disabled students. *Journal of Applied Developmental Psychology*, **4**, 149–161.

McKinney, J. D., & Speece, D. L. (1986). *Longitudinal stability and academic consequences of behavioral subtypes of learning disabled children*, **78**(5), 365–372.

Morris, R., Blashfield, R., & Satz, P. (1981). Neuropsychology and cluster analysis: Potentials and problems. *Journal of Clinical Neuropsychology*, **3**, 79–99.

Myklebust, H. R. (1978). Toward a science of dyslexiology. In H. R. Myklebust (Ed.), *Progress in learning disabilities* (Vol. 4). New York: Grune & Stratton.

Nichols, P. L., & Chen, T. C. (1981). *Minimal brain dysfunction: A prospective study.* Hillsdale, NJ: Lawrence Erlbaum.

Obrzut, J. E. (1979). Dichotic listening and bisensory memory skills in qualitatively diverse dyslexic readers. *Journal of Learning Disabilities*, **12**, 304–314.

Orton, S. T. (1937). *Reading, writing, and speech problems in children.* pp. 21–141. New York: Norton.

Paine, R. S., Werry, J. S., & Quay, H. C. (1968). A study of "minimal cerebral dysfunction." *Developmental Medicine and Child Neurology*, **10**, 505–520.

Petrauskas, R., & Rourke, B. (1979). Identification of subgroups of retarded readers: A neuropsychological multivariate approach. *Journal of Clinical Neuropsychology*, **1**, 17–37.

Pirozzolo, F. (1979). *The neuropsychology of developmental reading disorders.* New York: Praeger.

Pirozzolo, F. J., & Rayner, K. (1978). The neural control of eye movements in acquired and developmental reading disorders. In H. Whitaker & H. A. Whitaker (Eds.), *Studies in neurolinguistics* (Vol. 4). New York: Academic Press.

Ramey, C. T., & McKinney, J. D. (1981). Education of learning disabled children suspected of minimal brain dysfunction. In P. Black (Ed.), *Brain dysfunction in children: Etiology, diagnosis, and management* (pp. 203–220). New York: Raven Press.

Rayner, K. (1981). Eye movements and the perceptual span in reading. In F. J. Pirozzolo & M. C. Wittrock (Eds.), *Neuropsychological and cognitive processes in reading.* New York: Academic Press.

Rie, H. E., & Rie, E. D. (1980). *Handbook of minimal brain dysfunction.* New York: Wiley.

Ross, A. O. (1976). *Psychological aspects of learning disabilities and reading disorders.* New York: McGraw-Hill.

Rourke, B. P. (1975). Brain-behavior relationships in children with learning disabilities. *American Psychologist*, 30, 911–920.

Rourke, B. P. (1978). Neuropsychological research on reading retardation: A review. In A. L. Benton & D. Pearl (Eds.), *Dyslexia: An appraisal of current knowledge*. New York: Oxford University Press.

Rourke, B. P. (1982). Central Processing deficiencies in children: Toward a developmental neuropsychological model. *Journal of Clinical Neuropsychology*, 4(1), 1–18.

Rourke, B. P. (1983). Reading and spelling disabilities: A developmental neuropsychological perspective. New York: Academic Press.

Rourke, B. P. (Ed.). (1985). *Neuropsychology of learning disabilities: Essentials of subtype analysis*. New York: Guilford.

Rourke, B. P., Bakker, D. J., Fisk, J. L., & Strang, J. D. (1983). *Child neuropsychology: An introduction to theory, research, and clinical practice*. New York: Guilford Press.

Rourke, B. P., & Finlayson, M. A. J. (1975. Neuropsychological significance of variations in patterns of performance on the trail making test for older children with learning disabilities. *Journal of Abnormal Psychology*, 84(4), 412–421.

Rourke, B. P., & Finlayson, M. A. J. (1978). Neuropsychological significance of variations in patterns of academic performance: Verbal and visual-spatial abilities. *Journal of Abnormal Child Psychology*, 6(1), 121–133.

Rourke, B. P., & Strang, J. D. (1978). Neuropsychological significance of variations in patterns of academic performance: Motor, psychomotor, and tactile-perceptual abilities. *Journal of Pediatric Psychology*, 3,(2), 62–66.

Routh, D. K., & Roberts, R. D. (1972). Minimal brain dysfunction in children: Failure to find evidence for a behavioral syndrome. *Psychological Reports*, 31, 307–314.

Sarason, S. B. (1949). *Psychological problems of mental deficiency*. New York: Harper & Row.

Satz, P., & Fletcher, J. (1980). Minimal brain dysfunctions: An appraisal of research concepts and methods. In H. E. Rie & E. D. Rie (Eds.), *Handbook of minimal brain dysfunctions: A critical view*. New York: Wiley Interscience.

Satz, P., & Morris, R. (1981). Learning disability subtypes: A review. In F. J. Pirozzolo & M. C. Wittrock (Ed.), *Neuropsychological and cognitive processes in reading*. New York: Academic Press.

Satz, P., Morris, R., & Fletcher, J. M. (1985). Hypothesis, subtypes and individual differences in dyslexia: Some reflections. In D. Gray, J. Kavanagh (Eds.), *Biobehavioral measures of dyslexia*. Parkton, MD: York Press.

Satz, P., Taylor, H. G., Friel, J., & Fletcher, J. (1978). Some developmental and predictive precursors of reading disabilities: A six-year follow up. In A. L. Benton & D. Pearl (Eds.), *Dyslexia: An appraisal of current knowledge*. New York: Oxford University Press.

Satz, P., & Van Nostrand, G. (1973). Developmental dyslexia. An evaluation of a theory. In P. Satz & J. Russ (Eds.), *The disabled learner: Early detection and intervention*. Rotterdam: Rotterdam University Press.

Schaefer, E. S. (1981). Development of adaptive behavior: conceptual models and family correlates. In M. Begab, H. Garber & H. C. Haywood (Eds.), *Prevention of

retarded development in psychosocially disadvantaged children*. Baltimore MD: University Park Press.

Shankweiler, D., & Liberman, I. Y. (1976). Exploring the relations between reading and speech. In R. M. Knights & P. L. Bakker (Eds.), *Neuropsychology of learning disorders: Theoretical approaches*. Baltimore, MD: University Park Press.

Shepard, L. (1980). An evaluation of the regression discrepancy method for identifying children with learning disabilities. *Journal of Special Education*, 14, 79–91.

Siegel, L. S., & Linder, A. (1984). Short-term memory processes in children with reading and arithmetic disabilities. *Developmental Psychology*, 20, 200–207.

Skinner, H. A. (1978). Differentiating the contribution of elevation, scatter, and shape in profile similarity. *Educational and Psychological Measurement*, 38, 297–308.

Speece, D. L. (1987). Information processing subtypes of learning disabled readers. *Training Disabilities Research*, 2 (2), 91–102.

Speece, D. L., McKinney, J. D., & Appelbaum, M. I. (1985). Classification and validation of behavioral subtypes of learning disabled children. *Journal of Educational Psychology*, 77, 67–77.

Stanovich, K. E. (1981). Relationships between word decoding speed, general name-retrieval ability, and reading progress in first-grade children. *Journal of Educational Psychology*, 73, 809–815.

Strauss, A. A., & Kephart, N. C. (1955). *Psychopathology and education of the brain injured child. Vol. 11: Progress in theory and clinic*. New York: Grune and Stratton.

Strauss, A., & Lehtinen, L. (1947). *Psychopathology and education of the brain injured child*, New York: Grune and Stratton.

Swanson, H. L. (1984). Semantic and visual memory codes in learning disabled readers. *Journal of Experimental Child Psychology*, 37, 124–140.

Taylor, H. G., Satz, P., & Friel, J. (1979). Developmental dyslexia in relation to other childhood reading disorders: Significance and clinical utility. *Reading Research Quarterly*, 15, 84–101.

Torgesen, J. (1975). Problems and prospects in the study of learning disabilities. In E. M. Hetherington (Ed.), *Review of child development research* (Vol. 5). Chicago: University of Chicago Press.

Torgesen, J. K. (1982). The use of rationally defined subgroups in research on learning disabilities. In J. P. Das., R. F. Mulcahy and A. E. Wall (Eds.), *Theory and Research in Learning Disabilities*. New York: Plenum Press.

Torgesen, J. K., & Houck, D. G. (1980). Processing deficiencies of learning-disabled children who perform poorly on the Digit Span Test. *Journal of Educational Psychology*, 72, 141–160.

Torgesen, J., & Kail, R. V. (1980). Memory processes in exceptional children. In B. K. Keogh (Ed.), *Advances in special education. Vol. 1: Basic constructs and theoretical orientations*. Greenwich, CT: JAI Press.

Torgesen, J. K., & Licht, B. G. (1983). The learning disabled child as an inactive learner: Retrospect and prospects. In J. D. McKinney & L. Feagans, (Eds.), *Topics in learning disabilities*, Norwood, NJ: Ablex.

Torgesen, J. K., & Rashotte, C. A. (1980). Memory and comprehension of spoken discourse by learning disabled children with low digit span scores. Unpublished manuscript, Florida State University.

Torgesen, J. K., & Senf, G. M. (Eds). (1984). *Annual Review of Learning Disabilities*. New York: Professional Press.

Traub, M., & Bloom, F. (1975) *Recipe for reading*. Cambridge, MA: Educator's Publishing Service.

Vance, H. B., & Singer, M. G. (1979). Recategorization of the WISC-R subtest scaled scores for learning disabled children. *Journal of Learning Disabilities*, **12**, 487–491.

Vellutino, F. R. (1975). Alternative-conceptualizations of dyslexia: Evidence in support of a verbal-deficit hypothesis. *Harvard Educational Review*, **47**, 334–354.

Vellutino, F. R. (1978). Toward an understanding of dyslexia. Psychological factors in specific reading disability. In A. L. Benton & D. Pearl (Eds.), *Dyslexia: An appraisal of current knowledge*. New York and London: Oxford University Press.

Von Isser, A., Quay, H. C., & Love, C. T. (1980). Interrelationships among three measures of deviant behavior. *Exceptional Children*, **46**, 272–276.

Watson, B. V., Goldgar, D. E., & Ryschon, K. L. (1983). Subtypes of reading disability. *Journal of Clinical Neuropsychology*, **5**(4), 377–399.

Werry, J. S. (1968). Developmental hyperactivity. *Pediatric Clinics of North America*, **15**, 581–599.

Whalen, C. K., & Henker, B. (1980). *Hyperactive Children*. New York: Academic Press, Inc.

Wong, B. (1979). The role of theory in learning disabilities research, Part II. A selective review of current theories of learning and reading disabilities. *Journal of Learning Disabilities*, **12**, 649–658.

Social Competence and Motivational Characteristics of Learning Disabled Students

FRANK M. GRESHAM

Louisiana State University

Abstract—The social competence and motivational
characteristics of learning disabled students are
reviewed and discussed. Social skills and peer acceptance, two components of social competence, are emphasized in this chapter. Self-concept and the social
perceptual abilities of learning disabled students are also
discussed and evaluated. Several theories of human
motivation are used to differentially explain the social
competence deficits of learning disabled students.
Needs and recommendations are detailed at the conclusion of this chapter for researchers, practitioners, and
public policy makers.

Introduction

The field of learning disability historically has concerned
itself primarily with the identification, instruction, and
evaluation of *academic* problems of children and youth.
This, in part, is due to the definitional characteristics of
this handicapping condition. Unlike the categories of
mental retardation and behavior disorders, a specific
learning disability is defined exclusively in terms of
academic incompetence. That is, most states define a
specific learning disability in terms of an "educationally
significant" discrepancy between academic ability and
academic achievement (Keogh, this volume). In contrast, mental retardation is defined by deficits in both
academic and social adaptive behavior competencies
(Grossman, 1983). Similarly, behavior disorders typically refer to situationally inappropriate behaviors or
feelings under normal circumstances that adversely
affect academic performance (Epstein, Cullinan &
Sabatino, 1977; Gresham, 1982a, 1985b).

Recently, a number of researchers and educators have
concerned themselves with the social competence
characteristics of learning disabled students (Bryan,
1974a, b & c, 1976; 1982, Bryan & Bryan, 1978; Gable,
Strain, & Hendrickson, 1979; Gresham 1981b; Gresham
& Reschly, 1985; La Greca & Mesibov, 1979). This
interest in the social competencies of students with
learning disabilities has been prompted by the growing
realization that students with learning disabilities are
often poorly accepted by peers and consistently exhibit
deficits in positive social behaviors relative to their nonhandicapped counterparts (Bryan, 1982; Gable et al.,
1979, Gresham, 1981b, 1982a, 1983a; La Greca & Mesibov, 1979).

The purposes of the present chapter are to provide a
conceptualization and discussion of the social competence and motivational characteristics of students
with learning disabilities. Social skills and peer acceptance, two components of social competence, are emphasized in the chapter. In the author's view, identification
and remediation of social skill deficiences as well as
enhancing the acceptance of students by learning disabilities by peers and teachers are seen as critical aspects
of an "appropriate" education. As Hartup (1979b) so
aptly noted, "Peer relationships are not luxuries in
human development, but necessities" (p. 252).

The social competence and social acceptance
characteristics of students with learning disabilities will
be discussed in the context of the goals and focus of the
American education system and the increasing emphasis
upon instruction in less restrictive environments. Various definitions of social skills will be presented along
with a conceptualization and classification of social skill
deficiencies. Theoretical explanations of social skill
deficits will be presented using several major theories of
human motivation including *effectance motivation*
(Harter, 1978; White, 1959), *learned helplessness* (Seligman, 1975), *self-efficacy* (Bandura, 1977b), *operant
learning theory* (Skinner, 1953), and *ecological-
behavioral theory* (Hersh & Walker, 1983; Kantor, 1959;
Wahler & Fox, 1981). Future directions for research and
practice with learning disabled students will be discussed
and tied to public policy guidelines and curriculum planning as they relate to appropriate education in least
restrictive environments. Particular emphasis will be
given to the consideration of the *social acceptability*

(Wolf, 1978) of social skills instruction in regular education classrooms for students with learning disabilities.

Implications

The theory and research concerning the social competence and motivational characteristics summarized in this chapter provide state of the art information that should assist researchers, teachers, and public policy makers in improving the education of students with learning disabilities. Social competence is conceptualized as being an important subset of the global domain of personal competence (along with academic competence). Social skills and the peer acceptance status of students with learning disabilities are emphasized in this chapter along with theory and research concerning the motivational characteristics of students with learning disabilities.

This review of the research literature indicates that students with learning disabilities are poorly accepted, neglected, or rejected by their non-handicapped peers in regular classrooms and they have deficiencies in the areas of interpersonal behaviors, self-related behaviors, and task-related behaviors. Moreover, many students with learning disabilities can be characterized as having motivational deficits in the sense that they have histories of failure-based experiences in academic settings, low expectations for success, and deficits in perceived self-efficacy which results in the avoidance of situations and tasks in which they feel failure is probable.

A number of implications are detailed at the conclusion of this chapter for researchers, practitioners, and public policy makers. The chapter, as a whole, leads to the following major conclusions:

1. Students with learning disabilities experience significant problems in the areas of social skills, peer acceptance, and motivation;

2. Much additional research is needed in the area of social competence and motivational characteristics of students with learning disabilities;

3. Social competencies and motivation levels of potential learning disabled students should be evaluated as part of preplacement evaluations;

4. Preservice and inservice training should include the content areas of social competence and motivation;

5. Federal and state education agencies should fund research in the description, assessment, and instruction of social competence for students with learning disabilities; and

6. Social skills instruction should be considered as a prereferral intervention for potential learning disabled students which may have the effect of reducing the numbers of false positive classifications of students.

Personal Competence: A Global Perspective
Dimensions of Personal Competence

Personal competence can be described globally as being comprised of three subdomains: (a) academic

FIGURE 1
Personal Competence Domains and Response Classes for Children in Educational Settings

PERSONAL COMPETENCE

ACADEMIC COMPETENCE	SOCIAL COMPETENCE
• General Intelligence	• Adaptive Behavior
• Academic Achievement	• Social Skills
• Perceptual-Motor Skills	
• Language Skills	

competence, (b) social competence, and (c) physical competence (Greenspan, 1981). The first two of these; academic and social competence, are most germane to the current chapter and will be emphasized. Figure 1 graphically depicts the relationship of academic and social competence to the construct personal competence. It should be noted that there are at least moderate relationships between the domains of academic and social competence (Reschly, Gresham, & Graham-Clay, 1984). Figure 1 is presented to depict the domains of academic and social competence to the superordinate domain of "personal competence."

Academic competence. The construct of academic competence includes skill areas that can be labeled intellectual/cognitive skills, academic skills, perceptual-motor skills, and language skills. Students with learning disabilities are placed into special education, by guideline or law, on the basis of academic incompetence. Few, if any, students with learning disabilities get into the special education system primarily on the basis of social incompetence (Keogh, this volume; Reschly et al. 1984.)

Social competence. Social competence has long been regarded as a fundamental aspect of human capabilities. In a very early formulation, Thorndike (1927) suggested three kinds of intelligence, one of which was social intelligence or social competence. Social competence has also been a fundamental notion associated with conception of, definition, and classification criteria with handicapped persons. This is particularly apparent in the modern classification criteria in the area of mental retardation which have consistently, through several revisions, equally emphasized the importance of both cognitive/academic and social competence (Grossman, 1983).

Reschly et al. (1984) have conceptualized social competence as being comprised of two components: (a) *adaptive behavior* and (b) *social skills*. Adaptive behavior for children would include independent functioning skills, physical development, language development, and functional academic competencies. Social skills would include interpersonal behaviors (e.g., accepting authority, conversation skills, cooperative behaviors, etc.), self-related behaviors (e.g., expressing feelings, positive attitude toward self, ethical behavior, etc.), task-related behaviors (e.g., independent work, completing tasks, following directions, etc.), and peer acceptance.

Details regarding these social skills, particularly as they relate to students with learning disabilities will be provided in subsequent portions of this chapter and can be found in a number of recent publications (see Gresham, 1981b, 1982a, 1983a; La Greca & Mesibov, 1981; Stephens, 1978; Stumme, Gresham, & Scott, 1982, 1983). The following section will describe how the education system deals with the discovered academic and/or social incompetencies of its students.

Incompetence: Identification and Intervention in the School

The field of special education thrives upon and is positively reinforced by the discovery of personal incompetence in children (Gresham, 1984a, 1985b). Children found to be physically incompetent are placed into categories reflecting their incompetencies if their condition adversely affects educational performance (e.g., health impaired, orthopedically impaired, or sensory impaired). Similarly, students with learning disabilities are typically placed into special education on the basis of specific academic incompetencies.

Schools supposedly engage in the identification of personal incompetencies in students in order to provide them with special education and related services in "least restrictive environments" with the hope of remediating identified incompetencies. Hence, one way to view special education is that it is a system designed to identify incompetence in children, place them into "appropriate" educational programs that are "least restrictive" with the goal of having them emerge as competent individuals.

The relative success with which the special education enterprise accomplishes this goal is open to debate and depends upon what criteria are used to define success. However, there are little data to support the notion that special education effectively remediates the academic, physical, and/or social incompetencies of handicapped children. Few handicapped children ever become nonhandicapped as a direct result of special education other

than by administrative, legislative, or litigative declassification of fiat (Gresham, 1985b). Reasons for the failure of the special education system effectively to remediate personal incompetencies of handicapped students are beyond the scope of the present chapter. However, as will be discussed later, one reason has to do with the resistance of regular education to deal with the learning and behavior problems of mildly handicapped children in the regular classroom. Techniques used in mainstreaming become more of a problem in the social acceptability of interventions than in the effectiveness of given interventions to remediate learning and behavior problems in the regular classroom (Witt & Elliott, 1985; Wolf, 1978). The following section will provide several definitions of social skill followed by a heuristic classification system of social skill deficiencies.

Definitions of Social Skill

As previously discussed, social skill may be viewed as part of a broader construct known as social competence (Gresham, 1981a; Kazdin, 1979; McFall, 1982). Past conceptualizations of children's behavior have highlighted deviant aspects of social behavior (Foster & Ritchey, 1979). Recent interest in social skills has focused primarily upon building positive behaviors into the repertoire as well as eliminating negative behaviors (Asher & Hymel, 1981; Asher, Oden, & Gottman, 1977; Cartledge & Milburn, 1978, 1980; Greenwood, Walker, & Hops, 1977; Gresham, 1981a; 1981b, 1982a; Hops, 1983).

At least three general definitions can be distilled from the accumulated literature on children's social skills. One definition can be termed the *peer acceptance definition* in that researchers primarily use indices of peer acceptance or popularity (e.g., peer sociometrics) to define social skill. Using a peer acceptance definition, children and adolescents who are accepted by or who are popular with their peers in school and/or community settings can be said to be socially skilled. This definition has been implicit in the work of many prominent researchers in the social skills area (Asher & Hymel, 1981; Asher et al., 1977; Asher, Singleton, Tinsley, & Hymel, 1979; Gottman, 1977; Gottman, Gonso, & Rasmussen, 1975; Gottman, Gonso, & Schuler, 1976; Ladd, 1981; Oden & Asher, 1977).

In spite of the relative objectivity of this definition, the major drawback of it is that it cannot identify what specific behaviors lead to peer acceptance or popularity. As such, we are left with a group of children who are identified as poorly accepted (or well-accepted) without any knowledge of what social behaviors (or absence thereof) lead to their acceptance status.

This being the case, some researchers have opted for a *behavioral definition* of social skills. This approach essentially defines social skills as those situation-specific reponses that maximize the probability of maintaining reinforcement and/or decrease the probability of punishment contingent upon one's social behavior. Measures used to define social skills in this manner typically consist of observations of behavior in naturalistic or role-play situations and settings. Researchers adhering to a strict behavioral definition of social skills almost never utilize peer acceptance (via sociometric measures) as part of their criteria for defining social skills.

Many well-known investigators adopt primarily a behavioral definition of children's social skills (Bornstein, Bellack & Hersen, 1977; Combs & Slaby, 1977; Foster & Ritchey, 1979; Greenwood, Todd, Hops, & Walker, 1982; Greenwood, Walker, Todd, & Hops, 1981; Rogers-Warren & Baer, 1976; Strain, 1977; Strain, Cooke, & Apolloni, 1976). This definition has the advantage over the peer acceptance definition in that the antecedents and consequences of particular social behaviors can be identified, specified, and operationalized for assessment and remedial purposes. This definition, however, does not ensure that these social behaviors are in fact socially skilled, socially significant, or socially important. Merely increasing the frequency of certain behaviors that researchers define a priori as "social skills" may not impact upon goals of outcomes valued by society (Gresham, 1983b). A final and less-often discussed definition may be termed the *social validity definition*. According to this definition, social skills are those behaviors which, within given situations, predict important social outcomes for children. These so-called important social outcomes may be (a) peer acceptance or popularity, (b) significant others' judgments of social skills (e.g., parents, teachers, etc.), and/or (c) other social behaviors known consistently to correlate with peer acceptance and judgments of significant others. This definition used naturalistic observations of behavior, sociometric indices, and ratings by significant others to assess and define social skills. It has the advantage of not only specifying behaviors in which the child is deficient, but also can define these behaviors as socially skilled-based upon their relationships to socially important outcomes (e.g., peer acceptance, parental acceptance, teacher acceptance, etc.).

The social validity definition has received recent empirical support (Green, Forehand, Beck, & Vosk, 1980; Gresham, 1981b, 1982c, 1983b) as well as past indications of validity (Hartup, Glazer, & Charlesworth, 1967; Marshall & McCandless, 1957; McGuire, 1973; Moore & Updegraff, 1964; Singleton & Asher, 1977).

Conceptualization of Social Skills Problems

Social skills problems may be delineated into four types: (a) *skills deficits*; (b) *performance deficits*; (c) *self-control skill deficits*; and (d) *self-control performance deficits*. The basis for these distinctions rest upon whether or not the child knows how to perform the skill in question and the existence of emotional arousal reponses (e.g., anger, impulsivity, anxiety, etc.).

Although this conceptualization is primarily speculative at this point, there is some empirical support for the majority of social skills problems described (Camp, Blom, Herbert, & Van Doorninck, 1977; Gottman, 1977; Gresham, 1981a, 1981b; Gresham & Elliott, 1984; Meichenbaum, 1977). The purpose of this conceptualization is to provide a heuristic framework for social skills problems which should be useful in the assessment, classification, and remediation of social skill difficulties in students with learning disabilities.

Skills Deficits

Children with social skills deficits do not have the necessary social skills to interact appropriately with peers or they do not know a critical step in the performance of the skill. A social skills deficit is similar to what Bandura (1977a) refers to as an acquisition or learning deficit. Social skill deficits can be clarified by using an academic example. A child who does not know the "+" operation sign has a skill deficit in that he or she does not know what behavior to exhibit when seeing the operation sign for addition. This means that the child does not have this skill in the repertoire. Similarly, a child can know the "+" operation sign, but not know how to regroup when confronted with a problem (e.g., $32 + 19 = $ ————). This is a skill deficit in the sense that although the child knows what behavior to perform when seeing the operation sign for addition, he or she has left out a critical component in addition skills when responding to the problem $32 + 19 = 41$ (a regrouping error).

Performance Deficits

A social performance deficit describes the problem peculiar to children who have the social skills in their repertoires, but do not perform them at acceptable levels. Performance deficits can be thought of as a deficiency in the number of times a social behavior is emitted and may be related to a lack of motivation (i.e., reinforcement contingencies) or an absence of opportunity to perform the behavior (i.e., a stimulus control problem).

The key in determining whether a social skills problem is a performance deficit is whether or not the child can perform the behavior. Thus, if the child does not perform a behavior in a classroom situation but can perform the behavior in a behavioral role-play situation, it is a social performance deficit. Also, if the child has been observed to perform the behavior in the past, it is probably a performance rather than a skill deficit.

Self-Control Skill Deficits

A self-control skill deficit describes the problem peculiar to a child who has not learned a particular social skill because some type of emotional arousal response has prevented the acquisition of the skill. As such, one way to conceptualize this type of social skill problem is that it is a combination of a behavioral excess (emotional arousal response) and a behavioral deficit (the absence of a social skill reponse). This conceptualization would suggest that social skills are not learned because an interfering emotional arousal response prevents the acquisition of the social skill.

One emotional arousal response that interferes with learning is anxiety. Anxiety has been shown to prevent the acquisition of appropriate coping responses, particularly in the literature concerning fears and phobias (see Bandura, 1977a). Hence, children may not learn how to interact with peers because social anxiety or fear prevents social approach behavior. In turn, avoidance of or escape from social situations reduces anxiety thereby negatively reinforcing social withdrawal behaviors or social isolation.

Another emotional arousal response that may prevent the acquisition of social skills ia impulsivity (i.e., the tendency toward short response latencies in social situations). Children who exhibit impulsive social behavior fail to learn appropriate social interaction skills because their behavior often results in social rejection by peers. Therefore, peers avoid the impulsive child which results in the target child not being exposed to models of appropriate social behavior or being placed on an extinction schedule for his or her social responses.

Self-Control Performance Deficits

Children with self-control performance deficits have the specific social skill in their repertoires, but do not perform the skill because the presence of emotional arousal responses and problems in antecedent or consequent control prevents the child from exhibiting the skill at an acceptable level. That is, the child knows how to perform the skill, but does so infrequently or inconsistently. The key difference between self-control skill and self-control performance deficits is whether or not the child has the social skill in the repertoire. In the former case, the skill has never been learned; in the latter case, the skill has been learned but is not exhibited consistently. Two criteria are used to determine a self-control performance deficit: (a) the presence of an emotional arousal response, and (b) the inconsistent performance of the skill in question.

This classification of social skill deficits provides a useful heuristic for looking at the potential types of social skills difficulties of students with learning disabilities. Figure 2 provides a visual conceptualization of the aforementioned deficits. Although a given learning disabled student could fit into any of these categories, the literature on the social skills problem of students with learning disabilities suggests that they may be overrepresented in the bottom two quadrants of Figure 2. That is, they experience self-control skill and self-control performance deficits more than simple skill and performance deficits. The social competence deficits of students with

FIGURE 2
Classification of Social Skill Problems

	Learning Deficit	Performance Deficit
Emotional Arousal Response Absent	Social Skills Deficit	Social Performance Deficit
Emotional Arousal Response Present	Self-Control Skills Deficit	Self-Control Performance Deficit

Emotional arousal responses are internal responses such as anxiety, impulsivity, anger, etc., that prevent either the acquisition or performance of appropriate social behaviors.

learning disabilities are reviewed in the following sections.

Theoretical Explanations of Social Skills Deficits

A number of motivational deficits (e.g., low expectancy for success, learned helplessness, etc.) have been found to characterize handicapped children (Cromwell, 1963; Harter, 1978; Thomas, 1979). These motivational deficits, at least in part, have been cited as potential reasons for the failure of mainstreaming to bring about the instructional and social integration of handicapped children (Gresham, 1984a). Five theories of human motivation are useful in explaining the social deficits of students with learning disabilities: (a) effectance motivation (Harter, 1978; White, 1959), (b) learned helplessness (Seligman, 1975), (c) self-efficacy (Bandura, 1977a, (d) operant learning theory (Skinner, 1953), and (e) ecological-behavioral theory (Hersh & Walker, 1983; Kantor, 1959). The major components of each of these theories will be briefly described and related to the social skill deficits of learning disabled students.

Effectance Motivation

There are several psychological theories of human motivation which stress the importance of individuals' perceived effectiveness in mastering their environment. For example, the cognitive-developmental theory of Piaget (1952), the psychosocial theory of Erikson (1950), and the self-actualization theory of Maslow (1968) all recognize the importance of competence or "sense of mastery" in explaining human behavior.

White (1959) hypothesized that all individuals manifest an "urge toward competence" which he termed effectance motivation. Effectance motivation describes an individual's "need" to be successful, or otherwise deal effectively with the environment. The basic tenets of effectance motivation are as follows: (a) the organism desires to produce an effect on the environment, (b) the organism's goal is to deal effectively or competently with the environment, and (c) the results or effects of dealing effectively with the environment are feelings of efficacy.

Harter (1978) has reconceptualized and expanded White's (1959) original theory of effectance motivation. A major thrust of Harter's work has been to translate the effectance motivation contruct into researchable hypotheses. Several aspects of Harter's reconceptualiz-ation of effectance motivation are important.

First, Harter (1978) eschews the notion that effect-ance is a global construct and instead takes the stance that effectance may have a number of components. Based upon factor analyses of her own measure across various age levels, the *Perceived Competence Scale for Children*, Harter (1982) has differentiated three dimen-sions of competence or effectance motivation: (a) cogni-tive, (b) social, and (c) physical. It is important to isolate such effectance dimensions in order to assess individual differences in the degree to which a child invests energy in these different mastery domains and to consider the differential responses from a child's particular socializ-aing agents (e.g., parents, teachers, peers, etc.) for his or her efforts in these competence areas.

A second difference between Harter's (1978) recon-ceptualization of effectance motivation and White's original theory is her analysis of the effects of failure experiences on the individual. Whereas White (1959) focused primarily on the implications of success in deal-ing with the environment, Harter (1978) also examined the effects of failure on components of effectance motiv-ation.

How does the theory of effectance motivation relate to the social deficits of students with learning disabilit-ies? First, it is obvious that students with learning dis-abilities have derived their label on the basis of demonstrable academic incompetence, most probably not until they have reached the mid-elementary grades. According to the theory of effectance motivation, the effects of repeatedly failed mastery attempts are increased dependence on external approval, a perceived lack of competence of self-esteem, anxiety in mastery situations, and decrements in effectance motivation. By the time a student with learning disabilities is identified and labeled, he or she has a well-established pattern of responding to mastery situations.

Second, while it is possible to feel incompetent in one area (e.g., cognitive) and competent in other areas (e.g., social and physical), there is undoubtably some general-ization from one competence domain to other domains. Given that the school is clearly one of the strongest influences on a child's socialization history, it is not sur-prising that students with learning disabilities experi-ence a lack of perceived social competence as well as academic competence. Clearly, students with learning disabilities experience a series of failure-based mastery attempts related to academic tasks. The result or effect this has upon effectance motivation is quite predictable: (a) loss of interest (passivity), (b) refusal to attempt new tasks (noncompliance), (c) statements of self-doubt (e.g., "I can't do that"), and (d) overreliance on others (dependency).

Each of the above behaviors have social costs as well. Students who are uninterested in their work and who are noncompliant learners receive reprimands and pun-ishment from teachers. These reprimands, which are typically public, may communicate to the learning dis-abled child's peers that he or she is somehow less worth-while than others who comply and exhibit independent mastery attempts. Moreover, self-doubting statements and overreliance upon others eventually becomes pun-ishing to peers and teachers alike. Thus, the student with learning disabilities is typically caught in a vicious cycle of passivity, noncompliance, self-doubt, and external reliance which not only is counterproductive to aca-demic achievement, but also is damaging to interper-sonal relationships and social acceptance (Gresham & Reschly, 1985).

Effectance considerations may be utilized to explain motivational deficits in mainstreamed students with learning disabilities. By definition, such children have a history of failure in the regular education classroom. This history of failure-based experiences will most likely lead to low expectancy for success, fear of failure, and a high need for external reinforcement for mastery attempts. To the extent that mastery attempts have been extinguished previously in the regular classroom, main-streamed students with learning disabilities may be returned to an environment which stimulates anxiety and dependent behaviors concurrent with low perceived competence. These responses are certainly not adaptive in terms of successful academic or social functioning.

Learned Helplessness

Seligman's (1975) theory of learned helplessness (LH) represents another view of human motivation based upon an individual's perception of the relationship between his or her own behavior and its consequences or outcomes. The basic phenomenon in LH is the per-ception that one's behavior and its outcomes are inde-pendent. Hence, persons learn on the basis of past response-outcome interactions that their behavior is not effective in mastering the environment. That is, indivi-duals learn over a series of failure-based experiences that there is no relation between effort (behavior) and changes in surroundings or the attainment of a goal (out-comes).

Seligman (1975) has concluded from a number of studies that the LH phenomenon has three character-istics: (a) failure to intitiate responses, (b) failure to learn, and (c) emotional disturbance. Individuals in a state of LH will not initiate adaptive responses to remove themselves from aversive situations. In addition, persons in a state of LH have a striking inability to learn that they can control certain events in their environment. Evidence from a variety of sources (reviewed by Seligman, 1975) indicates that experiencing two events as independent (noncontingent) makes it extremely difficult at some later time to learn that they are dependent or related when they have been made contingent. Finally, Seligman (1975) reviews a number of studies demonstrating that this lack of controllability may produce anxiety and depression. Both anxiety and depression are complex psychological states that have been shown to have a very debilitating effect.

The concept of LH is relatively easy to apply to students with learning disabilities. The effects of failure in a variety of learning situations include poor self-esteem, low motivation and even depression (Thomas, 1979). Students with learning disabilities have been characterized by many of their teachers as no longer capable of believing they can learn. They learn over a series of failure-based experiences that there is no relationship between effort and outcome (i.e., they are in a state of learned helplessness). A great deal of initial teaching effort with learning disabled students focuses upon motivating them to expend sufficient effort in order to experience success (Haring, 1974). Many students with learning disabilities, however, continue to be easily frustrated, are unwilling to attempt tasks at their ability level, and become anxious in learning situations (Sabatino, 1976).

Although there have been few studies in the literature specifically addressing the effects of LH on the social behavior of students with learning disabilities, it stands to reason that many social problems of such students can be related back to the helplessness construct. Given the fact that individuals in a state of LH fail to initiate responses, fail to learn, and display a variety of emotional behaviors, one can see the potential negative impact this would have upon peer relationships, social interactions, and social acceptance. Future research should specifically address the phenomenon of LH as it relates to the social deficits of students with learning disabilities.

Self-Efficacy

The previously discussed concepts of effectance motivation and learned helplessness have been amended and reconceptualized by Bandura (1977a,) into a theory known as self-efficacy. The basic premise in self-efficacy, as in the theories of effectance motivation and learned helplessness, centers upon individuals' sense of personal efficacy to produce and to regulate events in their lives. According to Bandura (1977a), perceived self-efficacy is concerned with judgments of how well one can execute behaviors required to deal with prospective situations.

Perceived self-efficacy affects behavioral functioning by influencing an individual's choice of activities, effort, expenditure, and persistence in the face of difficulties. Self-percepts of efficacy can predict not only behavioral

choice, but also variations in coping behavior and even specific performance attainments (Bandura, 1977a). In addition, although self-efficacy is a situationally-specific variable, once perceived efficacy is enhanced, it tends to generalize to other similar situations requiring similar behaviors.

Bandura (1977a) differentiates between *efficacy expectations* and *outcome expectations* in his theory. Efficacy expectations reflect one's belief that one can successfully execute the behavior required to produce a given outcome. In contrast, an outcome expectation (sometimes referred to as a response-outcome expectation) reflects that belief that a given behavioral performance will produce a given outcome. Efficacy and outcome expectations are differentiated in this model because a person may believe that behaviors will produce certain outcomes (an outcome expectation), but that person may not believe that he or she can perform the requisite behaviors that will produce desired outcomes (an efficacy expectation).

The theoretical notions of effectance motivation and learned helplessness can be viewed as specific cases of self-efficacy. For example, efficacy expectations and effectance motivation both influence an individual's behavior based on motivation mastery beliefs. Accordingly, task choice and effort are mediated by the level of perceived competence or efficacy expected. Consistent with the perception of control encompassed by the LH construct, outcome expectations specifically address an invidual's belief that a certain outcome will result from a given behavior. As in LH, low outcome expectations result in low effort expenditure and low task persistence.

The regular education classroom and its curriculum often present situations in which students with learning disabilities feel they cannot perform certain behaviors to produce desired outcomes. Students with learning disabilities frequently remain in the regular classroom where they continue to experience academic and/or social failure.

The expectations that individuals hold about their ability to master certain tasks affect both the initiation and persistence of coping behavior. Moreover, the strength of these expectations predicts whether or not a person will even try to cope within given situations. This perceived self-efficacy also influences people's choice of behavior settings in that they avoid settings or situations that they believe exceed their coping skills, and approach settings and situations in which they believe they can successfully cope.

Students with learning disabilities have no choice of the setting in which they will be placed. These students are often forced to remain in the regular clasroom where failure-based experiences will continue to occur. The net result of this is that they come to believe that they cannot perform the behaviors that result in preferred outcomes (e.g., adequate academic achievement). Consequently, students with learning disabilities have a lowered sense of academic self-efficacy which, in all likelihood, generalizes to difficulties in peer acceptance and interpersonal relationships (Gresham, 1984a).

Operant Learning Theory

Many social interventions for students with learning disabilities have been based upon the principles of operant learning or, more accurately, applied behavior analysis (ABC) (Cooke & Apolloni, 1976; Gable et al., 1979; Gresham, 1981b; Hazel, Schumaker, Sherman, & Sheldon, 1982; Schumaker & Ellis, 1982). According to an ABA conceptualization, children experience difficulties in peer relationships because they either have not learned or they do not perform the behaviors that will lead to satisfactory interpersonal relationships. The definition of social skills used by Foster and Ritchey (1979) captures the essence of an ABA explanation of social skills deficits: "Those responses, which within a given situation, prove effective, or in other words maximise the probability of producing, maintaining, or enhancing positive effects for the interactor" (p. 626). Thus, social skills are those situationally-specific responses that maximize the probability of securing or maintaining reinforcement and decrease the probability of punishment or extinction contingent upon one's social behavior.

The previously described conceptualization of social skills problems into skill deficits, performance deficits, self-control skill deficits, and self-control performance deficits is based primarily upon an ABA or operant learning explanation. Social skill difficulties are viewed, depending upon the specific type of problem, as deficits in learning or performing the skill. Remediation focuses upon direct instruction for the skill in question using antecedent- and/or consequent-control techniques (see Gresham, 1981b for a comprehensive review).

While the ABA explanation of social skills difficulties has been extremely useful in conceptualizing and designing interventions, some see the operant model as being overly restrictive (Hersh & Walker, 1983; Wahler, 1975; Wahler & Fox, 1981; Wahler & Graves, 1983). An alternative model which takes into account a broader range of influences on the social competencies of children can be termed the *ecological-behavioral model*. This model is not only more comprehensive, but also provides a more adequate explanation of social skill deficiencies. It is discussed in the following section.

Ecological-Behavioral Theory

Wahler and Fox (1981) have suggested that a strict operant analysis of behavior provides limited access to the full range of environmental events that influence socially significant behavior. As such, we have perhaps a limited understanding of behavior in its ecological context.

A strict operant analysis of behavior emphasizes the importance of temporally brief associations between stimuli, responses, and consequences. An "adequate" functional analysis of behavior therefore limits itself to temporally contiguous associations between stimuli (discriminative, reinforcing, and/or punishing) and responses. Several researchers have made a distinction between so-called *stimulus events* and *setting events* in the analysis of behavior (Bijou & Baer, 1961; Wahler & Fox, 1981; Wahler & Graves, 1983). Setting events are more complex than the simple presence, absence, or change of a stimulus. Instead, a setting event is defined as a stimulus-response interaction which, because it has occurred, will influence other stimulus-response relationships which follow it. Setting events are made up of stimulus-response interactions (rather than durational condition or event) and can occur separate in time and space from the subsequent stimulus-response relationships which they influence (Wahler & Fox, 1981). For example, a child's interactions with parents before coming to school can influence to a great extent the child's behavior in the classroom that day. In this case, parent-child interactions can be said to function as setting events for future classroom behavior.

What does the notion of setting events have to do with the social behavior of students with learning disabilities in school settings? The standards, expectations, and tolerance levels that teachers hold for children's social behavior function as powerful setting events which influence subsequent stimulus-response interactions in the classroom. Research has shown that teacher expectations for students influence subsequent teaching behavior. For example, students perceived by teachers to be brighter or more competent receive more teacher attention, are given greater opportunities to respond, are praised more, and are given more verbal cues (Brophy, 1981; Brophy & Good, 1974; Good & Brophy, 1978).

Teachers hold expectations, standards, and tolerance levels for children's social behavior in the classroom (Hersh & Walker, 1983). Most teachers would consider a behavioral repertoire to be indicative of successful adjustment if it: (a) facilitated academic performance (e.g., listening to the teacher, following instructions, completing tasks, etc.) and (b) is marked by the absence of disruptive or unusual behaviors that challenge the teacher's authority and disrupt the classroom ecology (Hersh & Walker, 1983). The behavioral standards held by teachers function as setting events which indirectly control the teacher's behavior in the classroom. These setting events were most likely established on the basis of past stimulus-response interactions in the classroom that resulted in positively reinforcing (i.e., a quiet class and compliant students) and punishing (i.e., a noisy class and defiant students) consequences. Teachers probably evolved these social behavior standards which function as setting events on the basis of past learning history.

To summarize, the *model behavioral profile* for a student in the classroom would be a child who: (a) stays in his or her seat; (b) attends to instruction; (c) completes tasks independently (i.e., does not ask for teacher assistance); (d) complies with teacher commands, instructions, and directions; (e) follows classroom rules (which probably includes a–d above); and who does not: (a) defy the teacher, (b) behave in an aggressive or disruptive manner, (c) make loud noises or obscene gestures, (d) have tantrums, (e) steal, or (f) damage school property. This model behavioral profile does in fact contribute to school adjustment (as judged by teachers) and does in fact facilitate academic achievement. It also serves the convenience needs of classroom teachers for discipline, control, and preservation of authority (Hersh & Walker, 1983). It has little to do with development of interpersonal skills, social competencies, and the ability to cope effectively with peers.

Walker and Rankin (1983) developed an instrument for assessing teachers' standards and expectations for behavior in their classrooms called the *SBS Inventory of Teacher Social Behavior Standards and Expectations* (SBS). The SBS is an 107-item instrument designed to measure the teacher's behavioral standards and expectations in relation to adaptive and maladaptive classes of social behavior. The 10 highest- and 10 lowest-rated items of the SBS are presented as rated by 196 regular and special education teachers. The content of the 10 highest-rated items deal almost exclusively with classroom control, general discipline, and compliance with teacher commands supporting the earlier discussion of the model behavioral profile. The 10 lowest-rated items have a heavy peer social behavior content suggesting teachers do not assign a great deal of importance to social skills in their classrooms.

Clearly, students with learning disabilities do not fit the model behavioral profile described above. In fact, there is ample evidence in the literature to suggest that the behavior of students with learning disabilities is often quite the opposite of the model behavioral profile (Hallahan & Kauffman, 1976). Students with learning disabilities are often characterized as being noncompliant learners, distractible, poor listeners, and producing academic work of unacceptable quality. Note that the above characterization represents almost the exact opposite of the model behavioral profile expected (and often demanded) by most teachers. The behavioral profile of most students with learning disabilities is one which teachers find unacceptable and often intolerable. Gresham and Reschly (1985), for example, showed that teachers rated students with learning disabilities as being more deficient in academic-related social skills (e.g., task completion, independent work, on-task behavior, etc.) than peer-related social skills (e.g., cooperation with others, conversation skills, etc.). This would suggest that these behaviors subsumed in the model behavioral profile are the most salient for regular education teachers (Hersh & Walker, 1983; Walker & Rankin, 1983). Coupled with significant deficits in peer-to-peer social interactions skills and social acceptance, students with learning disabilities can be considered at risk

TABLE 1
Studies Demonstrating Poorer Sociometric Status of Students with Learning Disabilities

STUDY
Bruininks (1978)
Bryan (1974a, b, & c)
Bryan (1976)
Bryan & Wheeler (1972)
Deschler, Schumaker, Warner, Alley, & Clark (1980)
Gresham & Reschly (1985)
MacMillan & Morrison (1980)
MacMillan, Morrison, & Silverstein (1980)
Morrison (1981a)
Morrison (1981b)
Morrison, Forness, & MacMillan (1983)
Siperstein, Bopp, & Bak (1978)

for future problems in psychological and social adjustment (Gresham, 1981b, 1982a; La Greca & Mesibov, 1979, 1981).

Summary

The preceding theoretical explanations of learning disabled students' social deficits appear to be plausible based upon past research and logical extensions of each model. However, it should be noted that there is still not enough data-based research to conclude that the theories of effectance motivation, learned helplessness, self-efficacy, operant learning, or ecological-behavioral analysis adequately explain the social behavioral deficits of students with learning disabilities. Much additional research is needed to construct an adequate model for explaining the social-behavioral and peer acceptance difficulties of students with learning disabilities.

Social Competence Deficits of Learning Disabled Students: A Review of Literature

The following section will present evidence from empirically-based research attesting to the social competence deficits of students with learning disabilities. This review will be divided into four sections or topic areas: (a) sociometric status, (b) social behavior, (c) social perception, and (d) self-concept.

Sociometric Status

A number of studies in the special education literature have demonstrated that students with learning disabilities are poorly accepted and often rejected by their nonhandicapped peers (see Table 1 for a listing). The findings of these studies consistently show that children with learning disabilities in all elementary grades were less well-accepted and more frequently rejected than their nonhandicapped peers in the regular classroom.

A number of sociometric assessment procedures have been used to assess the sociometric status of students with learning disabilities. These have included: (a) peer ratings, (b) peer nominations, and (c) peer assessment methods (see Asher & Taylor, 1981, and Greenwood & Hops, 1982, for reviews). Variations in the administration and scoring of sociometric measures have limited the generalizability of the findings regarding the social status of students with learning disabilities. That is, not all studies cited in Table 1 have used similar sociometric assessment methodologies. Some have used positive peer nominations in which students are asked to nominate peers according to a prespecified positive criterion (e.g., "List your three best friends," "List three people in the class with whom you most like to play," etc.). Other studies have used a similar format but have asked children to nominate according to negative criteria ("List three people who are least liked by others"). It is important to point out that these two approaches (positive and negative criteria) are tapping two dimensions of sociometric status (Asher & Taylor, 1981). Positive nominations are used to determine those children who are isolated or ignored whereas negative nominations can be used to determine which children are actively rejected by peers. Morrison (1981a) presents an in-depth analysis of the issues involved in the sociometric classification of mildly handicapped children.

Other studies with learning disabled children have used peer rating formats in which children are asked to rate each other according to how much they like to play with or work with each other. Gresham and Reschly (1985) used this format and found that while there were significant differences between learning disabled and nonhandicapped students on both a "play with" and "work with" rating scale, the largest difference between students with and without learning disabilities was observed for a "work with" rating scale. This finding suggests that children make distinctions between different aspects of sociometric status and base these distinctions upon accurate perceptions of behavioral deficits (e.g., poor academic achievement).

Overall, it is indisputable that students with learning disabilities are more poorly accepted and more frequently rejected than their nonhandicapped peers. Collectively, the studies listed in Table 2 suggest that children with learning disabilities are one-half to a full standard deviation below that of nonhandicapped children. In other words, the "typical" child with learning disabilities is anywhere from the 15th to the 30th percentile of the sociometric distribution of nonhandicapped children. This suggests several things. First, children with learning disabilities experience poorer sociometric status than nonhandicapped children. Second, although their sociometric status is poorer, there is an overlap of the sociometric distributions of learning disabled and nonhandicapped students. This would indicate that there are a number of children with learning disabilities who are as well-accepted as nonhandicapped children. Finally, given the fact that some children with learning

TABLE 2
Studies Investigating the Social Behavior of Students with
Learning Disabilities

Study	Behaviors
Bryan (1974a, b, & c)	Task-oriented behavior; social interactions with peers & teachers
Bryan (1978)	Ratings of appearance, speech/language achievement; attractiveness to peers
Bryan & Wheeler (1972)	Task-oriented; social interactions with peers and teachers
Bryan, Wheeler, Felcan, & Henek (1976)	Cooperation, competition, helping, consideration, intrusiveness
Cooke & Apolloni (1976)	Smiling; Sharing; Positive Physical Contact; Verbal Complimenting
Gresham & Reschly (1986)	Teacher Ratings Environmental Behaviors Interpersonal Behaviors Self-Related Behaviors Task-Related Behaviors
Hazel, Schumaker, Sherman, & Sheldon (1982)	Giving Positive Feedback; Giving Negative Feedback; Accepting Negative Feedback; Resisting Peer Pressure; Negotiation; Problem-Solving
LaGreca & Mesibov (1981)	Conversational Statements, Conversational Topics; Number of Questions Asked; Proportion of Open-Ended Questions; Greetings; Conversational Comments
Odom, Jenkins, Speltz, & De Klyen (1982)	Isolate Behaviors: Interaction Behaviors; Negative Behaviors; Interactions with Teacher
Schumaker & Ellis (1982)	Asking Questions; Accepting Negative Feedback; Giving Negative Feedback; Following Instructions; Resisting Peer Pressure; Problem-Solving
Schumaker, Hazel, Sherman, & Sheldon (1982)	Accepting Negative Feedback; Conversation Behaviors; Following Instructions; Giving Negative Feedback; Giving Positive Feedback; Negotiation: Problem-Solving; Resisting Peer Pressure
Stark (1980)	Questions, Inviting Statements, Praise, Complimenting, Ignoring, Joining, Eye Contact, Smiling, Body Movement, Head Nods, Facial Expression, Speech Latency, Affect, Speech Disruptions, Voice Volume

disabilities are as accepted as their nonhandicapped peers, there may be a social skills explanation for the sociometric status of these children.

A standard deviation disparity in the average sociometric status of children with learning disabilities and their nonhandicapped peers indicates that one-sixth (approximately 17%) of children with learning disabilities are as well-accepted as average nonhandicapped children. Moreover, there is considerable evidence that the sociometric status of students with learning disabilities can be improved through social skills training (Gresham, 1981b, 1982a; La Greca & Mesibov, 1979, 1981; Odom, Jenkins, Speltz, & DeKlyen, 1982). As Gresham (1982a) points out, however, improvement in the sociometric status of children with learning disabilities requires more than mere physical placement of such children in regular classrooms: It requires programs specifically designed to teach social skills for peer acceptance.

Social Behavior

A number of studies have investigated differences between the social behaviors of learning disabled and nonhandicapped students. Table 2 lists the studies that have investigated the social behavior of students with learning disabilities. Most of these studies have utilized elementary-age students with three studies (Hazel et al., 1982; Schumaker & Ellis, 1982; Schumaker, Hazel, Sherman, & Sheldon, 1982) employing high school students or role-play situations. Only four studies have investigated the social behavior of students with learning disabilities in classroom settings using naturalistic observations of social behaviors (Bryan, 1974a, b, & c, 1978; Cooke & Apolloni, 1976; Odom et al., 1982).

Based upon a review of the above studies listed in Table 3, some consistent findings emerge. First, the student with learning disabilities does not appear to differ from the nonhandicapped student in terms of overall frequency of peer interactions. Instead, there appears to be a difference in the *quality* or kinds of social interactions between students with and without learning disabilities. For example, students with learning disabilities engage in more negative and rejecting interactions with peers than nonhandicapped children (Bryan, 1974, 1978). Moreover, students with learning disabilities are more likely to be ignored by peers than nonhandicapped students in the context of social interactions with peers.

Few studies have investigated differences in the positive social behaviors between learning disabled and nonhandicapped students. As such, the evidence for differences between these groups is somewhat less clear. The available evidence does seem to suggest, however, that students with learning disabilities display fewer positive social behaviors (e.g., complimenting, praising, etc.), show less initiative in peer situations, and display more distracting nonverbal behaviors than their nonhandicapped peers (La Greca & Mesibov, 1981).

An investigation by Gresham and Reschly (1985) studied differences between learning disabled and nonhandicapped students using teacher, parent, and peer ratings of social skills. Using the *Social Behavior Assessment* (Stephens, 1978), Gresham and Reschly showed that students with learning disabilities were rated by

TABLE 3
Studies Investigating Differences in Social Perception Between Learning Disabled and Nonhandicapped Students

Study	Social Perception Ability/Measure
Ackerman, Elardo, & Dykman (1979)	Role-Taking Moral Judgment; Intentionality
Bruno (1981)	Test of Social Inference
Bryan (1977)	Profile of Nonverbal Sensitivity
Dickstein & Warren (1980)	Cognitive Role-Taking; Affective Role-Taking; Perceptual Role-Taking
Fincham (1979)	Role-Taking; Conservation Tasks
Gerber & Zingraf (1982)	Test of Social Inference
Pearl & Cosden (1982)	Comprehension of Social Interactions
Wiig & Harris (1974)	Interpretation of Facial Expressions
Wong & Wong (1980)	Cognitive Role-Taking

both teachers and parents as having poorer social skills than nonhandicapped students. Specific differences were noted for interpersonal behaviors, self-related behaviors, and task-related behaviors. The largest differences between learning disabled and nonhandicapped groups were found for task-related behavior using both teacher and parent ratings. This class of behaviors included skills such as completing tasks, independent work, following directions, on-task behaviors, and the like. This finding would suggest that students with learning disabilities demonstrate deficits in task-related behaviors in both school and home settings. As such, remediation of these deficits should perhaps take place in both settings to ensure adequate generalization.

In summary, the research literature would suggest that students with learning disabilities interact with peers as frequently as nonhandicapped students; however, the nature or quality of these social interactions appear to be quite different. Learning disabled students' social interactions tend to be more negative in nature and are more likely to have a competitive or challenging quality to them. Although the evidence for differences in positive social behaviors is somewhat less clear, the recent research by Gresham and Reschly (1985) provides convincing evidence that students with learning disabilities are perceived as being deficient in positive social behaviors relative to nonhandicapped students by teachers and their parents. These findings hold true for teacher, parent, and peer ratings of social behaviors.

Social Perception

Social perception deficit, or the difficulty that individuals have with understanding and interpreting social cues, has been hypothesized as an explanation for the social deficits of students with learning disabilities. Johnson and Myklebust (1967) define social perception as the ability to identify, recognize, and interpret the meaning and significance of the behavior of others. The majority of studies in the area of social perception with learning disabled students have assessed either role-taking abilities or skills in comprehending nonverbal communication (La Greca & Mesibov, 1981). Table 3 lists the studies which have focused upon assessing differences between learning disabled and nonhandicapped groups in nonverbal communication and social inferences abilities (Bruno, 1981; Bryan, 1977; Gerber & Zinkgraf, 1982; Pearl & Cosden, 1982; Wiig & Harris, 1974). The majority of these investigations have focused upon the interpretation of emotional displays depicted in either facial expressions or through verbal paralanguage (Maheady & Maitland, 1982). In general, the results of these studies suggest that students with learning disabilities perform more poorly on measures of nonverbal communication than nonhandicapped peers. Although there are differences between learning disabled and nonhandicapped groups on measures of nonverbal communication and social comprehension/inference, the major methodological problem with all of these studies is the lack of external validity. That is, all of these studies have been conducted in analogue or laboratory-based settings which obviously severely limits the generalizability of these results. Given the fact that there have been no attempts to document the behavioral correlates of social perception deficits in naturalistic environments (e.g., the classroom), little can be said about how deficits in nonverbal communication affect overt behavioral performance in the classroom (Maheady & Maitland, 1982). As such, the social validity of this research for designing and implementing social skills interventions for students with learning disabilities is questionable (Gresham, 1983b).

Self-Concept

Self-concept, the general way in which one sees oneself, has been investigated in several studies comparing students with and without learning disabilities. In general, the investigation of self-concept differences between learning disabled and normally achieving children has yielded inconsistent results. Table 4 presents studies which have investigated the self-concepts of students with learning disabilities.

Most studies using global measures of self-concept such as the *Coopersmith Self-Esteem Inventory* (Coopersmith, 1967) and the *Piers-Harris Self-Concept Scale* (Piers & Harris, 1969) have produced no self-concept differences between learning disabled and nonhandicapped students (Boersma, Chapman, & Maguire, 1978; Rosenberg & Gaier, 1977; Silverman & Zigmond, 1981). One exception to this was the study by Thompson and Hartley (1980) who found differences between learning disabled and nonhandicapped English schoolchildren. Thus, it appears that learning disabled and

TABLE 4
Studies Investigating Self-Concept Differences Between Learning Disabled and Nonhandicapped Students

Study	Self-Concept Measure
Boersma & Chapman (1978)	Student's Perception of Ability Scale Piers-Harris Self-Concept Scale
Boersma & Chapman (1979)	Projected Academic Performance Scale
Chapman & Boersma (1979)	Student's Perception of Ability Scale Projected Academic Performance Scale
Hiebert, Wong, & Hunter (1982)	Projected Academic Performance Scale Student's Perception of Ability Scale
Kifer (1975)	Brookover Test of Self-Concept of Ability
Rosenberg & Gaier (1977)	Coopersmith Self-Esteem Inventory
Thompson & Harley (1980)	Coopersmith Self-Esteem Inventory

normally achieving students cannot be differentiated using global or general self-concept measures. This, however, may be more of an artifact of the psychometric inadequacies of the measures used, particularly for students with learning disabilities, rather than an indication of the lack of real differences between the groups.

One gets a very different picture when investigating the *academic* self-concept of students with learning disabilities. Using measures such as the *Student's Perception of Ability Scale* (SPAS), the *Brookover Test of Self Concept* (BTSC), and the *Projected Academic Performance Scale* (PAPS), significant differences have been found between students with and without learning disabilities.

For example, Boersma et al. (1978) were able to differentiate learning disabled and nonhandicapped groups using the SPAS, but no differences between the groups were found using the *Piers-Harris Self-Concept Scale*. These same results using the SPAS were found by Chapman and Boersma (1979) comparing groups of learning disabled and normally achieving students in grades 3-6. Similar results were obtained by Kifer (1975) using the BTSC.

Few studies have investigated the self-concept of adolescents with learning disabilities. Silverman and Zigmond (1981) found no differences in the general self-concept of learning disabled and nonhandicapped adolescents. However, Hiebert, Wong, & Hunter (1982) found significant differences in academic self-concept and academic expectations between learning disabled and nonhandicapped adolescents in grades 8 and 10. This finding replicates similar findings with learning disabled children in elementary grades (Boersma et al.,

1978; Chapman & Boersma, 1979; Kifer, 1975).

What do the results of the previous studies tell us about the self-concept of students with learning disabilities? Firstly, it indicates that constructs such as self-concept or self-esteem are vaguely defined and do not point to any clear operational definitions (Harter, 1978). Items on well-known self-concept scales such as the *Piers-Harris* and the *Coopersmith* tap a potpourri of skills dealing with physical abilities, popularity, personality traits, affective reactions, and many others. As such, responses to this conglomeration of items are summed to supposedly yield an index of self-worth or self-concept. The failure of researchers to find differences in total self-concept between students with and without learning disabilities is not surprising given the nature of the scales used.

Secondly, the data do indicate that students with learning disabilities have lower academic self-concepts using scales specifically designed to assess this construct. This finding would be expected given the fact that students with learning disabilities, by definition, are poor learners. Students with learning disabilities may have lower academic self-concepts because they have a history of failure in the mastery of academic skills (i.e., they are accurately perceiving reality). This interpretation is relatively straightforward and perhaps is a little simple-minded. When one looks at other areas in which students with learning disabilities experience difficulty, such as peer acceptance and social interactions, one gets a broader view of the difficulties such students experience in the social-affective domain. Deficits in academic self-concept usually co-exist with poor peer acceptance/rejection, deficits in positive social behaviors, and excessive negative social interaction patterns. Collectively, this suggests that students with learning disabilities are paying a high social-psychological price for their poor academic achievement (Hiebert et al., 1982).

Hypotheses Concerning Social Deficits of Students with Learning Disabilities

The foregoing review of the social deficits of students with learning disabilities indicates that these individuals experience significant deficits in peer acceptance, quality of social interactions, academic self-concept, communication skills, and social perception skills in laboratory settings. As previously discussed, the accumulated research evidence is more consistent in some areas of social deficiency (e.g., peer acceptance/rejection) than in other areas (e.g., social perception). However, given the relatively consistent evidence that students with learning disabilities do experience social-affective deficits, it becomes important to try to isolate specific causes or correlates of these deficiencies.

Two hypotheses have been formulated in the literature to account for the social deficits of students with learning disabilities (Bryan, 1982). Although there are a number of variations, essentially two hypotheses or

explanations for social deficits of students with learning disabilities can be found. One hypothesis, the *social skill deficit explanation*, states that the causes of learning disabled students' deficiencies in the social area are a direct result of social skills deficits. Thus, poor self-esteem, lower peer acceptance, peer rejection, dysfunctional social interaction patterns, and the like stem from deficiencies in social skills such as interpersonal behaviors, self-related social skills, and task-related social skills (Gresham, 1981b, 1982a, 1982b, 1985a, 1985b; Hops, 1983; Stephens, 1978; Strain, Odom, & McConnell, 1984).

A second hypothesis suggests that the social deficits of students with learning disabilities are caused by and/or associated with the same factors that cause or relate to academic deficiencies such as attention deficits, perception deficits, language deficits, listening skills, and so forth (Bryan, 1974a, b, & c; Johnson & Myklebust, 1967; Wiener, 1979). Thus, the same or similar processes that supposedly account for problems in the acquisition of reading skills, language skills, or computational skills can explain learning disabled students' social deficits. This hypothesis or explanation could be termed the *process explanation* since dysfunctional psychological processes (e.g., perception, attention, etc.) are used to explain the social deficits (e.g., poor acceptance, poor self-esteem, dysfunctional social interaction patterns, etc.) of students with learning disabilities.

There are data, some more consistent than others, to support the above hypotheses. The problem, however, is that there currently are not sufficient data to conclude that any one hypothesis is correct. Depending upon the theoretical orientation and interest of the researcher, one can find evidence to support either the skills deficit or process hypothesis. To evaluate more critically each of the above hypotheses, one must look to the specific kinds of research evidence that has been proffered to support each explanation. The research in this area can be grossly classified into two types: (a) basic or laboratory-based research and (b) applied or naturalistic research.

Most of the empirical support for the social skill deficit hypothesis comes from the applied research literature and has focused upon identifying, assessing, analyzing, and remediating overt social behaviors of learning disabled students as well as other handicapped students (Gresham, 1981b, 1983a; La Greca & Mesibov, 1979, 1981; Odom et al., 1982; Strain & Fox, 1981; Strain et al., 1984).

In contrast, much of the evidence for the process explanation of social deficits emanates from laboratory-based research which relies upon the use of cognitive-developmental tasks such as role-taking, facial perception, verbal communication, comprehension of nonverbal communication, and social problem-solving tasks (Bryan, 1977; Dickstein & Warren, 1980; Fincham, 1979; Gerber & Zinkgraf, 1982; Wiig & Harris, 1974; Wong & Wong, 1980). While this line of research has uncovered significant differences between students with and without learning disabilities, there have been few attempts systematically to assess *social behavioral characteristics* associated with social perception, nonverbal communication, and/or role-taking deficits in the natural environment. Most researchers pursuing this line of investigation develop somewhat artificial laboratory tasks, administer these tasks to learning disabled and nonhandicapped groups and typically conclude that the findings are generalizable to overt social behaviors in the naturalistic environment. As Maheady and Maitland (1982) point out, little can be inferred about the relationship between a child's performance in a laboratory-based setting and his or her behavior in the natural environment (e.g., the classroom).

Given the significant differences in the focus and methodology of these two lines of research with learning disabled students, legitimate comparisons between these two research areas cannot be made. In terms of social validity and relevance to educational programming, the skills deficit explanation is perhaps the most fruitful direction to take at this time. While the value and importance of basic research in the area should not be discounted, the skills deficit approach is most relevant to the educational and instructional needs of students with learning disabilities. This points up the problem of the discrepancy between research and practice. At present, we cannot translate the findings of basic research in the social characteristics of students with learning disabilities into viable educational practices.

State of the Art

The foregoing review indicates that students with learning disabilities are poorly accepted, neglected, or rejected by their nonhandicapped peers. Based upon the 12 studies listed in Table 2, it appears that the sociometric status of students with learning disabilities are from one-half to a full standard deviation below that of nonhandicapped children. This is consistent with the conclusion drawn by Gottlieb (1981) concerning the sociometric status of mainstreamed educable mentally retarded children. The poorer sociometric status of students with learning disabilities is perhaps the most consistent finding in the area of social competence with this population.

The literature regarding the classroom social behavior of students with learning disabilities is not as clear-cut. Few studies have assessed the social behaviors of students with learning disabilities in natural classroom settings (Bryan, 1974 a, b, & c, 1978; Cooke & Apolloni, 1976; Odom et al., 1982). The studies by Bryan (1974 a, b, & c, 1978) would suggest that students with learning disabilities engage in more negative social interactions with peers than do their nonhandicapped counterparts. There is a paucity of studies that have investigated differences in positive social behavior of children with learning disabilities although the reviews by La Greca and Mesibov (1979) and Gable et al. (1979) enumerate

a number of social skills in which students with learning disabilities are supposedly deficient. The study by Gresham and Reschly (1985), however, does indicate that students with learning disabilities have deficits in interpersonal behaviors, self-related behaviors, and task-related behaviors.

The weakest area of social competence concerning students with learning disabilities in terms of empirical evidence is that of social perception. The majority of studies in this area have been conducted in laboratory tasks as opposed to the natural classroom environment. Few empirical efforts have been made to corroborate the existence of social behaviors correlated with social perception deficits (Maheady & Maitland, 1982). Generally speaking, I am in agreement with the review in this area by La Greca & Mesibov (1981) who stated that "there does not appear to be much empirical support for the idea that LD children experience difficulties in social perception" (p. 413). As previously mentioned, the research in this area is primarily basic (as opposed to applied). In terms of practical considerations, the area of social perception has the least relevance for and applicability to remedial strategies in the classroom at this time.

Finally, there is no consistent evidence to show that students with learning disabilities have poorer *general* self-concepts than their nonhandicapped peers. However, there appears to be rather convincing support for the notion that students with learning disabilities have poorer *academic* self-concepts (Hiebert et al., 1982; Kifer, 1975). This is consistent with the motivational theories of effectance, self-efficacy, and learned helplessness which predict that students with learning disabilities would have feelings of ineffectance or helplessness in this area (Bandura, 1977a; Harter, 1978; Seligman, 1975; Thomas, 1979).

The following section will discuss the implications these findings have for public policy guidelines and curriculum planning for students with learning disabilities. This will be discussed in the context of the social acceptability of remediating social skill deficits of students with learning disabilities in the regular classroom.

Implications for Practice

There is enough evidence to suggest that students with learning disabilities are in need of specifically designed instructional programs to remediate social skill deficits to facilitate peer acceptance. A number of effective social skill training strategies exist (see reviews by Gresham, 1981b, Strain et al., 1984) to accomplish these goals. However, instructional procedures must be acceptable to teachers if they are to be implemented in the classroom (Witt & Elliott, 1985). Unfortunately, there are a number of behavior change strategies that are perceived as being unacceptable to teachers. Witt and Elliott (1985) have identified a number of factors that are related to a teacher's willingness to implement an instructional strategy in their classrooms. These include: (a) perceived effectiveness, (b) teacher time, (c) material resources, and (d) expertise required.

How acceptable would social skills training (SST) be to classroom teachers? Do classroom teachers consider school behaviors to be important skills to be taught in their classrooms?

The social acceptability of an intervention procedure forces one to ask the following questions: Do the ends justify the means? Do the participants, caregivers, and consumers consider the intervention procedure acceptable? *Acceptability* is a broad term which encompasses whether an intervention is appropriate for a given problem; whether it is fair, reasonable, or intrusive; and whether the intervention is consistent with conventional notions of what an intervention should be (Witt & Elliott, 1985). In short, acceptability consists of judgments from intervention consumers relating to whether or not they like (i.e., find acceptable) the intervention procedure.

How acceptable are social skills training (SST) strategies in the schools? To date, there has been no research to answer this question. Moreover, since teachers, school psychologists, guidance counselors, and school social workers would all conduct SST at any given time, the research needs to assess the differential acceptability of SST for these different school personnel.

Although there is no direct research regarding the acceptability of SST, past research on other intervention procedures indicates that acceptability is related to a host of factors such as time, complexity, risk to other children, risk to target children, and effectiveness (Witt & Elliott, 1985). There is no reason to believe that these same variables are not related in a similar manner to the acceptability of SST strategies.

A major problem facing the education of students with learning disabilities in regular classrooms is the design and implementation of procedures that are socially acceptable to regular education teachers. This is particularly true for social skill instruction procedures that may be novel and unacceptable to many teachers.

Needs and Recommendations

There are a number of needs and recommendations for future actions by researchers, practitioners, and public policy makers regarding the social competence and motivational characteristics of students with learning disabilities. For the sake of brevity and clarity, the most pressing needs and recommendations will be listed for research, practice, and public policy.

Research Needs

1. There is a clear need for much additional research into the causes and effects (both short-term and long-term) of social competence deficits of students with learning disabilities. The path analytic research by Morrison, Forness, and MacMillan (1983) is clearly exemplary in this respect and should be followed by similar research strategies that replicate, expand, and improve upon research in this area.

2. Although students with learning disabilities are approximately one standard deviation below the mean in peer acceptance, at least 16–17% of students with learning disabilities are average in terms of peer acceptance. Future research should address the extent to which students with learning disabilities who are average in peer acceptance differ in social competencies from poorly accepted students with learning disabilities. Presently, there is no research addressing this important topic.

3. Future research should validate the four-fold classification system of social skills deficits described earlier in this chapter (i.e., skill deficits, performance deficits, self-control skill deficits). For example, it is important to know the percentages of students with learning disabilities who fall into these four categories because each type of social skills problem would appear to merit somewhat different intervention approaches.

4. Consistent with the above recommendations, future research should be conducted using an aptitude X treatment interaction design to assess if different treatments interact with different social skills deficits depicted in Figure 2.

5. Past research with learning disabled populations has failed to consider developmental factors in assessing the social competence of students with learning disabilities. Much additional research is needed to determine the extent to which the social competence and motivational characteristics of students with learning disabilities changes from childhood through adolescence.

6. Future research is needed into the acceptability of social skills instruction of students with learning disabilities in regular classrooms. Preliminary data suggest that certain behavior change strategies may be viewed as unacceptable by many teachers because of lack of knowledge, lack of skill, time involved, and material resources required (Witt & Elliott, 1985). Much research needs to be done into the acceptability of social skills intervention by teachers and how to design more acceptable social skills interventions.

7. There are currently no norm-referenced measures of social skills for children and adolescents. Future research should focus upon developing normative data for children's social skills using a nationally representative sample. These measures should be developed for different informants such as teachers, parents, peers, and children themselves.

Practice Needs

1. There is clearly a need for teacher preparation institutions to implement social competence content in the curricula for both special and regular education teachers.

2. The assessment of learning disabled students' social competence (e.g., social skills, peer acceptance status, etc.) should be conducted as part of the preplacement evaluation. These assessment procedures can be used for classification decisions and for intervention purposes.

3. Social skills instructional procedures and social competence goals should be included in learning disabled students' individual education plans (IEPs) based upon the results of the preplacement evaluation in this area.

4. Social competence should be used as one basis for considering the appropriateness of "least restrictive environments" for students with learning disabilities.

5. Social competence should be used as one basis for evaluating the efficacy of resource room and regular classroom placements for students with learning disabilities.

6. Regular and special education teachers should be provided with inservice training in the areas of social competence and motivation as these relate to the student with learning disabilities.

7. Educational consultants, curriculum specialists, school psychologists, and other school personnel should pool their expertise in order to develop academic learning activities that impact upon social competence (e.g., cooperative learning).

8. The social behavior standards or expectations of regular classroom teachers should be assessed before students with learning disabilities are placed in their classrooms. This assessment will yield a profile of behaviors that the teacher considers critical to success in the classroom as well as a profile of behaviors that the teacher considers unacceptable. This information is crucial in identifying appropriate target behaviors for students with learning disabilities in regular classrooms and has the advantage of being ecologically valid. In addition, the technical assistance needs of regular classroom teachers should be assessed in order to provide them with the required technical and consultative assistance (see Walker & Rankin, 1983).

Policy Needs

1. There is a clear need for federal and state education agencies to fund research on the description, assessment, and instruction of social competence for students with learning disabilities. This funding should be for a broad base of activities in this area such as technical development of assessment procedures, curriculum development, instructional strategies, and program evaluation.

2. There is a need for federal and state education agencies to provide educational personnel with skills in the area of assessment, instruction, and evaluation of social skills and peer acceptance of students with learning disabilities.

3. Social skills training should be considered as a *pre-referral intervention* for potential learning disabled students. This may reduce the number of students inappropriately classified as learning disabled.

4. State education agencies should consider including social skill level, peer acceptance status, and motivational characteristics as part of the classification criteria for learning disability.

5. State and local education agencies should establish policies that redefine the roles of regular and special education personnel as the roles relate to the education of students with learning disabilities. In particular, both regular and special educators should be equally involved in promoting social competencies of students with learning disabilities through established social skills curricula and instructional procedures.

References

Ackerman, P., Elardo, P., & Dykman, F. (1979). A psychosocial study of hyperactive and learning disabled boys. *Journal of Abnormal Child Psychology, 7*, 91–99.

Asher, S. R., & Hymel, S. (1981). Children's social competence in peer relations: Sociometric and behavioral assessment. In J. D. Wine & M. D. Smye (Eds.), *Social Competence* (pp. 125–157). New York: Guilford Press.

Asher, S. R., Oden, S. L., & Gottman, J. M. (1977). Children's friendships in school settings. In L. G. Katz (Ed.), *Current topics in early childhood education* (Vol. 1). Norwood, N.J.: Ablex.

Asher, S. R., Singleton, L., Tinsley, B. R., & Hymel, S. A. (1979). A reliable sociometric measure for preschool children. *Developmental Psychology, 15*, 443–444.

Asher, S. R., & Taylor, A. R. (1981). The social outcomes of mainstreaming: Sociometric assessment and beyond. *Exceptional Education Quarterly, 1*, 13–30.

Bandura, A. (1977a). Self-efficacy: Toward a unifying theory of behavior change. *Psychological Review, 84*, 191–215.

Bandura, A. (1977b). *Social learning theory.* Englewood Cliffs, NJ: Prentice-Hall.

Bijou, S., & Baer, D. (1961). *Child development I: A systematic and empirical theory.* Englewood Cliffs, NJ: Prentice-Hall.

Boersma, F. J., & Chapman, J. W. (1978). Comparison of the Student's Perception of Ability Scale with the Piers Harris Self-Concept Scale. *Perceptual and Motor Skills, 47*, 827–832.

Boersma, F. J., & Chapman, J. W. (1979). Academic self-concept in elementary learning-disabled children: A study with the Student's Perception of Ability Scale. *Psychology in the Schools, 16*, 201–206.

Boersma, F., Chapman, J., & Maguire, T. (1978). *The Student's Perception of Ability Scale: An instrument for measuring academic self-concept in elementary school children.* Unpublished manuscript, University of Alberta, Canada.

Bornstein, M. R., Bellack, A. S., & Hersen, M. (1977). Social skills training for unassertive children: A multiple baseline analysis. *Journal of Applied Behavior Analysis, 10*, 183–195.

Brophy, J. (1981). Teacher praise: A functional analysis. *Review of Educational Research, 51*, 5–32.

Brophy, J., & Good, T. (1974). *Teacher-student relationships: Causes and consequences.* New York: Holt, Rinehart, & Winston.

Bruininks, V. L. (1978). Actual and perceived peer status of learning-disabled students in mainstream programs. *Journal of Special Education*, **12**, 51–58.

Bruno, R. M. (1981). Interpretation of pictorially presented situations by learning disabled and normal children. *Journal of Learning Disabilities*, **14**, 350–352.

Bryan, T. S. (1974a). An observational study of classroom behaviors of children with learning disabilities. *Journal of Learning Disabilities*, **7**, 25–34.

Bryan, T. S. (1974b). Peer popularity of learning disabled children. *Journal of Learning Disabilities*, **7**, 261–268.

Bryan, T. S. (1974c). Peer popularity of learning disabled children. *Journal of Learning Disabilities*, **7**, 621–625.

Bryan, T. S. (1976). Peer popularity of learning disabled children: A replication. *Journal of Learning Disabilities*, **9**, 307–311.

Bryan, T. S. (1977). Learning disabled children's comprehension of nonverbal communication. *Journal of Learning Disabilities*, **10**, 36–41.

Bryan, T. S. (1978). Social relationships and verbal interactions of learning disabled children. *Journal of Learning Disabilities*, **11**, 107–115.

Bryan, T. S. (1982). Social skills of learning disabled children and youth: An overview. *Learning Disability Quarterly*, **5**, 332–333.

Bryan, T. S., & Bryan, J. (1978). Social interactions of learning disabled children. *Learning Disability Quarterly*, **1**, 33–38.

Bryan, T. S., & Wheeler, R. (1972). Perception of children with learning disabilities: The eye of the observer. *Journal of Learning Disabilities*, **5**, 484–488.

Bryan, T. S., Wheeler, R., Felcan, J., Henek, T. (1976). "Come on dummy": An observational study of children's communications. *Journal of Learning Disabilities*, **9**, 53–61.

Camp, B. W., Blom, G. E., Herbert, F., & Van Doorninck, W. J. (1977). "Think Aloud": A program for developing self-control in young aggressive boys. *Journal of Abnormal Child Psychology*, **5**, 157–169.

Cartledge, G., & Milburn, J. (1978). The case for teaching social skills in the classroom: A review. *Review of Educational Research*, **48**, 133–156.

Cartledge, G., & Milburn, J. (Eds.). (1980). *Teaching social skills to children: Innovative approaches*. New York: Pergamon Press.

Chapman, J. W., & Boersma, F. J. (1979). Learning disabilities, locus of control, and mother attitudes. *Journal of Educational Psychology*, **71**, 250–258.

Combs, M. L., & Slaby, D. A. (1977). Social skills training with children. In B. B. Lahey & A. E. Kazdin (Eds.), *Advances in child clinical psychology* (Vol. 1), (pp. 161–203). New York: Plenum Press.

Cooke, T., & Apolloni, T. (1976). Developing positive emotional behaviors: A study in training and generalization effects. *Journal of Applied Behavior Analysis*, **9**, 67–78.

Coopersmith, S. (1967). *The antecedents of self-esteem*. San Francisco: W. H. Freeman.

Cromwell, R. L. (1963). A social learning approach to mental retardation. In N. R. Ellis (Ed.), *Handbook of mental deficiency* (pp. 215–247). New York: McGraw-Hill.

Deshler, D. D., Schumaker, J. B., Warner, M. M., Alley, G. R., & Clark, F. L. (1980). *An epidemiological study of learning disabled adolescents in secondary schools: Social status, peer relationships, activities in and out of school, and times uses*. (Research Report No. 19). Lawrence, KS:

The University of Kansas Institute for Research in Learning Disabilities.

Dickstein, E. B., & Warren, D. R. (1980). Roletaking deficits in learning disabled children. *Journal of Learning Disabilities*, **13**, 33–37.

Epstein, M., Cullinan, D., & Sabatino, D. (1977). State definitions of behavior disorders. *Journal of Special Education*, **11**, 417–425.

Erikson, E. (1950). *Childhood and society*. New York: Norton.

Fincham, F. (1979). Conservation and cognitive role-taking ability in learning disabled boys. *Journal of Learning Disabilities*, **12**, 33–37.

Foster, S. L., & Ritchey, W. L. (1979). Issues in the assessment of social competence in children. *Journal of Applied Behavior Analysis*, **12**, 625–638.

Gable, R. A., Strain, P. S., & Hendrickson, J. M. (1979). Strategies for improving the status and social behavior of learning disabled children. *Learning Disability Quarterly*, **2**, 33–39.

Gerber, P. J., & Zinkgraf, S. A. (1982). A comparative study of social-perceptual ability in learning disabled and nonhandicapped students. *Learning Disability Quarterly*, **5**, 374–378.

Good, T., & Brophy, J. (1978). *Looking into classrooms*. New York: Harper & Row.

Gottlieb, J. (1981). Mainstreaming: Fulfilling the promise. *American Journal of Mental Deficiency*, **86**, 115–126.

Gottman, J. M. (1977). The effects of a modeling film on social isolation in preschool children: A methodological investigation. *Journal of Abnormal Child Psychology*, **5**, 69–78.

Gottman, J. M., Gonso, J., & Rasmussen, B. (1975). Social interaction, social competence, and friendship in children. *Child Development*, **46**, 708–718.

Gottman, J. M., Gonso, J., & Schuler, P. (1976). Teaching social skills to isolated children. *Journal of Abnormal Child Psychology*, **4**, 179–197.

Green, K. D., Forehand, R., Beck, S. J., & Vosk, B. (1980). An assessment of the relationship among measures of children's social competence and children's academic achievement. *Child Development*, **51**, 1149–1156.

Greenspan, S. (1981). Social competence and handicapped individuals: Practical implications and a proposed model. *Advances in Special Education*, **3**, 41–82.

Greenwood, C., & Hops, H. (1982). Social skills deficits. In E. J. Mash & L. G. Terdal (Eds.), *Behavioral assessment of childhood disorders* (pp. 347–396). New York: The Guilford Press.

Greenwood, C., Todd, N., Hops, H., & Walker, H. (1982). Behavior change targets in the assessment and treatment of socially withdrawn preschool children. *Behavioral Assessment*, **4**, 237–297.

Greenwood, C. R., Walker, H. M., & Hops, H. (1977). Issues in social interaction/withdrawal assessment. *Exceptional Children*, **43**, 490–499.

Greenwood, C. R., Walker, H. M., Todd, N., & Hops, H. (1981). Normative and descriptive analysis of preschool free play social interaction rates. *Journal of Pediatric Psychology*, **6**, 343–367.

Gresham, F. M. (1981a). Social skills training with handicapped children: A review. *Review of Educational Research*, **51**, 139–176.

Gresham, F. M. (1981b). Validity of social skills measures for assessing social competence in low-status children: A multivariate investigation. *Developmental Psychology*, **17**, 390–398.

Gresham, F. M. (1982a). A model for the behavioral assessment of behavior disorders in children: Measurement considerations and practical application. *Journal of School Psychology*, **20**, 131–144.

Gresham, F. M. (1982b). Misguided mainstreaming: The case for social skills training with handicapped children. *Exceptional Children*, **48**, 422–433.

Gresham, F. M. (1982c). Social interactions as predictors of children's likeability and friendship patterns: A multiple regression analysis. *Journal of Behavioral Assessment*, **4**, 39–54.

Gresham, F. M. (1982d). Social skills instruction for exceptional children. *Theory Into Practice*, **20**, 129–133.

Gresham, F. M. (1983a). Social skills assessment as a component of mainstreaming placement decisions. *Exceptional Children*, **49**, 331–336.

Gresham, F. M. (1983b). Social validity in the assessment of children's social skills: Establishing standards for social competency. *Journal of Psychoeducational Assessment*, **1**, 297–307.

Gresham, F. M. (1984a). Social skills and self-efficacy for exceptional children. *Exceptional Children*, **51**, 253–261.

Gresham, F. M. (1984b). Social skills assessment and training. In J. Ysseldyke (Ed.), *School psychology: The state of the art* (pp. 57–80). Minneapolis, MN: National School Psychology Inservice Training Network.

Gresham, F. M. (1985a). Best practices in social skills training. In J. Grimes & A. Thomas (Eds.), *Best practices manual* (pp. 181–192). Cuyahoga Falls, OH: National Association of School Psychologist.

Gresham, F. M. (1985b). Strategies for enhancing the social outcomes of mainstreaming: A necessary ingredient for success. In J. Meisel (Ed.), *Mainstreamed handicapped children: Outcomes, controversies, and new directions* (pp. 193–218). Hillsdale, N.J.: Lawrence Erlbaum.

Gresham, F. M. (1986). Strategies for enhancing the social outcomes of mainstreaming: A necessary ingredient for success. In J. Meisel (Ed.), *The consequences of mainstreaming handicapped children* (pp. 193–218). Hillsdale, NJ: Lawrence Erlbaum.

Gresham, F. M., & Elliott, S. N. (1984). Advances in the assessment of children's social skills. *School Psychology Review*, **13**, 292–301.

Gresham, F. M., & Reschly, D. (1986). Social skills and peer acceptance differences between learning disabled and non-handicapped students. *Learning Disability Quarterly*, **9**, 23–32.

Grossman, H. J. (Ed.) (1983). *Classification in mental retardation*. Washington, D.C.: American Association on Mental Deficiency.

Hallahan, D., & Kauffman, J. (1976). *Introduction to learning disabilities: A psycho-behavioral approach*. Englewood Cliffs, N.J.: Prentice-Hall.

Haring, N. G. (Ed.) (1974). *Behavior of exceptional children: Introduction to special education*. Columbus, OH: Charles & Merrill.

Harter, S. (1978). Effectance motivation reconsidered: Toward a developmental model. *Human Development*, **21**, 34–64.

Harter, S. (1982). The Perceived Competence Scale for Children. *Child Development*, **53**, 87–97.

Hartup, W. W. (1979a). Peer relations and the growth of social competence. In M. W. Kent & J. E. Rolf (Eds.), *Primary prevention of psychopathology*: Vol. 3. Hanover, NH: University Press of New England.

Hartup, W. (1979b). The social worlds of childhood. *American Psychologist*, **34**, 944–950.

Hartup, W. W., Glazer, J. A., & Charlesworth, R. (1967). Peer reinforcement and sociometric status. *Child Development*, **38**, 1017–1024.

Hazel, S., Schumaker, J., Sherman, J., & Sheldon, J. (1982). Application of a group training program in social skills and problem solving skills to learning disabled and non-learning disabled youth. *Learning Disability Quarterly*, **5**, 398–408.

Hersh, R. H., & Walker, H. M. (1983). Great expectations: Making schools effective for all students. *Policy Studies Review*, **2**, 147–188.

Hiebert, B., Wong, B., & Hunter, M. (1982). Affective influences in learning disabled adolescents. *Learning Disability Quarterly*, **5**, 334–343.

Hops, H. (1983). Children's social competence and skill: Current research practices and future directions. *Behavior Therapy*, *14*, 3–18.

Hops, H., & Greenwood, C. R. (1981). Social skills deficits. In E. J. Mash & L. G. Terdal (Eds.), *Behavioral assessment of childhood disorders* (pp. 347–396). New York: The Guilford Press.

Johnson, D., & Myklebust, H. (1967). *Learning disabilities*. New York: Greene & Stratton.

Kantor, J. R. (1959). *Interbehavioral psychology*. Granville, OH: Principia Press.

Kazdin, A. E. (1979). Sociopsychological factors in psychopathology. In A. S. Bellack & M. Hersen (Eds.), *Research and practice in social skills training* (pp. 41–74). New York: Plenum Press.

Kifer, E. (1975). Relationship between academic achievement and personality characteristics: A quasi-longitudinal study. *American Education Research Journal*, **12**, 191–210.

Ladd, G. W. (1981). Effectiveness of a social learning method for enhancing children's social interaction and peer acceptance. *Child Development*, **52**, 171–178.

La Greca, A. M., & Mesibov, G. (1979). Social skills instruction with learning disabled children: Selecting skills and implementing training. *Journal of Clinical Child Psychology*, **8**, 234–241.

La Greca, A. M., & Mesibov, G. B. (1981). Facilitating interpersonal functioning with peers in learning disabled children. *Journal of Learning Disabilities*, **14**, 197–199, 238.

MacMillan, D. L., & Morrison, G. M. (1980). Correlates of social status among mildly handicapped learners in self-contained special classes. *Journal of Educational Psychology*, **72**, 437–444.

MacMillan, D. L., Morrison, G. M., & Silverstein, A. B. (1980). Convergent and discriminant validity of Project PRIME's Guess Who? *American Journal of Mental Deficiency*, **85**, 78–81.

Maheady, L., & Maitland, G. E. (1982). Assessing social perception abilities in learning disabled students. *Learning Disability Quarterly*, **5**, 363–370.

Marshall, H. R., & McCandless, B. R. (1957). A study in the prediction of social behavior of preschool children. *Child Development*, **28**, 149–159.

Maslow, A. H. (1968). *Toward a psychology of being*. New York: Van Nostrand Reinhold.

McFall, R. M. (1982). A review and reformulation of the concept of social skills. *Behavioral Assessment*, **4**, 1–33.

McGuire, J. M. (1973). Aggression and sociometric status with preschool children. *Sociometry*, **36**, 542–549.

Meichenbaum, D. (1977). *Cognitive behavior modification*. New York: Plenum Press.

Moore, S. G., & Updegraff, R. (1964). Sociometric status of preschool children related to age, sex, nurturance giving, and dependency. *Child Development*, **35**, 519–524.

Morrison, G. M. (1981a). Perspectives of social status of learning handicapped and nonhandicapped students. *American Journal of Mental Deficiency*, **86**, 243–251.

Morrison, G. M. (1981b). Sociometric measurement: Methodological consideration of its use with mildly learning handicapped and nonhandicapped children. *Journal of Educational Psychology*, **73**, 193–201.

Morrison, G. M., Forness, S. R., & MacMillan, D. L. (1983). Influences on the sociometric ratings of mildly handicapped children: A path analysis. *Journal of Educational Psychology*, **75**, 63–74.

Oden, S. L., & Asher, S. R. (1977). Coaching children in social skills for friendship making. *Child Development*, **48**, 496–506.

Odom, S., Jenkins, J., Speltz, M., & De Klyen, M. (1982). Promoting social integration of young children at risk for learning disabilities. *Learning Disability Quarterly*, **5**, 379–387.

Pearl, R., & Cosden, M. (1982). Sizing up a situation: LD children's understanding of social interactions. *Learning Disability Quarterly*, **5**, 371–373.

Piaget, J. (1952). *The origins of intelligence in children*. New York: International Universities Press.

Piers, E., & Harris, D. (1969). *The Piers-Harris Self-Concept Scale*. Nashville, TN: Counselor Recordings and Tests.

Reschly, D. J. (1981). Psychological testing in educational classification and placement. *American Psychologist*, **36**, 1094–1102.

Reschly, D. J., (1985). Mildly handicapped learning characteristics: Implications for classification, placement, and instruction. In M. Wang & M. Reynolds (Eds.) *Research of selected issues in the education of handicapped children*. Washington, DC: United States Department of Education.

Reschly, D. J., Gresham, F. M., & Graham-Clay, S. (1984). *Multifactored nonbiased assessment: Convergent and discriminant validity of social and cognitive measures with black and white regular and special education students*. Washington, D.C.: United States Department of Education, Grant No. G0081101156, Assistance Catalog No. CFDA: 84–023E.

Rogers-Warren, A., & Baer, D. (1976). Saying and doing: The verbal mediation of social behaviors. *Journal of Applied Behavior Analysis*, **9**, 335–354.

Rosenberg, B. S., & Gaier, E. L. (1977). The self-concept of the adolescent with learning disabilities. *Adolescence*, **12**, 490–497.

Sabatino, D. (Ed.) (1976). *Learning disabilities handbook: A technical guide to program development*. DeKalb, IL: Northern Illinois University Press.

Schumaker, J., & Ellis, E. (1982). Social skills training of LD adolescents: A generalization study. *Learning Disability Quarterly*, **5**, 409–414.

Schumaker, J. B., Hazel, J. S., Sherman, J. A., & Sheldon, J. (1982). Social skill performances of learning disabled, non-learning disabled, and delinquent adolescents. *Learning Disability Quarterly*, **5**, 388–397.

Seligman, M., (1975). *Helplessness: On depression, development, and death*. San Francisco: Freeman.

Silverman, R., & Zigmond, N. (1981). *Self-concept in learning-disabled adolescent*. Paper presented at the annual meeting of the American Educational Research Association, Los Angeles, CA.

Singleton, L. C., & Asher, S. R. (1977). Peer preferences and social interactions among third-grade children in an integrated school district. *Journal of Educational Psychology*, **69**, 330–336.

Siperstein, G., Bopp, M., & Bak, J. (1978). Social status of learning disabled children. *Journal of Learning Disabilities*, **11**, 98–102.

Skinner, B. F. (1953). *Science and human behavior*. New York: The Free Press.

Stark, P. A. (1980). *Development of a social skills role-play test for normal and learning disabled children*. Unpublished master's thesis. University of Miami.

Stephens, T. M. (1978). *Social skills in the classroom*. Columbus, OH: Cedars Press.

Strain, P. S. (1977). An experimental analysis of peer social initiations on the behavior of withdrawn preschool children: Some training and generalization effects. *Journal of Abnormal Child Psychology*, **5**, 445–455.

Strain, P. S., Cooke, R. P., & Apolloni, T. (1976). *Teaching exceptional children: Assessing and modifying social behavior*. New York: Academic Press.

Strain, P., & Fox, J. (1981). Peers as behavior change agents for withdrawn classmates. In A. Kazdin & B. Lahey (Eds.), *Advances in clinical child psychology* (vol. 4), (pp. 167–198). New York: Plenum Press.

Strain, P. S., Odom, S. L., & McConnell, S. (1984). Promoting social reciprocity of exceptional children: Identification, target behavior selection, and intervention. *Remedial and Special Education*, **5**, 21–28.

Stumme, V. S., Gresham, F. M., & Scott, N. A. (1982). Validity of social behavior assessment in discriminating emotionally disabled from nonhandicapped students. *Journal of Behavioral Assessment*, **4**, 327–342.

Stumme, V., Gresham, F. M., & Scott, N. (1983). Dimensions of children's classroom social behavior: A factor analytic investigation. *Journal of Behavioral Assessment*, **5**, 161–177.

Thomas, A. (1979). Learned helplessness and expectancy factors: Implications for research in learning disabilities. *Review of Educational Research*, **49**, 208–221.

Thompson, M. E., & Hartley, G. M. (1980). Self-concept in dyslexic children. *Academic Therapy*, **16**, 19–35.

Thorndike, E. L. (1927). Intelligence and its uses. *Harper's Magazine*, **140**, 227–235.

Wahler, R., & Fox, J. (1981). Setting events in applied behavior analysis: Toward a conceptual and methodological expansion. *Journal of Applied Behavior Analysis*, **14**, 327–338.

Wahler, R. & Graves, M. (1983). Setting events in social networks: Ally or enemy in child behavior therapy. *Behavior Therapy*, **14**, 19–36.

Walker, H., & Rankin, R. (1983). Assessing the behavioral expectations and demands of less restrictive settings. *School Psychology Review*, **12**, 274–284.

Weiner, B. A. (1979). A theory of motivation for some classroom experiences. *Journal of Educational Psychology*, **71**, 3–25.

White, R. W. (1959). Motivation reconsidered: The concept

of competence. *Psychological Review*, **66**, 287–333.

Wiig, E. H., & Harris, S. P. (1974). Perception and interpretation of nonverbally expressed emotions by adolescents with learning disabilities. *Perceptual and Motor Skills*, **38**, 239–245.

Witt, J. C., & Elliott, S. N. (1985). Acceptability of classroom intervention strategies. In T. R. Kratochwill (Ed.), *Advances in school psychology* (Vol. 4) (pp. 251–288). Hillsdale, NJ: Lawrence Erlbaum.

Wolf, M. M. (1978). Social validity: The case for subjective measurement or how applied behavior analysis is finding its heart. *Journal of Applied Behavior Analysis*, **11**, 203–214.

Wong, B. L., & Wong, R. (1980). Roletaking skills in normal achieving and learning disabled children. *Learning Disability Quarterly*, **3**, 11–18.

The Long-Term Consequences of Learning Disabilities

KENNETH A. KAVALE

University of Iowa

Abstract—A review of longitudinal research in learning
disabilities is presented. The review encompasses follow-up research reported for reading disorders, hyperactivity, and learning disabilities in order to enhance the
scope of the review. The literature on the natural history
of learning disabilities is chronicled by decade beginning
with the 1950s. Research reporting the nature and
characteristics of learning disabled samples over time,
the effects of intervention efforts, the social/emotional
adjustment, and the vocational status of identified learning disabled samples is synthesized. It was concluded
that learning disabilities are associated with a high risk
of lasting deficits especially the feeling that reading and
spelling are difficult, the high probability of repeating
one or more grades in school, and the possibility of
behavior problems, particularly low self-esteem.
Beyond these few generalizations, outcomes appear to
depend upon the nature and extent of the cognitive and
behavioral manifestations of the learning disability, the
intellectual level, and, to some extent, socioeconomic
status. Methodological concerns in follow-up research
are discussed as well as recommendations for research,
practice, and policy.

Introduction

When faced with a diagnosis of learning disability for
their child, parents frequently ask, "What will happen
to him (or her)?" The question is reasonable; our
responses usually are not. Although information can be
provided about the short-term (e.g., placement options,
remedial methods, auxiliary services, and the like), it is
difficult to provide adequate responses to questions
about the long-term consequences of learning disability.
The situation reflects the poor state of knowledge about
the outcome of the condition generally, and the factors
to consider in making a prediction (prognosis) for an
individual child. These concerns over the natural history
of learning disability are of more than theoretical interest since they reflect directly both upon the validity and
effectivness of the treatment programs. Furthermore,
examination of the natural history of learning disability

provides insight into whether or not observed changes
are due to treatment effects or maturation. Additionally, long term assessments, in addition to providing
information about treatment efficacy, also provide
insights into the extent to which the consequences of
learning disability may be attenuated or accentuated by
associated factors. The primary empirical means for
studying the natural history of learning disability is the
long-term follow-up study. Three types of information
may be obtained from follow-up studies: (a) perspective
over the duration of learning disability that reveals the
variations in its forms, the conditions out of which it
arises, and its variations over time; (2) assistance in evaluating the effectiveness of treatment approaches in
order to develop techniques for reducing learning disabilities; and (3) developing and testing hypotheses
about the relation of particular variables for adult status
(Robins, 1979).

Problems in Longitudinal Research on Learning Disabilities

While the goals stated above are important for understanding the nature of learning disability, it is surprising
that the natural history of the disorder has been so
poorly described. The diagnostic entity that emerged
not much over two decades ago has now become the
category containing by far the most children receiving
special education. More than two in five handicapped
children are considered to have learning disabilities
(USOE, 1984) which is more than 4% of all school-age
children. The number of children with learning disabilities has increased more than 100% since federal legislation (PL 94–142) mandating special education first
took effect. This rapid growth has been a source of consternation since learning disability is the category most
open to vague diagnostic interpretation and most likely
to contain children who do not require special services.
The problems are, at least, partially attributable to
inconsistencies surrounding definition, etiology and
treatment (see Kavale & Forness, 1985 for a discussion
of these issues), but also due to the lack of information

303

about the natural history of learning disability. Although the need for follow-up research has long been acknowledged (Bateman, 1966) and, recently, there is increased emphasis on learning disability at the secondary level (Deshler, 1978), a significant gap in understanding the long-term consequences (i.e., what happens to learning disabled children when they reach adulthood) of learning disability remains (Cronin & Gerber, 1982).

Long-term follow-up studies of individuals with learning disabilities do exist but come from diverse sources that differ markedly in their purposes, methodologies, and populations. For example, Robins (1977, 1979) discussed the common methodological problems found in follow-up studies. Conflicting findings appear to be the result of:

1. Failure to define precisely the sample included in the study;

2. Failure to provide a control group for legitimate comparisons;

3. Failure to control for attrition;

4. Failure to provide sufficient data in original assessment which prevents systematic comparison;

5. Failure to provide consistent data across subjects by relying on whatever data are available;

6. Failure to provide equivalent data at different assessment points;

7. Failure to predict adult outcome for individual children rather than a group of children.

The diversity and methodological difficulties make it difficult to arrive at an integrated picture of outcomes, and leads to widely variant claims about the ultimate fate of the child with learning disabilities including the possibility of (1) persistent academic problems, (2) dropping out of school, (3) developing emotional problems, (4) becoming delinquent, and (5) being in lower socioeconomic occupations. Yet, these findings have all been challenged; there exists no consensus regarding the long-term consequences of learning disability. Many of the findings are marked by enough equivocation to render them tentative, at best.

The many and varied findings appear to be related to the nature of longitudinal research. The diversity seems to be related to methodological variables, and the difficult pragmatic demands in conducting long-term studies. Because of the relative recency of the learning disability category, its course is still being chronicled. This is usually accomplished first by case histories. Although interesting, case studies usually lack the rigor necessary to generalize findings. Individual case studies are typically followed by more systematic research designs found in either retrospective studies or, the less common, prospective study. The latter two designs can be differentiated by the time at which the child becomes a subject. Retrospective studies diagnose children as learning disabled after the fact, and then assess these children and (usually) a control group to determine how the learning disabled group differs; while prospective

designs identify learning disabled subjects in early childhood and study subsequent behaviors as they occur. Again, a control group is usually used and may be either a comparison group of normal children or the learning disabled sample as their own control, comparing subsequent status with baseline data. Prospective studies are difficult to design and to implement so their numbers are small. Retrospective studies are more numerous but, when compared to prospective designs, possess a variety of problems that limit interpretation.

Schaie (1965) discussed problems inherent in longitudinal designs, especially retrospective studies. Longitudinal studies can include three kinds of independent variables: cohort (year of birth), chronological age, and date of measurement. The major research designs used in follow-up research allow the investigator to study only two of the three independent variables while the third always remains as a confounding factor. For example, a cross-sectional study which investigates whether there are differences between persons of different ages, confounds, as a consequence, chronological age and time of birth. Although it is assumed that measures on 5-year-olds born in 1960 are similar to measures on those born in 1980, many variables (e.g., height, weight) show generational changes as well as the influence of social forces.

The most typical longitudinal approach (retrospective study) involves another type of confounding: It is impossible to disentangle age changes and time of measurement. Is the child with learning disabilities different because he or she is 10 years older or because the environment has changed? With the typical use of repeated measures in follow-up studies, unequal carryover effects may become a source of confounding. Practice effects represent a subclass of carryover effects that confound any design aimed at discovering age, cohort, or time differences.

In sum, virtually all follow-up studies suffer from statistical inelegance with the most typical, retrospective studies, being especially suspect, not only because of sample bias and poor record keeping but also because of both cohort and time confounding. Retrospective studies suffer from additional disadvantages. In addition to problems of inconsistent and non-equivalent data, the reliability of data, especially from retrospective reports, is suspect because of the tendency either to forget selectively or to fake good. Rosenthal (1963), in a study investigating the accuracy of memories regarding relations with parents as well as adolescent social and emotional characteristics in adults aged 38–40, found the memories to be inaccurate generally, and suggested caution in using retrospective reports to relate adult characteristics to adolescent status.

Another disadvantage is the difficulty in establishing temporal relationships in retrospective studies. For example, learning disability is often marked by academic and social/emotional problems. But which comes first? Does the presence of social/emotional problems stemming from impaired relationships with parents, siblings, or peers make the child spend so much time and energy in seeking resolution of conflicts that academic pursuits become secondary and underachievement is the result? Or does the presence of academic problems cause the child so much stress and frustration that the social/emotional difficulties are a reaction to underachievement and are secondary to learning disability? It is often impossible in retrospective studies to establish time sequence clearly.

Perhaps the major disadvantage of retrospective studies surrounds the control group. Even when a control group is included, it is most often constituted after the fact, which makes it difficult to study one suspected cause while holding other variables constant. If a control group is chosen on the basis of either adolescent or adult outcome (e.g., nonhandicapped to contrast with learning disabled), there will most probably be many differences found in their childhoods. For instance, the learning disabled group may be found to have more birth complications, more environmental disadvantages, and more poor quality instruction. But there is no way to differentiate the relative influence of these three variables; it is impossible to tell which of the variables, if any, has contributed to the adolescent or adult outcome, and which is merely a corollary of the important variable among the three or of some other variables. If childhood is taken as the point of departure rather than adolescence or adulthood, then it is possible to provide control groups that test these variables independently. Cases, for example, with reported birth complications and less than optimal environments can be contrasted with cases possessing a history of birth complications but favorable environmental circumstances, to see which produce the larger proportion of learning disabilities. It will then be possible to know whether environmental factors appear to contribute to learning disability independently of the presence or absence of birth complications. The advantage here would be a learning disabled group characterized by the same attributes identified at the same time. The control group would then consist of subjects selected at the same time but without the attributes of the learning disabled group. It would then be possible to assess the changes in learning disabilities that occur over time. Thus, ideally all subjects are to be selected at the same time with the same set of attributes. Unfortunately, this type of methodological control is difficult to achieve.

Thus, the contradictory findings and tentative conclusions appear to be the consequences of differences in research methodologies, sample characteristics, outcome assessments, and intervening experience. These marked differences suggest that long-term follow-up research is marked by considerable method variance that masks much of the trait variance (i.e., learning disability) and leads to a variety of interpretations. The considerable methodological variance suggests that study outcomes need to be evaluated in the context of methodological issues. Despite the methodological difficulties, longitudinal research does possess advantages for the learning disability field. The primary advantage of follow-up research is that it provides information about learning disability over the long term. Alternative approaches (e.g., cross-sectional designs) cannot offer the same advantage particularly in a domain like learning disability where associated symptoms tend to change with age. Thus, for a perspective of the consequences of learning disability over time, longitudinal designs even with their problems can offer valuable information.

The Scope of Longitudinal Research in Learning Disabilities

Because the use of the diagnostic classification of learning disability is relatively new, follow-up studies limited to such children are few in number. Fortunately, follow-up research is available for other conditions that represent correlative conditions of learning disability and can be assumed to fall under the learning disability rubric. Consequently, literature dealing with reading disability (RD), minimal brain dysfunction (MBD), hyperactivity (HA), and attention deficit disorder syndrome (ADD) were included. The problems in defining learning disability as well as the heterogeneous nature of learning disability samples make it difficult to differentiate clearly these other diagnoses. Any arguments about the inclusion of any of these groups are largely semantic and would unnecessarily restrict the boundaries of the problem. The advantage is found in the more comprehensive picture provided about the long-term consequences imposed by disability centering around the problem of imparied school performance. Until the issue of learning disability definition is resolved, the boundaries of the disability will be clouded enough to warrant inclusion of correlative difficulties that at least circumscribe what is normally viewed as learning disability.

The purpose of this chapter then is to summarize findings of studies which have chronicled subsequent experiences of children who have been labeled learning disabled. To accomplish this purpose, the literature both published and unpublished was surveyed for studies dealing with the long-term consequences of learning disability (or the closely allied problems). The sources of studies included previous reviews in the areas, indexes and abstracts, and computerized literature search. The search located 254 studies.

Longitudinal Research in Reading Disability
The 1950s

Among the associated conditions of learning disability, reading disability (RD) possesses a sizable follow-up literature with the 1950s revealing the publication of a number of follow-up studies in RD. Many of these reports were from reading clinics and provided positive findings. For example, Birch (1949, 1950) reported that 64 children attending a clinic for 6 months made an average of 1.9 years of progress in reading: about four times the expected rate. Similarly, Bond and Fay (1950) followed 23 pupils and found that they gained five times as much as their previous achievement indicated they could be expected to gain. Longitudinal reports (Cosper & Kephart, 1955; Friedman, 1958; Mouly & Grant, 1956; Tufvander & Zintz, 1957; Valentine, 1951) of the effects of remedial treatment all suggested substantial improvement in reading disabled subjects which exceeded expectations.

These optimistic reports must be viewed with skepticism because of the absence of proper experimental design and analysis. In many cases there was a failure to discriminate genuine improvement in reading from a number of spurious effects. For example, it is difficult to attribute improvement to the remedial program in the Tufvander and Zintz (1957) study. Of the 82 cases studied, 40 were only provided with diagnostic testing and no remedial program but, of the 21 found to be making better than normal progress, 12 were from the tested only group. Conversely, in the 21 instances of less than normal progress, 14 were from the group receiving remedial instruction. Similarly, reading gains were not found uniformly across reading skills. Cosper and Kephart (1955), for example, found gains restricted to reading speed with no differences reported for recall of details, vocabulary, or comprehension. Additionally, a majority of these studies did not include a comparison (control) group or control for practice effects and statistical regression. Because Bond and Fay (1950), for example, used the same pre- and post-measure over a relatively short follow-up (6 months), practice effects are likely to account for a proportion of gain.

To overcome many of these difficulties, Curr and Gourlay (1953) conducted a controlled experiment with 128 children (mean chronological age 8.7) who were given remedial treatment and compared to a matched control group receiving no intervention. Results showed higher mean gains in reading age for the experimental group but only on one measure. But these results were offset by the negligible difference between groups on other reading measures. This suggests that remedial treatment appears to develop only isolated skills that do not transfer across reading measures but are restricted to measures similar in scope and content to the remedial program. Thus, although gains were impressive in isolation, they were not so in comparison with the gains of the control group particularly if practice and regression effects are taken into account. These findings were challenged (Birch, 1953; Kellmer-Pringle, 1953) making any conclusion problematic since it is difficult to separate real effects from design artifacts. The debate over the effects of treatment focused on design considerations and left unanswered the primary question: What are the long-term consequences of reading disability.

A majority of the studies conducted during the 1950s had relatively short follow-up periods which precluded

implications about the long-term (i.e., 3 or more years). The decade closed however, with a widely cited retrospective study by Hermann (1959) who followed 72 subjects over about a 15 year period to an average age of 24 years. A majority read at a level equivalent to about the sixth grade with a small percentage reading well ($n=10$). About one-third read poorly while another one-third read slowly and hesitantly but could manage a newspaper. Spelling and writing abilities were also generally poor for most which accounted for the overrepresentation of unskilled workers in the group. The lack of a control group tempers any conclusion but Hermann (1959) suggested that "complete resolution of the symptoms of congenital word blindness is rare" (p. 180).

This represents the most reasonable conclusion to be drawn from the studies conducted during the 1950s. Although lacking the design rigor for drawing firm conclusions, the studies suggested that, while reading disability responds to treatment and reading gains are possible, RD tended to be a persistent problem. Thus, the exact course of RD needed explication in terms of the subject variables most important and their interaction with treatment variables.

The 1960s

During the 1960s, the outcome of reading disability continued to be studied and most studies began to focus on the long-term consequences. For example, Curr and Gourlay (1960) followed their original 1953 group and found nonsignificant differences between remedial and control groups; the remedial subjects failed to maintain the advantages shown soon after (i.e., short-term) remedial teaching. With short-term effectiveness of remediation established, Adams (1960) studied "achievers" (i.e., subjects acquiring independent word attack). From a total public school remedial population of 1,374, 555 "achievers" were studied over 16 years. Among the 555 cases, 123 had graduated from high school, 104 enrolled in but did not finish high school, 102 were still in high school, and 59 were still in grade school (90 did not finish grade school and 77 did not finish high school in the area). These findings showed that about 70% of students who benefited from clinic remediation graduated from grade school while only 20% graduated from high school. Post-secondary education appeared to be only a remote possibility.

The Adams (1960) study reaffirmed the persistent nature of reading disability and less than optimistic prognosis. But it was still possible to find follow-up studies with more optimistic findings. In a 10-year follow-up of 44 pupils from a university clinic, Robinson and Smith (1962) found that all but three had completed high school. In fact, 11 were still enrolled in college, 3 had acquired an M.A. degree, and 2 were in Ph.D. programs. Only one subject was unemployed while the remainder were in a variety of professional or skilled occupations. Based on these findings, it was concluded that "able students who are retarded in reading can be rehabilitated educationally so as to fulfill their occupational ambitions" (Robinson & Smith, 1962, p. 25).

Similar optimism can be found in other reports. For example, Preston and Yarington (1967) followed 50 subjects for 8 years to an average age of 22 years. Using national averages for comparison, it was found that enrollment in and graduation from high school was no different from the general population. A comparable proportion gained admission to college. Their rates of employment in professional and skilled positions were no different from the general population and unemployment rates were no higher. Although this progress was slower. than normal, it was concluded that "retarded readers after a span of eight years fulfill educational and vocational roles comparable to those fulfilled by their age peers in the general population" (Preston & Yarington, 1967, p. 127). Even more optimistic was Rawson's (1968) report on 56 dyslexic boys followed for 23 years. All subjects pursued education beyond high school and 48 had earned college degrees. Forty-six subjects were occupationally in the two highest socioeconomic classes with the remainder in better than average occupations. These findings led to the conclusion that "dyslexic boys need not be considered poor risks for academic and occupational pursuits" (Rawson, 1968, p. 110).

Reconciliation of findings. How can these divergent findings be reconciled? The answer can be partially found in examining the samples selected. The recognition of sample variability is important; for example, Langman and Rabinovitch (1968) found considerable variability in reading performance in 96 pupils studied from first- to sixth-grade. Furthermore, reading success was more predictive than reading failure in the first-grade since 16 of 26 poor readers attained status in the average range after one or more years. It was concluded that maturation and environment work together to make every child uniquely different in reading performance.

There also appears to be some relationship with intelligence. For example, Robinson and Smith's (1962) sample had an average IQ of 120 while Rawson's (1968) sample had an average IQ of 131. In an analysis of their findings of the effect of remedial instruction (Bluestein, 1967; Cashdan & Pumfrey, 1969; Collins, 1961; Lovell, Bryne, & Richardson, 1963; Lytton, 1967), a positive correlation (average $r=0.52$) was found between IQ and remedial success. This suggests that intellectual ability is a significant factor in the outcome of remedial instruction and in the long-term outcome of reading disability. Without control for intellectual differences, it is difficult to differentiate the effects of remedial instruction and the effects of IQ on subsequent performance.

Besides the effects of intelligence, it is also important to determine the severity of the reading difficulties. The sample selected by Robinson and Smith (1982) averaged only somewhat more than one year of reading retardation. This sample was thus not severely disabled and

would fail to meet the required 2-year discrepancy level for learning disability. Yule (1973) demonstrated the importance of selection criteria by showing that, although prognosis for any reading disability is relatively poor, children with specific reading disability (i.e., reading underachievement is relation to chronological and mental age) have a poorer prognosis than backward readers (i.e., bottom end of reaching achievement continuum). Lloyd (1969) confirmed this differentiation in a study of 3,651 sixth-grade students who were defined on the basis of aptitude-achievement discrepancy as either under-, average-, or overachievers. Findings indicated that underachievers were significantly lower in reading performance in sixth-grade as well as over the subsequent middle and secondary school grades. Underachievers were consistently lower in grade point averages and standardized tests but no significant behavioral differences were noted.

Follow-up of remedial efforts. The nature of the remedial program may also affect outcomes for the selected samples. Niles (1966) studied the effects of three types of beginning reading programs on the reading achievement of 378 first-graders. Although no differences in second-grade reading achievement were found for average pupils, significant differences were found in the performance of 116 low achieving pupils who were found to favor a readiness program followed by reading trade books over a basal program. Although programmatic differences may be found, the actual number and type appear not to make a difference. While Lytton (1961) found the optimal situation to be frequent lessons in small groups, Cashdan and Pumfrey (1969) found no difference in a group receiving remedial efforts twice weekly as opposed to a group being given remedial treatment only once weekly over 7 months. In a later study, Lytton (1967) found that children followed up in the secondary school lost much more of their gains than those followed up in the primary school. It was postulated that the decreased emphasis on basic skills in the secondary school contributed to the relative decline in attainments.

Among the first studies which attempted to overcome many of the methodological difficulties found previously was that of Silver and Hagin (1964) who studied 24 children 10–12 years after receiving remedial instruction. At initial contact, the reading disabled children were subdivided into three groups: developmental, organic, and those with no perceptual or organic signs. A matched control group was established based on age, sex, and IQ. The disabled group (21 males and 3 females) had a median age of 19 at follow-up while the control group (8 males and 3 females) had a median age of 20 years. Of the 24 in the RD group, 15 (62%) were considered to have achieved reading proficiency. Most of this achieving group belonged to the developmental subgroup while the inadequate adult readers tended to come from the organic subgroup and retained a large proportion of perceptual problems. Later, Silver and Hagin (1966) reported that the perceptual difficulties that separated the control group from the RD group tended to persist and to distinguish the groups. In conclusion, Silver and Hagin (1964) suggested that "specific reading disability is a long-term problem in the life of an individual, the signs of which can be detected despite adequate educational, vocational, and social functioning" (p. 101). Thus, problems associated with reading disability were found to make a significant contribution and result in long-term negative consequences.

The finding of long-term negative consequences for reading disability, even in light of short-term gain, has been substantiated. Collins (1961) found that, three months after treatment, significant gains were still registered by the treated group (in word recognition but not comprehension). Retesting at 15 and 27 months later, however, showed no differences between groups on either occasion but both treated and control groups made similar progress toward reading attainment. Thus, treatment effects were not permanent and, over the long-term, treated children made the same progress as randomly selected controls. The progress seems to be primarily a function of maturation which was confirmed in several studies (Lovell, et al., 1963; Lovell, Johnson, & Platts, 1962). In the 1962 study, it was found that almost 60% of subjects receiving remedial treatment had attained a reading age of at least 9 years (about 3 years after having a reading age of approximately 6) at follow-up. But reading disability had serious implications on the children's educational future since not one was able to pursue a strict academic course of study. In the 1963 report, a controlled comparison indicated that after almost 4 years, no differences in mean reading ages were found between those attending remedial clinics and those who did not. It was concluded that regardless of the remedial arrangements, the long-term results appear to be the same: that is, the persistence of reading disability with negative implications for future status.

The persistence of reading disability may be partially associated with the general failure to improve attitudes towards reading. Balow and Blomquist (1965) assessed 32 reading clinic boys in young adulthood 10–15 years later. The group showed an average adult reading level of approximately 10th grade as compared to their second-grade level at the clinic. Of the 32, 27 graduated from high school while 23 had some post-high school education. Twelve subjects were in skilled jobs while 10 were in unskilled jobs (no information was available on the remaining 10). Through interviews, it was determined that most did not like school and felt that poor reading interfered with academic pursuits. A majority believed that the remedial efforts were not useful and, in general, the 32 subjects displayed a negative and slightly defeatist attitude about life. Collins (1961) supported this view by finding that remedial efforts had less effect on attitudes towards reading than on actual reading ability. Thus, it appears that long-term success is predicated on getting the reading disabled child to approach

the reading situation in a more positive way. Kellmer-Pringle (1961) made a distinction between "remedial education" and "coaching." Remedial education needs to involve a highly structured intervention program plus "emotional re-education" which focuses on attitude change and emotional re-adjustment. Coaching involves only more individual attention without programmatic changes or attention to reading attitudes. It was suggested that often the period of remedial intervention, while affecting reading performance, is too short for positively affecting attitudes, which requires an extended intervention period. The importance of attitudes particularly with respect to motivation was demonstrated by Crandall and Battle (1967) in a follow-up of 74 children over 27 years. The adult outcomes for this groups were positively related to academic and intellectual achievement effort and reveal the importance of acknowledging the influence of behavioral variables that mediate between intervention and outcomes.

The issue of subject characteristics was addressed in several studies which demonstrated how this variable is related to outcomes. Carter (1964) assessed 36 males, 19 years or older, who had attended a reading clinic while in either the third-, fourth-, fifth-, or sixth-grade. All were considered severely reading disabled and had been out of school for at least one year. Of the 36, 12 scored at or above grade level on a reading test administered just prior to high school entrance (Group A). The remaining boys ($n=24$) were reading one or more grade levels below expectation (mean IQ=105) upon entry to high school (Group B), despite similar remedial efforts. Group A subjects revealed a greater interest in and positive attitude toward reading. They also revealed higher levels of educational attainment and tended to continue their education with some ($n=5$) attending college. Group B, on the other hand, had a significantly greater number of dropouts and, when remaining in school, tended to pursue a less demanding curriculum (e.g., vocational rather than college preparatory). Subjects in Group A expressed higher vocational aspirations which were reflected in their greater numbers in skilled jobs and higher average annual incomes. A majority of Group B were found in unskilled occupations with several ($n=4$) being unemployed. An 11-item social adjustment scale revealed better social adjustment for Group A subjects. These findings point to the conclusion that better long-term results are found in those subjects who no longer manifest RD when entering high school. This implication is in accord with the suggestion that there may be an optimum age level (approximately 8–11 years of age) for providing remedial instruction to achieve maximum results (Bluestein, 1967; Chansky, 1963; Krippner, 1963; Lovell et al., 1962).

Howden (1967) followed 53 subjects for 19 years into their late 20s or early 30s. The sample was divided into three groups. The first ($n=9$) were those whose reading scores in the fifth or sixth grade were at least one standard deviation (1SD) above the grade mean and were designated "good readers." The second group ($n=22$)

were termed "average readers" and consisted of those whose reading performance closely approximated the grade mean. The third group (*n*=22) consisted of "poor readers" whose reading scores were at least 1*SD* below the class mean. At follow-up, poor readers performed less well than the other groups on all subtests of the *Gates Reading Survey*. Survey data on adult reading behavior showed that poor readers enjoyed reading less, and did not engage in as much reading activity as the other groups. The poor reading group accumulated less formal education which was reflected in their generally poor socioeconomic status. Although the outcome for poor readers was less favorable, definitive conclusions were confounded by the fact that the group differed on IQ with poor groups averaging 88 while the two other groups averaged 107.

Consequently, although achievement differences are an important outcome factor, they were related to intellectual differences which tend to confound findings unless the effects of IQ are controlled. With IQ not controlled, it is possible, for example, to reach a conclusion like Rawson (1968) who stated, "Given average or better intelligence . . . differences in educational and vocational achievement by adulthood on the part of non-dyslexic boys and dyslexic boys so diagnosed between the ages of six and twelve will not be greater than could be explained by chance alone" (p. 81). Was it the effect of intelligence or the remedial program which was responsible for the finding of no difference between groups? It is necessary to separate the effects of intelligence and the effects of reading disability independent of each other to determine their influence on outcomes. In the case of Howden's (1967) study, was it RD or lowered IQ that was responsible for the outcomes? Better control of these factors is required for firm conclusions, especially given the relationship between IQ and remedial success.

Hardy (1968a) followed 40 remedial cases seen between 1957 and 1961 whose average age was 11 years at referral and average IQ was 104. The RD group received individual instruction twice weekly which ranged from 3 to 50 months with an average of 10 months. Follow-up time averaged 6 years with subjects averaging 19 years old at follow-up. Although reading performance showed significant improvement at follow-up (compared to assessments at both time of referral and at the termination of remediation), 60% of subjects were still retarded in reading by an average of 20 months. In comparison, 40% were retarded by 20 months or more at referral while 23% were retarded at this level at the end of remediation. Clearly, reading disability is a persistent and pervasive problem.

With respect to specific improvement, it was found that gains in comprehension were related positively to IQ level. On the other hand, negative relationships were found between both chronological age and number of grades repeated, and reading gains. The duration

between end of remediation and follow-up was positively related to oral reading gains, suggesting the significant role of maturation on improvement. At follow-up, only 43% of subjects claimed that they enjoyed reading or read for pleasure. With respect to occupational status, 55% of subjects were classified as unskilled or semiskilled. Nevertheless, 65% reported being satisfied with their jobs and 95% reported satisfactory relationships with co-workers. Only two subjects were unemployed. Hardy (1968b) concluded that "although most severely disabled readers retain their difficulties in reading . . . they are able to make adequate academic adjustments if appropriate educational programs are provided in school" (p. 227).

These findings support clearly the persistent nature of reading disability. There is also an indication that, although reading gains are possible, the levels of improvement were not equal either to individual subjects' expected grade level gains or to gains made by pupils at comparable grade levels. Hardy (1970) also showed differences between subjects who finished school and those who were still in school at follow-up. The educational attainments of those who finished school were generally poor while subjects remaining in school were judged as making satisfactory academic progress. Thus, significant gains were typically found only during the period of remedial training with subjects tending not to maintain their improvement after termination of the remedial program (Buerger, 1968; Cashdan & Pumfrey, 1969; Lytton, 1967). For example, Lovell et al. (1962, 1963) found a significant relationship between progress made and length of time elapsed since remedial teaching ended. An increase in elapsed time was associated with decreased progress in reading. These findings led Silberberg and Silberberg (1969) to conclude that the efficacy of remedial reading was a "myth." Although there is typically improvement, sometimes quite large, at the end of remedial efforts, "this improvement quickly 'washed out' and the children seem to sink to a level commensurate with their preremedial experience" (p. 211).

In a study specifically designed to assess both the immediate effect of remedial instruction and the continued growth of pupils after termination of intensive remediation, Balow (1965) found that continued growth was dependent upon continued attention to the problem. While subjects given remedial assistance surpassed the normal growth rate of normal pupils by some five times, the cessation of supportive intervention was accompanied by no further growth for the subjects. Thus, severe reading disability was not corrected by short-term intensive remediation, even though it is ameliorated by such efforts. But there is evidence (Hillman & Snowdon, 1960) to suggest the possibility of an optimum length of remediation. For example, Bluestein (1968) found that most pupils appeared to have made maximum progress by the end of 2 years of remediation. Thus, RD is a chronic condition needing long-term treatment (Buerger, 1968). What is needed after an intensive remedial period (of about 2 years) is provision for supportive reading assistance which Balow (1965) found necessary to maintain the rate of growth in reading at approximately 75% of the normal rate (i.e., one month growth in reading skill for one month of instruction).

Besides intelligence, another significant variable appears to be socioeconomic status (SES). The studies (Rawson, 1968; Robinson & Smith, 1962) having better than average IQ subjects also revealed that these subjects came from a higher SES level. This factor may also explain partially the superior outcomes reported in these studies. The SES variable also appears to be related to the initial probability of developing reading disability. In an epidemiological study, Eisenberg (1966) found that 28% of public school children in sixth-grade in an urban system were reading 2 or more years below expectation. In comparison, only 3% of children in a suburban school system and no children in private schools in the area displayed a reading deficit of 2 or more years. It was concluded that sociopsychological factors were major contributors to reading disability. Thus, SES is related both to initial potential for RD and to academic prognosis. For example, although drawing samples from the same population, the Balow and Blomquist (1965) study sample was mostly middle SES and reported more favorable outcomes than the Balow (1965) study which included mostly lower SES subjects. Generally, studies including middle SES children (Carter, 1964; Hardy, 1968a; Howden, 1967, Preston & Yarington, 1967; Silver & Hagin, 1964) suggested that reading disability in elementary school will tend to be a persistent problem.

Conclusions. The decade of the 1960s found further development and insight from longitudinal research. The follow-up research suggested the following:

1. Reading problems tend to be persistent and represent chronic disabilities.

2. Even when reading gains were realized, subjects tended to still be retarded in reading even for individual expectations.

3. The more favorable the outcome, the more favorable were occupational status and social adjustment.

4. Besides extensive remedial efforts, reading problems require long-term supportive treatment.

5. Outcomes appear to be related to intelligence and to socioeconomic status.

6. Remedial programs should focus on reading skills and attitude changes in order to develop more positive feelings about reading.

7. The ages between 8 and 11 years appear to be the optimal time for remedial intervention.

8. Remedial programs lasting for approximately 2 years appear to provide maximum benefits.

These conclusions, however, must be approached with caution because, although representing methodological improvements, these follow-up studies were still marked by ambiguities and difficulties that temper any interpretations. The problems result from methodological weaknesses that reduce the merits of the individual studies. The studies from the 1960s were generally flawed on one or more methodological variables. For example, most studies failed to provide adequate and objective criteria for defining reading disability. Only four studies (Balow & Blomquist, 1965; Howden, 1967; Preston & Yarington, 1967; Rawson, 1968) provided at least some attempt at systematic definitional criteria. Compounding the problem of definitional criteria was the problem related to the source of samples. A majority of the studies drew their samples from a clinic population which tends to be biased by the nature and philosophy of the clinic. More desirable would be a sample drawn from a large school population, but only Howden (1967) sampled in this manner. Sample size is also important because of the probability of attrition in following subjects over extended time periods. Yet, only three studies (Howden, 1967; Preston & Yarington, 1967; Rawson, 1968) included samples of 50 or more subjects and would be reasonably protected against sampling artifacts.

The two most important considerations are control condition and length of follow-up period. For follow-up studies to be useful, they should reveal the adult outcomes of children early defined as reading disabled. Ideally, the study begins at school entry and follows the child until approximately 21 years of age. If the follow-up starts at an earlier age, then there is the possibility of biased sample while, if the study is terminated too soon, then information about ultimate outcomes in adulthood may be limited. Only the Rawson (1968) study met the ideal but suffers from the confounding influence of IQ and SES. The majority of the studies had follow-up periods of about 10 years while two studies (Hardy, 1968; Preston & Yarington, 1967) had follow-up periods of only about 5 years. Equally important in longitudinal research is the presence of a comparison group. This control condition is necessary to ascertain the relative outcomes for reading disabled children as measured against those of nonhandicapped children and to provide a more accurate prognosis for reading disabled children. For example, Balow and Blomquist (1965) were surprised to find that children reading at second-grade level at the end of elementary school were able to read at or near average adult levels 10 to 15 years later. Without adequate comparison data, such findings may appear surprising since there is nothing by which to judge the outcome. Additionally, a control group is necessary to determine the extent to which reading disability is either outgrown or overcome by, for example, maturation. Yet, only Howden (1967) included a matched comparison group of average readers while two (Preston & Yarington, 1967; Silver & Hagin, 1964) provided some means for comparison (e.g., previous data). The remainder included no control group. Thus, the longitudinal reports of the 1960s suffered from methodological difficulties that limits the confidence which can be placed in their conclusions. Thus, the interpretations should be considered suggestive and the conclusions need to be validated.

The 1970s

Reports about the long-term consequences of reading disability continued to be produced during the 1970s with greater insight into the issues of severity and outcome of reading disability, was provided by several studies. For example, Maginnis (1971) found that those children with the largest reading deficits were not necessarily those who profited most from remediation. There was a negligible correlation between degree of reading disability present 2 years earlier and the amount of gain in reading achievement at follow-up. Retrospectively, the correlation between reading disability at time of follow-up and reading improvement over 2 years was 0.60. Not one subject overcame the reading disability and 50% made only minimal progress. Similarly, Gottesman, Belmont and Kaminer (1975), in a 3–5 year follow-up of 58 reading disabled children, found that, as a group, these children revealed minimal reading gains and remained among the poorest readers for age. Approximately one-third of the children made sufficient progress to achieve a minimal degree of functional reading and this group represented the subjects with the highest initial scores. Conversely, the least improvement was shown by the subjects with the lowest initial scores.

Frauenheim (1978) found that a group of 40 dyslexic subjects had a mean adult reading grade level of 3.6 after 10 years. Additionally, equally severe deficits were noted in both spelling and arithmetic which resulted in a total 1.3 years of overall academic gain between diagnosis and follow-up. This level of reading retardation was more extensive than the mean adult reading levels of 10.2 (Balow & Blomquist, 1965) and 7.2 (Howden, 1967) found previously. The markedly lower reading outcomes can be attributed to the subject population which was precisely defined as primary reading retardation or developmental dyslexia (see Rabinovitch, 1968) and possessed the most severe reading disability. The carefully specified criteria for sample selection resulted in a severely disabled group who revealed persistent difficulties that limited their improvement. As Frauenheim (1978) concluded, "The fact that there was no relationship between the amount of special reading help and adult reading outcome also suggests that subjects reached what might be considered a plateau in reading skill development, and that further progress there became very difficult" (p. 483).

In another study using subjects carefully defined as having specific reading disability, Trites and Fiedorowicz (1976) found that deficits not only persisted with age but tended to grow larger relative to age and grade placement. At a 3-year follow-up, the average reading gain was 1.3 years which was discrepant by 2.4 years for actual grade placement and by 3.7 years for normal

age grade placement. This relationship between severity and outcome was also confirmed by Hunter and Lewis (1973) who found that, among 18 reading disabled males carefully selected according to definitional criteria, none had overcome the reading disability and, when compared to controls, displayed significantly lower reading achievement levels. At diagnosis, the mean reading deficit was 2.6 years while follow-up data showed a mean deficit of 2.9 years for the RD group. Similarly, Gottesman et al. (1975) found significantly poorer progress in a subgroup of language impaired children. Thus, these studies suggest that children with more severe reading disability made less progress and scored lower at follow-up than children who were less severely reading disabled.

Besides severity level, the age at which reading disability was diagnosed appeared to influence outcomes. It should be noted that age and severity may be related since it is reasonable to assume that only the more severely reading disabled children would be identified in the early grades. Gottesman et al. (1975) found that the most progress was made by the older subjects in their study (13 years of age or older). This finding was supported by Kline and Kline (1975) in a 4-year follow-up of 216 dyslexic children. Of the 216 subjects, 140 were treated with the Orton-Gillingham program and 96% were rated as improved while the 76 untreated (or school treated) subjects showed only 51% improvement. For both treated and untreated groups, the older subjects (age range = 12–17 years old) revealed more gain at follow-up. It cannot, however, be concluded that a positive relationship exists between age and reading status. Studies (e.g., Hardy, 1968b; Walker, 1963) have reported that the youngest children at the time of diagnosis revealed the greatest reading gains at follow-up. For example, Muehl and Forell (1973/1974) followed 43 reading disabled subjects from fifth-grade to tenth-grade. Although most subjects continue to be poor readers (only 4% read at average high school level), greater gain accrued to the younger subjects at follow-up. Thus, there is also some indication of a negative relationship between age and outcome.

While low IQ remained highly predictive for subsequent reading disability (Isom, 1975), the relationship between IQ and outcome was given further specification. For example, Yule and Rigley (1967), in a 4-year follow-up, indicated that when pupils making the most progress in reading were compared to those making least progress, the most progress group had significantly higher verbal IQ's on the *Wechsler Intelligence Scale for Children* (WISC). Although RD groups tended to have higher performance than verbal IQ (Belmont & Birch, 1966; Reed, 1967; Spache, 1957), Muehl and Forell (1973/1974) also found the verbal IQ at diagnosis was significantly correlated with later reading achievement. Additionally, verbal IQ score range better predicted the below-average range in which the subsequent reading scores fell than did performance IQ. For example, while

24 of 43 subjects had verbal IQs below average (<100), and 14 had verbal IQs less than 90, only 7 had performance IQs less than 100, and 2 less than 90 by contrast. Further specification was provided by Hunter and Lewis (1973) who found that large reading deficits at follow-up were associated with low scores on vocabulary and coding subtests while large gains were related to high scores on the Coding and Arithmetic subtests.

In a large-scale controlled study, Rutter, Tizard, Yule, Graham, and Whitmore (1976) surveyed children aged 9–10 who lived on the Isle of Wight, England, in 1964–1965. The subjects ($n=24$) were classified as reading backward (i.e., at least 28 months below age-level reading) or reading retarded (i.e., at least 28 months below their expected chronological and mental ages). A control group ($n=184$) of normal 9-10-year-old readers was randomly selected from the remainder of the population. Five years later, it was found that 56% of the backward group and 58% of the retarded were more than $2SD$ below the mean in reading achievement. Among those at or above age-level mean were only 4% of the backward and 2.5% of the retarded readers. The RD groups had an average reading level of 9 years with spelling achievement even worse but somewhat higher (although significantly lower than the control group) mathematics achievement. In fact, while showing less improvement in reading and spelling, the reading retarded group made the most improvement in mathematics.

This study again revealed the persistent nature of reading disability but sheds little light on the question of age relationships to outcome since the Isle of Wight sample fell in middle childhood (age 9–10) when identified. Also affirmed is the finding (Frauenheim, 1978) that reading disability may not be an isolated deficit, and may be associated with deficits in related academic areas. In general, the prognosis for academic achievement for severe reading disabled children is poor.

The Rutter et al. (1976) study also provided some insight into the relationship between reading and behavioral disorders. In the case where conduct disorders were first manifested between the ages 10–14, there was no higher incidence of previous reading disability than for the general Isle of Wight population. There was, however, a significant correlation between behavior problems beginning prior to age 10 and reading disability. Although the correlation reveals little about cause and effect, the finding does suggest that conduct disorders beginning after age 10 may not be the result of reading disability. Several other reports supported the age and behavioral disorders relationship. For example, Gottesman et al. (1975) found that a high proportion of their sample had psychiatric disorders at follow-up which were unrelated to the level of reading failure. While no differences between reading disabled and control groups existed at diagnosis, Hunter and Lewis (1973) found an emotional overlay in the reading disabled group at follow-up. On the basis of scores from a teacher rating scale, significant differences between

RD and control groups emerged with respect to ability to concentrate, oversensitivity, temper outbursts, and stubbornness. The RD group was also judged more excitable, selfish, quarrelsome, defiant, and attention-seeking. Thus, reading disability and behavioral disorders appear to be related but the nature of the causal relationships remain indeterminate. For more precise specification, longitudinal research must begin prior to the age of onset for either reading disability or behavioral disorders (i.e., no later than the beginning of first-grade). Furthermore, most studies did not assess emotional adjustment at diagnosis. For example, Balow and Blomquist (1965) used a valid outcome measure (*Minnesota Multiphasic Personality Inventory*) and found evidence of psychopathology even with reading gain but there was no comparison data. Consequently, most of the data on behavioral disorders is cross-sectional, and no insight into the causal relationship can be gleaned.

In a series of longitudinal investigations, Newman (1972, 1978, 1980) studied a group of students classified as low reading readiness when entering first grade and followed them through school. The 1972 study followed 230 likely underachievers to sixth-grade and found that first-grade reading achievement was a significantly more reliable predictor of sixth-grade achievement than first-grade readiness measures. This finding was supported by Isom (1975) who found that first-grade reading achievement provided the best prediction since, with few exceptions, the child who did not read well in first-grade will likely remain poor in reading achievement. In terms of the variables related to subsequent achievement, correlational analyses revealed a strong association between achievement and a g-factor for intelligence. Additionally, sex differences emerged with girls doing better in spelling and word study skills while boys performed better on vocabulary. Trites and Fiedorowicz (1976) also presented data related to sex differences. From diagnosis to follow-up, boys maintained their position in reading and spelling but lost about 10 percentile ranks in arithmetic. Girls, on the other hand, lost ground from initial to follow-up assessment in reading, spelling, and arithmetic. Thus, boys lost less ground than girls at follow-up (even though they were more disabled overall on an absolute basis).

In subsequent studies, Newman (1978, 1980) reported follow-up findings for the original sample when they were finishing high school and when they were involved in either more schooling or occupational pursuits. These reports were based on 20 students who showed the greatest contrast with original first-grade prognosis based on achievement data obtained at 9th and 12th grades. The purpose was to examine students' home and school environments in hopes of discovering the "whys" associated with improved reading achievement. Five variables—model, motivation, interest, perseverance, and pressure—were investigated to see if their influence might be greater than perhaps the previous identified variables like IQ or sex.

The 20 students selected were divided into four groups based on *Iowa Test of Educational Development* (ITED) scores and *Metropolitan Readiness Test* (MRT) results in first-grade. On the basis of 9th-grade ITED scores, two groups were formed: achievers who had scored at or above cohort mean on at least one subtest, and low achievers who had not scored at or above cohort mean on any subtest. The achievers were then divided into two groups: those who in first-grade had achieved raw scores between 1 and 39 on the MRT (below 22nd percentile in readiness) and those who had achieved MRT scores between 40 and 60 (22nd to 61st percentiles on national norms). These groups revealed differences with respect to the degree of influence of model, motivation, interest, perseverance, and pressure. The achieving group with the lowest readiness scores (1 to 39 on the MRT) had, by ninth-grade, greater achievement as measured by the ITED. They all attended postsecondary school and were gainfully employed. Newspapers were their primary sources of news and very generally had positive feelings about reading. All reported that their parents read to them regularly when they were children. Newman (1978) concluded:

> Student and parent interviews suggested that the achievment of these students was strongly supported by interest and positive pressure at home; intrinsic motivation seemed to evolve out of models, interests, and pressure; parent and teacher expectation played an important part. In other words, these were very average students who, given a stimulating and supportive home environment, were transformed into achievers (p. 84).

Thus, even with a poor prognosis in first grade, children were not doomed to failure, and academic achievement appeared to be fostered by the positive presence of four variables (model, motivation, interest, and perseverance), and by support, but low pressure, from the parents in the case of the fifth variable.

Finally, Newman (1980) investigated the impact of literacy on the occupations or postsecondary schooling of these 230 students, who had graduated from high school in 1976. Through questionnaires and personal interviews, it was concluded that the impact of literacy was considerable and, for the most part, positive. Sixty-one percent attended college, and 80% responded positively to the question, "What are your feelings about reading now?" As to occupation, 35% were students, 25% were in service positions, 20% were office workers, 10% were factory workers, one was a homemaker, and one was unemployed. These figures compared favorably with national averages and, rather than fulfilling the prophecy of failure for low readiness children, most of these subjects were highly motivated by a need for self-realization, and were pursuing satisfactory and reasonable individual goals.

Follow-up of remedial efforts. In examining the variables affecting outcomes, Newman (1972) investigated the effectiveness of four methods of teaching reading to low readiness children. The methods included a language-based program, a phonics program stressing letter sounds, a program stressing literature, and a program emphasizing skill development in perceptual and cognitive areas. The findings revealed no differences among treatment groups at first- or sixth-grade level. Similar findings were found for remedial reading methods. Although Schiffman (1964) found that remedial reading resulted in greater improvement after one year's instruction and one year later than either the regular developmental reading program or corrective reading, Silverberg, Iversen, and Goins (1973) found no long-term effects for any remedial reading method. A group of 102 students requiring remedial instruction when entering third-grade were given one of four remedial approaches: a visual-sight approach, an auditory-phonic approach, a kinesthetic approach, and a multisensory approach (Orton-Gillingham). Immediately after completion of the program, all methods improved reading levels dramatically (although the phonic method was slightly superior). By the middle of fourth-grade, follow-up assessments revealed that much of the gain had "washed out." These findings led to the conclusion that no one method of remedial reading instruction has any greater long-term effect than any other method. This finding is at variance with that of Kline and Kline (1975) who found great success with the Orton-Gillingham approach. Improvement was observed in 96% of the cases receiving the Orton-Gillingham program whereas only 45% of the school-treated cases showed some improvement. Despite the encouraging prognosis for subjects exposed to the Orton-Gillingham program, the results may be misleading. While all cases were referred for treatment, only part of that group actually received the Orton-Gillingham program and the remainder became the comparison group. This represents a confounding in the control group since it is not clear as to why the comparison group subjects did not participate. Additionally, despite improvement in the group receiving the Orton-Gillingham program, 40% of that group were still reading below grade level. Yet, they were classified as "showing some improvement" thereby possibly inflating their percentage of positive outcomes.

Rather than examining the effectiveness of a particular remedial reading method, Enfield (1976) studied, over 3 years, the efficacy of curriculum (i.e., sequential and hierarchical) and technology (i.e., multisensory and concrete) delivered through direct teaching in a district-wide remedial program (Project Read). The sample consisted of 665 children randomly selected from Grades 1, 2, and 3 who had average IQ but fell below the 25th percentile in reading and spelling measures. Comparisons on 10 measures of reading and spelling progress showed significant gains for the Project Read students. Furthermore, of the original 19 behavioral objectives, 12 (63%) were met or clearly surpassed while the remaining 7 revealed substantial progress towards attainment. The students in Project Read made greater yearly gains than a similar group who remained in a previously used tutoring program. Finally, on the basis of a district-wide testing program, there was a reduction of students who fell below grade level after the implementation of the 3-year project. Crosby (1977), however, failed to find such positive findings for 210 students enrolled in a special Reading Support Services Program. For remedial readers in the sixth-grade given the special program, ninth-grade reading comprehension and vocabulary scores were lower than counterparts who experienced only the regular school curriculum. The program also appeared to have little effect on producing more positive attitudes. The only positive effect was a lowered drop-out rate among students in the special program. This was similar to the findings of Rasmussen and Dunne (1962) who reported no significant academic gains in a group given corrective reading instruction but a reduction in drop-out rate among these students. Fiedler (1972), in a follow-up study of 29 high school students who received clinical reading assistance, found the greatest gains in attitudes towards reading. Although the group remained behind in reading, those who showed the greatest positive attitude change also showed the greatest academic gains. Thus, the drop-out rate reduction may be related partially to improved attitudes towards reading. In general, however, it remains unclear what effect the treatment program has on outcome. Perhaps Yule's (1973) observation on remedial efforts provides a partial explanation: Remedial work often comes too late and may be given over too short a time.

Long-term follow-up research. Satz, Taylor, Friel, and Fletcher (1978) conducted a longitudinal study on an entire population ($n = 426$) entering kindergarten in public schools in 1970. Based on measures of second grade reading achievement, the population was classified as severely retarded readers (N = 49), mildly retarded readers ($n = 62$), average readers ($n = 252$), and superior readers ($n = 63$). Follow-up was conducted 3 years later at the end of fifth-grade. Based on achievement measures, the sample was again classified into one of the reading groups. Of the 49 severely retarded readers at end of second-grade, only 6% were average or above average. Also, only 17.7% of the mildly retarded group were either average or above average at end of fifth-grade. Meanwhile, 30% of the average second-grade readers were mildly or severely disabled readers by the end of fifth-grade. Only 3% of the superior second-grade readers were seen as mildly disabled in fifth-grade. Despite the short follow-up period, the Satz et al. (1978) study affirmed the grim prognosis for children possessing reading disability as early as second-grade since very few who had difficulty in second-grade reached grade level by fifth-grade. Rourke and Orr (1977) also found minimal gain in a group of 19 reading disabled over a 4-year follow-up period. For example, only 5 of the 19 reading disabled subjects had made advances of 20 or more centile points on the *Metropolitan Achievement Test* (MAT) reading subtest while only 3 demonstrated such gain on the *Wide Range Achievement Test* (WRAT) spelling test, despite the expected "regression towards the mean" phenomenon. Thus, these findings supported the Rutter et al. (1976) finding that children with early reading disability are quite likely to encounter serious academic problems in reading, spelling, vocabulary, and mathematics.

In a 12-year prospective study, Bell, Abrahamson and McRae (1977) followed approximately 1,000 subjects from preschool through 12th grade. The findings indicated that an unevenness in specific developmental patterns (e.g., auditory, visual-motor, kinesthetic) present at school entry were significantly related to poor academic performance in the first school year. Furthermore, the percentage of poor readers increased in direct proportion to the number of specific anomalies present. Later academic performance (12th grade) was closely related to the rank order in achievement at the end of the sixth-grade ($r = 0.70$). Additionally, achievement levels were directly related to SES level. The failure rates were 71%, 18% and 3% for low, middle, and high SES levels respectively. This supported Isom's (1975) longitudinal finding that no predictor was as reliable as SES, and Muehl and Forell's (1973/1974) data indicating that the best high school readers came from high SES levels. With respect to remedial programs, Bell et al. (1977) found no significant effects for any particular program. It was found, however, that while the child may not be able to achieve at the norm for chronological age, remedial efforts do have positive effects on attitudes which may be reflected in fewer adjustment problems. This study is also unique with respect to the finding that more girls than boys had reading problems. It was suggested that this was found because the sample consisted of all children entering school at a particular period. In most studies, the samples are drawn from clinic referrals and may be different from those selected epidemiologically (Belmont & Birch, 1966). Additionally, clinic-referred children may possess a variety of problems in addition to reading disability (Cerny, 1976; Gilbert, 1957). Most especially, they possess behavior problems which are likely to cause difficulties both at home and school, and lead to a speedy referral.

Conclusions. The longitudinal research reported during the 1970s extended and refined understandings about the long-term consequences of reading disability. Most of the previously stated conclusions were validated but some differences emerged. In summary, the following generalizations appear warranted:

1. Reading disability is a chronic and persistent problem that has long-term consequences in terms of lowered academic status and reduced vocational status.

2. Reading disability tends to be a pervasive problem that affects all academic areas and is likely to be associated with adjustment problems and behavioral disturbance.

3. It is clear that the more severe the reading disability, the more severe the consequences.

4. The relationship to SES was substantiated and showed that less favorable outcomes are associated with low SES.

5. The relationship between age at diagnosis and outcome is not clear; both positive and negative relationships were noted.

6. The influence of IQ is positive, with higher IQs being associated with more favorable outcomes.

7. Interventions for reading disability show no differential effects; all programs are both effective and ineffective.

8. The development of positive attitudes is an important factor in outcomes, especially in preventing dropouts.

9. Success appears to be a consequence of variety of variables, both intrinsic and extrinsic, that operate to produce academic and occupational success.

Generally, the research from the 1970s was better designed than its predecessors and allowed for more firm conclusions. For example, the definitional criteria for reading disability was more objective and better defined (e.g., Frauenheim, 1978; Hunter & Lewis, 1973; Kline & Kline, 1975; Newman, 1978; Rourke & Orr, 1977; Rutter et al., 1976; Satz et al., 1978) which allowed for better generalization. Furthermore, several studies (Bell et al., 1977; Kline & Kline, 1975; Rutter et al., 1976; Satz et al., 1978) included large samples ($n > 100$) which provided more stability to outcome findings. Also improved were sampling methods with a greater number of studies either drawing samples from an entire school class or using an entire population as the study sample (e.g., Bell et al., 1977; Gottesman et al., 1975; Rutter et al., 1976; Satz et al., 1978) rather than clinic samples. Two areas were improved but still fell short of the ideal: control, and length of follow-up. A majority of the studies did not include a comparison group from which data may be placed in context. Several (e.g., Rourke & Orr, 1977; Rutter et al., 1976, Satz et al., 1978) did include, however, a matched control group of average readers that provided a basis for comparison. Most of the studies fell short in length of their follow-up period with a majority having a follow-up period of less than 5 years. The remainder fell between 5 and 10 years in length of follow-up with only the Newman (1978; 1980) reports reaching the ideal of following a sample from before age 8 to after age 20. Unfortunately, those reports did not meet the other methodological criteria and must be approached with caution. Generally, the research reported in the 1970s was improved but studies failed to meet the methodological requirements for unequivocal interpretation. Three studies (Bell et al., 1977; Rutter et al., 1976; Satz et al., 1978) appeared to meet most of the methodological criteria, and can be considered the best designed research from which valid conclusions may be drawn.

The 1980s

The 1980s showed increased specificity and diversity in longitudinal research. In a follow-up to a 1978 investigation, Frauenheim and Heckerl (1983) presented additional findings in the functioning of 11 subjects from their well-defined original dyslexic sample ($N = 40$). All subjects continued to experience significant difficulty in reading, spelling, and arithmetic. Also, despite remediation attempts, there was relatively little progress or change in basic academic skills. For example, at age 10 the mean reading level was 1.9 while, at age 27, the mean reading level was 2.6. The lack of gain was also found by Blackburn (1980) in six students followed over 3 years. Despite remedial instruction and initial gains (average = 1.4 years), only two students were found to have decreased the discrepancy between expected and actual reading achievement whereas four were found to have increased the discrepancy.

In the area of psychological test functioning, there remained a significant discrepancy between verbal and performance IQs in favor of the latter (Frauenheim & Heckerl, 1983). Further analysis using WISC subtest recategorizations found that this dyslexic group did quite poorly on the sequencing (freedom from distractibility) grouping whereas strengths were evidenced in the spatial and perceptual organization groupings. Again, the persistence of reading disability was reaffirmed, as well as the relationship with severity. The 11 subjects in this investigation represented the severe end of the reading disability continuum and, despite remedial efforts and an 8% high school completion rate, their reading deficits remained quite pronounced. In fact, although possessing adequate intelligence and educational opportunity, this group did not achieve functional literacy skills.

In their analysis of reading abilities in the dyslexic group, Frauenheim and Heckerl (1983) found marked deficits in sight vocabulary suggesting impaired memory for whole word units. Decoding skills were also poor particularly in sound-symbol association. Oral reading rate was very slow and marked by frequent substitutions. Subjects stated that their primary word recognition cue was context. While these findings provided insight into the adult reading abilities of dyslexic children, Fox and Routh (1983) found that first-graders with severe reading disability had marked deficits in phonemic analysis (i.e., process of segmenting spoken words into their component speech sounds). When followed over 3 years, all the reading disabled children were held back and were in third-grade while a matched control group of average readers were making normal progress and were in fourth-grade. When the reading performance of the RD group was analyzed at third-grade, all were now proficient at phonemic segmenting. The major difficulty, however, was found in the

315

spelling area where there was a marked tendency towards dysphasic spelling patterns which resulted in bizarre spelling errors. The comparison group, however, usually revealed good phonetic equivalents for misspelled words. In a 2-year follow-up, Aman and Mayhew (1980) provided additional insight into the cognitive functioning of children with specific reading retardation. In an analysis of non-IQ cognitive measures (e.g., *Matching Familiar Figures Test*, auditory-visual integration, short-term memory, *Continuous Performance Task*, seat movement, maze task, and graduated holes task), few improvements were noted on accuracy and response time measures but measures of response speed and motor steadiness improved significantly with maturation. It was concluded from a correlational analysis that perhaps more emphasis should be placed on temporal measures rather than solely on accuracy measures in assessing the educational progress of reading disabled children. This is in line with Kagan's (1965) suggestion for more attention to the temporal dimension in describing reading ability.

In the Colorado Family Reading Study, DeFries and Baker (1983) studied 69 pairs of reading disabled children and matched controls over 5 years. The carefully selected subjects averaged 9 years at diagnosis and 15 years at follow-up. All analyses clearly demonstrated the persistent nature of reading disability: The RD and control group subjects differed significantly on the average for composite measures of reading performance (i.e., *Peabody Individual Achievement Test* (PIAT): reading recognition, reading comprehension, and spelling) and symbol processing speed (i.e., WISC-Coding Subtest B and *Colorado Perceptual Speed Test*: rotatable letters and numbers) at both age levels.

Baker, Decker, and DeFries (1984) in further analyses found that both groups improved significantly between the two assessments which is in contrast to findings (Frauenheim, 1978; Satz et al., 1978, Trites & Fiedorowicz, 1976) suggesting that differences in reading achievement increased with age. The nature of the comparison groups and differences in remediation programs may account partially for these contradictory findings. Additionally, the rate of development in academic achievement and spatial reasoning measures were similar for the two groups as evidenced by the lack of a Group × Time interaction in the analysis. Meyer (1982), however, in an analysis of the same data, found that the correlation between progress rates in word recognition and reading comprehension was significantly greater for the RD group than the control group. This suggests that decoding skills were more systematically related to comprehension skills in the RD group. Furthermore, the relationship of the temporal aspects of remediation to follow-up achievement revealed that children who began receiving remediation later, as well as those who received fewer years of remediation, demonstrated greater achievement levels at follow-up.

With respect to prediction, Baker et al. (1984) found, although the groups were similar on average, longitudinal stability was less for the RD group, suggesting that performance across time is more variable in reading disabled children. This instability makes prediction of later performance in individual reading disabled children more tenuous when the prediction was based solely on earlier test results. This conclusion is at variance with the suggestion (Isom, 1975; Newman, 1978) that first-grade reading achievement is a good predictor of subsequent reading performance. De Fries and Baker (1983) did find, however, that, since parental influences play a more important role for reading disabled children, the accuracy of longitudinal prediction may be improved by the addition of parental information to predictive data. Finally, in an analysis of cognitive ability between groups, the performance IQ of the RD group was not significantly different from that of the control group (after covariance adjustment for differences in verbal IQ). Nevertheless, the RD group exhibited significantly poorer performance on achievement and symbolic processing tasks (even after verbal IQ covariance adjustments) suggesting that factors other than either verbal or performance IQs were responsible for the differences in contrast to the suggestion (Muehl & Forell, 1973/1974; Yule & Rigley, 1967) that verbal IQ is a prominent factor in producing group differences. This was particularly true for word recognition and spelling since the two groups differed in mean progress rate even when full scale IQ was used as a covariate which was not the case for reading comprehension progress (Meyer, 1982).

In an analysis of the residual effects of childhood reading disability, Rudel (1981) found some remaining difficulties among eight students who had received an extended period of remedial instruction. While their oral reading ability (measured by the *Gray Oral Reading Test*) was satisfactory (grade 12+), reading comprehension (*Iowa Silent Reading Test*) revealed much greater variability with percentile rankings ranging from 44 to 99 (mean=79). Although this group had better than average IQ (mean=122), they still displayed difficulties in reading, especially in phonetic decoding, and relied primarily on sight word reading and on context which is in accord with Frauenheim and Heckerl's (1983) findings. In conclusion, Rudel (1981) stated that:

> Reading disability may be considered "maturational lag," i.e., some children just learn to read later than others and require more (or different) teaching to enable them to read. However, the underlying deficits which make reading unexpectedly difficult for the intelligent child appear to plague some very intelligent adults who once required reading remediation (p. 100).

Spreen (1982) followed a group of 203 reading disabled children and their parents for 10 years, and they were compared to a group of 52 matched controls. At follow-up, with an average age of 19, the RD group displayed inferior academic performance in all areas of study, and had a poor attitude toward school. Additionally, the RD group exhibited a greater number of signs of personal maladjustment. In an analysis by sex, females were described as having more social and personality problems while males tended to show more "acting out" or antisocial behavior. It was also found that the RD group had a relatively poor chance for advanced training and skilled employment. The findings indicated that primary among the adult adjustment problems was occupational dissatisfaction as well as social and personal difficulties (although this was strongly influenced by SES). The occupational outcomes were more fully explored by Gottfredson, Finucci, and Childs (1984) who followed 579 severely dyslexic boys to determine differences in adult careers. The adult occupations of these boys, who were above average in IQ and SES, were compared to those of both a control group, and a general white male population. The RD group had higher level jobs than the average man but were much less likely than controls to become professionals. Instead, most were found to become managers or salesmen. The occupational differences between the RD and control group were related to their large differences in educational achievement. Given data on the competencies rated as critical to good job performance, reading disabled men were found to establish themselves in relatively high-level jobs emphasizing nonacademic rather than academic on-the-job skills. While nondisabled professionals rated reading among the most critical skills, managers and salesmen rated reading less important than such nonacademic competencies as initiative and persuasiveness. Thus, it appears that variations among jobs in their academic versus nonacademic skill requirements provide opportunities for reading disabled subjects, especially those with normal IQs, to obtain relatively attractive and high-level occupations.

Conclusions. In summary, the most recent longitudinal research affirmed many of the earlier findings but also provided some optimism. It is evident that reading disability is likely to be associated with long-term negative consequences. The problem of reading disability is persistent and chronic as well as pervasive in the sense of being associated with other academic achievement problems. Decoding skills remain poor and reading tends to be based on sight words and context. Unfortunately, remedial intervention may or may not be effective and no one type of program is superior to any other; nevertheless, any program needs to be administered over the long term (about 2 years) and should be followed by supportive interventions. Even under the best of circumstances, reading disabled children do not usually close the gap in their reading ability and may, in fact, become worse over time. Consistent with reading disability is the strong possibility of social and emotional

difficulties. To prevent their development, remedial efforts must also be directed at improving attitudes towards reading. The academic and social consequences of reading disability were most clearly reflected in reduced occupational status and less favorable attitudes about their station in life. Clarification of the effect of reading disability was found relative to severity, IQ, and SES; more negative outcomes were related to more severe disability while more positive outcomes were related to higher IQ and SES levels. The relationship with age of onset is unclear since both positive and negative associations were found but there was some suggestion that reading disability deficits do not necessarily increase with age and, although always lagging, reading disabled subjects may evidence the same rate of development as normal readers.

These conclusions all remain somewhat tentative, however, because of the presence of methodological difficulties in much of the reading disabilty longitudinal research. Although the sophistication and rigor in longterm studies improved over time, there remained enough methodological flaws to make definitive conclusions problematic. Specifically, while the criteria, selection, and size of samples improved thus allowing better generalization, the lack of comparison groups and short follow-up periods in many studies limited interpretation.

Despite the cautions imposed by methodological difficulties, reading disability represents a real problem in both the short- and long-terms. The fact that approximately 80% of learning disabled children manifest RD as a primary deficit (Kirk & Elkins, 1975; Norman & Zigmond, 1980) suggests that conclusions about reading disability are equally applicable to learning disability samples. Thus, the natural history of learning disabilities is likely to overlap substantially with that of RD. For the learning disabled child with reading disabilities, the reading difficulties are likely to be longstanding and may be associated with correlative social or emotional problems which, in turn, ultimately effect vocational outcomes. Thus, reading disability is a serious problem which, over time, produces adverse consequences for the affected child that may be only partially overcome even under optimal remedial circumstances.

Longitudinal Research in Hyperactivity/Minimal Brain Dysfunction

A condition closely allied to learning disability that possesses a sizable follow-up litarature is hyperactivity. The diagnosis of hyperactivity is vague and spans a wide continuum of conditions and terminology. But such differences do not necessarily signify actual differences in the target populations. Consequently, minimal brain dysfunction (MBD) and attention deficit disorder (ADD) are subsumed under the general rubric of hyperactivity. Ever since Clement's (1966) report, these conditions have been linked with learning disability and represent primary correlative symptoms. Much like reading disability, hyperactivity is common among children with learning disabilities so a description of its long-term consequences would add significantly to a comprehensive understanding of the natural history of learning disabilities. The common wisdom, drawn from early clinical experience, about hyperactivity suggests that, "In later years this syndrome tends to wane spontaneously and disappear. We have not seen it persist in those patients whom we have followed to adult life" (Laufer & Denhoff, 1957, p. 464). The primary question becomes one of whether this observation has been supported by subsequent longitudinal research.

The 1960s

In an early longitudinal study, Menkes, Rowe, and Menkes (1967) studied 14 subjects in a 25-year retrospective follow-up study. At time of referral, these patients ranged in age from 2 to 15 years and in IQ from 71 to 128. At follow-up, they were interviewed and had a neurological evaluation. Four subjects diagnosed as psychotic were in institutions; two were retarded and dependent upon their families, while eight were self-supporting but four of these eight had spent some time in an institution. For 11 subjects given neurological evaluations, eight had definite evidence of neurological dysfunction, one had equivocal evidence, and two had none. For three subjects, hyperactivity remained a problem since "they still felt restless, had a hard time settling down to anything including a television show, and changed jobs frequently" (Menkes et al., 1967, p. 396). These fairly negative outcomes were at odds with the more positive clinical evaluation and may be partially related to both IQ and SES. Of the 14 subjects, 4 had initial IQs of less than 80 and 6 came from the low SES strata. Without a comparison group to control for these possible confounding influences, no firm conclusions may be drawn.

The longitudinal literature can be divided into different time frames depending upon the age at which status was assessed. This type of analysis can provide greater insight into the nature of hyperactivity by revealing its natural history at specific points in time during the development of a child from early childhood through adulthood.

Follow-up of hyperactivity in preschool

In investigating the status of hyperactive preschoolers first identified in nursery school at age 4.5 years, Campbell, Schleifer, Weiss, and Perlman (1977), who were part of a Canadian group, followed 20 hyperactive children and 21 controls to a mean age of 6.5 years. The hyperactive children were classified as either "true" or "situational" depending upon the pervasiveness of their hyperactive behavior. The true hyperactive children were very active at all times and across all circumstances while the situational were moderately active and only in specific circumstances, usually home. For hyperactive versus control comparisons, both groups had above average WISC IQs with the controls significantly greater. The groups did not differ significantly on either the *Matching Familiar Figures Test* or the *Children's Embedded Figures Test*. Mean scores on a test of moral reasoning (Piaget story pairs) failed to separate the groups but true hyperactive children tended to show less mature reasoning than controls and situational hyperactive children. On *Conners' Parent Questionnaire*, both hyperactive groups were rated significantly worse than controls on the conduct problem factor and the impulsive-hyperactive factor. Situational hyperactive children were rated as more perfectionistic then both true hyperactive children and controls. This perfectionistic tendency appeared to reflect rigidity and unrealistic goals rather than an effort to be correct. In a series of interactions in a laboratory setting, the mothers of hyperactive children tended to make more suggestions about impulse control while the hyperactive children, especially true hyperactive, requested more feedback and made more comments on performance. It was concluded that young children diagnosed as true hyperactive remain so over time. This finding was later confirmed (Campbell, Breaux, Ewing, & Szumowski, 1984) in a one-year follow-up of parent-referred hyperactive preschool children. At intake, parent complaints focused on activity, inattentiveness, impulsivity, and noncompliant behaviors. One year later, mothers continued to rate these areas as problems and they were independently confirmed as persistent problems by laboratory assessments. In fact, there is the suggestion (Chapel, Robins, McGee, Williams, & Silva, 1982) that the number of hyperactive children shows a gradual increase between ages 5 and 7. In following a group of children from birth to 7 years of age, it was found that some high-risk children (11%) lost their hyperactivity by age 5 but a greater proportion (17%) demonstrated a problem when none was present before age 5. It was concluded that some original problems resurface as these children face the increasing demands of school and society.

In following the same group into elementary school at mean age of 7.5 years, Campbell, Endman, and Bernfeld (1977) found that hyperactive children received more negative feedback from teachers, engaged in more disruptive behavior, were rated by their teachers as more hyperactive, and expressed lower self-esteem than controls. The presence of hyperactive children was found to influence the interaction patterns between the teacher and the class as a whole. Maternal reports, however, did not reveal impressive continuity over the 3-year period (Campbell, Schleifer, & Weiss, 1978). Nevertheless, the distinction between true and situational hyperactivity appeared to have some prognostic utility since true hyperactive children were more often out-of-seat and off-task, and were rated as more inattentive. With the higher attrition rate among the situational hyperactive, it was suggested that the hyper-activity distinction may be related to district subgroups of reactive and constitutional hyperactivity.

A poor prognosis for children showing signs of MBD at the beginning of their school career was found in several studies. Eaves and Crichton (1975) found that among 39 subjects originally diagnosed as MBD, 60% were below grade level in academic achievement. Only 7 of the 39 had no school problems while only three of these seven were free of behavioral difficulties, especially at home. About one-third of these subjects were still distractable, restless, or overactive. Similarly, Gillberg, Gillberg, and Rasmussen (1983) found 80% of MBD children compared with 16% of a control group revealed school achievement difficulties. When the MBD group was divided into mild-moderate and severe groupings, 100% of the severe MBD group had academic problems. Although all MBD children were found to be at high risk for behavior problems (Gillberg & Gillberg, 1983), there was no difference along the mild to severe MBD continuum for the number and magnitude of behavior difficulties. With respect to IQ, the MBD group revealed considerable variability in WISC performance. Yet, there was little relationship between IQ and school achievement with just as many MBD children in IQ range of 85 to 126 showing academic difficulties as those with IQ levels below 85. Mednick (1977) found that children age 10–12 who showed transient neonatal symptoms (i.e., MBD) were more likely to manifest lowered IQ levels but there was no relationship with either academic or social functioning. Similarly, Rubin and Balow (1978) found that transitory neurological abnormality observed during the first year of life was a good indicator of risk for future impairment, especially in cognitive development. Thus, while lowered intellectual levels may be a concomitant symptom of MBD, it does not appear that it is the primary reason for achievement problems.

The reports of academic difficulties in MBD children all suggested that MBD was associated with language and speech problems. In examining this relationship, Hall and Tomblin (1978) followed 18 language-impaired and 18 articulation-impaired children for an average of 15 years and found that 9 language-impaired, compared to only one articulation-impaired, subjects continued to exhibit communication problems. Additionally, the language-impaired group consistently achieved at a lower level than the articulation-impaired group, particularly in reading. Further delineation of the language-impaired group was provided by Weiner (1972) who followed a group of dysphasic children and found that they continued to be deficient in auditory-vocal and oral-motor functioning, and in language comprehension. In contrast, they manifested no problems in visual-perceptual and visual-motor functioning when compared to a normal control group. The basic linguistic and perceptual dysfunction appeared to be the source of difficulty. Wepman and Morency (1971), for example, found that first-grade perceptual processing ability was related to

sixth grade achievement but no relationship was found between early articulation ability and school achievement. Thus, language impairment appeared to be the primary agent rather than speech difficulties like articulation problems. The presence of language impairment appears to be a persistent problem as further confirmed by Griffiths (1969) who found only 5 out of 26 subjects from a special remedial program were making satisfactory progress. Similarly, Garvey and Gordon (1973) confirmed the persistent nature of language disability on performance. Although language and speech attainments were within normal limits after treatment, they continued to experience academic difficulties. Consequently, MBD represents a hidden and persistent handicap that exerts a negative influence on performance even when there is a superficial appearance of normality.

Conclusions. 1. Hyperactivity in preschool is a real phenomenon with "true" hyperactivity manifesting itself as overactivity at all times and across all situations.

2. Hyperactivity appears to be associated with more conduct problems and greater impulsivity.

3. Hyperactivity appears to be persistent in early childhood and may even show an increase at school entrance.

4. Hyperactivity appears to be related to poor academic achievement and increased behavior problems which is independent of intellectual level and the presence of language and speech problems.

Follow-up of hyperactivity in elementary school

The antecedents of MBD and hyperactivity during the elementary school years were detailed in several prospective reports. Thomas, Chess, and Birch (1968), (see also Thomas & Chess, 1976) followed 108 New York children from early infancy over 10 years. Of the 108, 34 had been referred for behavior problems (see Rutter, Birch, Thomas, & Chess, 1964) of an "active" sort (i.e., anxiety, aggression, tantrums) and 8 for "passive" symptoms (i.e., withdrawal, nonparticipation). The remaining 66 were a nonclinical control group. Relative to the nonreferred group, the "active" group had been characterized in infancy by temperament that included excessive frequency of high activity, irregularity, low threshold, nonadaptability, intensity, persistence, and distractibility. Of the 42 clinical cases, 19 recovered, 5 improved, 3 were unchanged, and 15 became worse. In a later report, Thomas and Chess (1975) showed that the behavioral course, in children who became worse, could not be explained only in terms of motor dysfunction, intellectual deficit, patterns of parental attitudes, and more general environmental features, but also required a consideration of the constellation of temperamental factors.

In a similar prospective longitudinal study, Matheny, Dolan, and Wilson (1976) followed a large popu-

Kenneth A. Kavale

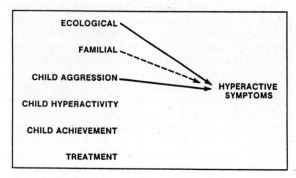

Figure 1. Predictors of Hyperactive Symptoms at Follow-up

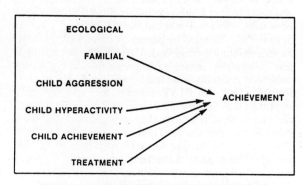

Figure 2. Predictors of Achievement at Follow-up

lation of twins from age 3 months to school. From the total population, 46 twins were studied who had been referred for poor academic performance. These twins were contrasted with a control group selected from the remaining twin sample. The experimental group had an average reading level about 2 years below the control group. From developmental information, it was found that the experimental group's *Bayley Mental Scale* scores were consistently, but never significantly, lower than controls. At 6 years of age, the groups differed significantly on the WISC (experimental = 94 and control = 102). Compared with controls, significantly more of the experimental twins had been reported as overly active children (87% vs. 26%), as more distractible (89% vs. 22%), and as more temperamental (67% vs. 30%). Thus, temperamental difficulties, specifically overactivity and distractibility, were predictive of later behavioral and academic problems.

Loney, Kramer, and Milich (1980) reported on a 3-year longitudinal study of 135 hyperactive boys in a multivariate analysis to predict symptoms and achievement at follow-up (mean age = 8.2 years). In a graphical display of predictors, hyperactive symptoms at follow-up are predicted as shown in Figure 1. (Arrows connect each category of independent variable with any outcome measure that it predicts. A dotted arrow shows a connection established from previous data while the absence of any arrow reveals no significant association between variables.) This analysis shows that ecological variables (e.g., SES, perinatal complications) and childhood aggression predict later hyperactivity. Furthermore, it was found that childhood aggression, and not childhood hyperactivity, was related both to ratings of self-esteem deficits and lowered scores on the *Piers-Harris Self-Esteem Scale* (Langhorne & Loney, 1979). Figure 2 shows predictors of achievement at follow-up. As might be expected, childhood achievement is the best predictor of later achievement followed by response to treatment. While childhood hyperactivity was not associated with behavioral outcomes, it was related to academic outcomes. Conversely, the best predictors of hyperactivity (i.e., ecological factors and childhood aggression) failed

to predict any academic outcome. These findings are in contrast to the suggestion that hyperactivity, as a general symptom, is an important determinant of the behavioral outcomes in MBD children (Cunningham & Barkley, 1978).

Follow-up of intervention efforts

The fact that treatment (i.e., stimulant medication) does not predict later behavioral symptoms (i.e., hyperactivity) is surprising since medication is effective, at least in the short-term, in reducing hyperactivity symptomatology (Kavale, 1982). But several other reports have noted that, over time, the optimistic therapeutic effects of drug treatment were not sustained (Blouin, Bornstein, & Trites, 1978; Woods, 1981). Despite continued medication, many problems were still present (e.g., school failure, antisocial behavior, psychiatric difficulties) although stimulants continued to reduce hyperactivity symptomatology. For example, Sleator, von Neumann, and Sprague (1974), in attempting to determine how long hyperactive children are likely to require medication, conducted a placebo-controlled follow-up. During one month, placebo was given which was "blind" to both subject and teacher. For 28 children given placebo trials, 17 showed deterioration during the placebo month while 11 could stop taking medication. In a 2-year follow-up of 72 hyperactive boys, Riddle and Rapoport (1976) found that the hyperactive group continued to manifest behavioral and academic difficulty. Off-drug classroom behavior revealed considerable stability from diagnosis to follow-up which did not appear to be influenced by change of school or interim stimulant drug treatment. When compared to a control group, the hyperactive group exhibited more academic difficulties, lower peer status, and more depressive symptoms.

The poor results of medication alone over the long term led Satterfield, Cantwell, and Satterfield (1979) to suggest that a combination of clinically useful medication with appropriate psychological treatments simultaneously directed to each of the hyperactive child's many disabilities might produce better outcomes. This was supported in a one-year follow-up of 84 hyperactive boys who, when re-evaluated, were significantly better behaviorally (as rated by parents, teachers, physicians, and the children themselves). They were less overactive, less distractible, more task persistent, and showed improved relations with family and peers. Their performance on the PIAT (except for spelling) was improved significantly more than predicted. Thus, multimodal treatment, rather than medication alone may provide the optimum intervention for hyperactive children. Later, this finding was supported in a 3-year follow-up (Satterfield, Satterfield, & Cantwell, 1981) comparing 3 years of treatment to 2 years or less. It was found that those who had received more treatment had a better outcome with respect to educational achievement and antisocial behavior than those who had received less treatment. These findings speak favorably for a comprehensive treatment plan (including stimulant therapy but not relying on medication alone) but require a cautious optimism since, in this study, subjects were not randomly assigned to a multimodality treatment group and some other comparison treatment group (e.g., group receiving medication alone).

Thus, these findings supported and provided some insight into the finding (e.g., Weiss, Kruger, Danielson, & Elman, 1975) that drug treated and untreated hyperactive children do not differ at follow-up. It is quite possible that drugs alone are not enough and a more comprehensive intervention program is necessary for improved status. Although drug treatment effects childhood hyperactivity over the short-term, behavioral outcomes directly and academic outcomes indirectly were determined more by conduct disorder (Milich & Loney, 1979). In a further analysis, Paternite and Loney (1980) found that aggressive symptomatology at diagnosis was the best outcome predictor, and that ecological factors also made a significant contribution. August, Stewart, and Holmes (1983) compared, over 4 years, a group of "pure" hyperactive children with a group who were both hyperactive and aggressive. It was found that aggressive and antisocial behavior continued in the latter group while, in the former, the conduct disorders were less marked and their primary symptoms continued to be overactive, inattentive, and impulsive behaviors. Thus, conduct problems in hyperactive children found at follow-up may reflect initial levels of agression and antisocial behavior rather than hyperactivity itself. The problem, however, is that conduct disorder is such an integral feature in hyperactivity diagnosis that it makes those designated as hyperactive practically indistinguishable in clinical terms from children with an unsocialized aggressive disorder (Stewart, Cummings, Singer, & de Blois, 1981).

In a clinical study of 70 MBD children seen for an average of 76 months in elementary school, Miller (1978) found that 5 had organic brain damage, 4 developed seizures, and 4 became psychotic. For the 12 who became adolescents, all were found to be doing poorly.

Most of the sample tended not to have been hyperactive prior to age 3 and came from unstable family environments. Parents were not concerned about the child's feelings and typically, one or both, parents had a psychological disorder. Moreover, 48% of the siblings of the hyperactive group had psychological problems. Parents generally wanted others to take responsibility for modifying the problems manifested by their children. It was concluded "that problems with handling anger within the family are central to the syndrome, and more long-term, intensive family observations are needed" (Miller, 1978, p. 222).

These family observations were provided in several other investigations. In an analysis of 74 subjects followed from childhood to adolescence and young adulthood, Battle and Lacey (1972) found that mothers of hyperactive boys were critical, disapproving, unaffectionate, and severe in their punishment while none of these maternal behaviors were associated with hyperactive girls. With respect to sibling and peer involvement, both sexes showed high levels of involvement but males were generally rejected while females were more accepted. Morrison and Stewart (1971) interviewed parents of 59 hyperactive and 41 control subjects and found a high prevalence of alcoholism, sociopathy, and hysteria in the parents of the hyperactive group. It was also suggested that significantly more of the hyperactive group parents were hyperactive as children. In comparison, these findings did not hold for adoptive parents of hyperactive children (Morrison & Stewart, 1973). Cantwell (1972) also found increased prevalence rates for psychiatric illness in parents of hyperactive children after conducting interviews with parents of 50 hyperactive children and 50 matched controls. The presence of psychiatric difficulties was particularly the case among parents who were thought to have been hyperactive children themselves. Thus, childhood hyperactivity may be a precursor for certain types of adult psychiatric illness. Hechtman (1981), however, found that the problems were not as severe as those described previously (Morrison & Stewart, 1971; Cantwell, 1972). In comparing 65 parents of young hyperactive adults with 43 parents of matched controls at both 5 year and 10–12 year follow-ups, the families of the hyperactive group continued to have more difficulties when compared to the normal control families. The difficulties were in mental health, marital relationships, and emotional climate at home but were relatively mild and seemed to improve with time.

Conclusions. 1. Hyperactivity appears to be a persistent problem with little reason for any optimism about positive outcomes.

2. The symptoms associated with hyperactivity appear to be positively related to severity level.

3. The primary symptoms of hyperactivity appear to be poor academic performance and increased conduct disorder in school.

4. Hyperactivity in and of itself appears to exert negative influences in functioning.

5. The antecedents of hyperactivity appear to be found in temperamental differences (e.g., overactivity, distractibility) observed in infancy.

6. The long-term consequences of hyperactivity appear to be resistant to treatment efforts although some positive results may be found over the short term.

Follow-up of hyperactivity in adolescence and young adulthood

The longitudinal literature next focuses on outcomes observed during the adolescent and young adult years. In a 12-year questionnaire follow-up of adolescents and young adults earlier referred for hyperactivity, Laufer (1971) found that some form of special schooling was required for 50 of the 66 respondents. For the respondents 19 years or older, 18 were employed and 14 were in college while 10 had military service. Of the total group, 59% were still hyperactive; for the 27 no longer hyperactive, most reported cessation of symptoms between 12 and 16 years of age. Psychiatric help was needed in 33% of the cases but only 5% required hospitalization. Although these findings were positive, they must be viewed with caution since 100 questionnaires were sent out originally and only two-thirds were returned which suggests the possibility of a positive response bias.

One positive aspect of the Laufer (1971) report which has received support is the finding that less than 10% of the sample reported problems with either alcohol or drugs. Similarly, Beck, Langford, MacKay, and Sum (1975) found no drug problems in a group of 30 adolescents who had been treated earlier with stimulant medication for 6 months or longer, while Oettinger, Majovski, and Gauch (1977) reported that a group of 25 males now 17 to 26 years of age who had been treated with stimulant medication more or less continuously from 4.5 to 16 years, still required medication to fulfill work demands but no increased dosage was necessary over the years (i.e., no evidence of addiction or physiological dependency). Thus, even with drug treatment over an extended period, there appears no long-term consequence as evidenced by the lack of drug-related difficulties (e.g., addiction, abuse) within the behavioral problems manifested by hyperactive children.

A retrospective study of 83 hyperactive children by Mendelson, Johnson, and Stewart (1971) was based on interviews of their mothers when the group was between 12–16 years of age. The findings indicated that, although 50% of the group had improved, 25% still required some form of special education, 22% displayed delinquent behavior, and about 75% had problems with restlessness, impulsivity, distractibility, excitability, and aggressiveness. These behaviors were associated with low self-esteem and poor school performance. When the

subjects themselves were interviewed (Stewart, Mendelson, & Johnson, 1973), more than 50% reported that they were restless, impatient, impulsive, and irritable. They found it difficult to study, and 40% showed evidence of poor self-esteem.

In a comprehensive 5-year prospective controlled follow-up study of 91 hyperactive subjects aged 10–18 ($M = 13.3$) (Minde, Lewin, Weiss, Lavigueur, Douglas, & Sykes, 1971; Minde, Weiss, & Mendelson, 1972; Weiss, Minde, Werry, Douglas, & Nemeth, 1971), it was found that, compared to a matched control group (age, sex, IQ, and SES), hyperactive adolescents, for the most part, continued to be distractible, impulsive, and emotionally immature, although less hyperactive. A majority had poor self-esteem. Achievement testing indicated that the hyperactive adolescents had a significantly higher failure rate in all academic subjects, and were rated, by teachers, as displaying more behavioral problems. Although learning disorders increased and lower IQ was associated with the hyperactive group, intelligence alone was ruled out as the primary contributor to underachievement supporting the findings of Gillberg et al. (1983) and Mednick (1977). Additionally, Cohen, Weiss, and Minde (1972) found that the hyperactive group continued to use impulsive rather than reflective approaches to cognitive tasks and, over the 5 years, showed no improvement on IQ tests. In a further analysis (Hoy, Weiss, Minde, & Cohen, 1978), on 11 cognitive tests, the hyperactive group performed significantly worse than controls on measures of sustained attention, visual-motor functioning, and motor performance as well as on two of four reading assessments. They also rated themselves lower on items related to self-esteem and sociability. It was suggested that hyperactive children at adolescence still possessed attentional and stimulus-processing difficulties that effected not only academic performance but also social functioning.

Dykman, Peters, and Ackerman (1973) followed 31 MBD/hyperactive youngsters and a matched control group from grade school to re-evaluation at age 14. The hyperactive group was inferior to controls on full scale IQ and on verbal IQ. Initially, the control group was only superior on verbal IQ. Subtest patterns showed the hyperactive group to be deficient in conceptual, sequencing, and symbolic abilities. Later, Ackerman, Dykman, and Peters (1977b) found that the hyperactive group had significantly more adjustment problems usually involving oppositional or delinquent behavior. They showed lower self-esteem and poorer self-image as evidenced by their lower scores on nearly all areas measured by the *Minnesota Counseling Inventory*: family relations, emotional stability, mood, reality, conformity, and leadership. They were generally discouraged and did not like school, which was reflected clearly in their academic progress which was several years behind controls in reading, spelling, and arithmetic. With respect to school progress:

Only nine had moved comfortably into the academic mainstream. Better than 40% of the LD returnees scored in the lowest quartile on all the WRAT subtests, i.e., performed more than 1.5 years below age expectancy. All children had made progress, but there were no dramatic spurts (Ackerman et al., 1977b, p. 295).

Thus, the hyperactive group had poorer academic performance when compared to the control group but not in comparison to other learning disabled groups. In a similar group comparison, Blouin et al. (1978) compared hyperactive adolescents to a group of children having difficulty in school for other reasons but who were matched with the hyperactive group for age, sex, and IQ. Five years later at follow-up, the hyperactive group consumed more alcohol, were more hyperactive, and had more conduct problems. Although the achievement level was poor generally, no differences in academic achievement or intellectual ability were found between groups. The presence of these behavioral and personality problems has been linked to MBD. For example, Kaste (1971) explored the effect of MBD on social and psychological development. In a 10-year follow-up, more than half the MBD subjects were still experiencing serious personality and behavioral problems, and their deviant behavior tended to persist. Peter and Spreen (1979) divided 177 learning handicapped children into 3 groups: brain damaged, minimally brain damaged, and learning disabled with no neurological signs. When followed-up 4 to 12 years later and compared to 67 normal controls, a significant relationship emerged between an earlier diagnosis of neurological impairment and later behavior deviance, even when the effects of sex, age, and IQ were taken into account. These behavioral problems tended to persist into adolescence and young adulthood but were found not to be associated with delinquency (Spreen, 1981).

In a 7-year follow-up study on a cross section of 501 children, Huessy and Cohen (1976) analyzed the progress of 95 high-risk children from identification in second-grade to ninth-grade. Selection was based on teacher questionnaire ratings that assessed social maturity, academic performance, general behavior and attitude, and neuromotor development. Based on percentile rankings, the upper (i.e., the worst) 20% were designated as hyperkinetic. The children were again rated on this questionnaire as fourth- and fifth-graders, and the 20% with the highest scores for either of the 3 years were later contrasted in ninth- and 12th-grades with controls.

It was found that those children who were identified in second-grade but not in fourth- and fifth-grades while frequently repeating a grade, had a good prognosis (in ninth-grade). Those children whose mean percentiles fell above the 80th percentile in second-, fourth-, and fifth-grades had the worst prognosis in high school, and

70% of that group had poor social adjustment in adolescence. Half of the high-risk group had repeated one or more grades while 10 children were no longer in regular classes. It was reported by teachers that the high-risk group continued to be inattentive, easily distractible, uncooperative, immature, unpredictable, attention seeking, and unable to settle down and follow directions. One major limitation, however, was the method of identifying hyperkinetic children. It is likely that the reliance solely on teacher ratings identified a heterogeneous group rather than those forming a pure group manifesting the hyperkinetic syndrome. Nevertheless, ratings by a variety of individuals may possess greater validity as demonstrated by Nichols and Chen (1981) who found that the most predictive characteristic of hyperactive children at age 7 were ratings at age 4 of hyperactivity, impulsivity, and short attention span. There is thus support for the finding that elementary school academic and behavioral performance has high predictive value for adolescence. Most findings confirmed the persistent nature of difficulties associated with childhood hyperactivity. For example, in a 5-year retrospective study of 81 adolescent hyperactive children (mean age = 15.5), Feldman, Denhoff, and Denhoff (1979) found that 57% were problem-free while 33% required continued drug treatment, counseling for emotional problems (e.g., poor self-esteem), or special educational arrangements. Similarly, Woods (1981), after following 64 hyperactive children into adolescence, found that a majority of the hyperactive group disliked school and performed poorly as a consequence. The hyperactive group had lower self-esteem and generally suffered from a pervasive sense of confusion about expectations.

Conclusions. 1. Symptoms of childhood hyperactivity tend to persist into adolescence and young adulthood.

2. The hyperactive child exhibits the symptoms of restlessness, impulsivity, and attention at the same level during adolescence and young adulthood.

3. During adolescence and young adulthood, hyperactivity is clearly associated with significant academic problems.

4. There is also increased social and conduct difficulties with parents, teachers, and peers during adolescence and young adulthood.

5. Hyperactivity during adolescence and young adulthood appears to be accompanied by poor self-esteem, poor self-image, and poor self-confidence.

Follow-up of hyperactivity in adulthood

The longitudinal literature has also followed hyperactive children into adulthood and offers insights into not only academic functioning but also vocational status as well as social functioning. Perhaps the most comprehensive analyses were reported by a Canadian group in a 10-

to 12-year follow-up study (Hechtman, Weiss, Perlman, Hopkins, & Wener, 1982; Weiss, Hechtman, Perlman, Hopkins, & Wener, 1979). The reports included 76 hyperactive subjects (mean age = 19.5) and 45 control subjects who were matched on age, sex, SES, and IQ. All hyperactive subjects were followed from the time they were between 6 and 12 years of age and met the following criteria: (a) restlessness and poor concentration were the primary complaints which had been present since their earliest years; (b) these primary complaints were a major source of difficulties both at home and at school; (c) IQ levels were at least 85; (d) none of the children were psychotic, epileptic, or cerebral palsied; and (e) all children were living at home with at least one parent.

In an analysis of demographic data (Weiss et al., 1979), it was found that the school histories of the hyperative group revealed less educational progress and more remaining in high school at follow-up. Their average marks were lower and more hyperactive students discontinued high school for this reason. They failed more grades in elementary and high school with academic failure not limited to any particular subject. The work history of the hyperactive group indicated no difference in job status between full-time working hyperactive subjects and controls. No difference was found between groups with respect to discrepancy between fathers' work status and that of the subjects. Vocational plans (or work aspirations) were not different between groups and were generally judged to be realistic. With respect to court referrals, there was a trend for the hyperactive subjects to have more court referrals during the 5 years preceding follow-up (47% vs. 32%). Difference between groups, however, were not significant in the year immediately prior to follow-up evaluation and tests of moral development indicated that the groups displayed similar levels of development (Hechtman, Weiss, & Perlman, 1984). A separate analysis, taking into account both the number and seriousness of different kinds of court referrals, showed no difference between the groups regarding the seriousness of such offenses (e.g., theft, aggression, disturbing the peace, traffic offenses, drug possession). Also, interestingly, the hyperactive group had significantly more car accidents (mean 1.3 vs. 0.07).

Psychiatric evaluation indicated that more hyperactive subjects displayed personality trait disorders, most frequently either impulsive or immature-dependent personality traits. Two hyperactive subjects were diagnosed as borderline psychotic. Significantly more hyperactive subjects felt restless and rated their childhood as unhappy. The most common responses as to what made their childhood unhappy included "feeling dumb," "family fights," and "being criticized."

Hechtman, Weiss, and Perlman (1978) found no difference between groups with respect to height, weight, blood pressure, or pulse rate. Serial comparison of electroencephalograms (EEG) of both groups at 10-year follow-up revealed no differences. Comparison of EEGs

of hyperactive subjects at diagnosis, 5-year follow-up, and 10-year follow-up indicated that normalization of the EEG tended to occur during adolescence (Hechtman, Weiss, & Metrakas, 1978).

In describing psychological test performance (Hopkins, Hechtman, & Weiss, 1979; Weiss, Hechtman, & Perlman, 1978), data were presented about subject ratings of self-esteem and social interaction (*California Psychological Inventory*), psychopathological traits (SCL-90), and experimental measures of self-esteem and self-concept. On measures of self-esteem, hyperactive subjects rated themselves as significantly inferior to controls. On ratings of psychopathology, however, no differences were found suggesting that hyperactive subjects do not perceive themselves as possessing classical psychopathological symptoms but, in general, did see themselves operating less optimally than controls. On social skill measures, hyperactive subjects performed less well on oral tasks but not on written tasks (*Situational Social Skills Inventory*) and the *Means-End Problem Solving Test*). Tests of cognitive style (MFFT, *Embedded Figures Test and Story Test*) indicated that the problems hyperactive subjects had during their childhood and adolescence persisted into adult life. Finally, rating scales were sent to employers and to teachers and revealed that teachers rated hyperactive subjects as inferior to controls while employers' ratings were identical for the two groups. This finding indicated that the demands of the social setting in which hyperactive subjects were evaluated influences the degree to which they were considered dormant.

The findings of the Canadian group have been confirmed by other follow-up reports. For example, Borland and Heckman (1976) followed 20 hyperactive males for 20–25 years and found that about half continued to show hyperactive symptoms with some showing psychiatric problems. Although a large majority completed high school and were employed steadily, which was also supported by Feldman, Denhoff, and Denhoff (1979), the hyperactive subjects had not achieved an SES level equal to that of their fathers or their brothers. This finding is in contrast to Weiss et al. (1979) and may be the result of Borland and Heckman's (1976) subjects being older. The Weiss et al. (1979) subjects were much younger and may indicate that time is on the side of control subjects. Beck (1976) also found lower occupational status among 22 subjects; the majority held jobs in semi-skilled or unskilled classifications (or unemployed), and related this to poor school achievement (mean reading level = 6.8; mean arithmetic level = 7.0). The primary hyperactive symptoms showed a reduction at follow-up (Beck, 1976) except for distractibility but the group was characterized by low self-esteem as found by Feldman et al. (1979). Despite hyperactive target symptom reduction, Beck (1976) suggested the presence of a number of "secondary symptoms" which puts this adult population at risk for later psychopathology. In general, emotional difficulties probably result from the persistence of hyperactive symptoms, and most social and possibly psychiatric consequences of the disorder relate to its presence in childhood as well as persistence in adulthood.

The conclusions about persistence into adulthood of childhood hyperactive behaviors have beem demonstrated in studies seeking evidence of a similar adult syndrome. An early entry (Quitkin & Klein, 1969) followed 105 psychiatric subjects who were characterized by least one of the following: (a) difficult birth history, (b) childhood hyperkinesis, (c) impulse disorder, (d) late speech, (e) clumsiness, (f) learning problems, (g) intellectual defect, (h) temper tantrums, or (i) organic indicator. The subjects were then classified into groups with or without "soft signs" and the group with "soft signs" were then judged in terms of current adult psychiatric status. Two syndromes were identified: a socially awkward withdrawn group and an impulsive-destructive group. This latter group was marked by hyperactivity in childhood and shows how hyperactivity was persistent and predictive of latter psychiatric difficulty. Wood, Reinherr, Wender, and Johnson (1976) selected 15 adults from a psychiatric clinic population whose major symptoms were restlessness, impulsivity, poor attention, and emotional lability. Parents were asked to complete the *Conner's Parent Rating Scale* based upon their memories of the children when they were 6–10 years old. Two-thirds of these parents' ratings placed the adult patients in the 95th percentile for hyperactivity during their childhoods. This suggested that these adult psychiatric patients were still manifesting continued problems of the hyperactive child syndrome.

In a similar type study, Shelley and Reister (1972) described 16 young adults serving in the Air Force who were having difficulty with fine and gross motor tasks, who showed problems of anxiety and low self-esteem, and who had problems with impulse control and concentration. When parents were interviewed, they reported a history of overactivity and academic difficulties during childhood. Finally, Gomez, Janowsky, Detin, Huey, and Clapton (1981) administered the *Wender-Utah Personality Inventory Adult Questionnaire* of childhood characteristics to 40 subjects. Of the 40 psychiatric subjects, about one-third reported symptoms compatible with childhood hyperactivity while, among 28 controls, only 4% reported compatible symptoms. Although interesting, these studies must be approached with caution because of the lack of a control group in some (e.g., psychiatric patient with different problems) and the questionable validity of parent and self ratings after some 10 years, which raises the problem of selective memory.

Morrison and Minkoff (1975) suggested that the "explosive personality" characterized by sudden outbursts of verbal or physical aggression and an inability to control overreaction to environmental pressures may be a sequel to the hyperactive child syndrome. Later, Morrison (1979, 1980) investigated 48 adult subjects (mean age = 29.7 years) who were hyperactive as children. When compared to a matched control group (i.e.,

age, sex, and SES), the hyperactive group revealed significantly more personality disorder, more sociopathy, and more alcoholism but less affective disorder than the control group. In terms of social characteristics, the hyperactive subjects' fathers were significantly more often employed in skilled and semi-skilled jobs rather than professional positions. As adults, the hyperactive groups averaged over one year less schooling and were less likely to attain a professional occupation. With respect to social characteristics, the hyperactive group had a history of more violence and more police contacts.

Mann and Greenspan (1976) suggested that adults who had MBD as children constitute a distinct diagnostic entity: *Adult Brain Dysfunction*. The primary diagnostic characteristics include: (a) a history of early learning disabilities with short attention span, (b) diffuse and severe symptoms in adulthood with anxiety and depression being primary, (c) a rapid and dramatic alteration in symptoms with drug treatment, and (d) cognitive processing characterized by rapid flow of speech and many subject shifts but without over indications of psychotic thinking.

In terms of long-term outcomes, Milman (1977, 1978) followed prospectively 73 children diagnosed as MBD into adult life. Among the 73 subjects, 38% were classified as having developmental lag, and 62% as having organic brain damage. The IQs ranged from 69 to 124, with 19% having IQs of 69. At follow-up, 10–20 years after diagnosis, subjects were 15–23 years of age (mean = 19.4 years). With respect to education, 84% completed high school, 27% attempted college, of whom 12% were still attending or had graduated. In terms of psychiatric status, 6% had no psychiatric disorder, 80% had personality disorders, and 14% were borderline psychotic. Global ratings of adjustment found 20% rated good or satisfactory, and 80% as marginal or poor. The poor outcomes were significantly correlated with: multiplicity of behavioral symptoms, multiplicity of "soft signs," low intelligence, learning problems (especially mathematics and spelling), and special class placement. Generally, a correlational analysis between initial status and adult outcome revealed strong positive correlation between childhood social problems and adult inadequate personality, and between childhood anti-social behavior and adult personalty disorder (particularly anti-social, passive-aggressive, and impulsive types), while there was a strong negative correlation between childhood hyperactivity and both school problems and normal psychiatric outcome. Although these findings were supportive of other long-term studies, they are particularly negative which may be influenced by the large proportion of subjects with organic brain damage and low IQ.

Conclusions. 1. Hyperactivity in adulthood is likely to reveal symptoms similar to childhood hyperactivity including restlessness, impulsivity, anxiety, inattention, and irritability.

2. Hyperactive adults are quite likely to possess childhood histories that included overactivity and school difficulties.

3. Hyperactive adults generally showed lower levels of academic attainment and vocational success but their vocational plans were generally realistic and reflected their abilities.

4. Hyperactive adults often displayed personality trait disorders including poor self-esteem and self-concept. These, in turn, were related to poor social skills manifested in impaired social interactions.

5. The persistence of childhood symptoms into adulthood led to the conclusion that adult hyperactivity may be considered a syndrome.

Methodological issues

Before summarizing the findings of longitudinal research in hyperactivity, it is necessary to examine several methodological issues to provide perspective. Although sample size varied considerably, a more important aspect was attrition rate, that is, the number of subjects intended for follow-up who either could not be located or refused to cooperate. Among the studies reviewed, the average attrition rate was almost 30% and ranged from 2% to 60%. No study, however, examined the difference between those hyperactive subjects followed up and those who were not. The problem is an inability to determine whether the hyperactive group not followed presented more or less hyperactivity than those finally evaluated. There is some suggestion from other disability areas (Cox, Rutter, Yule, & Quinton, 1977) that the missing groups, in general, manifest a worse comparative pathology. Thus, with some follow-up information missing, it is difficult to draw firm conclusions about the general population of hyperactive subjects.

Generalization of findings is also made problematic by the selection criteria used to sample both hyperactive and control subjects which makes it difficult to conclude unequivocally that similar groups of subjects are, in fact, being studied. For example, Barkley (1982), in reviewing 210 hyperactivity studies, found that 64% of those studies used nothing more than the opinion of the investigators in diagnosing hyperactivity without specifying any criteria that were used in making decisions about hyperactivity. A majority of the studies reviewed here did provide information on selection criteria (although not providing a detailed diagnostic scheme) but three studies failed to provide any such information (Huessy & Cohen, 1976; Laufer, 1971; Miller, 1978). Four studies which did provide sampling information did not detail either the source of information or the diagnostic procedures (Borland & Heckman, 1976; Mendelson et al., 1971; Menkes et al., 1967; Stewart et al., 1973). The remaining studies did a reasonable job in defining selection criteria, information sources, and diagnostic procedures; all the studies by the Canadian group (e.g., Campbell et al., 1977; Hechtman et al., 1982; Weiss et

al., 1971), the New York group (e.g., Thomas & Chess, 1968), the Iowa group (e.g., Loney et al., 1980), and the Arkansas group (e.g., Dykman et al., 1973) fell into this category.

Another problem related to selection criteria was the apparent overrepresentation of males in longitudinal samples. Safer and Allen (1976) reported that the proportion of boys in epidemiological and clinical samples is anywhere between 60% and 75%. Yet, although some studies did not report a sex distribution, those that did averaged almost 95% males (the lowest average was 86% while seven studies were 100% male). Thus, most studies reviewed appeared atypical with respect to sex distribution and casts doubt on whether the obtained findings can be generalized to the whole hyperactive population. Because boys tend to display conduct disorders, antisocial behaviors, and immaturity more frequently than girls (Shepherd, Oppenheim, & Mitchell, 1971), the overrepresentation of boys would tend to increase the chances of finding these behaviors, and may explain partially the finding that childhood hyperactivity (particularly when associated with aggression) is likely to result in similar behaviors at follow-up.

The presence of a control group is a primary methodological feature in longitudinal research. Some early studies (e.g., Huessy & Cohen, 1976: Laufer, 1971; Mendelson et al., 1971; Menkes et al., 1967; Minde et al., 1972; Stewart et al., 1973) had no controls but most later studies did include a control group. Some control conditions were poor, however, as in the case (Borland & Heckman, 1976) where siblings of hyperactive subjects were used as controls. This is not optimal because differences may be minimized because of similar environmental circumstances. There is, however, the possibility that differences may also be enhanced; for example, siblings may have inflexible perceptions from the time when hyperactivity was diagnosed in one of them which may result in the control sibling possessing a stable, but perhaps invalid, perception about the hyperactive sibling's overactivity, restlessness, and distractibility.

Another common problem is the selection of controls at a time later than the diagnosis of the hyperactive group (e.g., Cohen et al., 1972; Hechtman et al., 1982; Hopkins et al., 1979; Hoy et al., 1978; Riddle & Rapoport, 1976; Weiss et al., 1971.) Two difficulties are associated with this practice: (a) the absence of original comparison data which could be used to establish the uniqueness of the groups from the outset, and (b) the difficulties in making judgements about change over time since both groups do not share a common time frame. Additionally, it is also difficult to comment adequately on subjects lost over time. If assessed initially at the same time, then missing cases at follow-up can be evaluated in terms of the inititial assessment information.

The type of control subject selected may also be a source of difficulty. Studies including a comparison group (e.g., Borland & Heckman, 1976; Hopkins et al.,

1979; Hoy et al., 1978; Minde et al., 1971; Riddle & Rapoport, 1976; Weiss et al., 1971, 1979) almost always selected normal ones, that is, selected randomly from classmates of hyperactive children. Several studies (e.g., Cohen et al., 1972; Hechtman et al., 1982) attempted to improve upon this practice by not only selecting normal subjects randomly but also further screening this selected group to exclude subjects who possesses any cognitive or behavioral disturbance. But this practice makes it difficult to demonstrate that hyperactivity outcomes are different from that of other psychiatric conditions, not simply from normal comparison subjects. Otherwise, any differences found might simply reflect those expected in comparing groups with problems with those having no such problems. The derived findings may, in fact, reveal nothing specific about the outcomes of hyperactivity; the findings may be equally valid for groups labeled conduct disorders or immature personality. The further specification of control groups in terms of eliminating cognitive and behavioral factors may actually amplify the difficulties in isolating hyperactivity effects alone since the group differences are enhanced in an untypical fashion. The type of control conditions necessary were demonstrated in a study by White, Barratt, and Adams (1979) who used both psychiatric and normal controls to compare to a hyperactive group. The groups were matched for IQ, SES, sex, race, and age. When given a variety of assessments, the psychiatric control group, in general, performed more poorly than either the normal controls or hyperactive subjects. Thus, it is possible from such a design to conclude that cognitive difficulties were not necessarily either specific or unique to subjects with a history of hyperactivity but may be associated with other psychiatric disorders.

Conclusions. Despite a variegated picture of outcomes caused partially by both methodological variation (e.g., retrospective studies, family studies, cross-sectional research) and subject population (e.g., age differences, IQ differences, diagnostic differences), a synthesized view of the outcomes of childhood hyperactivity in adolescence and adulthood can be achieved. For a small proportion of hyperactive subjects, functioning in adolescence and adulthood is fairly normal, and no persistent difficulties are present. The majority of hyperactive subjects, however, do reveal continuing difficulties characteristic of the hyperactive child syndrome: in particular, restlessness, impulsivity, poor concentration, and poor social skills. These problems are often accompanied by lowered academic performance and vocational status. The hyperactivity symptoms often give rise to difficulties with work, interpersonal relationships, poor self-esteem, irritability, anxiety, and emotional lability. Finally, another small proportion of hyperactive subjects develop significant psychiatric problems or antisocial behavior. These subjects may be psychotic or borderline psychotic, severely depressed, and/or involved in drug or alcohol abuse. Although

gross psychopathology is not likely, there appears to be a propensity toward moderate personality disorder characterized by conduct disorder or immature-impulsive behavior. Thus, the outcome for children diagnosed hyperactive, in comparison to normal controls, is relatively poor since the child is likely to manifest a number of behavioral, social, personality, academic, and vocational difficulties.

Longitudinal Research in Learning Disabilities The 1970s

With the establishment of learning disability as a major category of special education during the 1960s, the 1970s saw the first appearance of follow-up literature with learning disabled children as subjects. Hinton and Knights (1971), in a 3-year follow-up of 67 children with learning disabilities, found a consistent pattern; early failure was highly related to later academic difficulties. In fact, WRAT scores for reading, spelling, and arithmetic were correlated about 0.60 between diagnosis and outcome assessment. This finding was later verified by Ackerman, Dykman, and Peters (1977a) who followed 93 boys with learning disabilities classified in grade school to age 14. The learning disabled group remained seriously retarded in reading, spelling, and arithmetic when compared to normal achievers. The learning disabled students who had the poorest outcomes at follow-up were those who had the most severe early reading problems and who scored poorly in the Information, Arithmetic, Digit Span, and Coding subtests of the WISC. The later achievement levels of the learning disabled group was independent of both earlier classification by activity level and neurological maturity.

Koppitz (1971) conducted a 5-year follow-up study of 177 children with learning disabilities aged 6–12 years. Most subjects had been experiencing school difficulty since kindergarten. Information was attained about the school district, sex, age, IQ, visual-motor perception, academic levels, behavior, developmental and medical history, and social background. For the sample studied, it was found: (a) there was a 6:1 ratio of boys to girls, (b) the mean IQ was 92, (c) 77% had visual-motor perceptual difficulties, (d) a majority showed behavior problems (which had been the major reason for referral to special class), (e) 84% were from unstable home environments, (f) 45% had MBD, and (g) 97% were hyperactive. At the end of 5 years, 40% remained in special classes, 15% had been referred for hospital or residential programs because of autism or psychosis, 24% had returned to regular classes, and 3% had been transferred to other special classes for the deaf or educable mentally retarded. The remaining 18% had either been withdrawn by their parents or moved.

It was found that among those returned to regular classes, success was more contingent upon behavior than achievement (although their reading levels were better from the beginning and their mean IQ was 98 versus 87 for those remaining in learning disability classes). There appeared to be a relationship with age: the younger the learning disabled subject, the more impaired and the longer special services were required. It was also noted that better progress was made if the learning disabled child's deficit was restricted to a single area. For example, a child with only impaired visual-motor difficulties was able to better compensate for the problem and show better progress. A child with learning disabilities, however, with both visual-motor and auditory-perceptual deficits (or any other combination of deficits) usually exhibited a more severe learning disability and exhibited little gain (if any). In fact, the learning disability sample as a whole displayed little improvement in academic achievement; the average gain was only 3–5 months for each year spent in the special class. Koppitz (1971) suggested that many reported gains were spurious and that academic progress typically levels off ("plateaus"). Therefore, pupils with learning disabilities require not just one or two years, but rather long-term, remedial efforts. Additionally, it was suggested that the value of intervention programs may be in improving self-concept and instilling more positive attitudes.

The Koppitz (1971) study, although widely cited, possessed difficulties, especially in sampling, that limits conclusions. The lack of a control group, of course, is a problem since no comparison can be made. The criteria used for sample selection, however, does not seem to discriminate children with learning disabilities from other conditions as evidenced by the inclusion of subjects who later became psychotic, mentally retarded, deaf, or required other special placement. Furthermore, the initial population may have been closer to a behaviorally disordered group than a learning disabled one since a large majority were referred for behavior difficulties, came from unstable home environments, and were placed outside their school districts. Consequently, it is questionable whether this study included a "typical" learning disabled population (even given the difficulties in defining what that might be). The characteristics and findings attributed to this sample may be unique and not applicable to the learning disabled population at large.

Gottesman (1978, 1979) followed 43 children with learning disabilities who were referred initially between ages 7 and 14 years, for a period of 5–7 years. Over half the sample received special help after evaluation, or were referred either to special classes or to special schools for children with learning disabilities. When their reading achievement was assessed at follow-up, the learning disabled sample, as a group, showed very small gains; they progressed, on average, at the rate of 4 months per year. The group in special education placements were more likely to have lower IQ levels, and to score lower on the achievement outcome assessment. But again, these findings must be approached with caution because of possible sampling difficulties. As a group, the selected sample revealed a higher incidence of neurological, psychiatric, and language disabilities. Additionally, their mean IQ level (88) fell within the low-average range.

Although reading achievement appears to be a major disability area for the child with learning disabilities (which was not unexpected given the persistent nature found for reading disability), several follow-up studies reported generally favorable outcomes. Abbott and Frank (1975) studied the outcome for 139 students with learning disabilities who had formerly attended a private school but who had since returned to regular class placement. Of the 139 students, about 75% were rated as making satisfactory progress with about the same percentage showing improved social and emotional status. It should be noted, however, that 50% required psychological counseling after leaving the special school. In a 10-year follow-up, Edgington (1975) found that, of 25 children with learning disabilities, 22 were still enrolled in school or had since graduated and three had dropped out (two were working full time and one was planning to re-enroll). Five students had not repeated a grade during their school history while 19 had repeated a grade prior to or concurrent with enrollment in a special program. Only one student had repeated a grade after enrollment in the special program. It was concluded that high school age children with learning disabilities are "rather indistinguishable from regular students in so far as successful completion of secondary school is concerned" (Edgington, 1975, p. 60). While these findings are positive, they must be approached with caution because of the large attrition rate. The original group consisted of 47 subjects with learning disabilities but follow-up data were gathered on only 25 which represents a self-selected group. Conceivably, the other 22 subjects might present a different outcome picture.

A positive tone was also found in the follow-up study reported by Lehtinen-Rogan and Hartman (1976) who assessed the adult attainments of 91 children with learning disabilities who received special education for an average of 3 years between the ages 6 and 13. The breakdown of academic accomplishments found 69% graduating from high school, 36% completing college, and 8% either completing or pursuing graduate study. About 70% were employed, with the following breakdown: professional (13%), clerical (33%), and unskilled (23%). Approximately 55% were independent of parental supervision. Only 6% showed evidence of delinquency. All IQs were in the average range but achievement levels were still depressed with mean grade scores of 10.4 in reading, 8.4 in spelling, and 6.7 in arithmetic. Although these were positive outcomes, almost 75% of the group reported some therapeutic or counseling experience at some point. Yet, personality testing showed them to be particularly vulnerable to stress; they were also found to possess low self-esteem, to be highly sensitive, and to be unable to form close interpersonal relationships. These were seen as the "hidden handicaps" of learning disability but were partially offset by a strong motivation toward academic achievement and productive work. While positive, the findings should be approached with some caution given the possible sampling bias caused by the selection of a private school population where families were supportive and sought remedial services.

Conclusions. 1. Learning disability, like reading disability and hyperactivity, is a persistent problem and is highly related to early school failure.

2. Learning disability tends to be a pervasive problem that affects adversely both academic and behavioral functioning.

3. There appeared to be a relationship with age; the younger the child with learning disabilities the more severe the disability and the more likely remediation is required over a long period.

4. Better progress is made by a learning disabled child with a deficit in only a single area as opposed to multiple deficits.

5. Better outcomes were associated with greater gains in behavioral functioning although academic remediation is also important.

6. A child with a learning disability is likely to need long-term services with much support given even after specific remedial efforts cease.

7. Generalizations are difficult given the heterogeneric nature of the learning disability samples used.

The 1980s

Even though some caution is necessary in interpretation, generally favorable outcomes have been reported in subsequent investigations. For example, White, Schumaker, Warner, Alley, and Deshler (1980), in a retrospective study comparing young adults diagnosed as having learning disabilities during their elementary school years with a group not labeled learning disabled, found a relatively small number of differences. Both groups were holding approximately the same number of full-time jobs and were earning about the same amount of money. In the social area, both groups had a number of friends and had frequent contact with parents and relatives. Generally then, the young adults with learning disabilities appeared to be adjusting as well as the non disabled group. There were, however, several differences that emerged. In the area of vocational adjustment, the learning disabled group were holding jobs with less social status and were less satisfied with their employment situation. Socially, the groups differed primarily with respect to their degree of involvement in recreational and social activities. Similarly, Fafard and Haubrich (1981) found that unemployment was not a problem at follow-up for 21 young adults who had received learning disability services. Most had graduated from high school and were involved in a variety of social relationships. Yet most still had residual reading disabilities and the vocational area was marked by concern and frustration. These findings led to the conclusion that an important component of learning disability programming is vocational education. Motivation was not

the problem but rather assistance was needed in (a) determining how to get a job, (b) identifying the types of jobs available to them, and (c) understanding what constitutes economic independence. Thus, the findings suggested a cautious optimism but also a cause for concern as stated by White et al. (1980)

> Although LD young adults are "making it" in a number of important areas, they seem to be much less satisfied with at least some areas of their lives. Personally, this can be related, in part, to the way in which past experiences have shaped their present attitudes and values, the difference between their expectations for adult life and what they have encountered, or a combination of these. In any case, the schools have neither adequately prepared the LD young adults for the social/affective facets of adult life nor taught them what to expect when they leave school. (p. 17–18)

Major-Kingsley (1982), in a 10-year retrospective study, attempted to analyze the achievement, adjustment, and aspirations of 40 boys with learning disabilities as young adults. By the age of 12, most of these subjects recognized that they had learning problems as evidenced by academic difficulties, especially in reading. In many cases, they reported feeling frustrated, depressed, hostile, inferior, alienated, and discouraged by their school difficulties. The learning disabled group, when compared to a normal comparison group, was far more likely to have received special education services. Yet nearly 80% felt that they continued to have a learning problem; these problems were described as primarily in reading, math, and writing. Most felt uneasy about their current reading ability (average reading score = ninth-grade), and tended to avoid situations that required reading. About 25% continued to experience feelings of low self-esteem, inadequacy, or frustration.

Despite the persistence of some academic difficulties, very few of the boys with learning disablities dropped out of school prior to high school graduation and more than half planned to complete college. Similar positive achievement findings were reported by Leone, Lovitt, and Hansen (1981) in a follow-up of 10 boys with learning disabilities 5–6 years after enrollment in a learning disability program. It was found that initial reading deficits (average 2 years below grade level in fourth- and fifth-grades) did not prevent the learning disabled group from being successful in high school. When compared to a control group, few differences were noted on general measures of high school performance (i.e., grade point average, attendance, class rank). The free-time activities and occupational interests of both groups were also found to be similar. As found in previous follow-up reports (e.g., White et al., 1980; Fafard & Haubrich, 1981), Major-Kingsley (1982) concluded that, "The overwhelming impression from this study is that individuals with learning disabilities in childhood function in young adulthood in much the same way as do individuals

Kenneth A. Kavale

who achieve adequately in school during childhood" (p. 116). Few differences between groups were found in either vocational or personal-social outcomes. Although generally setting lower educational and vocational goals than the non-disabled group, the learning disabled group, when considering the severity of their learning problems in childhood, were judged to have done remarkably well.

Positive conclusions were also drawn by Cobb and Crump (1984) in a retrospective follow-up of 100 young adults born before 1964 who were classified as having learning disabilities. That total sample included 25 identified as having learning disabilities but not placed and 75 identified and placed in a learning disability program. While the placed and nonplaced groups differed relatively little on outcome measures, the placed group were found to have poorer grades and seemed to evidence poorer coping skills. Yet, as a group, the total sample appeared to be functioning reasonably well as adults. About 85% were employed and a majority graduated from high school with many obtaining post-high school training and education. A wide variety of jobs were represented but a majority were in the skilled to semi-skilled areas. Reported incomes were generally low (average = $10,000/year) but interviews revealed the sample to be generally satisfied with their vocational choices. A majority reported that they no longer experienced reading problems but about 5% revealed that reading continued to be a source of difficulty. While the students with learning disabilities rated their regular class placement as beneficial, they were much more positive about learning disability classes and especially vocational education. In summary, Cobb and Crump (1984) concluded that, "The overall impression presented by the data is that these persons are fulfilling their adult roles quite well; they are, by and large, decent, productive citizens" (p. 143–144).

In a 4-year follow-up of 52 adolescents with learning disabilities who entered a special education program in the ninth-grade, Levin, Zigmond, and Birch (1985) added insight into the nature of the progress made by students with learning disabilities. At follow-up, the group should have been in the 12th grade but 16 were still enrolled in a special education program, seven were in a regular class, and 24 had stopped attending high school (five could not be located). Academic skills were assessed in 34 students (all those in school plus 11 dropouts). While school status was below expectation, academic gains over the 4-year period were impressive. Reading gains averaged about 2 years while math gains revealed about a 1 year gain on average. Further analyses, however, showed that about half of the achievement growth had taken place during the ninth grade with the remaining half spread over the following 3 years. Thus, after an initial spurt of academic growth, achievement tended to level off and, finally, reach a plateau. Interviews with the 11 dropouts found that only four felt the decision had been their own. The remainder reported that they had been encouraged to leave school

because of persistent academic and behavior problems.

Conclusions. 1. Most learning disabled subjects possessed residual academic difficulties as young adults but appeared to be well-adjusted.

2. The learning disabled group did not have a higher drop-out rate and most expressed a desire to attend college.

3. In terms of vocational adjustment, the learning disabled group possessed jobs with less social status and appeared less satisfied with their employment.

4. Considering the severity of their initial disability, most learning disabled subjects appeared to be doing well but most felt uneasy about their current reading ability and avoided situations that required reading.

5. Most learning disabled subjects, although finding the regular class beneficial, reported that learning disability classes and vocational (career) education were beneficial.

6. There tends to be an initial spurt of academic gain after remediation but this tends to level off over time.

Follow-up finding in learning disability versus reading disability

Thus, the studies using learning disabled samples reported a relatively optimistic view of outcomes and, although still possessing residual difficulties, the learning disabled subjects performed reasonably well given their earlier status. This favorable view is in contrast to the generally negative findings found for reading disability and hyperactivity. How could these seemingly contradictory outcomes be reconciled? The differences appeared to reflect specificity in diagnosis; the reading disabled and hyperactive groups were more precisely delineated while the learning disabled groups tended to be more globally defined. Given the difficulties surrounding learning disability definition (Kavale & Forness, 1985) and the problems in specifying learning disability identification criteria (Kavale & Nye, 1981), it is highly probable that any selected learning disabled sample will be diverse and reveal considerable variability. For example, Horn, O'Donnell, and Vitulano (1983) suggested that the severity factor may be masked by the initial referral source (clinic vs. school) with clinic populations possessing more severe (and multiple) problems while school-referred children may have less severe difficulties. Because most of the learning disability follow-up research was school-based, it is probable that a majority of the learning disability follow-up studies included a large proportion of mild learning disabled students. This means that they are less likely to manifest the reading disability and hyperactivity symptoms to the same degree and extent even though these are considered correlative conditions. Hence, the generally positive outcomes from learning disability follow-up research may reflect the mild nature of the disability caused by sampling from school-referred intact groups.

Follow-up of remedial efforts

The learning disability follow-up literature also focused on treatment approaches and assessed their efficacy over time. A large proportion of learning disability remedial services were delivered in a mainstream situation with resource room programming. For example, the positive findings reported by Edgington (1975) were based on a resource room model where daily attendance ranged from 25 to 90 minutes and small group instruction was scheduled throughout the school day. Weiner (1969) evaluated the effectiveness of a resource room for 72 children with learning disabilities. Results indicated significant growth in reading, spelling, and arithmetic over a 10 month period. Similarly, Sabatino (1971) investigated the use of a resource room as an alternative to the special class for 114 children with learning disabilities. Resource room programming, especially for students who attended daily, was found superior to either biweekly resource programming, the regular class, or the special class. Other efficacy studies (Pepe, 1974; Sindelar & Deno, 1978) have also shown the effectiveness of the resource room in increasing academic achievement and appropriate behaviors. These studies suffered from a short follow-up period which suggests caution in interpretation because of the possibility that the results may be due more to novelty effects than any programmatic variables (see Silberberg & Silberberg, 1969).

Bloomer (1978), in a 6-year follow-up of 163 children with learning disabilities in Grades 4-10 who were enrolled in a resource room, concluded that the resource room was an effective alternative special education service. The mean rate of gain in both reading and arithmetic was significantly greater than the rate of gain in the regular classroom after treatment. There was also a relationship with length of treatment: the greater the gain, the shorter the period of resource programming. Additionally, benefits from the resource room were associated with less severe learning disability, higher IQ level, and more perceptual integrity. It was also found that the first year in the resource room was most important in terms of later status; students who did best later achieved at a rate of one month of gain for every month of treatment during the initial year. Nevertheless, the average reading gain during the first year back in the regular classroom revealed a regression in reading achievement.

This finding was supported by Ito (1980, 1981) who found that, while resource room programming was effective for increasing reading rates of children with learning disabilities, the increased rates were not maintained in the regular classroom. Herr (1976) studied the effects of mainstreaming on the academic achievement of seven children with learning disabilities. The findings led to the conclusion that:

Mainstreaming had a serious detrimental effect on the academic achievement of six of the seven subjects. Although these subjects made significant gains during their enrollment at the Easter Seal Learning Center, they made no significant academic gains in the three years in public school and in some instances the data show that individual subjects lost ground on one or two of the WRAT subtests, (Herr, 1976, p. 27)

Similarly, Ritter (1978) found that although learning gains in reading and arithmetic were comparable for 20 learning disabled subjects during the mainstreamed year as found during enrollment in a special learning disability program, there was a significant decrease in gains for spelling. This finding led to the conclusions that regular classroom instruction alone may not be sufficient for children with learning disabilities, and supplemental programming seems necessary if prior learning rates are to be maintained. Ito (1980, 1981) suggested the following possibilities for supplemental programming: systematic fading of resource room services; follow-up services by the resource room teacher during the year following resource room placement; the training of regular classroom teachers to work more effectively with the returning learning disabled child; or the continued support of former resource room children through the itinerant/consultant teacher model.

Beside evaluating the resource room, the learning disability follow-up literature also evaluated other intervention programs. One option was the special class and program. Foster (1972), for example, followed 33 students with learning disabilities between 5 and 10 years after enrollment in a perceptual development program. About 67% had attained a level of functional literacy while nine were reading at or above their expectancy level. About 33% continued to experience reading problems. On the social side, the results were quite positive and most subjects showed significant school involvement. Generally, the students held realistic perceptions about their abilities and possessed appropriate levels of aspiration. In a similar perceptual development program, Gershman (1976) followed the 295 students with learning disabilities originally enrolled in 1971. By 1975, about 50% were in regular classes. Most appeared to be coping adequately in the regular class but generally remained in the bottom third of the class. They were rated, however, as quite similar to students of the same age and sex by teachers. The self-contained special class for learning disabled students was evaluated by Winter and Wright (1983) in a 5-year follow-up of the progress of 255 students with learning disabilities. In the academic area, significant gains were noted in reading, spelling, and arithmetic. A questionnaire about teaching style found teachers suggesting that individualization was an integral part of their program. Furthermore, positive changes in reading were found related to teaching methods that emphasized motor development and perceptual activities. Besides an emphasis on perceptual-motor development; precision teaching (Beck, 1977), structured phonetic and multisensory interventions (Mitchell, 1981), and team teaching (Schwartz, 1977) were all found effective over time in producing remedial gains. With the exception of precision teaching, however, the remedial gains tended to "wash out" over time and the learning disabled students generally continued to experience some academic difficulties. To prevent this regression in achievement, Silver, Hagin, and Beecher (1981) described an interdisciplinary school-based preventive program for learning disability (i.e., TEACH). Results from both 2- and 5-year follow-ups suggested that academic and behavioral gains can be sustained over the long-term with a program for secondary prevention so that former learning disabled students become indistinguishable from their "normal" peers.

In a comprehensive longitudinal analysis, McKinney and colleagues (McKinney & Feagans, 1984; McKinney & Krueger, 1974; McKinney & Speece, 1983) attempted to follow identified learning disabled children over the early elementary school years. In Project MELD (Models for Educating the Learning Disabled), McKinney and Krueger (1974) reported follow-up data on 97 children with learning disabilities and found that Project MELD had a significant impact on both academic and social competence. The models offered two alternatives: a deficit model that emphasized remediation of specific weaknesses through one-to-one instruction by a resource teacher, and an eclectic model that emphasized teacher consultation and attempted to build on strengths as well as remediate weaknesses. Follow-up data, however, indicated that during the second year the learning disabled group failed to progress academically at the same rate. Thus, again there was an indication of a slowing of achievement gain and the necessity of continued support if the learning disabled child is to maintain the same rate of gain.

McKinney and Speece (1983) followed 43 students with learning disabilities, over their second year, who were identified in Grades 1-3, of special education service. Teachers were asked to complete a behavior inventory on the 43 learning disabled students who were found to exhibit the same pattern of classroom behavior reported previously (Feagans & McKinney, 1981). Generally, teachers rated students with learning disabilities as deficient in behaviors that reflected academic competence (i.e., task-orientation, independence, verbal expression) as opposed to those reflecting social adjustment which also showed a consistency across time (McKinney, McClure, & Feagans, 1982). Findings from the *Schedule of Classroom Activity Norms* (SCAN) showed some consistency over time as evidenced by results showing that children with learning disabilities interacted with teachers more often than classmates. Thus, students with learning disabilities were shown to exhibit a relatively stable pattern of classroom behavior that distinguished them from average students. It

appeared that task-oriented behavior, independent functioning, and socially appropriate behavior were important elements in understanding the achievement difficulties of the child with learning disabilities.

In a 3-year follow-up, McKinney and Feagans (1984), using teaching rating scales, a classroom observational system (SCAN), and achievement tests, found that children with learning disabilities fall progressively further behind their normal peers in reading comprehension. In math, the learning disabled group remained about the same distance below their peers. With respect to behavior, the learning disabled group was found to exhibit more off-task and less on-task behavior suggesting that their classroom patterns were less efficient than normal peers in optimizing the learning situation (McKinney, Mason, Perkerson, & Clifford, 1975). Thus, children with learning disabilities do fall progressively further behind their peers, despite intervention aimed at making them approximate the academic status of their normally achieving peers. Although the behavior of the learning disabled group improved over time, this improvement was matched by the normal comparison group. The learning disabled group continued to exhibit the same maladaptive behaviors, particularly distractible, impulsive, and dependent/aggressive behaviors, in year 3 as they did in year 1.

These findings thus suggest more caution in interpreting the earlier optimistic findings. In fact, it appears that learning disability symptoms, particularly in academic and behavioral areas, are long-standing and possibly not as amenable to treatment as previously believed. The differences may again be related to sampling differences; the McKinney group carefully selected their learning disabled sample by specifying identification criteria in advance and assessing the extent to which the sample met those criteria. Consequently, the learning disabled group probably does include a large proportion of children who do manifest primary symptoms of reading disability and hyperactivity among the constellation of factors contributing to their learning disability.

Prospective research in learning disabilities

Two prospective reports provide support for a more tempered view of the long-term outcomes of learning disability. The Kauai Longitudinal Study (Werner, Bierman, & French, 1971; Werner & Smith, 1977, 1979, 1982) suggested that the long-term detrimental consequences of learning disability may be more debilitating in adulthood than other forms of exceptionality. The study followed a cohort of 1955 births who were scored on a 4-point scale for severity of perinatal complications. By age 10, 3% of the sample had been diagnosed as having learning disabilities because of severe reading and language problems (despite average or above WISC IQs), visual-motor impairment, hyperactivity, and difficulty in attention and concentration (Werner, Simonian, & Smith, 1967). The learning disabled group, at year 1, were rated by their mothers as "not cuddly," "not affectionate," and "not good-natured," "fretful." At 2 years, psychologists rated the learning disabled group as "awkward," "distractible," "fearful," "insecure," "restless," and "withdrawn." Additionally, IQ differences were now found and developmental ratings placed them "below normal." When evaluated at age 18, the learning disabled group was still underachieving in reading, writing, and language. The persistent academic difficulties were accompanied by behavioral difficulties (e.g., school misbehavior, frequent absences, delinquent behavior). A majority of the learning disabled group exhibited an external locus of control (i.e., lack of faith in the effectiveness of one's own actions) which prevented them from using their intellectual resources in scholastic achievement and influencing positive change in coping behavior. Thus, the learning disabled group revealed persistent and chronic deficits across two decades that did not seem to be affected significantly by either short- or long-term service, especially when based on strong biological and temperamental underpinnings.

In another prospective study based on a total cohort of 30,000, Nichols and Chen (1981) followed a subgroup of 2,476 children classified as learning disabled based on behavioral, cognitive, perceptual-motor, academic, and neurological identification variables during 7-year follow-up examinations. A factor analytic study identified learning disability as a factor and sample selection was based on variable scores falling in the extreme 8% of the distribution. These factor scores were then associated with more than 300 antecedent variables including SES, maternal, pregnancy, delivery, neonatal, infancy, preschool, and medical histories. These were all determined prospectively while some measures of physical and neurological status were determined concomitantly.

Analysis revealed that learning disabilities were strongly related to SES and demographic variables, particularly large family size, low SES, and frequent resident changes. Most of the 62 variables related to pregnancy, labor, and delivery periods were not significant except for hospitalizations and low blood pressure during pregnancy. Two infancy discriminators of the learning disabled group were small size at 1 year and an "unkempt" appearance at 8 months (independent of SES). Additionally, one-minute Apgar score, Bayley Score, and intensity of social response were other neonatal variables related to learning disability, but generally were found no longer significant when later performance measures were included. Finally, the children with learning disabilities in this sample of first- and second-graders were found to have started school at a younger age than the normal comparison group.

The 4-year examination revealed variables with strong association to learning disability. The learning disabled group had more failures on the *Porteus Mazes*, shorter attention spans, and greater level of activity than the comparison group. At age 7, learning disability discriminators included difficulty with right-left discrimination, refractive error, anaemia, and a history of measles. Given the importance of SES and demographic characteristics, learning disability was found to run in families with the best predictor being the average learning disability factor score of siblings. Because risks of learning disability to siblings of affected children were nearly identical, and since risks to other relatives did not vary systematically by degree of relationship, the strong familial association appeared to be environmentally rather than genetically determined.

A subgroup of the learning disabled group with hyperactivity were found, at age 4, associated with ratings of hyperactivity, impulsivity, and short attention span which were also related to hyperactivity at age 7. The hyperactive subgroup, like the learning disabled sample, also tended to fail the *Porteus Maze* test and had difficulty with right-left discrimination. There were also a variety of demographic, perinatal, and early developmental antecedents associated with later hyperactivity. Thus, these findings supported the suggestion of Alberman (1973) that learning disability was more strongly related to SES factors than with perinatal complications.

Follow-up of early identification research

The early identification of learning disability has also been investigated in several other follow-up studies. For example, Gottesman (1979) found that the best predictor of final achievement level was initial achievement level. Excluding initial and subsequent scores, WRAT outcomes were best predicted by initial age at testing, educational placement, and neurological history. Thus, the older child in a regular class with a negative neurological history was most likely to show the best reading performance. For the other outcome assessment (*Adult Basic Learning Examination*), final status was most related to initial age at testing, educational placement, and IQ. Thus, again an older child in a regular class with a relatively high IQ would most likely show the best outcome. Initial status as predictive of later status was confirmed by Francis-Williams (1976) in a 5-year follow-up of 42 children with learning disabilities who had been identified during the pre-school period. When compared to a control group, the learning disabled group scored more poorly on reading and arithmetic outcome assessments in which they had scored poorly in the preschool period. In fact, 11 of the 42 subjects were unable to read while 13 were retarded in reading by, at least, 12 months. Only nine learning disabled subjects were reading at or above their expected age-levels compared to 22 of the controls. During the preschool assessment, the learning disabled group were poorer than controls in language, copying ability, and concept formation, and follow-up assessments revealed a high correlation with initial scores in these areas.

Besides achievement scores, behavioral status has also been found predictive of later learning disability.

Forness and Esveldt (1975), using direct observation of kindergarten classes, were able to predict educationally high-risk children. At the end of first grade, Forness, Guthrie, and Hall (1976), through teacher ratings and achievement scores, found that the high-risk children were doing poorly. Later on, Forness, Hall, and Guthrie (1977) found that, in second-grade, the high-risk group continued to experience academic difficulties and had more special education assistance. The high-risk group were found to have been rated as more inattentive, more disruptive, more hyperactive, and more impulsive in kindergarten. These same off-task behaviors were predictive of later underachievement found by McKinney and Speece (1983). A multiple regression analysis indicated that behavioral ratings were predictive of academic progress over time. Thus, these findings suggested that learning disability has antecedents in early behavioral functioning and that off-task behaviors were predictive of later academic difficulties.

Conclusions

In summary, the learning disability follow-up literature generally corroborated the findings associated with its primary correlates (reading disability and hyperactivity) but also revealed some differences. The deficits associated with learning disability (both academic and behavioral) were found to be persistent. Yet, the outcome picture was generally more optimistic for learning disability than either reading disability or hyperactivity. This was partially due to sampling bias caused by the difficulties in defining learning disability and specifying identification criteria. Nevertheless, while a positive bias may have been inherent because of overrepresentation of mild learning disability, those studies using learning disabled subjects selected early tended to include more severely disabled subjects. In these studies, the age factor tended to influence outcomes; the youngest children at diagnosis generally showed the poorest outcomes while children older at diagnosis revealed better outcomes. There also appeared to be a relationship with age at follow-up. Those studies that followed children with learning disabilities into adulthood (i.e., beyond 25 years of age) generally had more positive outcomes. Unfortunately, a majority of the learning disability follow-up studies had subjects who were still in elementary school, high school, or only a year or so out of school. Thus, these outcomes were restricted in scope and may not reflect accurately the outcome picture for students with learning disabilities beyond the school years.

Besides age, outcomes appeared to be related to follow-up assessments. General measures of educational and vocational status based on level of schooling completed or occupational status, for example, revealed positive outcomes for students with learning disabilities. These global assessments yielded a majority of findings suggesting average (or better) attainment levels for

learning disabled subjects at follow-up. The positive picture did not emerge, however, when more specific academic assessments (e.g., achievement tests, reading tests) were the outcome measures. When the WRAT, MAT, or SAT were the measures used, for example, the learning disabled samples were found to possess continued deficits in reading, spelling, handwriting, and arithmetic. A proportion of studies not only found significant deficits but also found them to increase with age relative to age and grade placement. Basic skill deficits thus appeared to be persistent and enduring for the learning disabled child with no indication that they "catch-up" with normal peers. In the area of social/behavioral functioning, the follow-up literature presented a mixed picture: the studies were about evenly split between positive and negative outcomes. This finding appeared relatively independent of either educational/vocational or basic skill outcomes. Thus, outcome measure was an important variable in learning disability follow-up study since findings seem to be partially related to the type of outcome assessment used.

With respect to treatment, no one remedial practice or service appeared to be superior. All treatment practices appeared to result in some gain, particularly in the short-term. Regardless of the intervention, those initial gains tended to wash out over time and, if they were to be sustained, required supportive service over the long-term. The actual effectiveness of learning disability treatments was difficult to ascertain, however, because of the extensive variability encountered in learning disabled samples. Additionally, samples were not usually randomly separated into treatment and nontreatment conditions, which limited any conclusions about any positive or negative effect of intervention. Studies generally reported group statistics for either treatment effects or predictive antecedents which tended to mask individual outcomes that usually fell along a wide continuum. While some learning disabled subjects did well, others did not but, if global educational/vocational outcomes were positive and basic skill deficits persisted, then some learning disabled subjects had to develop strategies to compensate for the range of individual differences found. The nature of these strategies was not evident in the group statistics provided.

Finally, the learning disability follow-up literature needs to be approached with caution because of several methodological problems. Attrition appeared to be a problem; several studies approached a 50% attrition rate. These high rates always raise the question of whether the follow-up sample was similar to the sample selected at diagnosis. If the sample composition is altered significantly by attrition, then the outcome findings are not generalizable to the learning disabled population as a whole but rather the specific sample assessed. Few learning disability follow-up studies, however, addressed the issue of attrition. It is necessary for future research efforts to analyze the follow-up sample to determine whether the attrition has introduced a systematic bias.

A majority of the learning disability follow-up literature did not include a control group which limited interpretation since it was never certain that the outcome is related to the learning disability condition alone or to some other factors. For example, Hinton and Knights (1971) would require a control group where almost half the subjects had significant behavior problems so the effects of behavioral disorders could be controlled. A common method of control in learning disability follow-up studies was to compare learning disabled subjects' progress to estimated growth based on expected normal gain or test norms. Such a procedure is not recommended because these expectations are hypothetical and do not take into account variables that may influence outcomes (e.g., IQ, SES). Additionally, the use of estimated growth is likely to ensure that regression effects will influence outcome findings. Because learning disabled subjects were diagnosed on the basis of discrepancy scores (expected vs. actual achievement), at follow-up, any improvement in achievement levels is likely to reflect, at least partially, regression towards the mean. When actual rates of achievement gain are compared to expected rates, regression effects are likely to confound outcomes since the expected achievement gains are based upon the assumption that learning disabled subjects will maintain the level of discrepancy seen at diagnosis. If the same level is not maintained, especially for learning disabled subjects with the largest initial discrepancies, regression effects would probably overestimate improvement.

In some cases (e.g., Ackerman et al., 1977a), even though a control group was included, it is likely that there may have existed a bias in the control group that confounded comparison. When classroom teachers are asked to recommend nondisabled children from the same classroom from which the learning disabled sample was selected, it is possible that teachers may nominate children who differed from the learning disabled group not only in terms of the learning disability but also along other dimensions (e.g., behavior, IQ, SES) that confounded the effects of the learning disability. This problem can be overcome by random selection of the nondisabled group which then eliminates any potential bias introduced by the nominating process. Biasing factors may also be eliminated through the epidemiological approach (e.g., Nichols & Chen, 1981; Werner & Smith, 1977) wherein entire populations were studied rather than samples. This population is then divided at diagnosis into learning disabled and nondisabled groups. Through this procedure, biasing factors are minimized and any resulting group differences can be considered to have been based on valid comparisons.

Thus, the long-term consequences of learning disability defy a unilateral interpretation. Many findings were similar to those found for reading disability and hyperactivity but many of the findings were not similar. Consequently, answers to questions about learning disability outcomes remain tentative. The many and varied findings suggested that more longitudinal research is called for if the natural history of learning disabilities is to be fully understood. The present conflicting results makes it difficult to resolve basic policy issues for learning disability.

The State of Practice

Robins (1979) identified questions that follow-up studies can address. Most prominent were questions about the natural history of a disorder like learning disability. What are the symptoms? How early do they occur? How long do they last? Are there age-related exacerbations and remissions? Do symptoms change with age? Does childhood learning disability presage academic and behavioral difficulties later on? Another group of questions involves treatment: Does treatment alter the course of learning disability? Which treatments are most effective? What can parents do to ameliorate learning disability? What can teachers do? A related set of questions relates to etiology: Is childhood learning disability in part a genetic disorder? What is the role of sociocultural factors? What part do educational circumstances play in learning disability's development? Finally, questions about epidemiology can be addressed: What are the incidence and prevalence rates? What individuals or groups are at-risk?

Despite all of the variability and imperfections of method, the learning disability follow-up literature provided answers to some of the above questions. There was some consensus, for example, that children diagnosed as learning disabled continue to show impairment, at least, in those functions initially assessed as deficient. On the average, reading progress shown by children with learning disabilities was below normal expectation. For those learning disabled children with hyperactivity, it appeared that they continue to be somewhat more active than the average child. Even for very bright and successful subjects (i.e., Rawson, 1968), residual difficulties in reading and spelling were reported. When neuropsychological functions were assessed at follow-up, learning disabled subjects often showed reduced but still significant deficits in some areas (e.g., figure-ground discrimination, visual-motor skills). Although the evidence was scanty, the child with learning disabilities likely continues to have more difficulties coping with ordinary life stresses. There is likely to be lowered self-esteem accompanied by the development of self-critical reactions.

There appeared to be some consensus that children diagnosed as learning disabled have a great deal of difficulty subsequently in keeping up with their peers. Several studies found only a minority of the diagnosed learning disabled children in the appropriate grade for age at follow-up. These findings appeared to be independent of treatment effects since no appreciable differences emerged among intervention approaches. Although all treatments appeared effective in the short term, their efficacy tended to wane over time. Unlike the agreement found concerning the persistence of school problems, social and vocational adjustment after school years appeared highly variable from study to study. It does seem safe to conclude, however, that children with learning disabilities have an elevated risk of later emotional and behavioral difficulties but the ultimate impact of these problems on other aspects of the learning disabled child's life (e.g., work, marriage) is at present unclear.

Prediction of later adjustment and status for a child diagnosed as learning disabled is highly uncertain at present. Findings suggested, however, that a learning disabled child with a high IQ, high SES, and intensive systematic educational efforts has a relatively good prognosis for both academic achievement and vocational success. Conversely, learning disabled children with more modest IQ and SES do not necessarily have a poor prognosis but were likely to attain lower levels of achievement and occupational status. Prediction for children with learning disabilities is probably more difficult than for children in general because of the range restriction of scores for many predictors implicit in learning disability diagnosis and the generally more diffuse structure of abilities in learning disabled children (see Wallbrown, Wherry, Blaha, & Counts, 1974). Thus, individual children with learning disabilities may be idiosyncratic so that attempts to generalize statistically about deficits and outcomes may not be productive.

Finally, the learning disability follow-up literature contributed relatively little to understanding either the etiology or prevalence of learning disability. It also appears that it will be possible to obtain definitive and reliable information concerning the natural history of learning disabilities until a consensus definition can be achieved. All too often, the term learning disability was defined loosely and without operational specification. Consequently, there was an ambiguity surrounding the nature of the sample under study. The variety of terminology used such as dyslexia, minimal brain dysfunction, hyperactivity, attention deficit disorder, and the like sometimes referred to different children but, at other times, referred to the same children. There was no consistency which makes generalization difficult.

Besides definitional issues, other methodological considerations should be incorporated into future research. The ideal follow-up study for children with learning disabilities should use a longitudinal design, beginning with children selected prior to the onset of learning disability (i.e., probably during the preschool period). This procedure has proven valuable in the study of schizophrenia (e.g., Garmezy, 1974) and would be a good model for the learning disability field. The advantages would include the absence of bias in the target sample, the availability of a valid comparison group, and the availability of current (not exclusively retrospective) information. Such a methodology would provide data for cross-lagged panel designs (Campbell & Stanley, 1969) that would allow for the teasing out of cause and effect relationships between learning disabled child's symp-

toms and environmental events (e.g., does school failure lead to behavioral disorders or does behavioral disorders lead to school failure and learning disability?). Any future reserach should also use a wide array of outcome measures to examine the prognosis of learning disability in a variety of areas (e.g., academic, occupational, social, emotional, neuropsychological). These outcomes should be studied both separately and in interaction to determine the relationships, if any, among areas. These outcomes must also be more tightly controlled for IQ and SES. Presently, outcome differences cannot always be related to specific deficits because subjects often differed in general aptitude and family background. Finally, greater specification of treatment variables is necessary so comparisons can be made across studies. The variety of treatments in longitudinal research, even among the same sample, was a serious source of confounding since the interventions vary considerably in length, method, and intensity.

Needs and Recommendations

Although possessing a long and varied history, longitudinal research relating to learning disability has had only a modest impact on learning disability practice. The methodological difficulties have limited interpretation, and have prevented the research findings from modifying actions and attitudes in the learning disability field. Given the nature of the conclusions that may be drawn, needs and recommendations include:

Research

1. The need for more longitudinal research, especially with learning disabled samples, is clear. The quantity of research is impressive but has failed generally to provide definitive answers about the long-term consequences of learning disability. Therefore, more research is needed that is directed towards supplying comprehensive descriptions and conclusions about learning disability over time.

2. Future research should use a prospective design that defines the learning disabled sample precisely, provides a control group, collects consistent data, and controls for attrition. Longitudinal research is difficult to conduct and faces many pragmatic difficulties but future research must be directed towards meeting the standards of "ideal" research. The tenets of "good" longitudinal research are known and, although difficult to implement in practice, future studies should incorporate designs that meet the most rigorous standards.

3. Future research should span the years from preschool to adulthood in order to delineate completely the life history of learning disability. Past research has revealed outcome differences related to the age span investigated. The problem has been the too short age spans investigated which prevents a comprehensive description of learning disability over time. Therefore, research efforts need to investigate longer age spans that

include many different phases of a learning disabled child's life.

4. Future research should include a comprehensive array of outcome measures including academic, social, personality, and vocational assessments. This will insure a comprehensive description of learning disability outcomes that will provide a total picture of learning disability over time. Too often research efforts focused on only a single area that failed to uncover complex interactions among the outcome areas.

5. Secondarily to the primary outcome assessments, future research should investigate the efficacy of different treatment approaches, etiological considerations, and epidemiological questions. These variables are integral and critical components related to outcomes but are often not investigated. Consequently, longitudinal designs should include these factors to provide a total picture of learning disability over time.

Practice

1. There should be increased dissemination of longitudinal research findings to professionals in the learning disability field so they are better able to answer the parent's question, "What is to become of my child?" This is an important and fundamental question for parents but often the professional is provided with very little information about the long-term consequences of learning disability and cannot give satisfactory responses.

2. Research findings should be disseminated in popular form both to parents and to their secondary age students in order to prepare them for the long-term consequences of learning disability. Such dissemination will be useful in acquainting both parent and child with what we know about what is likely to happen in the future.

3. The child with learning disabilities should be provided with a realistic assessment of probable outcomes given the individual situations and programmatic possibilities. The child with learning disabilities must be realistically informed and made to understand that the condition does have long-term consequences. This will insure, at least, an awareness of learning disability and its effects over time so the child with learning disabilities is prepared for a variety of contingencies.

4. With greater insight into longitudinal research findings, Individualized Education Program meetings should reflect that awareness by providing a more realistic and detailed delineation of goals and objectives especially over the long term.

Policy

1. The learning disability field should not accept a status quo with respect to the state of longitudinal research. Although difficult to design and to implement, longitudinal research must be continued if the long-term consequences of learning disability are to be fully understood.

2. Funding agencies must be made aware of the importance of longitudinal research and provide a realistic funding mechanism for long-term studies. This means that more than a 5-year commitment is necessary if longitudinal research is to provide the desired outcomes.

3. It must be understood that longitudinal research is no longer in its infancy and future efforts need to be more sophisticated and comprehensive. This suggests that they will be more expensive and funding agencies must be ready to underwrite these increased costs.

4. The diversified nature of longitudinal research needed for comprehensive outcomes suggests that funding should be on an interagency basis. Furthermore, collaborative efforts among several disciplines would be useful so as to insure the necessary expertise for providing a total picture of learning disability over time.

5. With state agencies required to collect follow-up data (PL 98–199), more cooperative efforts among states should be arranged in order to insure the development of a national data base for longitudinal findings.

6. In terms of service delivery, the necessity of long-term service needs to be emphasized by policymakers. Furthermore, it must be understood that children with learning disabilities require different services at different times. Although many follow-up findings are equivocal, it is clear that any future success is contingent upon the presence of support services.

Conclusion

What then should we tell the parents of a child with learning disability? Although the data are by no means complete, there is a consistency indicating that he or she will possess a high risk of lasting deficits. With respect to outcome, there is a high risk of repeating one or more grades in school, and a somewhat elevated risk of some behavior problems (particularly low self-esteem). Beyond these few generalizations, outcomes appear to depend on the nature and extent of the cognitive and behavioral manifestations of learning disability, the child's IQ level, and to some extent the SES level. If the child with learning disabilities is fortunate enough to possess a high IQ, to have professional parents, and to have been exposed to intensive and long-term treatment, then the prognosis for academic and vocational success is good generally. Yet the child is likely never to lose the feeling that reading and spelling are areas of difficulty. On the other hand, if the child has a low IQ, a lower SES family, associated behavioral disorders and is subject to nothing but average intervention efforts, then the prognosis is poor, especially with regard to academic failure. Yet, prognosis for vocational and life adjustment, even with extensive school failure, is not totally gloomy. While risks for lowered SES and psychiatric contact are increased, the total social and occupational outcomes are as a rule not entirely negative. For the child in the middle, the "average" child with learning disabilities, any of the possible outcomes may occur. Parents should be advised that there is a high probability for some noticeable improvement but not enough to allay totally their expressed concerns about the child's future.

No matter the tentativeness of the conclusions drawn from past follow-up studies of children with learning disabilities, they have been worth doing since they have provided insights into the life history of learning disability. Longitudinal research so far has indicated that a childhood diagnosis of learning disability has substantial long-term significance but leaves unanswered many questions about the exact nature of learning disability and the reasons for its consequences. Therefore, follow-up research on children with learning disabilities conducted to date should be viewed as only a beginning. The many unanswered questions await more extensive and more rigorous investigation.

References

Abbot, R. C., & Frank, B. E. (1975). A follow-up of LD children in a private special school. *Academic Therapy*, **10**, 291–298.

Ackerman, P. T., Dykman, R. A., & Peters, J. E. (1977a). Learning-disabled boys as adolescents: Cognitive factors and achievement. *Journal of the American Academy of Child Psychiatry*, **16**, 296–313.

Ackerman, P. T., Dykman, R. A., & Peters, J. E. (1977b). Teenage status of hyperactive and nonhyperactive learning disabled boys. *American Journal of Orthopsychiatry*, **47**, 577–596.

Adams, V. L. (1960). *The Saint Louis public schools reading clinics: A follow-up study*. Unpublished doctoral dissertation, Saint Louis University.

Alberman, E. (1973). The early prediction of learning disorders. *Developmental Medicine and Child Neurology*, **15**, 202–204.

Aman, M. G., & Mayhew, J. M. (1980). Consistency of cognitive and motor performance measures over two years in reading retarded children. *Perceptual and Motor Skills*, **50**, 1659–1055.

August, G. J., Stewart, M. A., & Holmes, C. S. (1983). A four year follow-up of hyperactive boys with and without conduct disorder. *British Journal of Psychiatry*, **143**, 192–198.

Baker, L. A., Decker, S. N., & DeFries, J. C. (1984). Cognitive abilities in reading-disabled children: A longitudinal study. *Journal of Child Psychology and Psychiatry*, **25**, 111–117.

Balow, B. (1965). The long-term effect of remedial reading instruction. *The Reading Teacher*, **18**, 581–586.

Balow, B., & Blomquist, M. (1965). Young adults ten to fifteen years after severe reading disability. *Elementary School Journal*, **66**, 44–48.

Barkley, R. A. (1982). Guidelines for defining hyperactivity in children: Attention deficit disorder with hyperactivity. In B. B. Lahey & A. E. Kazdin (eds.), *Advances in clinical child psychology*, **5**, pp. 137–175. New York: Plenum.

Bateman, B. D. (1966). Learning disorders. *Review of Educational Research*, **36**, 93–119.

Battle, E. S., & Lacey, B. (1972). A context for hyperactivity in children, over time. *Child Development*, **43**, 757–773.

Beck, M. A. (1976). *A follow-up study of adults who were clinically diagnosed as hyperactive in childhood*. Unpublished doctoral dissertation, Wayne State University.

Beck, R. J. (1977). *Remediation of learning deficits through precision teaching: A follow-up study*. Unpublished doctoral dissertation, University of Montana.

Beck, L., Langford, W. S., Mackay, M. & Sum, G. (1975). Childhood chemotherapy and later drug abuse and growth curves: A follow-up study of 30 adolescents. *American Journal of Psychiatry*, **132**, 436–438.

Bell, A. E., Abrahamson, D. S., & McRae, K. N. (1977). Reading retardation: A 12-year prospective study. *Journal of Pediatrics*, **91**, 363–370.

Belmont, L., & Birch, H. G. (1966). The intellectual profile of retarded readers. *Perceptual and Motor Skills*, **22**, 787–816.

Birch, L. B. (1949). Remedial treatment of reading disability. *Educational Review*, **1**, 107–118.

Birch, L. B. (1950). The improvement of reading ability. *British Journal of Educational Psychology*, **20**, 73–76.

Birch, L. B. (1953). Comments on the article "An experimental evaluation of remedial education." *British Journal of Educational Psychology*, **23**, 56–57.

Blackburn, V. B. (1980). *A study of remedial reading students. Identification, reading achievement, and the follow-up of a select group*. Unpublished doctoral dissertation, Oklahoma State University.

Bloomer, C. H. (1978). *A six year follow-up study on learning disabled children in a resource room program*. Unpublished doctoral dissertation, Columbia University.

Blouin, A., Bornstein, L., & Trites, R. (1978). Teenage alcohol use among hyperactive children: A five year follow-up study. *Journal of Pediatric Psychology*, **3**, 188–194.

Bluestein, V. W. (1967). Factors related to and predictive of improvement in reading. *Psychology in the Schools*, **4**, 272–276.

Bluestein, V. W. (1968). Long-term effectiveness of remediation. *Journal of School Psychology*, **6**, 130–135.

Bond, G. L., & Fay, L. C. (1950). A report of the University of Minnesota reading clinic. *Journal of Educational Research*, **43**, 385–390.

Borland, B. L., & Heckman, H. K. (1976). Hyperactive boys and their brothers: A 25-year follow-up study. *Archives of General Psychiatry*, **33**, 669–675.

Buerger, T. A. (1968). A follow-up of remedial reading instruction. *The Reading Teacher*, **21**, 329–334.

Campbell, S. B., Breaux, A. M., Ewing, L. J., & Szumowski, E. K. (1984). A one-year follow-up study of parent-referred hyperactive preschool children. *Journal of the American Academy of Child Psychiatry*, **23**, 243–249.

Campbell, S. B., Endman, M. W., & Bernfeld, G. (1977). A three-year follow-up of hyperative preschoolers into elementary school. *Journal of Child Psychology and Psychiatry*, **18**, 239–249.

Campbell, S. G., Schleifer, M., & Weiss, G. (1978). Continuities in maternal reports and child behaviors over time in hyperactive and comparison groups. *Journal of Abnormal Child Psychology*, **6**, 33–45.

Campbell, S. B., Schleifer, M., Weiss, G., & Perlman, T. (1977). A two-year follow-up of hyperactive preschoolers. *American Journal of Orthopsychiatry*, **47**, 149–162.

Campbell, D. T. & Stanley, J. C. (1969). *Experimental and quasi-experimental decisions for research*. Chicago, Rand McNally.

Cantwell, D. (1972). Psychiatric illness in the families of hyperactive children. *Archives of General Psychiatry*, **27**, 414–423.

Carter, R. P. (1964). *A descriptive analysis of the adult adjustment of persons once identified as disabled readers*. Unpublished doctoral dissertation, Indiana University, Bloomington.

Carter, R. P. (1967). The adult social adjustment of retarded and non-retarded readers. *Journal of Reading*, **11**, 224–228.

Cashdan, A., & Pumfrey, P. D. (1969). Some effects of the remedial teaching of reading. *Educational Research*, **11**, 138–142.

Cerny, L. (1976). Experience in the reeducation of children with dyslexia in Czechoslovakia. *International Journal of Mental Health*, **4**, 113–122.

Chansky, N. M. (1963). Age, IQ, and improvement in reading. *Journal of Educational Research*, **56**, 439.

Chapel, J. L., Robins, A. J., McGee, R. O., Williams, S. M., & Silva, P. A. (1982). A follow-up of inattentive and/or hyperactive children from birth to 7 years of age. *Journal of Occupational Psychiatry*, **13**, 17–26.

Clements, S. D. (1966). *Minimal brain dysfunction in children: Terminology and identification*. Washington, DC: US Department of Health, Education, and Welfare. (NINDS Monograph No. 3, US Public Health Service Publication No. 1415).

Cobb, R. M., & Crump, W. D. (1984). *Post-school status of young adults identified as learning disabled while enrolled in public schools: A comparison of those enrolled and not enrolled in learning disabilities programs*. Washington, DC: US Department of Education, Research Projects Section.

Cohen, N. J., Weiss, G. & Minde, K. (1972). Cognitive styles in adolescents previously diagnosed as hyperactive. *Journal of Child Psychology and Psychiatry*, **13**, 203–209.

Collins, J. E. (1961). *The effects of remedial education*. London: Oliver & Boyd. (University of Birmingham, Institute of Education, Educational Monograph IV).

Cosper, R., & Kephart, N. C. (1955). Retention of reading skills. *Journal of Educational Research*, **49**, 211–216.

Cox, A., Rutter, M., Yule, W., & Quinton, D. (1977). Bias resulting from mising information: Some epidemiological findings. *British Journal of Preventive and Social Medicine*, **31**, 131–136.

Crandall, V. C. & Battle, E. S. (1969). The antecedents and adult correlates of academic and intellectual achievement effort. In J. P. Hill (Ed.), *Minnesota Symposia on Child Psychology*, (Vol. IV, pp. 36–93). Minneapolis: University of Minnesota Press.

Cronin, M. E., & Gerber, P. J. (1982). Preparing the learning disabled adolescent for adulthood. *Topics in Learning and Learning Disabilities*, **2**, 55–68.

Crosby, L. Y. (1977). *An investigation of the long-range effectiveness of a sixth-grade remedial reading program*. Unpublished doctoral dissertation, Wayne State University.

Cunningham, C. E., & Barkley, R. A. (1978). The role of academic failure in hyperactive behavior. *Journal of Learning Disabilities*, **11**, 15–21.

Curr, W., & Gourlay, N. (1953). An experimental evaluation of remedial education. *British Journal of Educational Psychology*, **23**, 45–55.

DeFries, J. C., & Baker, L. A. (1983). Colorado family reading study: Longitudinal analyses. *Annals of Dyslexia*, **33**, 153–162.

Deshler, D. D. (1978). Issues related to the education of learning disabled adolescents. *Learning Disability Quarterly*, **1**, 2–10.

Dykman, R. A., Peters, J. E., & Ackerman, P. T. (1973). Experimental approaches to the study of minimal brain dysfunction: A follow-up study. *Annals of the New York Academy of Sciences*, **205**, 93–108.

Eaves, L. C., & Crichton, J. U. (1975). A five-year follow-up of children with minimal brain dysfunction. *Academic Therapy*, **10**, 173–180.

Edgington, R. E. (1975). SLD children: A ten-year follow-up. *Academic Therapy*, **11**, 53–64.

Eisenberg, L. (1966). Reading retardation: I. Psychiatric and sociologic aspects. *Pediatrics*, **37**, 352–365.

Enfield, M. L. (1976). *An alternative classroom approach to meeting speical learning needs of children with reading problems*. Unpublished doctoral dissertation, University of Minnesota.

Fafard, M. B., & Haubrich, P. A. (1981). Vocational and social adjustment of learning disabled young adults: A follow-up study. *Learning Disability Quarterly*, **4**, 122–130.

Feagans, L., & McKinney, J. D. (1981). The pattern of exceptionality across domains in learning disabled children. *Journal of Applied Developmental Psychology*, **1**, 313–328.

Feldman, S., Denhoff E., & Denhoff, J. (1979). The attention disorders and related syndromes: Outcome in adolescence and young adult life. In E. Denhoff & L. Stern (Eds.), *Minimal brain dysfunction: A developmental approach*. New York: Masson.

Fiedler, M. (1972). Did the clinic help? *Journal of Reading*, **16**, 28–32.

Fletcher, J. M., & Satz, P. (1980). Developmental changes in the neuropsychological correlates of reading achievement: A six-year longitudinal follow-up. *Journal of Clinical Neuropsychology*, **2**, 23–37.

Forness, S. R., & Esveldt, K. C. (1975). Prediction of high-risk kindergarten children through classroom observation. *Journal of Special Education*, **9**, 375–388.

Forness, S. R., Guthrie, D., & Hall, R. J. (1976). Follow-up of high-risk children identified in kindergarten through direct classroom observation. *Psychology in the Schools*, **13**, 45–49.

Forness, S. R., Hall, R. J., & Guthrie, D. (1977). Eventual school placement of kindergarteners observed as high risk in the classroom. *Psychology in the Schools*, **14**, 315–317.

Foster, G. E. (1972). *A short-term follow-up study of the academic, social, and vocational adjustment and achievement of children five to ten years following placement in a perceptual development program*. Unpublished doctoral dissertation, Wayne State University.

Fox, B., & Routh, D. K. (1983). Reading disability, phonemic analysis, and dysphonetic spelling: A follow-up study. *Journal of Clinical Child Psychology*, **12**, 28–32.

Francis-Williams, J. (1976). Early identification of children likely to have specific learning difficulties: Report of a follow-up. *Developmental Medicine and Child Neurology*, **18**, 71–77.

Frauenheim, J. G. (1978). Academic achievement characteristics of adult males who were diagnosed as dyslexic in childhood. *Journal of Learning Disabilities*, **11**, 476–483.

Frauenheim, G. J., & Heckerl, J. R. (1983). A longitudinal study of psychological and achievement test performance in severe dyslexic adults. *Journal of Learning Disabilities*, **16**, 339–347.

Kenneth A. Kavale

Friedmann, S. (1958). A report in an L.E.A. remedial class. *British Journal of Educational Psychology*, **28**, 258–261.

Garmezy, N. (1974). Children at risk—the search for antecedents of schizophrenia: I. Conceptual models and research methods. *Schizophrenia Bulletin*, **1**, 14–90.

Garvey, M., & Gordon, N. (1973). A follow-up study of children with disorders of speech development. *British Journal of Disorders of Communication*, **8**, 17–28.

Gershman, J. (1976). *A follow-up study of graduates of the perceptual and behavioral special classes*. (Research Service No. 143). Toronto, Canada: Board of Education. (ERIC Document Reproduction Service No. ED 135 169).

Gilbert, G. M. (1957). A survey of "referral problems" in metropolitan child guidance clinics. *Journal of Clinical Psychology*, **13**, 37–42.

Gillberg, I. C., & Gillberg, C. (1983). Three-year follow-up at age 10 of children with minor neurodevelopmental disorders. I: Behavioral problems. *Developmental Medicine and Child Neurology*, **25**, 438–449.

Gillberg, I. C., Gillberg, C., & Rasmussen, P. (1983). Three-year follow-up at age 10 of children with minor neurodevelopmental disorders. II: School achievement problems. *Developmental Medicine and Child Neurology*, **25**, 566–573.

Gomez, R. L., Janowsky, D., Detin, M., Huey, L., & Clapton, P. L. (1981). Adult psychiatric diagnosis and symptoms compatible with the hyperactive child syndrome: A retrospective study. *Journal of Clinical Psychiatry*, **42**, 389–394.

Gottesman, R. L. (1978). *Follow-up study of reading achievement in learning disabled children*. Final Report. Washington, DC: Department of Health, Education, and Welfare. (ERIC Document Reproduction Service No. ED 155 883).

Gottesman, R. L. (1979). Follow-up of learning disabled children. *Learning Disability Quarterly*, **2**, 60–69.

Gottesman, R., Belmont, I., & Kaminer, R. (1975). Admission and follow-up status of reading disabled children referred to a medical clinic. *Journal of Learning Disabilities*, **8**, 642–650.

Gottfredson, L. S., Finucci, J. M., & Childs, B. (1983). *The adult occupational success of dyslexic boys: A large-scale, long-term follow-up*. Baltimore, MD: Johns Hopkins University, Center for Social Organization of Schools. (Report No. 334).

Gottfredson, L. S., Finucci, J. M., & Childs, B. (1984). Explaining the adult careers of dyslexic boys: Variations in critical skills for high-level jobs. *Journal of Vocational Behavior*, **24**, 355–373.

Griffiths, C. P. S. (1969). A follow-up study of children with disorders of speech. *British Journal of Disorders of Communication*, **4**, 46–56.

Hall, P. K., & Tomblin, J. B. (1978). A follow-up study of children with articulation and language disorders. *Journal of Speech and Hearing Disorders*, **43**, 227–241.

Hardy, M. I. (1968a). *Clinical follow-up of disabled readers*. Unpublished doctoral dissertation, University of Toronto, Canada.

Hardy, M. I. (1968b). Disabled readers: What happens to them after elementary school? *Canadian Education and Research Digest*, **8**, 338–346.

Hardy, M. I. (1970). The academic adjustment of disabled readers: A follow-up study. *Special Education in Canada*, **44**, 26–29.

Hechtman, L. (1981). Families of hyperactives. In R. Simmons (Ed.), *Research in Community and Mental Health* (Vol. 2), Greenwich, CT: JAI Press.

Hechtman, L., Weiss, G., & Metrakas, K. (1978). Hyperactive individuals as young adults: Current and longitudinal electroencephalographic evaluation and its relation to outcome. *Canadian Medical Association Journal*, **118**, 919–921.

Hechtman, L., Weiss, G., & Perman, T. (1978). Growth and cardiovascular measures in hyperactive individuals as young adults and in matched normal controls. *Canadian Medical Association Journal*, **118**, 1247–1250.

Hechtman, L., Weiss, G., & Perman T. (1984). Hyperactives as young adults: Past and current substance abuse and antisocial behavior. *American Journal of Orthopsychiatry*, **54**, 415–425.

Hechtman, L., Weiss, G., Perman, T., Hopkins, J., & Wener, A. (1982). Hyperactives as young adults: Prospective ten-year follow-up. In K. D. Gadow & J. Loney (Eds.), *Psychosocial aspects of drug treatment for hyperactivity*. Boulder, CO: Westview Press.

Hermann, K. (1959). *Reading disability*. Springfield, Il: Charles, C. Thomas.

Herr, C. M. (1976). Mainstreaming—Is it effective: A follow-up study of learning disabled children. *Division for Children with Learning Disabilities Newsletter*, **2**, 22–29.

Hillman, H. H., & Snowdon, R. L. (1960). Part-time classes for young backward readers. *British Journal of Educational Psychology*, **30**, 168–172.

Hinton, G. G., & Knights, R. M. (1971). Children with learning problems: Academic history, academic prediction, and adjustment three years after assessment. *Exceptional Children*, **37**, 513–519.

Hopkins, J., Hechtman, L., & Weiss, G. (1979). Cognitive style in adults originally diagnosed as hyperactives. *Journal of Child Psychology and Psychiatry*, **20**, 209–216.

Horn, W. F., O'Donnell, J. P., & Vitulano, L. A. (1983). Long-term follow-up studies of learning-disabled persons. *Journal of Learning Disabilities*, **16**, 542–555.

Howden, M. E. (1967). *A nineteen-year follow-up study of good, average, and poor readers in the fifth and sixth grades*. Unpublished doctoral dissertation, University of Oregon.

Hoy, E., Weiss, G., Minde, K., & Cohen, N. (1978). The hyperactive child at adolescence: Cognitive, emotional and social functioning. *Journal of Abnormal Child Psychology*, **6**, 311–324.

Huessy, H. B. (1977, March). *Behavior disorders and learning disabilities over 15 years in rural Vermont*. Paper presented at the Brown University Program in Medicine, "Minimal brain dysfunction: A closer look," Providence, RI. (ERIC Document Reproduction Service No. ED 167 325).

Huessy, H. R., & Cohen, A. H. (1976). Hyperkinetic behaviors and learning disabilities followed over seven years. *Pediatrics*, **57**, 4–10.

Hunter, E. J., & Lewis, H. M. (1973). The dyslexic child—two years later. *Journal of Psychology*, **83**, 163–170.

Isom, J. B. (1975). *A study of reading disability in the United States*. Washington, DC: National Institute of Education (DHEW). (ERIC Document Reproduction Service No. ED 141 746)

Ito, H. R. (1980). Long-term effects of resource room programs on learning disabled children's reading. *Journal of Learning Disabilities*, **13**, 322–326.

Ito, H. R. (1981). After the resource room—then what? *Academic Therapy*, **16**, 283–287.

Johnson, E. L., & Neumann, C. (1975). Multidisciplinary evaluation of learning and behavior problems in children: A follow-up study of 40 cases. *Journal of the American Osteopathic Association*, **74**, 168–174.

Kagan, J. (1965). Reflection-impulsivity and reading ability in primary grade children. *Child Development*, **36**, 609–628.

Kaste, C. M. (1971). *A ten-year follow-up of children diagnosed in a child guidance clinic as having cerebral dysfunction.* Unpublished doctoral dissertation, University of Minnesota.

Kavale, K. A. (1982). The efficacy of stimulant drug treatment for hyperactivity: A meta-analysis. *Journal of Learning Disabilities*, **15**, 42–51.

Kavale, K. A., & Forness, S. R. (1985). *The science of learning disabilities.* San Diego: College-Hill Press.

Kavale, K. A., & Nye, W. C. (1981). Identification criteria for learning disabilities: A survey of the research literature. *Learning Disability Quarterly*, **4**, 383–388.

Kellmer-Pringle, M. L. (1961). The long-term effects of remedial treatment: A follow-up inquiry based on the case study approach. *Educational Research*, **4**, 62–66.

Kellmer-Pringle, M. L., & Gulliford, R. (1953). A note on "An experimental evaluation of remedial education" *British Journal of Educational Psychology*, **23**, 196–199.

Kirk, S. A., & Elkins, J. (1975). Characteristics of children enrolled in the Child Service Demonstration Centers. *Journal of Learning Disabilities*, **8**, 630–637.

Kline, C. L., & Kline, L. C. (1975). Follow-up study of 216 dyslexic children. *Bulletin of the Orton Society*, **25**, 127–144.

Koppitz, E. M. (1971). *Children with learning disabilities: A five year follow-up study.* New York: Grune & Stratton.

Krippner, S. (1963). Correlates of reading improvement. *Education*, **84**, 30–35.

Langhorne, J. E., & Loney, J. (1979). A four-fold model for subgrouping the hyperkinetic/MBD syndrome. *Child Psychiatry and Human Development*, **9**, 153–159.

Langman, M. P., & Rabinovitch, R. D. (1968). The Hawthorne Center longitudinal reading study. In J. A. Figurel (Ed.), *Forging ahead in reading. Proceedings of the 12th annual convention, International Reading Association.* Vol. 12, Pt. I). Newark, DE: International Reading Association.

Laufer, M. W. (1971). Long-term management and some follow-up findings on the use of drugs with minimal cerebral syndromes. *Journal of Learning Disabilities*, **4**, 519–522.

Laufer, M., & Denhoff, E. (1957). Hyperkinetic behavior syndrome in children. *Journal of Pediatrics*, **50**, 463–474.

Lehtinen-Rogan, L. & Hartman, L. D. (1976). *A follow-up study of learning disabled children as adults.* Final Report. Washington, DC: Department Health, Education and Welfare (Bureau of Education for the Handicapped). (ERIC Document Reproduction Service No. ED 163728).

Leone, P., Lovitt, T., & Hansen, C. (1981). A descriptive followup study of learning disabled boys. *Learning Disability Quarterly*, **4**, 152–162.

Levin, E. K., Zigmond, N., & Birch, J. W. (1985). A follow-up study of 52 learning disabled adolescents. *Journal of Learning Disabilities*, **18**, 2–7.

Lloyd, D. N. (1969). *Reading achievement and its relationship to academic performance. Part I: Reading deficiency in elementary school and relationships to secondary school performance.* Bethesda, MD: National Institute of Health.

(ERIC Document Reproduction Service No. ED 034 660)

Loney, J., Kramer, J., & Millch, R. S. (1980). The hyperactive child grows up: Predictors of symptoms, delinquency and achievement at follow-up. In K. Gadow & J. Loney (Eds.), *Psychosocial aspects of drug treatment for hyperactivity.* Boulder, CO: Westview Press.

Lovell, K., Bryne, C., & Richardson, B. (1963). A further study of the educational progress of children who had received remedial education. *British Journal of Educational Psychology*, **33**, 3–9.

Lovell, K., Johnson, E., & Platts, D. (1962). A summary of a study of the reading ages of children who had been given remedial teaching. *British Journal of Educational Psychology*, **32**, 66–71.

Lytton, H. (1961). An experiment in selection for remedial education. *British Journal of Educational Psychology*, **31**, 79–94.

Lytton, H. (1967). Follow-up of an experiment in selection for remedial education. *British Journal of Educational Psychology*, **37**, 1–9.

Macy, D. J., & Carter, J. L. (1979, April). *The longitudinal effect of resource room intervention on school absenteeism of learning disabled students.* Paper presented at the annual meeting of the American Educational Research Association, San Francisco. (ERIC Document Reproduction Service No. ED. 170 986).

Maginnis, G. H. (1971). Reading disability and remedial gain. *Journal of Learning Disabilities*, **4**, 322–324.

Major-Kingsley, S. (1982). *Learning disabled boys as young adults: Achievement, adjustment, and aspirations.* Unpublished doctoral dissertation, University of California, Los Angeles.

Mann, H., & Greenspan, S. (1976). The identification and treatment of adult brain dysfunction. *American Journal of Psychiatry*, **133**, 1013–1017.

Maslow, P. (1979). Follow-up study of former learning disabled students: A summary. *Journal of Educational Therapy*, **1**, 101–110.

Matheny, A. P., Dolan, A. B., & Wilson, R. S. (1976). Twins with academic learning problems: Antecedent characteristics. *American Journal of Orthopsychiatry*, **46**, 464–469.

McKinney, J. D., & Feagans, L. (1984). Academic and behavioral characteristics of learning disabled children and average achievers: Longitudinal studies. *Learning Disability Quarterly*, **7**, 251–265.

McKinney, J. D., & Krueger, M. (1974). *Models for educating the learning disabled (MELD): Project period 1973–1974: Final evaluation report.* Washington, DC: Bureau of Elementary and Secondary Education (DHEW/OE). (ERIC Document Reproduction Service No. ED 108 402)

McKinney, J. D., Mason, J., Perkerson, K., & Clifford, M. (1975). Relationship between classroom behavior and academic achievement. *Journal of Educational Psychology*, **67**, 198–203.

McKinney, J. D., McClure, S., & Feagans, L. (1982). Classroom behavior patterns of learning disabled children. *Learning Disability Quarterly*, **5**, 45–52.

McKinney, J. D., & Spreece, D. L. (1983). Classroom behavior and the academic progress of learning disabled students. *Journal of Applied Developmental Psychology*, **4**, 149–161.

Mednick, B. R. (1977). Intellectual and behavioral functioning of ten- to twelve-year-old children who showed certain transient symptoms in the neonatal period. *Child Development*, **48**, 844–853.

Mendelson, W., Johnson, N., & Stewart, M. A. (1971). Hyperactive children as teenagers: A follow-up study. *Journal of Nervous and Mental Disease*, **153**, 273–279.

Menkes, M. M., Rowe, J. S., & Menkes, J. H. (1967). A twenty-five year follow-up study on the hyperkinetic child with minimal brain dysfunction. *Pediatrics*, **39**, 393–399.

Meyer, M. E. (1982). *A longitudinal study of 69 reading disabled children and a matched control group*. Unpublished doctoral dissertation, University of Colorado, Boulder.

Milich, R., & Loney, J. (1979). The role of hyperactive and aggressive symptomatology in predicting adolescent outcome among hyperactive children. *Journal of Pediatric Psychology*, **4**, 93–112.

Miller, J. S. (1978). Hyperactive children: A ten-year study. *Pediatrics*, **61**, 217–223.

Milman, D. H. (1977). *Minimal brain dysfunction in childhood: I. Outcome in late adolescence and early adult years*. Paper presented at the annual meeting of the American Psychiatric Association. (ERIC Document Reproduction Service No. ED 155 880)

Milman, D. H. (1978). *Minimal brain dysfunction in childhood: II. Late outcome in relation to initial presentation. III. Predictive factors in relation to late outcome*. Brooklyn, NY: State University of New York, Downstate Medical Center. (ERIC Document Reproduction Service No. ED 175 191)

Minde, K., Lewin, D., Weiss, G., Lavigueur, H., Douglas, V., & Sykes, E. (1971). The hyperactive child in elementary school: A 5 year, controlled, follow-up. *Exceptional Children*, **37**, 215–221.

Minde, K., Weiss, G., & Mendelson, N. (1972). A 5-year follow-up study of 91 hyperactive school children. *Journal of the American Academy at Child Psychiatry*, **11**, 595–619.

Mitchell, G. D. (1981). *School-related achievement of high risk learning disabled students: A follow-up study*. Unpublished doctoral dissertation, Duke University.

Morrison, J. R. (1979). Diagnosis of adult psychiatric patients with childhood hyperactivity. *American Journal of Psychiatry*, **136**, 955–958.

Morrison, J. R. (1980). Childhood hyperactivity in an adult psychiatric population: Social factors. *Journal of Clinical Psychiatry*, **41**, 40–43.

Morrison, J., & Minkoff, K. (1975). Explosive personality as a sequel to the hyperactive child syndrome. *Comprehensive Psychiatry*, **16**, 343–348.

Morrison, J. R., & Stewart, M. (1971). A family study of the hyperactive child syndrome. *Biological Psychiatry*, **3**, 189–195.

Morrison, J. R., & Stewart, M. (1973). The psychiatric status of legal families of adopted hyperactives. *Archives of General Psychiatry*, **28**, 888–891.

Mouly, G. J., & Grant, V. F. (1956). A study of the growth to be expected of retarded readers. *Journal of Educational Research*, **49**, 461–465.

Muehl, S., & Forell, E. R. (1973/1974). A follow-up study of disabled readers: Variables related to high school reading performances. *Reading Research Quarterly*, **9**, 110–123.

Newman, A. P. (1972). Later achievement study of pupils underachieving in reading in first grade. *Reading Research Quarterly*, **7**, 477–508.

Newman, A. P. (1978). *Twenty lives: A longitudinal study of the effects of five variables on the lives of 20 students who were low readiness in first grade (1964-1976)*. Bloomington, IN: Indiana University Press. (ERIC Document Reproduction Service No. ED 188 126)

Newman, A. P. (1980). *Twenty lives revisited: A longitudinal study of the impact of literacy on the occupations and schooling of students who were low reading readiness in first grade (1964-1978)—with special attention to model, motivation, interest, perseverance, and pressure*. Bloomington, IN: Indiana University Press. (ERIC Document Reproduction Service No. ED 188 125)

Nichols, P. L., & Chen, T. C. (1981). *Minimal brain dysfunction: A prospective study*. Hillside, NJ: Lawrence Erlbaum.

Niles, O. S. (1966). *A follow-up study in grade 2 of pupils who received special instruction in grade 1*. Washington, DC: Office of Education (DHEW), Bureau of Research. (ERIC Document Reproduction Service No. ED 037 329)

Norman, C. A., & Zigmond, N. (1980). Characteristics of children labeled and served as learning disabled in school systems affiliated with Child Service Demonstration Centers. *Journal of Learning Disabilities*, **13**, 542–547.

Paternite, C. E., & Loney, J. (1980). Childhood hyperkinesis and home environment. In C. K. Whalen & B. Henker (Eds.), *Hyperactive children: The social ecology of identification and treatment*. New York: Academic Press.

Oettinger, L., Majovski, L. V. & Gauch, R. R. (1977). Maturity and growth in children with MBD. In J. G. Millichap (Ed.), *Learning disabilities and related disorders* (pp. 72–89). Chicago Year Book.

Pepe, H. J. (1974). *A comparison of the effectiveness of itinerant and resource room model programs designed to serve children with learning disabilities*. Unpublished doctoral dissertation, University of Kansas. Dissertation Abstracts International.

Peter, B. M., & Spreen, O. (1979). Behavior rating and personal adjustment scales of neurologically and learning handicapped children during adolescence and early adulthood: Results of a follow-up study. *Journal of Clinical Neuropsychology*, **1**, 75–92.

Preston, R. C., & Yarington, D. J. (1967). Status of fifty retarded readers eight years after reading clinic diagnosis. *Journal of Reading*, **11**, 122–129.

Quitkin, F., & Klein, D. F. (1969). Two behavioral syndromes in young adults related to possible minimal brain dysfunction. *Journal of Psychiatric Research*, **7**, 131–142.

Rabinovitch, R. D. (1968). Reading problems in children. In A. H. Keeney & V. T. Keeney (Eds.), *Dyslexia: Diagnosis and treatment of reading disorders*. St. Louis, MO: C. V. Mosby.

Rasmussen, G. R., & Dunne, H. W. (1962). A longitudinal evaluation of junior high school corrective reading program. *The Reading Teacher*, **16**, 95–101.

Rawson, M. B. (1968). *Developmental language disability: Adult accomplishments of dyslexic boys*. Baltimore, MD: The Johns Hopkins Press.

Reed, J. C. (1967). Reading achievement as related to differences between WISC verbal and performance IQs. *Child Development*, **38**, 835–840.

Riddle, K. D., & Rapoport, J. L. (1976). A 2-year follow-up of 72 hyperactive boys: Classroom behavior and peer acceptance. *Journal of Nervous and Mental Disease*, **162**, 126–134.

Ritter, D. R. (1978). Surviving in the regular classroom: A follow-up of mainstreamed children with learning disabilities. *Journal of School Psychology*, **16**, 253–256.

Robins, L. N. (1977). Problems in follow-up studies. *American Journal of Psychiatry*, **134**, 904–907.

Robins, L. N. (1979). Follow-up studies of behavior disorders in children. In H. C. Quay & J. S. Werry (Eds.), *Psychopathological disorders of childhood*. New York: Wiley.

Robinson, H. M., & Smith, H. K. (1962). Reading clinic clients—Ten years after. *Elementary School Journal*, **63**, 22–27.

Rosenthal, I. (1963). Reliability of retrospective reports of adolescence. *Journal of Consulting Psychology*, **27**, 189–198.

Rourke, B. P., & Orr, R. R. (1977). Prediction of the reading and spelling performances of normal and retarded readers: A four-year follow-up. *Journal of Abnormal Psychology*, **5**, 9–20.

Rubin, R., & Balow, B. (1971). Learning and behavior disorders: A longitudinal study. *Exceptional Children*, **37**, 293–299.

Rubin, R. A., & Balow, B. (1978, August). *Infant neurological abnormalities as predictors of IQ and school performance*. Paper presented at the annual meeting of the American Psychological Association (36th), Toronto, Canada. (ERIC Document Reproduction Service No. ED 169 732)

Rudel, R. G. (1981). Residual effects of childhood reading disabilities. *Bulletin of the Orton Society*, **31**, 89–102.

Rutter, M., Birch, H. G., Thomas, A., & Chess, S. (1964). Temperamental characteristics in infancy and the later development of behavioral disorders. *British Journal of Psychiatry*, **110**, 651–661.

Rutter, M., Tizard, J., Yule, W., Graham, P., & Whitmore, K. (1976). Research report: Isle of Wight studies, 1964-1974. *Psychological Medicine*, **6**, 313–332.

Sabatino, D. A. (1971). An evaluation of resource rooms for children with learning disabilities. *Journal of Learning Disabilities*, **4**, 84–93.

Safer, D. J., & Allen, R. P. (1976). *Hyperactive children: Diagnosis and management*. Baltimore, MD: University Park Press.

Satterfield, J. H., Cantwell, D. P., & Satterfield, B. T. (1979). Multimodality treatment: A one-year follow-up of 84 hyperactive boys. *Archives of General Psychiatry*, **36**, 965–974.

Satz, P., Taylor, H. G., Friel, J., & Fletcher, J. M. (1978). Some developmental and predictive precursors of reading disabilities: A six year follow-up. In A. L. Benton & D. Pearl (Eds.). *Dyslexia: An appraisal of current knowledge*. New York: Oxford University Press.

Schaie, K. W. (1965). A general model for the study of developmental problems. *Psychological Bulletin*, **64**, 92–107.

Schiffman, G. B. (1964). *An investigation of the effectiveness of two pedagogical procedures in the remediation of remedial retarded readers*. Unpublished doctoral dissertation, University of Maryland.

Schwartz, J. S. (1977). *A longitudinal study to determine the effectiveness of a special program for the learning disabled child*. Unpublished doctoral dissertation, Fordham University.

Shelley, E., & Reister, A. (1972). Syndrome of minimal brain damage in young adults. *Diseases of the Nervous System*, **33**, 335–338.

Shepherd, M., Oppenheim, B., & Mitchell, S. (1971). *Childhood behavior and mental health*. New York: Grune & Stratton.

Silver, A. A., & Hagin, R. A. (1963). Specific reading disability: A twelve-year follow-up study. *American Journal of Orthopsychiatry*, **33**, 338–339.

Silver, A. A., & Hagin, R. A. (1964). Specific reading disability: Follow-up studies. *American Journal of Orthopsychiatry*, **34**, 95–102.

Silver, A. A., & Hagin, R. A. (1966). Maturation of perceptual functions in children with specific reading disability. *The Reading Teacher*, **19**, 253–259.

Silver, A. A., Hagin, R. A., & Beecher, R. (1981). A program for secondary prevention of learning disabilities: Results in academic achievement and in emotional adjustment. *Journal of Preventive Psychiatry*, **1**, 77–87.

Silverberg, N. E. Iversen, I. A., & Goins, J. T. (1973). Which remedial reading method works best? *Journal of Learning Disabilities*, **6**, 547–556.

Sindelar, P. T., & Deno, S. L. (1978). The effectiveness of resource programming. *Journal of Special Education*, **12**, 17–28.

Sixth Annual Report to Congress on The Implementation of Public Law 94–142: The Education for All Handicapped Children Act (1984). Washington, DC: Office of Special Education, U.S. Department of Education.

Spache, G. D. (1957). Intellectual and personality characteristics of retarded readers. *Journal of Psychological Studies*, **9**, 9–12.

Spreen, O. (1981). The relationship between learning disability, neurological impairment, and delinquency. *Journal of Nervous and Mental Disease*, **169**, 791–799.

Spreen, O. (1982). Adult outcome of reading disorders. In R. N. Malatesha & P. G. Aaron (Eds.), *Reading disorders: Varieties and treatments*. (pp. 473–498). New York: Academic Press.

Stewart, M. A., Cummings, C., Singer, S., & deBlois, C. S. (1981). The overlap between hyperactive and unsocialized aggressive children. *Journal of Child Psychology and Psychiatry*, **22**, 35–45.

Stewart, M. A., Mendelson, W., & Johnson, N. (1973). Hyperactive children as adolescents: How they describe themselves. *Child Psychiatry and Human Development*, **4**, 3–11.

Silberberg, N. E. & Silberberg, M. C. (1969). Myths in remedial education. *Journal of Learning Disabilities*, **2**, 209–217.

Thomas, A., & Chess, S. (1975). A longitudinal study of the three brain damaged children. *Archives of General Psychiatry*, **32**, 457–462.

Thomas, A., & Chess, S. (1976). *Temperament and development*. New York: Brunner/Mazel.

Thomas, A., Chess, S., & Birch, H. G. (1968). *Temperament and behavior disorders in children*. New York: New York University Press.

Trites, R. L., & Fiedorowicz, C. (1976). Follow-up study of children with specific (or primary) reading disability. In R. M. Knights & D. J. Bakker (Eds.), *The neuropsychology of learning disorders: Theoretical approaches* (pp. 41–50). Baltimore, MD: University Park Press.

Tufvander, E. A., & Zintz, M. V. (1957). A follow-up study of pupils with reading difficulties. *Elementary School Journal*, **58**, 152–156.

Valentine, H. B. (1951). Some results of remedial education in a child guidance centre. *British Journal of Educational Psychology*, **21**, 145–149.

Walker, K. P. (1963). *A follow-up study of two methods of treating retarded readers*. Unpublished doctoral dissertation, University of Iowa.

343

Wallbrown, F. H., Wherry, R. J., Blaha, J., & Counts, D. H. (1974). An empirical test of Myklebust's cognitive structure hypothesis for 70 reading-disabled children. *Journal of Consulting and Clinical Psychology*, **42**, 211–218.

Weiner, L. H. (1969). An investigation of the effectiveness of resource rooms for children with specific learning disabilities. *Journal of Learning Disabilities*, **2**, 223–229.

Weiner, P. S. (1972). The perceptual level functioning of dysphasic children: A follow-up study. *Journal of Speech and Hearing Research*, **15**, 423–438.

Weiss, G., Hechtman, L., & Perman, T. (1978). Hyperactives as young adults: School, employer, and self-ratings scales obtained during ten-year follow-up evaluation. *American Journal of Orthopsychiatry*, **48**, 438–445.

Weiss, G., Hechtman, L., Perman, T., Hopkins, J., & Wener, A. (1979). Hyperactives as young adults: A controlled prospective ten-year follow-up of 75 children. *Archives of General Psychiatry*, **36**, 675–681.

Weiss, G., Kruger, F., Danielson, V., Elman, M. (1975). Effect of long-term treatment of hyperactive children with methylphenidate. *Canadian Medical Association Journal*, **112**, 159–165.

Weiss, G., Minde, K., Werry, J. S., Douglas, V., & Nemeth, E. (1971). Studies on the hyperactive child: VIII. Five-year follow-up. *Archives of General Psychiatry*, **24**, 409–414.

Wepman, J. M., & Morency, A. S. (1971). *School achievement as related to speech and perceptual handicaps*. Final Report, Project # 70461, contract # OEG-2-7-070461-4543. Washington, DC: US Department of Health, Education & Welfare, Office of Education. (ERIC Document Reproduction Service No. ED 057 539)

Werner, E. E. Bierman, J. M., & French, F. E. (1971). *The children of Kauai: A longitudinal study from the prenatal period to age ten*. Honolulu: University of Hawaii Press.

Werner, E. E., Simonian, K., & Smith, R. S. (1967). Reading achievements, language functioning, and perceptual-motor development of 10 and 11 year olds. *Perceptual and Motor Skills*, **25**, 409–420.

Werner, E. E., & Smith, R. S. (1977). *Kauai's children come of age*. Honolulu: University of Hawaii Press.

Werner, E. E., & Smith, R. S. (1979). An epidemiologic perspective on some antecedents and consequences of childhood mental health problems and learning disabilities: A report from the Kauai longitudinal study. *Journal of the American Academy of Child Psychiatry*, **18**, 292–306.

Werner, E. E., & Smith, R. S. (1982). *Vulnerable but invincible: A longitudinal study of resilient children and youth*. New York: McGraw-Hill.

White, J., Barratt, E., & Adams, P. (1979). The hyperactive child in adolescence. *Journal of the American Academy of Child Psychiatry*, **18**, 154–159.

White, W. J., Schumaker, J. B., Warner, M. M., Alley, G. R., & Deshler, D. D. (1980). *The current status of young adults identified as learning disabled during their school career*. (Research Report No. 21). Lawrence, KS: University of Kansas, Institute for Research in learning Disabilities.

Winter, A., & Wright, E. N. (1983). *A follow-up of pupils who entered learning disabilities self-contained classes in 1981-1982*. (Research Report # 171), Toronto, Canada: Board of Education. (ERIC Document Reproduction Service No. ED 238 224).

Wood, D., Reimherr, F., Wender, P., & Johnson, G. (1976). Diagnosis and treatment of minimal brain dysfunction: A preliminary report. *Archives of General Psychiatry*, **33**, 1453–1460.

Woods, S. S. (1981). *Follow-up study of 64 hyperactive children in adolescence*. Unpublished doctoral dissertation, University of Michigan.

Yule, W. (1973). Differential prognosis of reading backwardness and specific reading retardation. *British Journal of Educational Psychology*, **43**, 244–248.

Yule, W., & Rigley, L. V. (1967). *A four-year follow-up of severely backward readers into adolescence*. In M. M. Clark & J. M. Maxwell (Eds.), *Reading: Influence of Progress, Proceedings of the Fifth Annual Study Congress of the United Kingdom* (Vol. 5).

Direct Academic Interventions in Learning Disabilities

JOHN WILLS LLOYD

Department of Curriculum, Instruction, and Special Education,
University of Virginia

Abstract—Although many specialized interventions such as perceptual-motor training have not generally proved effective in remedying the academic problems of learning-disabled pupils, a growing body of evidence indicates that specific alterations in the actual academic instruction these students receive can improve their acquisition and maintenance of skills. Simple intervention techniques such as reinforcing correct responding and correcting errors have been shown to be very helpful in many cases. Similarly, applications of effective teaching precepts such as providing frequent opportunities to respond and delivering instruction in smaller units are beneficial. However, more complex interventions are often necessary. Research about the nature of these interventions indicates that they must teach students strategies or operations for approaching and solving academic problems and that they must be complete. To be complete, an intervention must incorporate all components required for successful performance including those noted previously as well as others such as self-monitoring of performance.

The ultimate purpose of research in learning disabilities, including the work of those who study pupils' characteristics in laboratory situations, is the improvement of the learning performance of pupils with learning disabilities. The most direct path to this end, of course, is the study of interventions. In the case of achievement, the most immediate path to the improvement of performance is direct intervention in academic areas. In this chapter the evidence about direct academic interventions for students with learning disabilities is examined.

Overview

Although there have been many studies of effective methods for improving academic skills of learning disabled pupils, there have also been studies of ineffective methods. The evidence discussed in this chapter indicates that most indirect methods of intervention (i.e., those in which training does not focus on actual academic performance) do not reliably produce beneficial effects on achievement. Visual-perceptual training, optometric training, psycholinguistic process training, differentiation of instruction according to modality strengths and weaknesses, attention-to-task training, and social skills training are all examples of interventions or treatments that have not consistently improved academic performance. It is important to note that these interventions may sometimes improve academic performance or that they may have some other beneficial effects, but that they should not be considered effective means of remedying achievement problems.

In contrast, a substantial and growing body of evidence about effective interventions exists. This literature reveals that it is possible to influence the academic performance of learning disabled pupils by very simple techniques in some cases. These techniques include reinforcing specific aspects of academic performance (e.g., accuracy, rate) and modeling certain academic behaviors (e.g., fluent reading). However, these intervention strategies are ineffective when students do not know *how* to perform academic tasks; in such cases, it is necessary to adopt more complex interventions.

More complex interventions include multiple instructional components. Modeling and reinforcement are among these, but an additional component is required. Instruction must make explicit the steps through which students must go in order to perform given academic tasks successfully. In the case of thinking tasks such as are common in academic learning, it is important that the covert operations involved in the task be made overt and be taught systematically (often through modeling and reinforcement for imitating the model); then the separate operations are concatenated, smooth performance is developed through practice, and the requirement for overt performance is dropped. It may be that learning disabled and normally achieving pupils have differential needs for this more explicit instruction.

Simply teaching an operation itself in isolation is not a sufficient intervention, however. Instruction must convey all of the necessary parts of the performance to be learned and must integrate all of the parts. More complete interventions are more effective than less complete ones. For example, many academic operations are more likely to be performed accurately if the product of the operation is checked; therefore a self-evaluation component is beneficial in such operations. Such self-control components have become increasingly common in interventions.

In addition to knowledge about the structure of effective interventions, some evidence has emerged about the delivery of effective instruction. In general, this knowledge is consistent with the broader literature about effective teaching which has illuminated the importance of such variables as clear demonstrations, guided practice, feedback, and engagement in activities that are consistent with goals and objectives. Also, there is evidence accruing that it is important to deliver instruction in smaller segments and with additional practice opportunities in order to teach learning disabled pupils successfully.

The present state of knowledge about interventions makes it possible to describe how effective academic intervention programs may be designed and delivered. The next steps include (a) developing comprehensive intervention packages based on this knowledge, and (b) infusing this knowledge into practice in the field. The basic technology is available, but it must be used.

These conclusions represent the circumspect generalizations that can be made from the evidence. Some more specific and somewhat less stable conclusions can be drawn from this literature as well, and further research will help to confirm, deny, or modify these narrower conclusions. The evidence upon which my conclusions are based is presented in the body of the chapter. Before presenting this evidence, however, some general issues that frame the remainder of the treatment are described.

General Issues

The general issues discussed in this section include (a) the scope of the review, (b) research paradigms, (c) problems of aptitude-by-treatment interaction research, and (d) categories of interventions.

Scope of the Review

This review is restricted to examination of direct academic interventions, and this restriction is developed in the paragraphs immediately following. The contents of earlier reviews of learning disabilities including those by Bateman (1966), Lloyd, Hallahan, and Kauffman (1980), Torgesen (1975), and Wiederholt (1974) have not been extensively duplicated.

Only studies that involve frank experimental comparisons of an academic treatment program either to a control, baseline, or other treatment condition have been included. Furthermore, the emphasis has been placed on the study of interventions with immediate applied importance; thus, the studies included are ones in which

one of the dependent variables was some measure of achievement in an applied situation and the independent variable was some form of instruction in an academic area (speaking, reading, spelling, etc.).

This focus excludes several otherwise important areas of research. Some of these (e.g., social skills training), although clearly relevant to the problems of learning disabled students, usually include neither direct academic instruction nor dependent measures of academic performance. Others, such as *medical interventions* and *indirect interventions*, may have been studied using academic performance measures, but include nonacademic interventions. However, in order to establish the context for the research that is reviewed, medical and indirect interventions are discussed briefly here. In addition, because it has been frequently reviewed elsewhere, one area of direct academic intervention is briefly discussed here: *modality-matching* in reading instruction.

MEDICAL INTERVENTIONS

Medical interventions have a broad and somewhat controversial history in the area of learning disability. Psychopharmacological and dietary treatments have been studied extensively.

Psychopharmacological interventions. There have been many reviews of the effects of psychopharmacological interventions including narrative (e.g., Adelman & Compas, 1977; Whalen & Henker, 1976) and meta-analytic reviews (i.e., Kavale, 1982). Although they cover much of the same literature, the conclusions reached by the authors of these reviews differ. For example, Adelman and Compas (1977) present a frankly negative view about the effects of psychopharmacological interventions, but Whalen and Henker (1976) and Kavale (1982) are more positive. Of particular importance to the present analysts, however, is that the narrative reviews are not encouraging about the effects of psychopharmacological agents—particularly psychostimulants—on academic performance. This is not the case with the meta-analytic evaluation of drug studies; Kavale reported that the effect sizes for academic performance were smaller and more variable than those for ratings of behavior but that there are positive effects of drug therapy on various measures of achievement. (There is additional discussion of certain studies of psychopharmacological interventions in the later section on behavior modification.)

Dietary interventions. The K–P diet (Feingold, 1975), which obtained initial support from uncontrolled case studies (e.g., Feingold, 1976), has been subjected to more careful scrutiny in the ensuing years. Conners (1980), Kavale and Forness (1983), and Mattes (1983) have provided the most thorough and contemporary reviews of diet as a treatment program. Kavale and Forness (1983) used meta-analytic techniques to examine the evidence about the effects of the K–P diet treatment. Although their analysis indicated that the average child following the K–P diet would be better off than 55% of the subjects under a control condition for teacher's ratings of behavior, there is little encouraging evidence about the effects of this therapy on academic performance.

INDIRECT INTERVENTIONS

Indirect interventions include those in which learning disabled pupils are provided training or instruction in some area other than an academic one but the effects of the intervention on academic performance are considered. Although, when defined this way, there are other examples of indirect interventions (e.g., self-efficacy training, social skills training, art therapy, music therapy, and dressage), I shall briefly discuss only the more widely known of them: perceptual or perceptual-motor training, optometric training, psycholinguistic process training, and attention to task training.

Perceptual-motor training. The effectiveness of perceptual and perceptual-motor methods has been evaluated by many investigators. As would be expected because of the early interest in this type of intervention, these studies have been reviewed frequently. Among the reviews are those by Hallahan and Cruickshank (1973), Hammill and Goodman (1973), Hammill and Wiederholt (1973), Kavale and Mattson (1983), and Sabatino (1973). These reviewers all conclude that there is little evidence that perceptual and perceptual-motor training have demonstrable beneficial effects on learning disabled pupils' performance. At best, it appears that these interventions have effects on the measures with which they were associated (e.g., the Developmental Test of Visual Perception) and may have effects on other measures with similar formats and content; but they have no consistent effects on measures of academic performance.

Optometric training. On the whole, there is little evidence to support the use of optometric training programs with learning disabled pupils. In an early review, Keogh (1974) reported that the research evidence about the effectiveness of these programs was hampered by experimental problems (e.g., sample selection procedures) which made it difficult to draw definitive conclusions. More recently, Keogh and Pelland (in press) reviewed the literature on the effectiveness of optometric training and arrived at similar conclusions. They found that the available evidence did not permit a judgment that optometric training was effective. However, they mitigated the strength of their conclusion by noting that the wealth of case studies and testimonials in the

area suggested some possible effectiveness.

Psycholinguistic process training. During the early 1970s, many learning disability specialists questioned the value of training psycholinguistic processes. Hammill and Larsen (1974) reviewed studies on the effectiveness of psycholinguistic training and pronounced the evidence very weak. Their analysis was challenged by advocates of psycholinguistic training (e.g., Lund, Foster, & McCall-Perez, 1978). More recently, Kavale (1981) re-examined the evidence about the effectiveness of psycholinguistic training, using meta-analytic techniques. His results are not in complete agreement with the analysis of Hammill and Larsen (1974) and Larsen, Parker, and Hammill (1982) therefore replied with a critique of Kavale's analysis. Kavale analyzed 240 effects from 34 studies and found an average effect size of 0.39, a finding which would place the average pupil receiving psycholinguistic training at the 65th percentile of subjects who served in the control groups of the studies. Kavale considered this to be modest but clear evidence that psycholinguistic training programs do have effects on performance on a psycholinguistic test such as the Illinois Test of Psycholinguistic Abilities (ITPA). Larsen et al. (1982) challenged Kavale's review because it did not include six studies that had been part of the Hammill and Larsen (1974) review. When they computed effect sizes for these six studies they found that they yielded an average effect size of 0.03 which, when pooled with the results of Kavale's analysis, reduced the overall effect size to 0.34. Accordingly, Larsen et al. reaffirmed the conclusions of Hammill and Larsen (1974) that the effectiveness of psycholinguistic training remains undemonstrated. It should be noted that some advocates of psycholinguistic interventions (e.g., Kirk & Chalfant, 1984) consider this evidence irrelevant; they contend that the psycholinguistic training used in the studies was provided in isolation rather than in the context of academic instruction.

Attention training. It is often hoped that increasing attention to task will result in improved academic performance. Pupils have been put into study carrels where it was thought that the reduction of distracting stimulation would help them, but effects on academic performance were negligible (e.g., Sommerville, Warnberg, & Bost, 1973). Studies of reinforcement procedures have shown that academic performance is often not affected when reinforcement is contingent on attending behavior (e.g., Ferritor, Buckholdt, Hamblin, & Smith, 1972). Self-recording of attention, a third approach to improving attending which has been studied extensively with learning disabled pupils (e.g., Hallahan, Lloyd, Kneedler, & Marshall, 1982), has been found to have indirect effects on academic productivity in some but not all cases.

MODALITY MATCHING

In addition to multisensory training, a major role for the modalities in the area of learning disability has been their influence on adaptation of instruction according to "learning styles." This presents the clearest example in the field of learning disability of intervention based on an aptitude-by-treatment interaction model. In general, the advocates of this position contend that some pupils with auditory learning styles will learn better if instruction is presented in ways emphasizing auditory skills and that other learners with visual learning styles will learn better if instruction is presented in ways emphasizing visual skill.

The most common operationalization of this position is in the area of reading instruction. Auditory learners are expected to learn to read better when given instruction using an auditory approach (i.e., code-emphasis or phonics) than they would were they given instruction using a visual approach (i.e., look-say or sight-word). For visual learners, of course, the reverse would be expected. That is, the modality strength of the learner would be matched to the modality demands of the instructional program.

Reviewers of the evidence regarding modality-matched reading instruction have uniformly concluded that there is not evidence to support this view (Arter & Jenkins, 1977, 1979; Bateman, 1979; Larrivee, 1981; Tarver & Dawson, 1978; Ysseldyke, 1973). However, as this author has noted elsewhere (Lloyd, 1984), the recommendations about basing instruction on modality strengths and weaknesses continue to appear in the educational and special educational literature (Barbe & Milone, 1980; Carbo, 1983; Dunn, 1983).

Research Paradigms

An argument about the relative value of two approaches to experimental research will inevitably be confronted by anyone undertaking the analysis of treatment programs. It centers on the question: What constitutes acceptable evidence of the effects of a treatment program? One may place relatively more or less emphasis on the acceptability of many research paradigms. Do case studies provide evidence that permits strong inferences about an intervention's effects? Do studies using single-subject reversal designs permit strong inferences? Are between-groups designs using randomly assigned subjects who are clearly representative of the learning disabled population the only type of designs that permit strong inferences?

These and related questions pervade the clinical research methodology literature and need not be examined in detail here (c.f., Kazdin, 1980). The present review includes studies using either single-case or group research designs but omits case studies; that is, as noted above, only frankly experimental studies were examined. In the case of research using one or a few subjects, the following bases were used to discriminate between single-case experimental designs and case studies: Single-case designs include (a) repeated measurement of dependent variables, (b) repeated manipulation of independent variables, where these manipulations rule out threats to internal validity, and (c) comparison of the performance of an individual under one level of an independent variable to the performance of that same individual under another level of an independent variable (c.f., Kazdin, 1982). Case studies do not include all three of these attributes; they often (a) fail to provide repeated manipulations of the treatment program (e.g., do not include reversal phases or the time-lagged introduction of the treatment across baselines), and (b) limit repeated assessments to pretests and posttests.

Aptitude-by-Treatment Interactions

One of the most intuitively appealing and highly revered ideas in the field of learning disability is that interventions should be differentiated on the basis of individual learner characteristics. Indeed, the very existence of the categorical group is testament to the belief that instruction must be different for students with learning disabilities and nonhandicapped students. (The learning disability field's most often studied example of differentiation on the basis of learner aptitude, modality matching, was discussed in the previous section.) However, there is scant support available at present to indicate that matching types of learners to types of instruction will result in higher levels of achievement than undifferentiated instruction, either in the case of general education (Cronbach & Snow, 1977) or special education (Lloyd, 1984). Our failure to identify reliable interactions between learners' aptitudes and the instruction they receive may have been caused by many factors including the following: (a) differentiation among subtypes of pupils may be inadequate (but see McKinney's chapter in this volume); (b) differences in the types of interventions studied may be unreliable (the differences may be a function of the experimenters' opinions about the interventions rather than true differences in them); (c) examination of aptitudes may focus on irrelevant ones; or (d) other factors may interfere with identification of true interactions.

The limited empirical support for the adaptation of instruction on the basis of learner characteristics notwithstanding, a recurring theme of the following examination of the effects of interventions for students with learning disabilities will be that very few of the interventions have been studied with explicit attention to the possibility that some interventions may be differentially effective for learning disabled pupils or subtypes of them. Clinical hunches, self-reports, and other less rigorous forms of knowing continue to support the idea that different people may learn better when given one kind of instruction than they would were they given another kind of instruction. Furthermore, preliminary confirmatory evidence (e.g., Pascarella & Pflaum, 1981) encourages the continuation of the search for aptitude-by-treatment interactions.

Categories of Interventions

Earlier examinations of learning disability have divided intervention approaches into medical, process, and behavioral categories (Bateman, 1967; Lerner, 1976; Ysseldyke & Salvia, 1974). For two reasons, these categories are not useful for the present review. First, interventions such as those described by Pflaum and Pascarella (e.g., 1980) or Bryant (e.g., Bryant, Drabin, & Gettinger, 1981) clearly do not fit conceptually with the medical model, the process model, or the behavioral model. Second, as discussed above, the focus of the present review on direct academic interventions precludes further discussion of medical and process interventions.

I have grouped interventions into three categories and called these behavioral, instructional, and cognitive approaches. (I have used "approaches" as the higher order term and "interventions" as the lower order term.) These categories were derived according to the following rules: (a) if an intervention was based on constructs from the fields of cognitive psychology or information processing or both and depended only incidentally on reinforcement (in the operant sense of the word), it was considered to be a *cognitive* intervention; (b) if an intervention depended primarily on the constructs of "effective instruction," even though these constructs might be consistent with either a cognitive or a behavioral approach, it was considered an *instructional* intervention; (c) if an intervention was based on task analysis and recommended use of reinforcement, it was considered a *behavioral* intervention. Although one might consider these categories to be somewhat arbitrary divisions of points along a continuum—"cognitive behavior modification" is a good example of how the categories overlap—they serve to structure the remaining material.

Behavioral Approaches

The interventions included in this group—behavior modification and the Direct Instruction Model—share several features. In both cases, reinforcement is an integral part of interventions, observable behavior is the focus of treatments, academic tasks are treated as the summed products of component behaviors, and single-subject methodology is frequently used as a research strategy. Although behaviorists are usually thought to ignore the role of cognition in learning, the emphasis of some researchers in this group on teaching "thinking operations" is very similar to cognitive training.

Behavior Modification

Behavior modification has had a major effect on interventions in the area of learning disability. Early studies

TABLE 1
Applied Behavior Analyses Relevant to Learning Disabilities Interventions

Citation	Independent Variable(s)
Billingsley, 1977	Self- and externally imposed reinforcement
Blankenship, 1978	Modeling and feedback
Broden et al., 1978	Parental tutoring
Broughton & Lahey, 1978	Response cost
Fauke et al., 1973	Differential reinforcement
Fleisher & Jenkins, 1978	Forms of practice
Freeman & McLaughlin, 1984	Audiotaped modeling of reading words
Grimm et al., 1973	Modeling of solution process and reinforcement
Haring & Hauck, 1969	Programmed materials and token reinforcement
Hasazi & Hasazi, 1972	Teacher attention contingent on correctly written digits
Hendrickson et al., 1978	Modeling versus correction in reading
Jenkins et al., 1978	Reinforcement of accurate reading
Jenkins & Larson, 1979	Reading error correction techniques
Kauffman et al., 1978	Contingent imitation of errors
Knapczyk & Livingston, 1974	Promotion of question asking
Lahey et al., 1973	Reinforcement of accurate reading
Lahey et al., 1977	Differential reinforcement
Limbrick et al., 1981	Using context in reading
Lovitt & Curtiss, 1968	Reading aloud of arithmetic problems before solving them
Lovitt & Hansen, 1976	Skipping and drilling contingent on reading accuracy
Lovitt & Hurlburt, 1974	Phonics instruction
Lovitt et al., 1986	Modifications of science materials
Lovitt & Smith, 1974	Withdrawal of reinforcement
Lovitt & Smith, 1972	Verbal instructions
Luiselli & Downing, 1980	Correction and reinforcement
McKenzie et al., 1968	Token reinforcement
Roberts & Smith, 1980	Reinforcement of word reading accuracy versus reinforcement of comprehension question answering accuracy
Rose, 1985	Preview by reading silently to self versus preview by listening to teacher read passage aloud (elementary-age subjects)
Rose & Robinson, 1984	Illustrations in reading material
Rose & Sherry, 1984	Preview by reading silently to self versus preview by listening to teacher read passage aloud (adolescent subjects)
Smith, 1979	Teacher modeling of fluent reading

Smith & Lovitt, 1973	Differential reinforcement
Smith & Lovitt, 1975	Modeling
Smith & Lovitt, 1976	Reinforcement
Smith et al., 1972, Exp. 1	Withdrawal of positive reinforcement for arithmetic errors
Smith et al., 1972, Exp. 2	Manipulable teaching aids and modeling
Stromer, 1975	Modeling, practice, and differential reinforcement
Stromer, 1977	Modeling, practice, and differential reinforcement
Swanson, 1981a	Self-recording, token reinforcement, and contingent free time
Trice et al., 1981	Contingent free time
Van Houten & Little, 1982	Allocation of less work time

(e.g., Haring & Hauck, 1969; Zimmerman & Zimmerman, 1962) conducted with pupils who today would probably be considered learning disabled revealed that behavioral principles could be applied to matters of learning outside of the laboratory setting. More recently, researchers influenced by behavioral principles have conducted studies in each of the academic areas. Reviews by Lahey (1976) and Rose, Koorland, and Epstein (1982) are available.

The range of interventions that have been studied by behaviorally oriented researchers is not restricted to simple reinforcement and punishment procedures. Indeed, many of the interventions that have been examined using applied behavior analysis methodology (i.e., Kazdin, 1982) are more akin to other models of intervention. Both kinds of studies are considered in the following sections. Examples of these studies are shown in Table 1.

SPEAKING AND LISTENING

Behaviorally oriented educators and psychologists have worked extensively on the problems of receptive and expressive language and some valuable procedures and techniques may be available in the behavioral literature. For example, Garcia and Batista-Wallace (1977) trained parents to influence their children's use of the plural morpheme; Lahey (1971) used modeling techniques to increase the use of adjectives in Head Start pupils; and Hart and Risley (1974) increased the use of phrases and compound sentences using behavioral techniques and common teaching materials.

The Lovaas (e.g., 1977) and Monterey (e.g., Gray & Ryan, 1973) language programs are among the most clearly behavioral language intervention programs. They incorporate detailed control of reinforcement schedules, small step sequencing of tasks, and precise specification of teacher modeling behaviors. Evaluations of the Monterey language programs have revealed that they are effective (Gray & Ryan, 1973; Matheny & Panagos, 1978), but they have not been

evaluated with pupils expressly labeled learning disabled. Similarly, the Lovaas programs have extensive experimental support but they, too, have neither been designed for nor used with learning disabled students.

READING

One of the most ubiquitous findings in the behavior modification literature is that behavior can be influenced by its consequences. When one conceives of reading—particularly oral reading—as behavior, it is easy to understand why there are so many studies demonstrating the influence of reinforcement in reading.

Haring and Hauck (1969) examined changes in four elementary-age boys' reading performance. They compared the boys' skills under baseline conditions to their performance when programmed reading materials and token reinforcement were provided. Although their design was not frankly experimental, their results were consistent with much of the more recent research; when programmed learning materials, a more structured environment, and reinforcement were provided, the frequency of correct responding increased. Lahey, McNees, and Brown (1973a) evaluated the effects of simple reinforcement contingencies on the reading comprehension performance of two elementary-age pupils. Their single-subject analysis indicated that the accuracy of answers to reading comprehension questions could be increased by providing praise and rewards for correct answering. Similarly, Jenkins, Barksdale, and Clinton (1978) found that contingent reinforcement led to improvements in the reading rate and comprehension of elementary-age learning disabled boys and that the improvements transferred across settings and were maintained.

Clever arrangements of contingencies illustrate that the consequences controlling reading need not be tangible (e.g., tokens) or even social (praise). Lovitt and Hansen (1976) found that the reading performance of learning disabled boys could be substantially affected by making rapid progress contingent on performance; they established a program called "contingent skipping and drilling" in which rapid, accurate reading and answering of questions resulted in the opportunity to skip sections of the text but slow, inaccurate reading and answering resulted in required repetition and practice on materials. The skipping and drilling program resulted in substantial improvements in the pupils' reading performance.

Of course, not all behaviorally-based interventions require manipulation of consequences. For example, working with a boy and a girl from the primary grades who were identified as learning disabled, Smith (1979) found that rate of oral reading could be positively affected by simply having the teacher model fluent reading before requiring the students to read. In a second study she also observed that modeling influenced oral reading rate and accuracy of an elementary-age boy identified as learning disabled, but that additional interventions (e.g., corrections) enhanced these effects. Hendrickson,

Roberts, and Shores (1978) reported the results of their work with two primary-age boys with reading disabilities. They examined the effects of modeling and correction on the frequency with which the boys read words correctly and reported that modeling led to more rapid acquisition of word reading responses than did correction; however, although both procedures led to acquisition of the training words, neither procedure produced generalized word reading skills. Because these procedures are not instructional in the sense that they teach students *how* to read words, the absence of transfer to new words is understandable.

Lovitt and Hurlburt (1974) used behavioral procedures to study the effects of phonics instruction on the oral reading behavior of two elementary-age boys identified as dyslexic. In both cases, when phonics instruction (e.g., exercises based on Slingerland's program (Slingerland, 1974) or the Palo Alto readers) was implemented, the boys had higher correct oral reading rates and lower error rates than they did under baseline conditions.

Rose (1985; Rose & Sherry, 1984) used behavior analysis procedures to examine the effects of previewing procedures on oral reading performance. He reported that a procedure in which the teacher reads a passage aloud to students was superior to one in which the students may examine it silently prior to the time when they are required to read it aloud. The listening procedure resulted in fewer oral reading errors for both elementary (Rose, 1985) and secondary students (Rose & Sherry, 1984). Singh and Singh (1984) reported that another previewing procedure, in which the teacher used a brief discussion period to familiarize the students with the contents of a passage prior to their reading of it, reduced reading errors.

ARITHMETIC

Behavioral work in the area of arithmetic is equally diverse and extensive. The independent variables of some behavioral studies of arithmetic were shown in Table 1 and examples of these studies are discussed in the following paragraphs.

Smith and Lovitt (1976) demonstrated an important relationship between reinforcement and academic performance. In two studies, they assessed the arithmetic computation performance of 10 elementary-age boys (three in one study and seven in the other) identified as learning disabled. Their results indicated that reinforcement contingencies have little effect on rate or accuracy unless the pupils know how to perform the required operations. A similar finding is apparent in other studies (e.g., Grimm, Bijou, & Parsons, 1973).

In a widely cited study, Lovitt and Curtiss (1968) evaluated the effects of requiring an elementary-age boy identified as having behavior problems to read arithmetic problems aloud before writing his answers to them. The boy's performance improved on three types of arithmetic problems when this antecedent event was manipulated. However, the results were not reversible, as required by the experimental design used to assess these changes. Cullinan, Epstein, and Lloyd (1978) repeated the study using boys identified as learning disabled and using multiplication instead of subtraction problems but they did not obtain the results that Lovitt and Curtiss obtained. In addition to the differences between the studies just noted, the boy in the Lovitt and Curtiss study was clearly capable of performing the required operations but the boys in the Cullinan et al. study were still learning how to perform the operations required by the arithmetic problems.

WRITING

Handwriting. Handwriting problems have been extensively studied by behaviorally oriented special educators. They have developed what is nearly a "cure" for problems such as reversals despite having ignored psychological and physiological explanations of these problems. The procedure they have used is based on differential reinforcement contingencies: When the student writes a target letter, numeral, or word correctly, provide reinforcement (praise, for example); when the student writes an item incorrectly, require him or her to correct it. Six studies of this type of procedure or one very similar to it have repeatedly shown its effectiveness (Fauke, Burnett, Powers, & Sulzer-Azaroff, 1973; Hasazi & Hasazi, 1972; Lahey, Busemeyer, O'Hara, & Beggs, 1977; Smith & Lovitt, 1973; Stromer, 1975, 1977).

Composition. Behaviorally oriented special educators have also studied the modification of composing. Of course, rewards for changes in particular parts of compositions have been examined repeatedly (Brigham, Graubard, & Stans, 1972; Maloney & Hopkins, 1973; Maloney, Jacobson, & Hopkins, 1975). The outcomes of these studies are somewhat obvious: Reinforcement that is contingent on (a) writing more words increases the number of words written; (b) writing more action verbs (e.g., "run," and "swing," but not "are," and "want") increases the number of action verbs students use in their compositions; (c) using different words leads to essays that include a wider vocabulary. However, reinforcing a certain aspect of writing usually does not affect other parts.

To obtain broader effects using reinforcement, it probably will be necessary to design a system that reinforces different aspects of composing. Furthermore, it is unlikely that reinforcement will induce new forms (unless it is contingent on use of new forms), reemphasizing the recurring theme that learning disabled students must be shown *how* to write communicatively.

John Wills Lloyd

PSYCHOPHARMACOLOGY VERSUS BEHAVIOR THERAPY

The previous material does not address the question of the relative effectiveness of comprehensive behavioral interventions in relation to other specific interventions. However, studies comparing psychopharmacotherapy to behavior therapy have been conducted, particularly in the last decade, and provide additional information about both types of interventions (Ayllon, Layman, & Kandel, 1975; Christensen, 1975; Christensen & Sprague, 1973; Conners & Wells, 1979; Gittleman et al., 1980; Loney, Weissenburger, Woolson, & Lichty, 1979; Pelham, Schnedler, Bologna, & Contreras, 1980; Shafto & Sulzbacher, 1977; Whalen, Henker, Collins, Finck, & Dotemoto, 1979; Wolraich, Drummond, Salomon, O'Brien, & Sivage, 1978; Wulbert & Dries, 1977).

Many of these studies seem to reflect an "either-or" approach to the topic (i.e., only one treatment should be used and the studies were conducted in order to establish which one it should be, perhaps the one the authors favored). Few of them have included pupils expressly identified as learning disabled. However, there is sufficient overlap between the hyperactive subjects common in the studies and the learning disabled population to make it likely that the results would be substantially the same with learning disabled subjects.

Reviews and discussions of this evidence (O'Leary, 1980; Schroeder, Lewis, & Lipton, 1983; Sprague, 1983) indicate that there is no clear winner when pharmacological and behavioral interventions are compared. However, an emerging trend seems to be that some pupils react better to one or the other treatment (perhaps based on attributions for success) and that many pupils respond best to combinations of these treatments.

Direct Instruction Model

The Direct Instruction Model (DIM), which is most closely associated with the work of Engelmann, Carnine, Becker, and Bereiter (e.g., Becker, Engelmann, & Thomas, 1975; Bereiter & Engelmann, 1966; Carnine & Silbert, 1979; Engelmann, 1969b; Engelmann & Carnine, 1982), has generated much research in the field of learning disability. Although the generic term "direct instruction" (e.g., Rosenshine, 1976) gained great currency in the late 1970s and early 1980s, the Direct Instruction Model differs from it in some specific ways. In both the Direct Instruction Model and the generic direct instruction approach, there is emphasis on specific control of teacher behavior, particularly in the form of correction, reinforcement, and provision of practice opportunities, but in the DIM, relatively greater emphasis is placed on the logical analysis of instructional communications (Engelmann & Carnine, 1982). Indeed, direct instruction researchers have conducted many studies of these instructional programming principles both with normally achieving (e.g., Carnine, 1980b) and

handicapped learners (e.g., Gersten, White, Falco & Carnine, 1982).

The Direct Instruction Model has been shown to be effective in bringing about the acquisition of basic academic skills. Early indications of its effectiveness were reported by Engelmann (1969a), and substantial further evidence of effects on academic, cognitive, and self-concept measures is contained in the evaluation of the Follow Through program (Abt Associates, 1976, 1977; Becker & Carnine, 1981; c.f., House, Glass, McLean, & Walker, 1978). Furthermore, although not all reports are as clearly positive (e.g., Miller & Bizzell, 1984), desirable effects seem to persist into the later school years; Becker and Gersten (1982) reported that fifth and sixth grade children who had received their primary schooling under the Direct Instruction Model had higher achievement than children in comparison programs and White and Gersten (1983) reported that some effects were still apparent in high school.

Gersten, Becker, Heiry, and White (1984) examined the relationship between children's IQ at the beginning of schooling and their yearly academic growth under the Direct Instruction Model. They found that pupils with low IQs (i.e., those with IQs < 71) achieved at essentially the same rate as their peers with higher IQs (i.e., those with IQs between 71 and 90 and those with IQs > 90) during the first two years of schooling, but that at the third grade level the students with low IQs experienced significantly slower progress in reading in comparison with their peers. Of particular interest here is that the students who would traditionally be called "slow learners" or might have been classified as learning disabled (i.e., those in the IQ 71–90 group) acquired basic skills at about the same relative rate as their more capable peers, given instruction based on the Direct Instruction Model.

Research about the application of the Direct Instruction Model with handicapped learners has been extensive and has been reviewed by Gersten (1981). In a more recent review of much of the same literature, White (1987) reported a meta-analysis of 25 studies. He found an average effect size of 0.81 for academic measures, indicating that pupils receiving Direct Instruction were far better served than those in control or comparison conditions.

Although there are relevant studies in other areas such as spelling (e.g., Stephens & Hudson, 1984), this section shall treat only DIM studies in the areas of *speaking and listening*, *reading*, and *arithmetic*.

SPEAKING AND LISTENING

In addition to the Follow Through evidence showing that the Direct Instruction Model was the only sponsor to have significant effects on Metropolitan Achievement Test (MAT) language scores, Studies of DIM oral language programs have been conducted with mentally retarded and learning disabled pupils. The mental retardation studies include an investigation of the effects of

352

the DISTAR Language program in comparison to use of the Peabody Language Development Kit and other more general techniques. Maggs and Morath (1979) reported that the DIM program resulted in significantly greater development (as measured on the Stanford-Binet and other tests of development) than the comparison program and that the pupils progressed at a normal rate (i.e., one month increase in mental age for one month increase in chronological age) during the study. Gersten and Maggs (1982) recaptured these subjects five years later and reported that significant differences between groups persisted.

In other studies of the language skills, significant effects have also been reported. Weller (1979) evaluated the effects of a DIM intervention on the performance of preschool children who had language deficits. She reported that the DIM procedures had greater effects on acquisition of descriptor and functor words than did a comparison program (Blank, 1973). Similarly, research with elementary-age learning disabled students has revealed that DIM intervention has greater effects on vocabulary than a generic language program (Lloyd, Cullinan, Heins, & Epstein, 1980).

READING

Direct Instruction reading programs have been evaluated with learning disabled pupils in several studies. In one study, Serwer, Shapiro, and Shapiro (1973) reported that pupils identified as at risk who received DISTAR reading performed the same as pupils receiving perceptual-motor remedial training or both conditions on most criterion measures. Although the DISTAR group was poorer on two measures of motor skills and on measures of handwriting and arithmetic, it obtained a better score on the measure of wrong endings on words (as measured by the Gates-McKillop), the only significant difference on a measure of reading. Other studies are more supportive.

At the beginning reading level, a study by Stein and Goldman (1980) compared the DISTAR and Palo Alto reading programs with a sample identified as having "minimal brain dysfunction." The pupils given DISTAR reading instruction had significantly greater achievement as measured on the Peabody Individual Achievement Test (PIAT). At the remedial level, Lloyd, Epstein, and Cullinan (1981; Lloyd et al., 1981) reported the results of an intervention program based in part on the DIM. In their study, learning disabled pupils received reading instruction that included use of the Corrective Reading Program and their reading scores were compared to the reading scores of a randomly-assigned comparison group after six months of instruction. The pupils in the Direct Instruction groups had significantly higher scores on (a) word reading (as measured by the Wide Range Achievement Test), (b) passage reading (as measured by the Gilmore), (c) passage comprehension (as measured by the Gilmore). The authors reported that the effect sizes for these

measures were 0.71 or greater.

Other studies have investigated programmatic effects (e.g., Gregory, Hackney, & Gregory, 1982) and more specific aspects of DIM programming in reading (e.g., Carnine, Prill, & Armstrong, 1978; Darch & Gersten, 1974; Dommes, Gersten, & Carnine, 1984; Kameenui, Carnine, & Maggs, 1980), often using low-performing pupils as subjects.

ARITHMETIC

Direct Instruction studies of arithmetic have been conducted almost exclusively with nonhandicapped pupils. However, Lloyd, Saltzman, and Kauffman (1981) examined the effects of "strategy training," an instructional procedure based on the Direct Instruction Model principle of teaching cognitive operations by isolating and teaching a series of steps that lead to solution of a type of problem (cf., Lloyd, 1980). The authors found that transfer of training was predictable on the basis of the instruction provided learning disabled pupils. The results are consistent with the findings of Carnine (1980a) who reported that young nonhandicapped pupils provided instruction on the component skills of a multiplication strategy had more rapid acquisition of the strategy and greater transfer of it to untrained items than did young nonhandicapped pupils who were taught the component skills and the strategy at the same time.

Summary

The behavioral approach has provided substantial demonstrations that learning disabled pupils can be taught crucial academic skills. Furthermore, studies discussed in this section have illustrated several more refined conclusions: (a) although manipulation of consequences often improves performance, it is important that these pupils be shown *how to perform* as well; (b) contingencies that influence behavior need not be simplistic and brazen (e.g., M & Ms for each line read) because learning disabled pupils respond well to more "natural" contingencies, *provided that the contingencies are made clear* (as is done in contingent skipping and drilling, for example); (c) highly structured, carefully programmed instruction makes it possible to operationalize cognitive performances so that they can be successfully taught to learning disabled pupils with reasonable prospects of transfer.

Instructional Approaches

Many people have espoused what are essentially instructional approaches and their recommendations resemble the interventions of behaviorally oriented educators. But they would eschew, or at least be very uncomfortable with, the behaviorist label. They talk about teaching academic skills directly and so are kin to the Direct Instruction Model advocates, but do not adhere to the instructional programming principles of Engelmann and Carnine (1982).

This section distinguishes the work of these people from the behavioral and Direct Instruction approaches by using the term *instructional* to refer to their approach. Of course, advocates of other approaches would contend, rightly, that their interventions are instructional; this label is used simply to identify that interventions in this group do not share all of the characteristics that those in the behavioral group share or all of the characteristics that those in the cognitive group share. In practice, these interventions do have in common a basis in the research on effective instruction.

Three main interventions are included in this approach. One is the historically important *multisensory* interventions of Fernald and of Orton and Gillingham. (Although the multisensory programs were developed prior to effective-schools and teacher-effects research, their clinical realization bears similarity to effective instruction practices, e.g., frequent responding.) Another is the *direct teaching* work of people such as Bryant and Williams. The third is the *environmental modification* model, the clearest example of which is the Adaptive Learning Environments Model associated with Wang.

Multisensory Training

Multisensory interventions, although developed prior to the beginning of the use of the term learning disabilities, were based on modifying instruction in specific ways to improve the chances of learning by low-performing students. Clear examples of multisensory approaches have not been applied to all areas of achievement, but they have been quite popular in the language arts areas (i.e., reading and the handwriting and spelling components of writing).

Two of the most widely known and long standing approaches to reading instruction for children with learning disabilities, those of Fernald and of Orton and Gillingham (e.g., Gillingham & Stillman, 1965), incorporate emphasis on use of several sensory modalities. In addition, both the Slingerland (1974) program (based in large part on Orton and Gillingham's work) and the Remedial Reading Drills of Hegge, Kirk, and Kirk (1970) include use of multiple modalities during reading instruction.

Multisensory training in handwriting includes mostly the enhancement of the influence of some of the modalities. This is apparent in the use of writing instruments that increase the tactual or kinesthetic features of writing (e.g., tracing of sandpaper letters or use of pens that create greater drag). Indeed, at least one study (Massard & Etzel, 1972) indicates that having young children trace letters cut from sandpaper increases the speed with which the pupils attain mastery of writing those letters. (The studies by Massard and Etzel illustrate the careful examination of a phenomenon in which a series of studies eliminates alternative explanations by

systematically comparing independent variables. Such replication series are too rare in evaluation of special educational interventions.) But, the evidence in this area is not extensive. Research on the effects of various handwriting activities that incorporate additional or enhanced tactual or kinesthetic feedback would be advisable.

Silverberg, Iversen, and Goins (1973) examined the effects of the Fernald program with remedial readers and reported that it was less effective than a phonics-based approach on several measures of reading; however, it was more effective than the Orton-Gillingham program on one measure of reading accuracy. Within six months, however, the latter difference had dissipated but the former persisted. Myers (1978) reviewed the evidence about the effectiveness of the Fernald approach but did not find experimental support for it. Thus, despite the position of advocates who provide case studies of its successful use, research evidence does not indicate that the Fernald Visual-Auditory-Kinesthetic-Tactile approach has been effective.

Orton (1937) provided case studies about the successful use of his approach to remedial reading. Kline and Kline (1975) reported that pupils in a reading clinic sample who were provided Orton-Gillingham instruction were nearly twice as likely to show improvement as students in a comparison group. Silverberg et al. (1973) reported, however, that the Orton-Gillingham program was less effective than an auditory phonics program which did not incorporate multisensory training.

Another intervention that, in a way, augments sensory stimulation during instruction is the neurological impress method for reading. According to this method, the teacher (or tutor or parent) and student are to read text in unison. The idea is that the student will become accustomed to the fluency of mature reading, permitting the semantic aspects of the text to exert greater influence on his or her decoding performance. However, in a study with learning disabled pupils, Lorenz and Vockell (1979) found no beneficial effects of the method.

In all of these cases, where there have been successful uses of treatments, the question of what component or combination of components produced the effects resurfaces. It is entirely possible that the attributes of the instructional program which caused improvements were not emphasized in the theoretical base of the intervention. Research is needed to isolate the effective components of multisensory training—and of other interventions—if there are any dependable effects, in order both to assess theory and to develop more efficient treatments.

Direct Teaching Interventions

Over the last decade, many researchers who were not originally interested in learning disability began to work in the field; many had received formal training in psychology or some other area and came to the area of learning disability because of the opportunity to contrast normal and deviant academic development. Others who were originally special educators began their careers in the field with a cognitive process or other orientation. However, members of both of these groups drifted toward the modification of instruction as a format for approaching learning disabilities. The work of some of these researchers is described in this subsection.

READING

A report by Williams (1980) provides an excellent illustration of this type of intervention. Williams developed a program for teaching beginning reading which is based on extensive research on the component skills of pre-reading and reading. The program is very similar to other programs (e.g., those developed by Engelmann, 1969b, and Wallach & Wallach, 1976), but was designed expressly for use with pupils identified or likely to be identified as learning disabled. The program taught the skills of phonemic analysis, sound blending, and basic decoding during the primary grades and Williams' carefully conducted field test of it indicated that it was effective.

SPELLING

Similarly, Bryant et al. (1981) and Gettinger, Bryant, and Fayne (1982) developed means of modifying usual spelling instructional programs to increase their effectiveness with learning disabled children. Among the modifications they studied were (a) reductions in the number of words taught in any one lesson, (b) distribution of practice opportunities to increase retention, and (c) organization of spelling words to facilitate transfer from word to word. Their studies indicate that incorporations of these variables in spelling lessons improves the spelling performance of elementary pupils with learning disabilities. These modifications illustrate the application of effecting teaching precepts to instruction of students with learning disabilities. Although they bear on the structure of instruction, they bear more heavily on the delivery of instruction.

Environmental Modification

The third instructional approach is *environmental modification*. It differs from the interventions described in the previous two sections in that it—like the Direct Instruction Model—provides a comprehensive modification in the school environment rather than focusing primarily on teacher-student interactions and the organization of instructional.

The purpose of the Adaptive Learning Environments Model (ALEM) is to help atypical and normally achieving pupils to obtain greater benefits from their educational opportunities. ALEM takes a social-systems perspective which views schools as not responding appropriately to individual differences among pupils. To remedy this problem, ALEM seeks to modify the learning environment and build on each student's individual strengths. Modifying the environment makes it accommodate the needs and characteristics of individual students. Building on a student's strengths gives him or her a better chance of profiting from the school learning environment.

ALEM provides management and technical support to administrators and teachers. This support integrates effective instructional techniques into classroom practice. The techniques are based on research about variables such as proportion of time allocated to academic objectives, feedback about students' performance, and relationship between instructional activities and students' instructional objectives. It also includes reading and mathematics curricula from the Learning Research and Development Center (LRDC) that have substantial theoretical, research, and practical support. Characteristic of these programs are their detailed task analyses, specification of teaching actions, and provisions for continuous monitoring of student performance.

ALEM has been presented as a full-time mainstreaming program (Wang, 1981). It can be implemented within the context of the regular classroom and implementation is related to manifestation of predicted classroom activities (Wang & Birch, 1984b). Another study revealed that the ALEM program has significant beneficial effects on student attitudes and achievement in comparison to resource room programming (Wang & Birch, 1984a). However, the literature on ALEM cannot be considered conclusive because of shortcomings in research procedures used to evaluate it (Fuchs & Fuchs, in press; Hallahan, Keller, McKinney, Lloyd & Bryan, 1988).

Summary

The effectiveness of the interventions described in this section illustrate several important factors. First, principles of effective teaching are readily applicable to learning disabled pupils. More specifically, it appears that controlling such details of instruction as allocation of time to activities and presentation of instruction in small units will contribute to the acquisition of academic skills by learning disabled pupils. Second, it appears important that extensive, careful analyses of tasks be made when designing instructional materials for teaching basic academic skills to learning disabled pupils. Such analyses are at the core of programs developed by Williams (1980) and the LRDC and used by ALEM. Third, some of the features of effective interventions (e.g., repetition) were present in treatments that predate the official beginning of the field of learning disability.

Although there may be some intellectual antipathy between the advocates of these interventions and the advocates of behavioral interventions, it is important to note that there are striking similarities in the interventions proposed by each. For example, both the

Direct Instruction and the Adaptive Learning Environment Models emphasize control of the details of the classroom and school environments. Similarly, the programs advocated by Engelmann (1969b) and Williams (1980) both follow a code-emphasis approach to beginning reading. These and other confluences strengthen the case that there is an emerging technology of effective instruction for students with learning disabilities.

Cognitive Approaches

Cognitive approaches share an emphasis on the processes involved in human thinking, according these processes a role of greater importance than do behaviorists. Advocates of cognitive approaches vary as to what processes are considered important. Some emphasize the importance of *cognitive-behavior modification*, others emphasize *information processing* factors, and still others emphasize *psycholinguistic* factors (which are not necessarily associated with the indirect interventions related to the ITPA). Again, these divisions are arbitrary and inexact; there is a great deal of overlap among these interventions.

There have been a wide range of investigations in this area addressing several different intervention techniques under the rubric of cognitive training, self-control, or cognitive-behavior modification. Many of these studies are listed in Table 2. Selected studies are discussed in the following sections.

There are, of course, many omissions from this listing. For example, an extensive literature has developed regarding the teaching of keyword mnemonic strategies to learning-disabled students (cf., Mastropieri, Scruggs, & Levin, 1987). In brief, the keyword approach requires that students use simple mnemonics to help memorize keywords that are systematically related to facts that are to be remembered. For example, to remember that the mineral apatite is brown in color, is used for fertilizer, and has a hardness of 5, a pupil would be shown a picture of a brown (color of mineral) *ape* (shared letters at the beginning of ape and apatite), pouring fertilizer on a bee *hive* (rhyming words for degree of hardness). The approach has been studied extensively with learning disabled pupils. For example, Scruggs, Mastopieri, Levin, and Gaffney (1985) reported that the mnemonic strategy facilitated learning disabled junior high school students' acquisition of information about minerals, and Scruggs, Mastropieri, McLoone, Levin, and Morrison (1987) reported that the mnemonic strategy facilitated learning disabled high school students' learning of facts embedded in textual materials.

Cognitive-Behavior Modification

The cognitive-behavior modification (CBM) approach to learning disability is an outgrowth of a larger movement which accepted the empirical base of the behavioral approach but also accepted behaviorism's anathema, mentalism. Advocates of CBM also

TABLE 2
Studies of Cognitive Interventions Relevant to Learning Disabilities

Citation	Subjects[a]	Independent Variable(s)
Albion & Salzberg, 1982	5 EMR pupils 11–13 yrs	Self-instruction
Alley & Hori, 1981		
Bornstein & Quevillion, 1976	3 boys	Self-instruction
Bryant & Budd, 1982	3 HA boys 4–5 yrs	Self-instruction
Burgio et al., 1980	3 girls 2 boys, EMR 9–14 yrs	Self-instruction
Cameron & Robinson, 1980	3 HA boys 7–8 yrs	Self-instruction and self-correction
Camp et al., 1977	22 Aggressive boys 6–8 yrs	Self-instruction
Clark et al., 1981		
Douglas et al., 1976	29 HA boys 6–11 yrs	Self-instruction
Friedling & O'Leary, 1979	8 HA boys 6–8 yrs	Self-instruction
Gerber, 1981	32 LD children elementary	Self-assessment Self-guiding questions
Harris et al., 1988	32 LD boys 8 LD girls	Self-instruction
Harris & Graham, 1985	1 LD boy 1 LD girl 12 yrs	Self-instruction
Holman & Baer, 1979	2 LA boys 1 LA girl	Self-monitoring
Johnston et al., 1981	1 EMR girl 2 EMR boys 9–10 yrs	Self-instruction
Kosiewicz et al., 1982	1 LD boy 9 yrs	Self-instruction and self-correction
Lee & Alley, 1981		
Lesgold et al., 1975	62 elementary-age children	Self-imagery
Levin, 1973	54 elementary-age children	Self-imagery
Lloyd et al., 1982	1 LD girl 2 LD boys 8–10 yrs	Self-verbalization
Malamuth, 1979	33 elementary-age children	Self-instruction
McLaughlin et al., 1981	6 BD boys 10–12 yrs	Self-recording
Moran et al., 1981		Self-instruction
Palinscar & Brown, 1981	4 RD secondary-age pupils	Self-verbalization
Pacquin, 1978	1 BD girl 9 yrs	Self-graphing

Study	Sample	Intervention
Pflaum & Pascarella, 1980	40 LD elementary-age and secondary-age pupils	Self-evaluation
Pressley, 1976	32 RD elementary-age pupils	Self-imagery
Robin et al., 1975	30 normal kindergarteners	Self-instruction
Schumaker et al., 1982	9 LD secondary-age pupils	Self-correction and self-questioning
Seabaugh & Schumaker, 1981	8 LD adolescents	Self-regulation package
Smith & Alley, 1981		
Spates & Kanfer, 1977	45 elementary-age LA	Goal setting and self-evaluation
Swanson, 1981a	3 LD elementary-age pupils	Self-recording
Swanson, 1981b	1 LD boy	Self-recording and teacher praise
Varni & Henker, 1979	3 HA boys 8–10 yrs	Self-instruction Self-monitoring, and Self-reinforcement
Warner & Alley, 1981		Imagery
Whitman & Johnston, 1983	9 female 7 male EMR 10–13 yrs	Self-instruction
Wong & Jones, 1982	60 LD secondary-age pupils	Self-questioning

[a]BD = Behaviorally Disordered; EMR = Educable Mentally Retarded; LA = Low Achieving; LD = Learning Disabled; HA = Hyperactive; RD = Reading Disabled.

emphasised the role of meta-cognition (see discussion in the next section). But not only did cognitive-behaviorists contend that people's thoughts influence how they behave, they placed additional emphasis on such factors as a sense of personal effectiveness, student involvement in instruction, and so forth.

For the most part, CBM interventions are designed to increase self-awareness and self-control and, therefore, to improve academic behavior. Loper and Murphy (1985) and others have provided reviews of the literature in this area. Much of the research has been conducted in laboratories using nonacademic tasks and the data from it assessed by Gerber in Volume 1 of this series. Selected evidence about some applied investigations is discussed here.

READING

In the area of reading, there is a great deal of overlap among the cognitive approaches. For example, Brown (e.g., Brown et al., 1980) calls parts of her procedures "self-control" training, a term that evokes the idea of CBM. For this reason it is hard to designate an intervention as representative of only one type of intervention. However, there are some studies of interventions that seem to fit better here than under the other categories; they are those that reflect on the "self-treatments" (i.e., self-monitoring, self-instruction, self-verbalization, etc.).

Swanson (1981a & b) examined the effects of self-recording and reinforcement techniques on the reading of elementary-age, learning disabled pupils. In a series of three studies (Swanson 1981a), he found that self-recording and reinforcement contingencies influenced oral reading accuracy, silent reading rate, and comprehension question accuracy. Working with fifth-grade pupils reading two grade levels lower than their reading expectancy, Malamuth (1979) evaluated a broad-based self-management program. Using assorted materials, the students were shown how to direct themselves to scan materials during reading. Although conventional significance levels were not reached, Malamuth interpreted the results as indicating that pupils receiving the experimental program performed better on reading tasks than those in a control group. In contrast, Lloyd, Kneedler, and Cameron (1982) reported that requiring learning disabled pupils to verbalize the strategy they were to use in reading words did not facilitate word reading accuracy.

ARITHMETIC

Two particularly valuable studies of CBM have been conducted in the arithmetic area. Johnston, Whitman, and Johnson (1981) and Whitman and Johnston (1983) evaluated the effects of a self-instructional intervention for teaching arithmetic computation skills. In both studies, pupils were taught algorithms for solving specific types of arithmetic problems. The results indicated that this intervention had clear and substantial effects on the students' performance. One particular value of these studies is that they represent a systematic research effort with a clear theoretical basis and readily applicable results.

Many other studies (e.g., Grim, Bijou, & Parsons, 1973; Lovitt & Curtiss, 1968; Parsons, 1972) have investigated procedures that have been recommended for inclusion in CBM interventions. For example, Parsons (1972) studied the effects on arithmetic accuracy of having pupils both circle and name the operation symbol before performing addition and subtraction computations. The positive effects of this tactic have been interpreted as support for the idea that antecedent self-verbalization is a desirable component of CBM programs.

WRITING

In the area of handwriting, it has been recommended that pupils learning to write should verbally guide themselves through stroke sequences as they form letters.

(For example, while making the letter "m," pupils say, "First I make a short stick, then I make one hump and then another hump. And that makes an 'm' ".) Research by Hayes (1980) and Robin, Armel, and O'Leary (1975) has shown verbal self-guidance produces small, beneficial effects on handwriting. However, despite Hallahan's and Torgesen's theoretical positions about the passive learner (e.g., Hallahan & Reeve, 1980; Torgesen, 1977) which would suggest that this type of procedure may be particularly helpful to learning disabled students, there is not strong empirical support about its effects with learning disabled pupils (Graham, 1983; cf., Blandford & Lloyd, 1987).

Peer-editing and self-evaluation are techniques that have been found to be effective in teaching composition. Secondary-age students with low achievement learned to use an editing and rating system for evaluating their peers' essays. Students in the peer-editing condition had higher scores on a posttest than students in a comparable condition in which the editing of essays was done by teachers (Karegianes, Pascarella, & Pflaum, 1980). Also, third graders learned to check their own writing assignments according to guidelines (Ballard & Glynn, 1975). The self-evaluation procedure required them to count the number of sentences written, words written, various types of words used, and take other simple measures of writing; the students then assigned themselves points in a reward system depending on how they had done in their essays. Ballard and Glynn found that the combination of self-evaluation and self-reward had positive effects on the students' writing. Additionally, the Kansas group (e.g., Moran, Schumaker, & Vetter, 1981) has incorporated self-evaluation in their writing program for adolescents, as did Harris & Graham (1985).

Information Processing

Information processing, the contemporary version of how thinking works, grew out of systems approaches. The emphasis was on what happened to information between the stimulus and the response, inside the organism. There was concern about such variables as memory, organization, cognitive strategies, and so forth. Perhaps most central to this position is the idea of meta-cognition. Meta-cognition (e.g., Flavell, 1979) includes awareness of one's own thinking (self-awareness) and purposive direction of one's skills to achieve prespecified goals (self-control or self-regulation).

Since the beginning of what might be called the information processing boom, cognitively oriented researchers have studied reading programs intensively. The beginning of this interest is marked by volumes containing papers from conferences of cognitive psychologists (e.g., Kavanaugh & Mattingly, 1972).

Brown is one of the most influential cognitive researchers in the area of reading. In addition to conducting extensive laboratory research with retarded students (particularly in the area of memory, e.g., Brown,

1974) and on factors that influence reading (e.g., Brown & Smiley, 1978), Brown and her colleagues have conducted more applied studies of the effects of reading intervention procedures (e.g., Brown et al., 1980; Palinscar & Brown, 1983). Brown et al., (1980) described a study in which post-secondary age "normal" and "remedial" pupils were provided four different instructional conditions which varied in the comprehensivity of the training. In the least complete condition, pupils were "given encouragement to write a good summary, to capture the main ideas, to dispense with trivia and all unnecessary words" (p. 15), but in the most complete condition, they were given the same encouragement, shown *how* to do those things, and shown how to check whether they were doing so. Although all treatment conditions influenced some dependent variables roughly equally (e.g., deletion of trivial material), the most comprehensive intervention had greater effects on some dependent variables (e.g., invention of topic sentences).

Most importantly for the purposes of the present review, the most complete instruction condition had greater effects for the lower-performing students than did the less complete instructional conditions. This finding is consistent with other findings for cognitive treatments in which treatments incorporating thorough training have differentially greater effects on lower-performing subjects (e.g., André & Anderson, 1979; Pflaum & Pascarella, 1980).

Cognitive-Psycholinguistic Interventions

Cognitive-psycholinguistic interventions are closely associated with nativistic theories of language development. Although this perspective has many interesting theoretical components, in practice it usually translates into recommendations for less structured, more developmental, student-directed learning environments and programs.

SPEAKING AND LISTENING

Two programs—Sound-Order-Sense (SOS; Semel, 1970) and the Semel Auditory Processing Program (SAPP; Semel, 1976)—developed by Semel are consistent with a cognitive-psycholinguistic approach. The SOS program is designed to help children develop listening skills that will aid their comprehension of spoken language. The SOS program stresses perception of sounds, recall of the order of things that have been said, and semantics. The program also incorporates special features such as pupil books printed in a way that provides immediate feedback. The SAPP helps children develop language processing and interpretation skills. Activities provide work on auditory memory, morphology, syntax, semantics, and other types of language skills. Morphemic segmentation, sentence completion, and other activities which encourage learning of language skills are varied throughout the program to encourage general case learning. Semel and Wiig (1981) provided the results of an evaluation of the SAPP. In a pretest–posttest analysis, they found that elementary-age learning disabled pupils had substantially higher scores on several measures of language performance during the time that they were receiving the program.

READING

Cognitive-psycholinguistic interventions in the area of reading include two particularly noteworthy studies, those by Pascarella and Pflaum (1981) and Pflaum and Pascarella (1980). In these two studies, the authors investigated the effects of reading interventions that are consistent with cognitive and psycholinguistic perspectives on learning to read and examined the effects of the interventions on fairly clearly differentiated subgroups of pupils.

Pascarella and Pflaum (1981) assessed the effects of two different programs designed to teach students to use context clues in reading. One of the programs was mostly teacher-directed and the other required greater student self-direction. The results of their analysis indicated that elementary pupils whose attributions for success emphasized internal factors benefited relatively more from the self-directed than from the teacher-directed treatment. On the other hand, pupils with more external attributions for success benefited relatively more from the teacher-directed treatment.

Similar, but not altogether identical results were obtained in their previous study (Pflaum & Pascarella, 1980). In this study, they compared a highly-structured, teacher-directed reading program emphasizing beginning level reading skills to a less directive program emphasizing more advanced reading skills. They found that pupils who entered the experiment with lower levels of prior achievement benefited relatively more from the former program but that pupils with higher levels of prior achievement benefited relatively more from the latter program.

SPELLING

Bendall, Tollefson, and Fine (1980) identified an aptitude-by-treatment interaction similar to the one reported by Pascarella and Pflaum (1981). Bendall et al. found that adolescent learning disabled males with relatively internal attributions learned more spelling words in a program which allowed them to study the words in any way they wished than in one in which their study methods were prescribed for them. However, similar students with relatively external attributions for success learned more words in the high-structure than in the low-structure condition.

Summary

The cognitive interventions have provided valuable information about the kinds of interventions that are effective with learning disabled pupils. Taken together,

the results of these studies are encouraging. It is apparent that it is possible to base successful interventions on constructs about how thinking works; the interventions within the cognitive approach that have been successful have included systematic instruction in attacking and solving academic problems, tasks that we usually say reflect thinking. Furthermore, these results re-emphasize the importance of instruction that teaches cognitive operations systematically. Also, specific studies have revealed that the comprehensivity of an instructional intervention is important; it appears that more complete programs are important in teaching learning disabled and other low-performing students. However, although more directive and structured programs have been regularly found to be effective, it is possible to design programs that are somewhat less directive and structured but from which relatively higher-performing learning disabled students can still learn valuable skills. Furthermore, if the trend toward interactions between levels of prior achievement and program characteristics continues, then this area of research may make a very fruitful contribution to the practices of teaching learning disabled pupils. Such interactions are consistent with the evidence about comprehensivity of interventions; pupils who enter instruction with lower chances of success are better served by complete and carefully structured programs of teaching.

Conclusions

Interventions for pupils with learning disabilities have progressed a long way from the early emphasis of the field on modifying some aspect of pupils' moving, perceiving, or thinking. Researchers have clearly moved in the direction of studying interventions that focus directly on instruction. The predominant question in the studies reviewed here seems to be: How can we make instruction more effective for pupils with achievement deficits?

No one approach to academic interventions for students with learning disabilities can claim a corner on effectiveness. But there are common features among the myriad effective interventions. These features structure what I think will become the basic technology of academic interventions for students with learning disabilities. Future interventions will be:

1. Structured. That is, they will be characterized by a great deal of teacher direction in the initial stages. However, in the later stages they will probably emphasize increasing self-direction.

2. Goal-oriented. That is, they will closely correspond to terminal objectives.

3. Practice loaded. That is, they will provide adequate repetitions of actions to ensure that pupils acquire and maintain skills. This practice will take a massed form early in teaching and a distributed form later in teaching.

4. Strategy laden. That is, they will teach students processes or algorithms for performing academic tasks.

5. Independence-oriented. That is, successful interventions will teach students how to perform academic tasks on their own.

6. Detailed and comprehensive. Effective interventions will cover all the bases (e.g., include training about how to apply skills in atypical situations or to exceptional cases).

The present state of knowledge makes it possible to identify these features as common to successful interventions. But it is far less clear that these features are actually present in many classrooms. To be sure, where comprehensive intervention models (such as the Direct Instruction Model) have been adopted, it is more likely that instruction incorporates these features; but these sites are not, in my experience, common. Thus, perhaps the most pressing problem is getting what we know about effective instruction put into practice.

References

Abt Associates. (1976). *Education as experimentation: A planned variation model* (Vol. 3A). Cambridge, MA: Author.

Abt Associates. (1977). *Education as experimentation: A planned variation model* (Vol. 4). Cambridge, MA: Author.

Adelman, H. S., & Compas, B. E. (1977). Stimulant drugs and learning problems. *Journal of Special Education*, **11**, 377–416.

Albion, F. M., & Salzberg, C. (1982). The effect of self-instructions on the rate of correct addition problems with mentally retarded children. *Education and Treatment of Children*, **5**, 121–131.

Alley, G. R., & Hori, K. O. (1981). *Effects of teaching a questioning strategy on reading comprehension of learning disabled adolescents* (Research Report No 52). Lawrence, KS: University of Kansas Institute for Research in Learning Disabilities.

André, M. E. D. A., & Anderson, T. H. (1979). The development and evaluation of a self-questioning study technique. *Reading Research Quarterly*, **14**, 605–623.

Arter, J. A., & Jenkins, J. R. (1977). Examining the benefits and prevalence of modality considerations in special education. *Journal of Special Education*, **11**, 281–298.

Arter, J. A., & Jenkins, J. R. (1979). Differential diagnosis-prescriptive teaching: A critical appraisal. *Review of Educational Research*, **49**, 517–555.

Ayllon, T., Layman, & Kandel, H. (1975). A behavioral-educational alternative to drug control of hyperactive children. *Journal of Applied Behavior Analysis*, **8**, 137–146.

Ballard, K. D., & Glynn, T. L. (1975). Behavioral self-management in story writing with elementary school children. *Journal of Applied Behavior Analysis*, **8**, 387–398.

Barbe, W. B., & Milone, M. N., Jr. (1980). Modality. *Instructor*, **89**(6), 44–47.

Bateman, B. (1966). Learning disorders. *Review of Educational Research*, **36**, 93–119.

Bateman, B. (1967). Three approaches to diagnosis and educational planning for children with learning disabilities. *Academic Therapy*, **3**, 215–222.

Bateman, B. (1979). Teaching reading to learning disabled and other hard-to-teach children. In L. B. Resnick & P. A. Weaver (Eds.), *Theory and practice of early reading*

instruction (Vol. 1; pp. 227–259). Hillsdale, NJ: Erlbaum.

Becker, W. C., & Carnine, D. (1981). Direct instruction: A behavior theory model for comprehensive educational intervention with the disadvantaged. In R. Ruiz & S. W. Bijou (Eds.), *Behavior modification: Contributions to education* (pp. 145–210). Hillsdale, NJ: Erlbaum.

Becker, W. C., Engelmann, S., & Thomas, D. R. (1975). *Teaching 2: Cognitive learning and instruction*. Chicago: Science Research Associates.

Becker. W. C., & Gersten, R. M. (1982). A follow-up of Follow Through: The later effects of the Direct Instruction Model on children in fifth and sixth grades. *American Educational Research Journal*, **19**, 75–92.

Bendall, D., Tollefson, N., & Fine, M. (1980). Interaction of locus-of-control orientation and the performance of learning disabled adolescents. *Journal of Learning Disabilities*, **13**, 83–86.

Bereiter, C., & Engelmann, S. (1966). *Teaching disadvantaged children in the preschool*. Englewood Cliffs, NJ: Prentice-Hall.

Billingsley, F. F. (1977). The effects of self- and externally-imposed schedules of reinforcement on oral reading performance. *Journal of Learning Disabilities*, **10**, 549–559.

Blandford, B. J., & Lloyd, J. W. (1987). Effects of a self-instructional procedure on handwriting. *Journal of Learning Disabilities*, **20**, 342–346.

Blank, M. (1973). *Teaching language in the preschool: A dialogue approach*. Columbus, OH: Charles E. Merrill.

Blankenship, C. (1978). Remediating systematic inversion errors in subtraction through the use of demonstration and feedback. *Learning Disability Quarterly*, **1**(3), 12–22.

Bornstein, P. H., & Quevillion, R. P. (1976). The effects of a self-instructional package on overactive preschool boys. *Journal of Applied Behavior Analysis*, **9**, 179–188.

Brigham, T. H., Graubard, P. S., & Stans, A. (1972). Analysis of the effects of sequential reinforcement contingencies on aspects of composition. *Journal of Applied Behavior Analysis*, **5**, 421–429.

Broden, M., Beasley, A., & Hall, R. V. (1978). In class spelling performance: Effects of home tutoring. *Behavior Modification*, **2**, 511–530.

Broughton, S. F., & Lahey, B. B. (1978). Direct and collateral effects of positive reinforcement, response cost, and mixed contingencies for academic performance. *Journal of School Psychology*, **16**, 126–136.

Brown, A. L. (1974). The role of strategic behavior in retardate memory. In N. R. Ellis (Ed.), *International review of research in mental retardation* (Vol. 7; pp. 55–111. New York: Academic Press.

Brown, A. L., Campione, J. C., & Day, J. D. (1980). *Learning to learn: On training students to learn from texts*. Paper presented at the annual meeting of the American Educational Research Association meeting, Boston, April.

Brown, A. L., & Smiley, S. S. (1978). The development of strategies for studying text. *Child Development*, **49**, 829–835.

Bryant, L. E., & Budd, K. S. (1982). Self-instructional training to increase independent work performance in preschoolers. *Journal of Applied Behavior Analysis*, **15**, 259–271.

Bryant, N. D., Drabin, I. R., & Gettinger, M. (1981). Effects of varying unit size on spelling achievement in learning disabled children. *Journal of Learning Disabilities*, **14**, 200–203.

Burgio, L. D., Whitman, T. L., & Johnson, M. R. (1980). A self-instructional package for increasing attending behavior in educable mentally retarded children. *Journal of Applied Behavior Analysis*, **13**, 443–459.

Cameron, M. I., & Robinson, J. J. (1980). Effects of cognitive training on academic and on-task behavior of hyperactive children. *Journal of Abnormal Child Psychology*, **8**, 405–419.

Camp, B. W., Blom, G. E., Hebert, F., & van Doorninck, W. J. (1977). "Think Aloud": A program for developing self-control in young aggressive boys. *Journal of Abnormal Child Psychology*, **5**, 157–169.

Carbo, M. (1983). Research in reading and learning style: Implications for exceptional children. *Exceptional Children*, **49**, 486–494.

Carnine, D. W. (1980a). Preteaching versus concurrent teaching of the component skills of a multiplication problem-solving strategy. *Journal for Research in Mathematics Education*, **11**, 375–379.

Carnine, D. W. (1980b). Three procedures for presenting minimally different positive and negative instances. *Journal of Educational Psychology*, **72**, 452–456.

Carnine, D. W., Prill, N., & Armstrong, J. (1978). *Teaching slower performing students general case strategies for solving comprehension items*. Eugene, OR: University of Oregon Follow Through Project.

Carnine, D., & Silbert, J. (1979). *Direct instruction reading*. Columbus, OH: Charles E. Merrill.

Christensen, D. E. (1975). Effects of combining methylphenidate and a classroom token system in modifying hyperactive behavior. *American Journal of Mental Deficiency*, **80**, 266–276.

Christensen, D. E., & Sprague, R. L. (1973). Reduction of hyperactive behavior by conditioning procedures alone and combined with methylphenidate (Ritalin). *Behavior Research and Therapy*, **11**, 311–334.

Clark, R. L., Warner, M. M., Alley, G. R., Deshler, D. D., Schumaker, J. B., Vetter, A. F., & Nolan, S. M. (1981). *Visual imagery and self-questioning: Strategies to improve comprehension of written material* (Research Report No. 51). Lawrence, KS: University of Kansas Institute for Research in Learning Disabilities.

Conners, C. K. (1980). Artificial colors in the diet and disruptive behavior: Current status of research. In R. M. Knights & D. J. Bakker (Eds.), *Treatment of hyperactive and learning disordered children: current research* (pp. 234–259). Baltimore: University Park Press.

Conners, C. K., & Wells, K. C. (1979). Method and theory for pyschopharmacology with children. In R. Trites (Ed.), *Hyperactivity in children: Etiology, measurement, and treatment implications.* (pp. 141–157). Baltimore, MD: University Park Press.

Cronbach, L. J., & Snow, R. E. (1977). *Aptitudes and instructional methods*. New York: Irvington.

Cullinan, D., Epstein, M. E., & Lloyd, J. W. (1978). *Noneffects of self-verbalization on LD boys' multiplication performance*. Paper presented at the Annual Convention of the Association for Children with Learning Disabilities, Kansas City, KS.

Darch, C., & Gersten, R. (1984). *Comparison of two direction setting activities to increase the comprehension of high school LD students*. Unpublished manuscript, University of Oregon, Eugene.

Dommes, P., Gersten, R., & Carnine, D. (1984). Instructional procedures for increasing skill-deficient fourth graders' comprehension of syntactic structures. *Educational Psychology*, **4**, 155–165.

Douglas, V. I., Parry, P., Marton, P., & Garson, C. (1976). Assessment of a cognitive training program for hyperactive children. *Journal of Abnormal Child Psychology*, **4**, 389–410.

Dunn, R. (1983). Learning style and its relation to exceptionality at both ends of the spectrum. *Exceptional Children*, **49**, 496–506.

Engelmann, S. (1969a). The effectiveness of direct verbal instruction on IQ performance and achievement in reading and arithmetic. In J. Hellmuth (Ed.), *Disadvantaged child* (Vol. 3; pp. 339–361). New York: Bruner/Mazel.

Engelmann, S. (1969b). *Preventing failure in the primary grades*. Chicago: Science Research Associates.

Engelmann, S., & Carnine, D. (1982). *Theory of instruction*. New York: Irvington.

Fauke, J., Burnett, J., Powers, M. A., & Sulzer-Azaroff, B. (1973). Improvement of handwriting and letter recognition skills: A behavior modification procedure. *Journal of Learning Disabilities*, **6**, 296–300.

Feingold, B. F. (1975). *Why your child is hyperactive*. New York: Random House.

Feingold, B. F. (1976). Hyperkinesis and learning disabilities linked to the ingestion of artificial food colors and flavors. *Journal of Learning Disabilities*, **9**, 551–559.

Ferritor, D. C., Buckholdt, D., Hamblin, R. L., & Smith, L. (1972). The noneffects of contingent reinforcement for attending behavior on work accomplished. *Journal of Applied Behavior Analysis*, **5**, 7–17.

Flavell, J. H. (1979). Metacognition and cognitive monitoring: A new area of cognitive-developmental inquiry. *American Psychologist*, **34**, 906–911.

Fleisher, L. S., & Jenkins, J. R. (1978). Effects of contextualized and decontextualized practice conditions on word recognition. *Learning Disability Quarterly*, **1**(3), 39–47.

Freeman, T. J., & McLaughlin, T. F. (1984). Effects of a taped-words treatment procedure on learning disabled students' sight-word oral reading. *Learning Disability Quarterly*, **7**, 49–54.

Freidling, C., & O'Leary, S. G. (1979). Effects of self-instructional training on second and third grade hyperactive children: A failure to replicate. *Journal of Applied Behavior Analysis*, **12**, 311–319.

Fuchs, D., & Fuchs, L. S. (in press). An evaluation of the Adative Learning Environment Model. *Exceptional Children.*

Garcia, E. E., & Batista-Wallace, M. (1977). Parental training of the plural morpheme in normal toddlers. *Journal of Applied Behavior Analysis*, **10**, 505.

Gerber, M. (1981). *The effects of self-monitoring training on spelling performance of learning disabled and normally achieving students*. Unpublished doctoral dissertation, University of Virginia.

Gersten, R. (1981). *Direct instruction with special education students: A review of evaluation research*. Paper presented at the annual meeting of the Council for Exceptional Children. New York.

Gersten, R. M., Becker, W. C., Heiry, T. J., & White, W. A. T. (1984). Entry IQ and yearly academic growth of children in Direct Instruction programs: A longitudinal study of low SES children. *Educational Evaluation and Policy Analysis*, **6**, 109–121.

Gersten, R., & Maggs, A. (1982). Teaching the general case to moderately retarded children: Evaluation of a 5-year project. *Analysis and Intervention in Developmental Disabilities*, **2**, 329–343.

Gersten, R. M., White, W. A. T., Falco, R., & Carnine, D. (1982). Teaching basic discriminations to handicapped and non-handicapped individuals through a dynamic presentation of instructional stimuli. *Analysis and Intervention in Developmental Disabilities*, **2**, 305–317.

Gettinger, M., Bryant, N. D., & Fayne, H. R. (1982). Designing spelling instruction for learning-disabled children: An emphasis on unit size, distributed practice, and training for transfer. *Journal of Special Education*, **16**, 439–448.

Gillingham, A., & Stillman, B. (1965). *Remedial training for children with specific disability in reading, spelling, and penmanship* (7th ed.). Cambridge, MA: Educators Publishing Service.

Gittleman, R., Abikoff, H., Pollack, E., Klein, D. F., Katz, S., & Mattes, J. (1980). A controlled trial of behavior modification and methylphenidate in hyperactive children. In C. K. Whalen & B. Henker (Eds.), *Hyperactive children: The social ecology of identification and treatment* (pp. 221–243). New York: Academic Press.

Goodman, L., & Hammill, D. D. (1973). The effectiveness of the Kephart-Getman activities in developing perceptual-motor and cognitive skills. *Focus on Exceptional Children*, **4**(9), 1–9.

Gray, B., & Ryan, B. (1973). *A language program for the non-language child*. Champaign, IL: Research Press.

Gregory, R. P., Hackney, C., & Gregory, N. M. (1982). Corrective reading programme: An evaluation. *British Journal of Education Psychology*, **52**, 33–50.

Grimm, J. A., Bijou, S. W., & Parsons, J. A. (1973). A problem solving model for teaching remedial arithmetic to handicapped young children. *Journal of Abnormal Child Psychology*, **1**, 26–39.

Hallahan, D. P., & Cruickshank, W. M. (1973). *Psychoeducational foundations of learning disabilities*. Englewood Cliffs, NJ: Prentice-Hall.

Hallahan, D. P., Keller, C. E., McKinney, J. D., Lloyd, J. W., & Bryan, T. (1988). Examining the research base of the regular education initiative. Efficacy studies and the ALEM. *Journal of Learning Disabilities*, **21**, 29–35, 55.

Hallahan, D. P., Lloyd, J. W., Kneedler, R. D., & Marshall, K. J. (1982). A comparison of the effects of self- versus teacher-assessment of on-task behavior. *Behavior Therapy*, **13**, 715–723.

Hallahan, D. P., & Reeve, R. E. (1980). Selective attention and distractibility. In B. K. Keogh (Ed.), *Advances in special education* (Vol. 1; pp. 141–181). Greenwich, CN: JAI Press.

Hammill, D. D., & Larsen, S. C. (1974). The effectiveness of psycholinguistic training. *Exceptional Children*, **41**, 5–14.

Hammill. D. D., & Wiederholt, J. L. (1973). Review of the Frostig visual perception test and the related training program. In L. Mann & D. A. Sabatino (Eds.), *First review of special education* (Vol. 1; pp. 33–48). Philadelphia; JSE Press.

Haring, N. G., & Hauck, M. (1969). Improved learning conditions in the establishment of reading skills with disabled readers. *Exceptional Children*, **35**, 341–351.

Harris, K. R., Graham, S. (1985). Improving learning disabled students' composition skills: A self-control strategy training approach. *Learning Disability Quarterly*, **8**, 27–36.

Harris, K. R., Graham, S., & Freeman, S. (1988). Effects of strategy training on metamemory among learning disabled students. *Exceptional Children*, **54**, 332–338.

Hart, B., & Risley, T. R. (1974). Using preschool materials to modify the language of disadvantaged children. *Journal of Applied Behavior Analysis*, **7**, 243–256.

Hasazi, J. E., & Hasazi, S. E. (1972). Effects of teacher attention on digit-reversal behavior in an elementary school child. *Journal of Applied Behavior Analysis*, **5**, 157–162.

Hayes, D. J. (1980). The effect of guiding six-year-old kindergarten and nine-year-old third grade children to verbalize formational strokes upon their ability to reproduce letter-like forms. (Doctoral dissertation, University of Virginia, 1980.) *Dissertation Abstracts International*, **41**, 123A.

Hegge, T. G., Kirk, S. A., & Kirk, W. E. (1970). *Remedial reading drills*. Ann Arbor, MI: George Wahr.

Hendrickson, J., Roberts, M., & Shores, R. E. (1978). Antecedent and contingent modeling to teach basic sight vocabulary. *Journal of Learning Disabilities*, **11**, 524–528.

Holman, J., & Baer, D. M. (1979). Facilitating generalization of on-task behavior through self-monitoring of academic tasks. *Journal of Autism and Developmental Disabilities*, **9**, 429–446.

House, E. R., Glass, G. V., McLean, L. D., & Walker, D. F. (1978). No simple answer: Critique of the Follow Through evaluation. *Harvard Educational Review*, **48**, 128–160.

Jenkins, J. R., Barksdale, A., & Clinton, L. (1978). Improving reading comprehension and oral reading: Generalization across behaviors, settings, and time. *Journal of Learning Disabilities*, 1978, **11**, 607–617.

Jenkins, J. R., & Larson, K. (1979). Evaluating error-correction procedures for oral reading. *Journal of Special Education*, **13**, 145–156.

Johnston, M. B., Whitman, T. L., & Johnson, M. (1981). Teaching addition and subtraction to mentally retarded children: A self-instructional program. *Applied Research in Mental Retardation*, **1**, 141–160.

Kameenui, E., Carnine, D. W., & Maggs, A. (1980). Instructional procedures for teaching reversible passive voice and clause constructions to three mildly handicapped children. *The Exceptional Child*, **27**(1), 29–41.

Karegianes, M. L., Pascarella, E. T., & Pflaum, S. W. (1980). The effects of peer editing on the writing proficiency of low-achieving tenth grade students. *Journal of Educational Research*, **73**, 203–207.

Kauffman, J. M., Hallahan, D. P., Haas, K., Brame, T., & Boren, R. (1978). Imitating children's errors to improve their spelling performance. *Journal of Learning Disabilities*, **11**, 217–222.

Kavale, K. (1981). Functions of the Illinois Test of Psycholinguistic Abilities (ITPA): Are they trainable? *Exceptional Children*, **47**, 496–510.

Kavale, K. (1982). The efficacy of stimulant drug treatment for hyperactivity: A meta-analysis. *Journal of Learning Disabilities*, **15**, 280–289.

Kavale, K. A., & Forness, S. R. (1983). Hyperactivity and diet treatment: A meta-analysis of the Feingold hypothesis. *Journal of Learning Disabilities*, **16**, 324–330.

Kavale, K., & Mattson, P. D. (1983). "One jumped off the balance beam": Meta-analysis of perceptual-motor training. *Journal of Learning Disabilities*, **16**, 165–173.

Kavanaugh, J. F., & Mattingly, I. G. (1972). *Language by ear and by eye: Relationships between speech and reading*. Cambridge, MA: MIT Press.

Kazdin, A. E. (1980). *Research design in clinical psychology*. New York: Harper & Row.

Kazdin, A. E. (1982). *Single-case research designs: Methods for clinical and applied settings*. New York: Oxford University

Press.

Keogh, B. K. (1974). Optometric vision training programs for children with learning disabilities: Review of issues and research. *Journal of Learning Disabilities*, 7, 219–231.

Keogh, B. K., & Pelland, M. (in press). Vision training revisited. *Journal of Learning Disabilities*.

Kirk, S. A., & Chalfant, J. C. (1984). *Academic and developmental learning disabilities*. Denver: Love.

Kline, C. L., & Kline, (1975). A follow-up study of 216 dyslexic children. *Bulletin of the Orton Society*, 25, 127–144.

Knapczyk, D. R., & Livingston, G. (1974). The effects of prompting question-asking upon on-task and reading comprehension. *Journal of Applied Behavior Analysis*, 7, 115–121.

Kosiewicz, M. M., Hallahan, D. P., Lloyd, J., & Graves, A. W. (1982). Effects of self-instruction and self-correction procedures on handwriting performance. *Learning Disability Quarterly*, 5, 71–78.

Lahey, B. B. (1971). Modification of the frequency of descriptive adjectives in the speech of Head Start children through modeling without reinforcement. *Journal of Applied Behavior Analysis*, 4, 19–22.

Lahey, B. B. (1976). Behavior modification with learning disabilities and related problems. In M. Hersen, R. M. Eisler, & P. M. Miller (Eds.), *Progress in behavior modification* (Vol. 3, pp. 173–205). New York: Academic Press.

Lahey, B. B., McNees, M. P., & Brown, C. C. (1973). Modification of deficits in reading for comprehension. *Journal of Applied Behavior Analysis*, 6, 475–480.

Lahey, B. B., Busemeyer, M. K., O'Hara, C., & Beggs, V. E. (1977). Treatment of severe perceptual-motor disorders in children diagnosed as learning disabled. *Behavior Modification*, 1, 123–140.

Larrivee, B. (1981). Modality preference as a model for differentiating beginning reading instruction: A review of the issues. *Learning Disability Quarterly*, 4, 180–188.

Larsen, S. C., Parker, R. M., & Hammill, D. D. (1982). Effectiveness of psycholinguistic training: A response to Kavale. *Exceptional Children*, 49, 60–66.

Lee, P., & Alley, G. R. (1981). *Training junior high school LD students to use a test-taking strategy* (Research Report No. 38). Lawrence, KS: University of Kansas Institute for Research in Learning Disabilities.

Lerner, J. (1976). *Children with learning disabilities: Theories, diagnosis, teaching strategies* (2nd ed.). Boston: Houghton Mifflin.

Lesgold, A. M., McCormick, C., & Golinkoff, R. M. (1975). Imagery training and children's prose learning. *Journal of Educational Psychology*, 67, 663–667.

Levin, J. R. (1973). Inducing comprehension in poor readers: A test of a recent model. *Journal of Educational Psychology*, 65, 19–24.

Limbrick, E., McNaughton, S., & Glynn, T. (1981). Training low progress readers to use contextual cues: Generalized effects on comprehension, oral accuracy, and rate. *Educational Psychology*, 1, 221–229.

Lloyd, J. (1980). Academic instruction and cognitive-behavior modification: The need for attack strategy training. *Exceptional Education Quarterly*, 1(1), 53–63.

Lloyd, J. W. (1984). How shall we individualize instruction—or should we? *Remedial and Special Education*, 5, 7–15.

Lloyd, J., Cullinan, D., Heins, E. D., & Epstein, M. H. (1980). Direct instruction: Effects on oral and written language comprehension. *Learning Disability Quarterly*, 3(4), 70–76.

Lloyd, J., Epstein, M. H., & Cullinan, D. (1981). Direct teaching for learning disabilities. In J. Gottlieb & S. S. Strichart (Eds.), *Developmental theory and research in learning disabilities* (pp. 278–309). Baltimore, MD: University Park Press.

Lloyd, J., Hallahan, D. P., & Kauffman, J. M. (1980). Learning disabilities: Selected topics. In L. Mann & D. Sabatino (Eds.), *The fourth review of special education* (pp. 35–60). New York: Grune & Stratton.

Lloyd, J. W., Kneedler, R. D., & Cameron, N. A. (1982). Effects of verbal self-guidance on word reading accuracy. *Reading Improvement*, 19, 84–89.

Lloyd, J., Saltzman, N. J., & Kauffman, J. M. (1981). Predictable generalization in academic learning as a result of preskills and strategy training. *Learning Disability Quarterly*, 4, 203–216,

Loney, J., Weissenburger, R., Woolson, R., & Lichty, E. (1979). Comparing psychological and pharmacological treatments for hyperkinetic boys and their classmates. *Journal of Abnormal Child Psychology*, 7, 133–143.

Loper, A. B., & Murphy, D. M. (1985). Cognitive self-regulatory training for underachieving children. In D. Forrest-Pressley, G. E. MacKinnon, & T. G. Waller (Eds.), *Metacognition, cognition, and human performance* (Vol II, pp. 223–265). New York: Plenum.

Lorenz, L., & Vockell, E. (1979). Using the neurological impress method with learning disabled readers. *Journal of Learning Disabilities*, 12, 420–422.

Lovaas, O. I. (1977). *The autistic child: Language development through behavior modification*. New York: Wiley.

Lovitt, T. C., & Curtiss, K. A. (1968). Effects of manipulating an antecedent event on mathematics response rate. *Journal of Applied Behavior Analysis*, 1, 329–333.

Lovitt, T. C., & Hansen, C. L. (1976). The use of contingent skipping and drilling to improve oral reading and comprehension. *Journal of Learning Disabilities*, 9, 481–487.

Lovitt, T. C., & Hurlburt, M. (1974). Using behavior analysis techniques to assess the relationship between phonics instruction and oral reading. *Journal of Special Education*, 8, 57–72.

Lovitt, T., Rudsit, J., Jenkins, J., Pious, C., & Benedetti, D. (1986). Adapting science materials for regular and learning disabled seventh graders. *Remedial and Special Education*, 7(1), 31–39.

Lovitt, T. C., & Smith, D. D. (1974). Using withdrawal of positive reinforcement to alter subtraction performance. *Exceptional Children*, 40, 357–358.

Lovitt, T. C., & Smith, J. O. (1972). Effects of instructions on an individual's verbal behavior. *Exceptional Children*, 38, 685–693.

Luiselli, J. K., & Downing, J. N. (1980). Improving a student's arithmetic performance using feedback and reinforcement procedures. *Education and Treatment of Children*, 3, 45–49.

Lund, K., Foster, G. E., & McCall-Perez, F. C. (1978). The effectiveness of psycholinguistic training: A reevaluation. *Exceptional Children*, 44, 310–319.

Maggs, A., & Morath, P. (1976). Effects of direct verbal instruction on intellectual development of institutionalized moderately retarded children: A 2-year study. *Journal of Special Education*, 10, 357–364.

Malamuth, Z. N. (1979). Self-management training for children with reading problems: Effects on reading performance and sustained attention. *Cognitive Therapy and Research*, 3, 279–289.

Maloney, K. B., & Hopkins, B. L. (1973). The modification of sentence structure and its relationship to subjective judgment of creativity in writing. *Journal of Applied Behavior Analysis*, 6, 425–433.

Maloney, K. B., Jacobson, C. R., & Hopkins, B. L. (1975). An analysis of the effects of lecture, requests, teacher praise, and free time on the creative writing behaviors of third-grade children. In E. Ramp & G. Semb (Eds.), *Behavior analysis: Areas of research and application* (pp. 244–260). Englewood Cliffs, NJ: Prentice-Hall.

Massard, V. I., & Etzel, B. C. (1972). Acquisition of phonetic sounds by preschool children. I: Effects of response and reinforcement frequency. II: Effects of tactile differences in discriminative stimuli. In G. Semb (Ed.), *Behavior analysis and education—1972* (pp. 88–111). Lawrence, KS: University of Kansas Department of Human Development.

Matheny, N., & Panagos, J. M. (1978). Comparing the effects of articulation and syntax programs on syntax and articulation improvement. *Language, Speech, & Hearing Services in Schools*, 9, 57–61.

Mastropieri, M. A., Scruggs, T. E., & Levin, J. R. (1987). Mnemonic strategies in special education. In M. A. McDaniel & M. Pressley (Eds.), *Imaginal and mnemonic processes* (pp. 358–376). New York: Springer-Verlag.

Mattes, J. (1983). The Feingold diet: A current reappraisal. *Journal of Learning Disabilities*, 16, 319–323.

McKenzie, H. S., Clark, M., Wolf, M. M., Kothera, R., & Benson, C. (1968). Behavior modification of children with learning disabilities using grades as tokens and allowances as back up reinforcers. *Exceptional Children*, 34, 745–752.

McLaughlin, T. F., Burgess, N., & Sackville-West, L. (1981). Effects of self-recording and self-recording plus matching on academic performance. *Child Behavior Therapy*, 3, 17–28.

Miller, L., & Bizzell, R. P. (1984). Long-term effects of four preschool programs: ninth- and tenth-grade results. *Child Development*, 55, 1570–1587.

Moran, M. R., Schumaker, J. B., & Vetter, A. F. (1981). *Teaching a paragraph organization strategy to learning disabled adolescents* (Research Report No. 54). Lawrence, KS: University of Kansas Institute for Research in Learning Disabilities.

Myers, C. A. (1978). Reviewing the literature on Fernald's technique of remedial reading. *Reading Teacher*, 31, 614–619.

O'Leary, K. D. (1980). Pills or skills for hyperactive children? *Journal of Applied Behavior Analysis*, 13, 191–204.

Orton, S. T. (1937). *Reading, writing, and speech problems in children*. London: Chapman and Hall.

Pacquin, M. J. (1978). The effect of pupil self-graphing on academic performance. *Education and Training of Children*, 1(2), 5–16.

Palinscar, A. S., & Brown, A. L. (1981). *Training comprehension monitoring skills in an interactive learning game*. Unpublished manuscript, University of Illinois.

Palinscar, A. M., & Brown, A. L. (1983). *Reciprocal teaching of comprehension activities* (Tech. Rep. No. 269). Champaign, IL: University of Illinois Center for the Study of Reading.

Parsons, J. A. (1972). The reciprocal modification of arithmetic behavior and program development. In G. Semb (Ed.), *Behavior analysis and education—1972* (pp. 185–199). Lawrence, KS: Kansas University Department of Human Development.

Pascarella, E. T., & Pflaum, S. W. (1981). The interaction of children's attribution and level of control over error correction in reading instruction. *Journal of Educational Psychology*, 73, 533–540.

Pelham, W., Schnedler, R., Bologna, N., & Contreras, J. (1980). Behavioral and stimulant treatment of hyperactive children: A therapy study with methylphenidate probes in a within-subject design. *Journal of Applied Behavior Analysis*, 13, 221–236.

Pflaum, S. W., & Pascarella, E. T. (1980). Interactive effects of prior reading achievement and training in context on the reading of learning disabled children. *Reading Research Quarterly*, 16, 138–158.

Pressley, G. M. (1976). Mental imagery helps eight-year-olds remember what they read. *Journal of Educational Psychology*, 68, 355–359.

Roberts, M., & Smith, D. D. (1980). The relationship among correct and error oral reading rates and comprehension. *Learning Disability Quarterly*, 3(1), 54–64.

Robin, A. L., Armel, S., & O'Leary, K. D. (1975). The effects of self-instruction on writing deficiencies. *Behavior Therapy*, 6, 73–77.

Rose, T. L. (1985). The effects of two prepractice procedures on oral reading. *Journal of Learning Disabilities*, 16, 544–548.

Rose. T. L., Koorland, M. A., & Epstein, M. H. (1982). A review of applied behavior analysis with learning disabled children. *Education and Treatment of Children*, 5, 41–58.

Rose, T. L., & Robinson, H. H. (1984). Effects of illustrations on learning disabled students' reading performance. *Learning Disability Quarterly*, 7, 165–171.

Rose, T. L., & Sherry, L. (1984). Relative effects of two previewing procedures on LD adolescents' oral reading performance. *Learning Disability Quarterly*, 7, 39–44.

Rosenshine, B. (1976). Classroom instruction. In N. L. Gage (Ed.), *The psychology of teaching methods: Seventy-fifth yearbook of the National Society for the Study of Education* (Part I, pp. 335–370). Chicago: University of Chicago.

Sabatino, D. A. (1973). Auditory perceptions: Development, assessment, and intervention. In L. Mann & D. A. Sabatino (Eds.), *First Review of Special Education* (Vol. 1; pp. 49–82). Philadelphia: JSE Press.

Schroeder, S. R., Lewis, M. H., & Lipton, M. A. (1983). Interactions of pharmacotherapy and behavior therapy among children with learning and behavioral disorders. In K. D. Gadow & I. Bialer (Eds.), *Advances in learning and behavioral disabilities* (Vol. 2, pp. 179–225). Greenwich, CT: JAI Press.

Schumaker, J. B., Deshler, D. D., Alley, G. R., Warner, M. M., & Denton, P. H. (1982). Multipass: A learning strategy for improving reading comprehension. *Learning Disability Quarterly*, 5, 295–304.

Scruggs, J. E., Mastropieri, M. E., Levin, J. R., & Gaffney, J. S. (1985). Facilitating the acquisition of science facts in learning disabled students. *American Educational Research Journal*, 22, 575–586.

Scruggs, T. E., Mastropieri, M. A., McLoone, B. B., Levin, J. R., & Morrison, C. (1987). Mnemonic facilitation of text-embedded science facts with LD students. *Journal of Educational Psychology*, 78, 27–34.

Seabaugh, G. O., & Schumaker, J. B. (1981). *The effects of self-regulation training on the academic productivity of LD and NLD adolescents* (Research Report No. 37). Lawrence KS: University of Kansas Institute for Research in Learning Disabilities.

Semel, E. (1970). *Sound-order-sense* (Levels 1–2). Chicago: Follett.

Semel, E. (1976). *Semel auditory processing program*. Chicago: Follett.

Semel, E. M., & Wiig, E. H. (1981). Semel Auditory Processing Program: Training effects among children with language-learning disabilities. *Journal of Learning Disabilities*, **14**, 192–197.

Serwer, B. L., Shapiro, B. J., & Shapiro, P. P. (1973). The comparative effectiveness of four methods of instruction on the achievement of children with specific learning disabilities. *Journal Special Education*, **7**, 241–249.

Shafto, F., & Sulzbacher, S. (1977). Comparing treatment tactics with a hyperactive preschool child: Stimulant medication and programmed teacher intervention. *Journal of Applied Behavior Analysis*, **10**, 13–20.

Silverberg, N. E., Iversen, I. A., & Goins, J. T. (1973). Which remedial method works best? *Journal of Learning Disabilities*, **6**, 547–556.

Singh, N., & Singh, Y. (1984). Antecedent control of oral reading errors and self-corrections by mentally retarded children. *Journal of Applied Behavior Analysis*, **17**, 111–119.

Slingerland, B. H. (1974). *A multi-sensory approach to language arts for specific language disability children*. Cambridge, MA: Educators Publishing Service.

Smith, D. D. (1979). The improvement of children's oral reading rate through the use of teacher modeling. *Journal of Learning Disabilities*, **12**, 172–175.

Smith, D. D., & Lovitt, T. C. (1973). The educational diagnosis and remediation of written b and d reversal problems: A case study. *Journal of Learning Disabilities*, **6**, 356–363.

Smith, D. D., & Lovitt, T. C. (1975). The use of modeling techniques to influence the acquisition of computational arithmetic skills in learning-disabled children. In E. Ramp & G. Semb (Eds.), *Behavior analysis: Areas of research and application* (pp. 283–308). Englewood Cliffs, NJ: Prentice-Hall.

Smith, D. D., & Lovitt, T. C. (1976). The differential effects of reinforcement contingencies on arithmetic performance. *Journal of Learning Disabilities*, **9**, 21–29.

Smith, D. D., Lovitt, T. C., & Kidder, J. D. (1972). Using reinforcement contingencies and teaching aids to alter subtraction performance of children with learning disabilities. In G. Semb (Ed.), *Behavior analysis and education—1972* (pp. 342–360). Lawrence, KS: Kansas University Department of Human Development.

Smith, E. H., & Alley, G. R. (1981). *The effect of teaching sixth graders with learning difficulties a strategy for solving verbal math problems* (Research Report No. 39). Lawrence KS: University of Kansas Institute for Research in Learning Disabilities.

Sommerville, J. W., Warnberg, L. S., & Bost, D. E. (1973). Effects of cubicles versus increased stimulation on tasks performance by first-grade males perceived as distractible and nondistractible. *Journal of Special Education*, **7**, 169–185.

Spates, C. R., & Kanfer, F. H. (1977). Self-monitoring and self-reinforcement in children's learning: A test of a multistage self-regulation model. *Behavior Therapy*, **8**, 9–16.

Sprague, R. L. (1983). Behavior modification and educational techniques. In M. Rutter (Ed.), *Developmental neuropsychology* (pp. 404–421). New York: Guilford Press.

Stein, C. L'E., & Goldman, J. (1980). Beginning reading instruction for children with minimal brain dysfunction. *Journal of Learning Disabilities*, **13**, 219–222.

Stephens, M., & Hudson, A. (1984). A comparison of the effects of direct instruction and remedial English classes on the spelling skills of secondary students. *Educational Psychology*, **4**, 261–267.

Stromer, R. (1975). Modifying letter and number reversals in elementary school children. *Journal of Applied Behavior Analysis*, **8**, 211.

Stromer, R. (1977). Remediating academic deficiencies in learning disabled children. *Exceptional Children*, **43**, 432–440.

Swanson, L. (1981a). Modification of comprehension deficits in learning disabled children. *Learning Disability Quarterly*, **4**, 189–202.

Swanson, L. (1981b). Self-monitoring effects on concurrently reinforced reading behavior of a learning disabled child. *Child Study Journal*, **10**, 225–232.

Tarver, S. G., & Dawson, M. M. (1978). Modality preference and the teaching of reading: A review. *Journal of Learning Disabilities*, **11**, 17–29.

Torgesen, J. K. (1975). Problems and prospects in the study of learning disabilities. In E. M. Hetherington (Ed.), *Review of child development research* (Vol. 5; pp. 385–440). Chicago: University of Chicago Press.

Torgesen, J. K. (1977). The role of nonspecific factors in the task performance of learning disabled children: A theoretical assessment. *Journal of Learning Disabilities*, **10**, 27–34.

Trice, A. D., Parker, F. C., & Furrow, F. (1981). Written conversations with feedback and contingent free time to increase reading and writing in a non-reading adolescent. *Education and Treatment of Children*, **4**, 35–41.

Van Houten, R., & Little, G. (1982). Increased response rate in special education children following an abrupt reduction in time limit in the absence of a token economy. *Education and Treatment of Children*, **5**, 23–32.

Varni, J. W., & Henker, B. (1979). A self-regulation approach to the treatment of three hyperactive boys. *Child Behavior Therapy*, **1**, 171–192.

Wallach, M. A., & Wallach, L. (1976). *Teaching all children to read*. Chicago: University of Chicago Press.

Wang, M. C. (1981). Mainstreaming exceptional children: Some instructional design considerations. *Elementary School Journal*, **81**, 195–221.

Wang, M. C., & Birch, J. W. (1984a). Comparison of a full-time mainstreaming program and a resource room approach. *Exceptional Children*, **51**, 33–40.

Wang, M. C., & Birch, J. W. (1984b). Effective special education in regular classes. *Exceptional Children*, **50**, 391–398.

Warner, M. M., & Alley, G. R. (1981). *Teaching learning disabled junior high students to use visual imagery as a strategy for facilitating recall of reading passages* (Research Report No. 49). Lawrence, KS: University of Kansas Institute for Research in Learning Disabilities.

Weller, C. (1979). The effects of two language training approaches on syntactical skills of language-deviant children. *Journal of Learning Disabilities*, **12**, 470–479.

Whalen, C. K., & Henker, B. (1976). Psychostimulants and children: A review and analysis. *Psychological Bulletin*, **83**, 1113–1130.

Whalen, C. K., Henker, B., Collins, B. E., Finck, D., & Dote-moto, S. (1979). A social ecology of hyperactive boys: Medication effects in structured classroom environments. *Journal of Applied Behavior Analysis*, **12**, 65–81.

White, W. A. T. (1987). *The effects of direct instruction in special education: A meta-analysis*. Unpublished doctorial dissertation, University of Oregon, Eugene, Oregon.

White, W. A. T., & Gersten, R. M. (1983). The follow up of Follow Through students in high school: The Flint Mich. study. *Direct Instruction News*, **3**(1), pp. 1, 16.

Whitman, T., & Johnston, M. B. (1983). Teaching addition and subtraction with regrouping to educable mentally retarded children: A group self-instructional training program. *Behavior Therapy*, **14**, 127–143.

Wiederholt, J. L. (1974). Historical perspectives on the education of the learning disabled. In L. Mann & D. A. Sabatino (Eds.), *Second review of special education* (pp. 103–152). New York: Grune & Stratton.

Williams, J. P. (1980). Teaching decoding with an emphasis on phoneme analysis and phoneme blending. *Journal of Educational Psychology*, **72**, 1–15.

Wolraich, M., Drummond, T., Salomon, M. K., O'Brien, M. L., & Sivage, C. (1978). Effects of mythelphenidate alone and in combination with behavior modification procedures on the behavior and academic performance of hyperactive children. *Journal of Abnormal Child Psychology*, **6**, 149–161.

Wong, B. Y. L., & Jones, W. (1982). Increasing metacomprehension in learning disabled and normally achieving students through self-question training. *Learning Disability Quarterly*, **5**, 228–240.

Wulbert, M., & Dries, R. (1977). The relative efficacy of methylphenidate (Ritalin) and behavior modification techniques in the treatment of a hyperactive child. *Journal of Applied Behavior Analysis*, **10**, 21–31.

Ysseldyke, J. E. (1973). Diagnostic-prescriptive teaching: The search for aptitude-treatment interactions. In L. Mann & D. A. Sabatino (Eds.), *First Review of Special Education* (Vol. 1; pp. 5–32). Philadelphia: JSE Press.

Ysseldyke, J. E., & Salvia, J. (1974). Diagnostic-prescriptive teaching: Two models. *Exceptional Children*, **41**, 181–186.

Zimmerman, E. H., & Zimmerman, J. (1962). The alteration of behavior in a special classroom situation. *Journal of Experimental Analysis of Behavior*, **5**, 59–60.

Author Index

Subject Index